Time Out

Los Angeles

timeout.com/losangeles

Published by Time Out Guides Ltd, a wholly owned subsidiary of Time Out Group Ltd.
Time Out and the Time Out logo are trademarks of Time Out Group Ltd.

10 9 8 7 6 5 4 3 2 1

This edition first published in Great Britain in 2006 by Ebury Publishing
Ebury Publishing is a division of The Random House Group Ltd,
20 Vauxhall Bridge Road, London SW1V 2SA

Random House Australia Pty Limited 20 Alfred Street, Milsons Point, Sydney, New South Wales 2061, Australia
Random House New Zealand Limited 18 Poland Road, Glenfield, Auckland 10, New Zealand
Random House South Africa (Pty) Limited Isle of Houghton, Corner Boundary
Road & Carse O'Gowrie, Houghton 2198, South Africa

Random House UK Limited Reg. No. 954009

Distributed in USA by Publishers Group West
1700 Fourth Street, Berkeley, California 94710

Distributed in Canada by Penguin Canada Ltd
10 Alcorn Avenue, Toronto, Ontario, Canada M4V 3B2

For further distribution details, see www.timeout.com

ISBN 1-904978-99-1 (until January 2007)
ISBN 9781904978992 (after January 2007)

A CIP catalogue record for this book is available from the British Library

Colour reprographics by Wyndeham Icon, 3 & 4 Maverton Road, London E3 2JE

Printed and bound in Germany by Appl

Papers used by Ebury Publishing are natural, recyclable products made from wood grown in sustainable forests

Shutters on the Beach. *See p46.*

Time Out Guides Limited
Universal House
251 Tottenham Court Road
London W1T 7AB
Tel + 44 (0)20 7813 3000
Fax + 44 (0)20 7813 6001
Email guides@timeout.com
www.timeout.com

Editorial

Editor Will Fulford-Jones
Deputy Editor Edoardo Albert
Chief Consultant Editor Frances Anderton
Assistant Consultant Editor Matthew Duersten
Listings Editors Miranda Morton, Patrick Welch
Proofreader Nicholas Royle
Indexer Anna Raikes

Editorial/Managing Director Peter Fiennes
Series Editor Ruth Jarvis
Deputy Series Editor Lesley McCave
Business Manager Gareth Garner
Guides Co-ordinator Holly Pick
Accountant Kemi Olufuwa

Design

Art Director Scott Moore
Art Editor Pinelope Kourmouzoglou
Senior Designer Josephine Spencer
Graphic Designer Henry Elphick
Digital Imaging Dan Conway
Ad Make-up Jenni Prichard

Picture Desk

Picture Editor Jael Marschner
Deputy Picture Editor Tracey Kerrigan
Picture Researcher Helen McFarland

Advertising

Sales Director Mark Phillips
International Sales Manager Ross Canadé
International Sales Executive Simon Davies
Advertising Assistant Kate Staddon

Marketing

Group Marketing Director John Luck
Marketing Manager Yvonne Poon
Marketing & Publicity Manager, US Rosella Albanese

Production

Group Production Director Mark Lamond
Production Manager Brendan McKeown
Production Coordinator Caroline Bradford

Time Out Group

Chairman Tony Elliott
Managing Director Mike Hardwick
Financial Director Richard Waterlow
TO Magazine Ltd MD David Pepper
Group General Manager/Director Nichola Coulthard
TO Communications Ltd MD David Pepper
Group Art Director John Oakey
Group IT Director Simon Chappell

Contributors

Introduction Will Fulford-Jones. **History** Will Fulford-Jones (*Collective soul* Dan Epstein). **Los Angeles Today** Frances Anderton. **Architecture** Frances Anderton (*In the vernacular* Dan Epstein). **Fictional LA** Matthew Duersten. **Famous for 15 Minutes** Dan Epstein (*I wanna be elected, Have a little faith* Matthew Duersten). **On the Road** Will Fulford-Jones. **Where to Stay** Dylan Nugent; *additional reviews* Will Fulford-Jones (*Hotel babylon* Elisa Kronish). **Sightseeing** Will Fulford-Jones (*You Getty what you pay for* Frances Anderton; *Public art: Santa Monica to Venice* Shana Nys Dambrot; *We ♥ LA: Star maps* Will Fulford-Jones, Margaret Wappler; *Road trip* Margaret Wappler; *All dried out* Jade Chang; *We ♥ LA: The Great Wall of LA* Matthew Duersten; *The final frontier* Dee McLaughlin). **Restaurants** Katy Harris; *additional reviews* Will Fulford-Jones (*Designs for dining* Katy Harris; *We ⊛ LA: Cellphones, We ♥ LA: Taco trucks* Matthew Duersten; *Farmers Market favourites* Will Fulford-Jones; *Brunch bonanza* Dee McLaughlin). **Coffeehouses** Dee McLaughlin. **Bars** Matthew Duersten (*Walk: Hollywood's vintage bars* Will Fulford-Jones). **Shops & Services** Will Fulford-Jones, Katy Harris (*Spotlight: W 3rd Street* Will Fulford-Jones; *Spotlight: Abbot Kinney Boulevard* Miranda Morton; *Our daily bread* Katy Harris; *The get fresh crew* Matthew Duersten). **Festivals & Events** Isaac Davis (*Festivals: Music freebies* Miranda Morton). **Children** Frances Anderton. **Comedy & TV** Josh Forbes (*Come on down!* Dan Epstein). **Film** Dan Epstein. **Galleries** Shana Nys Dambrot. **Gay & Lesbian** Julian Hooper. **Music** Matt Diehl (*Artists in residence* Matthew Duersten; *Festivals: Music* Will Fulford-Jones). **Nightclubs** Matthew Duersten (*Are you ready for your close-up?* Dee McLaughlin). **Sports & Fitness** Will Fulford-Jones (*A tale of two owners* Dan Epstein). **Theatre & Dance** Rebecca Epstein. **Trips Out of Town** Will Fulford-Jones; *Palm Springs* Dan Epstein (*Meet George Jetson...* Dan Epstein). **Directory** Will Fulford-Jones.

Maps JS Graphics (john@jsgraphics.co.uk), except: page 320 used by kind permission of the Los Angeles County Metropolitan Transportation Authority.

Photography Max Malandrino, except: pages 10, 208 Getty Images; page 14 Bettmann/Corbis; page 16 Redferns; page 19 Corbis; page 21 LA Inc, the Los Angeles Convention & Visitors Bureau and AEG; page 33 Rex Features; pages 94, 122, 171, 175, 194, 235, 239, 246, 248 Amanda C Edwards; page 110 Ruth Wallace, USC; pages 134 (left), 135 © Knott's; page 134 (right) PEANUTS © UFS, Inc; page 150 Rob Greig; page 205 Robert Galbraith/Reuters; page 230 Erhard Pfeiffer; page 252 Reuters/Chris Pizzelo; pages 265, 267, 269, 273, 277 Heloise Bergman. The following images were provided by the featured establishments/artists: pages 30, 47, 61, 237, 261.

The Editor would like to thank Nyx Bradley, Lily Dunn, Robin McClain at LA Inc, Neil Sadler at Metro, and all contributors to previous editions of *Time Out Los Angeles* and *Time Out California*, whose work forms the basis for parts of this book.

Contents

The Valleys	**124**
Heading South	**131**

Eat, Drink, Shop   **137**

Restaurants	**138**
Coffeehouses	**166**
Bars	**170**
Shops & Services	**179**

Arts & Entertainment   **203**

Festivals & Events	**204**
Children	**210**
Comedy & TV	**215**
Film	**218**
Galleries	**222**
Gay & Lesbian	**228**
Music	**236**
Nightclubs	**245**
Sports & Fitness	**251**
Theatre & Dance	**260**

Trips Out of Town   **265**

Getting Started	**266**
Heading North	**267**
Heading Inland	**269**
Heading South	**278**

Directory   **283**

Getting Around	**284**
Resources A-Z	**293**
Further Reference	**302**
Index	**304**
Advertisers' Index	**310**

Maps   **307**

LA Overview	**308**
Santa Monica & Venice	**310**
Beverly Hills & Around	**311**
West Hollywood & Around	**312**
Hollywood & Midtown	**313**
East of Hollywood	**314**
Downtown	**315**
Street Index	**316**
Metro Rail Network	**319**
LA by Area	**320**

Introduction	**6**

In Context   **9**

History	**10**
LA Today	**19**
Architecture	**23**
Fictional LA	**30**
Famous for 15 Minutes	**36**
On the Road	**40**

Where to Stay   **43**

Where to Stay	**44**

Sightseeing   **67**

Introduction	**68**
Santa Monica & the Beach Towns	**73**
Brentwood to Beverly Hills	**83**
West Hollywood, Hollywood & Midtown	**91**
Los Feliz, Silver Lake & Echo Park	**103**
Downtown	**108**
East LA	**117**
South Central LA	**119**

Introduction

Remarked Mark Twain of Los Angeles, 'it's a great place to live, but I wouldn't want to visit there.' Sometimes also attributed to Will Rogers, it's a quip you'll have plenty of time to ponder as you sit at yet another everlasting rush-hour red light, or in yet another static traffic jam, before wondering, inevitably, how on earth people can bear to do this twice a day, five days a week.

Twain's thesis, while not wholly defensible, is nonetheless appealing. Certainly, while the city's innumerable individual neighbourhoods are easily approachable on their own terms, Los Angeles as a megalopolis explains itself only gradually, and certainly isn't easily grasped over, say, a long weekend. The sheer size of the place, sprawling out over five counties, is one obstacle, but it also takes time to understand how its component parts slot together, the relationships they have with each other, and the causes and effects that have led to this spreadeagled salmagundi of contradictions.

But, of course, LA's dazzling inexplicability is precisely its appeal, particularly for the visitor. Deterred from exploration by the ever-worsening traffic, many Angelenos have tried to counter the sprawl around them by building for themselves a smalltown life, breaking down the immensity of the city to two or three crucial neighbourhoods (where they live, where whey work, where they shop) and forgetting the remainder. The visitor, though, has no such excuse. Avoid the peak morning and afternoon periods on the road, and LA is easier to navigate than you might expect. And navigate it you should, to explore the always

fascinating, sometimes jarring collisions that give the city's enormity some perspective: between shiny West Hollywood and seamy Hollywood, between bourgeois Santa Monica and edgy Venice, between the largely untamed Griffith Park and the entirely bloodless suburbs beyond it, between the towering cloudbusters of the Financial District and the degradation on adjacent Skid Row.

It's an exciting place these days. The sun continues to shine and the entertainment industry continues to make entertainment; between them, they still define Los Angeles above all its other characteristics. But there are more interesting things happening elsewhere. A visual arts scene has sprung up almost out of nothing, galleries setting up shop everywhere from clean-cut Culver City to shady Chinatown. A welter of independent shops across the city are facing down homogenous mall culture and winning the battle, if not quite yet the war. The Downtown renaissance heralded by the arrival several years of Disney Hall has moved up a couple of gears, with two huge new developments set to change the face of the area. Excellent new restaurants are appearing all over town, further improving a dining scene that was already on the rise. And then there are the changes in the social and political landscape, reflected in the 2005 election of LA's first Latino mayor for more than a century.

In other words, things are happening here right now. And with any luck, this guidebook will help you find them. Smart guy, Twain. But from time to time, he didn't half talk some crap.

ABOUT TIME OUT CITY GUIDES

The fifth edition of *Time Out Los Angeles* is one of an expanding series of around 50 Time Out guides produced by the people behind the successful listings magazines in London, New York, Chicago and other cities around the globe. Our guides are all written by resident experts who have striven to provide you with all the most up-to-date information you'll need to explore the city or read up on its background, whether you're a local or a first-time visitor.

THE LOWDOWN ON THE LISTINGS

Above all, we've tried to make this book as useful as possible. Telephone numbers,

websites, transport information, opening times, admission prices and credit card details are included in our listings, as are details of selected other facilities, services and events. All were checked and correct at press time. However, owners and managers can change their policies with little notice. Before you go out of your way, we strongly advise you to call and check opening times, dates of exhibitions and other relevant particulars. While every effort has been made to ensure the accuracy of the information in this guide, the publishers cannot accept responsibility for any errors it may contain.

PRICES AND PAYMENT

Our listings detail the major credit cards – American Express (AmEx), Diners Club (DC), Discover (Disc), MasterCard (MC) and Visa (V) – taken by each venue. Many will also accept travellers' cheques issued by a major financial institution, such as American Express.

The prices we've supplied should be treated as guidelines, not gospel. Fluctuating exchange rates and inflation can cause prices to change rapidly, especially in shops and restaurants. If costs vary wildly from those we've quoted, then ask whether there's a good reason – and please email us to let us know. We aim to give the best and most up-to-date advice, so we always want to know if you've been badly treated or overcharged.

THE LIE OF THE LAND

While the various individual neighbourhoods and cities that make up Los Angeles are fairly easy to navigate, the metropolitan area as a whole is daunting for the first-time visitor. To help ease the stress, we've provided detailed driving directions for all establishments listed in the book, giving not only their address and cross street but also instructions on how to reach them from the most convenient freeway or major road. (The exit given might not be the nearest, but is the most straightforward.) For a primer on LA's layout, *see pp68-70*.

LA's neighbourhoods have very distinct characters, but the boundaries that separate them are occasionally fuzzy. We have used the most commonly accepted demarcations; see page 320 for a map that defines them. The back of this book also includes street maps of the most commonly visited parts of LA, along with a comprehensive street index. The street maps start on page 310, and pinpoint the locations of hotels (❶), restaurants (❶), coffeehouses (❶), and bars (❶) featured elsewhere in the guide. For all addresses throughout the book, we've given both a cross-street and a map reference, so finding your way around should be simple.

TELEPHONE NUMBERS

The LA region has myriad phone codes. All phone numbers in this guide are prefaced by a 1 and an area code: for example, 1-310 123 4567. If you are dialling from within that area, you can drop the 1 and the area code. If you're calling from outside the code, though, dial the 11-digit number as listed. For more, *see p295*.

ESSENTIAL INFORMATION

For practical information on the city, including visa, customs and immigration information, disabled access, emergency phone numbers, useful websites and the local transport network, see the Directory (*pp284-298*).

LET US KNOW WHAT YOU THINK

We hope you enjoy *Time Out Los Angeles*, and we'd like to know what you think of it. We welcome tips for places that you believe we should include in future editions and appreciate your feedback on our choices. Please email us at guides@timeout.com.

There is an online version of this book, along with guides to over 100 international cities, at **www.timeout.com**.

In Context

History	10
LA Today	19
Architecture	23
Fictional LA	30
Famous for 15 Minutes	36
On the Road	40

Features

We ♥ LA The Hollywood Sign	13
Collective soul	16
Live and direct	21
We ♥ LA Googie	27
In the vernacular	28
We ♥ LA Philip Marlowe	33
I wanna be elected	37
Have a little faith	39
We 🚫 LA Valet parking	42

Gehry House. See p27.

Main Street, 1948.

History

LA story.

Given Los Angeles's recent history, perhaps it shouldn't be surprising that human settlement here began with a series of Native American single-family suburbs scattered haphazardly across the landscape. Prior to the arrival of Spanish colonists in the latter part of the 18th century, what is now metropolitan Los Angeles was populated by 30,000 Native Americans. But they were not farmers – they relied on hunting and native plants for food – and, unlike the Iroquois and other tribes in North America, they hadn't organised into strong political confederations. Instead, they lived in small settlements surrounding the area's few rivers, each group adopting a separate identity.

The Spanish arrived in 1769 and, backed by military muscle and beginning with San Diego, established a string of Franciscan missions along the coast. The San Gabriel mission was founded in 1771, marking the first Spanish foray into the Los Angeles area. The supposed purpose was to spread the Christian faith; the early Franciscan missionaries, especially their leader Father Junipéro Serra, have been glorified over the centuries. In truth, though, mission life was feudal and even brutal. The reluctant Native American converts were rounded up from their small settlements and virtually enslaved by the Franciscans. Thousands died, forcing the missions to expand deep into the countryside in search of more converts.

The history of Los Angeles as a city dates to 1781 – the year the British surrendered to George Washington in Virginia, ending the War of Independence – when the Spaniards decided they needed a settlement, or *pueblo*, in Southern California to serve as a way station for the military. A site was selected nine miles east of the San Gabriel mission, where the Los Angeles River widened. California's military governor, Felipe de Neve, laid out a plaza measuring 275 feet by 180 feet (84 by 55 metres); lots were designated around it, each with a 55-foot (17-metre) frontage on the plaza.

De Neve commissioned his aides to recruit 24 settlers and their families from Sonora, over 350 miles north; on 18 August 1781, after a forced march of 100 days through desert heat, the 12 men, 11 women and 21 children who survived the trip arrived at the plaza. Thus did El Pueblo de Nuestra Señora la Reina de Los Angeles begin as it has always since grown: not with a hardy band of motivated settlers, but with a real estate agent looking for customers. (What is left of the plaza can be viewed at El Pueblo de Los Angeles Historical Monument, also known as Olvera Street, in Downtown LA.)

The new settlement remained a dusty cow town for decades; the population in 1800 was made up of 315 people and 12,500 cows. Other missions were added in what would become the Los Angeles metropolitan area, among them San Buenaventura, San Fernando and San Juan Capistrano. However, after Mexico declared itself independent from Spain in 1821 and annexed California the following year, Spanish-born priests were ordered out of the area. The mission system broke down, and powerful local families, eager to exploit mission land, received dozens of large land grants from the Mexican government. Most of these 'ranchos', typically several thousand acres in size, were recognised as valid claims of title when California entered the United States in 1850. Many remained intact into the 20th century, one of the many factors that allowed large-scale, mass-production land development to occur in Los Angeles.

Meanwhile Americans had been informally colonising Los Angeles throughout the era of Mexican rule, as wandering opportunists arrived in town, married into prominent 'Spanish' families and called themselves 'Don Otto' or 'Don Bill'. The actual transfer of the cow town into US hands occurred during the forcible annexation of California that triggered the Mexican-American war of 1846-48. Two months later, on 13 August, Commodore RF Stockton landed at San Pedro with 500 marines and started his march to the *pueblo*. With political support from the 'Dons', he captured the settlement without firing a shot. The US-Mexican treaty of 1848 confirmed US dominion over California and on 9 September 1850, it officially became the 31st state of the Union. (Its entry as a 'free' state, as opposed to a 'slave' state, was one of the precursor events leading to the American Civil War.)

BOOMS AND BUSTS

Los Angeles grew steadily but somewhat unspectacularly for the next 20 years, becoming a centre of California's 'hide and tallow' trade: raising cattle and selling the hides for coats and the fat for candle tallow to trading companies from the East Coast and Europe. California's first literary masterpiece, Richard Henry Dana's *Two Years Before the Mast* (1840), features memorable scenes of the author trudging through the shallow water of San Pedro harbour with cowhides on his back. When the gold rush hit Northern California, however, the cattle barons of Los Angeles discovered they could sell the cows for beef at $30 a head to the goldfields, rather than $3 a head to the traders. The 1872 publication of Helen Hunt Jackson's novel *Ramona*, which romanticised rancho life at the expense of historical accuracy, sparked a period of national publicity and interest in Southern California.

In 1886, the transcontinental railroad from St Louis to LA was completed, bringing with it the long-expected – but short-lived – boom. A price war broke out among the railroads, and the cost of a one-way ticket to LA dropped from $125 to a mere dollar. In 1887, the Southern Pacific Railroad transported 120,000 people to Los Angeles, at that time a city of 10,000 residents. The result was LA's first real estate boom, with more than 100 communities subdivided within a four-year period. Paper fortunes were made overnight, but then lost when the boom shrivelled in 1889. The population had grown dramatically, in part because many immigrants couldn't afford to leave. But, despite the crash, the 1880s had permanently transformed Los Angeles from a cow town into a fast-growing hustlers' paradise.

After the boom of the 1880s, the land barons and real estate operators who came to dominate the growth of Los Angeles were determined to build a more solid basis for expansion. Forming the Los Angeles Chamber of Commerce in 1888, they took the unprecedented step of embarking on a nationwide campaign, focused on the Midwest, to attract new immigrants. It was this campaign that led the journalist Morrow Mayo, writing in the 1930s, to conclude that Los Angeles was not a city but 'a commodity; something to be advertised and sold to the people of the United States like automobiles, cigarettes and mouthwashes'.

The Chamber of Commerce began sending speakers, advertisements and brochures to the Midwest. Then, in 1902, came the launch of the Rose Bowl (a college football game held on New Year's Day) and the preceding Rose Parade, designed to promote LA's sunny climate. It wasn't long before the advertisements took effect. As commodity prices rose in the first decade of the 20th century, thousands of Midwestern farmers sold up, moved west and set the wheels of a new boom in motion.

WATER, WATER EVERYWHERE

Duly encouraged by the influx of new residents, the city's land barons pulled off one of the most audacious and duplicitous schemes ever devised to ensure a city's greatness. In 1904, former LA mayor Fred Eaton went to the Owens Valley, a high-desert region 230 miles north of Los Angeles, claimed he was working on a dam project for the federal government and began buying land along the Owens River. Once the land was purchased, Eaton said the federal project was dead and revealed his true purpose: to divert the Owens River through an aqueduct to LA.

'LA in the 1920s had an irrepressible energy.'

Whipped into a frenzy by trumped-up fears of a drought, LA voters approved a bond issue in 1905 to build an aqueduct from the Owens Valley to the city. LA had enough water to serve the population at the time, but not enough to grow. As William Mulholland, the city's water engineer, put it at the time: 'If we don't get it, we won't need it.' Mulholland, a self-taught Irish immigrant, then accomplished one of the great engineering feats in US history. 'There it is,' he told the people of LA when the floodway opened in 1913. 'Take it.' A century after its completion, his 230-mile aqueduct still operates, without electrical power, entirely on a gravity system.

The aqueduct didn't come to LA proper, however. Instead, it went only as far as the San Fernando Valley, an adjacent farming region. In the last – and most masterful – part of the scam, Los Angeles's land barons had secretly bought the valley cheaply, annexed it to the city and then splashed Owens Valley water on to it for irrigation, greatly increasing its value. Today, the San Fernando Valley, population 1.5 million, is the prototypical US suburb, and its people chafe under the Los Angeles City controls that brought water to their valley in the first place.

MOTORS AND MOVIES

With the water in place, Los Angeles boomed in the 1910s and 1920s as did no other US city, partly on the strength of real-estate speculation, and partly on the rise of three new industries: petroleum, aircraft and movies. Due to its isolation, Los Angeles, with little natural wood and almost no coal, had regular fuel crises as severe as its water problem. However, the discovery of oil throughout metropolitan LA between 1900 and 1925, particularly around the La Brea Tar Pits and in Huntington Beach and Santa Fe Springs, put an end to that. The result was a plentiful supply of oil that enriched the region and helped to fuel the city's growing love affair with the automobile.

More dispersed than any other US city, Los Angeles took to the car more readily than anywhere except Detroit. Soon the city had its own thriving oil, automobile and tyre industries, each with their own monuments. In 1928, Adolph Schleicher, president of the Samson Tire & Rubber Co, constructed an $8-million tyre plant modelled after a royal palace once built by the king of Assyria. The plant (5675 Telegraph Road, City of Commerce) has since been reborn as a shopping Mecca known as the Citadel.

Movies and aircraft came to LA during the 1910s, and for the same reasons: the area's temperate weather, low rainfall and cheap land, the latter providing the wide open spaces that both industries needed in order to operate. Donald Douglas founded his aircraft company (a predecessor to McDonnell-Douglas) at Clover Field in Santa Monica – now the Santa Monica Municipal Airport – in 1921, while the Lockheed brothers started their company in Santa Barbara in 1914 before moving it to LA. Jack Northrop, who had worked with both Douglas and the Lockheeds, started his own company in Burbank in 1928. All three firms later formed the foundation of the US's 'military-industrial' complex.

Filming began in Los Angeles around 1910, and moved to Hollywood in 1911 when the Blondeau Tavern at Gower Street and Sunset Boulevard was turned into a movie studio. At the time, Hollywood was being marketed as a pious and sedate suburb, and the intrusion of the film industry was resented. The movie business was never really centred there; Culver City and Burbank, both of which were and are home to movie studios, have equally strong claims to being the capital of the film world. Nevertheless, Hollywood became the financial and social centre of the industry, growing from a population of 4,000 in 1910 to 30,000 in 1920 and 235,000 in 1930. The wealth of the period is still visible in the magnificent commercial architecture along Hollywood Boulevard between Cahuenga and Highland Avenues, although the town's early movie palaces, some still in operation today, were built not in Hollywood but on Broadway in Downtown LA.

PROGRESS OF SORTS

During the 1920s, a decade that saw the population of LA double, the city was a kind of 'national suburb' where the middle class sought

We ♥ LA The Hollywood sign

It seems wholly appropriate that LA's most famous landmark wasn't built out of civic pride or to improve the environment, but as a wildly ostentatious piece of advertising. Stuck for ideas as to how to promote their new real estate development in the Hollywood Hills, *LA Times* publisher Harry Chandler and Keystone Cops creator Mack Sennett hit upon an idea that was devastating in its simplicity. Some 50 feet tall, 450 feet wide and lit by 4,000 lightbulbs, their unmissable HOLLYWOODLAND sign was unveiled on 13 July 1923 and served its purpose brilliantly.

The sign was meant to stand for just 18 months, but it remained long after Chandler and Sennett had sold their properties. It briefly returned to the news in 1932, when 24-year-old British-born actress Peg Entwistle threw herself off the top of the 'H' after her career fell flat. But it was otherwise left to rot: into the late 1930s, when vandals lay waste to its lights, and the mid 1940s, when ownership of the land (and, it therefore follows, the sign) slipped into the hands of the local government.

Only when the 'H' collapsed in 1949 did the authorities start to realise they had to do something about its decay. Some lobbied to get rid of the sign, while others campaigned to keep it. In the end, a compromise of sorts was reached: the last four letters were removed, but the first nine were given a refurbishment (albeit without their lights). HOLLYWOODLAND was dead; hooray, instead, for HOLLYWOOD. Still, the decline was stemmed only temporarily: despite being granted landmark status in 1973, no effort was made to protect the sign. Graffiti was scratched on it, some parts were stolen, and, in 1977, an arsonist tried to torch the second 'L'.

It took an unlikely figure to restore a little star power to the landmark. When the Hollywood Chamber of Commerce estimated that a new sign would cost $250,000, Hugh Hefner hosted a fundraising gala at which individual letters were sponsored, to the tune of $27,700, by the likes of Gene Autry (the second 'L'), Andy Williams (the 'W') and Alice Cooper (the middle 'O', which he dedicated to Groucho Marx). The old sign came down in 1978, whereupon it was sold to a nightclub promoter named for Hank Berger for $10,000. Three months later, the new version, its letters 45 feet tall and between 31 and 39 feet wide, was unveiled amid much fanfare. It's this incarnation that still looks down over LA, protected by a security system following numerous unauthorised alterations: supporters of Oliver North covered the initial 'H' during the 1987 Iran-Contra hearings, two years after local punk band the Raffeys had managed to adapt it to read RAFFEYSOD.

In November 2005, the sign received its first all-over refurbishment in a decade. A San Diego-based firm sent 300 gallons of paint in a shade they tagged 'Hollywood White'; another company then moved in to do the five-week job, stripping back both the fronts and backs of the letters before giving them a fresh coat. In the same month, a gentleman named Dan Bliss put the original sign up for sale on eBay, having bought it from Berger two years earlier. The sale netted $450,400, roughly 20 times what the sign had cost to build 82 years earlier. Bliss's reason for selling? He needed to raise funds to invest in a movie.

● *For more on the sign's past, present and future, see www.hollywoodsign.org.*

Crowds packed the Coliseum at the **1932 Olympic Games**.

refuge from the teeming immigrant groups evident in other large metropolises. Civic leaders worked hard to build the edifices and institutions they thought a big city should have, including the Biltmore Hotel and the adjacent Los Angeles Central Library, Los Angeles City Hall, the University of Southern California and Exposition Park, and the Los Angeles Coliseum. And with the creation of the Los Angeles (now Pacific) Stock Exchange, LA also became the financial capital of the West Coast. The 'Wall Street of the West' was centred on Spring Street between 3rd and 8th Streets in Downtown; many of the original buildings remain today.

However, this same process of making Los Angeles the great 'white' city served to marginalise the minority groups that had long been a part of local life. The Mexican and Mexican-American population, which was growing rapidly to provide labourers for the city, was pushed out of Downtown into what is now the East LA barrio. And the African Americans, who had previously lived all over the city, found themselves confined to an area south of Downtown straddling Central Avenue, which became known as South Central. Both of these mini-migrations laid the foundation for serious social unrest in later decades.

Still, LA in the 1920s had an irrepressible energy. The arrival of so many newcomers created a rootlessness that manifested itself in a thousand different ways. Those in need of companionship were drawn to the city's many cafeterias (invented in LA), which served as incubators of random social activity. Those in need of a restored faith had (and still have) their choice of any number of faith healers. And those searching for a quick profit were drawn to the tantalising claims of local oil companies in search of investors.

Indeed, nothing captures a sense of the primal energy of Los Angeles during the 1920s as well as stories from the oil business. With a steady supply of gushers spouting in the suburbs (often in residential neighbourhoods), oil promoters had a ready-made promotional device, and with a stream of equity-rich farm refugees from the Midwest, they also had a ready-made pool of gullible investors. The promoters took out newspaper ads, held weekend barbecues at the gushers and used other strong-arm tactics to attract investment.

The most skilled promoter was a Canadian named CC Julian, who attracted millions of dollars to his oil company with a string of daily newspaper ads that had the narrative drive of a soap opera. When it became clear that he couldn't deliver on his investment promises, he was elbowed out of his own firm by an array of other swindlers who continued the scam and turned it into the longest-running scandal of the 1920s. By the time it was all over, Julian Petroleum had issued millions of bogus shares and the district attorney had been indicted on a bribery charge. The end came in 1931, when a defrauded investor opened fire in an LA courtroom on a banker who had been involved in the scam. The failed investor had ten cents in his pocket when he was arrested; the crooked banker had $63,000 in his pocket when he died.

GROWING UP

The 1930s was a more sober period for LA, as elsewhere in the US. With the boom over and the Depression settling in, the city's growth slowed, and the new arrivals were very different from their predecessors. Instead of wooing wealthy Midwestern farmers, LA now attracted poor white refugees from the Dust Bowl of Oklahoma and Texas, the 'Okies' made famous in John Steinbeck's novel *The Grapes of Wrath*. These unskilled workers wound up as farm labourers and hangers-on in the margins of society.

Dealing with these newcomers proved difficult for Los Angeles, but the problem was intertwined with another conundrum: how to handle the equally poor and unskilled Mexican and Mexican-American population. Since farm owners chose to hire Okies over Mexicans, LA County was overwhelmed with the cost of public relief, and resorted to forcibly repatriating even those Mexicans who were born and raised in Los Angeles.

The continued arrival of Okies and other 'hobos' caused a nasty public backlash. But it also built a liberal political mood among the have-nots, which culminated in the near-election of reformer and novelist Upton Sinclair as governor in 1934. Having moved to Pasadena in the 1910s, Sinclair wrote a diatribe called *I, Governor of California, and How I Ended Poverty*, going on to found the End Poverty in California (EPIC) movement and winning the Democratic gubernatorial nomination. Only a concerted effort by reactionary political forces (aided by movie-house propaganda from the film industry) defeated his bid. Afterwards, he wrote another book, this one called *I, Governor of California, and How I Got Licked*.

The region had other problems, such as the 1933 Long Beach earthquake, the first major quake to hit the city since it became populous.

But in the mid-1930s, optimism returned, heralded by the 1932 Olympic Games, held at the city's Coliseum. To celebrate the games, 10th Street was expanded, spruced up, renamed Olympic Boulevard and lined with palm trees, thus setting the fashion for palms in LA. In 1939, the first local freeway was built: the Arroyo Seco Parkway, now the Pasadena Freeway. An aqueduct bringing water from the Hoover Dam along the Colorado River opened in 1941. And World War II caused the biggest upheaval LA had seen to that point, setting the stage for the modern metropolis.

Already at the forefront of aviation, LA industrialised rapidly as it became a major military manufacturing centre and staging ground for the US fight against Japan in the Pacific. More than 5,000 new manufacturing plants were built in LA during the war, mostly in outlying locations. Dormitory communities sprang up to accommodate the workers. Many were 'model' towns sponsored by industrialists or the military, and they helped to establish the sprawling pattern of city development that came to characterise LA in the post-war period.

COLOUR CLASH

The city's population quickly diversified, laying more groundwork for the racial unrest that would later characterise the city. During the war, more than 200,000 African Americans moved to the city, mostly from Louisiana and Texas, to take advantage of job opportunities. But the South Central ghetto wasn't allowed to expand geographically to accommodate them, resulting in serious overcrowding. (In 1948, the Supreme Court threw out restrictive covenants, paving the way for an exodus of middle-class blacks west into the Crenshaw district.)

In need of labourers, Los Angeles welcomed the return of the Mexicans and Mexican Americans who had been pushed out a decade before. However, tensions between white Angelenos and Mexicans were widespread and constantly threatened to boil over. Some 600 Mexican Americans were arrested in connection with a murder in 1942; 22 were charged, and, in January 1943, 17 were eventually convicted after a trial thick with racial epithets. After a white sailor on shore leave was injured during a group brawl with a number of Mexican Americans four months later, more than 100 sailors left their ships and stampeded into East LA, gunning for Latinos in what became known as the Zoot Suit Riots after the baggy suits often worn by Mexican American men. A national civil rights outcry ensued and a committee was set up to investigate the trouble, but no punishment was ever meted out. Finally, on 2 October 1944, the

Collective soul

Al Bell, the chairman of Stax Records, conceived of 1972's **Wattstax** music festival as a way to thank LA's black community for its longtime support of the label and its musicians. Scheduled for 20 August 1972 at the Los Angeles Coliseum, the day-long event featured acts such as Isaac Hayes, the Staple Singers and the Bar-Kays, with Jesse Jackson acting as the MC. Though the size and scope of the event led to it being dubbed 'the Black Woodstock', Wattstax was less about peace and love than African-American empowerment, and had a far greater social impact than any of the dodgy Woodstock imitations that sprang up across America during the early 1970s.

Though seven years had passed since the 1965 Watts rebellion, the commercial and psychological wounds of the riots were still apparent. Bell believed a major concert could give African-American Angelenos a much-needed lift, raise money for local charities and hospitals, and demonstrate the potential socio-economic power of such black-run corporations as Stax (which, in the 1960s and early '70s, sold more soul music than any label save Motown).

Years before corporate sponsorship became an integral part of the concert business, Stax partnered with the Schlitz Brewing Company to cover the costs associated with the event, enabling promoters to cap ticket prices at only a dollar. The label's economic clout also allowed it to insist that only African-American police officers be used for security at the show, which went off without any violent incidents, and that black technicians be allowed to join the local motion picture labour unions so that they could work on a documentary film of the event.

The concert, which drew 100,000 to the Coliseum, and the subsequent live album were both commercial successes. However, the film – directed by Mel Stuart, best known for *Willy Wonka and the Chocolate Factory* – suffered from serious distribution problems, its 'radical' black pride message scaring off several national theatre chains. As a result, it wasn't widely seen until 2004, when an expanded version was re-released on DVD. In addition to the amazing Coliseum performances, among them a hot-pants-clad Rufus Thomas coaxing thousands of fans on to the field to do the Funky Chicken, the disc also features stand-up routines from a young Richard Pryor, musical interludes shot in local churches and clubs, and man-on-the-street interviews with locals. A vibrant and fascinating snapshot of black LA circa 1972, *Wattstax* is essential viewing for anyone interested in African-American music in general and LA history in particular.

The Bar-Kays, stars of Wattstax.

17 Mexican Americans found guilty at the 1943 murder trial had their convictions quietly quashed at appeal.

Discrimination against LA's growing Japanese community was yet more pronounced. Most Japanese Americans on the West Coast were interned in camps by the federal government during World War II, no matter how patriotic they were (indeed, in a supreme irony, some young men were permitted to leave the internment camps to join the US armed forces, which many did enthusiastically). Most Japanese lost their property, then concentrated in the Little Tokyo area of LA just east of City Hall. It took decades for Little Tokyo to return to prosperity, but an infusion of Japanese capital in the 1970s and 1980s has now created a thriving district.

When the many African Americans, Latinos and Japanese who fought for the US during the war returned to continued housing discrimination, police brutality and the general LA attitude that they were not 'real Americans', their sense of alienation grew further. But because Los Angeles was a highly segregated city, most whites could ignore the race problem; especially after the war, when the city reaped the benefits of industrialisation and a new suburban boom began.

AFTER THE WAR

The post-war era in LA is often recalled as an idyllic spell of prosperity and harmony. In fact, it was an unsettled period in which the city struggled to keep up with the demands of massive growth. Taxes rose in order to fund new facilities and heavily oversubscribed schools went on 'double-sessions', teaching two classes in the same classroom.

Most of all, the entire LA region devoted itself to building things. Freeway construction, which had been stymied by the war, exploded in 1947 when California imposed an additional petrol tax to pay for it. Virtually the entire freeway system, a marvel of modern engineering, was built between 1950 and 1970. Perhaps its most important long-term effect was to open up vast tracts of land in outlying areas for urban development, especially in the San Fernando Valley and Orange County, which was linked to Los Angeles by the I-5 (Golden State Freeway). A seminal event in this suburbanisation was the opening, in 1955, of Disneyland. It was the first theme park ever built and helped to popularise Orange County.

Other leisure attractions helped to establish LA as a major city during this period. In 1958, the city achieved 'major league' status by luring New York's Brooklyn Dodgers baseball team. But, as has so often been the case in LA's

history, even this event was marred by racial tension. To attract the team, the city gave the Dodgers a spectacular site in Chavez Ravine, overlooking Downtown LA. Located in a low-income Latino neighbourhood, the site had been earmarked for use as a public housing project. The project was never built; Dodger Stadium still stands today.

As suburbanisation continued in the 1950s and 1960s, more and more neglected areas were left behind as LA prospered. On a hot summer night in 1965, the pent-up frustrations of the black ghetto exploded into one of the first and most destructive of the US's urban disturbances. The Watts Riots began when an African American man was pulled over on a drink-driving charge; by the time they were over, dozens had been killed and hundreds of buildings had been destroyed (some estimates run the cost to $40 million). For many Angelenos living in their comfortable suburbs, the riots were the first indication that all was not well in their metropolis.

ONWARDS AND OUTWARDS

After the Watts Riots, Los Angeles began to suffer from an image problem for the first time, one with which the city struggled for the better part of a decade. National newspapers and magazines proclaimed the end of the California Dream. The Los Angeles Police Department, under a series of hard-line chiefs, continued to treat minority neighbourhoods as if they were occupied territories. As in other US cities, the breakdown of African American family life left black teenagers with few male role models, and they began to form gangs.

> **'Affluent whites found little in common with immigrants who were turning LA into a melting pot.'**

In 1966, Los Angeles actor Ronald Reagan, with no previous experience in politics, was elected state governor on a law-and-order platform. Three years later, the Charles Manson cult killed actress Sharon Tate and others at a home in Benedict Canyon, disturbing the sense of tranquillity and safety even in that high-end Beverly Hills suburb. In 1971, the city suffered its worst earthquake in 38 years, escaping a high death toll only because the quake struck at the early hour of 6am. Out of this troubled period, however, emerged a towering political figure: Tom Bradley, an African American police captain who had grown up in the segregated world of Central Avenue and later held his own in such white-dominated enclaves as UCLA and the LAPD.

In the 1950s, while at the LAPD, Bradley was assigned to improve relations with beleaguered Jewish shopkeepers in black neighbourhoods, a task he used to create the foundation for a cross-racial political alliance that sustained him for years. After retiring from the police, Bradley was elected to the City Council and, with strong support in South Central and the largely Jewish Westside, ran for mayor. He lost in 1969 but ran again in 1973 and won, becoming the first African American mayor of a predominantly white city (according to the 2000 census, the black population of the City of LA is only 12 per cent, and that of LA County a mere 10.5 per cent). By moving into the mayor's mansion, he helped desegregate the Hancock Park neighbourhood, which had violently resisted the arrival of Nat 'King' Cole some years before.

A low-key man with a calming personality, Bradley successfully ruled the city for 20 years through the power of persuasion. During the 1970s, he sought to heal racial wounds, while in the early 1980s, he turned his attention to development, reviving Downtown and courting international business; the 1984 Olympics were his greatest triumph. Bradley's efforts also benefited from a huge flow of Japanese capital into Los Angeles real estate in the 1980s. However, he lost popularity in the early 1990s, due in part to his handling of the Rodney King affair, and was replaced as mayor by Richard Riordan in 1993. He died five years later.

TROUBLED TIMES

However, this period proved to be a mere respite from LA's chronic social and racial tensions. The area became more polarised in the 1970s, as affluent whites grew more conservative and found little in common with the immigrants who were turning LA into a melting pot. Los Angeles had traditionally drawn its immigrants from the rest of the US. From the 1960s, however, most of its newcomers came from abroad. The decline of agriculture in Latin America made LA a magnet for immigrants – legal and illegal – from rural Mexico and elsewhere, while political strife in Central America also brought in hundreds of thousands. The city's position on the edge of the burgeoning Pacific Rim also attracted people (and capital) from Korea, the Philippines, Taiwan and Hong Kong.

The vast central areas of Los Angeles were re-energised by these newcomers. Tourism, trade and the garment industry boomed, as did the rapidly expanding Koreatown. But, as the neighbourhoods changed, friction grew. Latin American immigrants began crowding into historically black South Central, creating a culture clash with middle- and working-class homeowners. African Americans, in particular, felt more alienated than ever.

These tensions turned Los Angeles into a social tinderbox at the beginning of the 1990s. The arrest and beating of black motorist Rodney King by four LAPD officers in 1991, captured on tape by a home video enthusiast, proved to be the turning point. When a jury acquitted the officers of assault in 1992, it touched off a riot that lasted three days, during which 50 people died and 1,000 buildings were destroyed by fire and looting. Over 1,000 people were arrested, more of them Latino than black. The events were more widespread and destructive than the Watts disturbances of 1965; indeed, it was the worst urban riot in US history. Then, in 1995, the arrest and trial of OJ Simpson, an African American football star accused of killing his white ex-wife and another man, gripped the city. Simpson's acquittal stunned white residents, but reassured black locals that the legal system could be on their side.

INVENTING THE FUTURE

Yet despite racial tensions, an economic renaissance beginning in the mid 1990s has brought new life to Los Angeles. As the aerospace industry declined, the entertainment industry expanded rapidly. And, in 1997, house prices started to rocket again, just as they did in the 1970s and 1980s. Meanwhile, the Latino community has grown into the dominant racial group in LA County, a dramatic demographic change that has affected everything from shopping malls to city government. Indeed, Latinos are now the pivotal voting group in the city, as evidenced by the triumph of Antonio Villaragoisa in the mayoral elections of 2005. By defeating incumbent candidate James Hahn in a run-off election, Villaragoisa became the city's first Latino mayor for a century.

Regardless, Los Angeles continues to face the political tumult typical of a big American city, something only amplified by the preponderance of different governments here. Scandal never seems far away, though it's hard to imagine anything could top the events of 2003, which saw California's governor Gray Davis turfed out of office in the middle of his term and replaced by Arnold Schwarzenegger. As LA edges into the 21st century, it faces the substantial challenge of finding ways to harness its multicultural strengths.

▶ For more on **driving**, see p40.
▶ For more on **the history of the film industry in LA**, see p218.

Mayor **Antonio Villaraigosa**. See p21.

LA Today

Taking its cues from the East Coast, the City of Angels is approaching its future with focus. Frances Anderton reports.

While this book was being compiled in 2006, prisoners in an LA County jail were segregated on the basis of race, stripped naked and deprived of their mattresses. Prison guards had taken these seemingly extreme measures to prevent the inmates from fighting each other, following a week of violence between Latino and black inmates in crowded jails across the county that left hundreds injured and two dead.

It's hard to imagine such troubles when you land at cheerful LAX, greeted by palm trees and the sexy Theme Building silhouetted against blue skies. It's harder still to contemplate it while sipping a Margarita on the terrace of the Chateau Marmont, or zipping along the freeway on a sunny Sunday morning. But the bountiful land of vast horizons, generous houses and wide, smooth roads is disappearing. Like its jails, Los Angeles is overcrowded and seething with frustrations. The legendarily leisurely LA life does still exist, but it's available to fewer people than ever, and at an increasing price. And even people who can afford property here can't buy themselves extra space on the region's ever-more-packed roads.

LA County alone – that's excluding Orange, Riverside, San Bernardino and Ventura Counties, which help make up the vast megalopolis on a broader scale – is home to around ten million residents. Roughly six per cent of that number arrived in the last five years; half are new immigrants to the country. It's the most populous county in the US, and boasts a jumbled demographic: over one-third of LA County residents were born overseas, and over half of them speak a language other than English at home. Just as crucially, one-sixth of the population lives in poverty.

LA's wealthier residents feel their quality of life is under siege from these demographic shifts. Many have chosen to respond by incarcerating themselves in larger and more secure houses and cars; by setting up home in protected communities; and by voting for prison-building bond measures that send more and more youths to jail. Conversely, the less well-off are angry at the struggle to keep up, faced with a lack of affordable housing, decent public schools and healthcare. Many African Americans are especially frustrated at Latinos, whom they see as encroaching on their jobs, their neighbourhoods, their schools and, most upsetting of all, the political power they had only recently won for themselves.

GUESS WHO'S COMING TO DINNER?

The election in 1973 of Tom Bradley as the city's first African American mayor heralded an optimistic era of coalition-building between the city's black and white communities. Until

Live and direct

Just as the northern end of Downtown LA has come to be anchored by its refined cultural institutions (Disney Hall, MoCA), so its southern tip is to become a hub of popular entertainment. Due to be built over the next few years in the blocks around the Staples Center and the LA Convention Center, LA Live will be a $1.7-billion, four-million-square-foot 'sports-entertainment' complex with clubs and restaurants, a 14-screen cineplex and a 7,000-seat theatre. The Convention Center will get a 55-storey hotel, at last giving it a chance of competing with San Diego and Las Vegas. But the development will also include a sizeable residential element, in line with current trends Downtown.

'Awards shows, tourism and content are going to be the most important industries we have,' said Timothy Leiweke of AEG, the company responsible for LA Live. That assessment, galling to those who believe LA is also a centre for advanced medical research, space exploration and the visual arts, is based on statistics that suggest the public loves awards shows. No matter that the viewing figures for all such major shows have dropped in recent years: AEG's plans for the area even include a 30,000-square-foot 'museum experience' on the Grammys.

AEG proudly touts LA Live as a 'Times Square West'. Its critics say that's exactly what's wrong with it, arguing that it will be just another Disneyfied destination like the Grove, Universal CityWalk and, for that matter, modern-day, sanitised Times Square. There have also been grumbles about the government subsidies granted to the construction of the convention hotel and the inevitable rise in traffic. But its defenders argue that LA Live's substantial residential component will attract locals, who are already starting to move back to the area.

Since Downtown's decline in the 1950s, its boosters have argued that it could be revived as a genuine hub for the region. The opening of MoCA, the Staples Center and Disney Hall have helped; LA Live and the Grand Avenue Development, which promises a new 16-acre park and 2,500 new residential units in the area around the Music Center, are just the latest projects to be held up as the proof of Downtown's viability. This time around, though, the sheer volume of new housing might make them more than a tourist destination.

recently, LA's Latinos had been largely absent from positions of political power. But in 2005, the city elected its first Latino mayor in more than a century: the charismatic Antonio Villaraigosa, who comfortably ousted incumbent James Hahn. A year later, the city attorney, the president of the LA School Board, the chairwoman of the county Board of Supervisors, the county sheriff, the chairman of the MTA and the state Assembly speaker were all of Mexican heritage. The Latino inmates who jumped the blacks in the county jails outnumbered them in proportion to their numbers outside; black leaders throughout the city shuddered.

But for every frustrated cellmate, many others preferred simply to muddle along in the jail dorms as harmoniously as constant tension over beds, cigarettes and phone access can allow. And outside the jails, Angelenos are spending more time fornicating than fighting. Interracial dating and marriage is on the rise across all groups: around 20 per cent of Gen Xers now partner up with somebody out of their race, and each year sees nearly 5,000 inter-ethnic couples married in Los Angeles County. In terms of both music and fashion, hip hop is the lingua franca of LA youth, regardless of race. And so, too, is Hollywood, which keeps millions in work while also perpetuating the 'it could happen to *me*' mentality that drives people onwards, if it doesn't drive them crazy, in the city at large.

WHO'S GOING TO DRIVE YOU HOME?

One of the byproducts of mass growth in Los Angeles is the single issue that now unites virtually everybody in the area. The movie *Crash* ostensibly focused on combustible racial tensions in LA, but it was also about traffic. For good and bad, the city's smog-choked roads remain the one patch of common ground shared by Angelenos of all ethnicities and incomes.

It used to be that the freeways lived up to their name all day except rush hour, when smart drivers stuck to the surface streets to avoid the crush. Now, though, the freeways are crammed most of the time, and the surface roads are slower than ever. The influx of new residents and the concomitant addition of more cars has pushed traffic almost to a point of no return. Without a viable transit system as an alternative, people are simply gridlocked.

As a result, the city that built itself (and billed itself) as an auto-based alternative to the denser cities on the East Coast is now trying to ape the very towns it once decried. The current developmental buzzwords in LA are smart growth, densification and transit-oriented development. The terms don't always mean precisely the same thing, but in LA, they're simply different sides of the same mountain.

In recent years, the mayor has outlined visions of a city of skyscrapers scattered among green parks. In Downtown, no fewer than 25 new residential towers are at various stages of development; in a tidily ironic twist, the tallest is being built by KB Homes, a contractor that made billions in the last half-century turning the Los Angeles valley orange groves into tract-home sprawl. Where the city's commercial strips once more closely resembled one-storey main streets in Hollywood Westerns rather than the robust bastions of commerce in Chicago or San Francisco, LA is catching up with the older cities: increasingly, multi-storey residential apartments are being built above shops.

It doesn't seem to matter that after decades of nutty planning (or lack thereof), the city's different transit lines don't interconnect: the opening of a new bus or subway route is greeted by cheers. And in a significant sign of the changing times, wealthy homeowners along the Exposition line, a rail route linking Downtown and Culver City that shut down decades ago, have withdrawn their longtime opposition to re-opening it; the authorities hope that it'll be up and running again by 2010. Residents have realised that congested streets favour no one, least of all themselves.

COMMUNITY SERVICE

With the urbanisation of Los Angeles has come a huge shift in lifestyle. Where Angelenos used to hop in the car for meetings, dates or openings 25 miles away, they now weigh up whether such an occasion warrants spending maybe 90 minutes sitting in traffic. According to a recent study in the *LA Times*, even dating habits are changing: people can't be bothered with a romance more than a half-hour's drive away.

The unexpected upside to this change is a growing sense of community within individual neighbourhoods. Where much of LA has long been pedestrian-free and somewhat alienating, more of it than ever currently feels lived-in. From Leimert Park to Echo Park, new markets, coffeehouses, restaurants, stores and galleries are infusing life into formerly dispiriting areas.

In this regard, LA has been taking its cues from the East Coast by necessity, not desire. The reverse is true of its arts and culture: LA has long wanted its own arts institutions to equal those out East, and it's begun. Although its 2006 reopening was overshadowed by controversy over stolen antiquities and the resignation of free-spending head honcho Barry Munitz, the Getty Villa has assumed a curious gravitas and beauty after its lengthy remodelling. The Los Angeles County Museum of Art is also being redeveloped, albeit not as radically as originally proposed. The Jet Propulsion Laboratory and Cal Tech, two Pasadenan outposts of NASA that have long been a source of both local pride and Nobel prize winners, will add to their lustre with new buildings by Rem Koolhaas, Morphosis and Michael Maltzan. And how better to get over East Coast envy than by becoming the envy of the East Coast? A recent *New York Times* article declared that the LA Philharmonic, housed in Frank Gehry's astounding Walt Disney Concert Hall, is now the best orchestra in the country.

If the growth of Los Angeles is causing strife, it's at least partly because the city is choking on its own success. New arrivals continue to outnumber those leaving LA in frustration, because the city continues to sing its siren song. And as for the dark side: well, that's also part of LA's story, along with the earthquakes, the fires and the floods. If you want a sun-soaked paradise without the thrilling sense of pending apocalypse, there's always San Diego.

● *Frances Anderton is the host of* DnA: Design and Architecture *and the producer of* Which Way, LA? *and* To the Point, *on KCRW 89.9 FM.*

▶ For more on **Downtown**, *see p108.*
▶ For more on **the invisible Mexican workforce**, *see p213* **Nanny knows best.**

Downtown.

Architecture

Having built outwards, LA is now building upwards.

Los Angeles was founded and repeatedly reinvented by adventurers and fortune-seekers. While some showed up with 'nothing to declare but my genius', as Oscar Wilde told a US customs officer, others came laden with cultural baggage. It's this that explains why much of LA is a chaotic mishmash of borrowed styles, often executed with little finesse or imagination. But originality has flourished, ever since the arrival of the intercontinental railroad in 1887 turned a dusty cow town into a metropolis.

For the most part, LA appears bewilderingly vast, featureless and horizontal, at least from the freeways. And thanks in no small part to amnesiac developers, it also boasts relatively few major public buildings or landmark corporate structures. In fact, one really needs to explore the neighbourhoods to discover the city's architectural diversity. Topography offers

a clue: much of the best work is tucked away in the hills, clinging to 'unbuildable' sites that appeal to clients whose ambitions are matched by their budgets. LA, as it did all those decades ago, still rewards the explorer.

A CITY IS BORN

Only a few fragments remain from the original 18th-century settlement of El Pueblo de Nuestra Señora la Reina de Los Angeles. Misty-eyed preservationists blather on about the city's roots and the adobe tradition, but the evidence is unconvincing: dull, provincial buildings, rebuilt or prettified. There is, however, a rich legacy of buildings from the land boom of the late 1880s, notably the houses built in the Queen Anne and Eastlake styles on the 1300 block of **Carroll Avenue** (between Douglas Street and Edgeware Road) in Echo Park.

Close by, around the intersection of N Main and Arcadia Streets, north-east of US 101, is the newly restored **El Pueblo** district. The original city centre of 19th-century Los Angeles, it now consists of a patchwork of buildings around a square, La Placita, that's lit up at night like a Mexican plaza. Among them is the Italianate **Pico House**: built in 1870, it was LA's first hotel with indoor plumbing.

But perhaps the most remarkable Victorian structure in LA is the **Bradbury Building** (304 S Broadway, Downtown; *see p115*), erected as a garment factory by George Wyman in 1893. Behind its brick façade is a stunning sky-lit atrium ringed by tiled galleries with polished wood balustrades and open-cage lifts. Fittingly for a building reputedly inspired by a science fiction novel (Edward Bellamy's *Looking Backward*), it featured in the film *Blade Runner*. Today, it contains a variety of offices, but is open to the public.

At the foot of the San Gabriel Mountains lies Pasadena, a winter resort for rich Easterners at the turn of the 19th century. Remnants of the flamboyant hotels survive, as do many handsome bungalows built in the Craftsman style, an offshoot of the Victorian Arts and Crafts movement. The standout is Charles and Henry Greene's 1908 **Gamble House** (4 Westmoreland Place; *see p129*), a marvel of polished mahogany and Tiffany glass.

BETWEEN THE WARS

During the 1920s, Southern California embraced the Mediterranean tradition, building pocket haciendas, Churrigueresque car showrooms and abstracted Andalucian farmhouses. The city developed an indiscriminate appetite for all things foreign and exotic: George Washington Smith and Wallace Neff set the pace, but all Beaux Arts-trained architects were masters of period style, and every builder could run up a mosque, a medieval castle or an Egyptian tomb. The movies emerging from Hollywood legitimised this eclecticism, but the impulse came from newcomers who flocked to LA, dreaming of fortune or an easy life in the sun.

Perhaps the city's favourite fantasy house sits, appropriately, in Beverly Hills. The **Spadena House** (Walden Drive, at Carmelita Avenue, Beverly Hills; *see p88*), also known as the Witch's House, was built as a movie set in Culver City by Henry Oliver in 1921. Five years later, it was moved to its present location and

converted into a private residence. Yet LA's greatest personal fantasy was not a cinematic creation or a rich man's folly: the **Watts Towers** (1727 & 1765 E 107th Street, Watts; *see p122* **We ♥ LA**), a landmark to the irrational but heroic persistence of Simon Rodia, the Italian tilesetter who built them single-handedly over three decades.

Mass fantasies, meanwhile, found their outlet in exotic movie palaces. Hollywood Boulevard boasts a couple of classics: **Grauman's Chinese Theatre** (No.6925; *see p95*) and, opposite, the **El Capitan Theatre** (No.6838; *see p220*). Some old cinemas are now used for the performing arts, among them the **Pantages Theatre** (6233 Hollywood Boulevard, Hollywood; *see p260*) and the **Wiltern Theatre** (3790 Wilshire Boulevard, Koreatown; *see p238*). Some, though, lie derelict, such as the cluster in Downtown (*see p115*).

Other Downtown buildings embody the civic pride and Beaux Arts scholarship of the 1920s. Bertram Goodhue's **Central Library** (630 W 5th Street, Downtown; *see p114*) includes spirited murals and lofty inscriptions; likewise, the vast, pyramid-capped 1928 **City Hall** (200 N Spring Street, Downtown; *see p113*) was intended to impress to the point of pomposity. Its commercial counterpart was **Bullocks Wilshire** (3050 Wilshire Boulevard, near Koreatown), the grandest of the department stores. It's now a law school, with its art deco façades and ornament preserved.

On a smaller scale, a number of notable homes were built around this time, and have managed to survive today. The newly reopened **Hollyhock House** (Barnsdall Art Park, 4800 Hollywood Boulevard, Los Feliz; *see p104*) and the recently closed **Ennis-Brown House** (2655 Glendower Avenue, Los Feliz; *see p103*), are just two of several buildings Frank Lloyd Wright designed here in the 1920s. Two Austrian-born protégés of Wright, Rudolph Schindler and Richard Neutra, also made their mark. Schindler's notable buildings include his own live-work space, now the **MAK Center for Art & Architecture** (835 N Kings Road, West Hollywood; *see p92*), and the concrete-frame **Lovell Beach House** (13th Street, at Beach Walk, Balboa Island) in Orange County. And among Neutra's finest residences are the 1929 **Lovell House** (4616 Dundee Drive, at the southern end of Griffith Park; *see p103*) and the **Strathmore Apartments**, stacked up a hillside in Westwood (11005 Strathmore Drive).

The Los Angeles area fared better than most during the Depression, but the old extravagance vanished and New World 'streamline moderne' replaced European models for many public buildings and a few homes. In Downtown,

Union Station (p25)
The former booking hall doubles as Demi Moore's retreat in *Charlie's Angels: Full Throttle*

spy the **Coca-Cola Bottling Plant** (1334 Central Avenue), an ocean liner moored amid warehouses, and take a train from **Union Station** (800 N Alameda Street; *see p110*), the last of the great US passenger terminals.

POST-WAR GROWTH

The population of Southern California exploded in the 1950s. New suburbs obliterated fields and citrus orchards, extending, with the freeways, into the desert. Business interests spurred the renewal of Downtown, razing the decaying Victorian mansions atop Bunker Hill and creating, from the early 1960s, a corridor of office towers. But thanks to clogged freeways and abysmal public transport, Downtown never took off; Century City and other commercial hubs grew to serve the increasingly fragmented and suburban metropolis.

From 1945 to 1962, influential magazine *Arts + Architecture* sponsored the Case Study House programme, a visionary project with a mission to create prototypical low-cost houses using new prefabricated materials and building methods. Although they never achieved mass popularity, the houses stand as icons of Southern Californian design, characterised by the use of glass walls and doors – to make the exterior landscape flow into the interior, and vice versa – and open-plan glass-and-steel volumes. One of the best was the steel-framed **Eames House** (203 Chautauqua Boulevard, Pacific Palisades; *see p74*), a fusion of poetry and technology by famed husband-and-wife design team Charles and Ray Eames.

Several post-war LA architects were heavily influenced by Frank Lloyd Wright's organic modern tradition, chief among them John Lautner. Indeed, Lautner first came to LA in 1939 to supervise construction of Frank Lloyd Wright's **Sturges House** (441 Skyeway Road, Brentwood) and was sickened by the ugliness of the city. But it soon occurred to him, as it had to Wright in the 1920s, that he could realise his vision here, in the soft clay of a burgeoning community, as he never could in the tradition-bound East or Midwest. Among his daring properties was the 1960 **Chemosphere** (7776 Torreyson Drive, north of Mount Olympus). However, he did no more than scrape a living, and achieved widespread fame only in the few years before his death in 1994.

THIS IS THE MODERN WORLD

Los Angeles changed dramatically in the early 1990s. A bewildering succession of recession, riots, an earthquake and flooding jolted many architects into a sudden sense of civic responsibility. With tremendous zeal, they organised seminars, community workshops and

Lovell Beach House. *See p24.*

brainstorming sessions, out of which came numerous well-intentioned plans for LA.

Perhaps predictably, most of them gathered dust, and the devastated parts of the city were largely rebuilt by developers and politicians in the most expedient way possible. However, the brief period of reflection did produce some legacies. Among them was **Inner City Arts** (720 S Kohler Street, Downtown), which quickly came to life in a converted car repair shop in a post-riot rush of donations.

While the 1980s produced a recognisable architectural aesthetic, the 1990s proved less distinctive. The recession produced a shift away from the deconstructivist contortions that characterised much of the late '80s, but the

The house that Frank built: **Gehry House**. *See p27.*

'90s also saw a greater variety of styles. For Googie-style retro, check out Stephen Ehrlich's **Robertson Library** (1719 S Robertson Boulevard, Beverly Hills), the vibrant primary colours of Kanner Architects' **In-N-Out Burger** in Westwood Village (922 Gayley Avenue), or the slick **Hustler Casino** (1000 Redondo Beach Boulevard), built in the otherwise uninteresting city of Gardena by Godfredsen-Sigal Architects.

Recent years have also signalled a return to stark minimalism. Many of the current crop of thirty- and fortysomething architects have shunned elaborate design in favour of pared-down, elegant houses in the spirit of Schindler and the Case Study House architects. One of the leading exponents is Lorcan O'Herlihy, designer of the **Lexton-MacCarthy House** in Silver

Lake (3228 Fernwood Avenue), his own **Vertical House** (116 Pacific Avenue, Venice), and a forthcoming residential complex next door to, and inspired by, the Schindler House.

OPTIONS, OPTIONS

Just as LA started to emerge from recession in the early 1990s, so the town's most powerful industry decided to revitalise itself with a host of new projects. All the major studios embarked on expansion plans, developing restaurants, leisure centres and themed entertainment/retail destinations. There's no greater example of this trend than **Universal CityWalk**, an artificial street of noise and colour at Universal City (*see p126*) designed by the Jerde Partnership International. **CityWalk II**, a less imaginative variation on the theme, opened in 2000.

In another break from tradition, the hotel industry has been responsible for some of LA's most stylish design during the last decade. The most notable examples are the **Mondrian** (8440 Sunset Boulevard, West Hollywood; *see p57*), Philippe Starck's remodel of a '60s apartment building, and the two **Standard Hotels**, in

> **Chemosphere (p25)** Troy McClure lives in a cartoon version of Lautner's dazzling structure in a 1994 episode of *The Simpsons*

West Hollywood (8300 Sunset Boulevard; *see p59*) and Downtown (550 S Flower Street; *see p62*), which boast cheap, chic interiors by Shawn Hausman. However, not far behind are the hotels restored by designer Kelly Wearstler: the mid-century modernist **Avalon** (9400 W Olympic Boulevard, Beverly Hills; *see p56*); the Chinoiserie-inspired **Maison 140** (140 S Lasky Drive, Beverly Hills; *see p57*) and the **Viceroy** (1819 Ocean Avenue, Santa Monica; *see p46*), where English country house meets the future.

'LA's most interesting architecture continues to be residential.'

It was a very different colour of money that paid for perhaps the most exciting commission of the late 1980s and early 1990s. Richard Meier's **Getty Center** (1200 Getty Center Drive, Brentwood; *see p83*) cost over $1 billion, and introduced his brand of cool International Modernism to LA. Some visitors find the buildings a little too cool, but the outdoor areas are a real catch. The original **Getty Museum**, a replica Roman villa in Malibu, has been remodelled by Machado & Silvetti Associates as a centre for classical antiquities and comparative archaeology (*see p74*), and opened in early 2006. Other recent museum projects worth seeking out are the crisp, Meier-designed **Museum of Television & Radio** in Beverly Hills (465 N Beverly Drive; *see p89*), and the **Museum of Contemporary Art** in Downtown (250 S Grand Avenue; *see p115*).

Warehouse conversions have been popular in recent years, especially on the Westside. Two standouts are **Ground Zero** (4235 Redwood Avenue, Marina del Rey), by Shubin + Donaldson, and **TBWA Chiat/Day** (5353 Grosvenor Boulevard, Playa del Rey) by Clive Wilkinson Architects. Wilkinson outdid himself with the conversion of an Orange County warehouse into a new branch of the **Fashion Institute of Design and Merchandising** (17590 Gillette Avenue, Irvine).

TO BE PERFECTLY FRANK
Just as Frank Lloyd Wright inspired the first generation of modernists in Southern California, so Frank Gehry – born in Toronto, but resident in LA since childhood – has served as mentor to several generations of free-spirited architects. Although it took until 1997, and the opening of the voluptuous Guggenheim Museum in Bilbao, Spain, for him to attain worldwide fame, Gehry has been known to Angelenos for years.

Of his early work, perhaps the most notable is the 1964 **Danziger Studio/Residence**

(7001 Melrose Avenue, Hollywood), two bold, simple cubic structures. It wasn't long, though, before Gehry began to grow more experimental, drawing inspiration from artists rather than architects. Witness his 1978 remodelling of his own home (**Gehry House**, 1002 22nd Street, Santa Monica), a collage of chainlink fencing, plywood and exposed structure. Must-see examples from the 1980s and early 1990s include the **Loyola Law School** (1441 W Olympic Boulevard, Downtown); the **Edgemar Center for the Arts** (2437 Main Street, Santa Monica; *see p78 and p261*); **Santa Monica Place** (Broadway & 4th Street, Santa Monica), famous for its layered chainlink façade on the garage, visible from 2nd Street to the south; and the former **TBWA Chiat/Day** office (340 Main Street, Venice), with its eye-catching binoculars portico designed by Claes Oldenburg and Coosje van Bruggen.

In the 1990s, Gehry's work moved from raw, makeshift construction to complex, sensuous structures clad in rich materials, designed with the aid of sophisticated computer programmes. Two buildings in Anaheim – the **Team Disney** administration building (800 W Ball Road), with its undulating yellow façade, and

We ♥ LA Googie

When America emerged from the Depression and World War II, there was a mood of optimism and faith in technology. Cars were designed to look like jet fighters, while coffeehouses and car washes strove to look as though they were moving at warp speed. Lloyd Wright (Frank's son) and LA-based architect John Lautner led the charge; in 1949, Lautner designed an angular wood-and-glass coffeehouse called Googie's on the Sunset Strip.

It's since vanished, replaced by a pastel shopping-and-cinema complex, but the name Googie lives on as shorthand for the post-war generation of neon-topped, single-storey coffeehouses that epitomise the futuristic drive-by design of the 1950s and '60s. The furnishings within were a mix of cosy and gee-whizz: Naugahyde booths and space-age lamps. The best of the survivors may be **Pann's** (6710 La Tijera Boulevard, Inglewood; *see p161*) and **Ship's Culver City** (now a Starbucks; 10705 W Washington Boulevard, Culver City). The earliest surviving **McDonald's** (10807 Lakewood Boulevard, Downey), built in 1953, shares the aesthetic.

In the vernacular

Come on, own up: haven't you always wanted to eat a hot dog at a stand shaped like a giant hot dog? Or lick the jam out of a pastry at a donut shop crowned by a 20-foot donut? Well, welcome to LA, where you can make these worryingly Freudian fantasies come true at the **Tail-o'-the-Pup** (uprooted from its San Vicente Boulevard location, it'll hopefully be replanted in Westwood during 2006) and **Randy's Donuts** (805 W Manchester Boulevard, Inglewood). The pair are among LA's best-known examples of vernacular architecture: commercial buildings designed not only to grab your attention, but to notify you of the nature of the business within.

Back in the 1930s and '40s, such oddities abounded on most major LA thoroughfares. With automotive travel already a central part of Angeleno existence, local entrepreneurs quickly grew to understand the value of eye-catching roadside advertising. Untroubled by zoning laws or good taste – this was, after all, a city whose hottest dining spot was the hat-shaped Brown Derby – their whimsical, cartoonish buildings sprouted like dandelions. You could buy ice-cream from a towering ice-cream cone, grab a ham sandwich from the grinning mouth of a whale-sized pig, or even buy silk stockings inside a colossal leg.

Of course, like so much of Los Angeles, these buildings weren't built to last. What's more, those whose plaster-and-chicken-wire façades didn't crumble with age typically fell victim to the march of progress. Not even the Brown Derby was spared; its noble crown now sits dejectedly at the top of a hideous two-storey strip mall known as the **Brown Derby Plaza** (3377 Wilshire Boulevard).

But along with the Tail o' the Pup (moved in the 1980s to La Cienega Boulevard) and Randy's Donuts, traces of LA's past are still visible, from the tamale-shaped former tamale stand (now a beauty parlour) at **6421 Whittier Boulevard** in East LA to Hollywood's **Capitol Records Building** (1750 N Vine Street), reputedly built to resemble a stack of 45s on a spindle (and currently threatened with redevelopment), and the **Crossroads of the World** shopping centre (6671 Sunset Boulevard), whose 'international' flavour was reflected by its ocean liner-like centrepiece and its European-themed bungalows.

the muscular **Disney Ice Arena** (300 W Lincoln Avenue) – inspired and amazed. But even these eye-catching structures pale in comparison to the LA building, finally completed in 2003, for which Gehry will surely be best remembered.

The **Walt Disney Concert Hall** (135 N Grand Avenue, Downtown; *see p237*) was actually commissioned and designed a decade before the Guggenheim Museum in Bilbao which made Gehry's name internationally, but years of financial problems and construction delays nearly killed it. Its undulating aluminium exterior is similar to that of the Guggenheim (where the exterior is titanium), but the interior of the Concert Hall is arguably superior. The highlight is the auditorium, with warm wooden surfaces, a curved ceiling and marvellous acoustics.

Gehry's influence runs far and wide across LA, and there are several must-see buildings by architects working under his influence. The finest are in Culver City, where Eric Owen Moss has remodelled a succession of warehouses into cutting-edge workspaces on land known as the **Hayden Tract**. Among them are the **Box** (8520 National Boulevard) and **Samitaur** (3457 S La Cienega Boulevard). For more, *see p85*.

GOING DOWNTOWN

Some commentators have pinned Disney Hall as the spur for a developmental revolution in Downtown. In truth, though, it's been ongoing for a while. Gehry's **Geffen Contemporary** (152 N Central Avenue, Downtown; *see p115*), a remodelled police garage, is but one example; others include the aforementioned Museum of Contemporary Art, a complex of geometric solids and sky-lit galleries by Japanese architect Arata Isozaki; Rafael Moneo's austere **Catholic Cathedral of Our Lady of Angels** (555 Temple Street; *see p113*); and Pei Cobb Freed's soaring extension to the **Los Angeles Convention Center** (1201 S Figueroa Street).

A genuine revival of Downtown over the last decade has been fuelled by an explosion of residential development in remodelled commercial buildings. Since the **Los Angeles Conservancy**, an influential local pressure group, identified around 100 structures ripe for conversion, buildings dating from the 1910s through the 1970s have been transformed. A few are real treasures: the structures built in the early 1910s around 4th and Spring Streets; the **Pegasus Apartments** (612 S Flower Street), located in a 1940s office building by celebrated LA architect Welton Beckett; Claude

Beelman's **Eastern Columbia** building (849 S Broadway), an eye-catching zig-zag moderne building completed in 1930 and now an apartment block; and William Pereira's 1965 **Transamerica Building** (1149 S Broadway), due for regeneration soon.

However, with the well of existing buildings running dry, developers are starting to build upwards once more. KB Homes, one of the largest builders of the tract homes that turned LA into an endless sprawl, is now building a tower near the Staples Center, and both Frank Gehry and Morphosis have high-rise residential towers in the pipeline. The proposed Gehry tower is part of the **Grand Avenue Project**, a complex of cinemas, shops, offices, housing and a park to be built on some remaining parcels of land adjacent to the Walt Disney Concert Hall. The Morphosis tower, meanwhile, will be sited next to the **Herald Examiner Building** (1111 S Broadway), a Spanish Colonial revival building designed by Hearst Castle architect Julia Morgan that Brenda Levin, responsible for the restorations of the Bradbury Building and the **Griffith Observatory** (Griffith Park; see p105), is converting into offices and shops.

INTO THE 21ST CENTURY

As LA comes of age, it's being transformed from a city of single-family residences to one dotted with apartment blocks. The formerly shambling beach town of **Venice** has seen an explosion of such structures; to see the changes, head to the area circumscribed by Rose Avenue on the west, Abbot Kinney Boulevard on the south, 4th Avenue on the north and W Washington Boulevard to the east.

Another recent phenomenon is the emergence of a sustainable design sensibility, as designers try to integrate solar power and energy-efficient technologies into clean, modern buildings. Indeed, the trend has grown to such an extent that all new buildings tout their sustainability quotient. One of the more worthwhile examples is **Colorado Court** (502 Colorado Avenue, Santa Monica), a complex of affordable apartments with a wall of solar panels. Pugh Scarpa architects, who designed it, were also responsible for Larry Scarpa's own home in Venice: the **Solar Umbrella House** (615 Woodlawn Avenue), in which solar panels form a canopy over the house and wrap the southern side. Another proponent of green building is David Hertz, designer of his own **McKinley Residence** (2420 McKinley Avenue, Venice).

In recent years, architects have turned their attention to the public realm, and to schools in particular. The Los Angeles Unified School District has embarked on a massive building programme, which has built in great quantity but not great quality. Still, there are a few exceptions: the **Accelerated Charter School** (116 E Martin Luther King Boulevard, South Central LA), by Marmol Radziner and Associates (known mostly for restorations of mid-century Modern classics), and Morphosis's **Science Center School**, in the north-east corner of Exposition Park (see p119), an old Armoury remodelled to include a bamboo garden and a classroom building.

Morphosis, which earned a reputation in the late 1970s and early '80s for its ingenious custom houses, has come into its own in the new century with a number of public buildings. One is the marvellous **Diamond Ranch High School** (100 Diamond Ranch Road, Pomona), a striking sculptural building built high on a hill on a shoestring budget. The firm recently completed the **Caltrans District 7 Headquarters** in Downtown LA (100 S Main Street), its exterior skin comprised of operable aluminum panels on the east and west façades and photovoltaic cells on the south wall.

The schools programme has been largely unimpressive in architectural terms. Far more notable is a string of fine small buildings built over the last eight years as part of the Los Angeles Public Library branch library programme. Several new libraries are worth a look; perhaps the most notable is the **Hyde Park Miriam Matthews Branch Library** (2205 Florence Ave., Los Angeles) by Hodgetts + Fung, responsible for the most recent remodel of the **Hollywood Bowl** (see p98).

Still, despite these public works, LA's most interesting architecture continues to be residential. The region contains arguably some of the finest examples of 20th-century housing, and innovation has continued into the 21st. It's this that makes some recent phenomena both surprising and unwelcome. The most noticeable is the emergence of McMansions, oversized homes extending to the property line on lots that once contained a modest house and a generous garden. But just as unfortunate a trend, one symptomatic of the current housing boom, has been the razing of perfectly decent homes to make way for sometimes interesting but mostly banal overscaled properties. Though such demolitions have occurred piecemeal, they're adding up to a wholesale transformation of LA's residential neighbourhoods. Still, just as LA was founded by adventurers and fortune-seekers, so it continues to draw them.

▶ For more on **architecture tours**, see p71.
▶ For more on **modernism in Palm Springs**, see p273 **Meet George Jetson....**

In Context

Fictional LA

Los Angeles plays itself.

Literary Los Angeles

On 12 September 1884, 26-year-old Charles Fletcher Lummis began a 3,507-mile, 143-day walk from Cincinnati to LA. As he neared the city, he was met by Harrison Gray Otis, the owner of the *Los Angeles Times*; they walked the last ten miles together, discussing Lummis's new job as the first city editor of Otis's young newspaper. LA, gushed Lummis, is 'a standing riddle to the co-opted East, which cannot yet conceive of how a city so cultured and so beautiful could have sprung up here so quickly.'

If anyone 'invented' LA, it was this duo. Otis's paper championed the Anglo-Saxon 'booster' vision of a sun-kissed paradise; New England-born Lummis embodied the dream of coming west. Yet their source was a novel that wasn't even written about LA *per se*: *Ramona* (1884), by Massachusetts-born **Helen Hunt Jackson**, was intended as a critique of Manifest Destiny (the theft of Indian and Mexican land by white settlers), yet was appropriated as a romantic depiction of a mythical Southern California that never existed. Accepted at the time as truth, *Ramona* went through 135 printings in 50 years.

CRIME AND PASSION

LA didn't come into its own as a literary city until the 1920s, when novels such as **Upton Sinclair**'s *Oil!* (1922) and **Don Ryan**'s *Angels Flight* (1927) began to offer tougher indictments of the booster mentality, and writers including **Edgar Rice Burroughs** and **Myron Brinig** began using the scandal-hit movie industry as a way to satirise the town. The first crop of great LA novelists – **Louis Adamic, HL Mencken, Sinclair Lewis** – were all outsiders entering a primeval landscape that appeared to have no reason to its structure or history. Their work pioneered the paradoxical state of fascination and revulsion that gives LA fiction its edge.

The political and social scandals of the 1930s inspired what would come to be called 'hard-boiled' fiction. Its most famous outlet was the pulp mystery/adventure magazine *Black Mask*, founded in 1920 by Mencken (who hated both mystery stories and LA) and **George Jean Nathan** as a way to finance *Vanity Fair*. Editor Joseph T Shaw called the genre 'the New Wild West' and encouraged the editorial voice now associated with the genre: minimalist, fact-paced, slangy, racy, streetwise and, often, racist and homophobic. *Black Mask* ran for three decades, nurturing 'tough-guy' writers such as **Paul Cain**, **Dashiell Hammett**, **Raymond Chandler** and **Raoul Whitfield**, whose *Death in a Bowl*, serialised in *Black Mask* in 1930, is arguably the first of the LA private eye novels.

The genre spun off different approaches. **James M Cain** wrote existentialist noir about the consequences of murder, although *The Postman Always Rings Twice* (1934), *Double Indemnity* (1936) and *Mildred Pierce* (1941) were more influential in Europe than the US. Beginning in 1949 with *The Moving Target*, **Ross MacDonald**'s novels about Santa Barbara PI Lew Archer focused on man's violations of the natural landscape. And a little later, the LA police novel was further evolved by ex-cop **Joseph Wambaugh** in *The New Centurions* (1970) and *The Onion Field* (1973).

LA 'tecs of all types sit on the shelves, from **Robert Crais**'s bumbling, tai chi-practicing Elvis Cole and **Michael Connelly**'s pragmatic Hieronymus 'Harry' Bosch to **Paula L Woods**' black female cop Charlotte Justice and **Michael Nava**'s gay attorney Henry Rios. **Pete Dexter**'s golf-caddy thriller *Train* (2003) and **Terrill Lee Lankford**'s Hollywood noir *Earthquake Weather* (2004) are not private eye novels *per se*, but are still forays into Southern California's wicked netherworlds. But perhaps the oddest novel in the hard-boiled tradition is **Charles Willeford**'s *High Priest in California* (1953), about a sociopath who 'translates' James Joyce's *Ulysses* in his spare time.

The colour-coded noir of **Walter Mosley**, beginning with *Devil in a Blue Dress* (1990), acts as a vibrant cultural history of black LA through the eyes of World War II vet Ezekiel 'Easy' Rawlins. Like Mosley, **James Ellroy** composes his novels as historical narratives, in which real-life villains such as Mickey Cohen and Sam Giancana mix with the fictional likes of Ed Exley and Dudley Smith. His 'LA Quartet' (*The Black Dahlia*, *The Big Nowhere*, *LA Confidential* and *White Jazz*) offers the most hyper-realised and brutal dystopia imaginable.

LOOKING INWARDS

The Hollywood novel was perfected during the 1930s, but reached its flowering with **F Scott Fitzgerald**'s *The Last Tycoon* (1941), a fanciful account of the rise of MGM head Irving Thalberg. Two other novels take similar themes: **Budd Schulberg**'s *What Makes Sammy Run?*

(1941), whose title character became a potent symbol of Hollywood capitalism, and *The Day of the Locust* (1939) by **Nathaniel West**, a savage gallery of Hollywood grotesqueries.

Onwards from **Ludwig Bemelmans**' *Dirty Eddie* (1947), a story about a movie with a pig as the star, the Hollywood novel became a virtual industry in itself; **Peter Viertel**'s *White Hunter, Black Heart* (1953), **Terry Southern**'s *Blue Movie* (1970) and **John Gregory Dunne**'s *Playland* (1994) represent the tips of the iceberg. The tradition got a boost at the turn of the century with **Bruce Wagner**'s lacerating 'Cellular Trilogy' (*I'm Losing You*, *I'll Let You Go*, *Still Holding*), **John Blumenthal**'s *What's Wrong with Dorfman?* (2000), and **Jerry Stahl**'s *I, Fatty* (2004), a work of historical fiction about the Roscoe 'Fatty' Arbuckle case.

Even away from Hollywood, writers tapped their city for inspiration. **John Fante** wrote his LA quartet (*The Road to Los Angeles*, *Wait Until Spring, Bandini*, *Ask the Dust* and *Dreams from Bunker Hill*) about the Job-like plight of Arturo Bandini in Depression-era Downtown, while **Charles Bukowski** provided LA with its gutter Falstaff in the shape of Henry Chinaski, the star of novels such as *Post Office* (1971) and *Ham on Rye* (1982). With *City of Night* (1963), **John Rechy** turned noir on its ear with its tales of the Downtown hustler's paradise of Pershing Square; gay novels it inspired include **Peter Gadol**'s *Closer to the Sun* (1996).

But despite their financial advantage, LA's well-heeled were no better at dealing with the city. **Joan Didion**'s *Play It As It Lays* (1970) postulates that the intersection of La Brea and Sunset is 'the center of nothingness'. Later, **Bret Easton Ellis**'s *Less than Zero* (1985) and follow-up *The Informers* (1994) chronicled the lives of the privileged, suntanned LA youth in occasionally damning detail.

THE MELTING POT

From **Homer Lea**'s *The Valor of Ignorance* (1909), about a Japanese invasion of California, to **Andrew MacDonald**'s *The Turner Diaries* (1978), which inspired Timothy McVeigh, ethnic tensions in LA have inspired plenty of ugly fiction. However, a good deal of first-class writing has also charted the growths, pains and pyrrhic triumphs of LA's immigrants. **Arna Bontemps** penned *God Send Sundays* (1931) and *They Seek A City* (1945), glimpses of Watts when it was a rural village; **Chester Himes**' *If He Hollers Let Him Go* (1945) and *Lonely Crusade* (1947) were articulate responses to segregated LA; and the kids' books of Bunker Hill illustrator **Leo Politi**, especially *Pedro, The Angel of Olvera Street* (1946), are magical odes to the city's ethnic communities.

The Watts Writers Workshop, a grassroots organisation founded by Budd Schulberg after the Watts Riots of 1965, was an important stepping stone for many black writers. Among them were the Watts Prophets (**Richard DeDeaux**, **Otis O'Solomon**, **Anthony 'Made' Hamilton**), whose mixture of black-power consciousness and jazz predated rap and hip hop. Three decades later, more riots spurred a new breed into action: Mosley's *Always Outnumbered, Always Outgunned* (1997) and **Bebe Moore Campbell**'s *Brothers and Sisters* (1994) take place during and after the riots following the 1992 Rodney King trial. Still, it isn't all tragedy: *Straight Outta Compton* (1992) by **Ricardo Cortex Cruz** is a hip hop send-up of 'boyz 'n the hood' cliché, while former stand-up **John Ridley**'s brutally funny trio – *Love is a Racket* (1998), *Everyone Smokes in Hell* (1999) and *The Drift* (2002) – revel in the grit and gristle of a city that the author himself admits he 'hates worse than cancer'.

Mexican-Americans have been influenced by everything from magical realism to New Journalism. **Octavio Paz**'s *The Labyrinth of Solitude* (1950) offers a meditation on the East LA *pachuco*; also worth a look are **Thomas Sanchez**'s *The Zoot Suit Murders* (1978) and the newsreel-like *The Revolt of the Cockroach People* (1973) by **Oscar Zeta Acosta**, the real-life Dr Gonzo to Hunter S Thompson's Raoul Duke. Several novels by non-Mexicans feature convincing Mexican American characters: try **Kate Braverman**'s *Palm Latitudes* (1991).

APOCALYPSE NOW?

As early as Huxley's *Ape of Essence* (1948), fiction has dealt in apocalyptic visions of LA. But even scarier dystopian scenarios abounded in the latter part of the century, anchored by **Thomas Pynchon**'s superb post-riot essay 'A Journey to the Mind of Watts' and his novel *The Crying of Lot 49* (1966). **Carolyn See**'s *Golden Days* (1987) is perhaps the most disturbingly beautiful portrait of LA leading up to and after The End, asking the question, 'What if LA gave a nuclear war and no one came?'

LA's future has also proven fertile ground. The dense novels of **Steve Erickson**, *Days Between Stations* (1985) and *Our Ecstatic Days* (2005) in particular, have been described as 'science fiction without the science'. **Octavia E Butler**, meanwhile, is in a category all her own: a black woman who writes science fiction. Her 'Earthseed' series follows young survivalist cult leader Lauren Olamina and her struggle for survival in a depressed California in the 2030s.

More recently, LA fiction has exploded into a rainbow of subcultures that together offer a vibrant picture of a complex city. **Hillary**

Johnson's *Physical Culture* (1989) and **Kate Arnoldi**'s *Chemical Pink* (2002) dissect the perversities of the bodybuilding scene; **Craig Clark**'s graphic novel *Astrothrill* (1999) is a humorous cross-section of the insanities and inanities of the 1990s rock scene; and **Kem Nunn**'s *Tapping the Source* (1984) and **Allan Weisbecker**'s *In Search of Captain Zero* (2002) are fine novels about surfing culture. Since the *Sex and the City*/Bridget Jones-fuelled success of chicklit, female writers have forged a telling honesty about sex, dating and the mutual exclusivity of the two on the LA singles circuit: check out **Aimee Bender**'s *The Girl in the Flammable Skirt* (1998) or **Dana Johnson**'s *Break Any Woman Down* (2002).

Other writers have focused on specific LA enclaves. **David Ebershiff**'s *Pasadena* (2002) described the City of Roses as a Henry Jamesian world of easy elegance; in *Hoyt Street* (1993), **Mary Helen Ponce** tells of her San Fernando Valley youth; and **Michael Jaime Becerra** sets *Every Night Is Ladies' Night* (2004) among Latinos in the suburb of El Monte. **Michelle Huneven**'s *Jamesland* (2003) is a fractured love story based in Silver Lake, also the setting for **James McCourt**'s *Wayfaring at Waverly at Silver Lake* (2002); a nearby neighbourhood receives Felliniesque portraits in **Steve Scott**'s *Echo Park* (2000). **Alan Rifkin**'s *Signal Hill: Stories* (2003), meanwhile, spreads its net far and wide, from the scuffed streets of Long Beach up to the San Gabriel Valley.

Los Angeles on film

On 24 October 1907, a Chicago judge ruled that 'Colonel' William N Selig's movie equipment, acquired on the black market, infringed Edison Motion Picture patents. Banned from filming in Illinois, Selig read an LA Chamber of Commerce brochure promising '350 days a year of sunshine!', and duly sent Francis Boggs to film a scene for his adaptation of *The Count of Monte Cristo*. Boggs liked LA and stayed; his film **In the Sultan's Power** (1909), shot on a vacant Downtown lot (at 751 S Olive Street, now a parking garage), was the first dramatic film shot entirely in the city, and kicked off LA's 100-year reign as the most filmed town on earth.

Besides the open spaces and varied landscape, the region's most appealing draw for the filmmakers has been the remarkable light. LA's notorious thermal inversion – the result of extraordinarily stable air trapped between ocean, mountains and desert – results in a type of light whose quality is dreamlike rather than dramatic, a trancelike glow caused by the thickness of the sun and the shimmering of daylight that casts no shadows.

We ❤ LA Philip Marlowe

One of LA's great fictional characters, private eye Philip Marlowe has also proven one of its most filmable. Over the course of seven novels, starting in 1939 with *The Big Sleep* and finishing 19 years later with *Playback*, Raymond Chandler built a character both tough and weary, equally charming and cynical, a womanising, chess-playing drinker with an enviable line in wiseacre quips. Almost from the beginning, Marlowe leapt off the page, eventually landing in the arms of Hollywood.

The first Marlowe novel to reach the screen was *Farewell, My Lovely*, the second book in the series. Ageing matinée idol Dick Powell seemed an odd choice for the lead in Edward Dmytryk's 1944 movie, known both by its original title and as the more sinister *Murder, My Sweet*, but his tough yet vulnerable performance earned the approval of Chandler himself.

In Howard Hawks' sexy adaptation of *The Big Sleep* (1946), Humphrey Bogart's Marlowe is a relaxed professional, agile enough to play any angle he sees. However, the filming wasn't always straightforward. On set, Hawks and Bogart got into an argument as to whether one of the characters was murdered or committed suicide. When the scriptwriters, among them William Faulkner, couldn't figure it out, Hawks wired Chandler, who replied that he didn't know either. The question is left unresolved in both book and movie.

Actor/director Robert Montgomery chose a decidedly unusual camera-as-character approach to *The Lady in the Lake* (1946): apart from scenes in which he's caught in a window or a mirror, Marlowe remains unseen. This being the era before Steadicams, the result has dated badly, but critics who've tagged Montgomery's Marlowe as the worst ever plainly haven't seen macho B-movie actor George Montgomery (no relation) in *The Brasher Dubloon* (1947), adapted from *The High Window*.

Taking the lead in *Marlowe*, a 1969 adaptation of *The Little Sister*, James Garner satisfied the purists in part because he so closely resembled Chandler's descriptions of the detective: six foot tall and 199 pounds, with brown eyes and greying brown hair. However, the hardcore were outraged by Robert Altman's reinvention of *The Long Goodbye* (1973; *pictured*), which retooled their hero as a bow-legged, mumbling East Coast Jew, the ultimate fish out of water in the sun-baked, neon-washed purgatory of 1970s LA. Ignore them: casting Elliott Gould in the lead role was an inspired choice.

Robert Mitchum attempted to reinstate Marlowe's tough-guy roots in the atmospheric *Farewell, My Lovely* (1975). Unfortunately, the actor was already quite paunchy, and spent most of the movie looking as though someone had just roused him from a deep sleep. No one's brought Marlowe back to the cinema since then, but the character has been revived for the small screen, most notably by veteran jut-jawed tough guy Powers Boothe in *Philip Marlowe: Private Eye* (1984-86) and James Caan in *Poodle Springs* (1998).

COP SHOOT COP

Just as LA gave birth to noir literature, so Hollywood took up the mantle of filming it. **Double Indemnity** (1944), **Mildred Pierce** (1945) and **The Postman Always Rings Twice** (1946, remade 1981) are steamy tales of hapless schlubs done in by snaky femme fatales. Stephen Frears' rough-and-tumble **The Grifters** (1990) ploughs a similar furrow. And then there are the escapades of Chandler's Philip Marlowe (*see p33* **We ♥LA**).

Other crime films use LA in more opaque ways. Take **DOA** (1949, dismally remade in 1988), whose LA is edgy and artless, or **Heat** (1995) and **Collateral** (2004), Michael Mann's sumptuous travelogues; contrast them with **Memento** (2000), a dizzying puzzle of revenge, and **Training Day** (2001), which offers a vivid tour that hits East LA, Downtown, Echo Park and South Central in one day. David Lynch demonstrated that LA noir needn't be confined to the 'tec genre in **Mulholland Dr** (2001), arguably the best film about LA's incestuous relationship to the Hollywood fantasy machine.

Two crime films really stand out from the pack. Roman Polanski's creepy **Chinatown** (1974) follows the tough, well-meaning but ultimately ineffectual PI Jake Gittes (Jack Nicholson) through seedy, sun-kissed pre-war LA as he ties to unravel the mystery of a phony drought, a doomed mystery woman and her monstrous tycoon father. **LA Confidential** (1997), based on the Ellroy novel, is a more stylised but no less fascinating recreation of the seedy city in the 1950s. Its release imbued the city itself with a new iconography and cool.

Other filmmakers have been less concerned with making the city look stylish as with destroying it. There's been **War of the Worlds** (1953), **Escape from LA** (1996), **Earthquake!** (1974), **Volcano** (1997), the **Terminator** trilogy (1984-2003) and **Right At Your Door** (2006), but the finest musing on LA's demise remains Ridley Scott's **Blade Runner** (1982), which posits a mutated megalopolis of decaying technology and homicidal androids. Alex Cox's **Repo Man** (1984) is a sci-fi parody that manages to link car thiefs, aliens and LA punks; Kathryn Bigelow's **Strange Days** (1995) pictures the city on the eve of the millennium.

RICHER AND POORER

The 'gutter' school of LA films is distinguished by **Barfly** (1987), in which Mickey Rourke mumbles through a Bukowski script set in LA's fleabag hotels and odiferous dives. In John Cassavetes' **The Killing of a Chinese Bookie** (1976), a strip club is home to an extended family of lonely dancers, bartenders, and patrons; **Permanent Midnight** (1998) chronicles the heroin addiction of former TV writer Jerry Stahl (Ben Stiller); and **The Salton Sea** (2002) follows Val Kilmer's jazz trumpeter as he descends into a meth purgatory of LA 'tweakers'. Terry Zwigoff's **Ghost World** (2000) is a painfully funny tale of two cynical high school grads negotiating the rootless void of a pop culture-choked metropolis; a flipside of sorts is provided by the inarticulate hippies, sage-like cowboys and survivalist nuts of Joel and Ethan Coen's **The Big Lebowski** (1998).

Filmmakers, though, have had far more fun detailing the lifestyles of LA's rich and famous. Paul Bartel essays the perversions of the idle rich in **Scenes from the Class Struggle in Beverly Hills** (1989); Hal Ashby's **Shampoo** (1975) follows the romantic travails of a bed-hopping Hollywood hair stylist played by (who else?) Warren Beatty; and **Clueless** (1995) paints a satirical yet winning portrait of LA rich kids and their pampered lives. Indeed, teen life has been documented by numerous movie-makers. There's the classic **Rebel Without A Cause** (1955), whose famous rumble scene takes place at the Griffith Observatory. But there are also **Fast Times at Ridgemont High** (1982) and **Valley Girl** (1983), sweet but unflinching teen sex comedies that rise above their genres with pinpoint depictions of the LA mall culture. **Go** (1999) chronicles one night of sex and raving amid the E generation; **Thirteen** (2003) depicts LA teens growing up rather too quickly.

MOVIES AND MUSIC

Dreams of stardom have been tackled ad nauseum. Some of the best: **Sullivan's Travels** (1941); **In a Lonely Place** (1950); **The Bad and the Beautiful** (1952); **A Star is Born** (1954); **SOB** (1978); **Tapeheads** (1988); **The Big Picture** (1989); **Bugsy** (1990); **Postcards from the Edge** (1990); **Guilty by Suspicion** (1991); **Barton Fink** (1991); **The Player** (1992); **Chaplin** (1992); **Swimming With Sharks** (1994); **Get Shorty** (1995); **The End of Violence** (1997); **Gods and Monsters** (1998); and **The Cat's Meow** (2002).

Tim Burton's **Ed Wood** (1994) links the laughable films of 'the worst director of all time' with the underbelly of Hollywood's has-beens, wanna-bes and never-weres. The gothic vivisection of Hollywood's self-loathing detailed by Billy Wilder in **Sunset Boulevard** (1950) is still horrifying; Edgar G Ulmer's **Detour** (1945) plays like its cancerous brother. **Singin' in the Rain** (1952), which deftly recalls Hollywood's stumbling into the Sound Era, is almost enough to erase Wilder's bad juju. But only almost.

LA's music scene have spawned some inspired films, with the hippie hot-tub enclave of Laurel Canyon explored in both Alison Anders' **Sugar Town** (1999) and Lisa Cholodenko's **Laurel Canyon** (2002). Oliver Stone's **The Doors** (1991) falls sway to the insipid mythologising of Jim Morrison, but it's still a visually stunning film.

SOUTH CENTRAL REIGN

John Singleton's **Boyz N the Hood** (1991), released a year before the LA riots, and its undervalued follow-up **Poetic Justice** (1993), launched a trend of movies that indicted, glorified and poked fun at black LA culture. But where Singleton has affection for his 'hood, the Hughes Brothers' terrifying **Menace II Society** (1993) is a nightmare vision. Carl Franklin has been the most articulate sage of South Central: **Killer of Sheep** (1977), **To Sleep with Anger** (1990) and his adaptation of Walter Mosley's **Devil in a Blue Dress** (1995) are complex historical documents. Contrast them with **Bulworth** (1998), in which a US senator (Warren Beatty) dons gangsta wear and raps his way through America's ills.

> ## 'In film, LA became almost synonymous with urban fear and paranoia.'

East LA has exploded on to celluloid in the last two decades. **El Norte** (1983), **Mi Vida Loca** (1994), **My Family/Mi Familia** (1993), **Bread and Roses** (2000) and **American Me** (1992) are all fine films about Latino families struggling to stay afloat amid Anglo stereotypes; **Born in East LA** (1987) and **Up In Smoke** (1978) satirise the same stereotypes in alternately funny and stupid ways.

One of the best things about the ascension of Quentin Tarantino is his unabashed pride in depicting LA's heretofore unseen nooks and crannies, and the crooks and ninnies who inhabit them. The malls, diners and warehouses of Inglewood, Toluca Lake and Torrance take centre stage in **Reservoir Dogs** (1992), **Pulp Fiction** (1994) and **Jackie Brown** (1997). Others followed his lead in inferior imitations such as **The Usual Suspects** (1995).

With smut epic **Boogie Nights** (1997), the eye-popping **Magnolia** (1999) and the sweet, odd **Punch Drunk Love** (2002), Paul Thomas Anderson has become the John Cheever of the San Fernando Valley. He's not the first to film here. Robert Altman's **Short Cuts** (1993) views the stories of Raymond Carver through a Valley lens, but Altman protégé Alan Rudolph got here earlier with **Welcome to LA** (1977), which applies a *Nashville*-like structure to characters so obnoxious they could only be from LA.

A THIN LINE BETWEEN LOVE AND HATE

As LA entered the 1990s, it became almost synonymous with urban fear and paranoia. The New Agey **Grand Canyon** (1991) essays pre-Rodney King white malaise at the turn of the 1990s; and **Crash** (2005) updates the city's multi-ethnic tensions post-9/11.

Numerous films have depicted LA as smog-choked, monstrous and alienating; in Todd Haynes' **Safe** (1995), a rich LA wife even believes she's being poisoned by the modern world. But it's easy to forget the occasional love poem. **LA Story** (1991) is Steve Martin's Left Coast equivalent of Woody Allen's *Manhattan*; **Swingers** (1996) captures the rise of cocktail culture; and in the sleek, silky form of **Pretty Woman** (1990), LA found its *Pygmalion*.

Where would LA movies be without sex? Russ Meyer made **Beyond the Valley of the Dolls** (1970) specifically to get an X-rating, although it now seems passé. **The Rapture** (1991) follows Mimi Rogers through the bar- and bed-hopping world of swingers; Bob Fosse's **Star 80** (1983) is a depressing but skilled film about the 1980 murder of *Playboy* Playmate Dorothy Stratten. **The Fluffer** (2001) portrays heterosexual male actors working in gay porn; Paul Schrader's **Autofocus** (2002) tackles the sex addiction that led to the downfall and murder of *Hogan's Heroes* star Bob Crane; and **The Man From Elysian Fields** (2002), in which Mick Jagger plays the head of an escort agency, makes Schrader's **American Gigolo** (1980) seem positively glamorous.

Strangely, a city known for its pumped pecs has spawned few good sports flicks. Exceptions include **Big Wednesday** (1978), an intriguing study of Southern California surf culture, and its cheesy but fun 1991 counterpart **Point Break** (1991). The dog-eat-dog world of urban basketball is traversed in Ron Shelton's **White Men Can't Jump** (1992), while **Lords of Dogtown** (2005) documents the birth of 'extreme' skateboarding.

The 'sport' of car-stealing is essayed in the underappreciated B-movie classic **Gone in 60 Seconds** (1974; forget the insipid 2000 remake), whose bone-crunching stunts influenced the car chases in **Fletch** (1985), **Speed** (1994), **The Italian Job** (2003) and **To Live and Die in LA** (1985). Still, the last word on LA's car culture comes from **Falling Down** (1992), which tracks an Angry White Man (Michael Douglas) as he cuts a violent swath from East LA to Venice Beach after getting stuck in rush-hour gridlock. Don't follow his lead.

> ► For more on **books and films about LA**, see pp297-298.

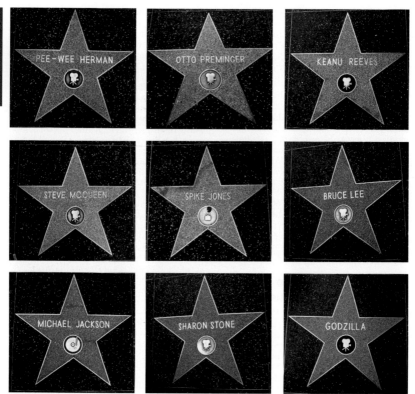

Famous for 15 Minutes

'It is strange to be known so universally and yet to be so lonely' – Albert Einstein.

America's appetite for celebrity is seemingly inexhaustible. Nonetheless, Hollywood is more than happy to feed it. One might think that the novelty of unknown amateurs and famous-for-once-being-famous faces would have worn off quickly, especially when there are more important things to occupy

the public consciousness; you know, like Brad and Angelina's baby. No such luck.

Los Angeles' role as the centre of the American entertainment industry goes hand in hand with its position as the world's largest star factory. And like any good factory, it has to meet public demand, regardless of whether it

I wanna be elected

Leland Stanford was sure his eyes weren't deceiving him. The former Governor of California was so convinced that all four hooves of a galloping horse are off the ground simultaneously that he reputedly engaged in a $25,000 wager with a friend. Now all he had to do was prove it. He found an ally in photographic pioneer Eadweard Muybridge.

After placing a series of cameras at the side of a racetrack, Muybridge attached trip wires to each shutter. As the horse galloped down the track, its hooves hit the wires, triggering the cameras. The series of photographs captured the horse in phases of action; run together, they gave the impression of motion. Muybridge's 'stop-action' photography delighted Stanford, who was proven correct by the footage. But it also astonished audiences, and became the forerunner of modern-day movie projection. Given Stanford's crucial role, it can thus be said that politics gave birth to the film industry. Ever since, the film industry has been trying to repay the debt.

The American obsession with celebrity dates back decades, and so celebrities have exploited their fame in a bid to kick-start political careers. Actor George Murphy was the first, becoming a US senator in 1965; two years later, Shirley Temple tried but failed to win election to Congess. Clint Eastwood was elected mayor of Carmel in 1986, two years before singer Sonny Bono did the same in Palm Springs (he later went on to the US Congress). Prior to his election as President in 1980, onetime B-movie actor Ronald Reagan served as the Governor of California. And then, of course, there's Der Governator.

With the arguable exception of Eastwood, Arnold Schwarzenegger is the only major entertainer to run for public office while still a major force at the box office. His gubernatorial campaign, in fact, seemed almost timed to coincide with the release of *Terminator 3: Rise of the Machines*. However, while he rode the fumes of his cinematic triumphs for his first two years in office, the love affair didn't last. After picking fights with the powerful state prison guards' union and the state tribal gaming industry, Schwarzenegger's standing in the polls fell further after a raft of measures he had proposed were defeated at statewide polls in late 2005.

One curiosity: while Hollywood is widely regarded as a bastion of liberal attitudes, the entertainers who've moved from its stages and screens into politics have all run on Republican tickets. Whoopi Goldberg, Barbra Streisand and George Clooney are just a handful of the many entertainers who've publically come out in support of the Democrats, but as yet, none has sought election. Schwarzenegger's low standing in the polls has led to many rumours about his possible opponents in the gubernatorial election due to be held in November 2006, with both Rob 'Meathead' Reiner and Warren 'Bulworth' Beatty mentioned in dispatches. But for now, at least, the only major Hollywood stars to find election as a Democrat remain Michael Douglas, who played the title role in Reiner's 1995 film *The American President*, and Michael Sheen, aka President Josiah Bartlet in *The West Wing*. Truth, it seems, really is stranger than fiction.

truly has the capacity to do so. Corners are cut in the manufacturing process, and perhaps a few cheaper ingredients are used in place of the higher-grade gear, but the products are thrown out on to the market regardless. Welcome to 21st-century Los Angeles, where no swimsuit model or karaoke-bar beefcake is insignificant enough to be kept off TV screens.

As the 'reality' trend continually rejuvenates itself with ever more banal permutations (*Skating with the Stars*, anyone?), and TV viewers combine an increasingly limited attention span with a disturbing willingness to embrace anyone with a half-decent Q Score, the ranks of the famous in LA have swollen to an all-time high. Anyone with a fan club and a

good-sized wad of cash can get a star on the Hollywood Walk of Fame these days; it's only a matter of time before said tourist attraction stretches all the way to Los Feliz.

BACK FROM THE DEAD

While the 'reality programming' explosion has put a whole generation of television writers out of work, it's been a veritable boon for celebrity has-beens and wannabes alike. Flava Flav, the formerly crack-addicted Public Enemy rapper, parlayed his wacky appearance on the third season of *The Surreal Life* into starring roles on not one but two other reality shows. Kristin Cavalleri of MTV's *Laguna Beach* boasts a skill set that doesn't stretch far beyond looking good in a swimsuit and talking crap about friends behind their backs, but she still somehow became the 'It' girl of late 2005 and early 2006, complete with a major feature in *Rolling Stone* and a show of her own (*Get This Party Started*). And *Newlyweds*, the fly-on-the-wall look at the (now-ended) marriage of former boy band member Nick Lachey and third-rate Britney Spears clone Jessica Simpson, not only resuscitated Simpson's career but led to a reality show and two chart-topping albums for her even less talented sister Ashlee. Can a series for CaCee Cobb, Simpson's 'best friend' and personal assistant, be far off?

> **'For star-spotting, try the intersection of Beverly and Robertson Boulevards in Beverly Hills. In 2005 alone, it was the site of two different Lindsay Lohan car crashes.'**

The current celebrity glut has, of course, done wonders for the circulation stats of trashy supermarket tabloids such as *The Star* and the *National Enquirer*. More celebrities means more potential for hot celeb-on-celeb love action (famous people seem to be most comfortable dating other famous people), not to mention more gossip and more scandal. After the tabloids reported that clean-cut, virginal *American Idol* singer Clay Aiken had been having sex with men he met online, several of his fans filed a class action fraud lawsuit against the performer. The incident speaks volumes about the power of the tabloids, not to mention the public's difficulty in distinguishing carefully manufactured image from reality.

SEEING STARS

If you feel that your trip to LA just won't be complete without indulging in a round of celebrity stalking, the aforementioned tabloids are an invaluable resource. Though you'll have to paw through page after page of creepy 'who's pregnant?' speculation to find it, they contain plenty of information about which LA hot spots are currently favoured by the famous. As a rule of thumb, if the same restaurant or nightclub is mentioned twice or more in the space of a single issue, you'll probably be able to see other celebs at those places on any given evening.

For daytime star-spotting, there's the Crunch gym in West Hollywood, whose close proximity to the Hollywood Hills makes it a popular workout destination for a number of stars. The Coffee Bean & Tea Leaf at the corner of Beverly and Robertson in Beverly Hills is especially popular with celebs, since it's located across the street from the Ivy, the perennial Hollywood power-lunch spot. Indeed, the intersection of Beverly and Robertson Boulevards itself has some serious celebrity mojo going on: in 2005 alone, it was the site of two different Lindsay Lohan car crashes.

Given Hollywood's eternal fascination with exotic religions (*see p39* **Have a little faith**), you might want to check the advertisement pages in the *LA Weekly* for details of local Kabbalah happenings – maybe you can spot Demi, Britney and, er, Rosie O'Donnell – or take a class at Golden Bridge Yoga, which boasts a very Hollywood-centric clientele. But while Scientology boasts an impressive number of celebrity adherents, it's probably best to give their events a wide berth; not only will you not get to ogle Tom Cruise, John Travolta or Beck, but someone will most likely pester you to take a 'Stress Test' or try to hook you up to an 'E-Meter'. You have been warned.

PUMPING HANDS, NOT IRON

However ridiculous it may sound, mindless celebrity worship remains an enormous part of life in Los Angeles, and in America in general. The 2003 election of Arnold Schwarzenegger to California's highest government office was a perfect example of the celebrity-over-substance principle in action; as absurd as they sounded, the ageing action star's campaign promises to 'terminate' the state's various woes actually found a surprisingly receptive audience.

Of course, while conservative pundits in the American media typically opine that left-wing Hollywood types such as George Clooney and Sean Penn are unqualified to air their political views in public because they're 'just actors', the idea of Republican celebs such as *Ah*-nold, Ronald Reagan, Sonny Bono and Fred 'Gopher from *The Love Boat*' Grandy holding public office doesn't seem to faze them one bit (*see p37* **I wanna be elected**). Sure, California's love affair with the Governor cooled considerably after he took office – his semi-disastrous term would have been ideal fodder for an American version of *I'm a Celebrity, Get Me Out of Here* – but there's no guarantee that he won't be re-elected in 2006. After all, he's famous, and in parts of America these days, that counts just as much as intelligence, vision or courage. Maybe the Dems should think about running Kristin Cavalleri against him? At least she's easier on the eye.

▶ For more on **tours of the stars' homes**, see p90.

▶ For more on the **Walk of Fame**, see p93.

Have a little faith

If there is one belief shared by all in Hollywood it's this: never put your own money into a film. That's what investors are for. So when Mel Gibson poured $30 million of his own hard-earned cash into an R-rated, subtitled film with dialogue in Latin, the smart money knew just where the moola was going: down the drain. Turns out the smart people weren't so smart after all. $612 million later, Gibson is now in a virtually unique position in Hollywood: free to make any movie he wants.

Rather than stick to Hollywood tradition and follow *The Passion of the Christ* with a sequel (an admittedly difficult proposition), Gibson ploughed $5 million of his *Passion* earnings into building the Holy Family Catholic Church near his home in Malibu (30188 W Mulholland Highway, Agoura Hills). News reports in 2006 suggested few parishioners, though that appears to be due less to the church's uncompromising interpretation of Catholic doctrine and more to Gibson's desire to keep it private.

Gibson's faith might be a little radical, but LA's celebrities have generally followed even more alternative religious paths, from Aimee Semple MacPherson's Angelus Temple to the Ojai-based Indian 'boy prophet' Krishnamurti. The patronage of stars can – indeed, almost invariably does – elevate the profile of a religious sect, most infamously with Kabbalah. For years an obscure school of Jewish mysticism, Kabbalah saw a huge spike in its popularity after A-list names such as Demi Moore, Lindsay Lohan, Paris Hilton, Mick Jagger, Britney Spears and (most famously, and openly) Madonna were all said to have signed up to it. So far, so good, but the religion's new-found fame has led to numerous articles and one absolutely damning BBC documentary that exposed some of its less savoury practices (selling cases of wildly expensive 'healing' water to vulnerable cancer patients, to name but one).

The media hype surrounding it has led to a bout of Kabbalah-fatigue of late, leading celebrities to turn their minds to other, more immediately fashionable religions. (And yes, fashion really does come into it. Signing up to the wrong religion is like wearing the wrong dress to the Oscars.) The best-known star Buddhist is Richard Gere, who once took advantage of an appearance at the Academy Awards to criticise Chinese repression of

Tibet. But there's also star Steven Seagal, whose enlightened status as a 'tulku' (a reincarnated lama) seems to have had little effect on his choice of film roles.

Scientology has drawn more scrutiny than any other religion because of its cult-like secrecy and its aggressive pursuit of any media outlet that criticises its teachings. Founded by science-fiction writer L Ron Hubbard, the religion is believed to have eight million disciples; among them are Beck, Isaac Hayes (formerly Chef on the TV show *South Park*), Kelly Preston, Lisa Marie Presley, Jenna Elfman and Kirstie Alley. Tom Cruise is the most famous Scientologist on the planet, but on the evidence of his outspoken and somewhat deranged comments about Scientology while promoting *War of the Worlds*, he seems to have learned nothing from fellow Scientologist John Travolta's public experiences. Travolta's *Battlefield Earth* (2000) was based on a novel by Hubbard, but the $100 million vanity project grossed barely a fifth of its costs at the box office, and is currently ranked by readers of the Internet Movie Database as one the 50 worst motion pictures ever made.

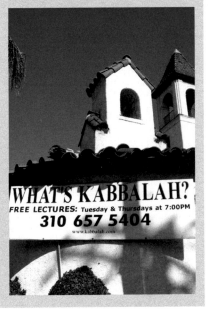

WHAT'S KABBALAH?
FREE LECTURES: Tuesday & Thursdays at 7:00PM
310 657 5404
www.kabbalah.com

On the Road

How Los Angeles learned to love the automobile.

Los Angeles wasn't entirely built around automobile travel. Not quite. The city had started to boom long before Henry Ford's Model T made car travel something other than a luxury for many Americans. Indeed, without the arrival of the transcontinental railroad in 1886 to what was then a dusty cow town, it's arguable that Los Angeles wouldn't have expanded to anything like the size that it has.

However, the city has since grown up around the possibilities of the motor car. As early as 1920, Los Angeles had more automobiles than any other US city. Four years later, despite a decent public transit network, more than half the commuters to what is now Downtown arrived by car. In a bid to discourage automobile use, the city council decided to outlaw street parking in the area between 11am and 6.15pm. After a massive outcry, the ban was revoked just 19 days later; it was the last time for several decades that local residents were dissuaded from driving.

LA's love affair with the car resulted in the sprawl that characterises it: the mile-wide boulevards and avenues, the low-rise, low-density tract homes that cover the suburbs and

exurbs, the drive-up and drive-thru consumer culture, and the wild, tentacular network of freeways. But how did it all come to pass?

LAND OF THE FREEWAY

As the photograph that opens our History chapter illustrates (*see p10*), sections of Los Angeles were once traversed by a network of streetcars and trolleys. Founded in 1901, the Pacific Electric Railroad linked Downtown LA with such disparate points as San Bernardino, Hollywood, Santa Monica and Long Beach. Ridership began to fall four decades before its closure in 1961, albeit with a huge spike in demand during World War II after gasoline was rationed and car production more or less ceased: in 1944, an astonishing 109 million people rode the network. Roughly 40 years after this halcyon time, construction began on an underground rail network that's still expanding today. However, it was what happened in between that has really defined modern-day LA.

By the late 1930s, the public were clamouring for major improvements in the road network. In 1940, with the opening of the much-heralded Arroyo Seco Parkway, they got them. Linking Downtown LA to Pasadena, the four-lane, crossing-free, 45mph-limit highway was modelled in part on the prettified parkways of New York, but with elements of modernity included in its design. An immediate hit, it proved the prototype for a network of roads that changed the very infrastructure of Los Angeles. (Aside from the conversion of the hard shoulders into traffic lanes, the stretch of road remains largely unchanged today; it's now called the Pasadena Freeway.)

The success of the Arroyo Seco Parkway inspired the local authorities to explore further the possibility of a citywide network of freeways. Various plans were brought to the table, and construction commenced in earnest soon after the end of World War II. The eight-lane Hollywood Freeway, linking Downtown to Hollywood and the San Fernando Valley, was the first major road to be constructed, and set the tone for the rest of the network. Construction of the road razed 2,000 buildings; all attempts at aesthetically pleasing landscape design, along the lines of that found on the Arroyo Seco Parkway, were eradicated between the drawing board and the building site. This was a purely functional road, and Heaven help anyone who stands in its way.

By the time President Eisenhower signed the Federal-Aid Highway Act of 1956, setting into motion the construction of the US-wide Interstate network, LA was well on the way towards building its own web of freeways. Over the following 15 years, more than 200 miles of them were constructed in LA, development that scarred the city while simultaneously opening it up. There's been little freeway construction since the mid 1970s, but the landscape of the city has changed beyond all recognition.

PASSING TRADE

On the maps, between La Brea and Fairfax Avenues, it's plain old Wilshire Boulevard. Its nickname, though, is the Miracle Mile, a nickname for which we owe thanks to a forward-thinking developer named AW Ross. When Ross bought this patch of land in 1920, there was virtually nothing there; the road itself wasn't even paved, and the land on either side was mostly given over to farming fields. Ross, though, not only predicted the increasing popularity of the car, but designed the entire road to suit it.

New buildings – department stores, mostly – were set tight against the roadside in order to attract passing traffic. At their sides, a revolutionary development, stood huge parking lots. By the 1930s, the mile-long stretch of road had become a sensation, attracting thousands of shoppers each day and revealing to Americans the true commercial possibilities of automotive

travel. The country in general, and Southern California in particular, might have grown up in a very different way without it.

One of Ross's theories was that buildings should be as attention-grabbing as possible: strong, bold and immediately appealing when seen from the driver's seat. It was this theory that eventually led architect John Lautner to table an extraordinary set of designs for a new coffee shop on Sunset Boulevard, to be called Googies. When it opened in 1949, its sharp angles, plate-glass frontage and exotic signage were unlike anything ever seen in the city, and customers flocked to it. The space-age structure moved from novelty to craze in months; the style became known as Googie architecture after Lautner's revolutionary design.

Googies has long since been demolished, but one imitator remains on the Miracle Mile. Built as Romeo's Times Square in 1955, Johnie's (6101 Wilshire Boulevard) served its last cup o' joe in 2000. However, it still stands by the side of the road as a monument to the 1950s boom in LA's automotive culture. Bulbs ripple on and off beneath a red neon sign designed to draw the eye of the passing motorist; inside, a handful of dim fingerspots pick out the counter and a handful of booths.

Other landmarks of roadside design remain from this era. Pann's Restaurant (*see pxxx*), which dates to 1956, is perhaps the finest piece of Googie architecture in the city, its prominent Inglewood lot helping it draw plenty of passing trade. Randy's Donuts (805 W Manchester Avenue, Inglewood) is a shambling 1952 shack topped with a 22-foot doughnut that can't help but catch the eye. And Bob's Big Boy (4211 Riverside Drive, Burbank), built to Wayne McAllister's design in 1949, is a dazzling affair, unmissable from the main road on which it sits.

Today, in a tribute to its early days, Bob's Big Boy offers car-hop service: waiters flit from auto to auto, taking orders and delivering food through the open windows. However, it was by no means the first place in LA to offer such convenience. Opening in Los Feliz in 1921, the same year Ross began developing what would become the Miracle Mile, Montgomery's Country Inn (later the Tam O'Shanter) opened as the first drive-in restaurant on the West Coast, a visionary move that took into account both the growing prevalence of the automobile and the sunny Southern Californian climate.

Imitators followed all over the country, but nowhere was the trend more prevalent than LA. Countless similar enterprises opened in the 1920s, '30s and '40s (a story told, with copious photographs, in Jim Heimann's book *Car Hops and Curb Service*), and have continued to open. However, where once such businesses were a

We 🚫 LA Valet parking

VALET PARKING STOP HERE

Service Charge $4.50

Gratuity Not Included

LA's valet-parking plague is built on a strange perception of hospitality, on the parts of both the business and their guest. 'We are a valuable hotel/restaurant/nightclub,' goes the argument of the former, 'and we value our guests so much we will take care of everything for them.' Of course, real hospitality would be to offer a choice of parking, but never mind. The car-owner is similarly keen to advertise his status. 'I valet-park,' reads the expression on the exec's face as he pulls up outside the hotel, 'because I am too important to walk.'

Self-parking is dear in LA, but tagging a valet-parking service on to your business is daylight robbery. At night, restaurants and bars set up (expensive) valet stands that result in the closure of (free) street-parking spaces. And one mid-range Downtown hotel charges $30 a night for the dubious privilege of having someone else park your car roughly 20 yards from where you drop it – even on weekends, when you can get a 24-hour pass in a nearby self-parking lot for five bucks.

Signs at the valet stands by most hotels make great play that guests get in-and-out privileges. Translation: you can have your car, if you ask nicely and tip well, and assuming you can find the damn valet in the first place. It's convenient, argue the valet parkers. No. It's convenient until you leave something in the car. Smokes, cellphones, perhaps even this book? That'll be a watch-checking wait outside and another fistful of singles. And crosstown journeys can take long enough without allowing an extra ten minutes for some disinterested scamp to locate your motor. *Yo! Valet! I can see it! RIGHT THERE!*

Sure, not every restaurant or hotel can have its own lot. That's fine; they're just trying to look after their guests. But businesses who prevent guests from parking in accessible lots have no such excuse. The best reason for valet parking? Though most valet parkers are Latino immigrants, there are also a lot more 'resting' actors and screenwriters in LA than there are bartending and table-waiting jobs. Creating valet jobs for them helps the economy and keeps them off the streets. Everyone's a winner. Except the driver.

novelty, they're now part of everyday life; entrepreneurs don't need to work so hard to attract attention, since the public are already expecting them to be there. Ringing Bob's Big Boy are innumerable drive-thru eateries, pharmacies, even banks. Not even their staff could tell you anything about their appearance.

THE FUTURE

In many regards, the Los Angeles area is continuing to grow. The city's borders seem to edge further out each year, and the population across the city is still on the rise. But for many locals, Los Angeles is shrinking. The traffic has grown so bad in recent years that residents are reluctant to travel any more than strictly necessary, and are spending more time than ever in their home neighbourhoods. In many regards, this is a welcome development: long-tired or neglected corners of the city are at last developing a genuine sense of community. But it also speaks ill of the city at large, gridlocked into submission. Just over a decade ago in

LA-set thriller *Speed*, a bomb on board Sandra Bullock's bus was set up to activate itself as soon as the vehicle exceeded 50mph. There's little danger of that happening here today.

There is an increasing sense in Los Angeles that the city's overarching reliance on the car is unsustainable. Long the poor relation of LA's car culture, the public transportation network is improving and growing for the first time since the glory days of the Pacific Electric Railroad, with plans on the drawing board for further expansion of the Metro system. To combat the city's awful smog, a few radical drivers around town run their vehicles on sustainable fuels such as biodiesel, and 2006 even saw the arrival of Bio-Beetle (www.bio-beetle.com), which rents cars that run only on recycled vegetable oil. And the fast-rising trend for urban living, especially Downtown, may yet see a decline in automotive commuting. Granted, you can't unring a bell: LA will always be a drivers' town. But something needs to be done, simply to get the city moving again.

Where to Stay

Where to Stay 44

Features

The chain gang 46
Hotel babylon 51
Hostels 55
Carry on camping 65

Hotel Figueroa. *See p63.*

Where to Stay

To sleep or not to sleep.

Deciding on a hotel in LA is all about location, location, location. The sheer size of the city means that where you choose to stay will greatly affect your time here. As such, even pretty basic hotels can charge a premium if they're on or near the beach; conversely, a room in an amenity-packed, business-friendly Downtown property can be had for a song on weekends. As a basic rule of thumb, the closer to the Pacific, the pricier the hotel, at least in relation to the level of service it offers.

A few classic old hotels have survived into the inexorable march of progress. Walking into the **Regent Beverly Wilshire** (*see p55*) or the **Beverly Hills Hotel & Bungalows** (*see p52*) is like striding into the 1940s: the decor is ostentatiously wealthy, but the service is immaculate, even classy. At the former, $185 buys you four Baccaratinis, a quartet of cocktails served in colour-coordinating Baccarat Martini glasses that guests can take as a souvenir; at the latter, regular guests get a gold key engraved with their name.

However, such relics are the exception rather than the rule these days. Having seen the trend for boutique hotels set in motion by the likes of **Avalon** (*see p56*) and the **Viceroy** (*see p46*), other properties are opening in previously unheralded parts of town: witness the 2005 arrival of **Shade** (*see p65*) in Manhattan Beach. Even corporate properties are getting wise to the virtues of independence: the **Delfina** (*see p47*) may be owned by Sheraton, but it was the Kor Group, owners of the Viceroy, who gave the hotel a dramatic rebranding. But if anonymity is fine, most of the countrywide chains are present: *see p46* **The chain gang**.

PRICES AND SERVICES

Accommodation prices vary a good deal here, both from hotel to hotel and within a single property: public holidays, big conventions and awards shows are just three events that affect prices. The rates we've quoted here, obtained from the hotels, reflect that disparity. Always shop around, and don't forget that quoted rates exclude a gasp-inducing 14 per cent room tax.

Always call a hotel directly when making a reservation. Better still, book online on the hotel's website: many hotels offer internet-only specials that can shave as much as $50 from the room rates. It's also worth checking reservation systems such as hotels.com and priceline.com,

which may have better deals. And always ask about cancellation policies when booking: most hotels require notice at least 24 hours ahead.

We've listed a selection of services for each hotel at the bottom of each review, everything from in-room entertainment options (all hotels have TVs unless stated, but others feature CD and/or DVD players) to the cost of parking. The vast majority of hotels feature dataports for dial-up users; however, many hotels also offer high-speed options for laptop-toters. 'Wireless' denotes a hotel that has a wireless connection throughout, while 'DSL' is used for hotels where a high-speed connection is available only via a cable. California law means that all hotels are required to provide accommodation for disabled visitors; all hotels also have no-smoking rooms.

Santa Monica & the Beach Towns

Malibu

Moderate

Casa Malibu Inn on the Beach

22752 Pacific Coast Highway, between Malibu Pier & Carbon Canyon, Malibu, CA 90265 (1-800 831 0858/1-310 456 2219/fax 1-310 456 5418/ casamalibu@earthlink.net). Bus 534/I-10, exit PCH north. **Rates** $99-$429 double. *Parking* free. **Credit** AmEx, MC, V.

This 1940s ocean-front motel attempts to emulate the typical Malibu beach house. Its 21 rooms, seven of which front on to the beach, are tastefully furnished; some have fireplaces, whirlpools, kitchens and/or private decks with patio furniture. The vine-covered buildings surrounding the garden are nice, but the real draw is the brick sun deck overlooking the hotel's private beach. Lana Turner used to hide in the Catalina Suite; Robert de Niro is rumoured to favour the Malibu Suite. Free continental breakfast includes pastries from nearby Granita.
Business services. DVD. Gym. Internet (wireless). Room service.

> ❶ Blue numbers given in this chapter correspond to the location of each hotel on the street maps. *See pp310-315.*

You may not want to close the **Shutters on the Beach**. *See p46.*

Malibu Beach Inn

22878 Pacific Coast Highway, between Malibu
Pier & Carbon Canyon, Malibu, CA 90265 (1-800
462 5428/1-310 456 6444/fax 1-310 456 1499/
www.malibubeachinn.com). Bus 534/I-10, exit PCH
north. **Rates** *$190-$410 double; $240-$525 suite.*
Parking $15. **Credit** AmEx, DC, MC, V.
Following a big brouhaha over public access near
his Malibu home, David Geffen quietly bought this
47-room hotel nearby. The Spanish architecture
revisits a time when Malibu was part of the
Spanish land grants; the ocean-front rooms are com-
plemented by 24-hour room service and a recently
added lobby bar. After long days in the sun and surf,
pick a DVD from the extensive library. Rates are
affordable for such an expensive community, even
before you factor in the complimentary continental
breakfast and afternoon tea.
Bar. DVD. Internet (wireless). Room service.

Santa Monica

Expensive

Casa del Mar

1910 Ocean Way, at Pico Boulevard, Santa Monica,
CA 90405 (1-800 898 6999/1-310 581 5533/fax
1-310 581 5503/www.hotelcasadelmar.com). Bus
33, 333, SM1, SM7, SM10/I-10, exit 4th-5th Street
south. **Rates** *$450-$725 double; $1,075-$3,200 suite.*
Parking $27. **Credit** AmEx, DC, Disc, MC, V.
Map p310 A3 ➊
This former Renaissance-style retreat started life as
an exclusive beach club frequented by silent film

stars, became a military hotel during World War II,
was converted into the headquarters of diet guru
Nathan Pritkin and served as HQ for Synanon, the
drug-rehab cult forced to disband in the '80s. Since
a $50-million facelift, Hollywood heavyweights such
as Oprah and Cher have been among the guests. The
129 rooms are dressed up in vintage beach decor:
bamboo headboards, Frette linens and wicker
chairs. The huge lobby, with its beautiful tiled floor,
has long been popular for drinks, thanks to its views
of the sunset through 20-foot windows.
Bars (2). Business services. CD. Concierge. DVD.
Gym. Pool. Restaurant. Room service.

Fairmont Miramar

101 Wilshire Boulevard, at Ocean Avenue, Santa
Monica, CA 90401 (1-800 441 1414/1-310 576
7777/fax 1-310 458 7912/www.fairmont.com).
Bus 20, 534, 720, SM1, SM7/I-405, exit Wilshire
Boulevard south. **Rates** *$289-$419 double; $349-$899*
suite. Parking $29. **Credit** AmEx, DC, Disc, MC, V.
Map p310 A2 ➋
Through wrought-iron gates and up a cobbled
driveway lies Santa Monica's oldest hotel. Nestled
on top of the bluffs overlooking the ocean, this
former estate was frequented by royalty from both
Hollywood (Garbo, Harlow) and the Beltway (JFK,
Clinton); photos in the lobby celebrate the history.
Renovations of the 32 bungalows were recently completed, and it seems no expense was spared; the 302
guestrooms aren't as posh, but the decor is tasteful
and some have views over the Pacific. In summer,
there's jazz in the outdoor Koi Pond Lounge.
Bar. Business services. CD. Concierge. Gym. Internet
(DSL). Restaurant. Room service.

The chain gang

The following hotel chains all have branches in and around LA.

Moderate

Hilton 1-800 445 8667/www.hilton.com.
Hyatt 1-888 591 1234/www.hyatt.com.
Marriott 1-888 236 2427/
www.marriott.com.
Radisson 1-800 333 3333/
www.radisson.com.
Sheraton 1-888 625 5144/
www.starwoodhotels.com.

Budget

Best Western 1-800 780 7234/
www.bestwestern.com.
Comfort Inn 1-877 424 6423/
www.comfortinn.com.
Holiday Inn 1-800 465 4329/
www.holiday-inn.com.
Motel 6 1-800 466 8356/
www.motel6.com.
Ramada 1-800 272 6232/
www.ramada.com.
Travelodge 1-800 578 7878/
www.travelodge.com.

Hotel Oceana

849 Ocean Avenue, at Montana Avenue, Santa Monica, CA 90403 (1-800 777 0758/1-310 393 0486/fax 1-310 458 1182/www.hoteloceana.com). Bus 534, SM4/I-10, exit 4th-5th Street north. **Rates** $350-$750 suite. *Parking* $26. **Credit** AmEx, DC, Disc, MC, V. **Map** p310 A2 ❸

The bright Oceana boasts a terrific location: directly across the street is Palisades Park, a prime sunset spot and the backdrop for numerous movies and ads. The colourful design of the 63 spacious suites pays tribute to hotels on the Côte d'Azur; all boast marble whirlpool baths, Aveda toiletries, kitchens with extensive honour bars, and either ocean-view balconies or a poolside location. Room service comes from a local Italian restaurant.
CD. Concierge. Gym. Pool. Internet (wirelesss). Room service.

Loews Santa Monica Beach Hotel

1700 Ocean Avenue, between Colorado Avenue & Pico Boulevard, Santa Monica, CA 90401 (1-800 235 6397/1-310 458 6700/fax 1-310 458 6761/ www.loewshotels.com). Bus 33, 333, SM1, SM7, SM10/I-10, exit 4th-5th Street north. **Rates** $315-$620 double; $625-$2,500 suite. *Parking* $26. **Credit** AmEx, DC, Disc, MC, V. **Map** p310 A3 ❹

Quintessential corporate California: light and airy, warm and beachy, casual but elegant in a bland way. The spectacular eight-storey glass atrium boasts giant palm trees and panoramic ocean views; some of the 340 luxury rooms also overlook the sea, and the beach is right across the street. A spa specialises in aromatherapy massages, Pilates classes and 'wellness weeks'. Other attractions include a spectacular Sunday brunch, revered French restaurant Lavande and the Papillon fireside lounge.
Bar. Business services. CD. Concierge. Gym. Internet (DSL in rooms, wireless in lobby). Pool. Restaurant. Room service.

Le Merigot

1740 Ocean Avenue, between Colorado Avenue & Pico Boulevard, Santa Monica, CA 90401 (1-888 539 7899/1-310 395 9700/fax 1-310 395 9200/ www.lemerigothotel.com). Bus 33, 333, SM1, SM7/ I-10, exit 4th-5th Street south. **Rates** $299-$449 double; $800-$1200 suite. *Parking* $21. **Credit** AmEx, DC, Disc, MC, V. **Map** p310 A3 ❺

Families are drawn to this contemporary European-style hotel by the beach location, while the top-notch business facilities attract corporate travellers. However, the main attraction at Le Merigot is one the largest health clubs/spas in Santa Monica, complete with a redwood sauna and a eucalyptus steam room. The 175 guestrooms are pretty luxurious, featuring Italian linens, down pillows and comforters. Quality Cal-French restaurant Cézanne is a draw for foodies, but is still usually very quiet and romantic.
Bar. Business services. CD. Concierge. DVD. Internet (DSL in rooms, wireless in lobby). Pool. Restaurant. Room service.

Shutters on the Beach

1 Pico Boulevard, at Ocean Avenue, Santa Monica, CA 90405 (1-800 334 9000/1-310 458 0030/ fax 1-310 458 4589/www.shuttersonthebeach.com). Bus 33, 333, SM1, SM7, SM10/I-10, exit 4th-5th Street south. **Rates** $355-$710 double; $1,075-$3,000 suite. *Parking* $27. **Credit** AmEx, DC, Disc, MC, V. **Map** p310 A3 ❻

Once a cool retreat for hot Hollywood stars, this old hotel reopened in 1993 as a chic resort. Although it's the sister hotel to Casa del Mar (*see p45*), Shutters eschews the French Riviera look in favour of Cape Cod couture. The lobby is all whitewashed wood, picture windows and shabby-chic couches; on foggy days, two fireplaces keep the guests warm. All 198 rooms have white shutters, balconies and whirlpool tubs. Guests can choose gourmet dining at One Pico, or people-watching at Pedals café on the beach. For some reason, the British love this hotel. **Photo** *p45.*
Bars (2). Business services. CD. Concierge. DVD. Gym. Pool. Restaurants (2). Internet (wireless). Room service. Spa.

Viceroy

1819 Ocean Avenue, at Pico Boulevard, Santa Monica, CA 90401 (1-800 622 8711/1-310 260 7500/fax 1-310 260 7515/www.viceroysanta monica.com). Bus 33, 333, SM1, SM7, SM10/I-10, exit 4th-5th Street south. **Rates** $319-$559 double; $519-$1,500 suite. *Parking* $26. **Credit** AmEx, DC, Disc, MC, V. **Map** p310 A3 ❼

The '60s façade is bland and the signage obscure, but that's the way the tragically hip like their boutiques. The interior, designed by Kelly Wearstler, is rather more interesting, its British Colonial theme enhanced by translucent tables and splashes of colour. The well-appointed rooms feature flat-screen TVs, custom armoires and marbled bathrooms. The two refreshing plunge pools are highlighted by surrounding private cabanas that double as exclusive hideouts from the Cameo Bar inside; PlayStations are available at the poolside. Although it's easier these days to get a table at chef Warren Schwartz's acclaimed Whist, the restaurant draws a crowd on weekends.
Bar. Business services. CD. Concierge. DVD. Gym. Internet (DSL in rooms, wireless in lobby). Pool. Restaurant. Room service.

Moderate

Ambrose

1225 20th Street, between Wilshire Boulevard & Arizona Avenue, Santa Monica, CA 90404 (1-877 262 7673/1-310 315 1555/fax 1-310 315 1556/ www.ambrosehotel.com). Bus 20, 720, SM2, SM11/ I-10, exit 4th-5th Street north. **Rates** $155-$245 double; $205-$265 suites. *Parking* free. **Credit** AmEx, DC, Disc, MC, V. **Map** p310 C2 ⑧
This boutique hotel is a mixture of sturdy Craftsman tradition and Asian chic; the living-room lobby, complete with crackling fire, is typical of the hotel's warm, familiar feel. Guestrooms, some with terraces and fireplaces, combine luxury and technology (there's free high-speed net access) with a bit of oriental panache: dark woods, green tea tones, bamboo

plants. This being Santa Monica, there's a health theme, represented through yoga classes and mini-bars packed with Chinese elixirs. The hotel is a little out of the way, but there's a complimentary shuttle service (in, of all things, a London black cab). *Business services. CD. Concierge. DVD. Gym. Internet (DSL & wireless). Room service.*

Channel Road Inn

219 W Channel Road, between PCH & Rustic Road, Santa Monica, CA 90422 (1-310 459 1920/fax 1-310 454 9920/www.channelroadinn.com). Bus 534, SM9/I-10, exit PCH north. **Rates** $195-$385 double. *Parking* free. **Credit** AmEx, MC, V. **Map** p310 A1 ⑨
Situated at the mouth of Santa Monica Canyon, this 14-room inn is a rustic little spot, complete with four-poster and sleigh beds. It's a block from the beach – getting there involves a tricky walk through a tunnel under the PCH – and is close to four beloved local restaurants, including the pricey celeb favourite Giorgio Baldi (*see p141*). Susan Zolla (who also owns the Inn at Playa del Rey; *see p50*) serves a hearty breakfast buffet of soufflés and scones. Book ahead for room six, with its own living room and jacuzzi. *Business services. CD. Concierge. Internet (wireless).*

Delfina

530 W Pico Boulevard, between 4th & 7th Streets, Santa Monica, CA 90405 (1-888 627 8532/1-310 399 9344/fax 1-310 399 2504/www.sheratonsanta monica.com). Bus 33, 333, SM1, SM7, SM10/I-10, exit 4th-5th Street south. **Rates** $259-$500 double; $359-$600 suite. *Parking* free. **Credit** AmEx, DC, Disc, MC, V. **Map** p310 B3 ⑩
Tucked away in a forgotten corner of Santa Monica, the Delfina has brought the lie to the old hotel-trade cliché about location, location, location. A recent $11

Delfina.

million renovation – by the Kor Hotel Group, which also owns the Viceroy, though the Delfina Hotel is branded as belonging to the Sheraton empire – has transformed a formerly moribund property into an attractive boutique-style hotel. However, even this careful redesign has been unable to escape the unmistakeable tang of corporate service. The rooms are calm, with blue accents providing a deliberate echo of the nearby ocean. The pool area is reminiscent of an upscale resort, complete with a Brazilian wood deck, elegant cabanas and tropical landscaping. *Bar. Business services. Gym. Internet (DSL in rooms, wireless in lobby). Pool (2).*

Georgian

1415 Ocean Avenue, at Santa Monica Boulevard, Santa Monica, CA 90401 (1-800 538 8147/1-310 395 9945/fax 1-310 451 3374/www.georgianhotel. com). Bus 4, 304, 534, SM1, SM7, SM8, SM10/ I-10, exit 4th-5th Street north. **Rates** *$235-$282 double; $300-$418 suite. Parking $21.* **Credit** AmEx, DC, Disc, MC, V. **Map** p310 A3 ⓫

The Georgian has a little more history than its Ocean Avenue neighbours: built when art deco was at its height, it wears its origins in pleasingly reserved fashion, tidily but not overdoing the schtick. Its most obvious link to the past is the stylish Speakeasy, underused as a breakfast room; it's certainly a more memorable space than the guestrooms, though that's not meant to demean their smartness, comfort and, in a number of cases, ocean views. Early-evening cocktails on the veranda are a doozy. *Bar. Business services. CD. Concierge. Gym. Restaurant. Internet (wireless). Room service.*

Hotel California

1670 Ocean Avenue, between Pico Boulevard & Colorado Avenue, Santa Monica, CA 90401 (1-866 571 0000/1-310 393 2363/fax 1-310 393 1063/www.hotelca.com). Bus 33, 333, SM1, SM7, SM10/I-10, exit 4th-5th Street north. **Rates** *$169-$189 double; $219-$279 suite. Parking £20.* **Credit** AmEx, Disc, MC, V. **Map** p310 A3 ⓬

It's immediately adjacent to the Loews, but this jaunty motel offers guests a very different type of Californian experience. Surfboards hanging from the wooden façade (and used as headboards) underline the location; surfers even get a 10% discount if they turn up with a board. However, the property is now under new management and plans are under way to revamp the 26 rooms, currently decorated with ceiling murals, hardwood floors and fridges. Like the song says, some guests never leave: there are nine long-stay apartments. *Internet (wireless).*

Shangri-La

1301 Ocean Avenue, at Arizona Avenue, Santa Monica, CA 90401 (1-800 345 7829/1-310 394 2791/fax 1-310 451 3351/www.shangrila-hotel.com). Bus 20, 534, 720, SM1, SM7, SM8, SM10/I-10, exit 4th-5th Street north. **Rates** *$170-$550 double; $215-$325 suite. Parking free.* **Credit** AmEx, DC, Disc, MC, V. **Map** p310 A2 ⓭

Located across from Palisades Park, just a few blocks from the Promenade and the beach, the Shangri-La prides itself on its spacious rooms and great ocean views. Built in the 1930s, the hotel's façade is an art deco glory; some of the fixtures and fittings in the guestrooms, renovated a few years ago, reflect this history. The property lacks a pool, a bar and a restaurant, but there is complimentary afternoon tea, continental breakfast and parking, the latter a real novelty in this corner of the city. *Internet (DSL).*

Budget

Bayside

2001 Ocean Avenue, at Bay Street, Santa Monica, CA 90405 (1-310 396 6000/fax 1-310 396 1000/ www.baysidehotel.com). Bus 33, 333, SM1, SM7, SM10/I-10, exit 4th-5th Street south. **Rates** *$79-$189 double.* **Credit** AmEx, DC, Disc, MC, V. **Map** p310 A3 ⓮

Across from the beach, the Bayside is something of a steal. The rooms are surprisingly comfortable: some have full kitchens, while others come with balconies and ocean views. The bathrooms, complete with original 1950s pink, green and blue tiles, are deliciously retro. There's air-con in the hotter, south-facing rooms; the rest rely on ceiling fans and sea breezes. *Business services. Internet (wireless).*

Hotel Carmel by the Sea

201 Broadway, at 2nd Street, Santa Monica, CA 90401 (1-800 445 8695/1-310 451 2469/fax 1-310 393 4180/www.hotelcarmel.com). Bus 4, 20, 304, 534, 720, SM1, SM7, SM8, SM10/I-10, exit 4th-5th street north. **Rates** *$79-$119 single; $109-$149 double; $189-$199 suite. Parking $10.* **Credit** AmEx, DC, Disc, MC, V. **Map** p310 A3 ⓯

The Carmel opened in 1929 and now looks its age. Still, that doesn't stop young visitors from packing the place, thanks to good rates and a prime location a block from the Promenade. The 102 rooms (16 with shared bathrooms) are clean but small and slightly gloomy; street-facing rooms can be noisy. But they're cheap, and the lively bar next door (Voda; *see p171*) will help take the edge off. *Internet (wireless).*

Venice

Moderate

Venice Beach House Historic Inn

15 30th Avenue, at Speedway Street, Venice, CA 90291 (1-310 823 1966/fax 1-310 823 1842/www. venicebeachhouse.com). Bus 108, C1/I-10, exit 4th-5th Street south. **Rates** *$130-$195 double. Parking free.* **Credit** AmEx, MC, V. **Map** p310 A6 ⓰

This landmark Craftsman-style inn, built in 1911, was the summer home of Venice Beach founder Abbot Kinney. Surrounded by a lush garden with cosy patio, the rustic bungalow is a sanctuary from the Venice circus, even though the beach is just at its back door. The nine rooms are named after famous guests; each comes with antiques and most have private bathrooms. A mobile day spa provides guests with a little pampering.

Business services. Internet (DSL). Room service.

Budget

Cadillac

8 Dudley Avenue, at Speedway Street & Ocean Front Walk, Venice, CA 90291 (1-310 399 8876/fax 1-310 399 4536/www.thecadillachotel.com). Bus 33, 333, C1, SM1, SM2/I-10, exit 4th-5th Street south. **Rates** $25 hostel bed; $89-$110 double; $130 suite. *Parking* free. **Credit** AmEx, MC, V. **Map** p310 A5 ⑰

This low-rise hotel, unmissable thanks to a pink and turquoise façade, sits in the thick of the Venice Beach freak show. However, things were a little calmer back in 1905, when it was built as Charlie Chaplin's summer home. Three hostel rooms each have two bunk beds and a shared bath; the 40 private rooms aren't overwhelmingly attractive, but you can't argue with the price. Common areas include a sun deck and a lounge with a pool table.

Gym. Internet (wireless).

Marina del Rey

Expensive

Ritz-Carlton Marina del Rey

4375 Admiralty Way, between Bali & Promenade Ways, Marina del Rey, CA 90292 (1-310 823 1700/ fax 1-310 823 2403/www.ritzcarlton.com). Bus 108/ Hwy 90, exit Mindanao Way west. **Rates** $279-$409 double; $379-$3,000. *Parking* $29. **Credit** AmEx, Disc, DC, MC, V.

Marina del Rey is hardly the most exciting part of LA: the neighbourhood's dining is mixed and the shopping is pretty unenticing. Stay here, however, and you might not want to set foot outside the front door. The Ritz-Carlton is already the most luxurious waterfront hotel in Los Angeles, but it's about to get even swankier: the property underwent a major $8-million renovation in 2006, and is soon to get a new spa. Savvy guests take advantage of the club level, where spectacular views of the Marina are combined with a complimentary private bar and five food presentations daily.

Bar. Business services. CD. Concierge. Internet (wireless). Pool. Restaurant. Room service. Spa.

Moderate

Inn at Playa del Rey

435 Culver Boulevard, at Pershing Drive, Playa del Rey, CA 90293 (1-310 574 1920/fax 1-310 574 9920/www.innatplayadelrey.com). Bus 220, 625/I-405, exit Culver Boulevard west. **Rates** $185-$285 double; $325-$385 suite. *Parking* free. **Credit** AmEx, MC, V.

Holed up in this Cape Cod-style beach cottage, you'd never guess you were just five minutes from LAX. Natural sunlight filters through the 21 rooms, each of which is decorated in a beachy theme and graced with fresh flowers; some have decks or fireplaces. A relaxing sun deck and jacuzzi almost make up for the lack of a pool. Playa del Rey's shops and surf are a breezy walk away, while the Ballona Wetlands, with 215 species of birds and hiking trails, is out the back door. A nice touch: the hotel rents out bicycles.

Business services. Concierge. Internet (wireless). Room service.

Brentwood to Beverly Hills

It's only fitting that Beverly Hills is home to some of the most luxurious hotels on the planet. Less expensive chains near UCLA and Century City push convenience over style.

UCLA & Westwood

Expensive

W

930 Hilgard Avenue, at Le Conte Avenue, Westwood, CA 90024 (reservations 1-800 421 2317/1-310 208 8765/fax 1-310 824 0355/www.whotels.com). Bus 2, 302, 305, 720, SM1, SM2, SM3, SM8, SM12/ I-405, exit Wilshire Boulevard east. **Rates** $289-$649 double. *Parking* $23. **Credit** AmEx, Disc, DC, MC, V.

Back in 2000, former set designer Dayna Lee turned the old Westwood Marquis into a hip, Starck-style haven with a dazzling white lobby. These days, the W chain is virtually ominpresent in American cities, but this branch, at least, is still both popular and fashionable. The rooms feature sleek furnishings, luxurious beds and down comforters; surrounded by two acres of lush garden, the pool area is a prime location on warm nights. Whiskey Blue, Rande Gerber's Polynesian hideaway, and the outdoor Backyard lounge fill with scenesters on weekends.

Bar (2). Business services. CD. Concierge. DVD. Gym. Internet (DSL). Pool. Restaurants (2). Room service. Spa.

Moderate

Angeleno

170 N Church Lane, at W Sunset Boulevard, Los Angeles, CA 90049 (reservations 1-866 264 3536/ 1-310 476 6411/fax 1-310 471 3667/www.hotel angeleno.com). Bus 2, 302, 761/I-405, exit Sunset Boulevard west. **Rates** $139-$309 double; $250-$349 suite. *Parking* $15. **Credit** AmEx, Disc, DC, MC, V.

In early 2006, the Hotel Angeleno became the first foray into the LA market by the Joie de Vivre chain, which runs no fewer than 18 boutique hotels in San

Hotel babylon

Few LA hotels have as much bacchanalian history attached to them as the **Continental Hyatt House** (now the Hyatt West Hollywood, 8401 Sunset Boulevard, 1-323 656 4101; *pictured*). In the 1960s and '70s, it was dubbed the 'Riot House': Keith Richards mooned onlookers from the window of room 1015, and Axl Rose held a barbecue on his balcony. But the prize for excess goes to Led Zeppelin: this is where Jimmy Page seduced groupies, where Robert Plant declared 'I am a golden God!' (a quote co-opted by Cameron Crowe for use in *Almost Famous*, parts of which were shot here), and where tour manager Richard Cole was once caught riding his Harley down the 12th-floor corridor.

But it's not all about riotous living: some LA hotels found their infamy through intimacy. At Bungalow 4 of the the legendary **Beverly Hills Hotel** (*see p51*), Clark Gable and Carole Lombard got it on while Gable was still married to Ria Langham. Goodness knows what went on in the Veranda Suite of the **Regent Beverly Wilshire** (*see p55*), but since it was home for several years to bachelor boy Warren Beatty, it's safe to say that it saw its share of star-on-starlet action.

Other hotels have grislier pasts. Singer Janis Joplin was found dead in room 105 of the **Landmark Hotel** (now the Highland Gardens; *see p61*) on 4 October 1970, having overdosed on heroin. And in the early hours of 5 March 1982, 33-year-old comedian John Belushi was found dead in Bungalow 3 of the **Chateau Marmont** (*see p57*) after mixing cocaine, heroin and alcohol in huge quantities.

Francisco. At 209 rooms, the Angeleno is probably a bit too big to really qualify as a boutique, but no matter: the building's landmark circular design carries with it a casual luxury that's exemplified in the penthouse-level restaurant and lounge. All the non-smoking rooms feature a private balcony with expansive views of the city. Be sure to take advantage of the complimentary wine reception each evening. For those concerned about good transport links, note that the hotel is located right by I-405.
Bar. Business services. CD. Gym. Internet (wireless). Pool. Restaurant. Room service. Spa.

Hilgard House
927 Hilgard Avenue, at Le Conte Avenue, Westwood, CA 90024 (1-800 826 3934/1-310 208 3945/ fax 1-310 208 1972/www.hilgardhouse.com). Bus 2, 302, 305, 720, SM1, SM2, SM3, SM8, SM12/I-405, exit Wilshire Boulevard east.
Rates $155 single; $160 double; $199-$320 suite. *Parking* free. **Credit** AmEx, DC, Disc, MC, V.
This European-style hotel offers one of the best deals in Westwood; the prices and its UCLA-friendly location make it popular with visiting academics. The three penthouse suites, each with full kitchen,

living room and dining area, are ideal for long-term guests. Don't expect amenities: there's no pool, gym, bar or restaurant. But the rates do include free continental breakfast and parking, the latter key in an area that desperately lacks decent parking facilities. *Business services. Internet (wireless). Room service.*

Where to Stay

Bel Air

Expensive

Hotel Bel-Air

701 Stone Canyon Road, at Bellagio Road, Bel Air, CA 90077 (1-800 648 4097/1-310 472 1211/ fax 1-310 476 5890/www.hotelbelair.com). I-405, exit Sunset Boulevard east. **Rates** $395-$600 double; $800-$3,700 suite. *Parking* $28. **Credit** AmEx, Disc, MC, V.

After the Sultan of Brunei bought the Beverly Hills Hotel (*see right*) in 1987, his brother decided he wanted a pink palace of his own. Five years later, he picked up this Mission-style '20s hotel in a wooded canyon; after a $16m facelift, it resumed service as a getaway for celebs and royalty. No two of the 91 guestrooms and recently renovated French-style bungalows are alike, but all carry with them the same worldly elegance. The grounds are a fairy tale, 12 acres of greenery dotted with fountains, flowers, mature redwood trees and even a small lake with its own swans. If you can't afford a room, come for high tea at the Terrace or treat yourself to a meal at Table One, located within reach of the chef's watchful eye. *Bar. Business services. CD. Concierge. Internet (DSL). Gym. Pool. Restaurant. Room service.*

Century City

Moderate

Hyatt Century Plaza Hotel & Spa

2025 Avenue of the Stars, Century City, CA 90067 (1-877 787 3452/1-310 277 2000/fax 1-310 277 3711/www.hyatt.com). Bus 4, 28, 316, 328, SM5/ I-405, exit Santa Monica Boulevard east. **Rates** $305 double; $455-$10,000 suites. *Parking* $29. **Credit** AmEx, Disc, DC, MC, V. **Map** p311 B4 ⑬

The Hyatt name implies something middlebrow, but don't be fooled: this 728-room property was a St Regis hotel until recently, and has retained a good deal of its former luxury. The building, like so many in Century City, is a pretty undistinguished tower; happily, the views from it, taking in everything from the Downtown skyline to the Pacific, are rather nicer than the views of it. Marble floors and warm colours make the lobby particularly inviting; especially the floor-to-ceiling glass walls, through which you can

> **Beverly Hills Hotel & Bungalows**
> Richard Gere takes his dates here in *American Gigolo*

see the lush gardens and serene pools. The rooms are handsome, if not especially dazzling. Amenities include Spa Mystique, the largest day spa in the city. *Bar. Business services. Concierge. Gym. Internet (DSL). Pool. Restaurant. Room service. Spa.*

Beverly Hills

Expensive

Beverly Hills Hotel & Bungalows

9641 Sunset Boulevard, at N Crescent Drive, Beverly Hills, CA 90210 (1-800 283 8885/1-310 276 2251/ fax 1-310 887 2887/www.thebeverlyhillshotel.com). Bus 2, 302/I-405, exit Sunset Boulevard east. **Rates** $410-$495 double; $900-$3,700 suite. *Parking* $28. **Credit** AmEx, DC, MC, V. **Map** p311 B2 ⑲

The fabled pink stucco façade, manicured grounds and sumptuous guestrooms of the Beverly Hills Hotel look as fresh and fanciful as they did on opening day over 90 years ago. The place oozes exclusivity: every screen legend from Valentino to Arnie has slept in this fabled hideaway or held court in its Polo Lounge. The biggest draw are the 21 bungalows, where Liz Taylor spent six of her honeymoons: No.5 has its own pool; No.7 is decorated to Marilyn's taste. The staff ratio here is three per guest, yet there's plenty of privacy. Frequent customers receive gold keys engraved with their names – and there are many. Take the time to hit backhands with the tennis pro (1959 Wimbledon champ Alex Olmedo) before hitting the spa. **Photo** *p53*. *Bar. Business services. Concierge. DVD. Gym. Internet (DSL). Pool. Restaurants (3). Room service. Spa.*

Four Seasons LA at Beverly Hills

300 S Doheny Drive, at Gregory Way, Beverly Hills, CA 90048 (1-800 332 3442/1-310 273 2222/fax 1-310 385 4927/www.fourseasons.com). Bus 20, 21, 28/I-10, exit Robertson Boulevard north. **Rates** $395-$515 double; $595-$5,100 suite. *Parking* $29. **Credit** AmEx, DC, MC, V. **Map** p311 D3 ⑳

The Four Seasons pampers its guests something silly. From the fragrant, flower-filled lobby to the immaculate rooms, every detail is calculated to spoil visitors. Lost bags? They'll whistle up an outfit from Saks. Fussy about pillows? Pick from body, neck and buckwheat varieties. Free cellphones and limos to Rodeo Drive are standard; on the rooftop terrace, cabanas come with a TV, a phone and a fully stocked refrigerator. The 285 high-tech rooms feature balconies, marble-topped desks and Frette linens. Fine dining is offered at Gardens, a highly regarded, highly priced restaurant serving Cal-Asian cuisine. *Bar. Business services. CD. Concierge. DVD. Gym. Internet (wireless). Pool. Restaurants (2). Room service.*

Luxe Hotel Rodeo Drive

360 N Rodeo Drive, between Brighton & Dayton Ways, Beverly Hills, CA 90210 (1-800 468 3541/ 1-310 273 0300/fax 1-310 859 8730/www.luxe hotels.com). Bus 4, 16, 20, 21, 304, 720/I-405, exit

Take to the **Beverly Hills Hotel & Bungalows**. *See p52.*

Wilshire Boulevard east. **Rates** $250-$359 double; $289-$1,400 suite. *Parking* $20. **Credit** AmEx, DC, Disc, MC, V. **Map** p311 C3 ㉑
The only Beverly Hills hotel with a Rodeo Drive address was redone by New York designer Vincente Wolf in 2002, and it's since become a magnet for film stars, fashionistas and shopaholics. The 88 rooms and suites blend the classic and the comfortable, utilising contemporary minimalist colours. If you need reminding where you are in the morning, most rooms face directly onto Gucci and Rem Koolhaas' Prada store, as much art installation as retail space. For those who need some respite from shopping on Rodeo, there's a sun deck and a gym. In addition, guests have free access to the tennis courts and spa at sister property Luxe Summit in Bel Air.
Bar. Business services. CD. Concierge. Gym. Internet (wireless). Restaurant. Room service.

Le Meridien at Beverly Hills

465 S La Cienega Boulevard, at Clifton Way, Beverly Hills, CA 90048 (1-800 543 4300/1-310 247 0400/ fax 1-310 247 0315/www.lemeridien.com). Bus 28, 105, 328/I-10, exit La Cienega Boulevard north. **Rates** $290-$549 double; $549-$1,800 suite. *Parking* $26. **Credit** AmEx, DC, Disc, MC, V. **Map** p312 B4 ㉒
Le Meridien hotels are generally favoured more by business travellers than vacationers, but this one boasts a location that's friendlier to those here on holiday: less than a mile north is the Beverly Center; just north-east are the shops of W 3rd Street, the

Farmers Market and the Grove, and a brisk walk east along Wilshire are the museums of the Miracle Mile. Recently renovated by French architect Pierre Yves Rochon, the guestrooms are plush and chic. Amenities include a business lounge, a 24-hour gym and a branch of famed steakhouse chain Morton's.
Bar. Business services. CD. Concierge. Gym. Internet (DSL). Pool. Restaurant. Room service.

Mosaic

125 S Spalding Drive, between Wilshire & Charleville Boulevards, Beverly Hills, CA 90212 (1-310 278 0303/fax 1-310 285 0896/www.mosaichotel.com). Bus 4, 16, 20, 21, 304, 720/I-405, exit Wilshire Boulevard north. **Rates** $350-$370 double; $600-$700 suite. *Parking* $25. **Credit** AmEx, DC, Disc, MC, V. **Map** p311 C3 ㉓
Following a 2003 facelift, the old Beverly Hills Inn is now chock-full of Botox babes, fashionistas and even the occasional celebrity. The intimate lobby bar and restaurant is popular for drinks at day's end, but also serves some well-regarded Asian fusion cooking. The 49 earth-toned rooms come complete with luxurious linens and Bose stereos with iPod connections. Summer 2006 will see the introduction of the Fab Four: four 2,500sq ft units with three bedrooms, three baths, a living room, a dining room and a family room with fireplace.
Bar. Business services. CD. Concierge. Gym. Internet (DSL in rooms, wireless in lobby). Pool. Restaurant. Room service.

THE ULTIMATE GUIDES TO LIVING IN LONDON

Peninsula Beverly Hills

*9882 Santa Monica Boulevard, between Wilshire
& Charleville Boulevards, Beverly Hills, CA 90212
(1-800 462 7899/1-310 551 2888/fax 1-310 788
2319/www.peninsula.com). Bus 4, 20, 21, 304,
720/I-405, exit Santa Monica Boulevard east.* **Rates**
$475-$625 double; $1,000-$3,500 suites. *Parking* $28.
Credit AmEx, DC, Disc, MC, V. **Map** p311 C3 ㉔
This French Renaissance palace, possibly LA's most
luxurious hotel, attracts a stream of celebrities and
professional athletes with white glove service and
award-winning cuisine. Rooms and villas include
antiques, marble baths and 24-hour personal valets,
plus a complimentary chauffered Rolls-Royce anywhere in Beverly Hills. Other highlights include the
Belvedere restaurant, the mahogany-lined Club Bar,
and the elegant Living Room, which serves the
area's best high tea. The spa recently reopened after
a $7m refit; the magnificent pool area and the Roof
Garden restaurant underwent renovations in 2006,
and will soon feature barbecues at the weekend.
*Bar. Business services. Concierge. Gym. Internet (DSL
& wireless). Pool. Restaurants (2). Room service.*

Raffles L'Ermitage Beverly Hills

*9291 Burton Way, at N Foothill Road, Beverly Hills,
CA 90210 (1-800 1-800 2113/1-310 278 3344/fax
1-310 278 8247/www.lermitagehotel.com). Bus 4,
16, 304/I-405, exit Wilshire Boulevard east.* **Rates**
$468-$548 double; $950-$5,000 suite. *Parking* $24.
Credit AmEx, DC, Disc, MC, V. **Map** p311 D2 ㉕
Hollywood bigwigs and fashionistas adore the sleek
L'Ermitage for its discreet staff, business perks and
gigantic guestrooms. The 124 Asian-influenced
rooms double as offices, but some executives like to
utilise the Writer's Bar and the Living Room to con-
duct informal meetings. The absence of housekeep-
ing carts (all items are carried by hand) is a nice
touch; nicer still are the high-tech rooftop poolside
cabanas with 360-degrees views of the city.
*Bar. Business services. CD. Concierge. DVD. Gym.
Internet (wireless). Pool. Restaurant. Room service. Spa.*

Regent Beverly Wilshire

*9500 Wilshire Boulevard, between S Rodeo & S El
Camino Drives, Beverly Hills, CA 90212 (1-800
427 4354/1-310 275 5200/fax 1-310 274 2851/
www.regenthotels.com). Bus 20, 21, 720/I-405, exit
Wilshire Boulevard east.* **Rates** $435-$900 double;
$625-$7,500 suite. *Parking* $31. **Credit** AmEx, DC,
Disc, MC, V. **Map** p311 D3 ㉖
This large 1928 hotel comprises two distinct envi-
ronments: the classic and historic Wilshire Wing,
on 10 floors, and the elegant, 14-floor Beverly Wing,
which overlooks Rodeo Drive. The hotel's location
makes it a major draw for the rich and the important,
though the old-world opulence – vaulted ceilings,
columns, oak panelling, pink marble floors – surely
helps. The hotel's new restaurant, a collaboration
between Wolfgang Puck and architect Richard
Meier, is due for completion in summer 2006.
*Bar. Business services. Concierge. Gym. Internet
(DSL in rooms, wireless in lobby). Pool. Restaurants
(2). Room service.*

Hostels

Like a lot of LA's bargain accommodation,
hostels here fill up well in advance;
when planning a visit, book as early as
you can. For more local hostels, see
www.hostels.com/en/us.ca.la.html.

Banana Bungalow Hollywood

*7950 Melrose Avenue, at N Hayworth
Avenue, West Hollywood, CA 90046
(reservations 1-800 446 7835/front
desk 1-323 655 1510/www.banana
bungalow.com). Bus 217, 218, LDF/
I-10, exit La Cienega Boulevard north.*
Rates $20-$22 dorm bed; $69-$100
private room. *Parking* free. **Credit** MC, V.
Map p312 C2.
This popular hostel is done out in
something of a retro style: all 32 rooms
are done up in funky colours, and the
lounge has been designed on a space-
age tip. The dormitories have six beds
per room with closets and baths or
showers; the private rooms have queen
beds, some come with two bunk beds too,
and balconies. There's a courtyard with
free Sunday barbecues, a movie lounge,
a café serving meals for around $5 and a
streetside patio to watch the world go by.
One word of warning: what with the garish
colours and the excruciating music, this
hotel has what might be the ugliest
website in California.

HI Santa Monica

*1436 2nd Street, at Santa Monica
Boulevard, Santa Monica, CA 90401
(reservations 1-888 464 4872 x137/
front desk 1-310 393 9913/www.hilos
angeles.org). Bus 4, 304, SM1, SM7,
SM8, SM10/I-10, exit 4th-5th Street
north.* **Rates** $26-$32 dorm bed; $78
double. **Credit** MC, V. **Map** p310 A3.
Book far in advance for this four-floor,
260-bed Santa Monica hostel: the
great location ensures that the demand
is always high. Following a $2-million
renovation the rooms more than cover
the basics: the dorms sleep between
four and ten while the private rooms come
with mirrors and dressers. The place is
spotless, though you might want to bring
flip-flops to wear in the shower (all the
bathrooms are shared). There's a café
open for breakfast, internet access,
video games, TV and movie rooms.

Moderate

Avalon

*9400 W Olympic Boulevard, at S Canon Drive,
Beverly Hills, CA 90212 (1-800 535 4715/1-310
277 5221/fax 1-310 277 4928/www.avalonbeverly
hills.com). Bus 28/I-10, exit Robertson Boulevard
north.* **Rates** *$259-$289 double; $359-$389 suite.*
Parking $26. **Credit** AmEx, DC, Disc, MC, V.
Map p311 D4 ②
The city's first and arguably still its best boutique
hotel, the former Beverly Carlton is, with the Viceroy
and Maison 140, part of a group of hotels set up by
Brad Korzen and designed by his wife, Kelly
Wearstler. The Avalon is a low-key, stylish remodel
of a mid-century building: through the lobby, hidden
behind a fabulous boomerang façade, is a kidney-
shaped pool and a kinetic bar-restaurant scene (*see
p172*). The 88 rooms are tastefully appointed with
vintage furnishings such as Eames cabinets and
Nelson bubble lamps. Pleasingly unflashy.
*Bar. Business services. CD. Concierge. Gym. Internet
(DSL in rooms, wireless in lobby). Pool. Restaurant.
Room service.*

Crescent

*403 N Crescent Drive, at Brighton Way, Beverly
Hills, CA 90210 (1-310 247 0505/fax 1-310 247
9053/www.crescentbh.com). Bus 4, 16, 304/I-405,
exit Santa Monica Boulevard east.* **Rates** *$175-$235
double. Parking $22.* **Credit** AmEx, DC, Disc, MC, V.
Map p311 D2 ②

This Beverly Hills boutique has gained a hip following since LA designer du jour Dodd Mitchell
reworked the old 1926 building in 2003. It's best
known for Boe: a casual spot for lunch, it thrives at
night, drinkers spilling out on to the deck as they
make the scene with a cocktail or a glass of wine.
The rooms aren't huge, but they are comfortable,
stocked with Italian linens, plush robes and flat-
screen TVs. Although there's no gym, guests can
book in-room massage and spa services. Building-
wide wireless access is another perk.
*Bar. Business services. CD. Concierge. DVD. Gym.
Internet (wireless). Pool. Restaurant. Room service.*

Loews Beverly Hills

*1224 S Beverwil Drive, at W Pico Boulevard, Los
Angeles, CA 90035 (1-800 235 6397/1-310 277
2800/fax 1-310 203 9537/www.loewshotels.com).
Bus SM5, SM7/I-10, exit National Boulevard,
Overland Ave.* **Rates** *$199-$299 double; $359-$429
suite. Parking $24.* **Credit** AmEx, DC, Disc, MC, V.
Map p311 D4 ②
Loews took over this property in 2003, and immediately set about attracting a younger crowd. Its 12-
storey figure stands tall in an area short on
skyscrapers, which means that its exterior is something of a blot on the landscape, but the comfortable,
inviting guestrooms come with both balconies and
excellent views of LA. There's a small-ish pool outside at ground level, and American dining in Lot 1224.
*Bar. Business services. CD. Concierge. Gym. Internet
(DSL). Pool. Restaurant. Room service.*

Worth appeasing: **Chamberlain West Hollywood.** *See p58.*

Maison 140

140 S Lasky Drive, at Charleville Boulevard, Beverly Hills, CA 90212 (1-800 432 5444/1-310 281 4000/ fax 1-310 281 4101/www.maison140beverlyhills. com). Bus 4, 16, 20, 21, 304, 720/I-405, exit Santa Monica Boulevard east. **Rates** *$199-$269 double. Parking $19.* **Credit** *AmEx, DC, Disc, MC, V.* **Map** *p311 C3* ③⓪

From the folks who brought you the terminally hip Avalon and Viceroy comes Maison 140, where the small, stylish rooms prove that form is more important than function. The decor, a chic return to 18th-century Paris with a few contemporary Asian twists, is every bit as glamorous as you'd expect from a building that was once owned by Lilian Gish. Rooms come equipped with spa treatments, flat-screen TVs and high-speed internet. There's free continental breakfast at the nearby lobby bar; guests receive pool privileges at the nearby Avalon (*see p56*).
Bar. Business services. CD. Concierge. DVD. Gym. Internet (DSL). Room service.

Budget

Beverly Terrace

469 N Doheny Drive, at Santa Monica Boulevard, Beverly Hills, CA 90210 (1-800 842 6401/1-310 274 8141/fax 1-310 385 1998/www.beverlyterracehotel. com). Bus 4, 304/I-10, exit Robertson Boulevard north. **Rates** *$115-$155 double; $209 suite. Parking free.* **Credit** *AmEx, DC, Disc, MC, V.* **Map** *p311 D2* ③①

Formerly a rather shabby little motel, the Beverly Terrace hotel now carries with it a casual, contemporary Asian theme, more demonstrably executed in some rooms than others. Some rooms have balconies, kitchens or views of the palm-fringed courtyard pool; all come with en suite bathrooms. Free continental breakfasts are served at the restaurant next door, Trattoria Amici. Good value, all in all, especially given the location.
Internet (wireless). Pool.

West Hollywood, Hollywood & Midtown

Always-trendy West Hollywood and once-grim Hollywood are teeming with stylish hotels, many at fair prices.

West Hollywood

Expensive

Chateau Marmont

8221 Sunset Boulevard, between N Harper Avenue & Havenhurst Drive, Hollywood, CA 90046 (1-800 242 8328/1-323 656 1010/fax 1-323 655 5311/

www.chateaumarmont.com). Bus 2, 302, LDHWH/ I-10, exit La Cienega Boulevard north. **Rates** *$335-$425 double; $1,700-$3,000 suite. Parking $25.* **Credit** *AmEx, DC, MC, V.* **Map** *p312 B1* ③②

This legendary 1929 hotel has always had a reputation for bad behaviour. Howard Hughes rented the penthouse to spy on starlets at the pool, and a steady stream of rock stars used to trash the place. But despite the notoriety, it's survived: after all, it was built as an earthquake-proof imitation of the Loire Valley's Château Amboise. In 1990, celebrity hotelier Andre Balazs restored it; today, it's a paparazzi-free zone for regulars such as Colin Farrell and Val Kilmer, who hang in the plush lobby lounge, lush gardens and the guest-only outdoor dining patio. The fabled Bar Marmont is undergoing a refit.
Business services. CD. Concierge. DVD. Gym. Internet (wireless). Pool. Restaurant. Room service.

Mondrian

8440 W Sunset Boulevard, at N Olive Drive, West Hollywood, CA 90069 (1-800 525 8029/1-323 650 8999/fax 1-323 650 5215/www.mondrianhotels. com). Bus 2, 302, LDHWH/I-10, exit La Cienega Boulevard north. **Rates** *$279-$425 double; $285-$445 suite. Parking $23.* **Credit** *AmEx, DC, Disc, MC, V.* **Map** *p312 B1* ③③

Celebs, models and wannabes still keep the attitude alive at invite-only SkyBar on weekends (*see p173*) and swanky Asia de Cuba restaurant, but this old Ian Schrager-Philippe Starck property is no longer the seven-day whirligig it was in the late 1990s. It should hardly need saying at this point, but Starck's decor won't be to everyone's taste, from the glowing glass walls of the lobby to the luxurious blinding whites of the guestrooms themselves (which can be noisy if you get a room facing Sunset Boulevard). The Agua Spa is a good way to work out the stress from the previous night's rumble on the strip.
Bar. Business services. Concierge. DVD. Gym. Pool. Restaurants (2). Spa. Room service.

Sunset Marquis Hotel & Villas

1200 N Alta Loma Road, between W Sunset Boulevard & Holloway Drive, West Hollywood, CA 90069 (1-800 858 9758/1-310 657 1333/fax 1-310 652 5300/www.sunsetmarquishotel.com). Bus 2, 302/I-10, exit La Cienega Boulevard north. **Rates** *$340-$500 suite; $600-$2,000 villa. Parking $23.* **Credit** *AmEx, DC, Disc, MC, V.* **Map** *p312 B1* ③④

The Sunset has been a hideaway for rock stars since 1963; indeed, it's Los Angeles' only hotel with a recording studio (David Arnold recorded the soundtrack to the remake of *Ocean's Eleven* here). The rooms are large and comfortable; suites feature kitchens and balconies, most overlooking the heated pool. Twelve villas, which come with their own private butler, surround a smaller pool complete with private cabanas. A $14m expansion project will add six new villas by spring 2007. Amenities include a small gym kitted out to the exact specifications of, of all people, Keith Richards.
Bar. Business services. CD. Concierge. Gym. Internet (wireless). Pools (2). Restaurants (2). Room service.

Orlando Hotel. *See p59.*

Moderate

Chamberlain West Hollywood

1000 Westmount Drive, at W Knoll Drive, West Hollywood, CA 90069 (1-800 201 9652/1-310 657 7400/fax 1-310 854 6744/www.chamberlainwest hollywood.com). Bus 2, 302/I-10, exit La Cienega Boulevard north. **Rates** $159-$349 double; $279-$539 suite. *Parking* $24. **Credit** AmEx, DC, Disc, MC, V. **Map** p312 B2 ③⑤

Another branch of the Kor Group, which also owns the Viceroy, Maison 140 and Avalon, this chic hotel has made quite a name for itself since opening in 2005. Its location on a tree-lined residential street lends it a casual, homey air; it continues inside the guestrooms, which come with comfortable couches and fireplaces. Settle down to work at one of the large in-room desks, or relax in the top-floor pool and the surrounding cabanas. The eponymous modern American bistro offers nice views of the lush garden patio. **Photo** *p56.* *Bar. Business services. CD. Concierge. DVD. Gym. Internet (DSL). Pool. Restaurant. Room service.*

Élan

8435 Beverly Boulevard, at N Croft Avenue, Los Angeles, CA 90048 (1-888 611 0398/1-323 658 6663/fax 1-323 658 6640/www.elanhotel.com). Bus 14, 16, 105, 316, LDF, LDHWH/I-10, exit La Cienega Boulevard north. **Rates** $139-$160 double; $195-$225 suite. *Parking* $14.50. **Credit** AmEx, DC, Disc, MC, V. **Map** p312 B3 ③⑥

The simplicity of the Élan's unabashedly modernist architecture, especially its concrete and plate glass façade, continues inside the 50-room hotel: the lobby is restrained and the guestrooms, done out in muted shades, are almost entirely free of clutter. The overall effect is Zen *Jetsons*; we mean that as a compliment. Unusually, there's no pool, restaurant or bar, but there is a complimentary wine reception on weekdays and a continental breakfast. *Business services. Concierge. Gym. Internet (wireless). Room service.*

Grafton on Sunset

8462 W Sunset Boulevard, between N Olive Drive & N La Cienega Boulevard, West Hollywood, CA 90069 (1-800 821 3660/1-323 654 4600/fax 1-323 654 5918/www.graftononsunset.com). Bus 2, 302, LDHWH/I-10, exit La Cienega Boulevard north. **Rates** $169-$349 double; $200-$450 suite. *Parking* $24. **Credit** AmEx, DC, Disc, MC, V. **Map** p312 B1 ③⑦

Formerly a speakeasy and then a transvestite hotel, the Grafton was given a huge makeover prior to reopening in 2000. It's now sleek and chic, but its four suites pay homage to Hollywood troublemakers of yore: the Rat Pack is – or attempts to be – a swingin' bachelor pad, while the Jane is dressed with come-hither satin sheets. Other rooms are decorated to attract the funseeking hipsters who are the hotel's real target audience. Funky services include free psychic readings and a shuttle to clubs and shops. *Bar. Business services. CD. Concierge. Gym. Internet (wireless). Pool. Restaurant. Room service.*

Le Montrose Suite Hotel

900 Hammond Street, at Cynthia Street, West Hollywood, CA 90069 (1-800 776 0666/1-310 855 1115/fax 1-310 657 9192/www.lemontrose.com). Bus 2, 105, 302/I-405, exit Santa Monica Boulevard east. **Rates** *$225-$375 suite. Parking $20.* **Credit** AmEx, DC, Disc, MC, V. **Map** p312 A2 ㉘

Le Montrose Suite is a residential-style hotel that offers those eponymous suites at decent prices. They're huge, too. The split-level rooms feature gas fireplaces, plush, European-style decor and serious art; larger suites, which come complete with kitchenettes, are good for families. There's a rooftop tennis court and saltwater pool surrounded by cabanas, and a guests-only restaurant, Privato. A sister property sits close by (1-310 855 8888).
Bar. Business services. CD. Concierge. DVD. Gym. Internet (wireless). Pool. Restaurant. Room service.

Orlando Hotel

8384 W 3rd Street, at Orlando Avenue, CA 90048 (1-800 624 6835/1-323 658 6600/fax 1-323 653 3464/www.theorlando.com). Bus 16/I-10, exit La Cienega Boulevard north. **Rates** *$209-$299 double. Parking $20.50.* **Credit** AmEx, DC, Disc, MC, V. **Map** p312 B3 ㉚

Converted and reopened in 2005, the Orlando is a European-style boutique hotel that is steps away from the terrific independent shops and cafés of W 3rd Street. The $4m renovation brought a tasteful design and cultured amenities to the property, including iPod speaker systems and wonderfully comfortable beds. The hotel's alliance with Ted Baker London has produced handsome uniforms for everyone from the front desk staff to the valet parking attendants. The property also boasts a sparkling saltwater rooftop pool and a high-quality restaurant, Gino Angelini's La Terza. **Photo** *p58.*
Bar. Business services. CD. Concierge. Internet (DSL & wireless). Pool. Restaurant. Room service.

Sofitel Los Angeles

8555 Beverly Boulevard, at N La Cienega Boulevard, West Hollywood, CA 90069 (1-800 521 7772/1-310 278 5444/fax 1-310 657 2816/www.sofitel.com). Bus 14, 16, 105, 316, LDF, LDHWH/I-10, exit La Cienega Boulevard north. **Rates** *$275-$325 double; $1,050 suite. Parking $18.* **Credit** AmEx, DC, Disc, MC, V. **Map** p312 B3 ㉚

A $35m makeover has this Beverly Boulevard hotel has turned the LA edition of the Sofitel chain into a real player on the local scene. Where did the money go? For starters, a Rande Gerber bar/lounge and a Kerry Simon restaurant; for a main course, 32-inch plasma-screen TVs in the 295 guestrooms; and to finish, the largest fitness facility in LA, open 24 hours and with a staff that includes the trainer who whipped Jennifer Lopez into shape. The decor combines cream, cinnabar and chartreuse lacquers with blonde and chocolate velvet upholstery, which isn't as bad as it sounds. The lobby and new spa continue the French theme elsewhere.
Bar. Business services. Concierge. Gym. Internet (wireless). Pool. Restaurant. Room service.

Standard Hollywood

8300 W Sunset Boulevard, at N Sweetzer Avenue, West Hollywood, CA 90069 (1-323 650 9090/fax 1-323 650 2820/www.standardhotel.com). Bus 2, 302, LDHWH/I-10, exit La Cienega Boulevard north. **Rates** *$150-$225 double; $450 suite. Parking $18.* **Credit** AmEx, DC, Disc, MC, V. **Map** p312 B1 ㊶

In 1998, at the height of *Austin Powers* mania, the Standard was converted from a '60s retirement home to a tongue-in-chic shag pad, and still draws ironic hipsters with its Jetsonian decor. The International Man of Mystery would feel at home among the cottage cheese ceilings and groovy lobby carpeting. The bright bedrooms come with minibars peddling condoms; the bathrooms, meanwhile, are a blinding acid orange. The place is so hip, in fact, that it sells its own-label CDs, so guests can take a little piece of stylish LA living home with them. One day the schtick will grow old, but for now the Standard still cracks a smile. For the Standard Downtown, *see p62.*
Bars (2). Business services. CD. Concierge. Internet (DSL). Pool. Restaurant. Room service.

Sunset Tower

8358 Sunset Boulevard, at N Sweetzer Avenue, West Hollywood, CA 90069 (1-800 225 2637/1-323 654 7100/fax 1-323 654 9287/www.sunsettowerhotel. com). Bus 2, 302, LDHWH/I-10, exit La Cienega Boulevard north. **Rates** *$245 double; $295-$345 suite. Parking $22.* **Credit** AmEx, DC, Disc, MC, V. **Map** p312 B1 ㊷

This building was in pretty good shape a few years ago, when it was known as the Argyle. Since then the new owners have chucked money at the place, trying to create the woodsy, cigar room feeling that accompanied the watering holes of Old Hollywood. They've spent an eight-figure sum on renovating the interior, restoring the gorgeous art deco façade and restoring the building's original name (it was built as an apartment block in 1931). The spacious rooms have been completely updated, with floor-to-ceiling windows, flatscreen TVs and wireless access throughout; the Tower bar and restaurant is just as chic. Book ahead for a treatment at the two-storey Argyle Salon & Spa. **Photo** *p61.*
Bar. Business services. Concierge. Gym. Internet (wireless). Pool. Restaurant. Room service. Spa.

Budget

Ramada West Hollywood

8585 Santa Monica Boulevard, between N La Cienega Boulevard & Rugby Drive, West Hollywood, CA 90069 (1-800 845 8585/1-310 652 6400/fax 1-310 652 2135/www.ramadaweho.com). Bus 4, 105, 304, LDHWH/I-10, exit La Cienega Boulevard north. **Rates** *$129-$199 double; $249-$400 suite. Parking $25.* **Credit** AmEx, DC, Disc, MC, V. **Map** p312 B2 ㊸

The Ramada's biggest draw is its prime location in the heart of Boystown. Formerly the Tropicana, the 175-room spot is popular with scene queens who want ringside seats for the nightlife along Santa Monica Boulevard (book early for a street-facing

room with balcony). Some suites come with refrigerator, minibar and microwave; two huge corner rooms have dramatic spiral staircases and giant beds.
Bar. Business services. Concierge. Gym. Internet (wireless). Pool. Restaurant. Room service.

Secret Garden B&B

8039 Selma Avenue, at Laurel Canyon Boulevard, West Hollywood, CA 90046 (1-877 732 4736/1-323 656 8111/fax 1-323 656 3888/www.secretgarden bnb.com). Bus 2, 218, 302, LDHWH/I-10, exit Fairfax Avenue north. **Rates** $125-$140 double; $165 cottage. *Parking* free. **Credit** AmEx, MC, V. **Map** p312 C1 ④
LA's best B&B is located a block from the Sunset Strip's hurly-burly, but inside, the pink, Spanish-style inn is pure serenity. Run by Raymond Bilbool, former maître d' of Chasen's restaurant, the hotel offers five individually decorated rooms and a fairy-tale garden setting. Only two rooms are en suite, but robes are provided for journeys down the hall. The guest cottage – with sleigh bed and jacuzzi bathtub – is very private. Bilbool serves up gourmet breakfasts, spiced up with gossip about Chasen's glory days. The cottage rate is negotiable.
Internet (wireless in lobby).

Hollywood

Moderate

Hotel Bamboo

2528 Dearborn Drive, at Winans Drive, Los Angeles, CA 90068 (1-323 962 0233/www.hotelbamboo.com). US 101, exit Cahuenga Boulevard north. **Rates** $275-$475 double. *Parking* free. **Credit** AmEx, MC, V.
Since it opened in 2003, this Hollywood Hills hideaway has become a word-of-mouth hit with showbiz insiders. As the name implies, the hotel is decorated in an Asian style, complete with Shoji screens, koi ponds and Japanese gardens. The five rooms have fireplaces, balconies and patios, plus swish granite bathrooms. There's no restaurant or room service, but there is a pool. The hotel's size means booking ahead is imperative.
CD. DVD. Internet (wireless). Room service.

Magic Castle

7025 Franklin Avenue, between N Sycamore Avenue & N Orange Drive, Hollywood, CA 90028 (1-800 741 4915/1-323 851 0800/fax 1-323 851 4926/ www.magiccastlehotel.com). Metro Hollywood-Highland/bus 212, 217, LDHWH/US 101, exit Highland Avenue south. **Rates** $179-$329 double. *Parking* free. **Credit** AmEx, Disc, DC, MC, V. **Map** p313 A1 ④
It was only a matter of time before this apartment-style hotel in the Hollywood foothills, once a fave among struggling actors and screenwriters, became a trendy boutique. All the spacious rooms have been redone in an Old Hollywood style, complete with smart bathrooms and luxury linens. With the exception of the singles, all rooms come with a full kitchen; most have balconies overlooking the pool. If you're looking for a room with a view, try the Hollywood Hills Hotel, the Magic Castle's sister property up the street (same website and reservations number). Although not nearly so nice, the 40 rooms have huge balconies and accompanying views over the city. Both properties are within walking distance of Hollywood Boulevard; guests receive entry to the Magic Castle, a private magician's club.
Business services. CD. Concierge. DVD. Internet (wireless). Pool.

Renaissance Hollywood

1755 N Highland Avenue, at Yucca Street, Los Angeles, CA 90028 (1-800 468 3571/1-323 856 1200/fax 1-323 856 1205/www.renaissance hollywood.com). Metro Hollywood-Highland/bus 210, 212, 217, 710/US 101, exit Highland south. **Rates** $149-$229 double; $219-$5,000 suite. *Parking* $12. **Credit** AmEx, DC, MC, V. **Map** p313 A1 ④
This stylish property, part of the massive Hollywood & Highland entertainment complex, is the first Marriott to make the cover of *Architectural Digest*. No wonder: its designers took the 'no brass, marble or beige' mandate to heart. The atrium lobby is a showy array of primary colours and retro furnishings, including Eames chairs, Noguchi tables and Miró-esque carpets; a grand staircase leads to the Hollywood and Highland mall. Upstairs, the large rooms are done up in snazzy 1950s-style decor; most have jaw-dropping views of the Hollywood sign. The rooftop pool recently received a $1m makeover, complete with cabanas and a bar.
Bar. Business services. Concierge. Gym. Internet (DSL). Pool. Restaurant. Room service.

Roosevelt

7000 Hollywood Boulevard, at N Orange Drive, Los Angeles, CA 90028 (1-800 950 7667/1-323 466 7000/fax 1-323 462 8056/www.hollywood roosevelt.com). Metro Hollywood-Highland/bus 210, 212, 217, 710, LDHWH/US 101, exit Highland Avenue south. **Rates** $179-$400 double; $279-$2,000 suite. *Parking* $23. **Credit** AmEx, DC, Disc MC, V. **Map** p313 A1 ④
After a lavish restoration by designer Dodd Mitchell in 2003, this 1927 landmark, a beautiful example of Spanish colonial design, is back where it belongs: firmly at the upper reaches of the A-list. The large rooms are now in beautiful shape, decorated in restrained colours with decent amenities and the occasional subtly placed nod to the starry Hollywood location. Downstairs, settle in for a drink at the Library bar or head to the esteemed Dakota steakhouse for dinner (*see p150*), but don't bank on

Roosevelt (p60) Masquerading as the Tropicana Motel, it's one of the places at which Leonardo DiCaprio narrowly avoids Tom Hanks in Steven Spielberg's *Catch Me if You Can*

Old Hollywood meets 21st century swank at the **Sunset Tower**. *See p59.*

being able to get into the Tropicana poolside lounge: it's so preposterously exclusive that even hotel residents aren't guaranteed entry. Still, a good Hollywood option regardless.
Bars (2). Business services. CD. Concierge. Gym. Internet (wireless). Pool. Restaurants (2). Room service.

Budget

Best Western Hollywood Hills
6141 Franklin Avenue, between N Gower Street & Vista del Mar Avenue, Hollywood, CA 90028 (1-800 287 1700/1-323 464 5181/fax 1-323 962 0536/ www.bestwestern.com). Metro Hollywood-Vine/bus 26, 180, 181, LDH/US 101, exit Gower Street south. **Rates** $109-$159 double. *Parking* free. **Credit** AmEx, DC, MC, V. **Map** p313 B1 ⓭
Ideally located just off US 101, this branch of the Best Western chain is a mere stroll from the bustling nightlife around Hollywood and Vine. The lobby walls are covered with murals and posters of movie stars; the guestrooms also provide decorative links to the movie world. Rooms come with refrigerators and microwaves, but you can also grab a midnight snack at the 101 Café, open until 3am. Rooms overlooking the pool are the quietest.
Internet (wireless). Pool. Restaurant.

Highland Gardens
7047 Franklin Avenue, at N Sycamore Avenue, Los Angeles, CA 90028 (1-800 404 5472/1-323 850 0536/fax 1-323 850 1712/www.highlandgardens hotel.com). Metro Hollywood-Highland/bus 212, 217,

LDHWH/US 101, exit Highland Avenue south. **Rates** $89-$99 double; $109-$119 suite. *Parking* free. **Credit** AmEx, MC, V. **Map** p313 A1 ⓰
The decor at the former Landmark Hotel may be unremarkable, but Hollywood's Walk of Fame is just outside, and within the hotel's boundaries, the lush gardens and teardrop pool provide respite from tourist madness seething just beyond the walls. It's a good place for a family, too: there are large two- and three-bedroom suites with kitchenettes, and ping-pong tables in the lobby.
Internet (wireless). Pool.

Fairfax District

Budget

Beverly Laurel Motor Hotel
8018 Beverly Boulevard, between S Laurel & S Edinburgh Avenues, Los Angeles, CA 90048 (1-800 962 3824/1-323 651 2441/fax 1-323 651 5225). Bus 14, 217, 218, LDF/I-10, exit La Cienega Boulevard north. **Rates** $98 double. *Parking* free. **Credit** AmEx, DC, MC, V. **Map** p312 C3 ⓾
This 1950s-era motel is one of the best buys on Beverly, its location making it popular with young movers and shakers. The rooms are funky, with black vinyl chairs and groovy '50s tables. Some have kitchens; all have microwaves and fridges. Potted plants spruce up the tiny pool area. The motel's coffee shop, Swingers, serves a mean meatloaf.
Internet (wireless). Pool. Restaurant.

Farmer's Daughter

*115 S Fairfax Avenue, at W 1st Street, Los Angeles,
CA 90036 (1-800 334 1658/1-323 937 3930/fax
1-323 932 1608/http://farmersdaughterhotel.com).
Bus 217, 218, LDF/I-10, exit Fairfax Avenue north.*
Rates $139-$159 single; $109-$169 double. $169
suite. *Parking* $12. **Credit** AmEx, MC, V.
Map p312 C3 ⑤①

You can tell simply by the shape of its buildings that
this place was once a pretty basic motel. It's a great
credit to the new owners of the gingham-giddy
Farmer's Daughter that in all other regards, it feels
fresh and new. The rooms have been duded up in
blue and yellow checks and denim bedspreads; farm
and barnyard humour abounds, with alarm clocks
that cry 'cock-a-doodle-doo'. Other amenities include
a DVD library at the front desk, a cosy little pool
and, as of 2006, Tart, a restaurant serving French-
influenced cuisine. Add in the great location and you
have one of the city's best bargains.
CD. DVD. Internet (DSL & wireless). Pool. Restaurant.

Downtown

Moderate

Millennium Biltmore

*506 S Grand Avenue, at W 5th Street, Los Angeles,
CA 90071 (1-800 245 8673/1-213 624 1011/
fax 1-213 612 1545/www.thebiltmore.com).
Metro Pershing Square/bus 14, 37, 76, 78, 79, 96/
I-110, exit 6th Street east.* **Rates** $189-$259 double;
$379-$2,000 suite. *Parking* $24. **Credit** AmEx,DC,
Disc, MC, V. **Map** p315 B3 ⑤②

Built in 1923, the Biltmore is the oldest hotel in
Downtown, and still maintains the Italian-Spanish
renaissance elegance that enticed such dignitaries
as Winston Churchill and JFK. The ground level is
striking, one gorgeous room after another peeling
off the exquisite lobby; a number of them, such as
the Crystal Ballroom and the Gold Room, are available only for private hire, but ask nicely at reception
and, if there's no event in there, someone'll show you
around. Next to such extravagance, the rooms themselves can hardly compete, but they're comfortable.
Downstairs is a handsome Roman-style pool.
*Bars (3). Business services. Concierge. Gym. Internet
(DSL & wireless). Pool (indoor). Restaurants (2).
Room service.*

Inn at 657

*657 W 23rd Street, at S Figueroa Street, Los
Angeles, CA 90007 (1-800 347 7512/1-213 741
2200/www.patsysinn657.com). Bus 81, 381/I-110,
exit Adams Boulevard west.* **Rates** $120-$135 double.
Parking free. **Credit** MC, V.

Millennium Biltmore (above)
The *Ghostbusters* catch their
first spook in the ballroom

This 11-room charmer is one of LA's best B&Bs.
Situated close to the University of California, it's
popular with visiting scholars. Rooms are elegantly
decorated in different period styles, with down comforters and a few needlepoint rugs. Teacher-
turned-lawyer-turned-innkeeper Patsy Carter serves
up a hearty breakfast in the intimate dining room or
on the patio. Free parking adds to the great value.
Business services. Internet (wireless).

Omni Los Angeles

*California Plaza, 251 S Olive Street, between W 2nd
& W 3rd Streets, Los Angeles, CA 90012 (1-800
442 5251/1-213 617 3300/fax 1-213 617 3399/
www.omnihotels.com). Metro Civic Center/bus, 14,
37, 76, 78, 79/I-110, exit 4th Street east.* **Rates**
$239-$260 double; $1,500 suite. *Parking* $26. **Credit**
AmEx, DC, Disc, MC, V. **Map** p315 C2 ⑤③

Located in Downtown's growing cultural district,
the Omni offers theatre and concert packages to
those wanting to come here to catch a show or attend
a party. In keeping with the theme, there's orches-
tral music in the lobby. The 453 bedrooms, elegantly decorated in taupe and olive, have free wireless
access; 'club level' guests (floors 15 and 16) get
butler service, free breakfast and cocktails. Family
suites have bunk beds, bean bags, toys and games.
*Bar. Business services. Concierge. Gym. Internet (DSL
& wireless). Pool. Restaurants (2). Room service.*

Standard Downtown

*550 S Flower Street, between W 5th & W 6th Streets,
Los Angeles, CA 90071 (1-213 892 8080/fax 1-213
892 8686/www.standardhotel.com). Metro 7th
Street-Metro Center/bus 16, 18, 55, 60, 62, 316/
I-110, exit 6th Street east.* **Rates** $95-$325 double;
$450-$500 suite. *Parking* $25. **Credit** AmEx, MC, V.
Map p315 B3 ⑤④

The Downtown version of the Sunset Strip shag pad
(*see p59*) pokes fun at jet-setting '60s bachelors and
James Bond culture, with the slick lobby setting the
tone. The swinger-style rooms come equipped with
platform beds, tubs for two and peek-a-boo showers. The rooftop bar, with DJs, vibrating waterbeds,
scantily clad waitresses and fantastic views – is a
tough ticket on weekends for non-guests; you'd do
as well to hang in the ground-level bar. In case you're
wondering about the artefacts in the lobby, the hotel
was once the HQ for Superior Oil.
*Bar. Business services. CD. Concierge. DVD. Gym.
Pool. Restaurant. Room service.*

Westin Bonaventure

*404 S Figueroa Street, at W 4th Street, Los Angeles,
CA 90071 (1-800 937 8461/1-213 624 1000/1-213
612 4800/www.starwoodhotels.com). Metro 7th
Street-Metro Center/bus 18, 53, 55, 62, 316/
I-110, exit 9th Street west.* **Rates** $139-$299 double;
$299-$599 suite. *Parking* $25. **Credit** AmEx, DC,
Disc, MC, V. **Map** p315 B2 ⑤⑤

In the extraordinary absence of a hotel near the convention centre, this five-tower, 35-storey, 1,400-room
monster does a pretty decent trade with those in the
city on business. Certainly, it looks the part: the huge

lobby features a central bar that specialises in coffee during office hours and alcohol when the day turns to evening. Several restaurants, including a steakhouse and a bistro, provide other opportunities for visitors to fill up their expense accounts and wine and dine business clients. The rooms, while not especially remarkable in themselves, are at least very comfortable and kept in excellent condition; needless to say, the views are terrific the higher your room. The pool is bigger than you'd expect, even though you do need a map to find it.

Bar. Business services. Concierge. Gym. Internet (DSL). Pool. Restaurants (3). Room service. Spa.

Wilshire Grand

930 Wilshire Boulevard, at S Figueroa Street, Los Angeles, CA 90017 (1-213 612 3900/1-213 688 7777//fax 1-213 612 3937/www.wilshiregrand.com). Metro 7th Street-Metro Center/bus 66, 81, 366, 381/ I-110, exit 6th Street east. **Rates** $99-$139 double; $250-$575 suite. *Parking* $24. **Credit** AmEx, DC, Disc, MC, V. **Map** p315 A3 ⑤⑥

The Wilshire Grand provides some of the better-value business accommodation to be found in the Downtown area, a fact that can presumably be ascribed in part to the Grand being also one of the district's biggest hotels. The rooms, while fairly anonymous, are at least a decent size and reasonably comfortable. Eating options include sushi at Kyoto and Korean eaterie Seoul Jung (the hotel is

Standard Downtown (p62) Jamie Foxx pulls a gun on a bystander outside the hotel in *Collateral*

popular with Asian business travellers); downstairs is Point Moorea, a mock tiki bar. As with many other Downtown hotels, rates plummet at the weekend.

Bar. Business services. Concierge. Gym. Internet (DSL & wireless). Pool. Restaurants (4). Room service.

Budget

Hotel Figueroa

939 S Figueroa Street, between W 9th Street & W Olympic Boulevard, Los Angeles, CA 90015 (1-800 421 9092/1-213 627 8971/fax 1-213 689 0305/ www.figueroahotel.com). Metro 7th Street-Metro Center/bus 66, 81, 366, 381/I-110, exit 9th Street east. **Rates** $98-$134 single; $124-$148 double; $175-$245 suite. *Parking* $8. **Credit** AmEx, DC, MC, V. **Map** p315 B4 ⑤⑦

This striking hotel is a dramatic mix of Morocco and Mexico, and oozes the kind of quirky but authentic character after which boutique hotel designers flail but so often fail to achieve. Built in 1925 as a YWCA, the Figueroa is now more exotic, but it's still an absolute bargain. The hotel's airy lobby is a potpourri of Moroccan chandeliers, huge cacti and

Morocco slugs it out with Mexico at the **Hotel Figueroa**.

A life on the ocean wave... The **Queen Mary**, moored in Long Beach. *See p65.*

woven rugs. Rooms vary in size, and are done out in funky casbah chic with Mexican-tiled bathrooms. Everyone loves the outdoor Veranda Bar.
Bar (3). Internet (wireless). Pool. Restaurant.

Ritz Milner

813 S Flower Street, at W 8th Street, Los Angeles, CA 90017 (1-877 645 6377/1-213 627 6981/fax 1-213 623 9751/www.milner-hotels.com). Metro 7th Street-Metro Center/bus 66, 81, 366, 381/ I-110, exit 9th Street east. **Rates** *$59-$89 double; $109-$119 suite. Parking $5.* **Credit** *AmEx, DC, MC, V.* **Map** *p315 B4* ⑤⑧

Once a luxury inn, later a Skid Row slum, the Ritz is now 'budget boutique'. It was overhauled in 2003, and boasts enough architectural details and services (including 24-hour security) to lure budget travellers. The hotel's 135 rooms won't win any design awards, but they do include high-speed internet access. The restaurant next door serves up brunch and lunch.
Bar. Business services. Internet (DSL). Restaurant.

The Valleys

San Fernando Valley

Moderate

Sportsmen's Lodge

12825 Ventura Boulevard, at Coldwater Canyon Avenue, Studio City, CA 91604 (1-800 821 8511/ 1-818 769 4700/fax 1-818 769 4798/www.slhotel. com). Bus 150, 167, 240, 750/US 101, exit Coldwater Canyon Avenue south. **Rates** *$165-$300 double; $195-$300 suite. Parking free.* **Credit** *AmEx, DC, Disc, MC, V.*

Relaxed and retro, the Sportsmen's Lodge is a Valley landmark that is popular with families and famous faces, thanks to its prime location near all the major studios (and free shuttle to Universal). The rooms are clean and comfortable, with flowery bedspreads and country pine furniture. Bathrooms are on the smallish side, but the Olympic-sized pool is a show-stopper, and the '50s-era coffee shop dishes out hearty, all-American breakfasts. There's also a modest gym and a bar with a lively happy hour. The moderate restaurant is at least blessed with views over a swan-filled lake and eight acres of gardens.
Bar. Business services. Gym. Pool. Restaurants (2). Room service.

San Gabriel Valley

Expensive

Ritz-Carlton Huntington Hotel & Spa

1401 S Oak Knoll Avenue, at Wentworth Avenue, Pasadena, CA 91106 (1-800 241 3333/1-626 568 3900/fax 1-626 568 3700/www.ritzcarlton.com). Bus 485/I-110, exit Glenarm Street east. **Rates** *$265-$400 double; $375-$3,000 suite. Parking $24.* **Credit** *AmEx, DC, Disc, MC, V.*

It's hard to believe that this idyllic, Mediterreanean-style retreat, built in 1907 and set on 23 landscaped acres, is just a few miles from the bustle and noise of Downtown. All of the 392 rooms and bungalows feature views of lush Japanese gardens, rolling hills and towering palm trees. The rooms are small but elegant, with plush robes and marble bathrooms. Splash in the large pool, unwind in the spa or simply enjoy the signature service.
Bar. Business services. Concierge. Gym. Pool. Restaurants (2). Room service.

Heading South

Near LAX

Moderate

Sheraton Gateway

6101 W Century Boulevard, between Airport & S Sepulveda Boulevards, Los Angeles, CA 90045 (1-888 544 8983/1-310 642 1111/fax 1-310 642 4048/ www.sheraton.com). Bus 117/I-405, exit Century Boulevard west. **Rates** $119-$279 double; $199-$399 suites. *Parking* $20. **Credit** AmEx, DC, Disc, MC.
After a recent $14m renovation under the watchful eye of the Kor Hotel Group (Avalon, Viceroy, etc), this tired airport hotel has been transformed into a hip, urban hotel in the airport corridor. The 802 rooms have been deliciously appointed with Lucite lamps and leather headboards, but the real draw is the outdoor pool terrace with black and white cabanas. The lobby's creative use of dark colours and the destination restaurant, Shula's 347, is a breath of fresh air for this corner of the city.
Bar. Business services. Concierge. Internet (DSL in rooms, wireless in lobby). Pool. Restaurant. Room service.

Manhattan Beach

Moderate

Shade

1221 N Valley Drive, at Manhattan Beach Boulevard, Manhattan Beach, CA 90266 (1-310 546 5552/fax 1-310 546 4985/www.shadehotel. com). Bus 126, 439/I-405, exit Manhattan Beach Boulevard. **Rates** $185-$219 double; $450-$600 suite. *Parking* $12. **Credit** AmEx, DC, Disc, MC, V.
Can't quite believe that long-forgotten Manhattan Beach is on the way up? Head to this sparkling new property, located within walking distance of some of the area's finest beaches. The 38 guestrooms

make use of the small space quite well: multi-purpose tables can be rolled back and forth over the bed for breakfast or for use as a desk. The modern aesthetic is enhanced by the lobby's Zinc Lounge, crowded daily with twentysomethings supping cocktails and knibbling small plates. There's a huge jacuzzi on the sky deck, offering views of the ocean.
Bars. Business services. Concierge. Gym. Internet (wireless). Restaurant. Room service.

Long Beach

Moderate

Queen Mary

1126 Queens Highway, Long Beach, CA 90802 (1-562 435 3511/fax 1-562 437 4531/www.queen mary.com). Metro Transit Mall/I-405, then I-710 south. **Rates** $109-$219 double; $360-$510 suites. *Parking* $10. **Credit** AmEx, DC, Disc, MC, V.
This grand cruise ship hasn't sailed since the 1960s; these days, it multitasks as a tourist attraction (*see p133*), an eating and drinking spot (the bar is an art deco glory) and a hotel. Unsurprisingly given the boat's age (it was built in 1936), the guestrooms aren't huge, and nor are they stocked with modern amenities. Still, that's hardly the point: they are, like most of the boat's public areas, handsome, historic and nicely maintained. Good value for what is perhaps the most spectacular hotel in LA. **Photo** *p64*.
Bar. Concierge. Gym. Internet (DSL in rooms, wireless in lobby). Restaurants (3). Room service.

Orange County

Expensive

Disney's Grand Californian Hotel

1600 S Disneyland Drive, between Ball Road & Katella Avenue, Anaheim, CA 92802 (1-877 700 3476/1-714 635 2300/www.disney.com). Bus OC205/I-5, exit Disneyland Drive south. **Rates** $350-$500 double; $510-$590 suite. *Parking* $11. **Credit** AmEx, DC, Disc, MC, V.

Carry on camping

Perhaps the most scenic camping in LA is at **Malibu Creek State Park** (four miles south of US 101 on Las Virgenes/Malibu Canyon Road). The park offers 4,000 acres for hiking, fishing and horseback riding, as well as 15 miles of stream-side trails. Not far away in Malibu is **Leo Carrillo State Park** (35000 PCH, Malibu), which has 1.5 miles of beach for swimming, surfing and fishing. Tent camping is allowed everywhere except the north side of the beach, which is open only

to camper vans. Bookings for both parks – staff recommend booking six months ahead for summer – can be made on 1-800 444 7275; see www.parks.ca.gov for more.
Private campsites tend to be less scenic than their state counterparts, but offer more amenities. One of many examples is the **Malibu Beach RV Park** (25801 PCH), where amenities include a jacuzzi. Aside from the RV park, there are 50 tent sites; to book, call 1-800 622 6052, or see www.maliburv.com.

Disney's grand entrance into the luxury hotel market celebrates California's redwood forests, mission pioneers and the painters of the Plein Air school. The grand lobby is a Frank Lloyd Wright-inspired gem, with stained-glass doors, wood panelling and a three-storey walk-in hearth with roaring fire. All of the bedrooms are non-smoking, smartly appointed and equipped with bunk beds, trundles and sleeping bags for overexcited children; some overlook the park. The hotel has its own private entrance to Disney's California Adventure, and is in walking distance of Disneyland itself.
Bar. Business services. Concierge. Gym. Internet (DSL). Pool. Restaurants (2). Room service.

Montage Resort & Spa

30801 South Coast Highway, Laguna Beach, CA 92651 (1-888 715 6700/1-949 715 6000/fax 1-949 715 6100/www.montagelagunabeach.com). Bus OC1/I-405, exit PCH south. **Rates** $535-$895 double; $1,100-$5,500 suite. *Parking* $29. **Credit** AmEx, DC, Disc, MC, V.
No expense was spared in building this 30-acre resort on a bluff overlooking the Pacific, fashioned after the work of California's Plein Air artists. Yet, unlike many other LA hotels, here the luxury is understated rather than flashy, a romantic blend of wood and stone, gables and porches, winding paths that lead to white sand beaches with luxurious beach furnishings. Rooms have private balconies with commanding ocean views and all the luxury trimmings you'd expect: deluxe beds, fine bed linens, goose-down pillows, flat-screen TVs with DVD players, marble bathrooms, candles and exotic toiletries. For body and soul, there's a glass-walled spa and three pools, one Olympic-sized.
Bars (3). Business services. CD. Concierge. DVD. Gym. Pool. Restaurants (3). Room service.

Ritz-Carlton Laguna Niguel

1 Ritz-Carlton Drive, at PCH, Dana Point, CA 92629 (1-800 241 3333/1-949 240 2000/fax 1-949 240 0829/www.ritzcarlton.com). Bus OC70, OC85, OC91/I-5, exit Crown Valley Parkway west. **Rates** $365-$705 double; $610-$3,200 suite. *Parking* $30. **Credit** AmEx, DC, Disc, MC, V.
Located where the OC meets the beach, the Ritz-Carlton draws a wealthy crowd who gather in the picture-window lounge for the dazzling sunsets. All rooms feature balconies (with ocean or pool views), plush furnishings, Frette linens and large marble bathrooms. A major renovation in 2005 updated the design from a stuffy traditional look to a contemporary California beach style. There's a great surfing beach directly in front of the property.
Bar. Business services. CD. Concierge. DVD. Gym. Internet (wireless). Pools (2). Restaurants (2). Room service.

St Regis Monarch Beach Resort & Spa

1 Monarch Beach Resort, at Niguel Road, Dana Point, CA 92629 (1-800 722 1543/ 1-949 234 3200/fax 1-949 240 0829/ www.stregismonarchbeach.com). Bus OC70, OC85, OC91/I-5, exit Crown Valley Parkway west. **Rates** $365-$695 double; $595-$3,200 suite. *Parking* $28. **Credit** AmEx, DC, Disc, MC, V.
This wonderful property competes with the Ritz-Carlton for the well-heeled dollar, with the St Regis's trump being an 18-hole Robert Trent Jones Jr-designed golf course. Set in 172 acres of grounds, including its own private beach, the St Regis also boasts three swimming pools, six restaurants and 400 rooms.
Bars (3). Business services. CD. Concierge. DVD. Gym. Internet (DSL). Pools (4). Restaurants (7). Room service.

Moderate

Disneyland hotels

Disneyland Hotel *1150 W Magic Way, between Ball Road & Katella Avenue, Anaheim, CA 92802 (1-714 520 5005/1-714 778 6600/fax 1-714 956 6597).* **Rates** $240-$320 double; $605-$2,000 suite. *Parking* $12.
Disney's Paradise Pier Hotel *1717 Disneyland Drive, at Katella Avenue, Anaheim, CA 92802 (1-714 999 0990/fax 1-714 776 5763).* **Rates** $215-$295 double; $350-$620 suite. *Parking* $12. **Credit** AmEx, DC, Disc, MC, V.
Both *www.disney.com. Bus OC205, OC430/I-5, exit Disneyland Drive.* **Credit** AmEx, DC, Disc, MC, V.
These two Disney hotels, both located in Disneyland and thus ideal for holidays to the Magic Kingdom, offer similar services at roughly similar prices, and both have had recent refits. The main change wrought by the Disneyland Hotel makeover is the huge new pool complex, complete with 110ft (33m) water slide. The boardwalk-themed pool area at Paradise Pier is less expansive, but the hotel still charms with its beachy theme. The common areas are full of Disneyland magic.
Bars. Business services. Concierge. Gym. Laundry. Pool. Restaurants. Room service.

Budget

Candy Cane Inn

1747 S Harbor Boulevard, at Katella Avenue, Anaheim, CA 92802 (1-800 345 7057/1-714 774 5284/fax 1-714 772 5462/www.candycaneinn.net). Bus OC205, OC430/I-5, exit Harbor Boulevard south. **Rates** $92-$164 double. *Parking* free. **Credit** AmEx, DC, Disc, MC, V.
There's hardly a stripe to be found at this hotel (the place was purchased on Christmas eve) a three-minute walk from Disneyland's main gate. However, it consistently wins Anaheim's most beautiful hotel award: set amid romantic gardens, it's deliciously nostalgic, with old-fashioned street lamps, cobblestone driveways and a hint of 1950s flair. The comfortable rooms are similarly old-fashioned, with French floral patterns and plantation shutters. A free Disneyland shuttle runs every half hour.
Internet (DSL). Pool.

Sightseeing

Introduction	68
Santa Monica & the Beach Towns	73
Brentwood to Beverly Hills	83
West Hollywood, Hollywood & Midtown	91
Los Feliz, Silver Lake & Echo Park	103
Downtown	108
East LA	117
South Central LA	119
The Valleys	124
Heading South	131

Features

Top ten Attractions	69
Street talk	70
You Getty what you pay for	74
Life's a beach	76
Public art Santa Monica to Venice	80
Walk UCLA campus	86
We ♥ **LA** Star maps	90
We ♥ **LA** Hollywood Walk of Fame	93
All dried out	104
Public art Downtown	110
We ♥ **LA** Watts Towers	122
We ♥ **LA** The Great Wall of LA	126
The final frontier	130

Getty Center. *See p83.*

Introduction

Welcome to Los Angeles.

The one sign you won't see when you arrive is the one directing you to the city centre, because there isn't one. Greater LA is an amorphous, sprawling agglomeration spread over a huge flood basin, subdivided by freeways and bound by ocean and hills: on its western edge by 160 miles of Pacific coastline, and then, clockwise, by the Santa Monica, San Gabriel, San Bernardino, San Jacinto and Santa Ana Mountains. Laid over this geography is a dizzying variety of cityscapes and neighbourhoods.

As you drive around, you may be confused by signs pointing to 'Los Angeles'. They're here because the City of Los Angeles is a distinct city within the County of Los Angeles; together with Riverside, Ventura, Orange and San Bernadino Counties, LA County is part of the Los Angeles Five-County Area, a colossal area of 34,000 square miles and 15 million people.

LA County contains 88 incorporated cities, each with its own downtown and jurisdiction; among them are Malibu, Santa Monica, Beverly Hills, Culver City, Pasadena and Los Angeles itself. To add to the confusion, some areas – East LA, for one– are unincorporated, meaning they're under the jurisdiction of the County of LA, but not the City. West Hollywood was incorporated into a city as recently as 1984, but Hollywood is just one of many neighbourhoods in the City of LA. And that's not even to mention broad titles such as the West Side (which, confusingly, contains a separate area called West LA) and South Central LA (comprising many black and Latino neighbourhoods).

To make exploring this mega-metropolis a little easier, we've split the LA region into a variety of different areas, which we've used not just in this Sightseeing section but throughout the book. We've summarised the areas over the next couple of pages and on a map on page 320; for more on how to get around, *see p284*.

SANTA MONICA AND THE BEACH TOWNS

Working north to south down the Pacific coast, desirable **Malibu** (*p73*), affluent **Pacific Palisades** (*p73*), comfortable **Santa Monica** (*p74*), arty **Venice** (*p79*) and tidy **Marina del Rey** (*p82*) all have their own distinct characters. The beach cities are not at their best in June, when they're swathed in morning cloud known as June Gloom. For information on the beaches themselves, *see p76* **Life's a beach**.

BRENTWOOD TO BEVERLY HILLS

Moving inland, LA soon reveals itself to be the glamorous city of popular legend, though you'll have to drive through (or around) fast-rising **Culver City** (*p85*), forgettable **West LA** and office-dominated **Century City** (*p88*) to find it. Wealthy, rustic **Brentwood** (*p83*) adjoins, to the west, university-dominated **Westwood** (*p87*) and, to the north, moneyed **Bel Air** (*p88*). To the east, **Beverly Hills** (*p88*) lives up to its reputation, from the impossibly posh shops around Rodeo Drive to the expansive, tree-lined residential streets that surround them.

WEST HOLLYWOOD, HOLLYWOOD AND MIDTOWN

Separated from Beverly Hills by Doheny Drive, parts of **West Hollywood** (*p91*) are nearly as swanky as its neighbour, although Beverly Hills doesn't have the nightlife to compete with WeHo's Sunset Strip. Due east is **Hollywood** (*p92*), less glamorous than its reputation but more popular than it's been for years. South of here are, variously, the shops and restaurants of the **Fairfax District** (*p98*); the museums of the **Miracle Mile** (*p99*); wealthy, residential **Hancock Park** (*p101*); earthy **Koreatown** (*p102*); and down-at-heel **Westlake** (*p102*).

LOS FELIZ, SILVER LAKE AND ECHO PARK

Set in an arc that starts north-east of Hollywood and ends on the edge of Downtown LA, these three districts make it on to few tourists' maps, which is just how the locals like it. **Los Feliz** (*p103*) is home to a number of funky shops and restaurants, and is the main entrance into vast Griffith Park; **Silver Lake** (*p106*) is scruffier, homier and artier; while **Echo Park** (*p106*) is home to Dodger Stadium.

DOWNTOWN

Stretching south from the eastern end of Sunset Boulevard, **Downtown** (*p108*) is the site of the original city and home to most of LA's political and financial institutions. Extreme wealth (the **Financial District**, *p113*) sits side by side with extreme poverty (**Skid Row**, *p111*); towering modern skyscrapers loom over old theatres (**Broadway**, *p115*) and art galleries. Also here is Latino-dominated **Olvera Street** (*p109*), a small-ish **Chinatown** (*p108*) and, nearby, **Little Tokyo** (*p111*).

EAST LA

East LA (*p117*), an unincorporated area east of Downtown, is the heartland of LA's Mexican community. Long the gateway for new migrants, it has crystallised into a Mexican hub: almost 90 per cent of its population is Latino, predominantly Mexican and mostly poor.

SOUTH CENTRAL LA

South Central's fluid boundaries have long been linked to the changing migratory patterns of black Angelenos. While popular cliché about South Central holds true in places (chiefly in long-troubled **Watts**; *p121*), it's blown out of the water in neighbourhoods such as affluent **Crenshaw** (*p123*) and cultured **Leimert Park** (*p123*). At the area's north-easternmost tip, close to Downtown, is the cultural hub of **Exposition Park** (*p120*) and the USC campus.

THE VALLEYS

The **San Fernando Valley** (*p124*), to the north-west of LA, and the **San Gabriel Valley** (*p127*), to the north-east, are often ridiculed for embodying the hot and smoggy horrors of West Coast suburbia. The cliché holds largely true in the former, but several of the San Gabriel Valley's neighbourhoods, chief among them **Pasadena** and **Claremont**, are very charming and more than a little historic.

HEADING SOUTH

When LA residents speak of the **South Bay**, they're usually referring to the coast-hugging cities south of LAX: **El Segundo**, **Manhattan Beach**, **Hermosa Beach** and **Redondo Beach** (*p131* for all), plus the landlocked suburb of Torrance to the east. Across the Vincent Thomas Bridge from **San Pedro** (*p131*) is **Long Beach** (*p132*), an old navy port that's now a relatively cosmopolitan city of nearly 500,000. To the south-east, **Orange County** (*p133*) attracts 40 million visitors a year, many heading directly to Disneyland.

Sightseeing tips

When sightseeing in Los Angeles, it doesn't necessarily pay to get up at the crack of dawn. Certainly, you should aim to arrive at the huge and hugely popular attractions (Universal Studios, Disneyland and Six Flags) as early as possible to beat the worst of the crowds. But otherwise, unless the museum or attraction you're hoping to visit is close to the hotel and can be easily reached without recourse to the freeway system, you may just find yourself stuck in horrendous rush-hour traffic.

If you're planning to visit a number of LA-area attractions, it may be worth thinking about investing in a **CityPass**. The Hollywood

Sightseeing

Top ten Attractions

The beaches
Some suit surfers, others attract hordes of gay men, while still others draw families out to play. Take your choice... See *p76*.

Disneyland
Whatever your hopes and fears, Southern California's most storied attraction lives up to them. See *p135*.

A walk around Downtown
LA's most pedestrian-friendly area is also its most varied, from Broadway's old theatres via myriad new galleries to the shiny glamour of Disney Hall. See *p108*.

Griffith Park
This sprawling park contains multitudinous attractions (the excellent Museum of the American West, the soon-to-reopen Griffith Observatory), but it's also a great place to escape the crowds. See *p105*.

Hollywood
Today's stars avoid the place, but the Walk of Fame, Grauman's Chinese Theatre and the Hollywood Forever Cemetery ensure their predecessors linger. See *p92*.

Huntington Library, Art Collections & Botanical Gardens
The library is terrific and the art strong, but the gardens at Henry Huntington's old estate are exceptional. See *p129*.

Japanese American National Museum
Don't think you'd be interested in the history of Japanese immigration to America? This enthralling museum will make you think again. See *p111*.

Museum of Jurassic Technology
Truth melds with the imagination and dreams collide with nightmares at David Wilson's mesmerising museum. See *p85*.

Norton Simon Museum
The **Getty Center** (*see p83*) has the buildings but not the collection. **LACMA** (*see p100*) has the collection but not the buildings. The Norton Simon Museum has both. See *p129*.

Watts Towers
The greatest piece of folk art in America? Almost certainly. See *p122*.

Street talk

LA is subdivided by numerous freeways and a loose grid of large arteries, the boulevards and avenues (aka surface streets). Boulevards typically (but not exclusively) go east to west, with street numbers in the City of LA itself starting at No.1 in Downtown and ascending westwards; avenues usually run north to south. Some boulevards and avenues are divided and prefixed with North, South, East or West, abbreviated throughout this guide to N, S, E and W; for example, N Fairfax Avenue and W Sunset Boulevard. To confuse matters further, the street numbering on some thoroughfares restarts at every city boundary; N Robertson Boulevard, for example, changes its numbering three times. Always check which stretch of road you want and watch the numbers carefully.

When planning a journey, make sure you find out the nearest cross-street; for example, Hollywood and Highland, or Sunset and San Vicente. If you're taking the freeway, find out the exit nearest to your destination. Unless you're sure of the district to which you're heading, it's also worth double-checking the specific city: the same street names do occur in different cities. Throughout this book, we've included cross-streets and a freeway exit for every listed establishment.

In the central portion of LA County, the geographical basin where you are likely to spend most of the time, **I-10** traverses LA from west to east and separates Hollywood, Beverly Hills and Midtown from South and South Central LA. **I-405** runs north to south on the west side of the City of Los Angeles, separating the affluent coastal and inland cities from the rest of LA. **I-110** goes north to south on the east side, separating Downtown and East LA from west and central LA. **US 101** and **I-5** head north-west from Downtown into the Valleys.

The freeways have names (often more than one) as well as numbers, and it helps to know both. The following are among the most popular and/or widely used:

I-5 Golden State Freeway/
 Santa Ana Freeway
I-10 Santa Monica Freeway/
 San Bernadino Freeway
US 101 Hollywood Freeway/Ventura Freeway
I-110/Hwy 110 Harbor Freeway/
 Pasadena Freeway
Hwy 134 Ventura Freeway
I-210 Foothill Freeway
I-405 San Diego Freeway
I-710 Long Beach Freeway

The coast road, **Highway 1**, is also known as the Pacific Coast Highway (aka PCH), becoming Lincoln Boulevard and Sepulveda Boulevard when it moves inland. Similarly, **Highway 2**, aka the Glendale Freeway, becomes Santa Monica Boulevard when it moves through the Westside.

An essential aid is the *Thomas Bros Street Guide to Los Angeles & Orange Counties*, an easy-to-use, annually updated map to the region. Now published by Rand McNally, it costs about $20 and is available from specialist shops such as **Traveler's Bookcase** (*see p183*), most general bookstores, superstores such as **Target** (*see p180*) and large drugstores including **Savon** and **Rite-Aid** (*see p199*). For updates on construction and road closures, call 1-800 427 7623. For websites providing traffic reports, route planning and handy shortcuts, *see p298*.

CityPass ($49, or $39 for 3-11s), includes admission to the **Hollywood Wax Museum** (*see p96*), a **Red Line Tours** walk (*see p71*), a **Starline Tour** (*see p71*) and either a tour of the **Kodak Theatre** (*see p260*) or entrance to the **Hollywood Museum** (*see p96*). The Southern California CityPass ($199, or $159 3-9s) includes a three-day pass to both **Disneyland** parks (*see p135*), and admission to **Universal Studios** (*see p126*), **San Diego Zoo** (*see p280*) and **SeaWorld** (*see p281*). Buy one from any participating attraction, or at www.citypass.com.

Look out, too, for the tidy **Maphawk** guides (www.maphawk.com) to various LA locales (Santa Monica, Venice, Hollywood and others), pinpointing local businesses of note. They're available free from local shops and cafés.

Guided tours

In addition to the organisations below, other tours are held less frequently. **Pasadena Heritage** (1-626 441 6333, www.pasadena heritage.org) runs a quarterly tour of Old Town Pasadena; the **City of Beverly Hills** run year-round trolley tours and occasional walking tours (1-310 285 2438, www.beverlyhills.org); and the **Friends of the LA River** (1-323 223 0585, www.folar.org) offers regular walks along and around it. *See also p225* **Festivals**.

Children's Nature Institute Family Walks

1-310 860 9484/www.childrensnatureinstitute.org.
Tours vary. **Cost** *Suggested donation* $7 family.
The CNI organises walks for under-8s in the Santa Monica Mountains and other areas near LA, introducing families to the outdoors while instilling respect for nature. Most are pushchair-accessible.

Los Angeles Conservancy Walking Tours

Information 1-213 430 4219/reservations 1-213 623 2489/www.laconservancy.org. **Tours** Sat, times and routes vary. **Cost** $10 non-members.
This praiseworthy organisation works first to preserve and revitalise LA's urban architectural heritage, and, secondly, to educate the public about it. To the latter end, it runs a wide variety of tours, taking in everything from Downtown's historic theatres (weekly) to architecture in San Pedro (quarterly). Reservations are required, the earlier the better.

Neon Cruises

1-213 489 9918/www.neonmona.org. **Tours** 7.30pm Sat, June-Oct only. **Cost** $45 non-members.
The Museum of Neon Art (*see p116*) run three-hour tours in an open-top double-decker bus during summer. The route Hollywood, Universal CityWalk and the faux pagodas of Chinatown. Book ahead.

Red Line Tours

1-323 402 1074/www.redlinetours.com. **Tours** *Historic Hollywood* 10am, noon, 2pm, 4pm daily. *Historic Downtown* 9.45am daily. *Contemporary Downtown* noon daily. **Cost** $20; $15-$18 discounts.
Red Line's two Downtown walking tours start at the Bradbury Building (304 S Broadway) and cover much of Downtown's interesting architecture; the Hollywood tour, which leaves from the Stella Adler Academy (6773 Hollywood Boulevard), visits many major Hollywood landmarks. Participants are given headphones and a small FM receiver tuned to pick up the guide, who speaks into a small transmitter; it's an inspired idea, perfect for blotting out traffic. Reservations are required for Downtown tours only.

Starline Tours

1-800 959 3131/1-323 463 3333/www.starlinetours. com. **Tours** check online. **Cost** $18-$103.
Starline run a broad range of tours around LA, from one-hour trolley rides to day-long tours. Their most popular tour is a 2hr loop around the homes of various stars; it leaves Grauman's Chinese Theatre (*see p95*) every half-hour. However, at $35 (plus a tip for the driver), it's not cheap, and you might be better off buying a map and guiding yourself (*see p90* We♥LA). Elsewhere, **LA Tours** (1-323 937 0999, www.la-tours.com) offers a similar service.

Take My Mother Please

1-323 737 2200/www.takemymotherplease.com.
Tours by appt. **Cost** *Half-day* $300 up to 3 people; $350 4 people; $400 5 people. *Full day* $475 up to 3 people; $550 4 people; $625 5 people.

For a personalised tour of LA, contact Anne Block, who ferries small groups around in the comfort of her silver Cadillac. The tailor-made tours are expensive but fun, and can cover all areas of the city.

Urban Shopping Adventures

1-213 683 9715/www.urbanshoppingadventures.com.
Tours call for details. **Cost** $32-$189.
Enthusiastic, knowledgeable shopaholic Christine Silvestri offers tours of the Melrose Heights boutiques and Downtown's Fashion District, sorting the wheat from the chaff and showing customers where to find the area's best bargains. The most popular are the walking tours, though there are also a variety of coach tours available. Call ahead to book.

Studio tours

The most famous studio tour in the US is at **Universal Studios** (*see p126*), but a number of other major studios also admit the public and offer them brief glimpses behind the scenes.

NBC Studios

3000 W Alameda Avenue, at W Olive Avenue, Burbank (1-818 840 3537/www.studioaudiences. com). **Tours** 9am-3pm daily. **Cost** $7; $3.75-$6.25 discounts; free under-5s.
The cheapest way to get behind the scenes in LA (legally, at least), this 70-minute walking tour takes in the set of *The Tonight Show* and a few other TV sound stages. Reservations aren't required.

Paramount Studios

5555 Melrose Avenue, at N Gower Street, Hollywood (1-323 956 1777/www.paramount.com).
Tours 10am & 2pm daily. **Cost** $35. **Map** p313 C3.
The only studio in Hollywood is once again welcoming visitors. The tours take roughly two hours, and reservations are required.

Sony Pictures

10202 W Washington Boulevard, at Jasmine Avenue, Culver City (1-323 520 8687/www.sony picturesstudios.com). **Tours** hourly 9.30am-2.30pm Mon-Fri. **Cost** $25.
Low-key walking tours, open only to over-12s, are offered during the week at this storied lot. Movies such as *The Wizard of Oz* were shot here in decades gone by; these days, it's used for both TV and film. Reservations are recommended.

Warner Brothers Studios

3400 Riverside Drive, at W Olive Avenue, Burbank (1-818 972 8687/http://www.wbsf.com). **Tours** *VIP* regular intervals, 8.30am-4.30pm Mon-Fri. *Deluxe* 10.30am Mon-Fri. **Cost** *VIP* $39. *Deluxe* $125.
The two-hour VIP tour of Warners' Burbank studios take in a goodly portion of the facility, before ending at a small museum; reservations are available only for the first three tours of the day. The Deluxe tours last five hours and go even further behind the scenes; reservations are recommended. Bring ID for both tours, and leave under-8s at home.

Sightseeing

Santa Monica & the Beach Towns

Oh, we do like to be beside the seaside.

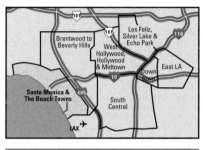

Malibu

Though it was officially incorporated as a city in 1990, Malibu is not a place so much as a 27-mile stretch of the Pacific Coast Highway that winds through some of Southern California's most magnificent coastal terrain. Parts of it are lined, on the ocean side, by beach houses of varying sizes and styles, with largely mediocre commercial buildings on the inland side nestling against the Santa Monica Mountains.

Malibu is such a desirable spot that its wildly wealthy locals, including privacy-hungry stars and publicity-shy industry moguls, are willing to live with the threat of seasonal fires and floods, and have formed a community dedicated to preventing new development from marring their lifestyle. Homeowners with properties backing on to Broad Beach have formed huge sand barriers, shrinking the public beach while simultaneously blocking access to their houses; others employ security guards to keep away the riff-raff and the paparazzi. However, they don't get it all their own way: in 2005, the courts finally ordered David Geffen to allow the public access to a beautiful stretch of sand he'd long regarded as his own. Carbon Beach is at 22132 Pacific Coast Highway; good luck finding it.

Leaving aside **Adamson House** (*see below*) and the reservation-only garden tours at **Ramirez Canyon Park** (5750 Ramirez Canyon Road, 1-310 589 2850), a 22-acre estate donated to the Santa Monica Mountains Conservancy by Barbra Streisand in 1993, Malibu has no sights as such. Its treats lie in

its beaches and canyons: within yards of the entrance to one of the many trails, you can be out of view of the city and communing with coyotes and red-tailed hawks. Others head here simply to eat: for local restaurants, *see p139*.

Adamson House

23200 Pacific Coast Highway (1-310 456 8432/ www.adamsonhouse.org). Bus 434/I-10, exit PCH north. **Open** *Tours* 11am-2pm Wed-Sat. **Admission** $3. **No credit cards**.
This striking 1929 Spanish-style building sits, along with the Malibu Lagoon Museum, inside the confines of Malibu Lagoon State Park. The major attraction at Adamson House is the array of decorative tiles manufactured at the once-celebrated but now-closed Malibu Tile Works. The guided tours allow visitors access to much of the property.

Malibu Chamber of Commerce

Suite 100, 23805 Stuart Ranch Road, at Civic Center Way, Malibu (1-310 456 9025/www.malibu.org). I-10, exit PCH north. **Open** 10am-4pm Mon-Fri.

Pacific Palisades

Between Malibu and Santa Monica lies Pacific Palisades, a small, rich community with a lower profile than its neighbours. The perfect, clipped, shiny green lawns and large bungalows of the area are straight out of *Leave It to Beaver*, but contained within its Santa Monica Mountains location are some wonderful, rugged places to visit; among them are **Rustic Canyon Park** (1-310 454 5734), **Temescal Canyon Park** (1-310 454 1395) and **Will Rogers State Historic Park** (*see p74*). Nearby are the **Self-Realization Fellowship Lake Shrine** (17190 Sunset Boulevard, 1-310 454 4114, www.yogananda-srf.org/temples/lakeshrine), a gorgeous, calming Buddhist retreat open to the public every day except Monday, and **Will Rogers State Beach**, a gay-friendly spot (*see p232* **Gay beaches**).

> **Will Rogers State Beach**
> Where Hasselhoff and Pammy filmed *Baywatch*

You Getty what you pay for

In 1974, oil magnate J Paul Getty opened a museum of his holdings in a faux villa in Malibu, based on the remains of the Villa dei Papiri in Herculaneum. The response: derision from architecture critics and ridicule from art experts, who called Getty's collection of antiquities, decorative arts and paintings mediocre. Billions of dollars will buy a lot of last laughs, and the Getty Museum grew into one of LA's most loved destinations. But in 1997, the decorative arts and paintings were moved to the **Getty Center** (*see p83*), and the villa was closed for conversion into a museum and study centre exclusively for the collection of Mediterranean antiquities.

When the **Getty Villa**, as it's now known, reopened in 2006, the response showed that history at least has a sense of humour: this time, the derision derived from the various scandals that enveloped the enterprise. Getty Trust president Barry Munitz was forced to resign after the *Los Angeles Times* reported that Munitz used Getty money to buy himself a Porsche, sold Getty-owned property to LA businessman and philanthropist Eli Broad for $700,000 below its appraised value, and had his staff express-mail umbrellas to him while he travelled. Marion True, the Getty's top curator, also quit, following reports that the Getty had bought stolen antiquities (a scandal that has now enveloped other US museums). And New York collector Barbara Fleischman quit her position on the Getty board three days before the villa's reopening, after it was revealed that she loaned money to True. The *LA Times* later reported that of the 42 items

being contested by the Italian government, around a dozen were donated or sold to the Getty by the Fleischmans, after whom an open-air amphitheatre at the Villa has been named.

Despite the scandal, the public has been agog see the reborn villa. Architects Jorge Silvetti and Rodolfo Machado have painstakingly restored the villa, repainting walls and laying down mosaic floors in vivid new colours. They've also transformed the entrance by creating a winding path through new buildings carved into the hillside, offering the visitor glimpses of the villa until, finally, the whole building comes into view.

A statue of Hercules, said to have inspired Getty to create the villa, presides over a round, shrine-like gallery, which leads into displays of 1,200 artefacts under such themes as Gods and Goddesses, Dionysos and the Theater, and Stories of the Trojan War. In addition, there are conservation laboratories for scholars, seminar rooms, a classroom and a research library.

Ever since Getty's death in 1976, his Trust has been trying to be taken seriously in the art world. Clearly, it still has a few problems in this area, but when you mix mountains of money with the classical world and then add LA into the mix, what can you expect? The whiff of scandal adds to the frisson of a place that otherwise may be just a little too earnest.

Getty Villa

17985 PCH, Pacific Palisades (1-310 440 7300/www.getty.edu). **Open** 10am-5pm Mon, Thur-Sun. **Admission** free; bookings required.

Eames House

203 Chautauqua Boulevard, off Pacific Coast Highway (1-310 459 9663/www.eamesoffice.com). Bus 434/I-10, exit PCH north. **Open** *Appointments only* 10am-4pm Mon-Fri; 10am-3pm Sat.
Charles and Ray Eames' landmark experiment in home design (*see p25*), built in 1949, is still used as a private residence by the Eames family. However, visitors are welcome to take a self-guided tour of the exterior on an appointment-only basis.

Will Rogers State Historic Park

1501 Will Rogers State Park Road, at Sunset Boulevard (1-310 454 8212/www.parks.ca.gov). Bus 2, 302, 476/I-405, exit Sunset Boulevard west. **Open** call for details. **Admission** call for details.
This 31-room house, set in 186 acres of grounds, has been maintained as it was in the 1930s, when Rogers – humourist, writer, 'cowboy philosopher',

trick-roper and the first honorary mayor of Beverly Hills – lived here. The property is once more in a glorious condition following the $5-million renovation that saw it reopen in April 2006. The grounds give access to some good hikes; one path takes you to Inspiration Point, from where you get a breath-taking view of mountains and sea. Polo matches are held here on weekends (www.willrogerspolo.org).

Santa Monica

Map p310

Denizens of scruffy Hollywood and cool Silver Lake see affluent Santa Monica as overpriced and uncool. They have a point but they're also missing one. Downtown Santa Monica is a white-bread-and-mayo kind of place, long on Starbucks, short on nightclubs and devoid of any sort of urban edge. But the chain-heavy centre of the city is hardly the whole story.

It's easy to see how people get drawn to Santa Monica, and why it's become the hub of Los Angeles's Westside. With the Santa Monica Mountains to the north and the shimmering Pacific to the west, the palm tree-lined cliffs and year-round sun tempered by ocean breezes, its natural surroundings couldn't be bettered. The roads, buildings and gardens that have grown up around it are immaculate: clean, tidy and easy on the eye. Outside of the 'June gloom' fog, it's always summertime in Santa Monica, and, if you've money in your pocket, the living is easy.

The area was inhabited for centuries by the Gabrieleno Native Americans, then by Spanish settlers who named the city and many of its major streets. Acquired by Anglo pioneers in the late 19th century, it soon snowballed from a small holiday resort into today's city, with a population of 84,000. Brits abound in Santa Monica, mixing with Iranians, retirees, health fanatics, beach bums, entertainment industry titans and entertainment industry wannabes.

As well as the tourist-oriented beaches, the amusement park on the pier and the strings of shops scattered in bunches around the neighbourhood, Santa Monica also boasts some of the best restaurants in the LA basin, thriving galleries and coffeehouses, and, perhaps most surprisingly, some excellent, daring modern architecture. Much of Frank Gehry's work is here, including his own house (*see p27*), but Santa Monica also contains art deco landmarks such as the **Shangri-La** hotel (*see p49*) and some fine 1950s architecture. The **Stick House** at 1911 La Mesa Drive, which falls into the latter category, is the only home in the country designed by Oscar Niemeyer, albeit from a distance: the architect never set foot in the US.

Lazing on a sunny afternoon: **Santa Monica Pier**. *See p77.*

Life's a beach

Ever since Vasco Núñez de Balboa first laid eyes on the Pacific Ocean in 1513, the world has gazed upon the Southern California coastline with wonder. With its gorgeous interface of sea and sky against a chiselled, lush mountain backdrop, the 30-mile stretch of beaches along Los Angeles County's coastline – from Malibu in the north, through famous Santa Monica and Venice, and on to the South Bay – is incomparable.

Despite LA's surf city reputation, the Pacific is chillingly cold nine months of the year. But in July and August, when oceanside temperatures hover around 90°F (32°C), the water can reach 70°F (21°C). The further you are from Santa Monica Bay, where waste is pumped into the ocean, the cleaner the water. That said, even the water in Santa Monica has improved under the auspices of Heal the Bay (1-310 453 0395), an environmental outfit devoted to monitoring

pollution levels. Swimming is permitted on all LA County beaches, but strong currents and pounding waves make it difficult.

Beaches officially open at sunrise and close at sunset. Many have space and rental gear for inline skating, roller-hockey, cycling,

Montana Avenue

Running four blocks north of Wilshire Boulevard, the city's main east–west artery, Montana Avenue is situated towards the northern, wealthier end of Santa Monica, bordering on the Santa Monica Canyons. A drab commercial strip during the 1970s, the street has since metamorphosised into the Rodeo Drive of the coast, although here conspicuous consumption comes with a little more subtlety and a lot less flash. Designer stores sit alongside little fashion boutiques and the sort of clean-cut Californian restaurants favoured by casually-clad ladies who lunch and the gentlemen who love them. It's a very agreeable sort of place in which to while away a lazy afternoon.

The blocks north of Montana are chiefly, smartly residential. A few blocks north is **San Vicente Boulevard**, a wide street lined with grass verges that's usually populated with fit specimens getting their jog on to a soundtrack beamed in by iPod. The east end of San Vicente, around the junction with Bundy Drive and edging into Brentwood, features some popular eating haunts, among them **Vincenti** (No.11930; *see p143*). A block north of its western tip, meanwhile, are the **4th Street Steps** (4th Street and Adelaide Drive), 189 concrete steps that function as a cliffside Stairmaster and a pick-up place for low-fat singles.

Third Street Promenade

Drifting south from Montana Avenue, Santa Monica gets steadily more commercial until you reach traffic-soaked **Wilshire Boulevard** and then, eventually, the **Third Street Promenade**. A four-block pedestrianised stretch that runs down 3rd Street from Wilshire to Colorado Avenue, it's anchored by the Frank Gehry-designed **Santa Monica Place** mall, a three-storey mix of independent shops and over-familiar chains (Gap, Sunglass Hut, Victoria's Secret). Approach the mall from Main Street to the south for a surprising façade, but be quick: it looks likely to be demolished soon to make way for an open-air mall.

The Third Street Promenade is a handsome affair, though the pride the locals take in it is rather out of proportion to its appeal. Street entertainers try to live up to their job title with mixed results, while henna tattooists ink passers-by too sensible for the real thing. College kids pick up threads from **Urban Outfitters** (No.1440) and **Diesel** (No.1340; for both, *see p186*); their elder siblings settle down with a good book in the obligatory branches of **Barnes & Noble** (No.1201) and **Borders** (No.1415; for both, *see p182*). You get the picture.

Santa Monica Beach (p77) The *Lords of Dogtown* take to the surf

surfing and volleyball, as well as refreshment stands, showers and toilets. Alcohol, pets and nudity are prohibited; bonfires are permitted only at Dockweiler State Beach in Vista del Mar and Cabrillo Beach in San Pedro, and then only in designated fire rings. Lifeguards are on duty year round. Occasionally, due to rough rip tides, shark sightings and pollution, beaches may be closed by lifeguard crews, but such occurences are rare. In summer, check the LA Times for ratings of all the local beaches.

Though there is limited free parking on the Pacific Coast Highway, parking can be difficult and sometimes expensive. Still, it's better to pay for a legit space than have your vehicle towed. For more information on beaches, call the Department of Beaches & Harbors on 1-310 305 9546, or check its website at http://beaches.co.la.ca.us. The following are the pick of LA's beaches, from north to south.

El Matador State Beach

Small, beautiful and dominated by rocky outcrops, El Matador looks not unlike a European beach. Six miles north of Malibu and roughly 25 miles up the coast from Santa Monica (the approximate street address is 32350 Pacific Coast Highway), it's just past Zuma Beach (see p78), accessible via a steep gravelly path. Wear shoes and don't bring too much heavy gear or picnic paraphernalia. There are no lifeguards or other facilities, so you should be able to find some privacy on the beach; spread your towel in the cupped hands of the rocks.

Arriving early or staying late should reward you with a memorable dawn or sunset. El Matador and nearby El Pescador and La Piedra beaches collectively form the Robert H Meyer Memorial Beaches; both its neighbours are worth a visit. ▶

But amid this parade of the familiar are some welcome streaks of individuality. Foodies and top local chefs head here on Wednesdays and Saturdays for the fine farmers' markets (see p194). **Puzzle Zoo** (No.1413; see p202) charms all and sundry with its engaging array of child-pleasers, and comes as welcome evidence that not all of Santa Monica is vanilla flavoured.

Angels Attic Museum

516 Colorado Avenue, between 5th & 6th Streets (1-310 394 8331/www.angelsattic.com). Bus 4, 304, SM2, SM3, SM4, SM5, SM9/I-10, exit 4th-5th Street north. **Open** 12.30-4.30pm Thur-Sun. **Admission** $6.50; $3.50-$4 concessions. **Credit** MC, V. **Map** p310 A3.
One of Los Angeles's most charming museums, this delightful Victorian property is home to more than 60 antique dolls' houses, along with an array of dolls from around the world, in seven separate galleries. The museum celebrated its 20th birthday in 2004.

Santa Monica Historical Society Museum

1539 Euclid Street, between Broadway & Colorado Avenue (1-310 395 2290/www.santamonicahistory. org). Bus 4, 304, SM1, SM5, SM10, SM11/I-10, exit 4th-5th Street north. **Open** 10am-4.30pm Tue-Fri; 1-4pm 2nd & 4th Suns of mth. **Admission** $5; $2 discounts; free under-12s. **Credit** MC, V. **Map** p310 B3.
This small museum, founded in the 1970s and located several blocks east of the Third Street Promenade, contains an assortment of displays detailing the history of the city. Among its most precious holdings are some 500,000 photographs; the

majority are from the Santa Monica Outlook newspaper, which closed in 1998 after over 120 years of publication. Space constraints mean that the majority of the museum's exhibits are in storage, but in 2007 the situation should improve when it moves to a larger space in the Santa Monica Public Library at 6th Street and Santa Monica Boulevard.

Santa Monica Beach

For a different perspective, head a block north and a block west from the Third Street Promenade to the Rooftop bar and restaurant at the **Huntley Hotel** (1111 2nd Street, 1-310 394 5454, www.thehuntleyhotel.com). On a clear day, you can see all the way to Santa Catalina Island and the endless lizard's back of the jagged San Bernardino Mountain peaks.

Continuing a couple of blocks west will bring you to hotel-lined **Ocean Avenue** and, across the road, lovely Santa Monica Beach. The focal point is **Santa Monica Pier** (at Colorado Avenue), a pleasingly traditional operation stocked with all the usual fairground games (including a Ferris wheel) and cotton-candy stands. On warm weekends, the whole stretch is busy with revelling families and sun-bleached beach bums. Those who'd rather not get sand between their toes hole up at the posh terrace bar at **Shutters on the Beach** (see p46) to watch sunset, before adjourning across Ocean Avenue to the **Viceroy** (see p46) to sup Cosmos with the beautiful people.

Life's a beach (continued)

Zuma Beach

The four-mile sprawl of immaculate sand that makes up Malibu's family-friendly Zuma Beach (at 30000 PCH) is ideal for surfing, swimming, volleyball, sunbathing and long walks; the water is clean and the sand soft beneath your feet. Zuma can get crowded, and getting there along the traffic-congested PCH can be a challenge. There are lifeguards, toilets and showers. You can buy food from stands, but packing a picnic basket is a better idea.

Malibu

Most beaches in Malibu are legally required to have public access, but finding the routes to them can be very difficult. The public beaches, spotted with commercial restaurants, are nothing out of the ordinary but still prove popular for swimming, sunning and watching the do-or-die surfers at Surfrider Beach. There are also tidepools, a marine preserve, and volleyball and picnic areas. Drive out towards Point Dume to see the opulent houses of the rich and famous, some sitting precariously on the edge of rocky bluffs.

Santa Monica State Beach

This big beach is usually crowded and has a festive, summer-holiday feel to it. The big attraction is Santa Monica Pier, about three city blocks in length and packed with typical and endearingly low-tech distractions: pier fishing, video arcades, free twilight dance concerts in summer, fortune tellers, fairground games, rides and an 11-storey Ferris wheel.

Venice Beach

People-watching is the raison d'être at Venice Beach. Seawards from the Walk, jump into the flow of the winding Venice Boardwalk, where you can skate or

Santa Monica Pier Aquarium

1600 Ocean Front Walk, at Colorado Avenue (1-310 393 6149/www.healthebay.org/smpa). Bus 33, 333, SM1, SM4, SM7, SM8, SM10/I-10, exit 4th-5th Street north. **Open** 2-5pm Tue-Fri; 12.30-5pm Sat, Sun. **Admission** $2-$5. **Credit** MC, V. **Map** p310 A3.

Now run by environmental charity Heal the Bay after UCLA had to pass it up due to funding difficulties, the Santa Monica Pier Aquarium takes an avowedly educational tack; indeed, it's closed during the morning to allow for school field trips. A nice diversion for parents who can't bear the raucous atmosphere on the pier, the museum is located at beach level, directly beneath the pier's carousel.

Ocean Park & Main Street

Main Street begins at the bottom of the Third Street Promenade and ends a little over two miles south-east in the heart of Venice. However, its most interesting stretch runs between Pico Boulevard and Rose Avenue. This is the hilly, bohemian neighbourhood of **Ocean Park**, immortalised often in paintings by Richard Diebenkorn, one of its famous denizens.

The street, one of Santa Monica's three main commercial thoroughfares (along with Montana Avenue and the Third Street Parade), is an upmarket strip populated with coffeehouses, shops, restaurants and, of course, the ubiquitous joggers. However, its highlight is

the **Edgemar Center for the Arts** (No.2437), a Frank Gehry-designed sculptural mall that houses the MOCA store and a branch of **Peet's Coffee & Tea** (*see p166*), considered by coffee snobs to offer the best java around.

All those highlights are on Main Street between Strand and Rose Avenues, which runs through the most charming part of Ocean Park. The large commercial chain stores are notable largely by their absence; these pedestrian-scale buildings, dating from the early 20th century, instead house a number of intriguing clothes and bric-a-brac stores, plus the **Eames Office Gallery** (No.2665, 1-310 396 5991, www. eamesoffice.com), founded by Charles and Ray's grandson, Eames Demetrios.

Inland Santa Monica

Though inland Santa Monica is chiefly residential, it does hold pockets of interest for the visitor. Chief among them is **Bergamot Station**, a complex of art galleries created at a former Red Trolley terminus (2525 Michigan Avenue, at Cloverfield Boulevard, www. bergamotstation.com; *see also p222*). Its most famous tenant is the **Santa Monica Museum of Art** (*see p79*), but many of its other galleries merit attention. The area's other major museum is the currently closed **Museum of Flying** (*see p79*) at the **Santa Monica**

cycle, watch or play volleyball or basketball, and check out the pumped-up men and women who work out at Muscle Beach. Street parking is usually jammed, but there are several beachside parking lots; try the end of Rose Avenue or Windward Avenue, off Pacific Avenue.

Manhattan & Hermosa Beaches

These neighbouring spots south of LAX are right out of a Southern California postcard, offering clean water, sand that stretches out of sight, small piers and all kinds of activities: volleyball (Manhattan Beach hosts an annual Volleyball Open each August), sailing and ocean-front paths for walking, cycling and inline skating. The charm of these beaches is the local flavour; visitors can swim, picnic and bask in the sun alongside residents and local fishermen. The surf isn't bad either.

Huntington State Beach

Essentially, more of the above, just further south (Huntington Beach is about 15 miles south of Long Beach). Its chief attraction is its surfing: Huntington Beach picks up swells from a variety of directions, which makes for good waves, and the water is often less crowded than at Malibu's Surfrider Beach.

Airport, itself home to a monthly antiques market (fourth Sunday of the month) and the well regarded **Hump** restaurant (*see p141*).

California Heritage Museum

2612 Main Street, at Ocean Park Boulevard (1-310 392 8537/www.californiaheritagemuseum.org). Bus 33, 333, SM1, SM2, SM8, SM10/I-10, exit 4th-5th Street south. **Open** 11am-4pm Wed-Sun. **Admission** $5; $3 discounts; free under-12s. **Credit** MC, V. **Map** p310 A3.
An engaging, enthusiastically run operation, housed in an 1894 Summer P Hunt house and devoted, for the most part, to the decorative arts. The exhibits take the shape of a number of rooms decorated in period style, among them a Victorian-era dining room and a 1930s kitchen. This permanent collection is supplemented by temporary displays; past shows have been devoted to Santa Catalina Island and masks from around the globe. For the weekly farmers' market held here, *see p194.*

Museum of Flying

Santa Monica Airport (1-310 392 8822/www. museumofflying.com). Bus SM8/I-10, exit Bundy Drive south. **Open** call for details. **Admission** call for details. **Credit** AmEx, MC, V. **Map** p310 D5.
Devoted to the history of aviation, this small museum closed in 2004 to move into new premises. The process has proven more time-consuming than the museum anticipated, but it hoped to move into a new aircraft hangar on the north side of Santa Monica Airport by early 2007. Call before setting out.

Santa Monica Museum of Art

Building G1, Bergamot Station, 2525 Michigan Avenue, at Cloverfield Boulevard (1-310 586 6488/ www.smmoa.org). Bus SM7/I-10, exit Cloverfield Boulevard north. **Open** 11am-6pm Tue-Sat. **Admission** free; suggested donation $3. **Credit** AmEx, MC, V. **Map** p310 D3.
Greater LA's best contemporary art gallery occupies a corner of Bergamot Station, a former trolley stop on the LA–Santa Monica red line, and attracts sizeable crowds to its openings and lively temporary exhibitions by local and international artists. Shows have included collages and drawings by the late Fluxus-Happenings artist Al Hansen and his grandson, singer Beck, and Portuguese architect Alvaro Siza. Keep an eye out for the regular special events (lectures, discussions, concerts and the like) that accompany the shows.

Santa Monica Visitor Center

1920 Main Street, at Pico Boulevard (1-310 393 7593/www.santamonica.com). Bus 33, 333, SM1, SM4, SM7, SM8, SM10/I-10, exit 4th-5th Street south. **Open** 9am-6pm daily. **Map** p310 A3.

Venice

Map p310

Despite the gentrification in and around it, its touristy atmosphere, and the fact that its name long ago passed into popular cliché as a byword for hippydom, Venice retains its edge. Its most visible population is what it's been for decades

Sightseeing

Public art Santa Monica to Venice

Appropriately, much of LA's public art was designed to be seen through a car windscreen. Murals pace alongside the freeways and streets, from the East LA *barrio* to Santa Monica and Downtown to Venice Beach; outdoor sculptures sit by the side of the road. However, along the beaches in and around Santa Monica, there's a vast slew of public art that's best seen from two feet rather than four wheels. Taking a zig-zag path southwards along the shoreline from the Third Street Promenade (*see p76*) to Venice will bring you past a wildly varied array of murals, sculptures and spectacles.

The topiary dinosaur fountains of sculptors Claude and François LaLanne join Seward Johnson's lifelike cast-bronze figures along the Third Street Promenade. On the beach, just north of the Santa Monica Pier, sits Carl Cheng's imposing *Walk on LA*; under the pier is Manfred Muller's *Twilight and Yearning*. Heading back inland, Paul Conrad's *Chain Reaction*, a copper and stainless steel chain-link mushroom cloud, sits outside the Santa Monica Civic Auditorium, just north of the intersection of Main Street and Pico Boulevard. Back on the beach (near where Pico Boulevard hits it) sit Doug Hollis's *Singing Beach Chairs*, a set of full-scale musically tuned lifeguard chairs.

As you cross into Venice, the artistic aesthetic becomes less refined, more organic and often exuberantly bizarre. At the corner of Rose Avenue and Main Street, Jonathan Borofsky's iconic *Ballerina Clown* (*pictured*) sits diagonally across from the equally iconic but less subversive *Binoculars* by Claes Oldenburg, incorporated into the Frank Gehry-designed TBWA Chiat/Day building. Head back to the boardwalk for a long stretch of murals; including, at Speedway and 18th Avenue, *Jim Morrison* by legendary Venice denizen Rip Cronk.

Along the beach, keep an eye out for Noel Osheroff's stone bench medallions, mosaic inlays on public restrooms by William Attaway and, of course, the dozens of artists and craftsmen plying their wares along the route to the turnabout at Windward Circle (look for the 60-foot steel sexton by Mark di Suvero). Indeed, public art in Venice is generally performative, and the people are the heart of the experience. The lively graffiti pit at Windward changes every hour, with spray can artists from all over the city engaged in a perpetual game of tag.

Several websites provide information on the constantly evolving public art landscape of the Westside, among them the Mural Conservancy of Los Angeles (www.la murals.org), SPARC (www.sparcmurals. com) and Public Art in LA (www.publicart inla.com). In addition, the Santa Monica authorities have published an 'Art Trek' map that pinpoints the galleries and works of public art around the city. You can pick it up from the visitor centre (*see p79*), or download it from www.santamonica.com.

– hippies, bums, artists and students – but in recent years, they've been joined by young creatives who can't afford a place in Santa Monica (and, in some cases, wouldn't want one if they could). However, even they're being priced out of the market these days: the stratospheric rise in property prices has given rise to new condo developments offering a kind of faked loft-living for moneyed newbies. The uneasy mix is completed by low-income black and Latino communities beset by social problems; the Oakwood area (circumscribed by Lincoln and Venice Boulevards and Sunset and Electric Avenues) is a bit sketchy after dark, though it's far safer than it was a decade ago.

Venice owes its existence to entrepreneur Abbot Kinney, who founded the once-independent city (it's now under the jurisdiction of Los Angeles) in 1904, hoping that it would become the hub of an American cultural renaissance. The canals (complete with two dozen gondoliers imported from Italy), lagoon and Venetian-style buildings were all his doing, and though he failed to achieve the cultural rebirth, he did create a successful resort known, in its heyday, as the 'Playland of the Pacific'.

It wasn't until later, after many of its canals were tarmacked, that Venice developed as a cultural hotbed. Artists have been attracted to the area for decades, drawn by the sense of community and cheap rents. Among those who've long maintained studios here are Laddie John Dill, Ed Moses and Chuck Arnoldi, now wealthy on their landholdings as well as their art. If you're here in May, look out for the annual Venice Artwalk, a fundraiser for the Venice Family Clinic that offers visitors the opportunity to tour more than 60 artists' studios. Year-round, though, keep your eyes peeled for the public art around Venice; Jonathan Borofsky's *Ballerina Clown*, on the corner of Main Street and Rose Avenue, is the most striking, but Ocean Front Walk and its surrounding streets are home to many more examples, including a number of murals.

But while the artistic community is long established, it wasn't until the 1980s that Venice became a hotbed of architectural activity. The neighbourhood punches well above its weight with regard to the design of its buildings, and an enjoyable few hours can be spent touring its more notable spots. Frank Gehry's **Norton and Spiller Houses** (2509 Ocean Front Walk and 30 Horizon Avenue) are overshadowed only by his **Chiat/Day Building** (340 Main Street), its entrance marked by a gigantic pair of Claes Oldenburg-designed binoculars. Among other striking buildings are the **Sedlak and 2-4-6-8 Houses** by Morphosis (Superba Court,

Amoroso Court); Brian Murphy's **Hopper House** (Indiana Avenue); the John Friedmann/Alice Kimm reworking of swank bar the **Brig** (1515 Abbot Kinney Boulevard); and several new apartment buildings by such notable local architects as Fred Fisher (the **Hampton Studio Lofts**, 800-804 Hampton Drive), Stephen Ehrlich (the **Venice Beach Loft**, 25 Brooks Avenue), Koning Eizenberg (the **Electric Artblock**, 499 Santa Clara Avenue) and Mark Mack (the **Abbot Kinney Lofts**, 1200 Abbot Kinney Boulevard).

As expected for such a residential area, Venice is low on traditional attractions; its streets are its sights. The area west of Lincoln Boulevard has rows of clapboard beachhouses on 'walk-streets' (pedestrian-only alleyways leading to the beach) and, at the more affluent southern end, one of LA's best-kept secrets: an idyllic enclave of eclectic architecture, waterways, bridges and motormouth ducks known as the Venice Canals.

Its founder is commemorated in the name of its main thoroughfare, the increasingly chichi **Abbot Kinney Boulevard**. On it sits a varied collection of galleries, shops, cafés (chiefly the **Abbot's Habit** at No.1402 and **Jin Patisserie** at No.1201; for both, *see p166*) and restaurants such as popular, fashionable **Axe** (No.1009; for both, *see p142*). The area's other key strip is **Rose Avenue**, an east–west commercial street at the north end of the neighbourhood. It holds a few interesting second-hand shops, but the main attraction is the **Rose Café** (No.220, 1-310 399 0711), a self-serve and sit-down restaurant with an attractive garden and craft store.

Near the corner of Rose Avenue and Main Street sit two of LA's most famous gyms – **Gold's** (*see p259*) and the **World Gym** (812 Main Street, 1-310 827 8019) – although you won't have to visit either to see their buff clientele, who can often be spied showing off their beefy biceps at many Venice locales. The most famous is Muscle Beach, home each day to assorted steroid-stuffed individuals who see their exercise as entertainment.

Muscle Beach just a small corner of **Venice Beach** (*see p78* **Life's a beach**), long known as a mecca for kooky California culture. These days, the innumerable henna tattooists, ropey buskers and cheap sunglasses retailers recall nothing so much as Greenwich Village or Camden Market under the sun; it's unlikely that

Venice Pier Michael Douglas finally gets his comeuppance in *Falling Down*

Venice Boardwalk.

a 2006 ordinance aimed at limiting the number of vendors and entertainers on the Boardwalk will change the character of the place too much. Still, the Boardwalk entertains, whether for people-watching (skateboarders, couples, the area's few remaining unhinged goofballs), lunch-munching (at the **Figtree Café**, 429 Ocean Front Walk, 1-310 392 4937, *p46*) or book-browsing (at the excellent **Small World Books**, 1407 Ocean Front Walk; *see p182*).

Marina del Rey

Considering its location next to the largest area of open water on the planet, one strangely unsung aspect of life in LA is its sailing. Many Angelenos keep boats – and some even live in them – at **Marina del Rey Harbor**, a resort and residential complex just south of Venice in an area bounded by Washington Boulevard, Admiralty Way, Fiji Way and Via Marina. Conceived a century ago and finally completed in 1965, the Marina consists of an artificial harbour with eight basins named to evoke the South Seas (Tahiti Way, Bora Bora Way) and filled with bobbing yachts, motor boats and flashy cruisers; around the outside sit low- and high-rise apartment blocks, generic hotels and touristy restaurants.

**Venice High School
(1300 Venice Boulevard, Venice)**
Rydell High School in *Grease*

Perceived as a haven for swinging singles, the Marina is actually home to many retirees and young families for whom the complex is a reasonably priced and slightly charming place to live. Its sterility is enlivened enormously by a motley crew of impecunious, old-school boat-dwellers; indeed, if only to see a true 1970s period piece, the Marina is worth a visit.

The Marina's attractions are all recreational. Picnic, jog and cycle (the Marina is a link in the 21-mile coastal bike path) in the **Burton W Chace Park** and **Admiralty Park** at the northern end; fish from a dock at the west end of Chace Park or rent a boat to go ocean-fishing at **Fisherman's Village** (13755 Fiji Way, at Lincoln Boulevard; Green Boathouse); or join whale-watching excursions run during winter by any number of charter companies. But otherwise, save your money: the shopping is touristy (concentrated in Fisherman's Wharf, a cheesy replica of a New England fishing town), and most eateries are more to be recommended for their waterside charm rather than the actual food that they serve.

At the south end of Marina del Rey, just north of LAX, is **Playa del Rey**, a largely residential beach neighbourhood and artificial lagoon. The area is a magnet for nature-lovers and birdwatchers, who come to observe the great grey herons, white egrets and other creatures that converge on the **Ballona Wetlands**, the last remaining large, coastal wetland ecosystem in LA county, just east of Playa del Rey, in Playa Vista.

Brentwood to Beverly Hills

Money can't buy you love. Here's what it can buy you instead.

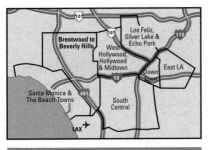

Brentwood

Brentwood consisted of farms and fields until 1915, when a real-estate agent named Bundy saw its residential potential. Landscape architects and engineers were commissioned to create 'flora, arbor and artistic park attractions', and everything that suggested a formal city street was avoided. As such, Brentwood resembles a small town; the main road, **San Vicente Boulevard**, has running down its centre a line of coral trees, the official tree of LA.

In years gone by, Raymond Chandler wrote *High Window* and *Lady of the Lake* while living at 12216 Shetland Place, and Marilyn Monroe died a lonely death down the road at 12305 5th Helena Drive. However, it was another star who really put Brentwood on the map, although the exact parts he put on it are no longer there. The condo of murdered Nicole Brown Simpson on S Bundy Drive has been relandscaped to deter ghoulish sightseers, while OJ Simpson's house on N Rockingham Avenue was bulldozed in summer 1998 for similar reasons.

Getty Center
1200 Getty Center Drive, at I-405 (1-310 440 7300/ www.getty.edu). Bus 761/I-405, exit Getty Center Drive. **Open** 10am-6pm Tue-Thur, Sun; 10am-9pm Fri, Sat. **Admission** free.

Los Angeles's acropolis occupies the top of a hill on land once destined to be the site of a co-operative housing development. The complex was conceived as a home for the hitherto disparate entities of the J Paul Getty Trust, but that's the only straightforward thing about it. Architect Richard Meier was hired to

build it in 1984, but it took 13 years, several additional designers (to work on the interior and the landscaping) and $1 billion to complete. The surprise is that it turned out to be a remarkable set-up, a complex of travertine and white metal-clad pavilions that resembles a kind of monastic retreat designed for James Bond (or, say critics, a high-end office park). Its relative inaccessibility is more than compensated for by the stupendous panoramic views, from the hills and the ocean in the west all the way around to Downtown in the east.

Once you've parked at the bottom of the hill and taken the electric tram ride up to the museum complex, one thing quickly becomes apparent: it's a big place. To the west of the plaza is a café and a restaurant, both excellent, and the circular Research Institute, which houses a private scholarly centre and a changing roster of public exhibits. North are the other institutes (some off-limits to the general public) and the Harold M Williams Auditorium, where lectures and symposia alternate with less academic fare. And to the south, up a grand Spanish Steps-style stairway, is the museum lobby, an airy, luminous rotunda that opens to a fountain-filled open courtyard surrounded by six pavilions housing the permanent collection and temporary shows. Still, the art can't compete with the buildings in which it's housed, the Central Garden (designed by Robert Irwin to a mixed reception, but nonetheless a focal point), the Cactus Garden on the South Promontory, and, most of all, *those* views.

Collections
The Getty Center's acquisitions budget is the envy of museums the world over. However, it was a Johnny-come-lately to European art; until, say, the Vatican has a fire sale, the collections won't be a match for the museums of the Old World. This point was drilled home in 2004, when London's National Gallery raised £22 million to keep Raphael's *The Madonna of the Pinks* in the UK after the Getty had offered £7 million more for it. Still, that's not to write off its holdings. Certain aspects – post-Renaissance decorative arts and, especially, its ever-expanding photography selection – are magnificent.

> **Mount St Mary's College (12001 Chalon Road, Brentwood)**
> Harbor High School on *The OC*

Billions of dollars + love of art = **Getty Center**. *See p83.*

The collections are spread over four two-level pavilions, all linked on both levels by walkways. The art is displayed more or less chronologically: the **North Pavilion** contains pieces from prior to 1600; the **East and South Pavilions** feature works from the 17th and 18th centuries; and the **West Pavilion** begins in 1800 and runs up to the present day. The plaza level of each pavilion contains sculpture and decorative arts, along with temporary exhibits in other disciplines (illuminated manuscripts in the North Pavilion, drawings in the East Pavilion, photography in the West Pavilion); the first floor of each pavilion is given over to paintings. There's a lot to see.

On the ground floor of the **North Pavilion**, room N104 contains an eye-catching array of glass objects dating from the 15th century, while N105 is home to a rotating series of small-scale displays drawn from the Getty's collection of illuminated manuscripts. Upstairs is dominated by Italian religious painting of the 15th and 16th centuries, with highlights being a vast altarpiece by Bartolomeo Vivarini (N202) and a scintillating *Venus & Adonis* believed to have come from Titian's workshop (N205).

The selection of paintings in the **East Pavilion** is heavy on the Dutch and Flemish masters, albeit with few major works. Notable pieces include Gerrit van Honthorst's *Christ Crowned with Thorns* (E201); works by Rubens, among them *The Entombment* (E202); a minor Frans Hals (E204); and Gerrit Dou's intensely detailed *Astronomer by Candlelight* (E205). The ground floor is given over to so-so European sculpture (E101) and displays from the drawings collection (E202 & E203).

One of the museum's strengths is the collection of 17th- and 18th-century decorative arts, most of it French, that monopolises the ground-floor galleries in the **South Pavilion**. Some rooms contain individual exhibits (seek out the glorious long-case clock in S103, and the immense, luxuriant bed in S109); others are virtual reconstructions of French drawing

rooms, complete with original panelling. Next to this opulent array, the galleries upstairs can't compete, but they do contain three Gainsborough portraits (S204) and Odilon Redon's *Baronne de Domecy*, an amazing, dream-like piece that overshadows the rest of the pastels and watercolours in S206.

The ground-floor galleries in the **West Pavilion** are given over to unremarkable European sculpture and decorative arts from the late 18th and 19th centuries plus, in W104-W106, changing exhibits from the excellent photography holdings. Upstairs is a strong-ish selection of paintings, mostly from the 19th century. Delacroix's fierce *Moroccan Horseman Crossing a Ford* (W201) is terrific, and room W202 contains a seascape by Turner, but the key exhibits are in W204: several Monet pieces, a Cézanne still life, a delightfully raffish Renoir portrait of composer Albert Cahen d'Anvers, and Van Gogh's *Irises*.

Skirball Cultural Center & Museum

2701 N Sepulveda Boulevard, at I-405 (1-310 440 4500/www.skirball.org). Bus 761/I-405, exit Skirball Center/Mulholland Drive north. **Open** noon-5pm Tue, Wed, Fri, Sat; noon-9pm Thur; 11am-5pm Sun. **Admission** $8; $6 discounts; free under-12s and to all Thur. **Credit** MC, V.

An offshoot of the Hebrew Union College located six miles north of the Getty Center, the Skirball has become quite a powerhouse. The permanent displays include a reconstruction of a Middle Eastern archaeological dig and a collection of pieces chronicling Jewish migration to America, but the emphasis is on temporary shows, a mix of social history displays and art exhibitions that have taken in such varied topics as the history of the American Dream and folk photography in LA. The Skirball also offers lectures, readings and a variety of performances.

Incidentally, the Hebrew Union College should not be confused with the University of Judaism across the I-405 (15600 Mulholland Drive, 1-310 476 9777, www.uj.edu), whose smallish Platt Gallery shows work by mainly Jewish local artists.

Culver City

Located at the intersection of the I-10 and I-405 , Culver City was once the home of three major motion picture studios – MGM, Hal Roach and Selznick International – and produced half the films made in the US. Movies such as *The Wizard of Oze* were shot here, but the old glamour has evaporated. MGM, which claimed to have 'more stars than there are in heaven', sold up to the producers of *Dallas*; the area is now dominated by **Sony Studios**, squeezed in on part of the old MGM lot between W Washington and Culver Boulevards east of Overland Avenue. For tours, *see p71*.

However, thanks to forward-thinking city planners, Culver City is back on the up. Downtown, at the junction of Main Street and Culver Boulevard, is a low-key collection of shops, galleries and restaurants. **Town Plaza**, around the junction of Culver Boulevard and Irving Place, is surely the only block in the city with two fountain sculptures: Eric Orr's nameless triangular granite pole, and Douglas Olmsted Freeman's more eye-catching *Lion's Fountain*. A few yards to the west are a couple of historic structures: the **Culver Hotel**, built in the 1920s, and the **Kirk Douglas Theatre** (*see p262*), an old 1940s cinema. North of here, across Culver Boulevard, are the tidy **Media Park** and the extraordinary **Museum of Jurassic Technology** (*see below*).

Away from Downtown, Culver City's main attractions are architectural. Local bakers Helms may have baked their last loaf in 1969, but the **Helms Bakery** remains. An 11-acre complex located at the corner of Venice Boulevard and Helms Avenue, it now houses furniture shops and the **Jazz Bakery** (*see p244*).

Not far from here, on the 3500 block of **Hayden Avenue** close to the junction with National Boulevard, is perhaps the most eye-catching architectural project in LA.

In the 1940s and '50s, the **Hayden Tract** was a thriving industrial area, but by the '80s the businesses had largely moved out. Enter Frederick Smith, an entrepreneur with a vision of how to regenerate the area, and Eric Owen Moss, the experimental architect he chose to give it life. Some of the old factories remain, but others have been replaced by Moss's odd yet dazzling office buildings.

Park outside the daunting black hulk of the **Stealth** building (3528 Hayden Avenue); walk under it and into the parking lot to see Moss's singular style in full effect. In one corner stands the **Umbrella** (No.3542), its crazed exterior staircase leading nowhere; across the way is another building with a frontage that leans precariously forward, echoing the angles of the Stealth building. Back on the main road sits the demented façade of **3535 Hayden Avenue**, all spiky wood and awkward concrete. Just around the corner on **National Boulevard** are **8522 National**, a complex of five renovated warehouses, and the **Box**, whose meeting room sticks out like a sore (and square) thumb. And over on La Cienega Boulevard sits the strangely graceful **Samitaur** building (No.3457).

Museum of Jurassic Technology

9341 Venice Boulevard, at Bagley Avenue (1-310 836 6131/www.mjt.org). Bus 33, 220, 333, C1, C4, C5/I-10, exit Robertson Boulevard south. **Open** 2-8pm Thur; noon-6pm Fri-Sun. **Admission** free; suggested donation $5. **No credit cards.**

Don't be fooled by the name: this is not some kind of Spielbergian dinosaurland. It's far more interesting than that. Hidden behind an unassuming, windowless storefront, David Wilson's Museum of Jurassic Technology presents itself as a repository of curiosities (opera singer Madelena Delani, who suffered from terrible memory failings), scientific wonders (a bat that can fly through walls) and artistic miracles (the so-called 'microminiatures' of Soviet-Armenian refugee Hagop Sandaldjian, who painted impossibly tiny sculptures that fit within the eye of a needle with plenty of room to spare).

Sightseeing

Greystone Mansion. *See p89.*

Walk UCLA campus

As befits one of America's most highly regarded academic institutions, the campus of **UCLA** (the University of California at Los Angeles) is a grand, handsome place. A walk around it is a pleasant way to spend an hour or two, diverse architectural styles and noteworthy public art blending in beautifully landscaped grounds that together highlight the school's huge wealth and influence. Before you stroll, though, pick up a campus map and a parking permit ($8) from the booth on Westwood Plaza: parking tickets are dispensed here with alarming enthusiasm.

Once you've parked, walk north from the information booth past the **Ackerman Student Union Building** and you'll come to **Bruin Plaza**, a buzzing spot for most of the day. Political and social groups campaign here, under the gaze of the fearsome **Bruin Bear** statue. There's more activity further north past the **Ashe Center** (named in honour of Arthur Ashe, a Davis Cup player while still a student here), but of a very different kind: in fine weather, **Wilson Plaza** is covered with students playing football, tossing Frisbees or flicking through textbooks.

Tucked away in the north-east corner of Wilson Plaza is the **Fowler Museum of Cultural History** (1-310 825 4361, www.fowler.ucla.edu), which presents temporary exhibitions on diverse ethnographic themes. Although the subjects can be a little esoteric, they're presented in an approachable way that draws in the cultural gadfly. The one permanent display is of 250 pieces from the Francis Fowler silver collection.

From here, make your way up the **Janss Steps**, but be careful – a long-held superstition runs that treading on the sixth step dooms the walker to bad luck and, perhaps, an extra year in college. At the top is **Dickson Terrace**, an indelibly handsome patch of green named for Edward Dickson, the university's founding father. To your right is **Royce Hall**, home to many events in the university's excellent UCLA Live series (see p264). And on your left is the **Powell Library**, handsome from the outside and beautiful from within. Both buildings were completed in 1929 and modelled, to some degree, after Italian churches: Royce Hall on the Basilica Sant'Ambrogio in Milan, and the Powell Library after the Basilica di San Zeno in Verona. Along with **Kinsey Hall** and **Haines Hall**, which also flank Dickson Terrace, they're the oldest buildings on the campus.

Continue past the flagpole and turn left past **Dodd Hall** and the **Luvalle Commons** building (stop here for a snack if you're hungry), and skip quickly past the horrible **Public Policy Building** on your right. You're now in the **Franklin D Murphy Sculpture Garden**, which holds works by the likes of Barbara Hepworth (*Elegy III*), Joan Miro (*Mère Ubu*) and Henry Moore (*Two-Piece Reclining Figure*). Don't be alarmed if you see a few students talking expansively to themselves: they're probably theatre students rehearsing for plays to be staged in one of two theatres in **MacGowan Hall**. To the north-east corner of the garden sits the new **Edye & Eli Broad Art Center**, due to open in late 2006.

Fact is mixed with the fantastical through the elaborate treatment (dramatically lit vitrines, audiovisual displays) accorded everything from the history of trailer parks to 17th-century Renaissance man Athanasius Kircher. Which exhibits, if any, are bona fide? Which, if any, are satirical? And does it matter? A subversive, witty and brilliant enterprise, it challenges the very nature of what a museum is or should be, while also taking its place as one of the city's most fascinating attractions. Unique and unreservedly recommended.

Star Eco Station

10101 W Jefferson Boulevard, between Overland & Duquesne Avenues, Culver City (1-310 842 8060/ www.ecostation.org). Bus 220, C3, C4/I-10, exit Overland Avenue south. **Open** 1-5pm Fri; 10am-4pm Sat, Sun. **Admission** $7; $5-$6 discounts. **No credit cards**.

This new wildlife rescue centre in Culver City provides care for unwanted exotic animals donated by the public or confiscated by governmental agencies. Families are welcome to pet an alligator or stroke a snake as they learn about endangered species, environmental concerns and how kids can make a change.

Westwood & around

The Westwood neighbourhood is dominated by **UCLA**. The 400-acre campus makes for an agreeable diversion. To reach it, drive up Westwood Boulevard and follow the right-hand fork as it turns into Westwood Plaza. *See above* **Walk** for a tour.

South of UCLA and north of Wilshire Boulevard is **Westwood Village**. This small pocket of commerce, centred around Westwood

Walk down Charles E Young Drive East and you'll come to the **Founders Rock**, a 75-ton boulder dragged here from Perris Valley (halfway between LA and San Diego) and dedicated in 1946 on the 20th anniversary of the founding of UCLA. Head past **Murphy Hall**, outside which are sculptures by Gordon Newell and Fritz Koenig, and then walk south to the **Schoenberg Hall**; it's named in honour of exiled German composer Arnold Schoenberg, who served as professor here (having previously taught at USC). To the west of the building is a model for Robert Graham's *Duke Ellington Memorial* in New York, Duke at the piano balanced on the heads of nine nude muses. And just south is perhaps the most striking piece of public art on the campus: Jere Hazlett's **Inverted Fountain**, inspired by the hot springs of Yellowstone.

From here, you could wander further south to the **Mathias Botanical Garden** (1-310 206 6707, www.botgard.ucla.edu), a seven-acre, 5,000-species habitat; alternatively, cut back through the campus, where your car awaits. Hopefully, it won't have a parking ticket on it.

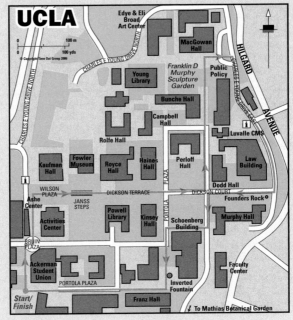

Boulevard and Broxton Avenue, is walkable, but the restaurants and shops are bland; a surprise, perhaps, given the high population of students. There's less to buy but more to see at the **UCLA Hammer Museum** (*see below*) and **Westwood Memorial Park** (1218 Glendon Avenue, at Wilshire Boulevard, 1-310 474 1579), the final resting place of Marilyn Monroe, Billy Wilder and Frank Zappa (in an unmarked grave next to actor Lew Ayres).

South of here, the area rather peters out. Wilshire Boulevard itself is dominated by uninteresting skyscrapers; below it, Westwood Boulevard contains a few ethnic restaurants but not much else. The most powerful presence in the area is the **Mormon Temple** (10777 Santa Monica Boulevard, at Overland Avenue), topped by a 257-foot (84-metre) tower that's

itself crowned with a gold-leaf statue of the angel Moroni. The temple, the largest Mormon house of worship outside Salt Lake City, is open only to church members (there's a visitor centre for those who don't claim to be Latter Day Saints; 1-310 474 1549), but the manicured lawn and white stone building, lit at night, are an awe-inspiring sight. Similarly expansive, but rather less impressive, is the **Westside Pavilion**, a classic 1980s LA mall.

UCLA Hammer Museum

10899 Wilshire Boulevard, at Westwood Boulevard (1-310 443 7000/www.hammer.ucla.edu). Bus 20, 21, 720, SM1, SM2, SM3, SM8, SM12/I-405, exit Wilshire Boulevard east. **Open** 11am-7pm Tue, Wed, Fri, Sat; 11am-9pm Thur; 11am-5pm Sun. **Admission** $5; $3 discounts; free under-17s. Free to all Thur. **Credit** AmEx, MC, V. **Map** p311 A4.

Rich industrialist Armand Hammer founded this museum in his Occidental Petroleum building primarily to house his personal collection. Now, under the ownership of UCLA and the leadership of Annie Philbin, the Hammer stages fascinating themed shows of modern art, photography and graphic design. The former have included everything from video installations to educative shows on the development of American comic art, while the latter are often drawn from UCLA's Grunwald collection of graphic arts. Shows are supplemented by the Hammer Projects series, which focuses on emerging artists, and works from Hammer's own collections.

Bel Air

After it was developed by Alphonzo E Bell in the early 1920s, the sleepy hillside community north of Westwood rapidly became a favoured location among stars who valued privacy and a good view. Celebs abound, but there's not much for the outsider to see along the winding roads. The **Hotel Bel-Air** on Stone Canyon Road (No.701, at Bellagio Road; *see p52*) mirrors the tranquil, dripping-with-money locale, with its beautifully manicured gardens and luxuriant lake.

Century City

Tiny Century City was once a movie backlot, where Tom Mix filmed his Westerns. Bought by Alcoa from 20th Century Fox in 1961, it's still dominated by Fox Studios and a skyline-dominating overabundance of high-rise office buildings: 8.6 million square feet (800,000 square metres) of office space on only 176 acres of land. Most of the buildings are nondescript, but there are two exceptions, both by Minoru Yamasaki: the triangular **Century Plaza** towers and the **Century Plaza Hotel** (2025 Avenue of the Stars), a huge, high-rise ellipse. The main reason to visit is the **Westfield Shoppingtown** mall (*see p181*), which received an overhaul in 2006 to help it compete with the Grove.

Beverly Hills

Map p311

There is Big Money in many LA neighbourhoods. However, nowhere is the local wealth displayed with quite such panache as it is in Beverly Hills. Its commercial thoroughfares are lined with high-end shops and eateries, its residential streets are immaculately manicured, and both foot and motor traffic are pristine. It is, in other words, the Los Angeles of popular imagination.

The area has been a magnet for the famous for decades. Star couple Douglas Fairbanks and Mary Pickford were the first to move here in 1920, to a Wallace Neff-designed mansion at 1143 Summit Drive they called Pickfair. (It was demolished in 1988 by Pia Zadora, who built a less distinguished home in its place.) There are still a number of stars here, but immigrants from Iran and Israel make up an increasingly high proportion of the local population.

North of Santa Monica Boulevard

The best way to experience Beverly Hills is to drive the residential streets in the area bounded by **Sunset Boulevard**, **Doheny Drive**, **Santa Monica Boulevard** and **Walden Drive**. There's an eerie quiet throughout: traffic is sparse, while the only people on foot are gardeners. Still, if you get the feeling you're being watched, that's because you probably are: as tiny signs on almost every fencepost detail, security firms patrol these streets. You can't see them, but rest assured that they can see you.

The area is anything but homogenous. When you have as much money as the folks round here, you don't just buy a house: you build your own. And, of course, you build it exactly as you please, which might not be in anything like the same way as your neighbours. As a result, the architecture is a magpie blend of styles: everything from squat modernist boxes to palatial mansions and Spanish villas, often all on the same street. Still, nothing is quite as wild as the fairytale folly of the 1921 **Spadena House**, also known as the Witch's House (516 N Walden Drive, at Carmelita Avenue). Built in Culver City to house a movie studio's offices, the fantastical structure was moved here in 1934. Its owner is currently giving it a much-needed renovation, but you can still get an idea of its lunacy from a glance at the exterior.

At the north-eastern junction of Santa Monica and Wilshire Boulevards sits another landmark of old Beverly Hills. Harnessing **Beverly Gardens**, a pleasant but unremarkable stretch of greenery, stands the **Wilshire Electric Fountain**, built by architect Ralph Flewelling and sculptor Merrell Gage. Upon completion in 1931, the dramatic water displays and neon lighting stopped traffic. These days the traffic doesn't need any extra slowing down, but the fountain is still a fine sight. Its focal point is a Native American praying for rain.

Two Beverly Hills landmarks sit on Sunset Boulevard, by the junction with Beverly Drive. Known as the 'Pink Palace', the **Beverly Hills**

Hotel (No.9641; *see p52*) was one of the first buildings to be constructed in the city. Close by, at the intersection of Beverly and Sunset, is **Will Rogers Memorial Park**; it was here, in the park's public toilets, that George Michael was arrested in 1998.

The houses north of here, around Benedict and Coldwater Canyons, are even grander than those south of Sunset. None is more imposing than the **Greystone Mansion** (905 Loma Vista Drive, 1-310 550 4796, pictured p85), a 55-room Tudor-style home that's featured in films including *The Witches of Eastwick* and *Indecent Proposal*. The mansion was built in 1927 by oil millionaire Edward L Doheny for his son, who was shot dead within weeks of moving in. The house is closed to the public, but its 18 acres of landscaped gardens are open 10am-5pm daily.

South of Santa Monica Boulevard

While the streets north of Santa Monica Boulevard are where the locals live, the roads south of it are where they spend their money. The pocket bounded by Wilshire Boulevard, Canon Drive and Little Santa Monica Boulevard that includes **Rodeo Drive**, **Dayton Way** and **Brighton Way** is known as the **Golden Triangle**, and is home to every high-end fashion designer you'd care to name. **Two Rodeo Drive**, a $200-million ersatz European cobbled walkway, is always busy with window-shopping tourists and serious spenders. In contrast to the residential streets further north, this area is very pedestrian-friendly;

Where to park the Rolls? **Rodeo Drive**.

find a parking spot and pound the pavement to really get a handle on the area.

Signs of wealth abound along Little Santa Monica Boulevard. The **Peninsula Beverly Hills** (No.9882, at Charleville Boulevard; *see p54*) is a good place for celebrity-spotting; next door stands the IM Pei-designed **CAA** (Creative Artists Agency) building, all white marble and cantilevered glass. **Beverly Hills Rent-A-Car** (No.9732, at S Linden Drive) deals not in Fords and Chevys but Porsches and Ferraris, while **Sprinkles** (No.9635, at S Bedford Drive, 1-310 274 8765) sells delicious $3.25 cupcakes to Hillbillies who are watching their figure only *so* closely. Other women sit in shop windows getting their hair coiffed. And at Little Santa Monica Boulevard and Rexford Drive sits the Spanish baroque-style **Civic Center**, as carefully maintained as any film set. However, it's not as exclusive as it might first appear. While the area is still dominated by spendy stores, a few chains have arrived in recent years; there's even a **Gap** on Beverly Drive. What's more, numerous remnants of old Beverly Hills have survived intact. **Nate 'n Al's** (414 N Beverly Drive, at Brighton Way; *see p146*) is a too-Jewish-to-be-true deli that draws a mixed crowd of young bucks and ancient ladies who lunch; south, the stretch of **Beverly Drive** between Wilshire and Pico Boulevards is a wonderful example of classic LA 1950s architecture. Close by Civic Center, the **Union 76** gas station on the corner of Little Santa Monica Boulevard and Rexford Drive boasts an amazing 1950s cantilevered concrete canopy. And a few blocks west is tobacconist **Al Kramers** (9732 Little Santa Monica Boulevard) – in modern-day LA, there's nothing quite as old fashioned as smoking.

Beverly Hills Visitors Bureau

239 S Beverly Drive, between Charleville Boulevard & Gregory Way (1-800 345 2210/1-310 248 1015/www. bhvb.org). Bus 20, 21, 720/I-10 exit S Beverly Drive north. **Open** 8.30am-5pm Mon-Fri. **Map** p311 D3.

Museum of Television & Radio

465 N Beverly Drive, at Santa Monica Boulevard (1-310 786 1000/www.mtr.org). Bus 4, 14, 16, 22, 304/I-10, exit Robertson Boulevard north. **Open** noon-5pm Wed-Sun. **Admission** free; suggested donation $5-$10; $3-$4 concessions. **No credit cards. Map** p311 C3.
The MTR's permanent collection consists of 100,000 TV and radio programmes, duplicating the holdings of its New York counterpart. The collection is accessible to the public for on-site viewing (simply search the computer database and request a tape), but the museum, designed by Getty Villa architect Richard Meier, also organises regular screenings in its main theatre, on anything from the CMA awards to the Muppets, plus seminars and discussions.

Sightseeing

We ♥ LA Star maps

Gawking at people with some degree of celebrity is a national pastime in the US. Gawking at their houses, though, is the only-in-LA equivalent. Los Angeles is rife with guided tours of movie star homes (the exterior only, mind), but most cost a preposterous $30-$40 for 90 minutes spent being ferried around in a garish minibus by an unemployed and otherwise unemployable actor. You're best off guiding yourself.

Sourcing the data seems straightforward. In summer, an assortment of vendors set up stalls on streetcorners in Hollywood, Beverly Hills and Bel Air, hawking map guides that purport to pinpoint the homes of La-La-Land's elite. Fork over a ten-spot (credit cards not accepted), and you too can peek into Dr Phil's front garden or take a photograph of Burt Reynolds' fence. Or, perhaps, the garden of a house where Dr Phil may once have lived, and a fence that used to belong to Burt Reynolds. Though some of the so-called 'Star maps' are kept in good order (the edition sold kerbside at Sunset Boulevard and Baroda Drive in Beverly Hills is regarded as the market leader), others are best served with a pinch or six of salt.

And even assuming you do wind up with a relatively accurate map, don't expect to see a thing. While this is LA and anything could happen, you'll be incredibly fortunate if you catch a glimpse of a star scurrying into a dark car; indeed, you may be lucky if you catch even a glimpse of the property behind all the shrubbery. And wherever you go, don't linger too long, stare through binoculars, knock on doors, shout anyone's name repeatedly, barrel down private driveways or climb over any gates. A deeply embarrassing arrest will surely follow.

Museum of Tolerance at the Simon Wiesenthal Center for Holocaust Studies

9786 W Pico Boulevard, at Roxbury Drive (1-310 553 8403/Simon Wiesenthal Center 1-310 553 9036/www.wiesenthal.com/mot). Bus SM5, SM7, SM13/I-10, exit Overland Avenue north. **Open** 11am-6.30pm Mon-Thur; 11am-3pm Fri; 11am-7.30pm Sun. Last entry 2-2½hrs before closing. **Admission** $10; $6-$8 discounts. **Credit** AmEx, MC, V. **Map** p311 C4.

When it opened in 1993, the Museum of Tolerance was seen as a daring enterprise: a museum devoted to an abstract concept rather than a specific type of artefact. However, while it's an adventurous conceit, it's also extremely enlightening, not least because the set-up is careful to leave it to the visitor to come up with their own definition of the word.

The main exhibit is a deeply involving hour-long walk-through on the Holocaust, which blends taped narration with photographs, film footage, personal testimonies, dioramas and World War II artefacts. At the start of the exhibit, you're given a 'passport' with a child's photograph; their fate is revealed to you at the end of the tour. You can explore the subject further on the computers in the museum's Multimedia Center (the material is online at http://motlc.wiesenthal.com), via displays of other Holocaust documents, and in conversation with a number of World War II survivors, who regularly visit the museum to give talks and host discussions.

Elsewhere in the museum, the Tolerancenter is an interactive exhibit that aims to spur visitors into thinking about their attitudes and prejudices. As well as attracting members of the public, it's used as an educational aid by the local schools system, and as a crucial part of LAPD officer training. The newest of the three major exhibits is Finding Our Families, Finding Ourselves, a multimedia exhibit in which the likes of Carlos Santana, Maya Angelou, and Billy Crystal tell of their family heritages as immigrants and children of immigrants.

Beverly Hills City Hall (450 N Crescent Drive) The police station in *Beverly Hills Cop*

West Hollywood, Hollywood & Midtown

Could another golden age be on the way for LA's most storied neighbourhood?

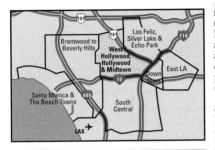

West Hollywood

Map p312

An independent city since 1984, West Hollywood is actually three bustling communities in one. Most famously, the tiny city – a little under two square miles – is the epicentre of gay and lesbian life in LA, with Santa Monica Boulevard as its main strip (*see p229*). However, it's also home to the (straight) nightclubs of the fabled Sunset Strip (*see p240*), and, in the east of the city, a community of immigrant Russians.

Sunset Strip, the stretch of W Sunset Boulevard that runs from Doheny Drive to Laurel Canyon, was developed in 1924. By the 1930s, it was Hollywood's playground: at the Trocadero and Ciro's, singers such as Lena Horne belted out sets for celebs, businessmen and mobsters (Mickey Cohen and Bugsy Siegel both called the area home in the 1940s and '50s).

However, it was a very different type of nightlife that gave the Sunset Strip something approaching iconic status. Located at 8901 W Sunset, the **Whisky A Go-Go** (*see p243*) became the first discothèque on the West Coast when it opened in 1964, and was a hit almost from the moment it opened. Other clubs followed, and the area became the centre of LA youth culture during the 1960s, with everyone from the Byrds to the Doors playing here.

The area still has its nightlife, though it's all a bit forlorn these days. The **Comedy Store**, on the site where once stood Ciro's (No.8433; *see p215*), helped to break stars such as Robin Williams, but these days offers a rather less

notable roster of comics. The venerable **Roxy** (No.9009; *see p241*) and the younger **House of Blues** (No.8430; *see p240*) continue to host fine acts, but the booking policy at the Whisky long ago lost its spark. The legend of the Strip is otherwise kept alive by hotels such as the practically legendary **Chateau Marmont** (No.8221; *see p57*).

While **Sunset Plaza** (W Sunset Boulevard, east of La Cienega Boulevard) offers the area's best shops, the area's main points of interest during daylight are its billboards and buildings. Sunset Strip is a veritable gorge of amazing billboards as big as the buildings they're on. As for those buildings, not all catch the eye for the right reasons: the copper-coloured **Directors Guild of America** building (7920 W Sunset Boulevard) and the **Beverly Center** mall (8500 Beverly Boulevard; *see p180*) are both vast, undistinguished structures that dominate their respective horizons. Halfway between them is the even larger **Pacific Design Center** (8687 Melrose Avenue, 1-310 657 0800, www.pacific designcenter.com). César Pelli's monstrosity may be striking on the outside, with a third red building scheduled to join the existing blue and green behemoths, but it's irredeemable within. Built to house outlets for the interior design trade, it's underused for its size, though **MoCA** (*see p115*; 1-310 289 5223) does leave its Downtown base to stage exhibitions here.

Away from Sunset and Santa Monica Boulevards, it's a different architectural story. A far cry from the huge avenues of nearby Beverly Hills, the residential streets of West Hollywood are cosy, densely packed and pleasingly free of pretence. A quick detour off the main drag, on wheels or on foot (as evidenced by the numerous dog-walkers, this is a very pedestrian-friendly area), is an agreeable way to spend a half-hour or so. You might need a car to climb up steep **Sunset Plaza Drive**, but it's worth the effort simply to see how the other half live.

> **565 N Cahuenga Avenue,**
> **Hollywood** The Cunningham
> house in *Happy Days*

Rudolf Schindler's old home now houses the **MAK Center for Art & Architecture.**

Two buildings are notable. The angular **Lloyd Wright Home & Studio** (858 N Doheny Drive) was designed by Frank's eldest son; it remains closed to the public. But the real gem, one of the city's best buildings, is at 835 N Kings Road: built as a live-work space by Rudolf Schindler, the extraordinary, secluded structure now houses the **MAK Center for Art & Architecture** (see p92). Given the building's undisputed architectural importance, it was little surprise when plans for a sizeable condominium complex next door caused controversy when they were revealed in 2003. However, Lorcan O'Herlihy's sensitive design eventually gained planning approval; the building is expected to be completed in 2007.

MAK Center for Art & Architecture

Schindler House, 835 N Kings Road, between Waring & Willoughby Avenues (1-323 651 1510/ www.makcenter.com). Bus 4, 105, 304/I-10, exit La Cienega Boulevard north. **Open** 11am-6pm Wed-Sun. *Tours* hourly 11.30am-2.30pm Sat, Sun. **Admission** $7; free-$6 discounts. Free to all 4-6pm Fri. **Map** p312 B2.
Constructed in 1922 by radical Austrian architect Rudolf Schindler, this landmark is a dazzling combination of concrete walls, redwood partitions, rooftop 'sleeping baskets' and outdoor living rooms. Tours of the house are offered on weekends, but, in keeping with Schindler's adventurousness, the building also hosts a variety of interesting exhibitions, talks and concerts based on decidedly non-mainstream themes.

West Hollywood Convention & Visitors Bureau

Pacific Design Center, 8687 Melrose Avenue, at N San Vicente Boulevard (1-800 368 6020/ 1-310 289 2525/www.visitwesthollywood.com). **Open** 8.30am-5.30pm Mon-Fri. **Map** p312 A2.

Hollywood

Map p313

It took LA's city fathers a long time to realise that Hollywood wouldn't sell itself. For years, tourists arrived in the fabled neighbourhood expecting to walk on to a movie set: camera crews on every corner, paparazzi crowding the sidewalks, stars of the silver screen parading down Hollywood Boulevard. What they found was a shabby collection of streets and alleys left to crumble by locals, almost every vestige of glamour drained from its pallid face. Granted, the floodlit paradise of filmic immortality conjured up by the name was the creation of imaginative press officers: movies haven't been filmed in Hollywood for decades, and the continued use of its name as shorthand for the movie industry is misleading, to say the least. Still, few visitors were prepared for what they found. Word spread; people stopped coming

Things, at last, are getting better. Since the late 1990s the city has made an effort to restore a little glitter to the long-beleaguered area, and both tourists and locals are beginning to return. The regeneration hasn't been without its critics, but the local authorities haven't been deterred, and further improvements seem inevitable.

Hollywood Boulevard

Riots, earthquakes and construction work during the 1990s added extra layers of decay to the stretch of **Hollywood Boulevard** between La Brea Avenue and Vine Street, already one of the city's seamier thoroughfares. In the last ten years, it's made a comeback, re-dubbed the **Hollywood Entertainment District** after a billion-dollar makeover. Tourists are once more

We ♥ LA Hollywood Walk of Fame

It's a question that has baffled Hollywood stargazers for years: what *do* Donald Duck, Mötley Crüe, Emilio Estefan, Shecky Greene, Steve Martin, Destiny's Child and Judge Judy have in common? No, they haven't all had hot dogs named after them at Pink's. And nor have they been signed up as contestants for the next series of *I'm A Celebrity Get Me Out of Here!* The answer is rather more instructive: in 2005 and 2006, along with such luminaries of pop culture as DJ Wink Martindale, superannuated singing duo the Righteous Brothers and *Wheel of Fortune* hostess Vanna White, all of them received stars on the Hollywood Walk of Fame.

From Bud 'Who's on first?' Abbott to bearded Texan bluesmen ZZ Top, more than 2,000 greats from the world of entertainment have been immortalised on the Walk since Oscar-winning actress Joanne Woodward received the first honour in 1960. Well, perhaps 1,000 showbusiness greats, and 1,000 or so others. Nominations are made via an application form available from the Hollywood Chamber of Commerce, before Johnny Grant, a longtime producer and the Honorary Mayor of Hollywood, convenes a mysterious committee to award the stars. Assuming you're successful, you (or, more likely, your record label, movie producers or TV company) need to stump up $15,000 to pay for the ceremony.

Made of pink terrazzo inset with gold lettering and one of five symbols denoting the recipient's profession (film, TV, radio, music or stage), the stars run along Hollywood Boulevard between La Brea Avenue and Gower Street, as well as along a small stretch of Vine Street. Walking the Walk of Fame is a lesson in Hollywood history, but also a pop quiz of sorts. Paul Newman – wow! Franklin Pangborn – who? (A bit-part player from the black and white days.) Tom Jones, Quincy Jones and Spike Jones need no introduction; Allan Jones, an undistinguished actor from the 1930s and '40s, probably will. Dogs honoured include Lassie, best remembered for a string of TV shows, and Strongheart, solely remembered for stumbling into a blazing hot studio light and dying in 1929.

As with the entertainment world in general, marketing appears to have played a major part in the Walk of Fame of late, with many big names receiving their stars just as their new series airs, their new album emerges or their new movie hits cinemas. There's no better example of this trend than the 2005 decision to allow companies on to the Walk, provided they were at least 50 years old. The first to receive a star was Disneyland, three days prior to their 50th anniversary. You scratch my back...

And yet despite all its quirks and mysteries, the Walk of Fame is one of LA's great glories, and precisely the landmark that Hollywood and its fans deserve. It is alternately dazzling and bewildering; it is by turns sentimental and laughable; and, perhaps most pertinently, it is far, far too big. It is where the entertainment industry nails its true colours to the mast, albeit without really realising it, and offers the most blatant illustration of a truth that's dominated Hollywood for a century: talent will take you to the top of your profession, but a big pile of cash, a bulging contacts book and a great agent will get you there quicker.

KEVIN SPACEY

Sightseeing

---

starting to spend time and money in Hollywood, but – crucially – so are the locals.

The centrepiece of the regeneration is the four-storey **Hollywood & Highland** centre, which opened in 2001 but is only now finding its feet. Billing itself, with surprising modesty, as a 'shopping and entertainment centre', the development mixes around 40 high-end mall favourites (Aveda, Banana Republic, Mac; *see p181*) with eating options, a bowling alley

(see p255), the disheartening **Hollywood Pop Academy** (www.hollywoodpopacademy.com) and the **Kodak Theatre**, the 3,300-seat home of the annual Academy Awards (for tours, *see p260*). Despite various alterations to the layout in 2005, it's still a confusing place, hampered by bewilderingly poor signage.

For any evidence of Hollywood glamour, you'll need to head next door to the legendary **Grauman's Chinese Theatre** (*see p95 and*

Road trip

In 2001, David Lynch's *Mulholland Dr.* won the auteur both the Cannes Film Festival prize for Best Director and some of the best reviews of his life. The movie, indeed, is boggling, dazzling and brilliantly unhinged. Is there anything that can compare? Only, of course, Mulholland Drive itself, a swooping, curving, enigmatic road that's more stunning than any film.

A confluence of Hollywood-style spectacle and wild SoCal bramble, Mulholland Drive springs to existence near the Hollywood Bowl and dies out at Leo Carrillo State Beach. (By then it's the Mulholland Highway, the road splitting into two in Woodland Hills just east of Topanga Canyon Boulevard; if you're driving west along Mulholland Drive, take the left.) The views along LA's spine encompass the great dichotomies for which the city is known, from the pivoting views of the ocean and the scalloped edges of the Santa Monica Mountains on the road's west side to the softly blinking grid of the Valley and the puncturing tops of Downtown buildings out east. Best of all, seven miles of the road – betwee Canoga Avenue and Encino Hills Place – is closed to cars. Informally known as Dirt Mulholland, it's a small but pointy thorn into that inflated expression that the City of Dreams is only auto-accessible.

The road, which opened in 1924 to one of the biggest celebrations in LA's history, was named for William Mulholland, the man who wrangled the Owens River away from Owens Valley farmers so he could irrigate the San Fernando Valley. Mulholland was a hero at the time; yet, a few years later, his reputation was washed up in the massive flood caused by the breaking of the St Francis Dam that took more than 500 lives. He died in 1935, isolated and depressed.

Even as teenagers flocked to it for make-out sessions under a blanket of stars (the road has long had a reputation as LA's primary Lovers' Lane), a darker side to the road emerged. In 1948, Caryl Chessman, tagged by the press as the Red Light Bandit, robbed and sexually assaulted women parked in their cars by the roadside. In later years, the road became a magnet for drag racers, who topped speeds of 100mph as they tore down the jagged road. After a 12-year-old boy was killed in 1982, there was serious talk of closing the road; in the event, a compromise was struck by erecting barricades at peak racing times.

The past decade has seen the road flourish, thanks to the efforts of the Mountains Recreation and Conservation Authority and some of Mulholland's more famous and outspoken residents (Jack Nicholson has not one but two mansions on the road). Beating development plans and some short-lived talk of paving Dirt Mulholland, the road is the gateway to the nation's largest metropolitan wildlife area: the Big Wild, 20,000 acres of parkland anchored by Topanga State Park and populated by coastal sage, walnut and oak trees.

To cover all of Mulholland Drive should take somewhere around three hours, though reserving a whole day is recommended; don't forget to bring hiking boots or a mountain bike in order to tackle Dirt Mulholland. To pick up the road's east end, exit US 101 northbound (just north of Hollywood) at Barham Boulevard, turn left at Barham and left again on Cahuenga Boulevard. At the Mulholland stoplight, turn right then immediately veer left. To access the road's west end, take a right from the Pacific Coast Highway close to the Leo Carillo State Beach.

Ripley's Believe it or Not!.

p220), which got a much-needed restoration as part of the area's overall redevelopment. Indeed, virtually the only buildings that exude any star quality are the old cinemas that have somehow survived the years: almost opposite the Chinese Theatre sits the **El Capitan** (No.6838; *see p220*), for whose glorious makeover we have Disney to thank; and down the road sits the historic **Egyptian Theatre** (No.6712; *see p221*), home to the American Cinematheque. The **Hollywood Entertainment Museum**; (*see below*) adds context, with a little 21st-century glitz coming courtesy of the resurgent **Hollywood Roosevelt** (No.7000; *see p60*): built in 1927 and the host of the first Academy Awards, the hotel is once again a hot hangout.

East of Highland Avenue, it's all a little depressing, as unattractive attractions (the **Hollywood Wax Museum** and **Ripley's Believe it or Not!**; *see pp96-97*) compete with souvenir shops, panhandlers and an enormous scientology centre for attention. The enjoyable **Hollywood Museum** (*see p96*) and 80-year-old restaurant/bar **Musso & Frank** (No.6667; *see p174* **Walk**) offer a link

> **Chateau Alto Nido, 1851 N Ivar Avenue** William Holden's home in *Sunset Boulevard*

to cinema's golden age; conversely, the **Erotic Museum** (*see below*) connects visitors to a time when adult theatres still stood in the area. And all along Hollywood Boulevard are the pink stars that collectively make up the **Hollywood Walk of Fame** (*see p93*).

If you look up while walking Hollywood Boulevard, you'll regularly spy signs above the sidewalk that mark sites of historical or architectural significance. Taken individually, they're an interesting diversion; taken as a group (46 in total), they make for an excellent self-guided tour. Among the sites omitted from the list are two lingerie shops: **Frederick's of Hollywood** (No.6751, 1-323 957 5953) and **Playmates** (No.6438, 1-323 464 7636).

Erotic Museum

6741 Hollywood Boulevard, between N Highland & N Las Palmas Avenues (1-323 463 7650/www.theerotic museum.com). Metro Hollywood-Highland/bus 210, 212, 217, 310, LDH, LDHWH/US 101, exit Highland Avenue south. **Open** *11am-8pm Mon-Thur, Sun; 11am-11pm Fri, Sat.* **Admission** *Over-18s only* $12.95; $9.95 discounts. **Credit** MC, V. **Map** p313 A1. Provocatively sited in the heart of newly family-friendly Hollywood, the Erotic Museum opened in January 2004 with the mission statement to 'educate the public about human sexuality by creating entertaining exhibitions regarding the broad range of mankind's erotic endeavour through the ages'. In effect, this means everything from ancient pleasure machines and Picasso etchings to Tom Kelly's 1953 photographs of Marilyn Monroe and clips of John Holmes in all his 13 and a half inches of glory. Don't get too excited: this is meant to be educational.

Grauman's Chinese Theatre

6925 Hollywood Boulevard, between N Orange Drive & N Highland Avenue (1-323 464 8111/ www.manntheatres.com). Metro Hollywood-Highland/bus 210, 212, 217, 310, LDH, LDHWH/ US 101, exit Highland Avenue south. **Tickets** $9; $6 discounts. **Credit** MC, V. **Map** p313 A1. It's still a great place to catch a movie (*see p220*), but most people come to the Chinese Theatre for the hand and/or foot imprints of around 200 Hollywood stars. As legend has it, Norma Talmadge accidentally stepped into the wet cement outside the new building during construction; in response, theatre owner Sid Grauman fetched Mary Pickford and Douglas Fairbanks to repeat the 'mistake' with their feet and hands, beginning the tradition. The courtyard is usually choked with snap-happy tourists measuring their own extremities against the likes of John Wayne and Judy Garland; it's just a pity that its appeal is tempered by the tour hawkers and the ticket agents who clutter the forecourt. **Photo** *p96*.

Hollywood Entertainment Museum

7021 Hollywood Boulevard, between N Sycamore Avenue & N Orange Drive (1-323 465 7900/www. hollywoodmuseum.com). Metro Hollywood-Highland/

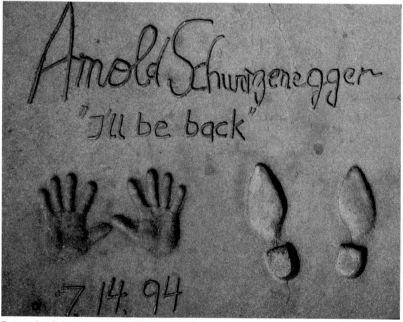

bus 210, 212, 217, 310, LDH, LDHWH/US 101, exit Highland Avenue south. **Open** *Memorial Day-Labor Day* 10am-6pm daily. *Labor Day-Memorial Day* 11am-6pm Mon, Tue, Thur-Sun. **Admission** $12; $5-$10 discounts; free under-4s. **Credit** AmEx, MC, V. **Map** p313 A1.

This below-ground museum has little of its subject's pzazz, but it's still more enjoyable than you might expect. TV groupies are drawn chiefly by its original TV show sets, highlighted by *Star Trek* and the bar from *Cheers*, but there's also plenty of Tinseltown memorabilia (including stars' wigs and cosmetics from the Max Factor Museum of Beauty, which the Entertainment Museum incorporates), a delightful miniature model of 1940s Hollywood by Joseph Pellkofer, and even an educational wing. Temporary shows could cover anything from Polish film posters to the blaxploitation movies of the 1970s.

Hollywood Museum

1660 N Highland Avenue, between Hawthorn Avenue & Hollywood Boulevard (1-323 464 7776/ www.thehollywoodmuseum.com). Metro Hollywood-Highland/bus 210, 212, 217, 310, LDH, LDHWH/ US 101, exit Highland Avenue south. **Open** 10am-5pm Thur-Sun. **Admission** $15; $5-$12 discounts. **Credit** AmEx, MC, V. **Map** p313 A2.

Built as the headquarters of the Hollywood Fire & Safe Building in 1914, this structure was converted in 1928 into a beauty salon by Max Factor.

A refurbishment by Factor seven years later turned it into an Art Deco classic; after a recent renovation, it's now the Hollywood Museum.

The ground floor of the museum has been decorated to resemble the original Factor shop, its walls lined with memorabilia related to stars of the 1930s, '40s and '50s. Out the back sits Cary Grant's 1965 Silver Cloud Rolls Royce, gleaming even today. The top two floors bring things closer to the present day: among the ephemera are Stallone's boxing gloves from *Rocky* and all manner of Streisand-related stuff. The basement, meanwhile, holds a mock-up of Hannibal Lecter's cell from *The Silence of the Lambs*.

Hollywood Information Center

6231 Hollywood Boulevard, at Argyle Avenue (1-323 467 6412/www.lacvb.com). Metro Hollywood-Vine/bus 180, 181, 210, 212, 217, 310, LDH, LDHWI/US 101, exit Vine Street south. **Open** 10am-10pm Mon-Sat; 10am-7pm Sun. **Map** p313 B1.

Hollywood Wax Museum

6767 Hollywood Boulevard, at N Highland Avenue (1-323 462 8860/www.hollywoodwax.com). Metro Hollywood-Highland/bus 210, 212, 217, 310, LDH, LDHWH/US 101, exit Highland Avenue south. **Open** 10am-midnight daily. **Admission** $12.95; $6.95-$8.50 discounts; free under-6s. *Joint ticket with Guinness World of Records* $14.95; $8.95 discounts; free under-6s. **Credit** AmEx, Disc, MC, V. **Map** p313 A1.

But as the Governor? **Grauman's Chinese Theatre**. *See p95.*

Hollywood might be pushing itself into the 21st century with vim and vigour, but some attractions remain stuck firmly in the past. The Hollywood Wax Museum harks back, not altogether intentionally, to days long past, when a poorly proportioned wax model of someone famous was liable to draw gasps of astonishment from entertainment-starved crowds. There's fun to be had trying to recognise the stars, but perhaps not 13 bucks' worth. Combined tickets are available for the Wax Museum and the equally tacky **Guinness World of Records Museum** (No.6764, 1-323 462 5991) across the street.

Ripley's Believe it or Not!

6780 Hollywood Boulevard, at N Highland Avenue (1-323 466 6335/www.ripleys.com). Metro Hollywood-Highland/bus 210, 212, 217, 310, LDH, LDHWH/US 101, exit Highland Avenue south. **Open** 10am-10.30pm Mon-Thur, Sun; 10am-11.30pm Fri, Sat. **Admission** $11.95; $7.95 5-12s; free under-6s. **Credit** AmEx, MC, V. **Map** p313 A1.
One of 15 Ripley's Believe it or Not!s around the US, and if you've been to any of the others, you can skip this. Indeed, if you haven't been to any of the others, you can skip this, a parade of bizarre 'facts' that stretch the definition of the word 'museum' to breaking point. Eminently avoidable. **Photo** *p95*.

South of Hollywood Boulevard

Few visitors wander much off Hollywood Boulevard during their visit to Hollywood; few locals blame them. Still, though there's less obvious tourist appeal away from the main drag, and though pockets of the area are a little on the seamy side, it's a relief to escape the throngs and get into a neighbourhood with a little more dirt under its fingernails.

The junction of Hollywood and Vine is as far as most go along Hollywood Boulevard, whether for a drink at the dimly lit, boozy and utterly fantastic **Frolic Room** (No.6245; *see p174* **Walk**) or to spy the 13-storey **Capitol Records Building** (1750 N Vine Street, just north of Hollywood Boulevard). Instantly recognisable, it's shaped like a stack of records and topped with a stylus, reputedly the idea of songwriter Johnny Mercer and singer Nat 'King' Cole. When it emerged in 2006 that EMI might sell the building to a condo developer, there was a public outcry, but it may not be enough to save one of LA's most distinctive landmarks.

Otherwise, walking two blocks south down Vine Street will take you to **W Sunset Boulevard** which, while not as seedy as it once was (prostitutes are less prevalent than when Hugh Grant met Divine Brown on the corner of Sunset and Courtney Avenue), still retains its edge. The main attraction isn't even on Sunset: rather, it's the view from the corner of Sunset and N Bronson Avenue, one of the best vantage points from which to see the **Hollywood Sign** (*see p13*). South of here is the **Hollywood Forever** cemetery (*see below*); just by it is **Paramount Studios**, the only working studio in Hollywood. For tours, *see p71*.

Back on Sunset, and heading west, the attractions are largely commercial. While the tourists wander Hollywood & Highland hoping to see a star, the in-the-know celeb-hunters are at the **ArcLight** cinemas (No.6360; *see p219*). Adjacent to it sits **Amoeba Music** (No.6400; *see p201*), capable of reducing even the most jaded record collector to a bug-eyed lunatic.

A few blocks west sits **Crossroads of the World** (No.6671), a charming outdoor shopping plaza (now offices) built in 1936 that pre-dates LA's strip mall explosion by 50 years. Too bad its successors couldn't follow the example of its eye-catching mixture of English, French, Moorish and Spanish architecture. There's more peculiar architecture a block south of Sunset at 1416 N La Brea Avenue: these incongruous Tudor-style buildings now provide a home for Henson Productions, but for years were **A&M Studios**. Among the thousands of acts that recorded here down the decades are the Rolling Stones and the Carpenters, but its musical history is equalled by its cinematic past: its core was built in 1918 by Charlie Chaplin, who used it as his movie studio and whose footprints are (allegedly) visible in concrete outside Studio 3.

Back west on Sunset sits another musical landmark, the **Guitar Center** (No.7425; *see p202*). The selection of axes is dizzying in the extreme, and it's entertainment enough just to listen to the 'Hey, dude!' patois of the shop assistants and customers. If you've made it this far down Sunset, though, you're back on the edges of West Hollywood, for which *see p91*.

Hollywood Forever Cemetery

6000 Santa Monica Boulevard, between N Gower Street & N Van Ness Avenue (1-323 469 1181/www. forevernetwork.com). Bus 4, 156, 304/US 101, exit Santa Monica Boulevard west. **Open** *Summer* 8am-7pm daily. *Winter* 8am-6pm daily. **Admission** free. **Map** p313 C2.
Where better to look for the Ghost (or Ghosts) of Hollywood Past? The owners of the cemetery have come in for some criticism for promoting the place as a tourist attraction, but any place that houses the remains of such celluloid luminaries as Tyrone Power, Cecil B DeMille, Jayne Mansfield and Peter Lorre would probably become one regardless. The cemetery is also the final resting place of Rudolph Valentino; legend has it that a mysterious 'Woman in Black' still stalks the place, mourning the demise of Hollywood's original Latin lover. Mel Blanc's headstone says 'That's All, Folks!'; Johnny Ramone's has quotes from Vincent Gallo and Lisa Maria Presley. Douglas Fairbanks Sr and Jr are in a huge

Sightseeing

tomb in front of a lake guarded by a fountain and three black swans. But William Andrews Clark Jr, founder of the LA Philharmonic, has an even bigger mausoleum in the middle of a lake. **Photo** *p99*.

The Hollywood Hills

Rising up north of Franklin Avenue, the Hollywood Hills are the fag-end of the Santa Monica Mountains, which divide LA from the San Fernando Valley (*see p124*). As well as providing a perch for the iconic Hollywood sign (*see p13*), they're home to residents not quite as rarefied as those of the more exclusive canyons to the west. Celebrities who do move here are more youthful: they get a secluded pad and easy access to louche Los Feliz without actually having to live there.

North of the West Hollywood strip, **Runyon Canyon Park** is a strip of canyon wilderness running from Mulholland Drive to Franklin Avenue (entrances on Fuller Avenue and Vista Street; www.runyon-canyon.com). As well as some genuine nature (coyote, deer), it contains a ruined mansion, the foundations of a Frank Lloyd Wright pool house and the recumbent but intact Outpost sign, sister real-estate billboard to the Hollywood sign. Trails of varying lengths and difficulty take you to great 360° viewpoints.

Between Runyon Canyon and US 101 is the architecturally affecting **Hollywood Bowl**. The Bowl and its hillside surroundings are best experienced at a concert, but the area is open for exploration, picnicking and museum visits at other times. Across US 101, the **Hollywood Reservoir** provides a shoreline circuit and a chance to muse on LA's debt to piped-in water and dam-builder William Mulholland. To the east are the hills of Griffith Park (*see p105*); one way to access these is to rent yourself a horse from Sunset Ranch near the park's western boundary (*see p255*).

Hollywood Bowl Museum

2301 N Highland Avenue, at US 101 (1-323 850 2058/www.hollywoodbowl.com). Bus 156/US 101, exit Highland Avenue north. **Open** *LA Phil season* 10am-8.30pm Tue-Sat; 2hrs prior to concert Sun. *Off-season* 10am-4.30pm Tue-Sat. **Admission** free.
This fine little museum presents a lively account of the Hollywood Bowl's history, through archival film footage, audio clips, photography and all manner of other memorabilia.

Hollywood Reservoir & Dog Park

Lake Hollywood Drive, Hollywood Hills. Bus 156, 163, 426/US 101, exit Barham Boulevard north.
Formed in 1924 when the Mulholland Dam was built, the Hollywood Reservoir was a landmark piece of engineering, both physical and social. Holding 2.5 billion US gallons, it provided the drinking water to facilitate the city's spread, piping it in from over 300

miles away through the landmark Owens River Aqueduct system. Now most of its water storage is underground, but the pretty lake attracts runners, walkers and the occasional cyclist to its waterside trails, which offer a fantastic view of the Hollywood sign. Tucked behind the reservoir up Beachwood Canyon is the Hollywood Dog Park. It's not uncommon to catch a glimpse of jogging celebs who think they're incognito under their baseball caps.

Fairfax District

Map p312

Although LA's first major Jewish community settled in the East LA neighbourhood of Boyle Heights, the stretch of **Fairfax Avenue** between Beverly Boulevard and Melrose Avenue has been LA's main Jewish drag since the 1940s. If you're in the market for a new menorah or the latest in Israeli pop music, you're in the right place. Kosher grocers, butcher's shops, restaurants and bakeries line the street; all are excellent, and, naturally, almost all are closed on Saturdays. Open 24-7, however, is the legendary **Canter's Deli** (No.419; *see p153*), a World War II-era kosher restaurant, deli and bakery. Adjoining it is the divey **Canter's Kibitz Room** (*see p175*); across the street sits **Largo** (No.432; *see p241*), a haven for KCRW-friendly singer-songwriters.

Just south of the Beverly-Fairfax intersection lies **CBS Television City**, built in 1952 and still used as a filming location for shows such as *The Price is Right* (*see p217* **Come on down!**). Looking at the vast complex, you'd never guess the site once held a major sporting stadium: Gilmore Field, built in 1939 and home to the minor-league Hollywood Stars baseball team until their demise in 1957 (CBS bought the lot, razed the stadium and expanded their facilities). Next door, at the junction of W 3rd Street and Fairfax Avenue, is the tag-team retail experience of the **Grove** (*see p180*) and the **Farmers Market** (*see p154*). The former is dominated by all the usual chains, but its spacey, open-air layout helps make it one of the most pleasant shopping centres in LA.

The Farmers Market, which predates the Grove by more than 60 years, no longer lives up to its name. Still, though the farmers who set up here for the first time in 1934 have long since moved their wares elsewhere (*see p194*), food continues to dominate this wonderfully old-fashioned commercial corner. Some of the stalls here are shops, selling fruit and fudge and assorted sundry temptations; others are full-service food counters, hawking everything from pizza to gumbo for the benefit of a cheerily ravenous crowd. For the best places to eat here, *see p154* **Farmers Market favourites**.

Where are they now? **Hollywood Forever Cemetery.** *See p97.*

Miracle Mile & Midtown

Map p312

The Miracle Mile, which stretches along Wilshire Boulevard between Fairfax and La Brea Avenues, gained its nickname because of its astonishing growth during the 1920s (*see pp40-42*). It doesn't live up to that moniker any more, but after a spell in the 1990s, when businesses shut left, right and centre, the area seems to be on the rise again. The May Co department store (No.6067), a mainstay for half a century before closing in 1993, is now part of **LACMA** (*see p100*). Nearby diner **Johnie's** (No.6101) is no longer open, but this glorious example of 1950s Googie architecture at least remains, restored by local preservationists and frequently hired out to movie crews.

This stretch of Wilshire is also known as Museum Row, and for good reason. The **Los Angeles County Museum of Art** (*see p100*), the **Petersen Automotive Museum** (*see p101*), the **Craft & Folk Art Museum** (*see below*), the **A+D Museum** (opening in summer 2006; *see below*) and the **Page Museum** (*see p101*) are all within walking distance of each other, the latter with the added attraction of the **La Brea Tar Pits**, a huge, bubbling swamp of primordial ooze.

A+D Museum

5900 Wilshire Boulevard, at S Spaulding Avenue (1-310 659 2445/http://aplusd.org). Bus 20, 21, 720/I-10, exit Fairfax Avenue north. **Open** call for details. **Admission** call for details. **No credit cards. Map** p312 C4.

Having spent the last few years bouncing around the city (in late 2003, it moved from Downtown's Bradbury Building to a short-lived tenancy in West Hollywood), the A+D Museum is scheduled to reopen in summer 2006 on the Miracle Mile. As before, the museum plans to stage a roster of temporary exhibitions devoted to various aspects of architecture and design (hence the museum's name).

Craft & Folk Art Museum

5814 Wilshire Boulevard, between S Curson & S Stanley Avenues (1-323 937 4230/www.cafam.org). Bus 20, 21, 720/I-10, exit Fairfax Avenue north. **Open** 11am-5pm Tue, Wed, Fri; 11am-7pm Thur; noon-6pm Sat, Sun. **Admission** $5; $3 discounts; free under-12s. **Credit** AmEx, MC, V. **Map** p312 C4.

Since having been saved from oblivion by the city, which took it over in 1998 after financial troubles, LA's only public showcase devoted entirely to functional

> **Johnie's Coffee Shop**
> Where Mr Orange signs up to the
> heist in *Reservoir Dogs*

Sightseeing

Page Museum at the La Brea Tar Pits. *See p100.*

and informal art has broadened its programming. Charming and informative shows of Slovenian craft, Venetian Carnivale masks and musical instruments 'of trance and ecstasy' have appeared at the resurrected museum, which has an interesting gift shop.

Los Angeles County Museum of Art

5905 Wilshire Boulevard, at S Spaulding Avenue (1-323 857 6000/www.lacma.org). Bus 20, 21, 720/I-10, exit Fairfax Avenue north. **Open** noon-8pm Mon, Tue, Thur; noon-9pm Fri; 11am-8pm Sat, Sun. **Admission** $9; $5 discounts; free under-17s. Free after 5pm daily, & 2nd Tue of mth. **No credit cards. Map** p312 C4.

Back in 2002, funding difficulties and public outrage at the proposed demolition forced the board of the Los Angeles County Museum of Art to abandon plans for Dutch architect Rem Koolhaas to rebuild almost its entire complex of buildings. Renzo Piano has since been engaged to remodel parts of the site, a three-phase plan that will initially include the construction of a 70,000sq ft contemporary art museum, an underground parking lot and a new entrance pavilion, and an overhaul for the museum's façade. This work is scheduled for completion in late 2007; phases two and three call for the renovation of the museum's various galleries and the former May Co department store, now known as LACMA West.

Architecture critics have been enthusiastic, but Piano will have his work cut out if he's to turn this cluster of buildings into a cohesive whole. Although LACMA commands a huge amount of public affection, the existing LACMA buildings are an aesthetic jumble; combined as a single museum, they're infuriating. The chaotic variety of buildings is one problem, but the substandard signage and mapping is another. It's a real pity, because the museum's collections are actually quite impressive.

The museum's main holdings are currently kept in the **Ahmanson Building**. On the ground floor sit the collections of American and African art; upstairs are a section of the European art and decorative art holdings; and on level three sits an engaging selection of Islamic art. However, visitors should note that most sections of the Ahmanson Building will be closed at one time or another during the renovations of 2006 and 2007; when the work is complete, the building will be entirely given over to European holdings. Call or look online before setting out to check the status of construction.

The **Hammer Building**, linked to the adjacent Ahmanson, is currently best approached for its collection of Impressionist and post-Impressionist art. Highlights include works by Cézanne (*Boy with a Straw Hat*), Gauguin (*The Red Cow*), Toulouse-Lautrec (various minor works), Degas (an incredibly striking portrait of *The Bellelli Sisters*) and Monet, represented by such contrasting works as the relatively plain *The Beach at Honfleur* and the considerably more colourful *In the Woods at Giverny* (1887). Right by the Hammer Building is the **Japanese Art Pavilion**, which does pretty much what you might expect.

The **Modern & Contemporary Art Building** features a marquee selection of artists: works by Rothko, Ruscha, Pollock, Liechtenstein, Picasso, Kelly and Mondrian are all on show. Look out, in particular, for David Hockney's *Mulholland Drive*, a crazed, colourful hymn to his former home city. (And note, too, the proximity of the Bank Of America Robert F Maguire Foundation Gallery to the Steve Martin Gallery (Russian avant-garde art, of all things), which itself adjoins the Chevron USA Gallery. It's an entertaining lesson in the ways in which LACMA goes about its fundraising.)

Temporary exhibitions are regularly held here, too: check online for details. But do note that opening hours, already a little variable due to special events in the evenings, may change further with the progress of the building work. Always call ahead.

Page Museum at the La Brea Tar Pits

5801 Wilshire Boulevard, between S Stanley & S Curson Avenues (1-323 934 7243/www.tarpits.org). Bus 20, 21, 720/I-10, exit La Brea Avenue north. **Open** 9.30am-5pm Mon-Fri; 10am-5pm Sat, Sun. **Admission** $7; $2-$4.50 discounts; free under-5s. Free 1st Tue of mth. **Credit** AmEx, Disc, V. **Map** p312 C4.
Back in 1875, a group of amateur palaeontologists discovered animal remains in the pits at Rancho La Brea, which bubbled with asphalt from a petroleum lake under what is now Hancock Park. Some 130 years later, the pros are still at work here, having dragged more than 3.5 million fossils from the mire in the intervening years. Some are up to 40,000 years old; the museum estimates that about 10,000 animals, dipping their heads in search of water before becoming trapped in the sticky asphalt that bubbles from the ground, met their deaths here.

Many of these specimens are now on display in this delightfully old-fashioned museum, which can't have changed much since it opened in 1972. Interactivity is limited to several windows on to the labs where scientists work on bone preservation; the bulk of the museum is made up of simple, instructive displays of items found in the pits. Most are bones – of jackrabbits, gophers, a 160lb bison, skunks and a 15,000lb Columbian mammoth, plus an extraordinary wall of 400 wolf skulls – though there are also early cave drawings and human accoutrements such as bowls and hair pins. Outside, the pits still bubble with black goo; in summer, you can watch palaeontologists at work in the excavation of Pit 91 and inhale the nasty tang of tar in the air. **Photo** *p100*.

Petersen Automotive Museum

6060 Wilshire Boulevard, at Fairfax Avenue (1-323 964 6315/1-323 930 2277/www.petersen. org). Bus 20, 21, 720/I-10, exit Fairfax Avenue north. **Open** 10am-6pm Tue-Sun. **Admission** $10; $3-$5 discounts, free under-5s. **Credit** AmEx, MC, V. **Map** p312 C4.
The Miracle Mile was the first commercial development in LA designed expressly for the benefit of drivers, and thus makes an apt home for this museum of automobile culture. The story of how Los Angeles – and, for that matter, much of the west coast – was built around the needs of drivers is a fascinating and instructive tale. Unfortunately, though, the Petersen Museum doesn't tell it in any great detail, preferring instead to dazzle visitors with an admittedly impressive collection of autos from the last century.

Some of the vehicles on display wear their history with pride: a maroon 1942 Lincoln Continental, a delivery truck from Culver City's iconic Helms Bakery, even an old Vincent motorcycle. Others look ahead: Batmobiles from both the original TV series and the Tim Burton movies, a relatively tasteful hot rod conversion by Ed 'Big Daddy' Roth, and a taxi designed by Syd Mead for *Blade Runner*. While the life-size dioramas of garages and diners evoke the early days of the American car obsession, the museum misses its chance to tell a story that really warrants telling. But, hell, the cars are lovely.

Hancock Park

Map p313

A handsome residential neighbourhood dating back to 1910 (not to be confused with the park of the same name, west on Wilshire Boulevard), **Hancock Park** is home to some of LA's most palatial mansions, at least outside Beverly Hills and Bel Air. Historically an Anglo enclave, Hancock Park excluded blacks and Jews (who moved west) until 1948, when Nat 'King' Cole was the first African-American to move to the neighbourhood. He wasn't to be the last, but Hancock Park remains a bastion of wealthy middle-class Anglo values and attitudes.

Bounded by Wilshire Boulevard and Van Ness, Highland and Melrose Avenues, the area is at its best around Christmas, when local homeowners try to outdo each other with decorative displays of festive jollity. Some are delightful, subtle strings of white fairy-lights highlighting the perfect geometry of these wildly expensive homes. Others, though, are more demonstrative, such as **Youngwood Court** (at the south-east corner of W 3rd Street and S Muirfield Road, *pictured*). The 20-plus

From left: David, David, David, David, David, David... **Youngwood Court**.

Sightseeing

**357 S Lorraine Boulevard,
Hancock Park** Home of the Baker
family in *Cheaper By the Dozen*

replicas of Michelangelo's *David*, arranged in
a semi-circle around the front lawn, catch the
eye all year round. But at Christmas, when the
ranch-style home is covered from tip to toe in
white lights and the statues are topped with
Santa hats, it's an extraordinary sight.

The area's main commercial drag is **N
Larchmont Boulevard**, between Beverly
Boulevard and W 1st Street and informally
known as **Larchmont Village**. A little snatch
of Main Street middle America in the heart
of LA, the two-block stretch is lined with
bourgeois restaurants, antique shops and the
like, some chains (including, with terrifying
inevitability, Starbucks) but others owned
independently and established for years. Many
are housed in buildings built in the 1920s.

Koreatown & around

Map p313 & p314

Torched during the 1992 riots, Koreatown –
the Midtown neighbourhood roughly bordered
by Wilshire and Pico Boulevards, and N
Western and N Vermont Avenues – has made
a comeback. Tensions between the Korean and
African-American communities (and, to a lesser
extent, the area's Central American population)
haven't exactly abated, but an accord of sorts
seems to have been reached, especially as
blacks are perhaps now more concerned with
their grievances against Latinos.

Korean businesses are still visible: some
predating the riots, others established only in
the last decade. Banks, men's clubs and shop-
front grocers abound along Pico and Olympic
Boulevards, and the area is dotted with Korean
restaurants such as **Dong Il Jang** (3455 W
8th Street; *see p156*). However, despite its
name, the neighbourhood's character comes
more from the Latin Americans who now live
here, and outnumber the Koreans by around
four to one. Among Anglos, **El Cholo** (1121
S Western Avenue) is the most popular
Mexican restaurant, but you'll find more
authentic food at colourful **Guelaguetza**
(3337½ W 8th Street). For both, *see p156*.

Koreatown's north-western corner,
Wilshire Boulevard and N Western Avenue, is
dominated by the **Wiltern Center**. A green
art deco pile built in 1931, it lingered in a state
of advanced decrepitude during much of the
1970s and '80s before being rescued and turned
into a performing arts and commercial centre.

The **Wiltern LG** (*see p238*) hosts regular rock
shows and the occasional club night; fans meet
before or after for 'food and grog' at the **HMS
Bounty** (3357 Wilshire Boulevard; *see p176*),
a convivial gathering place for local soaks.

Across the street from the Bounty sits the
site of the old **Ambassador Hotel** (No.3400,
www.theambassadorhotel.com), a once-
glamorous resort built in the 1920s but known
to most as the site of Robert F Kennedy's
assassination. Despite numerous protests, the
hotel was demolished in 2006 to make way for
a new high school. However, another landmark
has survived the wrecking ball: **Bullocks
Wilshire** (No.3050), one of the first department
stores to open outside Downtown (in 1929), has
been transformed into a law school.

Westlake

Map p314

Two parks anchor the down-at-heel area of
Westlake just west of Downtown: **Lafayette
Park** (on Wilshire Boulevard, by the junction
of S Hoover Street), and its larger neighbour,
MacArthur Park (also on Wilshire, between
S Alvarado and S Park View Streets). For
years populated chiefly by gang members,
drug dealers and the homeless, MacArthur
Park is safer now than it's been for a while
and jammed with Latino families. Its former
grandeur is only fleetingly apparent, even
after the restoration of its lake and 500-foot
(150-metre) high water spout, but it's still not
difficult to see how the park could have inspired
Jimmy Webb to pen his epic (if, to be honest,
somewhat nonsensical) song in its honour.

If you'd like to leave a cake out in the rain
here, your best bet is to head to **Langer's
Delicatessen** (704 S Alvarado Street, 1-213
483 8050); considered by many to have the
best pastrami sandwich in town, it also has a
kerbside takeaway service for customers too
scared to park their cars on the surrounding
mean streets. Burger fans should seek out
Cassell's (3266 W 6th Street; *see p155*).

Grier Musser Museum

*403 S Bonnie Brae Street, between W 4th & W 5th
Streets (1-213 413 1814/www.griermussermuseum.
com). Metro Westlake-MacArthur/bus 18, 200/US
101, exit Alvarado Street south.* **Open** noon-4pm
Wed-Sat. **Admission** $6; $4-$5 discounts.
No credit cards. Map p314 C6.

This Victorian house, located on a fairly unremarkable residential street just north-east of MacArthur
Park, has been maintained to reflect its origins, and
is thus stuffed almost to bursting with antique fixtures, fittings and general ephemera. Special events,
including annual presentations at Hallowe'en and
Christmas, keep things ticking over.

Los Feliz, Silver Lake & Echo Park

Three tales of urban bohemia.

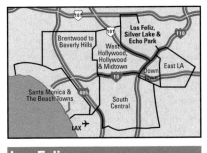

Los Feliz

Map p314

Desirable but never flashy, cool rather than fashionable, Los Feliz is a fluid melding of yuppie demand, hipster distinction and ethnic influence. Drive around the blocks leading to **Griffith Park** and you'll find huge mansions, luscious flora and fauna and signs from the Los Angeles City Fire Department directing you to not indulge in cigarettes while 'in the hills'. Life moves at a mellower pace here, and not solely due to the multitude of speed bumps.

Los Feliz is named for José Feliz, a soldier who claimed the area in the early 19th century and whose family held on to it for 50 years until they lost it in a legal snafu. The area housed a number of film studios in the silent era, including a set for DW Griffith's *Intolerance* at the Sunset Boulevard and Hillhurst Avenue site now occupied by the single-screen, Egyptian-flavoured **Vista** cinema. Walking north-west from here up Hollywood Boulevard will lead you past a scattering of shops towards **Barnsdall Art Park** (*see p104*).

The stretch of Vermont that runs north of here, between bustling Hollywood Boulevard and bucolic Franklin Avenue, is one of Los Feliz's two main streets. It's a very pedestrian-friendly area, its hipster boutiques and good-value eateries best approached on foot. Shops include the **SquaresVille** (No.1800; *see p190*) and **Atmosphere** (No.1728; *see p186*) clothing outlets, and 'fiercely independent' (their words) bookstore **Skylight** (No.1818; *see p182*); eating

options include **Fred 62** (No.1850; *see p156*); bars include the **Dresden Room** (No.1760; *see p176*), where you'll find ultra-campy lounge duo Marty and Elayne. The arty vibe is completed by the **Los Feliz Three Cinemas** (No.1822, 1-323 664 2169). Parallel to Vermont Avenue lies the similarly wanderable **Hillhurst Avenue**. Once you're done roaming the shops, swing by **Yuca's Hut** (No.2056; *see p157*) for tacos or **Mexico City** (No.1948; *see p156*) for something a bit more substantial.

The residential streets in Los Feliz are almost entirely handsome, but a couple of properties stand out from the crowd. One is the **Ennis-Brown House** (2655 Glendower Avenue, north-east of Vermont Avenue, www.ennishouse.org), a boxily exotic Frank Lloyd Wright concrete construction from 1924. Unfortunately, the city declared it unsafe in 2004 and ordered it closed; it's currently raising funds for a renovation. The other major home here, in better shape, is the **Lovell House** (4616 Dundee Drive). Richard Neutra's International Modern gem was built in 1929, but is most famous for its starring role in *LA Confidential* 70 years later.

Play ball! **Griffith Park**. See p105.

All dried out

The T-Birds and the Scorpions raced their souped-up jalopies here in *Grease*, and Arnie chased the good guys along its concrete banks when he was still the Terminator. But, movies apart, the **Los Angeles River** is something of a laughing stock. As LA grew its river was lined in concrete by zealous engineers in order to contain flash floods. The Los Angeles River soon became a city-wide in-joke, the river that's anything but.

Until now. After years of promises left unkept, the efforts of local activists have finally paid off. Parts of the 52-mile waterway are actually full of – yes! – water, and its environment is more accessible than ever to the public. Take the Los Angeles Riverwalk (accessible where Dover Street meets the river in Atwater Village, or from the equestrian trail in North Atwater Park), a 1.3-mile trail along a stretch of the river dotted with pocket parks that make innovative use of limited space.

The river is also more welcoming to wildlife than it has been for years. The frogs are starting to make a comeback in Frogtown, near where the I-5 crosses the river at the north-eastern corner of Elysian Park; over 100 species of bird also make their homes here. Locals catch crayfish in the shallows, and parks line the west bank of the river as it heads towards the Elysian Valley. Meanwhile, up at the Sepulveda Basin (near the intersection of US 101 and I-405 in the San Fernando Valley), cottonwoods and willows grow untamed and the occasional swimmer takes the plunge. It's a change from the time when the only creatures you'd see were river cats, painted on the river's flood-proofing duct-covers (which look like giant cat heads) by guerilla artists.

A fine introduction to the river is provided by the non-profit Friends of the Los Angeles River, aka FoLAR (1-323 223 0585, www.folar.org), which leads free walking tours once a month. If you choose to go unaccompanied, beware during flood season (February and March): flash flooding does occur.

Barnsdall Art Park & Hollyhock House

4800 Hollywood Boulevard, between Edgemont Street & Vermont Avenue (1-323 660 4254/ Hollyhock House 1-323 644 6269, www.hollyhock house.net/Junior Arts Center 1-323 644 6275, www. fojac.org). Metro Sunset-Vermont/bus 26, 204, 754, LDH/US 101, exit Sunset Boulevard east. **Open** *Barnsdall Art Park* noon-5pm daily; 6-9pm first Fri of mth. *Hollyhock House* noon-4pm Wed-Sun. *Junior Arts Center* 9am-5pm daily. **Admission** free-$5. **Map** p314 A2.

After philanthropist and eccentric Aline Barnsdall bought this cute little hill during World War I, she immediately engaged Frank Lloyd Wright to build her a group of buildings at its summit. The complex was designed to include a cinema, a theatre and an array of artists' studios, but was never completed. Judging by the speed with which Barnsdall moved elsewhere (she donated the land and its buildings to the city in 1927, just four years after she moved in), Barnsdall was no great fan of Wright's work. Happily, the city was more appreciative, and has recently restored Hollyhock House, Barnsdall's former home, to a very handsome state. Tours are conducted five days a week; booking is advisable.

Barnsdall originally donated the land to the city for it to be used as a public art park, and it still fulfils that role seven decades later. Temporary exhibitions are staged in a variety of galleries, there's a Junior Arts Center and the annual indie rock festival ArthurBall is also held here.

Griffith Park

Back in 1896, mining tycoon Griffith J Griffith donated 3,015 acres (five square miles) of land to the city for use as a public park. Since expanded by a third thanks to other land donations and purchases down the decades, **Griffith Park** is the largest city-run park in the US (five times the size of New York's Central Park), its vastness separating Los Feliz and the Hollywood Hills from Glendale and Burbank.

It's an unexpectedly dramatic place, immense and largely untamed. Some patches are flat, packed with picnickers, football-tossers, drumming circles and Frisbee-throwers on warm weekends. Other sections have been civilised by golf courses (no fewer than four of them), tennis courts, soccer pitches and even the occasional museum. But much of the park remains surprisingly wild and rugged.

The 53 miles of hiking trails around the park offer far more variety than you'd expect from an urban park. The most popular walk is the half-hour schlep from Griffith Observatory to the 1,625-foot (495-metre) peak of **Mount Hollywood**, and not without good reason: the views from the top are awesome, the city spreadeagled around you in all its hazy majesty. Details of all the park's walks can be gleaned from the Ranger Station in the park's south-east corner (4730 Crystal Springs Drive, 1-323 913 4688), but be warned: the only hiking maps available are poorly photocopied and, in places, partly illegible. New maps are promised in due course, but don't hold your breath.

The manmade attractions include the **Los Angeles Zoo**, **Griffith Observatory**, the **Museum of the American West**, the open-air **Greek Theatre** and a gorgeous 1926 merry-go-round, open daily in summer and weekends in winter (1-323 665 3051). Those interested in Hollywood of yore should scamper up to the **Forest Lawn Memorial Park** (6300 Forest Lawn Drive, 1-800 204 3131; for the Glendale park, *see p124*), the final resting place for stars including Buster Keaton, John Ritter, Telly Savalas, Stan Laurel and Tex Avery.

Griffith Park is open 6am-10pm daily. For more information, call 1-323 913 4688 or check www.ci.la.ca.us/RAP/grifmet/gp; to reach park rangers, call 1-213 665 4372.

Autry National Center: Museum of the American West

4700 Western Heritage Way, opposite LA Zoo, Griffith Park (1-323 667 2000/www.museum oftheamericanwest.org). Bus 96/I-5, exit Zoo Drive west. **Open** 10am-5pm Tue-Sun. **Admission** $7.50; $3-$5 discounts. *Joint ticket with Southwest Museum (see p97)* $12; $5-$8 discounts. **Credit** AmEx, MC, V.

You might expect this Griffith Park museum to be a kitschy exploration of the life and works of the famous singing cowboy. However, though there's usually some sort of Autry memorabilia on display in the foyer, it's actually a fascinating exploration of the western US, outlining its history and detailing the myths that came to surround it.

The museum is bigger than it looks, spread over two floors with permanent exhibits on the right and temporary shows on the left. The downstairs galleries tell the story of Western migration by different communities, with illuminating exhibits on how they lived, what they hunted, where they settled and the like. Due homage is paid to the Spanish *vaqueros*, the original pioneering cowboys of the Old West whom Hollywood largely wrote out of the history books. However, fans of Western myth and legend will enjoy catching sight of Doc Holliday's revolver from the shootout at the OK Corral, John Wesley Hardin's business card (complete with imitation bulletholes) and the 200-strong Colt Firearms Collection.

The ground-floor galleries offer a collection of iconographic cowboy art, plus ephemera from the golden age of the western. Across the hall are the George Montgomery and Showcase Galleries, which host a series of excellent temporary shows; from June 2007 to January 2008, there's a major exhibition on Autry himself, scheduled to coincide with the 100th anniversary of his birth. The museum is twinned with the Southwest Museum (*see p107*).

Griffith Observatory

2800 E Observatory Road (1-323 664 1181/www. griffithobs.org). Bus 180, 181, 380/I-5, exit Los Feliz Boulevard west. **Open** *Observatory* closed until late 2006; call for details. *Satellite* 1-10pm Tue-Fri; 10am-10pm Sat, Sun. **Admission** *Observatory* call for details. *Satellite* free. **Map** p314 A1.

'If every person could look through that telescope,' declared Griffith J Griffith, 'it would revolutionise the world.' The formidable deco-modern building, which opened in 1935, houses a triple-beam solar telescope and a 12in (30.5cm) Zeiss refracting telescope, and its outside deck provides excellent views of the city's sprawl. On a more ephemeral level, the building has starred in many films, from the acclaimed (*Rebel Without a Cause*) to the disdained (*Flash Gordon*).

In early 2002, the Observatory closed for renovation and expansion. During the closure, staff have set up a 'satellite' operation in the north-east corner of Griffith Park just south of the LA Zoo's parking lot, containing a handful of astronomy displays and a telescope for night viewing. The facility will shut when the main Observatory reopens, hopefully in late 2006: check online or call the Observatory's 'Renovation Hotline' on 1-323 664 0155 for details on how the works are progressing.

4616 Greenwood Place, Los Feliz
Otherwise known as *Melrose Place*

Los Angeles Zoo

5333 Zoo Drive (1-323 644 4200/www.lazoo.org).
Bus 96/I-5, exit Zoo Drive west. **Open** *June-Labor
Day* 10am-6pm daily. *Labor Day-May* 10am-5pm daily.
Last entry 1hr before closing. **Admission** $10; $5-$7
discounts; free under-2s. **Credit** AmEx, Disc, MC, V.

The LA Zoo's greatest asset is its location, within
the isolated hills of Griffith Park. It's a pretty popular place, receiving around 1.4 million visitors every
year, but the zoo's size – 80 acres, plus a huge parking lot – means it rarely feels too busy. Highlights
include a labyrinthine aviary, a pair of hippos, a
young Sumatran tiger (born in late 2005) and gangs
of lively, crowd-pulling monkeys, along with the
new-ish Sea Lion Cliffs just inside the entrance.

Still, there could – and, perhaps, should – be an
awful lot more here. A huge swathe of land in the
centre of the park has been cleared for a number of
new attractions, among them a gorilla reserve and
a habitat for a much-touted pair of golden monkeys
from China. However, construction has been delayed
by funding problems, and labourers are conspicuous by their absence. If you only visit one zoo in
California, make it the one in San Diego (*see p280*).

Travel Town Museum

5200 Zoo Drive (1-323 662 5874/www.cityofla.org).
Bus 96, CE549/Hwy 134, exit Forest Lawn Drive.
Open 10am-4pm Mon-Fri; 10am-5pm Sat, Sun.
Admission free.

This endearing outdoor museum in Griffith Park's
north-west corner is made up of restored railroad
cars from the Union Pacific, Atchison and Santa Fe
lines, an early 20th-century milk delivery truck, and
more than a dozen steam and diesel locomotives.
Adjacent to the museum is the LA Live Steamers
(1-323 664 9678, www.lals.org), a club of rail enthu-
siasts that constructs and runs scale replicas of
diesel, steam and electric engines. Free rides are run
around a small track on Sundays, 11am to 3pm.

Silver Lake

Map p314

Gang activity still nibbles at its southern edges,
and the clothes on sale in its boutiques won't
confuse anyone into thinking they're on Rodeo
Drive. But not even *Vanity Fair* tagging Silver
Lake as the 'coolest neighbourhood in LA' has
stopped its rise. Its blend of art schoolers, left-
of-centre industry folk and ethnic communities
have managed to stave off the chain stores.
Instead, Silver Lake is dominated by bijou
independent shops, restaurants and bars that
stop it collapsing into Hollywood brashness.

The convergence of W Sunset Boulevard and
Santa Monica Boulevard – known as **Sunset**

> **Silvertop** Home to a wealthy family
> in *Less Than Zero*

Junction – is the axis of Silver Lake. Between
here and the junction of Silver Lake Boulevard,
Sunset Boulevard is dotted with small shops,
the majority selling quirky gifts (try **Serifos** at
No.3814, 1-323 660 7467) or fashion items (at
No.3938, **Kicks** hawks the kind of sneakers
you don't wear to the gym; *see p192*). To see
the locale in all its glory, visit the **Sunset
Junction Street Fair** in August (*see p206*).

The neighbourhood's namesake boulevard
is worth driving if only for the curves around
Silver Lake itself (it's actually a reservoir),
glittery at night and enveloped by some of the
area's nicest homes. Sights are at a premium;
this is a residential neighbourhood, pure and
simple. However, the surrounding streets are
bastions of refined old LA glamour: some of the
city's finest architects worked here in the 1920s
and 1930s. The many RM Schindler properties
include the **Droste** and **Walker Houses** at
2025 and 2100 Kenilworth Avenue, and the
daunting **Olive House** at 2236 Micheltorena
Street. Also on Micheltorena are two buildings
by John Lautner: **Silvertop** (No.2138) and
Lautner's own residence (No.2007). Austrian-
born architect Richard Neutra is represented by
a cluster of buildings on Silver Lake Boulevard
and a handful on Neutra Place.

Echo Park

Map p314

In the early 1900s, a suburb called Edendale
became a real film industry hotbed, attracting
movie-makers with its bright sun and clear
days. Now known as Echo Park, the area is
still a draw, albeit for different reasons: it's the
gateway neighbourhood to LA's predominantly
Latino east side, but is also home to a major-
league baseball stadium, two fine parks and
some deliciously restored century-old buildings.

Echo Park is sometimes defined as the area to
the north of US 101 and east of Alvarado Street,
but many locals mark the border with the giant
'Happy Foot/Sad Foot' sign at the Sunset Foot
Clinic, on the corner of Benton Street and W
Sunset Boulevard. This area, with Alvarado
and Sunset as its nucleus, supports many of
Echo Park's best cafés and shops, plus the
Echo Park Film Center (No.1200, 1-213 484
8846, www.echoparkfilmcenter.org). Sunset
offers several clothing boutiques, some fine
antiques stores and eating options including
the **Brite Spot** (No.1918; *see p158*).

To the south-east of the junction of Sunset
and Alvarado sits the green space from which
the neighbourhood takes its name. **Echo Park**
was laid out in the 1890s by architect Joseph
Henry Taylor to resemble an English garden; it

The architecture is eye-catchingly modern in **Silver Lake**. *See p106.*

does, albeit not in wholly convincing fashion. In the summer, it hosts festivals presented by the area's Filipino, Vietnamese, Cuban and Samoan communities. If you've time, take a paddle-boat ride through the blossoming lotuses in the lake.

Emerging on the west side of Echo Park will lead you into **Angelino Heights**, an enclave noted for its beautifully restored Victorian mansions. There's scarcely an ugly building within its confines (loosely bordered by W Sunset Boulevard, Boylston Street, US 101 and Echo Park), but the 1300 block of **Carroll Avenue** is especially attractive. North-east is **Dodger Stadium**, the handsome home of the perennially underachieving LA Dodgers baseball team (*see p253*). Beyond the outfield bleachers lies the vast **Elysian Park**; less scenic than Griffith Park, granted, but not without worthwhile trails and picnic spots. It also features the somewhat bizarre environs of the **Los Angeles Police Academy** (1880 N Academy Drive). Established in 1920 as a private shooting club for LAPD officers, it boasts an exotic rock garden, chapel, café and gift shop that are accessible to the public. Don't forget to view the Jack Webb Memorial or the brass-knuckle collection.

Scattered throughout Echo Park are a number of quaint stairways – some from the 19th century, others reconstructed – that provide pedestrians with a route from the streets to their hillside or canyon homes. A couple are especially notable: at 232 steps, the **Baxter Steps** (at Baxter and Avon Streets) are believed to be the city's tallest, while at

923-927 N Vendome Street are the steps up which Laurel and Hardy try to drag a piano in their 1932 film *The Music Box*.

Although it's less than 200 yards long and slightly isolated from Echo Park's other points of interest, one further thoroughfare merits a visit. With a gradient of 33 per cent, **Fargo Street** is said to be the steepest road in all of California. For 30 years, the LA Wheelmen cycling club (www.lawheelmen.org) have organised a ride up its incline. It's usually held in March, but be warned: on average, barely half the participants make it to the top.

Autry National Center: Southwest Museum of the American Indian

234 Museum Drive, at Marmion Way, Mount Washington (1-323 221 2164/www.southwest museum.org). Metro Southwest Museum/bus 81, 83/I-110, exit Avenue 43 north. **Open** 10am-5pm Tue-Sun. **Admission** $7.50; $3-$5 discounts; free under-6s. **No credit cards.**

Located in Mount Washington, a couple of miles north-east of Elysian Park, LA's oldest museum is approaching its 2007 centenary with renewed energy, having safeguarded its future by joining forces with the Museum of the American West (*see p105*) to form what's now known as the Autry National Center. The museum's collection takes in some 250,000 items from the last 2,000 years, including textiles, jewellery and other Southwest-related artefacts (careful: some anthropologists believe some of the items to be still inhabited by gods or ancestor spirits). The highlights are divided into four permanent galleries, each exploring the history of a different native American culture.

Downtown

From Skid Row to high art, via Chinatown and Little Tokyo, all human life is here.

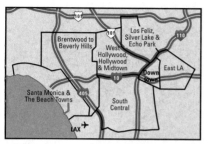

By day, Downtown LA is a great many things: a crisp political district, a bustling centre of finance and commerce, a Mexican shopping mall, a convention hub, a multi-billion-dollar fashion market and plenty more besides. By night, at least until a few years ago, it wasn't much at all: once the workers left their offices, only Skid Row's 7,000 homeless prevented the place from becoming a total ghost town.

But things are changing here, and quickly. The Staples Center and Disney Hall have brought people back to Downtown at night, and Gallery Row (along Main and Spring Streets between 2nd and 9th Streets; *see p227*) has added a little grass-roots culture. All this is well and good, but for an area to be properly renewed what it needs is not transient visitors, no matter how cultured, but people. That is, city residents choosing to make their homes and lives in the area, and thus having a real stake in its continued habitability. This is now beginning to happen in Downtown. Once-neglected old skyscrapers are being converted into snazzy apartment blocks, dormant offices are becoming residential properties, and two major new commercial developments – one around Grand Avenue, the other down by the Staples Center – both include substantial provision for residential accommodation.

Provided you take care around its shadier corners, especially at night, Downtown is very pedestrian-friendly. Several groups run walking tours (*see p71*), but the more independently minded might be interested in the self-guided Angels Walk: for details, pick up a leaflet from the LACVB (*see p296*) or see www.angelswalk la.org. Don't be surprised if you see movie crews at work: Downtown is the single most filmed neighbourhood in LA.

Chinatown

LA's original Chinatown sprang up in the 1850s around Alameda Street. A thriving area at the turn of the 20th century, it began to fade soon after, and the land that held it was redeveloped as Union Station in the 1930s. (One remaining building from the original Chinatown holds the **Chinese American Museum**; *see p110*.)

However, although the Chinese community leaders had failed to secure a future for their neighbourhood, their children soon managed to establish a second Chinatown. Led by Peter Soo Hoo, the local Chinese population bought land at 75¢ per square foot in an area just north-west of Union Station in what was once Little Italy, and set about constructing a new Chinatown that would serve the local Chinese American community while also, they hoped, appealing to tourists. In June 1938, Chinatown's **Central Plaza**, an inauthentic yet strangely exotic confection, opened to the public.

Almost 70 years later, Central Plaza is still the focal point of Chinatown, but Chinatown is no longer the focal point of LA's Chinese American communities: that role falls to Monterey Park, north-east here. The small district feels a little forlorn these days, the buildings ragged and the streets often quiet outside of **Chinese New Year** (*see p209*), yet it has undergone a revival of late: the arrival of a cluster of galleries and new bars makes for an interesting juxtaposition with the dusty old Chinese-owned bric-a-brac stores.

N Broadway and, to a lesser extent, **N Spring Street** are the main roads, home to banks, grocers, bakeries (try the **Phoenix**, at 969 N Broadway), medicine stores and a new Metro station. However, the heart of Chinatown remains **Central Plaza** (947 N Broadway), one of the nation's first pedestrian malls. These days, its businesses are a mix of old-fashioned restaurants and bars such as **Hop Louie** (950 Mei Ling Way, 1-213 628 4244), tacky souvenir shops on **Gin Ling Way**, and new businesses

> **Foo Chow (949 N Hill Street)**
> Reads the sign on the side
> of the restaurant: 'Jackie Chan's
> *Rush Hour* – A Best Seller Movie
> Was Shot Here'

such as hipster-friendly Asian eaterie **Café Via** (451 Gin Ling Way, 1-213 617 1481). A statue of Republic of China founder Dr Sun Yat-Sen oversees proceedings with a stern expression.

North of Central Plaza, the volunteer-run **Chinese Historical Society** (411 Bernard Street, 1-323 222 0856, www.chssc.org, open 11am-3pm Wed-Fri, noon-4.30pm Sun) contains information on Chinatown's past. To the west, **Hill Street** holds more Chinese businesses; on Thursdays from 2pm to 7pm, a farmers' market sets up shop in the parking lot adjacent to the United Commercial Bank (727 N Hill Street). But perhaps the area's most interesting street is skinny **Chung King Road**, just behind it. Some of its old Chinese shops remain, while others have been taken over by Anglos and converted into tiny galleries. Among them are the **Happy Lion** (No.963) and **Black Dragon Society** (No.961); for details of these and others, *see p227*.

Olvera Street & the Plaza

Just across Cesar E Chavez Avenue from Chinatown is **El Pueblo de Los Angeles Historical Monument**, a restored 44-acre historic park that purports to be on the site of the original settlement of LA. In fact, the first settlement was half a mile from here, but no trace of it remains; LA's official birthday is 4 September 1781, the day that the first Spanish settlers began farming and building ranches.

It's a curious jumble of buildings, most built in the late 19th and early 20th centuries and used today for all manner of purposes. Your first stop should be to collect a map from **Sepulveda House** on the east side of N Main Street (No.622, 1-213 628 1274, www.cityofla. org/elp, 10am-3pm Mon-Sat), a 19th-century house converted into a visitors' centre and small museum about the area's history.

Right by Sepulveda House, running east of Main Street, is **Olvera Street**, a narrow, pedestrianised thoroughfare. Renovated in 1930 as a Mexican marketplace, it's now just a tourist trap, albeit a generally enjoyable one. In between the odiferous taco stands and the stalls hawking colourful hats and shirts, keep an eye out for **Avila Adobe**, the oldest house in LA. Built in 1818, this small ranch-style home has been restored, and now operates as a museum.

At the southern end of Olvera Street sits the circular **Plaza**, the bustling focal point of El Pueblo. The sizeable bandstand in the centre hosts shows by dancers and musicians, and a number of festivals, such as the **Blessing of the Animals** (*see p204*) and **Las Posadas** (*see p209*). South of the Plaza is a cluster of old and not-so-old buildings; one, a 19th-century fire station, now houses a diverting collection of old firefighting equipment. And just across Main Street from the Plaza are more historic buildings, including the oldest Catholic church in LA: **Our Lady, Queen of the Angels**, commonly known as La Placita.

There's rarely big trouble in Downtown's little **Chinatown**.

Sightseeing

Public art Downtown

Some corners of it are decades-old; others were built only last week. However, the one characteristic that links virtually every part of Downtown LA is the preponderance of public art: outside corporate skyscrapers, on the walls of public buildings, even in the form of bicycle racks. The Public Art in LA website (www.publicartinla.com), maintained by USC librarian Ruth Wallach, is an unbeatable resource to the hundreds of works around the area. Here, though, are six of the best...

Hammering Man – Jonathan Borofsky (1988)
California Market Center, 110 E 9th Street
Borofsky is best known for his *Ballerina Clown* (see p80 **Public art**). But this hulking silhouette, bashing unenthusiastically with a hammer in his left hand, is just as effective. For his *Molecule Man*, see p113.

Source Figure, by Robert Graham.

Mind, Body and Spirit – Gidon Graetz (1986)
south-west corner of 4th & Hope Streets
This vast, twisty horn, made from stainless steel and bronze by Israeli artist Graetz in his Italian studio, is one of a number of sculptures commissioned by the YMCA.

Source Figure – Robert Graham (1991)
Hope Place, between 4th & 5th Streets
This three-foot bronze nude stands proudly atop a column in a fountain halfway up the Bunker Hill Steps. The 'source' of the name is a nod to the water that flows from the pool down towards the Central Library.

Friendship Knot – Shinkichi Tajiri (1972)
2nd & San Pedro Streets, Little Tokyo
Born in Los Angeles in 1923 but based in the Netherlands since the 1950s, Tajiri has long favoured knots in his works, which include paintings, drawings and sculptures such as this towering fibreglass object in Little Tokyo.

**Ed Ruscha Monument –
Kent Twitchell (1978-87)**
on the side of 1031 S Hill Street
One adopted Angeleno artist pays tribute to another in this slightly creepy six-storey mural. Clad in a red shirt and grey slacks, the very realistic-looking Ruscha gazes out over the vehicles of an ordinary parking lot. The title itself is perhaps a little previous: as of 2006, Ruscha was still with us.

Bicycle Rack – Randall Wilson (1998)
corner of College & Yale Streets, Chinatown
Wilson's pair of inverted hearts are one of ten Downtown bike racks designed by students at the Southern California Institute of Architecture as part of a project entitled *The Bike Stops Here*; others stand in Pershing Square, outside the Geffen Contemporary and by the Times-Mirror Building. Two years later, a further 32 racks were installed on Hill Street between Civic Center and Pico Boulevard.

Visible from the Plaza is **Union Station** (800 N Alameda Street). Opened in 1939 on the site of the original Chinatown, it was the last of the great American rail stations to be built (at a cost at the time of $11 million). The terminus unified the three railroads that then served LA. By 1971 however, just seven passenger trains a day were running through here, but thankfully it's a bit busier today. Its distinctive, Mission-style exterior, marble floors, high ceilings and decorative tiles make it an evocative place. However, don't confuse it with the Spanish colonial architecture that stands next to it. That's the post office.

Chinese American Museum

425 N Los Angeles Street, at Arcadia Street (1-213 485 8567/www.camla.org). Metro Chinatown/ bus 76/US 101, exit Los Angeles Street south. **Open** 10am-3pm Tue-Sun. **Admission** $3; $2 discounts. **No credit cards. Map** p311 C1.

While the CAM's location in El Pueblo might seem a little incongruous, it's actually very aptly sited in LA's original Chinatown. The Garnier building, in which part of it sits, is the most historic Chinese building in the area: built in 1890, when Chinese immigrants dominated in this part of town, it's been home to a number of major community organisations. Exhibits spotlight both the history of LA's Chinatown and the more general experience of Chinese-Americans in the US.

Little Tokyo & south

Head south down Alameda Street, past Temple Street to Central Avenue, and you'll reach the **Geffen Contemporary** wing of the **Museum of Contemporary Art** (*see p115*), housed in a warehouse converted – impressively – by Frank Gehry. Right by the museum, Roger Yanagita's **Go for Broke Monument** commemorates the Japanese American soldiers who fought in World War II, experiences dramatised in the 1951 movie *Go for Broke*. Further down Central Avenue is the **Japanese American National Museum** (*see below*), in a grand plaza designed by sculptor Isamu Noguchi; opposite, partly housed in the 1925 Nishi Hongwanji Buddhist Temple, is the JANM's **National Center for the Preservation of Democracy**.

It's at this corner that Little Tokyo really begins. Just across the road, running between 1st and 2nd Streets just west of Central Avenue, is the **Japanese Village Plaza**, a two-storey mini-mall with restaurants, shops and karaoke bars. Across from the Japanese Village Plaza are the **James Irvine Gardens**, a lovely, romantic example of a traditional Japanese garden. The gardens are accessible by taking an elevator to the basement of the **Japanese-American Cultural & Community Center** (244 S San Pedro Street, 1-213 628 2725).

There's more to see to the east of Japanese Village Plaza. **Astronaut Ellison S Onizuka Street**, which runs diagonally south between 1st Street and the corner of 2nd and San Pedro Streets, is named for one of the astronauts who died in the *Challenger* crash in 1986. Amid assorted shops and restaurants, a model of the shuttle commemorates his life. A little further west is the 19th-century St Vibiana's Cathedral (114 E 2nd Street), recently converted into a performing arts centre named **Vibiana Place**. West of the Japanese Village, meanwhile, is the **Higashi Honganji Buddhist Temple** (505 E 3rd Street), which blends neatly and sweetly into its otherwise Western surroundings.

South-west of Little Tokyo is a thrilling little shopping district centred on **Wall Street** between 3rd and 5th Streets. Crammed together like sardines, dozens of shops and stalls sell everything from kids' toys to air pistols to crowds of Asian and Latino customers. Signs in windows read 'Wholesale only', but most shopkeepers don't seem fussy, and bargains abound. On 3rd Street by San Pedro Street, look out for a wall painted, charmingly, with American corporate logos (Tylenol, Colgate, Swisher Sweets) from days of yore.

Japanese American National Museum

369 E 1st Street, at N Central Avenue (1-213 625 0414/www.janm.org). Bus 30, 31, 40, 42, 58, 340/ US 101, exit Alameda Street south. **Open** 10am-5pm Tue, Wed, Fri-Sun; 10am-8pm Thur. **Admission** $8; $4-$5 discounts; free under-5s. Free to all 10am-8pm 3rd Thur of mth, 5-8pm all other Thurs. **Credit** AmEx, MC, V. **Map** p311 C2.

The story of Japanese immigration to the US really begins in 1882, when bosses were barred from importing cheap Chinese labour by the Chinese Exclusion Act. Thousands of Japanese arrived to take their place; many settled in the San Joaquin Valley and became farmers. But then the Japanese were excluded from American life in much the same way as the Chinese had suffered before them: prevented from owning land in 1913, banned from immigrating in 1924 and sent to brutal internment camps during World War II. Only in 1952 were people born in Japan allowed to become American citizens.

This excellent museum, one of the city's best, tells the story of Japanese immigration to the US in lucid, engaging fashion; even if you've no prior interest in the subject, you'll be drawn in to it by the perfectly pitched displays. Aside from the permanent exhibition, the museum stages an engaging roster of documentary and art exhibitions, including a wrenching yet beautiful display of images and artefacts from the aforementioned internment camps. To cap it all off, there's a lovely gift shop.

In 2006, the museum opened the **National Center for the Preservation of Democracy** (111 N Central Avenue, 1-213 830 1880, www.ncdemocracy.org), an educational institute aimed at preserving and promoting democracy in the US. For details of its public programmes, check online.

Skid Row

Walking further south will bring you to LA's most infamous area: **Skid Row**, centred around 5th Street between Main and Alameda Streets. The homeless have long congregated here; several missions offer food handouts and a roof for the night. But the area has also become both a magnet for lowlifes of every stripe and a dumping ground for the souls that the city has forgotten, or would like to forget. Dealers come from across town to sell drugs; users come from across town to buy them. One of the missions is rumoured to run a bus service from a nearby jail, collecting homeless convicts as they're

Airline flights are one of the biggest producers of the global warming gas CO_2. But with **The CarbonNeutral Company** you can make your travel a little greener.

Go to **www.carbonneutral.com** to calculate your flight emissions then 'neutralise' them through international projects which save exactly the same amount of carbon dioxide.

Contact us at **shop@carbonneutral.com** or call into the office on **0870 199 99 88** for more details.

CarbonNeutral®flights

freed; several local hospitals have admitted doing the same with patients, many mentally ill, if the hospital has no place to put them and the patient has no place to go.

Despite the best efforts of the missions, the scene along 5th Street seems almost beyond the law. Crack is sold in broad daylight; excrement drips from sidewalk to roadway to drain; empty liquor bottles tumble along the sidewalk like logs on a river. Dementia is everywhere. The LAPD have begun to crack down on the drug trade, unarguably the main problem, but the area has largely resisted improvement thus far.

Civic Center & around

Civic Center

Just north-east of Little Tokyo, there's a neat intersection of immigrant communities: **Judge John Aiso Street**, named for the highest-ranking *nisei* to serve for the Allies during World War II, connects to Temple Street and the **Edward R Roybal Federal Building** (255 E Temple Street), named for California's first Mexican American congressman. Outside the latter is Jonathan Borofsky's sculpture *Molecule Man*, a quartet of huge metal figures.

The majority of LA's administrative and political institutions are based in this area, known as **Civic Center**. Just north of the Federal Building, at Aliso and Los Angeles Streets, is the **Metropolitan Detention Center**, LA's newest prison. Designed to blend in with the office blocks around it, the building looks nothing like a conventional jail; legend has it that a group of Japanese tourists once tried to check in, thinking it was a hotel. To the east is the art deco-styled **City Hall** (200 N Spring Street), LA's tallest building until 1957. Other landmarks include Thom Mayne's amazing new **Caltrans Building** (100 S Main Street); the slightly tatty 1930s **Times-Mirror Building** (202 W 1st Street), home to the *Los Angeles Times*; and the **Los Angeles County Courthouse** (210 W Temple Street), scene of the OJ Simpson trial in 1995.

Disney Hall & around

Though Downtown contains a surprising number of historic buildings, it's best known for two of its newest. The **Cathedral of Our Lady of the Angels** (555 W Temple Street) has had a number of nicknames pinned to it since its dedication in 2002: perhaps the most memorable is 'Our Lady of the 101', after the freeway from which it can clearly be seen.

It's a fine structure, but it's overshadowed by its neighbour. The **Walt Disney Concert Hall** (111 S Grand Avenue; *see p237*) finally opened in 2003 after an odyssey of promises, delays, starts, stops, shutdowns, ego battles, funding problems and structural concerns. Yet it was all worth it: bold, brash and even sensual in its reflective glory, Frank Gehry's building sits like a reclining steel butterfly, its wings fanning languidly atop Bunker Hill. It's just as wonderful inside: the acoustic of the hall is among the best in the US. Still, not everyone is happy: those who live in its wake have formally complained about the tremendous glare the exterior gives off during the day.

Disney Hall adjoins several other buildings, which officially shelter under the umbrella term of the Performing Arts Center. The **Dorothy Chandler Pavilion** was, until Disney Hall opened, the home of the LA Philharmonic, and now contents itself with staging opera and dance. The **Mark Taper Forum** and the **Ahmanson Theatre**, meanwhile, are two of LA's better playhouses. For all three, *see p296*. To the west of the Music Center sits the bold, horizontal edifice of the **Department of Water & Power** (111 N Hope Street) with its 120,000-square-foot (11,000-square-metre) moat and beautiful water conservation garden.

This area looks set to change dramatically in the next five or six years, at least if the **Grand Avenue Authority** gets its way. The ongoing revival of Downtown has so far happened by stealth, Disney Hall the only new building expressly designed to lure visitors. The GAA, though, have sought and found approval for a $2-billion construction project centred on the development of a 16-acre park stretching between the Music Center and City Hall (if the relocation of two forgettable civic buildings is given the green light, the park would be 26 acres). The development is also set to include 2,600 apartments, a 275-room hotel, retail space and even a high school. For more, see www.grandavenuecommittee.org.

The Financial District & Bunker Hill

South of Disney Hall, art meets commerce head on. At Grand Avenue and 3rd Street sits the **Museum of Contemporary Art** (*see p115*), part of the billion-dollar **California Plaza**. The museum itself is unmissable – there's a

Promenade Towers (123 S Figueroa Street) Edward Norton watches his apartment in this block go up in flames during *Fight Club*

Sightseeing

huge Swiss Army knife, designed by Claes Oldenburg, in front of it – but the plaza is by no means unmemorable, whether for the computer-operated fountain spraying 40-foot geysers in the Watercourt, or the daily concerts in summer. Across the road, meanwhile, sits the **Wells Fargo Center** (333 S Grand Avenue); as well as being a banking powerhouse, it's home to the engaging **Wells Fargo History Museum** (1-213 253 7166), which tells the story of the bank founded in the heyday of the Gold Rush.

Popularly known as **Bunker Hill**, this area was where LA's rich built their houses a century ago. While the fringes of the area are slowly growing more residential, the grand old mansions are long gone, and the only remnant of the old Bunker Hill neighbourhood is **Angels Flight** (Hill Street, between 3rd & 4th Streets): built in 1901, closed in 1969, reopened 27 years later and shut again after a fatal accident in 2001, it's the world's shortest railway.

A couple of blocks south sits **Pershing Square**. A public meeting place since 1866, it was renamed in 1918 after the commander of the US Army in World War I. It's now a restful place, hosting concerts in summer and an ice rink in winter. Dominating its edge is the **Millennium Biltmore** hotel (*see p62*), built in 1923 and one of the grandest hotels in Los Angeles. Another art deco prize sits just south of Pershing Square in the shape of the **Oviatt**

Building (617 S Olive Street), designed in 1928 to house an exclusive men's haberdashery.

A little west of here is the **Richard J Riordan Central Library** (630 W 5th Street). Completed in 1926, it's a fine library but also a striking *beaux arts* building, with a dramatic, tiled pyramid tower. After a fire in the 1980s, it was refurbished with money stumped up by the developers of **US Bank Tower**, formerly Library Tower (633 W 5th Street); built by IM Pei in 1990 and towering 1,018 feet (310 metres) into the Downtown sky, it's the tallest building in LA. (Al Qaeda is well aware of its height: it was reportedly one of its targets in a botched 9/11 style plot.) In front of the library is the oasis of the **Robert F Maguire Gardens**; the wide, graceful sweep of the 103 **Bunker Hill Steps**, linking 5th and Hope Streets.

Heading west from here along 5th Street and turning left down Flower Street will bring you in sight of two hotels. The **Standard** (550 S Flower Street; *see p178*) is Downtown's hippest hang, a bright, sleek hotel with an impressive rooftop bar (*see p178*). Almost opposite is the **Westin Bonaventure** (404 S Figueroa Street; *see p62*), the most distinctive skyscraper in Downtown. With its interior pools and bubble-shaped elevators, it's a refreshing change to the uniformity of most nearby tall buildings.

Abandoned for years by Angelenos outside of office hours, the streets around here are

Richard J Riordan Central Library.

gradually being resettled by moneyed twenty- and thirtysomethings hungry for something LA has been unable to provide: an urban lifestyle. The **Pegasus Lofts** (Flower Street, between 6th Street and Wilshire Boulevard) is a typical piece of high-style living for these new Downtowners. 'The Urban Habitat, Unbound' reads the sign on the side; the other corner of the structure holds the Daily Grill, an upscale restaurant/bar filled with local workers.

Heading south down Figueroa Street will bring you to the **Downtown Farmers' Market** (S Figueroa & W 7th Streets), held here from 10am until 4pm on Thursday, Friday and Saturday. No matter which day you wander here, though, you'll see one of LA's best-known sculptures: Terry Allen's *Corporate Head*, a lifesize effigy of a corporate executive with its head disappearing into the side of the Citicorp office building (725 S Figueroa Street). It's the highlight of **Poet's Walk**, an assortment of verse inscriptions and public art.

Museum of Contemporary Art & Geffen Contemporary

MOCA *250 S Grand Avenue, at 3rd Street (1-213 621 2766). Metro Civic Center/bus 2, 4, 10, 11, 14, 48, 92, 302/I-110, exit 3rd Street east.* **Map** p311 B2.
Geffen Contemporary *152 N Central Avenue, at 1st Street (1-213 621 2766). Bus 30, 31, 40, 42, 58, 340/US 101, exit Alameda Street south.* **Map** p311 C2.

Both *www.moca.org.* **Open** 11am-5pm Mon, Fri; 11am-8pm Thur; 11am-6pm Sat, Sun. **Admission** *Combined ticket* $8; $5 discounts; free under-12s. Free to all 5-8pm Thur. **Credit** AmEx, MC, V.

The city's – and, arguably, the American West's – premier showcase for post-war art, MoCA started life in a humongous bus barn on the edge of Little Tokyo. It's now the Geffen Contemporary, its spacious, raw interior designed by Frank Gehry in the 1980s; it's considered by some to be one of his gutsiest spaces. When MoCA's main building, designed by Japan's Arata Isozaki, was completed a block from the Civic Center, the museum was able simultaneously to mount ambitious survey exhibitions and to showcase items from its fine permanent collection, which includes pieces by Rauschenberg, Rothko, Twombly, Mondrian and Pollock.

Upwards of half a dozen shows can be viewed at any single time between the two galleries; MoCA stages the more mainstream exhibits, leaving the Geffen Contemporary to concentrate on more esoteric art. Recent shows have included a display of Warhol drawings and a show that attempted to expand upon Frank Gehry's design processes. A programme of talks and performance events round out the scene. A free bus runs between the two sites.

Broadway

If you want to see what a real Mexican shopping street looks like, as opposed to the tourist tack of Olvera Street, head to **Broadway**. Running the length of Downtown, it's the most fascinating street in the area, a place where decrepit old Downtown meets both the increasingly Hispanic modern city and the affluent creatives who are returning to the area in droves.

Start at 2nd and Broadway and wander south; a block away, you'll find the **Bradbury Building** (304 S Broadway, 1-213 626 1893; *see p24*), a turn-of-the-century masterpiece in brick and iron lacery. The building has been sold to a Hong Kong real estate developer, who's reputed to have plans to add a restaurant to the ground floor. Across the street sits the enclosed **Grand Central Market** (*see p195*), a perpetually busy Mexican-style market with stalls selling everything from fresh meat to fruit smoothies.

Nearby is the **Million Dollar Theatre** (No.307), where Sid Grauman launched his West Coast operations. Broadway was once LA's own Little White Way: it's the first and largest Historic Theatre District listed in the National Register of Historic Places. Its six blocks have drawn renewed interest of late; it's been spearheaded in part by the **Los Angeles Conservancy** (www.laconservancy.org), whose weekly theatres tour (*see p71*) and annual **Last Remaining Seats** festival (*see p220* **Festivals**) offer access to many of the usually-closed theatres. Others on Broadway include the

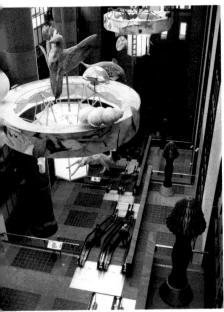

Sightseeing

Los Angeles Theatre (No.615), built in 90 days during 1931 at a cost of a million dollars; the **Pantages/Arcade Theatre** (No.534), now retail space; the **Tower Theatre** (No.802), the exterior of which is referred to by many as LA's first depiction of the casting couch; the **Orpheum** (No.842), which cost an astonishing $3 million in 1926; and the **United Artists Theatre** (No.933), now a church.

Across the street from the **Orpheum** is the **Eastern Columbia Building**, a key link between old and new Downtown. Built in 1929 by Claude Beelman, the building is a gorgeous, 13-storey, turquoise art deco pile. Like many old buildings Downtown, it's been converted into desirable loft apartments in recent years by the Kor Group, also responsible for the Pegasus Lofts and for a slew of hyper-fashionable hotels across LA. By now, you've reached Downtown's **Jewelry District** (Hill Street and Broadway, between 6th and 8th Streets), a polyglot's delight: expect to hear anything from Hebrew to Armenian, as the stallholders, shop owners and repairers go about their exotic business.

The Fashion District & South Park

South-east of the Jewelry District is another bustling commercial hub. Known for years as the Garment District, the roads around Los Angeles Street south of 7th Street received a rebranding in the 1980s when real estate owners got together in an attempt to modernise the area. It seems to have worked: the **Fashion District** (www.fashiondistrict.org) pulses with activity these days. Clothes are still made here in decades-old warehouses, but a great many more are brought in from elsewhere and sold: the area does $7 billion a year in wholesale trade, with a further $1 billion in retail to the public.

The four main market centres are all grouped together; spread over three 13-storey buildings housing 1,000 showrooms, the **California Market Center** (110 E 9th Street, www. californiamarketcenter.com) is the biggest. However, outside of the excellent ground-floor fashion bookstore and Jonathan Borofsky's sculpture *Hammering Man*, or unless you're here for one of the sample sales (held on the last Friday of some months), there's not much to see. Instead, start pounding the pavements in search of bargains at the 150-plus shops around

Grand Olympic Auditorium (1801 S Grand Avenue)
Where Hilary Swank took on all-comers in *Million Dollar Baby*

the area that mix wholesale and retail trade. Chaotic, relentless **Santee Alley**, between Maple Avenue and Santee Street, deals mostly in cheap Gucci and Versace knock-offs, but there's far nicer stuff elsewhere, much of it at extremely nice prices. For an insider's guide to the area, take one of the regular tours with **Urban Shopping Adventures** (*see p71*).

The northern tip of the Fashion District is flagged by the **Flower District** (www.laflowerdistrict.com) and the **Los Angeles Flower Market** (on Wall Street, between 7th and 8th Streets). Get here pre-dawn for a colourful riot of activity, as wholesalers unload truckloads of snapdragons, lilies, roses, orchids and tulips. The southwestern edge of the Fashion District is marked by the **Coca-Cola Building** (1334 S Central Avenue), built in 1937 and designed by Robert Derrah to resemble an ocean liner.

West of here, there's less to see, at least once you've passed the **Herald Examiner Building** (1111 S Broadway). Built to house William Randolph Hearst's newspaper in 1912, it's no longer functional for anything other than movie shoots. Regardless, its long, squat façade is worth the diversion, as is the more decorous frontage of the **Mayan Theatre** a block away (1038 S Hill Street), its bizarre bas-relief warriors – designed by Mexican artist Francisco Cornejo – impossible to pass without stopping. Continuing north-east is the kid-friendly **Grand Hope Park** (at S Hope and W 9th Streets), home to the **Museum of Neon Art** (*see below*).

Continuing west brings you to **South Park**, which isn't a park at all. The area is anchored by the intersection of US 110 and the I-10. Nestled within their arcs are two hulking structures: the **Staples Center** (1111 S Figueroa Street; *see p238 and pp253-254*), and the adjoining **LA Convention Center** (1201 S Figueroa Street; *see p289*). The latter has struggled to attract business in recent years, but the area is set for some dramatic changes in future years courtesy of **LA Live**; *see p21* Live and direct.

Museum of Neon Art

Grand Hope Park, 501 W Olympic Boulevard, at S Grand Avenue (1-213 489 9918/www.neonmona.org). Metro 7th Street-Metro Center/bus 14, 37, 38, 71, 76, 78, 79, 96/I-110, exit W 9th Street east. **Open** 11am-5pm first Tue of mth, Wed-Sat; noon-5pm Sun. **Admission** $5; $3.50 discounts. **Credit** AmEx, MC, V. **Map** p311 B4.
If you've made a side-trip to Las Vegas during your stay, you might be a little underwhelmed by a visit here; and if not, then you may be slightly disturbed by some of the museum's art, which lurches from the affecting to the disgusting. Still, there's plenty to enjoy, including a programme of shows that has included works by neon sculptor Richard Ankrom and exhibitions on the neon of Vegas and Reno.

East LA

Latino lessons.

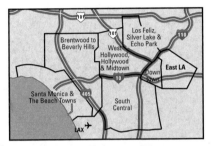

East LA is LA's own Ellis Island. Many non-Anglo immigrant groups arrived here first, starting with Jews in the early 20th century, followed by Asians, blacks, Italians and, finally, Mexicans, who have dominated the area since the 1960s. And while Latinos have much more power in the 21st century – exemplified by the 2005 election of Antonio Villaraigosa, a native of Boyle Heights and the city's first Hispanic mayor since 1872 – the area's political clout was so negligible in the 1960s that it was torn asunder by freeway construction.

However, it remains a lively area, with a vibrant street life and strong sense of Latino identity. Some of LA's best murals, dating from the Chicano movement in the 1960s, are here and on **Broadway** in Downtown, which many consider East LA's Main Street.

East LA encompasses the hilly district of Boyle Heights (part of the City of Los Angeles) and extends, unofficially, east from the Los Angeles River to just beyond Atlantic Boulevard, and from Olympic Boulevard north to I-10. Officially, it starts even further east at Indiana Avenue, but the true spiritual starting point is **Olvera Street**, at the corner of Cesar E Chavez Avenue and Alameda Street in Downtown. Pretty much all that remains from the days of first Spanish and then Mexican rule, it's now a touristy stretch of mariachi singers and stalls selling Mexican trinkets (*see p109*).

Much of the action in East LA takes place on **1st Street**, **Whittier Boulevard** and **Cesar E Chavez Avenue**. The latter, named after the United Farm Workers Union president, is actually a continuation of Sunset Boulevard, and runs from north of Downtown through Boyle Heights into East LA. At the intersection of Cesar E Chavez and Soto Street in Boyle

Heights, you can see several murals by local artists. Also here is the **Paseo of Peace**, a landscaped memorial walkway honouring local veterans of the Vietnam War.

Chavez Avenue is home to immigrant Latino street vendors, selling bargain silver items, bootleg tapes and mangoes and papayas, and strolling musicians, who will play a romantic bolero or two on their well-worn guitars for a reasonable fee as you dine at **La Parilla** (2126 E Cesar E Chavez Avenue; *see p160*). For fresh Mexican pastries, try the family-run **La Mascota Bakery** (2715 Whittier Boulevard, at Orme Avenue).

Just east of Downtown, at 1st Street and Boyle Avenue, is the famous **Mariachi Plaza**, one of the largest congregations of freelance mariachi musicians outside Mexico City's Garibaldi Square. Sporting traditional black ranchero outfits, they gather here and wait for passing drivers to hire them to play at social and family events. Also on 1st Street is the relatively expensive **La Serenata de Garibaldi** (No.1842, between N State Street & N Boyle Avenue; *see p161*), which specialises in Mexican haute cuisine, and, further east, **El Mercado** (No.3425, at Cheesebroughs Lane), a multi-level market reminiscent of those found in Mexican cities. Upstairs are restaurants with duelling mariachi bands, each seeking to lure clientele from the others, while downstairs teems with stalls selling all manner of goods.

On Cesar E Chavez Avenue, you'll find one of East LA's best-known arts institutions: print specialists **Self-Help Graphics** (No.3802, at N Herbert Avenue, 1-323 881 6444), with its distinctive façade of multicoloured pottery encased in plaster walls. The gallery shows work by established and up-and-coming Latino artists and runs community art workshops. Despite recent budget problems that have left the facility in temporary limbo, the gallery still holds its annual **Día de Los Muertos** (Day of the Dead) celebration each autumn (*see p208*). The event has become an East LA tradition, presenting the cream of the Latino counter-culture crowd of poets, performance artists and

Weingart Stadium, East Los Angeles College, Monterey Park
'Run, Forrest! Run!'

Sing for your supper at **Mariachi Plaza**. *See p117.*

agit-prop theatre groups; it's a must-be-seen-at event for Latino and other local hipsters. For breakfast or lunch, head west on Chavez to N Evergreen Avenue and the always crowded **El Tepeyac Café** (No.812; *see p161*) for a Hollenbeck Special, an oversized burrito that could choke a horse. Alternatively, amble south to **Ciro's** (No.705, at Malabar Street) for more traditional Mexican food.

East LA also boasts three very pleasant parks, the largest being **Lincoln Park**. Located at 3540 N Mission Road, just north of the I-10, it contains statues of Mexican revolutionary heroes and the Plaza de la Raza, a popular arts centre in a converted boathouse by the lake that offers arts classes to children after school and hosts evenings of music, dance and theatre. The area's other parks are less impressive: **Hollenbeck Park** (at 4th and Cummings Streets), built to an English model, and the heart-shaped **Prospect Park** (off Chavez Avenue, at Echandia Street), a legacy of the local Jewish community. One final open space worth visiting in the area is the **Evergreen Cemetery**, with its grand Beaux Arts gates and handsome Ivy Chapel. Located at 1st and Lorena Streets and dating from 1877, it's one of the oldest cemeteries in LA; among its memorials is a towering one to the Japanese-American 442nd Regimental Combat Team that fought in World War II and has since become the most decorated unit in US military history.

South of Highway 60, in the southern end of East LA, is **Whittier Boulevard**, aka 'the

Boulevard'. The stretch of the street heading east towards Atlantic Boulevard offers a wealth of clothes shops, restaurants, *botánicas* (selling herbs and incense), bakeries, nightclubs and bars. On 29 August 1970, the Boulevard was the scene of a 'police riot' when a Chicano anti-war demonstration was attacked by police. Chicano journalist Ruben Salazar was killed in the Silver Dollar bar (No.4945, at S La Verne Avenue) by a police tear-gas pellet to the head. Salazar's death was thought by many to be retribution for his criticism of the sheriff's department's abusive behaviour towards people of colour; the park – renamed **Salazar Park** in his honour – is a symbol of the 1970s Chicano Movement.

Until police put a stop to it, Whittier Boulevard used to be the main drag for locals to display their low-rider hot rods. But East LA continues to be the LA capital of hot rod design and, if you're lucky, you'll see a spectacular example cruising the street. Look out, too, for customised low-rider motorbikes.

East LA life spills over into its north-eastern neighbour, the city of **Monterey Park**. Try **Luminarias** (E 3500 Ramona Boulevard; 1-323 268 4177) for dinner, salsa and merengue music. The **Vincent Price Gallery** at East Los Angeles College (1301 Cesar E Chavez Avenue) takes its name from the horror film icon and art enthusiast who donated over 2,000 works of art from his personal collection because, as he put it, 'this is where it's needed'. However, the neighbourhood as a whole is dominated not by Latinos but by Asians; *see p128.*

South Central LA

The heart of African American Los Angeles is changing.

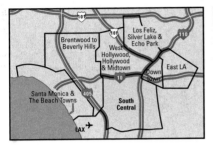

South Central owes its black identity to the era of restrictive covenants, legal restrictions on who could reside in a neighbourhood or property that were instituted in the early 20th century and finally repealed in 1948. These laws, which also restricted Jews, Chinese and Mexicans, confined African Americans to a tight area around Central Avenue.

The area enjoyed a cultural boom in the jazz age, but following the lifting of restrictive covenants, blacks gradually moved west, making the Crenshaw district their cultural and commercial centre. In the past two decades, African Americans have vacated South Central in growing numbers to head to the suburbs. Into their homes have moved Latino families, who've made their mark in the form of a vibrant sidewalk culture (especially on weekends).

Between the mid 1970s and the LA Riots of 1992, South Central developed an unenviable reputation as one of the most deprived and violent areas in the US. Gang warfare was rife, and it sometimes felt as though the drugs trade was the area's biggest employer. Indeed, South Central LA had developed such a bad name that, in 2003, the city council passed an ordinance that officially changed it to South LA. It hasn't really caught on: most still know it by its more infamous moniker.

Whichever name you use, South Central is not necessarily dangerous, and it's unlikely you'll get caught in the crossfire between the rival gangs that riddle the area. However, it can be bleak. Many of the homes and gardens in the area are quite pretty, but largely missing are attractive shops, high-end restaurants, public landscaping and decent parks. Unrelieved by hills or sea, South Central seems to consist of relentless flatlands of concrete and asphalt.

Sightseeing

Exposition Park & around

Los Angeles's love affair with farmers' markets has blossomed in recent years. However, it's actually been present since the late 19th century: farmers sold food and plants in an open-air market for around four decades at Agricultural Park, south of Downtown LA. By 1910, the park had become a haven for deadbeats, gamblers and prostitutes; William C Bowers, a local attorney, began a campaign to reclaim the land and build on it a public park and educational centre. In 1913, his vision became reality with the opening of the renovated and renamed **Exposition Park**.

If you approach the park from Downtown along Figueroa Avenue, you may be alarmed by the sight of a large plane directly in front of you, seemingly in the middle of the road. Don't worry: the decommissioned DC-8 is merely the frontage of the **California ScienCenter's** Air & Space Exhibits (*see p120*). Close by is the **Californian African American Museum** (*see below*). However, the park's main attraction is also its oldest: the **Natural History Museum of Los Angeles County** (*see p120*).

The park's northern frontier is home to the seven-acre **Rose Garden**, home to around 100 varieties of rose and close to 10,000 individual plants. However, the stretch of land directly in front of the museums, in the centre of the park, is plain and scruffy. To the newcomer, it almost looks unfinished, but there are no immediate plans to tidy it up.

The south side of the park is dominated by the hulking **Los Angeles Coliseum**, built in 1923 and the main stadium for the Olympics of both 1932 and 1984. The Coliseum suffered major damage in the 1994 earthquake, just months before the LA Raiders NFL team, who had been using it as their home for a dozen years, moved back to Oakland. These days, it's used in autumn by the University of Southern California's all-conquering Trojans football team, but otherwise remains mostly dormant.

California African American Museum

600 State Drive, between S Figueroa Street & S Vermont Avenue, Exposition Park (1-213 744 7432/ www.caamuseum.org). Bus 40, 42, 102, 550/I-110, exit Exposition Boulevard west. **Open** 10am-4pm Wed-Sat. **Admission** free; donations requested.

From microscope to telescope: the **California ScienCenter.**

Bigger than it looks from the outside, this handsome museum and research library focuses on the artistic and historical achievements of African Americans. The small but tidy permanent exhibit loosely tells the story of African Americans' journey from Africa, through emancipation and into the 20th century, using an assortment of paintings, textiles, photographs, ceremonial objects, personal testimonies and other memorabilia. Included among the exhibits are substantial displays on Ella Fitzgerald, former LA Mayor Tom Bradley and William Spiller, the first African American admitted into the PGA. The museum's other galleries host engaging temporary exhibits, some historical and some artistic, supplemented by a programme of talks, screenings and even the occasional concert.

California ScienCenter

700 State Drive, between S Figueroa Street & S Vermont Avenue, Exposition Park (1-213 744 7400/ IMAX 213 744 2014/www.casciencectr.org). Bus 40, 42, 102, 550/I-110, exit Exposition Boulevard west. **Open** 10am-5pm daily. *Air & Space Gallery* 10am-1pm Mon-Fri; 11am-4pm Sat, Sun. **Admission** *Museum* free. *IMAX* $8; $4.75-$5.75 discounts. **Credit** *IMAX* MC, V.

A fusion of two longstanding prior facilities, the California Science Center opened in 1998 in a bright, airy building directly in front of the Rose Garden in Exposition Park. The main building is split into two loosely themed wings: Creative World, which focuses on technology (and has a little catching up to do), and World of Life, an engaging if sometimes slightly queasy selection of exhibits on all manner of living things. The top floor also features a Science Court, a fairly disparate jumble of interactive playthings, and the ever-popular High-Wire Bicycle, which allows the brave and the trusting to ride a bike along a one-inch wire some 43 feet above the ground in order to demonstrate the powers of gravity. Two supplementary exhibits, Worlds of Ecology and Worlds Beyond, are scheduled to open

in 2010; already here is an IMAX cinema, screening the usual array of dazzling, quasi-educative, nature-slanted films. Entrance to the museum is free, which might explain why the main attraction on the ground floor is an enormous shop.

Next door, in a hulking, Frank Gehry-designed building, sits the Air & Space Gallery. Among the exhibits are a replica of a Wright Brothers glider, a decommissioned police helicopter, and Explorer 1, the first American spacecraft to orbit the earth.

Natural History Museum of Los Angeles County

900 Exposition Boulevard, between S Figueroa Street & S Vermont Avenue, Exposition Park (1-213 763 3466/www.nhm.org). Bus 40, 42, 102, 550/I-110, exit Exposition Boulevard west. **Open** 9.30am-5pm Mon-Fri; 10am-5pm Sat, Sun. **Admission** $9; $2-$6.50 concessions; free under-5s. **Credit** AmEx, Disc, MC, V.

Housed in a handsome Spanish-Renaissance building that opened with Exposition Park itself back in 1913, and containing an amazing 33 million exhibits (not all of them are on display at any one time), the Natural History Museum of LA County claims to be the largest museum of natural history in the US. That may be true, but both the description and the name of the museum are somewhat misleading: the institution's remit stretches beyond the natural world, albeit in rather random directions.

It's an immense place, so it's worth planning your visit. Those with only a little time to spare should head directly to the truly dazzling collections in the Hall of Gems & Minerals, where the exhibits include a 4,644-carat topaz, a 2,200-carat opal sphere and a quartz crystal ball which, with a diameter of 10.9in and a weight of 65lb, is one of the biggest on earth. Other highlights include the small but fascinating exhibit on chaparral, which includes an artful film about how fire regenerates landscapes; the effectively creepy and dauntingly crawly Insect Zoo; and the Ancient Latin America gallery, easily the most interesting of the anthropological exhibits.

As befits a museum that's been around for almost a century, some of the exhibits are showing their age a little. The designated dinosaur exhibit, which includes a stegosaurus, a T-rex skull and a mamenchisaurus with a ludicrously huge neck, isn't especially dynamic, while the three main mammal galleries, featuring an array of stuffed creatures packed into quaint little dioramas, are a bit forlorn. Still, there's plenty here to please the kids and educate the adults, or vice versa.

USC (University of Southern California)

Fans of the aforementioned USC Trojans don't have far to travel for home games. The college itself is just north of Exposition Park, bounded by Figueroa Street, Exposition Boulevard, Vermont Avenue and Jefferson Boulevard.

The campus of the university, established here in 1880, is tidy but unspectacular when compared to the sculpture-studded home of UCLA (*see p86* **Walk**). Still, a few corners of the campus are worth a peek, chiefly the **Doheny Library** (1-213 740 2328). The first-floor Treasure Room offers an interesting roster of free exhibitions on everything from vaudeville to Antarctica. Those wishing to explore the campus in more detail should head here on Mondays, when free 50-minute campus tours leave on the hour between 10am and 3pm from the Admission Center in Trojan Hall, just off Figueroa Street at Child's Way.

Directly north of USC sits the 80-year-old, 6,500-capacity **Shrine Auditorium** (665 W Jefferson Boulevard). This huge, Moorish structure has recently had its role as host of the Oscars taken over by the Kodak Theatre in Hollywood, but still stages the Emmys each September. East of USC is predominantly a warehouse and freight industrial area, particularly the town of Vernon, which also used to be a hub for the city's gritty boxing-gym culture documented in the Oscar-winning film *Million Dollar Baby*.

Central Avenue

The significance of **Central Avenue** in the history of black LA can't be overestimated. Between the 1920s and the '50s, it was home to some of the first financial enterprises, theatres, churches and social institutions established exclusively to serve blacks; to get a picture of pre- and post-war Central Avenue, read Walter Mosley's Easy Rawlins detective mysteries.

The road was also famous for the music that boomed out of its bars and nightclubs: jazz at first, then R&B. This heritage is celebrated every August with the **Central Avenue Jazz**

Festival (*see p242* **Festivals**), but at most other times of year, modern-day Central Avenue is unalluring. Many of its buildings are vacant and in disrepair; the **Dunbar Hotel** (4225 S Central Avenue), the first hotel built by and for African Americans, is now operated as a complex of low-income residential units.

Watts

After the jazz era, blacks continued their migration south along Central Avenue towards Watts. The district is notorious for the riots of 1965 and 1992, but it also contains an LA landmark in the shape of the **Watts Towers** (*see p122* **We ♥ LA**). The adjacent **Watts Towers Arts Center** (1727 E 107th Street, 1-213 847 4646) hosts exhibitions, workshops, festivals and concerts.

Though much of the area is still neglected, Watts is re-emerging as a focal point for black pride, a development embodied by the **Watts Labor Community Action Committee** (10950 S Central Avenue, 1-323 563 5639, www.wlcac.org). The centre was destroyed during the riots in 1965 and 1992, but it's now been rebuilt as a social and cultural centre. The centre's *The Mother of Humanity* is the largest bronze sculpture of a black woman in the world, and the building's main façade is the setting for *Mudtown Flats*, a mural showing historic sites on Central Avenue. The centre runs historical and cultural bus tours of Watts; run on a by-appointment basis and costing $10 (kids go half-price), you can book on 1-323 357 0819.

Where it's in **Exposition Park**. *See p119.*

We ♥ LA Watts Towers

When Italian-born tilesetter Simon Rodia moved to Watts, the neighbourhood was ethnically mixed. Three decades later, when he left, it was predominantly black and Latino, widely seen as the heart of LA's African-American community. In the intervening years, though, Rodia had constructed its single iconic structure, an extraordinary piece of folk art that's one of only four National Historic Landmarks in the entire city of Los Angeles.

Rodia started work on constructing what have become known as the Watts Towers shortly after purchasing a triangular lot in the area and moving on to the site in 1921. Using nothing but found objects (salvaged metal rods, cast-off pipe structures, broken bed frames), Rodia sent his towers inching gradually skywards over several decades, reinforcing them with steel and cement to prevent interference from both neighbours and the authorities.

Scaling the towers on a window-washer's belt and bucket, Rodia gradually decorated his towers with a patchwork of yet more found materials that inadvertently act as a reliquary of early and mid 20th-century consumer objects. The glass is mostly green and comes from bottles of 7-Up or Canada Dry; the tiles came from Malibu Pottery, where Rodia was employed in the late 1920s. Other objects clearly visible on the towers' coarse, gaudy 'skin' include jewellery, marble and an estimated 25,000 seashells.

The towers' construction, by a single pair of hands over a 33-year span, are part of their legend. But so is their wan, spectral beauty. Like skeletal echoes of Antoni Gaudí's voluptuous Barcelona church steeples, the towers reach for the sky in an elaborate network of spindly, curved tendrils, connected with equally playful, decorous webs. There are 17 of them in all, the tallest stretching 99 feet into the Los Angeles sky.

The locals, though, were never especially supportive of his endeavours. Miscreant kids regularly smashed the towers' glass and tiling; during the war, a rumour even started that Rodia was sending classified information to the Japanese through the towers, which didn't endear him to his neighbours. In 1954, after years of abuse and vandalism, the 75-year-old Rodia abruptly gave the land to a neighbour and moved away, apparently not caring what happened to the towers he'd spent 34 years constructing.

After Rodia's departure, the towers changed hands several times, but were issued with a demolition in 1957 on the basis that they were structurally unsound. A public outcry ensued, and two years later the city agreed to run stress tests on the towers to test their stability. A stress load of 10,000 pounds was applied to the towers, but they didn't budge an inch... Unlike the crane applying the stress, which buckled under the strain. The towers' future was assured.

It's not all been plain sailing. The towers gradually deteriorated over the years, and were damaged in the 1994 earthquake. However, after a decade-long programme of renovations, they're now in better shape than ever. For details of tours, call 1-213 847 4646.

Leimert Park

Leimert (pronounced 'Luh-murt') Park is LA's most appealing black neighbourhood. Anchored by the park itself and Degnan Boulevard, the area has undergone a cultural renaissance in recent years, with art galleries, jazz clubs, speciality shops and restaurants springing up all over the place. Simultaneously, property prices have soared: the average price of a home here more than doubled between 2000 and 2005.

Leimert Park Village, a pedestrianised area bordered by Crenshaw Boulevard, 43rd Street, Leimert Boulevard and Vernon Avenue, is the cultural centre of African American life in LA. There's live music nightly, whether approachable blues at **Babe & Ricky's Inn** (*see p244*), freestyle rap at **KAOS Network** (4343 Leimert Boulevard) or uncompromising jazz at **World Stage** (*see p244*). On Degnan Boulevard sit a number of Afrocentric art galleries; the **Museum in Black** (No.4331, 1-323 292 9528) is the most notable. On the food front, try **The Kitchen** (3347½ 43rd Place, 1-323 299 7799). Also off Degnan is the famous **Phillip's Barbecue** (4307 Leimert Boulevard, 1-323 292 7613): prepare to queue for a take-out order of some of the best ribs in town.

Crenshaw

Crenshaw, the area surrounding the eponymous boulevard south of I-10 to Florence Avenue, is today one of the few mainly black communities in LA County. But the site of the 1932 Olympic Village and LA's first airport had a different profile after World War II, when many Japanese returning from internment camps settled here and established themselves as landscape gardeners; their legacy is still visible.

The Hills (Baldwin Hills, Windsor Hills, Fox Hills, View Park and Ladera Heights), which lie west of Crenshaw Boulevard around Slauson Avenue, are home to some of LA's most prominent upper middle-class and professional blacks. The five connected neighbourhoods are said to have the highest concentration of black wealth in the US. Balancing this affluence at the base of these manicured hills is an area known as the Jungle: the name originally derived from the neighbourhood's lush tropical plantings, but it is better known these days as a haven for drug dealing and other illicit activities.

In the 1940s, the first shopping plaza in the US was built at the intersection of Martin Luther King Jr (aka 'King') and Crenshaw Boulevards. Now transformed into the **Baldwin Hills Crenshaw Plaza** (3650 W Martin Luther King Jr Boulevard), it's the centre of the Crenshaw community, which finds a cultural anchor in the shape of the **Magic Johnson Theaters** (4020 Marlton Avenue; *see p221*). Part-owned by the former NBA great, the cinemas have the friendliest staff in LA, and the rowdiest crowds: the audience joins in on the action, shouting advice to the actors.

For a rousing religious experience, visit the **West Angeles Church of God in Christ** (3600 Crenshaw Boulevard, 1-323 733 8300, www.westa.org). Presided over by bishop Charles Blake, it's one of the most popular black Pentecostal churches. With the help of huge donations from Denzel Washington and the aforementioned Johnson, both members of the church, Blake built this massive $40 million cathedral, which hosts services at 8am and 11am every Sunday.

On the far west side of Crenshaw, sprawling between La Cienega Boulevard and La Brea Avenue, is the **Kenneth Hahn State Recreation Area** (1-323 298 3660), one of the city's most undervalued attractions. Named after a popular former city councilman, it's a huge, delightful place, with a fishing pond, ducks, swans, a Japanese bridge over a waterfall, undulating hills and basketball courts. Take one of the hiking trails for spectacular views of the city.

North of the park is the Historic West Adams district (formerly known as 'Sugar Hill', extending from Figueroa Street to Crenshaw Boulevard and from Venice to Jefferson Boulevards), a lovingly preserved collection of Victorian, Craftsman and Colonial Revival houses laid out after the 1880s.

Inglewood

Although it's located outside the LA city limits, Inglewood is often considered part of South Central. It's best known as the home of two LA institutions: the **Great Western Forum**, where the LA Lakers basketball team and LA Kings hockey team played before they moved to the Staples Center, and **Randy's Donuts** (*see p28* **In the vernacular**), an architectural classic that's been dishing up majestically calorific donuts since 1952. South of the Forum is the **Hollywood Park Race Track & Casino** (*see p254*), which features horse-racing and, each weekend, live music. Just east of Inglewood, in Hyde Park, sits the quiet intersection of Florence and Normandie Avenues, the flashpoint for the 1992 riots.

Phillips' Barbecue (2619 S Crenshaw Boulevard, Crenshaw)
The gang gather for a feast in *SWAT*

The Valleys

Betrothed and divine…

San Fernando Valley

Located directly north of the Hollywood Hills, the San Fernando Valley is most famous for its girls. The gum-popping, air-headed Valley Girl – immortalised by the Frank Zappa song and the Martha Coolidge movie of the same name – is a quintessential 1980s phenomenon, but the local porn industry both pre- and post-dates it. While *The Brady Bunch* was being filmed in a split-level 1960s ranch house, other San Fernando backyards found girls in curls and guys in tight polyester trousers doing a lot more than playing ball. Paul Thomas Anderson, the Valley's latest self-appointed chronicler, exposed suburbia's sordid past (and present) in *Boogie Nights*.

The earlier history of the valley, fictionalised in the movie *Chinatown*, is a colourful tale of betrayal and greed. At the start of the 20th century, LA's land barons hoodwinked voters into approving bonds for an aqueduct and then diverted the water away from the city to the San Fernando Valley so they could cash in on the increased land values. Despite this shady past, many older residents remember only a pastoral yesteryear full of horses and orange groves; a desire to recapture it led to a secession movement, which lost a 2002 campaign for the San Fernando Valley to become its own city.

The San Fernando Valley's two main cities sit more or less side by side, north of Griffith Park. Crisply pressed **Glendale** is larger than dreary Burbank, but both are ultimately forgettable places that bring to mind Mark Twain's famous quote that 'Los Angeles is a great place to live, but I wouldn't want to visit there'. After all, Glendale's main attraction is a cemetery, the **Forest Lawn Memorial Park**, (1712 S Glendale Avenue, 1-800 204 3131, www.forestlawn.com; for the Hollywood Hills location, *see p105*), the final resting place of celebrities such as Lon Chaney, Walt Disney, Errol Flynn, Spencer Tracy, Nat 'King' Cole, Clark Gable and Harold Lloyd.

The film industry cuts so deep in **Burbank** that the name was used as the last name for Jim Carrey's titular character in *The Truman Show*. However, the area is only really worth a visit for a snack at **Bob's Big Boy** (4211 Riverside Drive, 1-818 843 9334), said to have invented the double-decker hamburger, or if you've got audience tickets for one of the TV shows filmed

in the area (*see p217*). Warner Brothers (for tours, *see p71*), NBC and Disney have studios here, with Disney's impossible to miss; the animation building, designed by postmodernist Robert Stern, is topped by a two-storey wizard's hat similar to the one worn by Mickey Mouse in *Fantasia*'s Sorcerer's Apprentice sequence, and the word 'animation' spelt out in 14-foot-high letters. Burbank's so-called Media District, along Riverside Drive, studio execs power-lunch the days away, but really, there's nothing to see here; better to drive to **Universal Studios** (*see p126*), both studio and theme park.

Things don't get much more interesting elsewhere. Due north-west of Burbank sit **Mission Hills** and the **Mission San Fernando Rey de España** (*see p281* **On a mission**), founded in 1797 and rebuilt after the 1971 earthquake; **Sylmar** boasts the two Nethercutt museums (*see below*); and, a short ride up I-5, **Santa Clarita** is home to the ever-popular **Six Flags** park (*see p125*). To the west, **Sherman Oaks**, once Valley Girl Central but now more diverse; **Northridge**, whose most notable features are the Googie-style **First Lutheran Church of Northridge** (18355 Roscoe Boulevard, 1-818 885 6861), aka the 'First Church of Elroy Jetson'; and **Simi Valley**, where those who dress to the right may enjoy the **Ronald Reagan Library & Museum** (*see p125*).

Suburbia aside, though, the San Fernando Valley is also the gateway to the **Santa Monica Mountains**, one of the country's most beautiful and environmentally fragile urban mountain ranges. Separating the Valley from the city basin and the ocean, the mountains are covered with hiking and biking trails, and contain many ranches that once belonged to movie stars and the studios that employed them. The **Paramount Ranch** (2813 Cornell Road, off Kanan Road, Agoura), has stood in for Tombstone and Dodge City, and was used for the TV series *Dr Quinn, Medicine Woman*. For more information on the area, contact the **Santa Monica Mountains National Recreation Area** (401 W Hillcrest Drive, Thousand Oaks, 1-805 370 2301, www.nps.gov/samo).

Nethercutt Collection

Nethercutt Museum *15151 Bledsoe Street, at San Fernando Road, Sylmar (1-818 367 2251).* **Open** 9am-4.30pm Tue-Sat.

Santa Monica Mountains. *See p124.*

San Sylmar *15200 Bledsoe Street, at San Fernando Road, Sylmar (1-818 367 2251).* **Open** *Tours* 10am, 1.30pm Tue-Sat. Booking essential. **Both** *www.nethercuttcollection.org. Bus 94, 394/ I-5, exit Roxford Street east.* **Admission** free.

The collection of eccentric cosmetics heirs and philanthropists Dorothy and JB Nethercutt makes for a striking pair of museums. The San Sylmar site houses a huge collection of old, fancy but functional objects, all in working order: anything from gorgeous old cars and Steuben Glass hood ornaments to French furniture and automated musical instruments. Among the sporadic events are recitals on the Mighty Wurlitzer Pipe Organ. Shorts and jeans are prohibited out of respect for the fancy merchandise. The Nethercutt Museum, meanwhile, provides a handsome home for 100 of the Nethercutts' 230-plus classic cars: Daimlers, Lincolns, Packards and Duesenbergs, all kept in immaculate order.

Ronald Reagan Library & Museum

40 Presidential Drive, at Madera Road, Simi Valley, Ventura (1-805 522 8444/www.reaganlibrary.net). **Open** 10am-5pm daily. **Admission** $5; $3 discounts; free under-15s. **No credit cards.**

This place is great for fans of the Gipper, but liberal types will probably see red. The museum has a CD-Rom display containing Reagan's most endearing quips, photos of him as a young ladykiller and a replica of the Oval Office, plus awesome gifts received over the years, such as a White House-shaped tissue box made from white yarn.

San Fernando Valley Conference & Visitors Bureau

Suite 200, 5121 Van Nuys Boulevard, between Magnolia Boulevard & Otsego Street, Sherman Oaks (1-818 379 7000/www.valleyofthestars.org). Bus 183, 233, 237, 761/US 101, exit Van Nuys Boulevard north. **Open** 8.30am-5pm Mon-Fri.

Six Flags California

Magic Mountain Parkway, off I-5, Valencia (1-818 367 5965/www.sixflags.com). I-5, exit Magic Mountain Parkway. **Open** *Magic Mountain: Summer* from 10am daily. *Winter* from 10am Fri-Sun. Call for closing times. *Hurricane Harbor: Summer* from 10am daily; call for closing times. *Winter* closed. **Admission** *Magic Mountain* $59.99; $29.99 discounts; free under-2s. *Hurricane Harbor* $29.99; $20.99 discounts; free under-2s. *Combined ticket* $69.99. **Credit** AmEx, Disc, MC, V.

Comprising Magic Mountain and newer watery cousin Hurricane Harbor, Six Flags delivers for all but the most joyless (and, in summer, crowd-phobic) holidaymaker. The park offers rollercoasters and water rides for every level of screamer; the most famous include the Colossus, billed as 'the tallest and fastest wooden coaster in the West', and the Viper, which soars 188ft (56m) in the air.

Engineers at Six Flags spend their days thinking of different ways to scare the living crap out of you. Test their success on X, the five-ton coaster that has independent 360-degree spin action, or try Scream, which guarantees you'll do just that as you ride a unique floorless train while it executes a zero-gravity loop. The newest attraction, which opened in 2006, is Tatsu, a four-minute coaster lurch through four areas of the park at speeds of up to 60 miles an hour. 'Fly at the speed of fear', goes the tagline, which sounds about right. Note that many rides have height requirements starting at about 48in (1.22m). Set scenically on the hip of the San Fernando Mountains, this is fun with a capital 'F'.

Universal Studios & CityWalk

100 Universal City Plaza, Universal City (1-800 864 8377/www.universalstudios.com). Metro Universal City/bus 96, 156, 166/US 101, exit Universal Center Drive. **Open** *Studios* Summer 10am-6pm Mon-Fri; 9am-7pm Sat, Sun. Winter 10am-6pm Mon-Fri; 10am-7pm Sat, Sun. *Citywalk* 11am-9pm Mon-Thur, Sun; 11am-11pm Fri, Sat. **Admission** $59; $49 discounts; under-3s free. **Credit** AmEx, DC, Disc, MC, V.

Most attractions have the decency to save their souvenir shops until the end. Not here. You can't reach Universal Studios without strolling down CityWalk, a loud, colourful and oppressive pedestrianised street crammed with souvenir hawkers and junk-food retailers. If you've got children, don't be surprised to find your finances severely depleted before you've even reached the gates of the studios.

Once you're safely inside Universal Studios, you'll find an attraction whose overall entertainment value is more than the sum of its parts. Certainly, the rides, while fun, aren't as exciting as you might expect. You're here for the illusion of glamour, the memories brought back by the rides rather than the rides themselves. Adults will enjoy going back to the past with the *Back to the Future* stomach-churner, while

young teenagers may be charmed by the *Jurassic Park* ride. Other films brought to something approaching life include *Terminator 2*, *Backdraft* and, bizarrely, *Waterworld*, but the pick of the themed attractions, for both grown-ups and kids, is the cheeky *Shrek 4-D* movie.

Similarly, the studio tour is more about association than excitement. Despite all the advance hype boasting of how you're being let behind the scenes at a working Hollywood studio, the closest you'll likely get to seeing some actual action is spying the occasional spark's car parked behind an otherwise faceless sound stage. However, once you've resigned yourself (and your kids) to a star-free afternoon, there's a great deal to enjoy, from old movie sets seemingly left lying around by careless stagehands, to the cheesily compiled set pieces (was that Jaws in the water?) and a dazzling new chase sequence inspired by the Vin Diesel movie *The Fast and the Furious*. The excellent tour guides, riffing enthusiastically on a crisp and amusing script, were joined in 2006 by a Whoopi Goldberg narration beamed in via TV sets.

A cheap-as-chips special-effects demonstration here, a live band there, and that's pretty much the deal. But still, it's hard not to have a decent measure of fun here, assuming you arrive early (especially in summer) to avoid the worst of the crowds. The ticket prices detailed above are for basic admission only; a variety of queue-jumping tickets are also available, starting at $79 for an off-season 'Front of Line' pass to $149 for the VIP ticket. Check online for a full list of ticket options.

We ♥ LA The Great Wall of LA

The longest standing mural in the world is located in an ignominious location: a drainage canal in the San Fernando Valley. No matter: it would still make Diego Rivera whistle in amazement. Truly, it's the Big Picture: a landmark 40-panel pictorial representation of Californian and American history from prehistoric times to the 1950s, much of it devoted to ordinary Americans and minority groups rather than famous public figures. The mural was started in 1976 by artist and Pacoima native Judith Baca with $1 million in public funding to help rehabilitate at-risk juveniles, many of whom were falling into street gangs.

Eventually, with the advice of hundreds of artists, scholars and residents, 400 youths aged between 14 and 21 (all paid) covered the bare concrete with vibrant colours and designs. They produced more than 2,700 feet (approximately half a mile) of acrylic-based murals in segments over seven summers,

finishing in 1984. The mural itself is visually dazzling – a clothes-line links 1930's Dust Bowl refugees to Japanese-Americans in a World War II internment camp – and even contains a wry sense of humour. Dodger Stadium is depicted as a flying saucer dropping on top of the old Chavez Ravine, the old Latino shanty town that was obliterated by its construction.

Baca and her Venice-based Social and Public Arts Resources Center (www.sparc.org) are currently engaged in restoring the damage done from exposure to 30 years of the Southern Californian climate. Meanwhile, you can still view it by taking the Ventura Dreeway north and exiting on Coldwater Canyon, where you then head north. The mural is located in the Tujunga Wash flood control channel on Coldwater Canyon Avenue between Burbank Boulevard and Oxnard Street in the area called Valley Glen, near Grant High School and Los Angeles Valley College.

Sculptures by Edgar Degas (left) and Henry Moore at the **Norton Simon Museum**. *See p129.*

San Gabriel Valley

Though crowded with suburban development and often choked with traffic, the San Gabriel Valley at least boasts a picturesque location, set against the striking San Gabriel Mountains to the north. Unlike the San Fernando Valley, the San Gabriel Valley is not part of the City of Los Angeles, an independence that's reflected, by accident and design, in its neighbourhoods: it's a more charming place than its neighbour, ethnically more diverse and architecturally less homogenous. You can reach it from LA via a series of east-west freeways, including I-210 (Foothill Freeway), I-10 (San Bernardino Freeway) and US 60 (Pomona Freeway), as well as the north-south I-110 (Pasadena Freeway).

First settled by wealthy retired farmers from the Midwest, **Pasadena** is one of the most attractive towns in the area, and one of the few parts of southern California where having 'old money' still means something. Its focal point is **Old Town Pasadena** (centred on Colorado Boulevard and bounded by Arroyo Parkway, De Lacey Avenue and Holly and Green Streets), a 1920s-meets-1990s retail district. As late as the mid 1980s, it was a rundown collection of boarded-up buildings; today, packs of teenagers mingle with families and couples in what is an immaculately all-American retail experience. Inevitably, then, chains dominate, but a number of independent stores and eateries do thrive here, and it's still a world away from the Valley mall culture of myth and legend.

Pasadena's other visitor attractions are varied and worthwhile. Among its museums are the **Norton Simon Museum** (*see p129*), the **Pacific Asia Museum** (*see p130*), the **Pasadena Museum of California Art** (*see p130*) and **Kidspace** (*see p129*); slightly lower key, but arguably more interesting, are the **Gamble House** (*see p129*) and NASA's **Jet Propulsion Laboratory** (*see p130* **The final frontier**). If you're in town over New Year, try and make time for the **Rose Parade** (*see p209*), a jolly celebration so firmly ensconced in the calendar that it now has its own spoof, the **Doodah Parade** (*see p209*).

Two perfectly pleasant communities adjoin Pasadena. North-west is the picturesque hillside town of **La Cañada Flintridge**, home of the peaceful **Descanso Gardens** (*see p128*). And just south of the town is the expensive suburb of **San Marino**, developed by land and railroad baron Henry Huntington at the start of the 20th century. His former estate (*see p129*) now houses a world-class collection of books and manuscripts, and has some astonishingly beautiful gardens. Near here, Pasadena's Lake Street district and the Fair Oaks area of **South Pasadena** are both very pleasant walking and shopping areas.

Heading east, points of interest become fewer and further between. In **Arcadia** sits an elegant 1930s racetrack, **Santa Anita Park** (*see p254*), and the **Los Angeles County Arboretum & Botanical Garden** (*see p129*). Beyond are acres of suburbia, enlivened only by a handful of older foothill communities along the Foothill Freeway. Both **Sierra Madre** and **Monrovia**, which lie in the shadow of the San Gabriel Mountains, have charming early 20th-century downtown areas.

Continuing east on I-210, you'll eventually reach **Claremont** and the Claremont Colleges, a collection of six educational institutions near East Foothill Boulevard. The campus offers shady streets and an academic vibe reminiscent of East Coast Ivy League schools. The town's 'Village' (east of Indian Hill Boulevard, between 1st and 4th Streets) is another delightful downtown area, featuring buildings from the 1920s. South-east of Claremont is **Pomona**, home to another college (California State Polytechnic University) and, each autumn, the two-week **LA County Fair** (*see p206*). The area remains an important agricultural centre, so you'll get to see the same giant vegetables and prize-winning pigs as you would in the Midwest.

The area directly south of Pasadena holds greater variety. The bustling suburbs of **Monterey Park**, **Alhambra** and **San Gabriel** have largely Chinese or Chinese-American populations, a great many of them immigrants from Taiwan and Hong Kong. Forget Chinatown, just north of Downtown LA (*see p108*): this is actually one of the largest Chinese settlements in America. As a result, the commercial strips of Atlantic Boulevard and Garfield Avenue contain Chinese restaurants of every sort, as well as groceries, bakeries and herb shops. For a crash course in Chinese food, visit the **Universal Shopping Plaza**, a garish behemoth of a mall on Del Mar Avenue and Valley Boulevard.

Descanso Gardens

1418 Descanso Drive, at Oakwood Avenue & Knight Way, La Cañada (1-818 949 4200/www.descanso .com). I-210, exit Gould Avenue north. **Open** 9am-5pm daily. **Admission** $7; $5 discounts; free under-5s. **Credit** AmEx, MC, V.
This delightful tribute to the horticultural magic of southern California includes more than 600 varieties of camellia (these are best seen between the middle of February and early May, when there are around 34,000 of the plants in bloom). The gardens are also notable for their five acres of roses. In addition, there lilac, orchid, fern and California native plant areas, as well as an oriental tea house donated by the Japanese-American community. For body and soul, the gardens offer yoga classes amid the greenery.

Huntington Library, Art Collections & Botanical Gardens. *See p129.*

Gamble House

4 Westmoreland Place, at Walnut Street, Pasadena (1-626 793 3334/www.gamblehouse.org). Bus 177, 267/I-10, exit Orange Grove Boulevard north. **Tours** hourly noon-3pm Thur-Sun. **Admission** $8; $5 discounts.

This stern but handsome property, built by Charles and Henry Greene in 1908, is perhaps the leading example of southern California's 'Craftsman' bungalow style, influenced – in typical fashion – by both Japanese and Swiss architecture. The property received a long-awaited restoration in 2003/2004. The Greenes also built other houses in adjacent streets, notably Arroyo Terrace and Grand Avenue.

Huntington Library, Art Collections & Botanical Gardens

1151 Oxford Road, off Huntington Drive, San Marino (1-626 405 2100/www.huntington.org). Bus 79/I-110, exit Atlantic Boulevard north. **Open** *June-Aug* 10.30am-4.30pm Tue-Sun. *Sept-May* noon-4.30pm Tue-Fri; 10.30am-4.30pm Sat, Sun. **Admission** $115; $10-$12 discounts; free under-5s. Free to all 1st Thur of mth. **Credit** MC, V.

Set in the wealthy suburb of San Marino, the bequest of entrepreneur Henry E Huntington is now one of LA's most enjoyable attractions. The main library, which holds more than six million items, is open only to researchers (apply for credentials in advance of your visit). However, some of its holdings, which include a Gutenberg Bible and the earliest known edition of Chaucer's *Canterbury Tales*, are usually on display. The art collection is almost as notable; encompassing 18th- and 19th-century French and British art (including Gainsborough's *The Blue Boy*,

alongside paintings by Blake, Reynolds and Turner) and a fine selection of American works, it's supplemented by temporary exhibitions. While the main gallery is being renovated, highlights from the collection are on show in the new Erburu Gallery

Though all this high culture can overwhelm, take time to explore the botanical gardens, arguably the most glorious in the entire region. The 150 acres are divided into a variety of themes: the Desert Garden is packed with cacti and other succulents; the Shakespeare Garden evokes a kind of Englishness rarely seen in England these days; and the Japanese garden is magical. Two tips: get there early, and don't plan on seeing everything. **Photo** *p128*.

Kidspace Children's Museum

Brookside Park, 480 N Arroyo Boulevard, at W Holly Street, Pasadena (1-626 449 9144/www.kidspace museum.org). Bus 177, 267/I-210, exit Mountain Street west. **Open** 9.30am-5pm. **Admission** $8; under-1s free. **Credit** AmEx, Disc, MC, V.

Housed for two decades in a school gym, this popular interactive children's museum moved to a new site in 2004 after a successful $18-million funding drive. There's a wide variety of exhibits and entertainments, from educational gardens to the Splash Dance water feature in the central courtyard, the perfect way to cool down on a baking Valley afternoon. A sizeable new structure, Building Bigger, will add further attractions when it opens in 2007.

Los Angeles County Arboretum & Botanical Garden

301 N Baldwin Avenue, between W Colorado Boulevard & Campus Drive, Arcadia (1-626 821 3222/www.arboretum.org). Bus 79, 264, 268/I-210, exit Baldwin Avenue south. **Open** 9am-4.30pm daily. *Library* 9am-5pm daily. **Admission** $7; $2.50-$5 concessions; free under-5s. **Credit** AmEx, MC, V.

These gorgeous grounds in Arcadia, very close to the Santa Anita racetrack, have been designed as an educational facility (the plants are mostly arranged by region, and tours are available), but many people simply come here for a little peace and quiet. You could wander these gardens for hours; many do, taking in tropical forests and waterfalls, trees and fish. A quiet, unheralded delight.

Norton Simon Museum

411 W Colorado Boulevard, between N Orange Grove Boulevard & N St John Avenue, Pasadena (1-626 449 6840/www.nortonsimon.org). Bus 177, 180, 181, 256, 380/I-110, exit Colorado Boulevard west. **Open** noon-6pm Mon, Wed-Sun. **Admission** $8; $4 discounts; free under 18s & students. **No credit cards**.

The Norton Simon's Gehry-helmed makeover in the late 1990s raised the museum's profile. But it also helped the museum expand the range of its collection, giving it more space and creating a calm, simple environment in which to display it. The museum's directors have taken the ball and run with it: this is a beautifully designed museum, its collection sympathetically mounted and immaculately captioned.

The final frontier

In 1958, they controlled and built the satellite Explorer I, America's first foray into space. A few years later, they built the robot that first went to the Moon, paving the way for NASA's astronaut lunar landings. They're behind all the Mariner spacecrafts, which have flown by Venus, Mercury and Mars, and the Voyager project, which flew by Jupiter, Saturn, Uranus and Neptune. They are the scientists at the **Jet Propulsion Laboratory**, managed for NASA by the California Institute of Technology.

Based on a 177-acre site in Pasadena, the JPL has led the US's planetary space exploration for decades. Employing 5,500 people, and equipped with an annual budget of $1.4 billion, it's the JPL that designed, built and now operates NASA's Deep Space Network, and which is responsible for the Mars Pathfinder and the recent mission to Mars, the successful Spirit rover. Its exploratory exploits are matched by its protective work; the laboratory maintains an asteroid-tracking system, monitoring any large mass in outer space that could threaten our planet, while its cameras and sensors are on satellites circling Earth, sending back vital data about our ozone and oceans. And it doesn't stop at space exploration. Back in the 1970s, the lab pioneered solar energy for the US Department of Energy, and developed electric vehicles for the Department of Transportation. They also work for the US Department of Defense, though this work is necessarily rather more secretive.

Roughly once a week, the Jet Propulsion Laboratory opens its doors to the public; the two- to two-and-a-half-hour tour begins with a multimedia overview of the laboratory, after which the public are shown around the Space Flight Operations Facility and the Spacecraft Assembly Facility. Demand, predictably, is high, and booking is essential. Security concerns dictate that US citizens need to bring a passport or driver's licence, while citizens of other countries must declare their nationality prior to booking and bring a passport and/or green card on the day. For reservations, write to the Public Services Office, Mail Stop 186-113, Jet Propulsion Laboratory, 4800 Oak Grove Drive, Pasadena, CA 91109, or call 1-818 354 9314; for more information, check www.jpl.nasa.gov.

The museum is still best known for its impressive collection of Old Masters, notably pieces by 17th-century Dutch painters such as Rembrandt (a particularly rakish self-portrait), Brueghel and Frans Hals. The French impressionists are represented by, among others, Monet, Manet and Renoir. Other valuable holdings include a generous array of Degas's underappreciated ballerina bronzes, some excellent modern works – including a haunting Modigliani portrait of his wife, some Diego Rivera paintings, and plenty of works by the so-called Blue Four (Feininger, Jawlensky, Klee and Kandinsky), and large collections of European prints, Far Eastern art and Buddhist artefacts. After you've checked out the temporary shows, head into the excellent sculpture garden. All told, a terrific museum. **Photo** *p127*.

Pacific Asia Museum

46 N Los Robles Avenue, at E Colorado Boulevard West, Pasadena (1-626 449 2742/www.pacificasia museum.org). Metro Memorial Park/bus 180, 181, 267, 687/I-110, exit Colorado Boulevard east. **Open** 10am-5pm Wed, Thur, Sat, Sun; 10am-8pm Fri. **Admission** $7; $5 discounts; free on 4th friday of month. **No credit cards**.

Art and artefacts from Asia and the Pacific Rim are displayed in the historic Grace Nicholson Building, a re-creation of a northern Chinese palace with a charming Chinese Garden Court to match. Displays include both contemporary and traditional Asian arts, but the museum's most popular events are its family-oriented festival day. A new Japanese gallery opens towards the end of 2007.

Pasadena Convention & Visitors Bureau

171 S Los Robles Avenue, at Cordova Street, Pasadena (1-626 795 9311/www.pasadenacal.com/ visitors.htm). Metro Del Mar/bus 180, 181, 267, 687/I-210, exit Los Robles Avenue south. **Open** 8am-5pm Mon-Fri; 10am-4pm Sat.

Pasadena Museum of California Art

497 E Colorado Boulevard, between S Los Robles & S Lake Avenues, Pasadena (1-626 568 3665/www. pmcaonline.org). Metro Memorial Park/bus 180, 181, 267, 687/I-210, exit Lake Avenue. **Open** noon-5pm Wed, Thur, Sat, Sun; 10am-8pm Fri. **Admission** $6; $4 discounts; free under-12s. **Credit** AmEx, MC, V.

An open-air staircase beautified by moody lightplay from an oculus above it creates a striking entrance into this three-storey facility. The museum is dedicated to California art and design from the last 150 years; since opening in 2002, it has staged exhibitions of work by the likes of mid 20th-century artist Edward Biberman, and modernist painter and poet Yun Gee, a Chinese emigrée to San Francisco when he was 15. The PMCA also run a Design Biennial, featuring the best design emanating from California; the next one is scheduled for 2007.

Heading South

When you wish upon a star…

The South Bay & Long Beach

The South Bay

El Segundo, Manhattan Beach, Hermosa Beach & Redondo Beach

Getting to the South Bay is half the fun. The Vista del Mar road, which runs along the beach, starts about a mile south of Marina del Rey, off Culver Avenue at Dockweiler State Beach. Zip past LAX airport and you're in the district of **El Segundo**. The best non-aquatic attraction here is an old-fashioned cinema: the **Old Town Music Hall** (140 Richmond Street, 1-310 322 2592, www.otmh.org), open weekends only, features pre-1960s movies and organ concerts.

Continue south on Vista del Mar (which becomes Highland Avenue) until you reach Manhattan Beach Boulevard and then make a right towards the ocean. On sunny weekends, **Manhattan Beach** is mobbed with skaters, cyclists and sun-worshippers. Cleaner than Venice, the strands in Manhattan offer the same sort of people-watching pleasures, but without the ethnically diverse crowds. After a day at the beach, there's good casual dining at the **Kettle** (1138 Highland Avenue, 1-310 545 8511), one of the best 24-hour restaurants in the LA area.

The surfside flavour continues southward into nearby **Hermosa Beach** and **Redondo Beach**, the latter boasting one of the area's most developed piers in the shape of **King Harbor** (at the end of Portofino Way). Purists might find its shops, restaurants, fish markets and marina rather naff, but Redondo is the most family-oriented of the South Bay's beaches.

Palos Verdes & San Pedro

One of the best drives in Southern California is the loop around scenic Palos Verdes Peninsula. Take the Pacific Coast Highway (Highway 1, aka the PCH) south to Palos Verdes Boulevard (at Redondo State Beach, a mile or so south of the eponymous city), go south again to Palos Verdes Drive West and then Palos Verdes Drive South. On the way, stop at the lovely glass and

stone **Wayfarer's Chapel** (5755 Palos Verdes Drive South), the most visited building by architect Lloyd Wright (Frank's son), and the **South Coast Botanic Garden** (26300 Crenshaw Boulevard, 1-310 544 6815, www.southcoastbotanicgarden.org).

Ironically, ritzy Palos Verdes shares the peninsula with one of LA's most colourful working-class communities. The traditional home of fishermen, dockers, Navy staff and immigrants, **San Pedro** – also home of the massive Port of LA – used to seem more Boston than Burbank. Gentrification and cuts in defence spending have changed that, but a walk along quaint 6th Street and a Greek meal at **Papadakis Taverna** (301 W 6th Street, 1-310 548 1186) or a classic film at the **Warner Grand Theatre** (478 W 6th Street, 1-310 548 7672, www.warnergrand.org), a restored 1931 movie palace, can make the years vanish.

There's a spectacular view of the ocean from nearby **Angels Gate Park** (3601 S Gaffey Street), home to the giant Korean Friendship Bell, a bicentennial gift to the US from South Korea. Below this bluff, **Point Fermin Park**, with its 1874 wooden lighthouse, is a great picnic spot. The **Cabrillo Marine Aquarium** (*see below*) and the **Los Angeles Maritime Museum** (*see p132*) are both fun for families.

Cabrillo Marine Aquarium

3720 Stephen White Drive, at Pacific Avenue, San Pedro (1-310 548 7562/www.cabrilloaq.org). Bus 445, 446/I-110, exit Harbor Boulevard west. **Open** noon-5pm Tue-Fri; 10am-5pm Sat, Sun. **Admission** free; donations requested (suggested donations: $5; $1 discounts). **No credit cards.**
This aquarium, dedicated to California marine life, is home to a jellyfish farm, a hands-on tidal pool exhibit and 30 ocean-life tanks. Special seasonal events include two-hour whale-watching trips, occasional guided walks to the tidal pools at Point Fermin Marine Life Refuge and grunion runs (held during the migrating season of this small, pencil-sized fish).

International Surfing Museum

411 Olive Avenue, between Main & 5th Streets, Huntington Beach (1-714 960 3483/www.surfing museum.org). Metro 5th Street/bus LB181, LB182/I-405, exit Beach Boulevard south. **Open** *Summer* noon-5pm daily. *Winter* noon-5pm Mon, Thur-Sun. **Admission** $2; $1 discounts; free under-6s. **Credit** AmEx, MC, V.

Aquarium of the Pacific. *See p133.*

This small museum honours Duke Kahanamoku, the godfather of surfing, and celebrates surf music, surf life-saving and – of course – surf babes. It's staffed with volunteers full of stories; ask to hear the one about Dick Dale's guitar, stolen from the museum's original building but now hanging in the rear gallery. Other exhibits include old masks, spear guns and tritons, and an array of surfboards.

Los Angeles Maritime Museum

Berth 84, end of W 6th Street, San Pedro (1-310 548 7618/www.lamaritimemuseum.org). Bus 446, 447/I-110, exit Harbor Boulevard west. **Open** 10am-5pm Tue-Sat; noon-5pm Sun. **Admission** $3. $1 discounts **No credit cards**.

The largest maritime museum in California contains, among other displays, a potted history of fishing in the state and an array of model boats and ships. Upstairs is the radio room, in which members of the United Radio Amateur Club demonstrate maritime radio communications. There's also an exhibition about the building in which the museum is housed, a fine 1940s Streamline Moderne structure that once acted as a ferry terminal.

Long Beach

Long Beach has been given short shrift by its more well-heeled neighbours to the north and south; the Long Beach of popular imagination is one of dockers, swing shifts and drunken sailors on leave. But since the factories closed and Navy work dwindled in the 1980s, it's changed almost beyond recognition. The area is smarter than it's ever been, and more cultured; however, those in search of its old edge can still find it; turf wars between rival blacks, Latinos and Cambodians keep up tensions.

The city's turnaround was heralded by the opening of the **Aquarium of the Pacific** (*see p133*) in 1998, one of the US's largest and most spectacular aquariums. It is, though, just a part of the redevelopment of the area known as Queensway Bay, now dotted with shops and restaurants. An anchor's toss from the Aquarium is the **Queen Mary** (*see p133*). One of the largest passenger ships ever built, it now houses a variety of attractions, restaurants and bars, and even a hotel.

Other worthwhile diversions in the area include the small but ambitious **Long Beach Museum of Art** (*see p133*), the **Museum of Latin American Art** (*see p133*) and the extremely avant-garde **Long Beach Opera** (*see p236*), arguably the most eccentric opera company in the US. If you're here in April, you'll have your ears blown clean off by the noise from the **Long Beach Grand Prix** (*see p204*). But one big no-no is a day at the beach: pollution is a problem in this industrial town, especially since the breakwaters were built years ago to hold back the (cleansing) waves.

The nightlife here has improved. Downtown Long Beach has some fine restaurants, among them popular steakhouse **555 East** (555 E Ocean Boulevard, at Linden Street, 1-562 437 0626). The stretch of Broadway between

Sightseeing

Alamitos and Ximeno Avenues holds a few more worthwhile eateries, while you'll find some decent thrift stores on 4th Street (near Cherry Avenue). The Belmont Shore region (2nd Street, from Park to Bayshore Avenues) has a younger feel, thanks to the students from nearby Cal State. Among its highlights are record shop **Fingerprints** (4612 2nd Street, 1-562 433 4996) and **Lucille's BBQ** (4828 E 2nd Street, 1-562 434 7427, www.lucillesbbq.com). If it all feels a little sterile, go grab a beer at either of Long Beach's two most worthwhile bars: **Joe Jost's** (2803 E Anaheim Street, 1-562 439 5446, www.joejosts.com), a wizened old tavern, and punk haven **Alex's Bar** (2913 E Anaheim Street, entrance at the back, 1-562 434 8292, www.alexsbar.com).

Naples (off 2nd Street, between Bay Shore and Marina Avenues) is an expensive neighbourhood laid out around picturesque canals; it's similar to Venice up the coast, but with none of the latter's decay. Gondola rides are offered by **Gondola Getaway** (5437 E Ocean Boulevard, 1-562 433 9595, www.gondola getawayinc.com, reservations required).

Aquarium of the Pacific

100 Aquarium Way, at Shoreline Drive (1-562 590 3100/www.aquariumofpacific.org). Metro 1st Street/bus 60, 232, 360/I-710, exit Shoreline Drive east. **Open** 9am-6pm daily. **Admission** $19.95; $11.95-$16.95 discounts. **Credit** AmEx, MC, V.

This spectacular $117m aquarium, with its wave-shaped profile, has been open since 1998, saving parents the drive down to Seaworld in San Diego in order to give the kids their fill of watery fun. Inevitably, the Shark Lagoon is the most popular exhibit, the bite of the oddly becalmed residents presumably worse than their non-existent bark. Much of the rest of the aquarium is divided geographically: the lovable sea lions in the Southern California section, all kinds of garish fish in the tropical Pacific area. If the real thing isn't enough for the little brats, they may enjoy an animated and exaggerated version of same in the shape of *AnimalVision 3-D* ($3). **Photo** *p132*.

Long Beach Convention & Visitors Bureau

1 World Trade Center, at E Ocean Boulevard (1-562 436 3645/www.visitlongbeach.com). Metro Transit Mall/bus 60, 232, 360/I-710, exit Shoreline Drive east. **Open** 8am-5pm Mon-Fri.

Long Beach Museum of Art

2300 E Ocean Boulevard, at Kennebec Avenue (1-562 439 2119/www.lbma.org). Bus LBA, LBD/I-405, then I-710 south. **Open** 11am-5pm Tue-Sun. **Admission** $7; $6 discounts; free under-12. Free to all 1st Fri of mth. **Credit** MC, V.

Though only true connoisseurs will reckon it worth the drive down in itself, the Long Beach Museum of Art nonetheless keeps its locals entertained with a

cultured roster of temporary exhibits. The permanent collection includes some notable Californian pieces and an extensive library of video art. The building's an intriguing one: completed in 1912, it was designed and originally used as a summer home by philanthropist Elizabeth Milbank Anderson.

Queen Mary

1126 Queens Highway (1-800 437 2934/1-562 435 3511/www.queenmary.com). Metro Transit Mall/I-405, then I-710 south. **Open** 10am-6pm daily. **Admission** $17-$32; $12-$27 discounts. **Credit** AmEx, DC, Disc, MC, V.

Having retired from active duty in 1967, the majestic *Queen Mary* is now a popular tourist attraction and hotel (for the latter, *see p65*). Attractions range from a low-key display of photographs outlining the boat's history to temporary shows and the rather more adventurous Ghosts & Legends attraction, which plays up to the boat's reputation as a home for myriad old spooks. Steady your nerves afterwards with a Martini in the gorgeous bar.

Museum of Latin American Art

628 Alamitos Avenue, at E 6th Street, Long Beach (1-562 437 1689/www.molaa.com). Metro 5th Street/bus 60, 232, 360, LB7/I-710, exit Alamitos Avenue north. **Open** 11.30am-7pm Tue-Fri; 11am-7pm Sat; 11am-6pm Sun. **Admission** $5; $3 discounts; free under-12s. **Credit** AmEx, DC, MC, V.

The Museum of Latin American Art is located in the developing East Village Arts District of Long Beach, on a site that was once the home of Balboa Amusement Producing Company, the most productive silent film studio of its day. The permanent collection is supplemented by a range of temporary shows and a new 15,000sq ft sculpture garden. A new building is scheduled to open towards the end of 2006.

Orange County

The South Coast

Seal Beach and **Sunset Beach**, near the Los Angeles County border, begin the 50-mile expanse of beach bliss that is coastal Orange County. The Pacific Coast Highway (aka PCH, or Highway 1) runs the length of it. While Seal Beach and Sunset Beach are decent fun, the real action starts to the south in **Huntington Beach**, aka 'Surf City'. Hang out at the pier (Main Street, off PCH) or on the sand and you'll see how the city got its nickname; from dawn to dark, surfers are searching for the perfect wave. The refurbished Main Street is home to numerous surfboard shops and bars.

Newport Beach, to the south, is something else altogether. From the lavish homes overlooking Newport Harbor to the outdoor **Fashion Island** mall and the **Orange**

Sightseeing

County Museum of Art (850 San Clemente Drive, 1-949 759 1122, www.ocma.net), which specialises in California art, Newport Beach is where the American leisured class live out their days in splendour. Balboa Island (Jamboree Road Bridge, near PCH) and Balboa Peninsula (Balboa Boulevard and PCH) are both prime walking areas; a ferry ushers visitors between the two. The island is full of shops, restaurants and homes; just off the ferry on the peninsula is a carnival with a Ferris wheel and arcade.

Laguna Beach began as an artists' colony and is the home of the admired Laguna Art Museum (307 Cliff Drive, 1-949 494 8971, www.lagunaartmuseum.org). The city hosts a Festival of the Arts in August and September. Main Beach, with its pick-up basketball and volleyball games, is a must for people-watching.

Down the coast, San Juan Capistrano is famous for the swallows that return to Mission San Juan Capistrano (see p281 On a mission) each spring. But the structure, built in 1776, is worth visiting on its own account. At the county's end, San Clemente has all the sun and waves but few of the crowds of its neighbours. Richard Nixon's western White House, the Spanish-inspired Casa Pacifica, can be seen from San Clemente State Beach.

Central Orange County

Costa Mesa, which isn't on the coast, likes to bill itself as an arts-friendly city, thanks to the presence of the Orange County

Performing Arts Center (600 Town Center Drive, 1-714 556 2787, www.ocpac.org) and the admired South Coast Repertory (655 Town Center Drive, 1-714 708 5500, www.scr.org). However, it's really a city of commerce above all else: among its malls are South Coast Plaza (off I-405 at Bristol Avenue, 1-800 782 8888, www.southcoastplaza.com), one of the largest in the world; Triangle Square (intersection of Highway 55 and Harbor Boulevard, 1-949 722 1600, www.triangle square.com), a huge altar to consumerism; and the hipster-tilted Lab (2930 Bristol Street, 1-714 966 6660, www.thelab.com), which bills itself as an 'anti-mall' and counts Urban Outfitters, Buffalo Exchange and the Subject Matter gallery among its tenants.

To the north, Santa Ana is a distinctively Latino city. Strolling along busy 4th Street, between French and Ross Streets, with its colourful storefronts and hum of Spanish, is like walking through a small city in Mexico. Santa Ana is also home to the Bowers Museum of Cultural Art (2002 N Main Street, 1-714 567 3600, www.bowers.org), which has a strong collection of Latin and African arts and crafts, and a budding artists' district between Broadway, Bush, 1st and 3rd Streets.

Another lively neighbourhood is Little Saigon in Westminster, the largest Vietnamese community outside Vietnam. It's worth a visit for the south-east Asian foods served at restaurants such as Seafood Paradise (8602 Westminster Boulevard, 1-714 893 6066).

Anaheim & inland

Anaheim and its surrounds are filled with icons of middle Americana, of which **Disneyland** is king. The area around it, for years known for cheap motels and strip-mall seediness, has been revitalised, though at the cost of much of its wacked-out 1950s Googie architecture. A couple of sports teams – baseball's Angels (*see p252*) and the hockey-playing Mighty Ducks (*see p254*) – provide the locals with further diversions.

For a more traditional slice of American pie, hop over to Beach Boulevard near La Palma Avenue in **Buena Park**, where you'll find **Knott's Berry Farm** (*see p135*) and the **Movieland Wax Museum** (7711 Beach Boulevard, 1-714 522 1154, www.movieland waxmuseum.com). If you're in the area, two other shrines to the American way of life deserve a visit. The **Crystal Cathedral** (12141 Lewis Street, Garden Grove, 1-714 971 4000, www.crystalcathedral.org), an all-glass house of worship, is a marvel of sheer excess, built by Philip Johnson and John Burgee for preacher Dr Robert H Schuller and his ministry. The **Nixon Library & Birthplace** in Yorba Linda (*see p135*), meanwhile, is a combination of library and pro-Nixon propaganda machine.

Anaheim/Orange County Visitor & Convention Bureau

800 W Katella Avenue, at N Batavia Street (1-714 765 8888/www.anaheimoc.org). **Open** 8am-5.30pm Mon-Fri.

Disneyland

1313 S Harbor Boulevard, between Katella Avenue & Ball Road, Anaheim (1-714 781 4000/recorded information 1-714 781 4565/www.disneyland.com). Bus OC205, OC430/I-5, exit Disneyland Drive. **Open** *Disneyland: Summer* 8am-midnight daily. *Winter* 10am-8pm Mon-Thur; 8am-midnight Fri, Sat; 9am-9pm Sun. *California Adventure: Summer* 10am-8pm Mon-Thur; 10am-9pm Fri-Sun. *Winter* 10am-6pm Mon-Thur; 10am-8pm Fri; 10am-9pm Sat, Sun. Hours vary: check online. **Admission** *One park for one day* $59; $49 discounts; free under-3s. Call or check online for details of combination tickets. **Credit** AmEx, DC, Disc, MC, V.

The Disneyland resort isn't just a set of theme parks; it's a spectacular piece of pop art that's as bright or dark as you'd like it to be. Incorporating two parks – the 50-year-old, near-mythic **Disneyland** and the younger, less celebrated **Disney's California Adventure** – the resort calls itself 'The Happiest Place on Earth'. If you bring the right mood with you, it certainly can be.

Certainly, Disney does all it can to get you in the right mood. Disneyland is not so much a park as its own separate world; there are even three Disney-operated hotels (*see p66*) in the resort, so you need not have the illusion shattered at the end of the day. The hotels, though, do bring to attention the main drawback to spending time here: the sheer expense. You can save hundreds of dollars staying at one of the non-Disney hotels just outside the property, and you may need to do so in order to afford the steep prices of food, drink and admission. It's worth noting, though, that ticket prices drop if you visit for multiple days, recommended if you want to get a real feel for the place and ride all the rides.

Knott's Berry Farm. *See p136.*

Sightseeing

Both parks boast dozens of dining spots, with cuisine ranging from burgers and pizza to pastas and seafood. Still, you may want to dine at **Downtown Disney**, a pedestrian-only avenue of nightclubs (including a House of Blues) and restaurants between the two parks. It's not that the food is that much better, but if you're going to be paying Disney's high prices, you might as well be able to order a drink or two to soften the blow: liquor sales were banned from Disneyland by Walt himself, citing the undesirable 'carnie atmosphere' booze might have created.

The other main demerit against Disneyland is the crowds: they can be overwhelming, particularly in summer. (Top tip: few visit on Super Bowl Sunday.) But the crowds can't be helped, and they're unlikely to change: Disneyland is popular for a reason.

Disneyland

Disneyland is packed with must-do attractions spread over seven 'lands', all immaculately themed in every detail. **Main Street USA** embodies turn-of-the-19th-century America, while **Frontierland** takes on Westward expansion (the John Wayne version) and **New Orleans Square** is just like its namesake, minus the booze. **Adventureland** offers thrills of the jungle variety; **Tomorrowland** is a kitschy look into the future; **Critter Country** is the wooded home of Winnie the Pooh and Br'er Rabbit; and **Fantasyland** is where Disney's animated films come to life. It's here you're most likely to find Mickey Mouse, scurrying about in Toontown.

The secret of Disneyland's charm lies in its history. Unlike the company's other parks, Disneyland was largely designed by Walt himself, and it's the only one in which he ever set foot. As a result, Disneyland is practically a biography of its creator's life, if you know where to look. Try reading the names in Main Street's upper-level windows; you'll find many of Disney's collaborators and artists listed. *The Walt Disney Story* features artefacts from Disney's entertainment career. And in Frontierland, you'll find the petrified tree Walt once gave his wife as an anniversary present.

But most people, of course, are here for the rides. Among the best are **Space Mountain** (in Tomorrowland), a legitimately thrilling indoor rollercoaster ride through 'deep space'; the epic **Indiana Jones Adventure** (in Adventureland), based on the Spielberg adventure movies; **Pirates of the Caribbean** (in New Orleans Square), the basis for the hit Johnny Depp film and one of the most detail-packed and atmospheric rides in the park; and the **Matterhorn** (in Fantasyland), a breakneck bobsled ride around and through a scaled-down replica of the Swiss peak. Beyond that, there are dozens of carnival-style 'dark' rides, boat trips, rollercoasters, flume rides and Audio-Animatronics shows, each telling its own story and holding charms for young and old alike.

Disney's California Adventure

Located in the former Disneyland car park, this decent little park, while no match for Disneyland in terms of size or attention to detail, does a decent job of celebrating the geography, culture and history of its namesake state. Plus, unlike Disneyland, it serves wine, beer and cocktails, and has done so since opening day with little or no carnie interference.

While DCA doesn't have anything as engrossing as Pirates of the Caribbean, it does feature some decent rides. The **Twilight Zone Tower of Terror**, a special effects-packed 'drop'-ride based on the classic TV show and housed in the **Hollywood Pictures Backlot** section of the park, is worth a look, as is **Soarin' Over California**, a beautiful flight simulator. Soarin' Over California is located in the **Golden State** section, itself split up into separate areas that pay homage to (among other places) San Francisco and Wine Country. The highlight of the **Paradise Pier** section, meanwhile, is the **California Screamin'** rollercoaster, the tallest and fastest coaster ever built in a Disney park. Not every ride is suitable for kids of all ages, but very young children are welcome in **A Bug's Land**.

Knott's Berry Farm

8039 Beach Boulevard, at La Palma Avenue, Buena Park (1-714 220 5200/www.knotts.com). Bus OC29/I-5, exit Beach Boulevard south. **Open** *Knott's Berry Farm: Jan-Apr, Sept-Dec 10am-6pm Mon-Fri; 10am-10pm Sat; 10am-7pm Sun. May 10am-6pm Mon-Fri; 9am-11pm; 10am-7pm Sun. June-Aug 10am-10pm Mon-Fri, Sun; 9am-11pm Sat. Soak City USA: May-Oct 10am-7pm daily.* **Admission** *Knott's Berry Farm* $40; $15-$35 discounts; free under-3s. *Soak City USA* $17; $15 discounts. **Credit** AmEx, DC, Disc, MC, V.

Knott's Berry Farm started as a farm selling the home-made preserves of one Mrs Cordelia Knott. Although Ma Knott and her family are long gone, her jams are still on sale, as are tasty fried chicken dinners at the restaurant outside the gates. Inside the park, which portrays an idealised, kinder America, there are water rides, the 20-storey Sky Jump parachute ride and Montezooma's Revenge, a stomach-churning rollercoaster ride. Many of the buildings in the park have been transplanted from old mining towns, which heightens the feeling of nostalgia. Next door to the Berry Farm sits **Soak City**, a mammoth water park; combination tickets are available for the two attractions. Hours for both parks vary; call or check online to find out hours for the day on which you plan to visit. **Photo** *p134.*

Richard Nixon Library & Birthplace

18001 Yorba Linda Boulevard, at Imperial Highway, Yorba Linda (1-714 993 3393/www.nixonfoundation.org). Bus OC26/Hwy 90, exit Yorba Linda Boulevard west. **Open** 10am-5pm Mon-Sat; 11am-5pm Sun. **Admission** $8; $3-$6 discounts; free under-7s. **Credit** AmEx, Disc, MC, V.

Located in the suburb where Nixon was born, this library offers a walk through his presidency as well as a tour of the modest house, built from a kit by his father, in which Tricky Dick was born. The gifts section includes a gun from Elvis Presley, as well as the usual assortment of buckles and paintings. Dick and Pat are enjoying their afterlife in the gardens.

Eat, Drink, Shop

Restaurants	**138**
Coffeehouses	**166**
Bars	**170**
Shops & Services	**179**

Features

The best Restaurants	139
Designs for dining	148
We 🚫 **LA** Cellphones	150
Farmers Market favourites	154
We ♥ **LA** Taco trucks	161
Brunch bonanza	164
The best Coffee	166
Get connected	169
The best Bars	172
Walk Hollywood's vintage bars	174
Where to shop	181
Spotlight W 3rd Street	187
Spotlight Abbot Kinney Boulevard	188
Our daily bread	193
The get fresh crew	194

Restaurants

Get stuffed.

Hang with the hipsters at **Wilshire**. *See p142.*

Whether in old-school steakhouses or 21st-century high-concept restaurant-clubs, eating out has never been more de rigueur here. LA was a fairly ordinary culinary town until the early 1990s, its restaurants dominated more by fashion than by food, but the city has been steadily improving ever since. There are still numerous style-over-content spots around town, sure, but great food is a lot easier to find. As, for that matter, is a late-opening kitchen: the old cliché that Angelenos are early to rise and quick to bed is as out of date as smoking in restaurants. That said, looking young and thin are still prerequisites in many places: the natives may order tons, but they don't always clear their plates.

The old idea of chef as celebrity is still very much in evidence. Indeed, several of the town's top toques have branched out and taken their careers into their own hands: Michael Cimarusti has left the **Water Grill** to open **Providence**, L'Orangerie's Chrisotophe Eme is now in charge at **Ortolan**, and Jared Simons has started **Violet**. After the near-constant staff,

menu and now design re-shuffling at Bastide, once LA's most innovative French restaurant, it seems a smart move.

Other chef/owners have added to their portfolios. Suzanne Goin of **Lucques** and **AOC** has joined forces with hubby David Lentz, formerly of **Opaline**, to open the **Hungry Cat**; Liza and Tim Goodell, the couple behind **Meson G**, have introduced **Dakota** and **25 Degrees** into the Hollywood Roosevelt. Most intriguingly, David Myers of **Sona** has joined forces with sushi star Kazunori Nozawa (of **Sushi Nozawa**) to start a late-night Japanese joint in West Hollywood called **Sokyo**; it's due to open in July 2006. Check local listings for other openings when you're in town: there's always another trend just waiting to burst…

> ❶ Purple numbers given in this chapter correspond to the location of each restaurant on the street maps. *See pp310-315.*

Eat, Drink, Shop

INSIDE INFORMATION

Competition for tables in LA can be fierce, especially at the hipper restaurants, so make reservations if possible (and be sure to call if you're running late). Note that some white-tablecloth establishments take credit card details in order to hold the table. If there's space for walk-ins, you should still be primed to hang at the bar and wait. If you're happy with the service, tip a bare minimum of 15 per cent; it isn't unheard of for waiters to chase customers down the street for less.

The term 'California casual' was invented here, but don't push your luck: some of the finer eateries draw the line at shorts and jeans. Smoking is banned in all restaurants, although it's sometimes permitted on patios.

Santa Monica & the beach towns

Malibu

Allegria

22821 Pacific Coast Highway, at Coastline Drive (1-310 456 3132). Bus 534/I-10, exit PCH north. **Open** 11.30am-2.30pm, 5-10pm daily. **Main courses** $10-$32. **Credit** AmEx, DC, MC, V. **Italian**
LA is the city of dreams, so it makes perfect sense that you can scoot up to Malibu and sit down for supper in what appears to be a Tuscan villa. Naturally, it's popular with the dream weavers themselves, but ordinary locals swear by the place, particularly the pumpkin tortelloni with sage.

Geoffrey's

27400 Pacific Coast Highway, west of Latigo Canyon Road (1-310 457 1519/www.geoffreysmalibu.com). Bus 534/I-10, exit PCH north. **Open** 11am-10pm Mon-Thur; 11.30am-11pm Fri; 10am-11pm Sat; 11.30am-3.30pm Sun. **Main courses** *Lunch* $16-$30. *Dinner* $18-$30. **Credit** AmEx, MC, V. **Californian**
Geoffrey's offers another chance to dine the world in California: sitting on its cliffside deck, you'd swear you were on the French Riviera. However, the menu, the wine list and the coolly casual waiting staff will soon set you straight: all are classically Californian. The quality of the food, the views and the service all make the drive worthwhile.

Moonshadows

20356 Pacific Coast Highway, west of Big Rock Drive (1-310 456 3010/www.moonshadowsmalibu. com). Bus 534/I-10, exit PCH north. **Open** 11.30am-10.30pm Mon-Thur; 11am-1am Fri, Sat; 11am-11.30pm Sun. **Main courses** $9-$27. **Credit** AmEx, DC, MC, V. **Fish & seafood**
This old Malibu surf-and-turf has lately been infused with new life, courtesy of a resident DJ and a modernised menu. Some things don't change, though: it's still a great place for slurping oysters while waiting for the sun to set into the Pacific.

Nobu

Malibu Country Mart, 3853 Cross Creek Road, north of PCH (1-310 317 9140/www.noburestaurants.com). Bus 534/I-10, exit PCH north. **Open** 5.45-10pm Mon-Thur, Sun; 5.45-11pm Fri, Sat. **Main courses** $15-$40. **Credit** AmEx, DC, MC, V. **Japanese**
Nobuyuki Matsuhisa's Malibu restaurant is small but very starry. A long sushi bar is stocked with the freshest fish. However, most come for the trademark Tokyo-meets-Lima fusion dishes: fish and beef laced with chillis, garlic and an array of surprising sauces. Booking a month ahead or wait for the sushi bar. For Matsuhisa, his other LA restaurant, *see p145*.

Santa Monica

Counter

2901 Ocean Park Boulevard, at 29th Street (1-310 399 8383/www.thecounterburger.com). Bus SM8/I-10, exit Centinela Boulevard south. **Open** 11am-10pm Mon-Thur; 11am-11pm Fri, Sat; noon-9pm Sun. **Main courses** $7-$13. **Credit** AmEx, MC, V. **Map** p310 D4 ❶ **Cafés & diners**
The Counter manages the difficult feat of being hip and child-friendly at once by allowing both the

The best Restaurants

For Californian cuisine

Campanile (*see p155*); **Grace** (*see p153*); **Joe's** (*see p142*); **Vermont** (*see p156*).

For American classics

Apple Pan (*see p144*); **Cassell's** (*see p155*); **Kate Mantilini** (*see p146*); **Roscoe's House of Chicken & Waffles** (*see p151*).

For star-studded dining

Geisha House (*see p150*); **Ivy** (*see p148*); **Lodge Steakhouse** (*see p148* **Designs for dining**).

For a Euro-blowout

AOC (*see p153*); **La Cachette** (*see p145*); **Patina** (*see p159*); **Sona** (*see p150*).

For a Mexican feast

Chano's (*see p158*); **La Serenata di Garibaldi** (*see p161*); **Tlapazola Grill** (*see p145*).

For modern design

Dakota (*see p150*); **Meson G** (*see p154*); **Orchid** (*see p141*).

For vegetarians

Leaf Cuisine (*see p144*); **Mao's Kitchen** (*see p142*); **India Sweet House** (*see p153*).

Eat, Drink, Shop

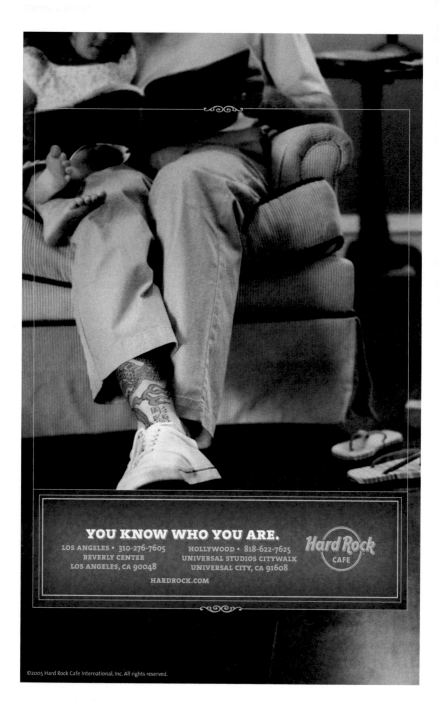

self-consciously ironic and ravenously hungry to build their own burgers with an array of cheeses and toppings. If that's not enough, desserts include a chocolate burger made from doughnuts and mousse.

Drago

2628 Wilshire Boulevard, at 26th Street (1-310 828 1585/www.celestinodrago.com). Bus 20, 720, SM2/ I-10, exit Cloverfield Boulevard north/20th Street north. **Open** 11am-3pm, 5.30-10.30pm Mon-Fri; 5.30-10.30pm Sat, Sun. **Main courses** $12-$34. **Credit** AmEx, MC, V. **Map** p310 D2 ❷ **Italian**
Celestino Drago's place has been around for more than 15 years, and has been popular with foodies and discerning celebrities for virtually as long. The reasons: good pasta, a convivial, luxurious atmosphere, and warm Italian service from the old school.

Giorgio Baldi

114 W Channel Road, at PCH (1-310 573 1660/ www.giorgiobaldi.com). Bus 534, SM9/I-10, exit PCH north. **Open** 6-10pm Tue-Sun. **Main courses** $15-$35. **Credit** AmEx, MC, V. **Map** p310 A1 ❸ **Italian**
This simple, family-run trattoria is one of only a few Italian restaurants by the beach; get a patio seat for some fresh Pacific air, and hope that the waiters can hear you above the din. The food is superb but pricey. Still, you know you're getting the real thing: the restaurant flies in its seafood from Italy.

Hump

Santa Monica Airport, 3221 Donald Douglas Loop South, off Stewart Avenue (1-310 313 0977/www. typhoon.biz). Bus SM14/I-10, exit Bundy Drive south. **Open** noon-2pm, 6-10.30pm Mon-Thur; noon-2pm, 6-11pm Fri; 6-11pm Sat; 6-10pm Sun. **Sushi** $5-$16. **Credit** AmEx, DC, MC, V. **Map** p310 D5 ❹ **Japanese**
The Hump overlooks the runway at Santa Monica Airport, and its Japanese food is as expansive as the views. Aficionados claim it's the freshest sushi in LA, a claim you'll believe when you notice the lobster moving as it arrives at the table. The specials prices can be hard to swallow, but if you stick with the regular sushi/sashimi menu, you won't be disappointed.

Josie

2424 Pico Boulevard, at 25th Street (1-310 581 9888/www.josierestaurant.com). Bus SM7/I-10, exit Cloverfield Boulevard south/20th Street south. **Open** 6-10pm Mon-Fri; 6-11pm Sat; 5.30-9pm Sun. **Main courses** $21-$36. **Credit** AmEx, Disc, MC, V. **Map** p310 D4 ❺ **American**
You'll find Josie and two other female chefs labouring in the kitchen, while husband Frank manages front of house. Progressive American, French and Italian influences abound, producing combinations such as buffalo foie burger with truffle fries, or campfire trout with beans. Desserts are indulgent.

> **Geoffrey's (p139)** Where Harrison Ford meets Martin Landau for lunch in *Hollywood Homicide*

Lemon Moon

12200 W Olympic Boulevard, at S Bundy Drive (1-310 442 9191/www.lemonmoon.com). Bus SM5, SM14/I-10, exit Bundy Drive south. **Open** 8am-3pm Mon-Fri. **Main courses** $3-$13. **Credit** AmEx, DC, Disc, MC, V. **American**
LA takes on NYC with this Big Apple-style eaterie, run by Josiah Citrin of Mélisse (*see below*) and JiRaffe's Raphael Lunetta. The menu offers market-fresh American food with a Mediterranean twist for breakfast and lunch. The salads are excellent.

Mélisse

1104 Wilshire Boulevard, at 11th Street (1-310 395 0881/www.melisse.com). Bus 20, 720, SM2, SM11/ I-10, exit Lincoln Boulevard north. **Open** 6-10pm daily. **Main courses** $27-$45. **Credit** AmEx, DC, Disc, MC, V. **Map** p310 B2 ❻ **French**
Josiah Citrin's classic-with-a-twist Provençal fare is presented with panache. Try the egg caviar, in which a poached egg is laced with lemon crème fraîche, returned to its shell and served in a silver egg cup, or the roasted Maine lobster, which comes in a swirl of Thai green curry. The garden room or the perimeter booths are exquisite.

Orchid

119 Broadway, at W 2nd Street (1-310 395 6037). Bus 4, 304, 534, SM1, SM7, SM8, SM10/I-10, exit 4th-5th Street north. **Open** 11.30am-3pm, 5-10pm daily. **Main courses** $10-$23. **Credit** AmEx, DC, Disc, MC, V. **Map** p310 A3 ❼ **Thai**
Orchid's owners are recent émigrés from Thailand; their background is clear from the sublime quality of their Thai food: try Asian fettuccine with calamari, roast duck curry and scallion-crusted cod in a tamarind sauce. The slick modern design, done out in clean aubergines and greens, comes with a wave-like sculptural ceiling and large booths.

Sushi Roku

1401 Ocean Avenue, at Santa Monica Boulevard (1-310 458 4771/www.sushiroku.com). Bus 4, 304, 534, SM1, SM7, SM8, SM10/I-10, exit 4th-5th Street north. **Open** 11.30am-2.30pm, 5.30-11.30pm Mon-Fri; noon-11.30pm Sat; 4.30-10.30pm Sun. **Sushi** $10-$20. **Credit** AmEx, DC, Disc, MC, V. **Map** p310 A3 ❽ **Japanese**
Still LA's hippest sushi joint, Sushi Roku is designed in an odd Zen-meets-Frank-Lloyd-Wright style, with grey stone, black granite and bamboo. The sushi ranges from basic dishes to unusual fare: crispy tuna sashimi spring rolls with a chilli oil and beurre blanc sauce, and seared yellow tail with balsamic dressing. **Other locations**: 8445 W 3rd Street, West Hollywood (1-323 655 6767); 333 Miller Alley, Pasadena (1-626 683 3000).

Violet

3221 Pico Boulevard, at 32nd Street (1-310 453 9113/www.violetrestaurant.com). Bus SM7, 534/ I-10, exit Centinela Avenue south. **Open** 11.30am-2pm, 6-11.30pm Mon-Fri; 5.30-11.30pm Sat, Sun. **Main courses** $9-$16. **Credit** AmEx, MC, V. **Map** p310 D4 ❾ **American**

Chef/owner Jared Simons has managed a rare trick with Violet: it's a new restaurant that's both fashionable and unpretentious. In large part, that union of contraries is down to Simon's own charm, which spreads from the kitchen to the valet stand (he's been known to open diners' car doors for them as they arrive or leave). In the dining room, small plates ('promiscuous dining', Simon says) vary from mac 'n' cheese to scallops with vanilla risotto. Three courses on Sunday night go for just $25.

Wilshire
2454 Wilshire Boulevard, between Chelsea Avenue & 25th Street (1-310 586 1707/www.wilshirerestaurant.com). Bus 20, 720, SM2/I-10, exit Cloverfield Boulevard north/20th Street north. **Open** 11.30am-2pm, 6-10pm Mon-Fri; 6-10pm Sat; 6-9pm Sun. **Main courses** $24-$55. **Credit** AmEx, DC, Disc, MC, V. **Map** p310 D2 ➓ **American**
Choose your seats carefully at this hipster hangout: you can go indoors or out, at a secluded table or in full view of the other diners. The loungey vibe – complete with now-ubiquitous fire and water elements – encourages diners to linger over their high end, organic New American fare: short ribs, lobster or wood-grilled beef, for example. **Photo** *p138.*

Venice

Axe
1009 Abbot Kinney Boulevard, at Broadway Avenue (1-310 664 9787/www.axerestaurant.com). Bus 33, 333, SM1, SM2/I-10, exit 4th-5th Street south. **Open** 11.30am-3pm, 6-10.30pm Tue-Fri; 9am-3pm, 6.30-10.30pm Sat; 9am-3pm Sun. **Main courses** $8-$22. **Credit** AmEx, DC, Disc, MC, V. **Map** p310 A5 ➊ **Californian**
The interior at Axe (pronounced 'ah-shay') is fabulously minimalist: industrial chic mixed with sleek wood. Service is erratic and the acoustics are terrible, but the food and atmosphere are both winners. The lunch menu is a healthy, organic mix: salads, sandwiches and hearty bowls of chicken and rice. At night, things get more sophisticated: try black mussels drenched in a broth of green curried coconut.

Brick House
826 Hampton Drive, at Brooks Avenue (1-310 581 1639). Bus 33, 333, SM1, SM2/I-10, exit 4th-5th Street south. **Open** 8am-3pm Mon-Fri; 8am-5pm Sat, Sun. **Main courses** $5-$10. **Credit** AmEx, MC, V. **Map** p310 A5 ➋ **Cafés & diners**
Where Venice has breakfast; or, at least, where they should. There aren't many surprises on the menu here at this matey little hangout, but nor does there need to be: this is just top-quality comfort food (sandwiches, omelettes, etc), served with a grin.

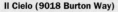

> **Il Cielo (9018 Burton Way)**
> Reece Witherspoon gets dumped
> here in *Legally Blonde*

Joe's
1023 Abbot Kinney Boulevard, between Broadway & Westminster Avenues (1-310 399 5811/ www.joesrestaurant.com). Bus 33, 333, SM1, SM2/ I-10, exit 4th-5th Street south. **Open** 11.30am-2.30pm, 6-11pm Tue-Fri; 11am-2.15pm, 6-11pm Sat, Sun. **Main courses** $11-$24. **Credit** AmEx, MC, V. **Map** p310 A5 ➌ **Californian**
Opened in 1991 by chef Joseph Miller, Joe's began life as an unassuming neighbourhood place. After a slew of accolades, Miller expanded, but the place has retained its low-key feel, and the French-Californian food remains exquisite. Our favourite table is in front of the open kitchen; if you're lucky, you'll be fed a few extras. The prix-fixe lunch is a steal.

Lilly's French Café & Wine Bar
1031 Abbot Kinney Boulevard, at Broadway (1-310 314 0004/www.lillysfrenchcafe.com). Bus 33, 333, SM1, SM2/I-10, exit 4th-5th Street south. **Open** noon-2.30pm, 6-10pm Mon-Fri; noon-2.30pm, 6-10.30pm Sat, Sun. **Main courses** $16-$24. **Credit** AmEx, Disc, MC, V. **Map** p310 A5 ➍ **French**
A modest French bistro with a charming patio. Not everything on the menu is good, but the appetisers, desserts and wine list are more than serviceable. Try the frisée salad *avec* lardons and poached eggs, or the garlic-redolent snails.

Mao's Kitchen
1512 Pacific Avenue, at Windward Boulevard (1-310 581 8305/www.maoskitchen.com). Bus 33, 333, SM1, SM2/I-10, exit 4th-5th Street south. **Open** 11.30am-10.30pm Mon-Thur, Sun; 11.30am-3am Fri, Sat. **Main courses** $6-$10. **Credit** AmEx, MC, V. **Map** p310 A5 ➎ **Chinese**
The late weekend hours and lively atmosphere make up for the infamously bad service from the tattooed and pierced staff at this Venice staple. Big portions of solid 'country-style' Chinese grub and lots of vegetarian options have helped make it a popular local hangout at all hours.

Wabi Sabi
1635 Abbot Kinney Boulevard, at Venice Boulevard (1-310 314 2229). Bus 33, 333, SM1, SM2/ I-10, exit 4th-5th Street south. **Open** 5.30-10.30pm Mon-Thur; 5.30-11pm Fri, Sat; 5.30-10pm Sun. **Main courses** $18-$24. **Credit** AmEx, DC, Disc, MC, V. **Map** p310 A5 ➏ **Japanese**
Sushi/sashimi joints are as common as cars in LA, but this one stands out. Wabi Sabi has a fun, bustling vibe to go with its casually stylish design, but this means you could face a weekend wait.

Marina del Rey

Aunt Kizzy's Back Porch
4325 Glencoe Avenue, between Mindanao Way & Maxella Avenue (1-310 578 1005). Bus SM1/ Hwy 90, exit Mindanao Way north. **Open** 11am-10pm Mon-Thur; 11am-11pm Fri, Sat; 11am-9pm Sun. **Set menus** $7.95-$19.95. **Credit** AmEx, MC, V. **American**

The Deep South comes to LA at Aunt Kizzy's, and covers the wall with signed celebrity photos. Eating the fried chicken, cornbread and meat loaf, you might believe you were in rural Georgia, at least until you catch a glance of the mini-mall outside.

Café del Rey

4451 Admiralty Way, between Bali & Promenade Ways (1-310 823 6395/www.cafedelreymarina.com). Bus 108/Hwy 90, exit Mindanao Way west. **Open** 11.30am-3pm, 5.30-9.30pm Mon-Thur; 11.30am-3pm, 5.30-10pm Fri, Sat; 10.30am-2.30pm, 5-9pm Sun. **Main courses** $10-$39. **Credit** AmEx, DC, Disc, MC, V. **Californian**
The setting, overlooking the marina, is beautiful; the light and airy interior oozes class; and the menu is an excellent fusion of French, Californian and Pacific Rim cuisine, rounded off by an award-winning selection of Californian wines.

Sakura House

Marina Plaza, 13362 Washington Boulevard, at Glencoe Avenue (1-310 306 7010). Bus 108, C1/Hwy 90, exit Mindanao Way west. **Open** 5.30-10pm Mon, Wed-Sun. **Main courses** $18-$25. **Credit** AmEx, Disc, MC, V. **Japanese**
Hidden away in a humdrum mini-mall, the excellent Sakura House specialises in *kushiyaki* (grilled things on skewers, for the uninitiated): try the prime rib with spinach and shiso leaf pinwheels, squid with garlic and the jalapenos filled with potato. Leave room for dessert: grilled banana and chocolate sauce.

Brentwood to Beverly Hills

Brentwood

Literati II

12081 Wilshire Boulevard, at S Bundy Drive (1-310 479 3400/www.literati2.com). Bus 20, 720, SM2/ I-10, exit Bundy Drive west. **Open** 11am-2.30pm, 6-11pm Mon-Thur; 11am-2.30pm, 5.30-11pm Fri; 10am-2pm, 5.30-11pm Sat, Sun. **Main courses** $12-$34. **Credit** AmEx, DC, Disc, MC, V. **Californian**
In LA, even a literary-themed café has Hollywood photos on the walls. Still, how else would the screenwriters, tapping at their laptops, feel at home? If the deal comes through, Literati is formal enough for business meetings. If not, it's relaxed enough for a commiseratory whine about philistine execs over steak-frites and more Californian dishes.

Pecorino

11604 San Vicente Boulevard, at Mayfield Avenue (1-310 571 3800). Bus 20, 720, SM2, SM4/I-10, exit Bundy Drive north. **Open** 11.30am-2pm, 5.30-11pm Mon-Sat; 5.30-11pm Sun. **Main courses** $11-$21. **Credit** AmEx, DC, Disc, MC, V. **Italian**
This particular corner of LA isn't exactly short of Italian eateries, but brothers and owners Mario and Rafaele work to make the place feel like a hospitable gentlemen's club. Try the bruschetta dusted with spiced ricotta and cherry tomatoes.

Eat Italian at **Pecorino**.

Takao

11656 San Vicente Boulevard, at Darlington Avenue (1-310 207 8636). Bus 20, 720, SM2, SM4/ I-10, exit Bundy Drive north. **Open** 11.30am-5.30pm Mon-Sat; 5-10pm Sun. **Main courses** $9-$24. **Credit** AmEx, DC, MC, V. **Japanese**
An alumnus of master-chef Nobuyuki Matsuhisa, the eponymous chef-owner of Takao, Takao Izumida serves up delicate and inventive seafood dishes and sushi, among other excellent Japanese dishes, at this Brentwood staple. Expect the best in service, a celebrity sighting or two, and a steep bill at the end of the evening.

Vincenti

11930 San Vicente Boulevard, between S Bundy Drive & Montana Avenue (1-310 207 0127/ www.vincentiristorante.com). Bus SM3, SM4/I-405, exit Sunset Boulevard west. **Open** 6-10pm Mon-Thur, Sat; noon-2.30pm, 5-10pm Fri. **Main courses** $16-$40. **Credit** AmEx, MC, V. **Italian**
Favoured by the local haute bourgeoisie, Vincenti is a contemporary Italian restaurant that looks extremely sleek, and has some rather smart food to match its appearance. The pastas are decent, but there are also excellent meat and fish dishes, cooked in a wood-burning rotisserie. All in all, it makes for a pleasant spot to while away an evening.

Culver City

Beacon

3280 Helms Avenue, between Venice & Washington Boulevards (1-310 838 7500/www.beacon-la.com). Bus 33, 220, 333, C1/I-10, exit Robertson Boulevard south. **Open** 11.30am-2pm Mon; 11.30am-2pm, 5.30-11pm Tue-Sun. **Main courses** $10-$15. **Credit** AmEx, MC, V. **Pan-Asian**

Eat, Drink, Shop

Burger, fries and a soda? As American as **Apple Pan**.

Steaming bowls of miso, well-priced bento boxes, sashimi or grilled hanger steak whizz out of the kitchen to a hungry throng of locals and curious visitors at this great little spot. The dark wood tables, concrete walls and high ceilings serve as simple adornments to the food in this modern Asian café.

Café Brasil

10831 Venice Boulevard, at Westwood Boulevard (1-310 837 8957/www.cafe-brasil.com). Bus 33, 333, C1, C3/I-10, exit Overland Avenue south. **Open** 11am-10pm daily. **Main courses** $7-$18. **Credit** MC, V. **Brazilian**

This funky shack prides itself on its low-cost, authentic Brazilian food: fish and meat marinated and then grilled, served with rice and beans, and Brazilian salsa. Feijoada, a traditional pork stew that's cooked overnight, is served on weekends. **Other locations:** 11736 Washington Boulevard, West LA (1-310 399 1216).

Ford's Filling Station

9531 Culver Boulevard, at Cardiff Avenue (1-310 202 1470/www.fordsfillingstation.com). Bus 220, C1/I-10, exit Overland Avenue south. **Open** 11am-11pm daily. **Main courses** $14-$26. **Credit** AmEx, MC, V. **American**

The Ford is chef Benjamin, Harrison's son. Chew on that with your halibut, clams and mashed potatoes. The Filling Station offers an American take on a British gastropub: expect some fine local wines and beers to accompany the food, the brick façades, the exposed ducts and the leather club chairs.

Leaf Cuisine

11938 W Washington Boulevard, between Marcasel & Atlantic Avenues (1-310 390 6005/www.leaf cuisine.com). Bus C2, SM14/I-10, exit Bundy Drive south. **Open** 8am-9pm daily. **Main courses** $5-$9. **Credit** AmEx, Disc, MC, V. **Vegetarian**

Time to eat your greens, folks. As the name suggests, the restaurant makes its meals from the kingdom of chlorophyll: organic salads or wraps, concocted from croquettes made of chick peas, to lentils cocooned in collard green and then seasoned with curry, pesto or guacamole. **Other locations:** 14318 Ventura Boulevard, Sherman Oaks (1-818 907 8779).

West LA

Apple Pan

10801 W Pico Boulevard, at Glendon Avenue (1-310 475 3585). Bus C3, SM7, SM8, SM12, SM13, SM16/I-10, exit Overland Avenue north. **Open** 11am-midnight Tue-Thur, Sun; 11am-1am Fri, Sat. **Main courses** $5-$7. **No credit cards.** **Map** p311 A5 ⑰ **Cafés & diners**

The Apple Pan was born in 1947, when the Baker family bought a vacant lot and built the place from the ground up. The formula was simple: sandwiches, burgers and home-made pies served on paper plates and washed down with Coke, Dr Pepper or rootbeer. Sixty years later, it's hardly changed: at lunchtime, the 26 counter stools are as coveted as ever.

Bombay Café

12021 W Pico Boulevard, between S Bundy Drive & S Westgate Avenue (1-310 473 3388). Bus SM7, SM10, SM14/I-10, exit Bundy Drive north. **Open** 11.30am-3pm, 5-10pm Mon-Thur; 11.30am-3pm, 5-11pm Fri; 5-11pm Sat; 5-9.30pm Sun. **Main courses** $12-$18. **Credit** AmEx, MC, V. **Indian**

In a city with more than its fair share of mediocre Indian restaurants, the Bombay Café has built a loyal following for its masala dosas, rice pudding and mango kulfi, all washed down in time-honoured fashion by Indian beer or a cup of chai.

Monte Alban

*11927 Santa Monica Boulevard, between Brockton
& Armacost Avenues (1-310 444 7736). Bus 4,
304, SM1, SM10/I-10, exit Bundy Drive north.*
Open 8am-11pm daily. **Main courses** $5-$10.
Credit AmEx, DC, Disc, MC, V. **Mexican**
This family-run Mexican restaurant is certainly an
amiable place to spend an evening, but we're pleased
to report that the food is also terrific. The flavourful
Oaxacan specialities are well regarded here, particularly the array of complex mole sauces. Try the
sweet plantain or flan for dessert.

Mori Sushi

*11500 W Pico Boulevard, at Gateway Boulevard
(1-310 479 3939/www.morisushi.org). Bus SM7/
I-10, exit Bundy Drive north.* **Open** 11.45am-2.15pm,
6-10pm Mon-Fri; 5.30-10pm Sat. **Sushi** $2-$12.
Credit AmEx, MC, V. **Japanese**
One of the city's classier Japanese restaurants with
exotic sushi and sashimi dishes delivered in a minimalist but inspired setting with service that borders
on charming. Definitely worth the indulgence.

Tlapazola Grill

*11676 Gateway Boulevard, at S Barrington Avenue
Boulevard (1-310 477 1577). Bus SM7/I-10, exit
Bundy Drive south.* **Open** 11am-10pm Tue-Thur,
Sun; 11am-11pm Fri, Sat. **Main courses** $8-$14.
Credit MC, V. **Mexican**
Having graduated from the kitchens of Santa
Monica's Röckenwagner, a group of old friends from
Oaxaca, Mexico headed east to open their own place.
Don't be put off by the nondescript mini-mall loca-
tion: the food here is a delicious and affordable culi-
nary hybrid. Dishes such as grilled salmon with
pumpkin seed sauce and masa pancake with achiote
shrimp are served with lashings of warmth.

UCLA & Westwood Village

Nanbankan

*11330 Santa Monica Boulevard, at Corinth Avenue
(1-310 478 1591). Bus 4, 304/I-405, exit Santa
Monica Boulevard west.* **Open** 5.30-11pm daily.
Main courses $20-$25. **Credit** AmEx, Disc, MC, V.
Japanese
LA's original *robatayaki* restaurant, where chefs
labour over hibachis cooking up everything from
New Zealand lamb chops to chicken gizzards and
okra. Sit at the bar and order up a storm, but don't
be surprised if you end up overeating.

Native Foods

*1110½ Gayley Avenue, at Kinross Avenue
(1-310 209 1055/www.nativefoods.com). Bus 2,
20, 21, 302, 305, 761.* **Open** 11am-10pm daily.
Main courses $4-$9. **Credit** AmEx, DC, MC, V.
Vegetarian
Despite being part of a new-ish chain, this vegan
eaterie carries with it a quite old-fashioned earnest-
ness and frill-free ambience. Happily, the food is a
lot more enticing: even diehard carnivores might
enjoy the salads, seitan and tempeh on offer.

Tanino

*1043 Westwood Boulevard, between Weyburn
& Kinross Avenues (1-310 208 0444/www.tanino.
com). Bus 2, 302, 305, 761/I-405, exit Crenshaw
Boulevard north.* **Open** 11am-3pm, 5-11pm Mon-Fri;
5-11pm Sat; 4.30-10pm Sun. **Main courses** $12-$32.
Credit AmEx, Disc, MC, V. **Italian**
Genial Sicilian Tanino Drago – brother of Celestino,
for whose restaurants *see p141 and p163* – presides
over this elegant Westwood dining room, built in
1929 by Paul Revere Williams. The pasta dishes are
exceptional, though don't be surprised if you don't
have room for dessert.

Bel Air

Hotel Bel-Air

*701 Stone Canyon Road, at Tortuoso Way (1-310
472 1211/www.hotelbelair.com). I-405, exit Sunset
Boulevard east.* **Open** 7-10am, noon-2pm, 6.30-9.30pm
Mon-Sat; 7am-2pm, 7-10pm Sun. **Main courses**
Breakfast $11-$21. *Brunch* $54. *Lunch* $15-$25. *Dinner*
$30-$45. **Credit** AmEx, DC, Disc, MC, V. **Californian**
Driving up Stone Canyon Road to this 1920s hotel
(*see p52*) is romantic enough, but wait until you
get to the grounds. The restaurant is similarly ver-
dant: take a leisurely brunch, lunch or dinner on the
bougainvillea-draped terrace. Food includes great
hamburgers and very good pasta, fish and salads.

Century City

La Cachette

*10506 Little Santa Monica Boulevard, at Thayer
Avenue (1-310 470 4992/www.lacachetterestaurant.
com). Bus 4, 16, 304/I-405, exit Santa Monica
Boulevard east.* **Open** noon-2pm, 6-10pm Mon-Fri;
6-10pm Sat, Sun. **Main courses** $28-$35. **Credit**
AmEx, DC, MC, V. **Map** p311 A4 **⑱** **French**
This romantic, high-end restaurant serves some of
LA's finest French cuisine. Chef Jean François
Meteigner, who apprenticed in Michelin-starred
restaurants in Paris, plies his trade with deftness and
restraint. Try his provocative tasting menu, which
might include the likes of foie gras on fruit bread and
roasted squab pigeon in a red wine reduction.

Beverly Hills

Fountain Coffee Shop

*Beverly Hills Hotel, 9641 Sunset Boulevard, at N
Crescent Drive (1-310 276 2251/www.thebeverlyhills
hotel.com). Bus 2, 302/I-405, exit Sunset Boulevard
east.* **Open** 7am-7pm daily. **Main courses** $9-$16.
Credit AmEx, DC, Disc, MC, V. **Map** p311 B2 **⑲**
Cafés & diners
This cute pink-and-pistachio soda bar is just about
as legendary as the hotel's Polo Lounge (*see p147*).
Perch on a stool at the counter (built in 1949) and
order omelettes, pancakes or waffles for breakfast,
or salads, sandwiches or burgers for lunch/dinner.
Top it all off with a float. For the hotel, *see p52*.

Eat, Drink, Shop

Nate 'n Al's: a little slice of New York in the heart of Beverly Hills.

Eat, Drink, Shop

Grill on the Alley

9560 Dayton Way, at Wilshire Boulevard (1-310 276 0615/www.thegrill.com). Bus 20, 21, 720/I-405, exit Wilshire Boulevard east. **Open** 11.30am-10.30pm Mon-Thur; 11.30am-11pm Fri, Sat; 5-9pm Sun. **Main courses** $23-$40. **Credit** AmEx, DC, Disc, MC, V. **Map** p311 C3 ② **American**

Book one of the Grill's booths for lunch, then settle back for some serious anthropological research into the behaviour of Hollywood's powerbrokers. Everyone from A-list actors to their even more influential agents eats here, chowing down on the well-prepared steaks and burgers.

Kate Mantilini

9101 Wilshire Boulevard, at N Doheny Drive (1-310 278 3699). Bus 20, 21, 720/I-10, exit Robertson Boulevard north. **Open** 7.30am-midnight Mon; 7.30am-1am Tue-Thur; 7.30am-2am Fri; 11am-2am Sat; 10am-midnight Sun. **Main courses** $8-$30. **Credit** AmEx, DC, MC, V. **Map** p311 D3 ㉑ **American**

A true trend-setter, from the dressed-up American menu to the specially commissioned Morphosis-designed building in which it's served. Sit at the counter or in a booth and hunker down to Caesar salads, oversized onion rings, cheeseburgers and eggs benedict. For healthy types, there are a few low-fat chicken dishes.

Mastro's Steakhouse

246 N Canon Drive, at Dayton Way (1-310 888 8782/www.mastrosteakhouse.com). Bus 20, 21, 720/I-405, exit Wilshire Boulevard east. **Open** 5-11pm daily. **Main courses** $33-$84. **Credit** AmEx, Disc, MC, V. **Map** p311 D3 ㉒ **American**

It's loud and it's meaty, and thus, on the surface, it's more a place for cigar-chomping agents than the beautiful people. However, the A-list flood here, drawn by the old-school glamour and the great food: try the steak sashimi and the bone-in filet.

Matsuhisa

129 N La Cienega Boulevard, between Wilshire Boulevard & Clifton Way (1-310 659 9639/www. nobumatsuhisa.com). Bus 20, 21, 220, 720/I-10, exit La Cienega Boulevard north. **Open** 11.45am-2.15pm, 5.45-10.15pm Mon-Fri; 5.45-10.15pm Sat, Sun. **Main courses** $5-$28. **Credit** AmEx, DC, Disc, MC, V. **Map** p312 B4 ㉓ **Japanese**

Chef Nobuyuki Matsuhisa's merging of Japanese and Peruvian cuisines attracts expense-account eaters and celebrities. Traditional sushi is available, but Matsuhisa is most famous for his fusion dishes. For Nobu in Malibu, *see p139.*

Nate 'n Al's

414 N Beverly Drive, between Santa Monica Boulevard & Brighton Way (1-310 274 0101/ www.natenal.com). Bus 20, 21, 720/I-405, exit Wilshire Boulevard east. **Open** 7am-9pm daily. **Main courses** $7-$15. **Credit** AmEx, Disc, MC, V. **Map** p311 C3 ㉔ **Jewish**

After six decades in the heart of Beverly Hills, just about the only things that have changed at Nate 'n Al's are the prices. Eightysomething Jewish matrons and twentysomething hotshot producers chow down on blintzes and corned beef hash next at this none-more-Jewish deli. It'll be just the same in 2066.

Nic's

453 N Canon Drive, between Brighton Way & Santa Monica Boulevard (1-310 550 5707/www.nics beverlyhills.com). Bus 4, 16, 304/I-405, exit Santa Monica Boulevard east. **Open** 5-11pm Mon-Sat. **Main courses** $15-$20. **Credit** AmEx, Disc, MC, V. **Map** p311 C2 ㉕ **American**

Nic's restaurant and bar sits at the edge of Beverly Hills both geographically and metaphorically, attracting everyone from punks to politicians. The moneyed boho vibe is reflected in the food: chef Larry Nicola calls it American with ethnic flair. Check out the Vod Box, a top-shelf vodka-tasting freezer.

Polo Lounge

Beverly Hills Hotel, 9641 Sunset Boulevard, at N Crescent Drive (1-310 276 2251/www.thebeverlyhills hotel.com). Bus 2, 302/I-405, exit Sunset Boulevard east. **Open** 7am-2am daily. **Main courses** *Breakfast* $6-$16. *Lunch* $15-$34. *Dinner* $23-$40. **Credit** AmEx, DC, MC, V. **Map** p311 B2 **㉖ American**

A not-to-be-missed piece of Old Hollywood, where the power breakfast was invented and having a phone brought to your table became a legendary Hollywood ruse. The hotel was left intact: million-dollar deals are still sealed over eggs benedict, while romantic interludes are shared on the charming patio.

Porta Via

424 N Canon Drive, at Brighton Way (1-310 274 6534). Bus 4, 20, 21, 304, 720/I-405, exit Wilshire Boulevard east. **Open** 7.30am-3pm Mon; 7.30am-10pm Tue-Sat; 9am-3pm Sun. **Main courses** $10-$25. **Credit** AmEx, Disc, MC, V. **Map** p311 C2 **㉗ Californian**

The Californian-Italian cuisine served here includes Denzel Washington's favourite burger, along with chopped salads and daily fish and meat specials. You can eat at the bar, or take a sidewalk table and eat while watching the well-heeled strut by.

Spago of Beverly Hills

176 N Canon Drive, between Clifton Way & Wilshire Boulevard (1-310 385 0880/www.wolfgangpuck. com). Bus 4, 20, 21, 304, 720/I-405, exit Wilshire Boulevard east. **Open** 11.30am-2.15pm, 5.30-10.30pm Mon-Thur; 11.30am-2.15pm, 5.30-11pm Fri; noon-2.30pm, 5.30-11pm Sat; 5.30-10.30pm Sun. **Main courses** $20-$50. **Credit** AmEx, DC, Disc, MC, V. **Map** p311 D3 **㉘ Californian**

Wolfgang Puck closed the original Spago in 2001, but this version had opened three years earlier. It's a huge extravaganza, with Italian glass chandeliers, Hockneys and Picassos on the walls, and a wall of glass that shows the chefs at work. The food is classic Puck: designer pizzas, light California cuisine with Far East influences, and modern Austrian dishes.

West Hollywood, Hollywood & Midtown

West Hollywood

Ago

8478 Melrose Avenue, at N La Cienaga Boulevard (1-323 655 6333). Bus 10, 11, 105, 705/I-10, exit La Cienega Boulevard north. **Open** noon-2.30pm, 6-11pm Mon-Thur; noon-2.30pm, 6-11.30pm Fri, Sat; 6-10pm Sun. **Main courses** $24-$44. **Credit** AmEx, DC, Disc, MC, V. **Map** p312 B2 **㉙ Italian**

Celebrities, Italian American gents and beautiful women converge on Ago nightly: some for the excellent Italian menu, others for the extensive wine list, others still for the energetic atmosphere. You may have to wait for your table, but you'll be treated like a long-lost family member by way of compensation.

Blue Bamboo

359 N La Cienega Boulevard, between Oakwood Avenue & Beverly Boulevard (1-310 854 0622/ www.bluebamboo.cc). Bus 14, 105, 705, 714. **Open** noon-10pm Tue-Thur; noon-11pm Fri, Sat; 5-10pm Sun. **Main courses** $12-$18. **Credit** AmEx, Disc, MC, V. **Map** p312 B3 **㉚ Thai**

Don't let its proximity to a girlie bar put you off: the family-run Blue Bamboo offers the freshest, spiciest and most authentic Thai food in town. A good place to start is with the chicken larb served in crisp lettuce leaves. Other fine choices include the green papaya salad and the tom yum kai soup, or pick from myriad entrées and noodle dishes.

Dan Tana's

9071 Santa Monica Boulevard, between N Doheny Drive & Nemo Street (1-310 275 9444/www. dantanas.com). Bus 4, 304/I-10, exit Robertson Boulevard north. **Open** 5pm-1am daily. **Main courses** $17-$40. **Credit** AmEx, Disc, MC, V. **Map** p312 A2 **㉛ Italian**

A local favourite since 1964, this late-night restaurant is still a vivacious place, frequented by film and TV stars, sports personalities, the rank and file of the movie industry and those just after a bit of Hollywood history. The food is simple, hearty Italian fare, and the staff are terrific fun.

Dominick's

8715 Beverly Boulevard, between San Vicente Boulevard & Robertson Boulevard (1-310 652 2335/ www.dominicksrestaurant.com). Bus 14, 220, 305, 550, 714, exit Robertson Boulevard north. **Open** 6-11.30pm Mon-Thur; 6pm-12.30am Fri-Sun. **Main courses** $14-$41. **Credit** AmEx, Disc, MC, V. **Map** p312 A3 **㉜ Italian**

The Rat Pack gathered in the original Dominick's in the 1950s, which may be why diners tend to prefer the vintage leather booths to the patio tables. The whole place hums at night with young revellers stuffing themselves with simple Italian American fare (stuffed mushrooms, fettucine carbonara).

Griddle Café

7916 W Sunset Boulevard, at Fairfax Avenue (1-323 874 0377/www.thegriddlecafe.com). Bus 2, 217, 302, 717/I-10, exit Fairfax Avenue north. **Open** 7am-4pm Mon-Fri; 8am-4pm Sat, Sun. **Main courses** $6-$13. **Credit** AmEx, Disc, MC, V. **Map** p312 C1 **㉝ Cafés & diners**

A greasy spoon as only West Hollywood knows how, which is to say that it's not in the least bit greasy. Buff young hunks and hunkettes munch breakfast standards and lunchtime sandwiches; they're watching your figure, even if you're not.

Cajun Bistro (8301 Sunset Boulevard) When it was Source, Woody Allen tries the mashed yeast and unsuccessfully proposes to Diane Keaton in *Annie Hall*

Eat, Drink, Shop

Designs for dining

Dodd Mitchell has designed more restaurants than he's had bad dinners. A high-school dropout with no formal design training, Mitchell worked as a set designer on music videos before applying his signature look – sensual and dramatic, with elemental Zen moderne materials – to everything from the **Sushi Roku** chain (see p141) to the **Hollywood Roosevelt Hotel** (see p60). In a city where a celebrity sighting sometimes takes precedence over the food, decor is important. Says Mitchell: 'I follow my heart and then it somehow falls together.'

There's always a stop-you-in-your-tracks element in Mitchell's designs. At the hip Japanese hangout **Katana** in West Hollywood (8439 W Sunset Boulevard, 1-323 650 8585, www.katanarobata.com), it's an infinity waterfall; at Hollywood Italian **Dolce** (8284 Melrose Avenue, 1-323 852 7174, www.dolceenoteca.com), the fire-illuminated bar catches the eye. And at **Dakota** (see p150), the leather lace curtain separating the hostess station from the restaurant was inspired, claims Mitchell, after he watched a woman unlace her thigh-high boot on an adult movie. The designer's resumé also includes **Balboa** at the Grafton (see p58); the **Falcon** restaurant-lounge in Hollywood (7213 W Sunset Boulevard, 1-323 850 5350, www.falconslair.com), co-designed with architects John Friedman and Alice Kimm; and the **Lodge Steakhouse** (14 N La Cienega Boulevard, Beverly Hills, 1-310 854 0024; pictured), a 1950s spin on a log cabin theme.

Mitchell is generally hired to produce designs that will attract a hip and spendy crowd. And if he's unavailable, then Thomas Schoos steps into the breach with his own brand of Asian Moderne stylings. **Koi** (see p149) is a case in point, a restaurant where the scenesters come to be seen against a backdrop that melds indoor and out.

Schoos is also responsible for the sweeping, fabric-draped cabañas at **O Bar** (8279 Santa Monica Boulevard, West Hollywood, 1-323 822 3300, www.obarrestaurant.com) and **Citizen Smith** (1600 N Cahuenga Boulevard, Hollywood, 1-323 461 5001, www.citizen smith.com), an industrial loft that looks like it belongs on Bleecker Street.

When innovative chef Suzanne Goin teamed up with hubby David Lentz to open the **Hungry Cat** (see p151), they hired Johnston MarkLee to design it. The result is a whimsical take on the East Coast seafood joint: old world materials, curved walls, a zinc bar, solid oak furniture. It's both hip and contemporary without the noise of a Mitchell design. But then the two restaurants have different clients.

Hirozen

8385 Beverly Boulevard, between N Orlando Avenue & N Kings Road (1-323 653 0470/www.hirozen. com). Bus 14/I-10, exit La Cienega Boulevard north. **Open** 11.30am-2.30pm, 6-10pm daily. **Main courses** $5-$20. **Credit** AmEx, DC, Disc, MC, V. **Map** p312 B3 ㉞ **Japanese**
If you ever drive past this mini-mall and spy a long line, the chances are everyone's waiting to get into Hirozen. On top of the traditional sushi, iconoclastic chef Hiroji Obayashi conjures up some quietly inventive dishes. Try to book ahead.

Il Sole

8741 Sunset Boulevard, between N La Cienega & San Vicente Boulevards (1-310 657 1182). Bus 2, 105, 302, 705/I-10, exit La Cienega Boulevard north. **Open** 6-10pm daily. **Main courses** $25-$50. **Credit** AmEx, DC, MC, V. **Map** p312 A1 ㉟ **Italian**
Authentic Tuscan cooking – filet with shaved truffles, lightly dressed lobster salad – is served in this multi-room Sunset Plaza restaurant. We prefer to dine amid the dusty bottles of priceless wine down in the cellar while watching everyone from Mick Jagger to Steven Spielberg get stuck in.

Ivy

113 N Robertson Boulevard, at Alden Drive (1-310 274 8303). Bus 14, 16, 220, LDF, LDHWH/I-10, exit Robertson Boulevard north. **Open** 11.30am-11pm Mon-Fri; 11am-11pm Sat; 10am-11pm Sun. **Main courses** $20-$50. **Credit** AmEx, DC, Disc, MC, V. **Map** p312 A3 ㊱ **Californian**
LA's ultimate star-spotting restaurant is still going strong. Diners continue to grumble about the rude service, but that doesn't seem to affect its status: the celebs still flock here (especially for lunch), the plebs follow. Good bets include the excellent salads and fresh fish dishes, but the real forte are desserts.

Jar

8225 Beverly Boulevard, at N Harper Avenue (1-323 655 6566/www.thejar.com). Bus 14/I-10, exit Fairfax Avenue north. **Open** 5.30-10pm Mon-Thur, Sun; 5.30-11pm Fri, Sat; 10am-2pm Sun. **Main courses** $19-$41. **Credit** AmEx, MC, V. **Map** p312 B3 ㊲ **American**
Headed by chef Suzanne Tracht, this classy chophouse has gained a deserved reputation for its New York steaks and braised pork belly. Sauces run from lobster béarnaise to tamarind; superior side dishes include duck-fried rice and braised mustard greens.

In another brief, the firm created a calm and fresh environment for **Orchid** in Santa Monica (*see p141*). The designers came up with a palette of forms and colours rooted in Eastern cultures but made from unconventional materials. The custom-made ceiling panels pack the biggest punch, forming a canopy that diffuses light through translucent, undulating organic shapes that suggest the patterns and shapes of orchids.

At **Meson G** (*see p154*), multi-talented chef/owner Liza Goodell and designer Sandy Davidson combined 1960s mod with 21st-century chic to produce one of LA's most eye-catching restaurants. The stainless steel counter is striking; other light-hearted modern elements include Hermès orange banquettes, a marble bar and a delightful twig sculpture that stretches across the dining room.

'The last four or five years, restaurants have been very brown and conservative,' says Goodell. 'We didn't want to create a holier-than-thou temple, where you have to be quiet while you order your Martinis. We would love [patrons] to dance on the tables. But fun for me isn't going to a nightclub. I'm not 20! I didn't want dark bathrooms, firewalls or fountains.'

Perhaps ironically, Liza and husband Tim now preside over Dakota and **25 Degrees** (*see p151*), but they only took over after Dodd Mitchell's designs were in place. And in any case, as Mitchell points out, a restaurant's appearance can only take it so far. 'Ultimately, if the food isn't good and the staff aren't friendly, what the restaurant looks like doesn't matter.'

Eat, Drink, Shop

Koi

730 N La Cienega Boulevard, between Melrose Avenue & Santa Monica Boulevard (1-310 659 9449). Bus 10, 11, 105, 705/I-10, exit La Cienega Boulevard north. **Open** 6-11pm Mon-Wed, Sun; 6-11.30pm Thur; 6pm-midnight Fri, Sat. **Main courses** $12-$29. **Credit** AmEx, Disc, MC, V. **Map** p312 B2 ❸ **Japanese**

One of designer Thomas Schoos' dramatic Zen creations, this cavernous restaurant features a cool bar, several outdoor patios and lots of stone and fire elements. The food is Japanese nightclub fare, big on presentation but smaller on content. If you like to gawk at LA scenesters, you're in the right place.

Lucques

8474 Melrose Avenue, at N La Cienega Boulevard (1-323 655 6277). Bus 10, 11, 105, 705/I-10, exit La Cienega Boulevard north. **Open** 6-10pm Mon; noon-2.30pm Tue; noon-2.30pm, 6-11pm Wed-Sat; 5-10pm Sun. **Main courses** $14-$44. **Credit** AmEx, DC, MC, V. **Map** p312 B2 ❸ **French**

Suzanne Goin's restaurant is one of the most delightful in town. The inventive French-Mediterranean seasonal food (such as roasted beet salad with fried chickpeas, suckling pig with pabada astrurianna) is inventive; the lunch and Sunday dinner *prix fixe* menus are easier on the pocket. Trivia: the restaurant is in Harold Lloyd's former carriage house.

Orso

8706 W 3rd Street, at S Hamel Road (1-310 274 7144/www.orsorestaurant.com). Bus 16, 220/I-10, exit La Cienega Boulevard north. **Open** 11.45am-11pm daily. **Main courses** $14-$28. **Credit** MC, V. **Map** p312 A3 ❹ **Italian**

Sitting on the becalmed, casually elegant back patio at Orso, it's easy to forget you're in LA. Or, at least, it would be if it weren't for all those celebs: Faye Dunaway's a regular, while shy Jennifer Jason Leigh chooses a corner table by the foliage. And the food? The pizzas are thinner than the girls, the liver and onions are tremendous and the pasta is superb.

Palm

9001 Santa Monica Boulevard, at Doheny Drive (1-310 550 8811/www.thepalm.com). Bus 4, 304/I-10, exit Robertson Boulevard north. **Open** noon-10.30pm Mon-Fri; 5-10.30pm Sat; 5-9.30pm Sun. **Main courses** $16-$38. **Credit** AmEx, Disc, MC, V. **Map** p312 A2 ❹ **American**

We ⊘ LA Cellphones

In LA, a city always on the move (or, at least, stuck in traffic), cellphones are a necessity, as vital as comlinks on the *Starship Enterprise*. Unfortunately, this means that LA is the world's capital of wireless rudeness. Keep an eye out for cellphone-happy drivers steering with their knees, or pedestrians standing in the middle of traffic talking on their phones even after the lights have changed.

Worst of all, though, inconsiderate phone etiquette has invaded LA's restaurants. Sit down for lunch at any restaurant in Beverly Hills or West Hollywood, and it won't be long before you see and hear TV types breaking off their power-lunch to set up a power-dinner, doctors loudly discussing their latest stomach surgery, even loved-up couples calling each other from the restrooms.

Many restaurateurs see such ill-mannered behaviour as a necessary evil – honestly, would you like to tell Tom Cruise he has to get off the phone with Katie? – but some have had enough and created 'cellphone only' areas modelled after smoking sections (remember them?). **Millie's** in Silver Lake (*see p158*) took a more aggressive tack several years ago, displaying a 'No Cellphones!' sign on the front of its menu. Perhaps a little extreme, but, in this town at least, still wholly laudable. Turn 'em off, people. It's not important. It can *wait*.

Eat, Drink, Shop

Given the transient nature of the city and its main business, a sense of history is rare in LA restaurants. All the more reason then to visit the Palm. However, historically minded vegetarians should stay away: eating here involves being able to deal with over-sized slabs of red meat, the rarer the better. This is the sort of restaurant where men come to celebrate a deal being struck, over simple American fare and with familial service by staff who've been in situ for years. Many of the diners are regulars, and tables are like well-fought-over real estate.

Sona

401 N La Cienega Boulevard, between Oakwood & Rosewood Avenues (1-310 659 7708/www. sonarestaurant.com). Bus 10, 11, 105/I-10, exit La Cienega Boulevard north. **Open** 6-10.30pm Tue-Thur; 6-11.30pm Fri; 5.30-11.30pm Sat. **Main courses** $32-$38. **Credit** AmEx, DC, Disc, MC, V. **Map** p312 B3 **㊸ French**

Sona's design is downright dreamy, but David Myers' modern French food is even more impressive. Served on Bernadout china, it's full of lovely touches: a nasturtium leaf floats atop cold poached salmon; tapioca adorns the roasted line-caught cod. The tasting menu is worth the sticker price. His wife Michele wows with her desserts: try the strawberry rhubarb strudel with mascarpone sorbet.

Hollywood

Ammo

1155 N Highland Avenue, between Lexington Avenue & Santa Monica Boulevard (1-323 871 2666/ www.ammocafe.com). Bus 4, 156, 304/US 101, exit Highland Avenue south. **Open** 11am-3pm, 6-10pm Mon-Thur; 11am-3pm, 6-11pm Fri; 10am-3pm, 6-11pm Sat; 10am-3pm Sun. **Main courses** $9-$25. **Credit** AmEx, MC, V. **Map** p313 A2 **㊸ American**

Ammo's gritty location lends it a certain cred. Stylists, editors and other industry folk flock to the groovy, low-key space for simple, well-prepared comfort food: turkey burgers, brown rice with chicken stir fry and chopped vegetable salad, all chased down with home-made ice-cream sandwiches.

Dakota

Hollywood Roosevelt, 7000 Hollywood Boulevard, at Orange Drive (1-323 769 8888/www.dakota-restaurant.com). Metro Hollywood-Highland/bus 156, 212, 217, 312, 717, LDHWH/US 101, exit Highland Avenue south. **Open** 6-11am, 11.30am-2.30pm, 6-11pm Mon-Thur, Sun; 6-11am, 11.30am-2.30pm, 6-11.30pm Fri, Sat. **Main courses** $13-$50. **Credit** AmEx, DC, Disc, MC, V. **Map** p312 A1 **㊹ American**

Tim and Liza Goodell's retro American steakhouse is a good-looking place, designed by Dodd Mitchell in stone, black leather and dark wood. However, it's not just the design and the location – in the hip Hollywood Roosevelt hotel (*see p60*) – that draws a glamorous crowd: the food is excellent.

Geisha House

6633 Hollywood Boulevard, at Cherokee Avenue (1-323 460 6300/www.geishahousehollywood.com). Metro Hollywood-Highland/bus 156, 212, 217, 312, 717/US 101, exit Highland Avenue south. **Open** 6pm-2am daily. **Main courses** $12-$42. **Credit** AmEx, MC, V. **Map** p313 A1 **㊺ Japanese**

Your mother probably told you it's rude to watch TV while eating. But you're in Hollywood now, where a large screen and myriad smaller ones relay flicks to a sometimes heaving bar. A wall of fireplaces is the centrepiece of the bi-level dining room; celebrities join the bridge-and-tunnel crowd nightly, as eye-catching as the immaculate fish atop the plain white rice they pop into perfect mouths.

Hungry Cat

1535 N Vine, at W Sunset Boulevard (1-323 462 2155/www.thehungrycat.com). Metro Hollywood-Vine/bus 2, 210, 302, 710, exit Cahuenga Boulevard south. **Open** 5.30pm-midnight Mon, Sat; 11.30am-2.30pm, 5.30pm-midnight Tue-Fri; 11am-3pm, 5.30pm-midnight Sun. **Main courses** $9-$12. **Credit** AmEx, Disc, MC, V. **Map** p313 B2 **46 American**
Lacquered walls, a snaking zinc bar and oak furniture work in juxtaposition with David Lenz and spouse Suzanne Goin's spin on East Coast seafood. It's a fun place to enjoy a full raw bar, succulent lobster rolls or a hearty bowl of little neck clams, accompanied by a fine muscadet from the Loire Valley.

Mario's Peruvian Seafood

5786 Melrose Avenue, at N Vine Street (1-323 466 4181). Bus 10, 11, 210, 710/I-10, exit La Brea Avenue north. **Open** 11.30am-8.30pm Mon-Thur, Sun; 11.30am-10pm Fri, Sat. **Main courses** $7-$13. **Credit** AmEx, Disc, MC, V. **Map** p313 B3 **47 Peruvian**
No wonder there's often a line outside this Peruvian hole-in-the-wall: the food at Mario's is both cheap and delicious. Highlights include siete mares (seven seas seafood soup), lomo saltado (strips of beef sautéed with onions and tomatoes, served with French fries) and a hot guacamole sauce. Worth the wait.

Memphis

6541 Hollywood Boulevard, between Whitley Avenue & Schrader Boulevard (1-323 465 8600/ www.memphishollywood.com). Metro Hollywood-Highland/bus 2, 156, 210, 212, 217, 302, 312, 717, LDHWH/US 101, exit Cahuenga Boulevard south. **Open** 6pm-1am Mon-Sat; 11am-4pm, 6pm-1am Sun. **Main courses** $18-$34. **Credit** AmEx, DC, Disc, MC, V. **Map** p313 B1 **48 American**
This newcomer is tucked away in a two-storey house that seems out of place on the West Coast. Tricked out in a deep burgundy and black palette, downstairs holds a relaxing two-room bar; upstairs, tables are scattered throughout more rooms. The food is hearty Southern fare – fried chicken, baby back ribs – and the service attentive.

Providence

5955 Melrose Avenue, at Cole Avenue (1-323 460 4170/www.providencela.com). Bus 10, 11/US 101, exit Cahuenga Boulevard south. **Open** 6-10pm Mon, Tue; noon-2.30pm, 6-10pm Wed-Fri; 5.30-10pm Sat; 5.30-9pm Sun. **Main courses** $32-$38. **Credit** AmEx, DC, Disc, MC, V. **Map** p313 B3 **49 Fish & seafood**
Together with partner and maître d' Donato Poto, Michael Cimarusti has created an exquisite dining experience, where flavour and presentation are paramount. The five- or nine-course tasting menus are superlative, offering such delights as a single Santa Barbara spot prawn, served alongside a shot glass of blood orange gelée with sweet peas and olive oil. For dessert, Pink Lady apples roasted in honey, served with hazelnuts, goat's cheese ice-cream and rosemary, is immaculate.

Roscoe's House of Chicken & Waffles

1514 N Gower Street, at W Sunset Boulevard (1-323 466 7453/www.roscoeschickenandwaffles.com). Metro Hollywood-Vine/bus 2, 302, LDHWI/US 101, exit Gower Street south. **Open** 8.30am-midnight Mon-Thur, Sun; 8.30am-4am Fri, Sat. **Main courses** $4-$10. **Credit** AmEx, Disc, MC, V. **Map** p313 B2 **50 American**
The dimly lit, carefully under-decorated Hollywood branch of this funky southern joint (there are four others in town, from Pasadena to Long Beach) delights locals for its late opening hours and low prices, but most of all for its fantastic fried chicken. On a diet? Don't even think about it.
Other locations: throughout the city.

25 Degrees

Hollywood Roosevelt, 7000 Hollywood Boulevard, at N Orange Drive (1-323 785 7244/www.25degrees restaurant.com). Metro Hollywood-Highland/bus 156, 212, 217, 312, 717, LDHWH/US 101, exit Highland Avenue south. **Open** 5pm-1am daily. **Main courses** $10-$13. **Credit** AmEx, Disc, MC, V. **Map** p313 A1 **51 American**
Tim and Liza Goodell (of Dakota; *see p150*) here present their twist on the trad burger joint. The beef is sirloin, the cheese doesn't come in packets, there are

Hollywood's **Hungry Cat.**

OUR CLIMATE NEEDS
A HELPING HAND TODAY

Be a smart traveller. Help to offset your carbon emissions from your trip by pledging Carbon Trees with Trees for Cities.

All the Carbon Trees that you donate through Trees for Cities are genuinely planted as additional trees in our projects.

Trees for Cities is an independent charity working with local communities on tree planting projects.

www.treesforcities.org   Tel 020 7587 1320

Trees for Cities
Charity registration number 1032154

over 20 dipping sauces, and the drinks list includes more than 50 imported and domestic wines to sip, by the glass or half bottle. Not exactly McDonald's. Oh, and the name? That's the temperature difference between meat medium rare and well done.

Fairfax District

AOC

8022 W 3rd Street, at S Laurel Avenue (1-323 653 6359/www.aocwinebar.com). Bus 16, 217, 218, LDF/ I-10, exit Fairfax Avenue north. **Open** 6-11pm Mon-Fri; 5.30-11pm Sat; 5.30-10pm Sun. **Main courses** $9-$18. **Credit** AmEx, DC, Disc, MC, V. **Map** p312 C3 ⓢ **French**
The name stands for Appellation d'Origine Contrôlée, which is the system for certifying the regional origin of food and wine in France. AOC might be a long way from France, but the food, served in small, tapas-like portions, is exquisite: dishes might include salad of arugula, persimmon and hazelnut strewn with pomegranate seeds, or braised pork cheeks with a mustard gremolata. The wine selection is strong, particularly the reds. Reservations are hard to come by; if all else fails, ask for a seat at the bar.

Angelini Osteria

7313 Beverly Boulevard, at Poinsettia Place (1-323 297 0070/www.angeliniosteria.com). Bus 14, 714/ I-10, exit La Brea Avenue north. **Open** noon-2.30pm, 5.30-10.30pm Tue-Fri; 5.30-10.30pm Sat, Sun. **Main courses** $18-$32. **Credit** AmEx, Disc, MC, V. **Map** p312 D3 ⓢ **Italian**
What this *boîte* lacks in atmosphere, it makes up for in lively, more-ish food. At lunchtimes, it's awash with local workers; the evenings, on the other hand, see a mix of families and couples settling in to a simple, well-prepared menu that might include a wheatberry salad with red onions, and cherry tomatoes with olive oil and balsamic dressing.

Canter's Deli

419 N Fairfax Avenue, at Oakwood Avenue (1-323 651 2030/www.cantersdeli.com). Bus 14, 217, 218/ I-10, exit Fairfax Avenue north. **Open** 24hrs daily.
Credit Disc, MC, V. **Map** p312 C3 ⓢ **Jewish**
Like many of its regulars, this restaurant is more than 70 years old but still going strong regardless. Knishes, kishkas, blintzes and bagels are all on the menu, served around the clock in an austere but by no means unpleasant room. Classic old LA.

Cobras & Matadors

7615 Beverly Boulevard, between N Curson & N Stanley Avenues (1-323 932 6178). Bus 14, 714/ I-10, exit Fairfax Avenue north. **Open** 6-11pm Mon-Thur, Sun; 6pm-midnight Fri, Sat. **Tapas** $6-$18. **Credit** MC, V. **Map** p312 C3 ⓢ **Spanish**
Expect to wait for a table at this hip Spanish tapas bar, owned by Steven Arroyo. Inside, it's noisy but fun; outside on the sidewalk, you can dine under heat lamps. Ensure you pick up a bottle of something suitably Spanish from their nearby wine store.

Doughboys

8136 W 3rd Street, at Crescent Heights Boulevard (1-323 651 4202/www.doughboys.net). Bus 16, 218, 316, LDF/I-10, exit Fairfax Avenue north. **Open** 7am-midnight daily. **Main courses** $7-$10. **Credit** AmEx, Disc, MC, V. **Map** p312 C3 ⓢ **Cafés & diners**
Some argue that this bakery/café is a victim of its own success; certainly, it's packed on weekends, and not only with shoppers trawling the boutiques of W 3rd Street. Still, though you may have to hang around for your food, the exquisite sandwiches and naughty cakes are worth the wait. Just.

Grace

7360 Beverly Boulevard, between N Martel & N Fuller Avenues (1-323 934 4400/www.grace restaurant.com). Bus 14/I-10, exit La Brea Avenue north. **Open** 6-10.30pm Tue-Thur; 6-11pm Fri, Sat; 6-10pm Sun. **Main courses** $18-$32. **Credit** AmEx, DC, Disc, MC, V. **Map** p312 D3 ⓢ **Californian**
Michael Berman's design provides a good-looking backdrop for one of LA's best-looking crowds. Chef Neil Fraser's cooking is ambitious, probably best sampled via the tasting menu. Offerings might include Dungeness crab salad or wild boar tenderloin.

India Sweet House

5992 W Pico Boulevard, at Stearns Drive (1-323 934 5193/www.isweethouse.com). Bus 105, 217, SM5, SM7/I-10, exit La Cienega Boulevard north. **Open** 11am-9pm daily. **Main courses** $3-$15. **No credit cards. Map** p312 B5 ⓢ **Indian**
Indian restaurants are common in this neighbourhood, but despite being more take-out vegetarian café than restaurant, India Sweets is a maharajah among them. Try the thali, and leave room for the sugary (of course) and irresistible desserts.

Joan's on Third

8350 W 3rd Street, between S Kings Road & S Flores Street (1-323 655 2285/www.joansonthird. com). Bus 16, 316, LDF/I-10, exit Fairfax Avenue north. **Open** 10am-8pm Mon-Sat; 11am-6pm Sun. **Main courses** $6-$20. **Credit** AmEx, MC, V. **Map** p312 B3 ⓢ **Cafés & diners**
This friendly, family-run deli and café is a superb lunch spot, but also a fab place to stock up for an impromptu picnic. Favourites include soups, salads, chicken and rib dishes, fine imported cheeses and charcuterie, bonbons and legendary cupcakes. They've expanded next door, making dining a more commodious affair, and now offer breakfast.

M Café de Chaya

7119 Melrose Avenue, at N La Brea Avenue (1-323 525 0588). Bus 10, 11, 212, 312/US 101, exit Highland Avenue south. **Open** 9am-9pm daily. **Main courses** $9-$15. **Credit** AmEx, MC, V. **Map** p312 D2 ⓢ **Health food**
About as healthy as you can get while stuffing your face: organic, macrobiotic-style eating in a cafeteria ambience. Still, that doesn't mean the food is dull: the Korean-style bibimbap seems positively sinful.

Farmers Market favourites

Now well into its eighth decade of operation, the Farmers Market is still going strong. That said, it's changed considerably over the years. Its origins were humble indeed: in 1934, local farmers began selling produce on this site, then a derelict lot, from the backs of their trucks.

A handful of stalls do still sell fresh groceries here, but they're now far outnumbered by restaurant operations: more than 30 in total, offering a virtual round-the-world culinary road trip on the corner of 3rd and Fairfax. Alongside the historic **Du-Par's** restaurant (1-323 933 8446, www.dupars.com), once again serving home-style specials after a refurbishment, here are our favourite stands...

● **Bryan's Pit BBQ** (#740, 1-323 931 2869) serves good old-fashioned Texas 'cue transplanted to LA. Get a pork sandwich with a side of baked yam.

● **Deano's Gourmet Pizza** (#310, 1-323 935 6373). Patsy Amore's (#448) dishes up more basic NY-style pizza, but we prefer the fare at Deano's: healthy options, headily topped.

● **Gumbo Pot** (#312, 1-323 933 0358, www.thegumbopotla.com) offers a little bit Nawleens food. Jambayala and po'boys.

● **Lotería! Grill** (#322, 1-323 930 2211, www.loteriagrill.com) doesn't quite live up to some of its wilder plaudits, but the Mexican food here is very decent indeed.

● **Tusquella's Fish & Oyster Bar**'s (#436, 1-323 939 2078) not inconsiderable appeal can be summed up in three glorious words: catfish and chips.

Once you're done, get dessert at **Bennett's Old-Fashioned Ice-Cream** (#548, 1-323 939 6786), and then wash it down with something from the good range of beers sold at **326** (#326, 1-323 549 2156) or **EB's** (#408, 1-323 549 2157). Smokers will be delighted to learn that since the market, while covered, is classed as open air, puffing is permitted.

The Farmers Market is located on the corner of W 3rd Street and S Fairfax Avenue, and it is open from 9am-9pm during the week, 9am-8pm on Saturdays and 10am-7pm on Sundays. For more details, see www.farmersmarketla.com.

Eat, Drink, Shop

Meson G

6703 Melrose Avenue, at N Citrus Avenue (1-323 525 1415/www.mesongrestaurant.com). Bus 10, 11, 212, 312/US 101, exit Highland Avenue south. **Open** 6-11pm daily. **Main courses** $22-$38. **Credit** AmEx, DC, Disc, MC, V. **Map** p313 A3 ⑥ **Mediterranean**

Meson is one of the city's prettiest restaurants, but the food more than matches the aesthetics. Crispy pork belly, avocado, serrano ham and fried egg played with our minds, while sashimi of yellow tail, blood orange and mint toyed with our hearts. Try, if you can, one of the two tasting menus of either five or nine courses: they're dear, but worth every cent.

Ortolan

8338 W 3rd Street, between S Kings Road & Flores Street (1-323 653 3300/www.ortolanrestaurant.com). Bus 16, 218, 316, LDF/I-10, exit Fairfax Avenue north. **Open** 6-10pm Mon-Sat. **Main courses** $28-$38. **Credit** AmEx, DC, Disc, MC, V. **Map** p312 B3 ⑥ **French**

The decor is eye-catching – white on white rooms, a parade of overhanging chandeliers, antique wooden floors – but wait until you see the food presentation. The soup arrives in test tubes; the palette-cleansing sorbet comes in paper-wrapped wafers. The less splashy dishes are even better: try lamb pastilla for two. The name? A small, rare bird eaten on the sly by French gourmands. **Photo** *p155*.

Table 8

7661 Melrose Avenue, between N Stanley & N Spaulding Avenues (1-323 782 8258/ www.table8la.com). Bus 10, 11, 217, 218, LDF/ I-10, exit Fairfax north. **Open** 6-10.30pm Mon-Thur; 6-11pm Fri, Sat. **Main courses** $17-$30. **Credit** AmEx, DC, Disc, MC, V. **Map** p312 C2 ⑥ **Mediterranean**

Named for the table at Chadwick's where entrepreneur Chris Heyman and chef Govind Armstrong first hatched plans to open a restaurant together, Table 8 manages to be both elegant and hip. The upscale international/Mediterranean food really grabs the attention: start with the green bean salad with duck prosciutto, and be sure to follow it with the flatiron steak.

Toast

8221 W 3rd Street, at Harper Avenue (1-323 655 5018). Bus 16, 316, LDF/I-10, exit Fairfax Avenue north. **Open** 7.30am-6pm daily. **Main courses** $8-$12. **Credit** AmEx, MC, V. **Map** p312 B3 ⑥ **Cafés & diners**

As the name implies, breakfast is the main thing at this fashionable, lively hangout on W 3rd Street: options range from the healthy to the sinful, all served in impressive portions to a good-looking crowd fresh from the shops or the gym. However, it's not the only thing: the lunch menu includes some perfectly extravagant sandwiches.

Miracle Mile & Midtown

Campanile
*624 S La Brea Avenue, between W 6th Street &
Wilshire Boulevard (1-323 938 1447/www.campanile
restaurant.com). Bus 20, 21, 212, 720/I-10, exit La
Brea Avenue north.* **Open** 11.30am-2.30pm, 6-10pm
Mon-Wed; 11.30am-2.30pm, 5.30-11pm Thur, Fri;
9.30am-1.30pm, 5.30-11pm Sat; 9.30am-1.30pm Sun.
Main courses *Brunch* $6-$15. *Lunch* $14-$18.
Dinner $24-$45. **Credit** AmEx, DC, Disc, MC, V.
Map p312 D4 **65** **Californian**
Campanile is gorgeous to look at, with graceful
arches, skylights and an atrium. And owner chef
Mark Peel, a Spago alumnus, serves up some of the
city's most reliable Cal-Med fare with esoteric wine
pairings. The recently renovated bar, by young
architect Ana Henton, is another option.

Inaka
*131 S La Brea Avenue, between W 1st & W 2nd
Streets (1-323 936 9353/www.inakarestaurant.com).
Bus 14, 16, 212/I-10, exit La Brea Avenue north.*
Open noon-12.30pm, 6-9.45pm Tue-Fri; 5.30-9.45pm
Sat; 5.30-9pm Sun. **Main courses** $9-$19. **Credit**
AmEx, MC, V. **Map** p312 D4 **66** **Japanese**
This macrobiotic restaurant, tarted up in a Zen style,
is a tranquil spot for a healthy lunch or dinner (albeit
a rather bland one). The menu includes soups, salads, beans, seafood, vegetables and fish. Part of its
ethos is to take time with the preparation of the food,
so come prepared to wait.

Versailles
*1415 S La Cienega Boulevard, between W Pico
Boulevard & Alcott Street (1-310 289 0392).
Bus 105/I-10, exit La Cienega Boulevard south.*
Open 11am-10pm daily. **Main courses** $9-$15.
Credit AmEx, MC, V. **Map** p312 B5 **67** **Cuban**
A funky no-frills Cuban joint, boasting decent food,
blink-and-you'll-miss-it service and keen prices – no
wonder the LAPD love it. Try the garlic chicken
served with sweet raw onion and fried plantains on
white rice with black beans.
Other locations: 10319 Venice Boulevard, at Motor
Avenue, Culver City (1-310 558 3168).

Hancock Park

Girasole
*225½ N Larchmont Boulevard, between Beverly
Boulevard & W 1st Street (1-323 464 6978). Bus
14, 210, 710, 714/I-10, exit La Brea Avenue north.*
Open 5.30-11pm Tue, Sat; noon-3pm, 5.30-11pm
Wed-Fri. **Main courses** $14-$22. **Credit** AmEx,
MC, V. **Map** p313 B4 **68** **Italian**
This relatively authentic trattoria is one of the
better restaurants on a strip with a few too many
mediocre eating options. Ermanno takes care of
things out front, while Sonia cooks up a storm in the
back. The rigatoni with sausage, olives and piquant
tomato sauce is especially good. Bring a bottle of
wine, or get one from the wine store next door.

Prado
*244 N Larchmont Boulevard, between W 1st
Street & Beverly Boulevard (1-323 467 3871).
Bus 14, 210, 710, 714/I-10, exit La Brea Avenue
west.* **Open** 11.30am-3pm, 5.30-10pm Mon-Sat;
4.30-9.30pm Sun. **Main courses** $12-$25.
Credit AmEx, DC, Disc, MC, V. **Map** p313 B4 **69**
Southwestern
Prado is split into two sections, with the twin themes
of night and day depicted on the walls and ceilings.
The menu is pan-American, from which we suggest
the Prado sampler: moist corn tamales served with
sour cream, caviar and tomatillo sauce, shrimp in
black pepper sauce, crab cakes with tartare sauce
and a portion of Pacifico-style chilli relleño.

Koreatown & around

Cassell's
*3266 W 6th Street, between S Berendo Street & S
New Hampshire Avenue (1-213 480 5000). Metro
Wilshire-Vermont/bus 20, 21, 204, 720, 754/I-10,
exit Vermont Avenue north.* **Open** 10.30am-4pm
Mon-Sat. **Main courses** $5-$7. **No credit cards**.
Map p314 A6 **70** **Cafés & diners**
Hamburgers are to Americans what pizzas are to
Italians: there are endless arguments about where
to find the best patty of meat slapped between baps.
When the question comes up you can earn yourself
serious insider points by rooting for Cassell's. Many
Angelenos are faithful to this lunch-only joint, which
serves up a mean and greasy burger with home-
made mayonnaise and a great potato salad.

Ortolan. *See p154.*

Eat, Drink, Shop

El Cholo

1121 S Western Avenue, between W Olympic & W Pico Boulevards (1-323 734 2773/www.elcholo.com). Bus 30, 31, 207, 330, 757/I-10, exit Western Avenue north. **Open** 11am-10pm Mon-Thur; 11am-11pm Fri, Sat; 11am-9pm Sun. **Main courses** $7-$15. **Credit** AmEx, Disc, MC, V. **Map** p313 D6 **⑦ Mexican**

Granted, the food here doesn't come across as authentically Mexican, but who cares? The Mex-American grub churned out of the kitchen at this colourful hangout is both rich and tasty, and the Margaritas are strong enough to stun an ox.

Dong Il Jang

3455 W 8th Street, at S Hobart Boulevard (1-213 383 5757). Metro Wilshire-Western/bus 20, 21, 66, 366, 720/I-10, exit Western Avenue north. **Open** 11am-10pm daily. **Main courses** $10-$25. **Credit** AmEx, MC, V. **Map** p313 D5 **⑦ Korean**

One of the more upmarket Korean restaurants in Koreatown. Dine at the sushi bar, in a booth, or sitting on cushions on the floor. Of the Korean barbecued fare, try the galbi-marinated beef short ribs, which arrives with myriad side dishes: pickled vegetables, sweet potatoes, glass noodles and rice.

Guelaguetza

3337½ W 8th Street, at Irolo Street (1-213 427 0601). Metro Wilshire-Normandie/bus 20, 21, 66, 366, 720/I-10, exit Vermont Avenue north. **Open** 8am-10pm daily. **Main courses** $4-$14. **Credit** AmEx, Disc, MC, V. **Map** p313 D5 **⑦ Mexican**

Oaxaca is a Mexican region famed for its seven types of moles (sauces). At this casual, colourful Koreatown restaurant, you can try at least four: mole negro, made with four types of chilli; red mole coloradito, with chocolate, sugar and peanuts; or the more standard green and yellow moles. Service is brisk. **Other locations**: 3014 W Olympic Boulevard, Koreatown (1-213 427 0608).

Las Delicias Chapinas

3731 W Pico Boulevard, between 4th & 5th Avenue (1-323 731 6995). Bus 30, 31, 210, 710/I-10, exit Arlington Avenue north. **Open** 8am-9pm daily. **Main courses** $6-$12. **No credit cards.** **Map** p313 C6 **⑦ Guatemalan**

A fun little Guatemalan neighbourhood *boîte*, Chapinas entertains its customers with live marimba music. Dishes include carne asada, sausages and pork tamales; portions are sizeable and prices are extremely keen. You may need to book at weekends.

Soot Bull Jeep

3136 W 8th Street, between S Berendo & S Catalina Streets (1-213 387 3865). Metro Wilshire-Western/ bus 20, 21, 66, 366, 720/I-10, exit Vermont Avenue north. **Open** 11am-11pm daily. **Main courses** $16-$19. **Credit** AmEx, Disc, MC, V. **Map** p314 A6 **⑦ Korean**

All the sizzling goes on right in front of you here, at one of the best Korean barbecue joints in LA. Before you're seated, a waitress will scatter a trowel full of glowing coals into a pit set in the middle of your table.

Taylor's Steak House

3361 W 8th Street, at S Ardmore Avenue (1-213 382 8449/www.taylorssteakhouse.com). Metro Wilshire-Normandie/bus 66, 206, 366/I-10, exit Western Avenue north. **Open** 11.30am-9.30pm Mon-Thur; 11.30am-10.30pm Fri; 4-10.30pm Sat; 4-9.30pm Sun. **Main courses** $16-$34. **Credit** AmEx, Disc, MC, V. **Map** p313 D5 **⑦ American**

It's not as old as it looks: having opened on the corner of Olympic and Western in 1953, Taylor's only moved to this location in 1970. Still, the loungey decor is purely vintage, and so is the meat-dominated menu. The prime rib is exquisite, but you can't go wrong with any of the steaks. **Photo** *p157.*

Los Feliz, Silver Lake & Echo Park

Los Feliz

Electric Lotus

4656 Franklin Avenue, at N Vermont Avenue (1-323 953 0040/www.electriclotus.com). Bus 26, 180, 181, 204, 754/US 101, exit Vermont Avenue north. **Open** 11am-midnight daily. **Main courses** $8-$18. **Credit** AmEx, Disc, MC, V. **Map** p314 A2 **⑦ Indian**

A hip, late-night Indian restaurant with a chic and contemporary interior but a fairly familiar menu. There's electronica-inspired DJs or traditional live music most evenings, with Friday and Saturday nights the best for a partying crowd.

Fred 62

1850 N Vermont Avenue, at Franklin Avenue (1-323 667 0062/www.fred62.com). Bus 26, 180, 181, 204, 754/US 101, exit Vermont Avenue north. **Open** 24hrs daily. **Main courses** $6-$15. **Credit** AmEx, DC, Disc, MC, V. **Map** p314 A2 **⑦ Cafés & diners**

Done out like a '50s diner, but with '60s design influences and a soundtrack that runs through '70s funk and '80s alt-rock, this round-the-clock Los Feliz eaterie defies easy categorisation. The menu is stylised fast food with a slight health-conscious and vegetarian focus, but also includes LA's best meat loaf.

Mexico City

2121 Hillhurst Avenue, at Avocado Street (1-323 661 7227). Bus 180, 181/I-5, exit Los Feliz Boulevard west. **Open** 5-10pm Mon, Tue; noon-3pm, 5-10pm Wed-Fri; noon-11pm Sat, Sun. **Main courses** $9-$15. **Credit** AmEx, MC, V. **Map** p314 B1 **⑦ Mexican**

The decor at Mexican City is Mexican retro and so, for the most part, is the menu. Still, the food is certainly zesty – enchiladas with interesting sauces, and Yucatan specialities including carne and shrimp – and enthusiastically scoffed up by the young hipsters who hang out here.

Vermont

1714 N Vermont Avenue, at Hollywood Boulevard (1-323 661 6163/www.vermontrestaurantonline. com). Metro Vermont-Sunset/bus 26, 180, 181, 204, 206, 754/US 101, exit Vermont Avenue north.

Open 11.30am-3pm, 5.30-10.30pm Mon-Thur,
Sun; 11.30am-3pm, 5.30-11.30pm Fri, Sat. **Main
courses** $15-$30. **Credit** AmEx, DC, Disc, MC, V.
Map p314 A2 ⑳ **Californian**
Everything about Vermont is warm, from the welcome extended by owners Michael and Miguel to the
offerings on the menu, a mostly excellent mishmash
of American and French comfort food. Michael's
salad, a couple of perfectly poached eggs perched
atop bacon and frisée with a warmed vinaigrette, is
hard to beat; also excellent is lamb shank with apricots, root veggies and couscous.

Yuca's Hut

*2056 Hillhurst Avenue, at Ambrose Avenue
(1-323 662 1214). Bus 180, 181, 780/US 101,
exit Vermont Avenue north.* **Open** 11am-6pm
Mon-Sat. **Main courses** $2-$4. **No credit cards.**
Map p314 B2 ㉛ **Mexican**
Blink and you'll miss this roadside shack. Best keep
your eyes peeled, then: the tacos and burritos here
are absolutely top of the range, stuffed to bursting
with immaculately cooked meat. **Photo** *p159*.

Silver Lake

Café Stella

*3932 W Sunset Boulevard, between Sanborn &
Hyperion Avenues (1-323 666 0265). Bus 2, 4, 175,
302, 304/US 101, exit Silver Lake Boulevard north.*
Open 6-11pm daily. **Main courses** $19-$25.
Credit AmEx, MC, V. **Map** p314 B3 ㉜ **French**

This casual French bistro and bar is immensely popular with locals. The menu is far from fussy nouvelle:
poulet à l'estragon, and excellent steak au poivre with
pommes lyonnaise or translucent pomme frites and
ratatouille are highlights. Pavement seating is available; booking is strongly advised.

Cliff's Edge

*3626 Sunset Boulevard, at Edgecliff Drive (1-323
666 6116). Bus 2, 4, 302, 304/US 101, exit Silver
Lake Boulevard north.* **Open** 6pm-midnight Mon-Sat;
11am-3pm Sun. **Main courses** $12-$22. **Credit**
AmEx, DC, MC, V. **Map** p314 C3 ㉝ **Italian**
A wonderful patio, strewn with Indonesian parasols
and teak benches, makes this a cool place to take a
date. The service can be spotty and the Italian small
plate dishes are a little inconsistent, but when it's on
good form, this is a fine place.

Edendale Grill

*2838 Rowena Avenue, between Auburn & Rokeby
Streets (1-323 666 2000/www.edendalegrill.com).
Bus 92, 201/I-5, exit Hyperion Avenue west.*
Open 5.30-10pm Mon-Thur; 5.30-11.30pm Fri, Sat;
10am-3pm, 5.30-10pm Sun. **Main courses** $8-$18.
Credit AmEx, MC, V. **Map** p314 D2 ㉞ **American**
Hip locals come to this former fire station as much
for the atmosphere – the happening bar stays open
two hours after the kitchen closes – as for the food,
which tends towards hearty American fare. Typical
dishes include iceberg lettuce wedges smothered in
blue cheese dressing and Berkshire pork chops with
roasted parsnips and brandy shallot glaze.

Eat, Drink, Shop

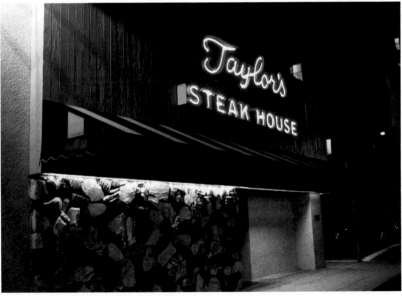

Meat the locals at historic **Taylor's Steak House**. *See p156.*

> **Cha Cha Cha (656 N Virgil Avenue)**
> Paul Walker takes Vin Diesel's sis
> here in *The Fast and the Furious*

Gingergrass

2396 Glendale Boulevard, at Brier Avenue (1-323 644 1600/www.gingergrass.com). Bus 92/US 101, exit Glendale Boulevard north **Open** 11am-3pm, 5-10pm Mon-Thur, Sun; 11am-3pm, 5-10.30pm Fri, Sat. **Main courses** $6-$15. **Credit** AmEx, DC, Disc, MC, V. **Map** p314 D2 ⑮ **Vietnamese**

This modern and modestly priced Vietnamese-inspired joint offers a strong range of changing blackboard specials. Take your time and linger over wok tossed pork chops, tofu sandwiches, banana leaf fish, lemon grass chicken and noodle bowls, washed down with a basil lime elixir served chilled.

Jade Café

1521 Griffith Park Boulevard, at W Sunset Boulevard (1-323 667 1551/www.jadecafe.org). Bus 2, 4, 302, 304/US 101, exit Silver Lake Boulevard north. **Open** 11am-10pm daily. **Main courses** $12-$16. **Credit** AmEx, MC, V. **Map** p314 B3 ⑯ **Fusion**

Jade Café pulls off a neat conjuring trick, fusing Mexican, Italian and Thai elements to surprisingly sinful effect. Don't believe us? Try the red pepper stew or ginger coconut noodles, chased down by marmalade chocolate cake and apricot chiffon cream.

Malo

4326 W Sunset Boulevard, between Fountain & Bates Avenues (1-323 664 1011/www.malo restaurant.com). Metro Vermont-Sunset/bus 2, 4, 26, 302, 304/US 101, exit Highland Avenue south. **Open** 6-10pm Mon, Sun; 6-11pm Tue-Thur; 6pm-midnight Fri, Sat. **Main courses** $18-$33. **Credit** AmEx, MC, V. **Map** p314 B3 ⑰ **Mexican**

Steven Arroyo of Cobras & Matadors (*see p153*) usually manages to attract a hip crowd to his ventures, and Malo is no exception. This time he's gone back to his roots, serving up small dishes of Mexican staples to a raucous and fashionable crowd in a setting defined by black tiles and flock wallpaper.

Millie's

3524 W Sunset Boulevard, at Maltman Avenue (1-323 664 0404). Bus 2, 4, 302, 304/US 101, exit Silver Lake Boulevard north. **Open** 7.30am-4pm daily. **Main courses** $4-$10. **Credit** MC, V. **Map** p314 C3 ⑱ **Cafés & diners**

It's Silver Lake, which means it's packed with hipsters. But the food at Millie's is straight from the old school: vast, pretension free breakfasts, brunches and lunches, cooked before your eyes and served with never-ending cups of coffee and glasses of teas.

Pho Café

2841 W Sunset Boulevard, at N Occidental Boulevard (1-213 413 0888). Bus 2, 4, 201, 302, 304/US 101, exit Silver Lake Boulevard north. **Open** 11am-midnight daily. **Main courses** $7-$10. **No credit cards.** **Map** p314 C4 ⑲ **Vietnamese**

Less is more would seem to be the dictum here, in terms of both design (by trendy architects Escher GuneWardena) and food. Bright orange plastic chairs and fishbowl pendant lights face a stainless steel kitchen and wood bar; the menu is pretty much confined to rice noodles in classic pho broth, spring rolls and a handful of other vegetarian options.

Tantra

3705 W Sunset Boulevard, at Edgecliffe Drive (1-323 663 8268/www.tantrasunset.com). Bus 2, 4, 302, 304/US 101, exit Virgil Avenue north. **Open** 5-11pm Tue-Sun. **Main courses** $13-$19. **Credit** AmEx, DC, Disc, MC, V. **Map** p314 B3 ⑳ **Indian**

This still-fashionable restaurant-cum-nightclub features high ceilings, pink walls, Bollywood movies and decent food: the curries are solid, as are the wafer-thin naans. Bring a flashlight to see what you're eating, or to check out the good-looking crowd.

Echo Park

Brite Spot

1918 W Sunset Boulevard, at Alvarado Street (1-213 484 9800). Bus 2, 4, 200, 302, 304, 603/US 101, exit Glendale Boulevard north. **Open** 6am-4am Mon-Fri; 7am-4am Sat, Sun. **Main courses** $7-$14. **Credit** AmEx, Disc, MC, V. **Map** p314 D5 ㉑ **Cafés & diners**

Echo Park might be getting livelier, but this vintage late-opening diner is still the best eating option. Chow down on a variety of comfort-food dishes, cooked with haste and served with insouciance.

Downtown

Chano's

3000 S Figueroa Street, at W 30th Street (1-213 747 3944). Bus 81, 381/I-10, exit Maple Avenue/San Pedro Street south. **Open** 8am-5pm daily. **Main courses** $2-$5. **No credit cards.** **Mexican**

There are several burrito huts along Figueroa, but this is arguably the best. You wouldn't confuse the stuffed burritos with health food, but no matter. Great horchata, too. Park in the tiny lot and eat at an outdoor table, or use the drive-through service.

Ciudad

445 S Figueroa Street, between W 4th & W 5th Streets (1-213 486 5171/www.ciudad-la.com). Metro 7th Street-Metro Center/bus 16, 18, 53, 55, 62, 316/I-110, exit 9th Street west. **Open** 11.30am-3pm, 5-8.45pm Mon, Tue; 11.30am-3pm, 5-9.45pm Wed, Thur; 11.30am-3pm, 5-10.45pm Fri; 5-10.45pm Sat; 5-8.45pm Sun. **Main courses** *Lunch* $7-$20. *Dinner* $15-$30. **Credit** AmEx, DC, Disc, MC, V. **Map** p315 B3 ㉒ **Southwestern**

Chefs Susan Feniger and Mary Sue Milliken, aka the Too Hot Tamales, researched this tribute to Latin American cuisine by touring South America. The decor is colourful and fun, and so is the lively, mouthwatering menu. Concentrate on the appetisers and the cocktails.

Empress Pavilion

*Bamboo Plaza, 988 N Hill Street, at Bamboo Lane
(1-213 617 9898). Bus 81, 90, 91, 94, 96, 381,
394/I-110, exit Hill Street east.* **Open** 10am-2.30pm
Mon-Fri; 9.30am-2.30pm Sat, Sun. **Main courses**
$11-$18. **Credit** DC, MC, V. **Chinese**
Bring a crowd with you to this outstanding – and
vast – Cantonese-style restaurant: the more people
you bring, the more dim sum waitresses you can flag
down. The main menu is pretty fine, though you'll
pay less at any number of nearby restaurants.

Engine Co No.28

*644 S Figueroa Street, between Wilshire Boulevard
& 7th Street (1-213 624 6996/www.engineco.com).
Metro 7th Street-Metro Center/bus 26, 51, 52, 60,
352/I-110, exit 3rd Street east.* **Open** 11.15am-9pm
Mon-Fri; 5-9pm Sat, Sun. **Main courses** $15-$30.
Credit AmEx, Disc, MC, V. **Map** p315 B3
🌐 **American**
The Downtown renaissance is in full swing, but this
stylish restaurant has a jump start on its newly
arrived competitors: housed in an old fire station
(hence the name), it's been serving American comfort food since the late 1980s. There's a complimentary shuttle to Disney Hall and the Staples Center.

Kendall's Brasserie & Bar

*Dorothy Chandler Pavillion, 135 N Grand Avenue, at
W 1st Street (1-213 972 7322/www.kendallsbrasserie.
com). Metro Civic Center/bus 2, 4, 10, 11, 14, 48,
92, 302, 714/I-110, exit 3rd Street east.* **Open**
11.30am-2.30pm Mon; 11.30am-10pm Tue-Sun.
Main courses $13-$23. **Credit** AmEx, MC, V.
Map p315 B2 🌐 **French**
If you need food fast before a concert at the Music
Center or Disney Hall, you're in luck: Kendall's has
had lots of practice at feeding and seeing off patrons
in time for the conductor's entrance. It's a jolly joint
with lovely old wood panelling, serving lobster to
steak with the usual roster of beers and wines.

Koshiji

*123 Astronaut Ellison S Onizuka Street, at E 1st
Street (1-213 626 4989). Metro Civic Center/bus
30, 31, 40, 42, 330/I-110, exit 3rd Street east.*
Open 11.30am-2pm, 6-10pm daily. **Menus** $5-$22.
Credit AmEx, MC, V. **Map** p315 D2 🌐 **Japanese**
Koshiji prepares well-presented *kushiyaki* (grilled
meats, fish and vegetables) and serves it against a traditional Japanese canvas. Try eggplant and green
beans encased in pork belly or the good prix fixe menu.

Ocean Seafood

*747 N Broadway, at Ord Street (1-213 687 3088/
www.oceansf.com). Metro Union Station/bus 45, 46,
81, 83, 84, 85/I-110, exit Hill Street east.* **Open**
9am-10pm daily. **Main courses** $5-$15. **Credit**
AmEx, Disc, MC, V. **Map** p315 C1 🌐 **Chinese**
During the day, Ocean in Chinatown is a bustling dim
sum operation, but by night, the atmosphere is more
relaxed. Squeamish diners would note that you'll get
the chance to see your food waving its claws at you
in the tanks on the way in to the restaurant.

Original Pantry

*877 S Figueroa Street, at 9th Street (1-213 972
9279). Metro 7th Street-Metro Center/bus 66, 81,
366, 381/I-110, exit 9th Street east.* **Open** 24hrs
daily. **Main courses** $9-$17. **No credit cards.**
Map p315 B4 🌐 **Cafés & diners**
Original? They got that right – it's now owned by former mayor Richard Riordan, but this corner café has
been here since the 1920s. It looks it, too, but then
when you're open 24 hours a day, there's not much
opportunity for decorating. The menu fits the surroundings: lumps of meat, puddles of grease and
omelettes as big as your head. Long may it thrive.
Photo *p160.*

Patina

*Walt Disney Concert Hall, 141 S Grand Avenue,
between W 2nd & W 3rd Streets (1-213 972 3331/
www.patinagroup.com). Metro Civic Center/bus 2, 4,
10, 11, 14, 48, 92, 302, 714/I-110, exit 3rd Street
east.* **Open** 11.30am-1.30pm, 5-11pm Mon-Fri;
5-11pm Sat, Sun. **Main courses** $17-$40. **Credit**
AmEx, Disc, MC, V. **Map** p315 B2 🌐 **Italian**
The best of the restaurants serving Disney Hall con-
certgoers; in fact, it's one of the best in the whole city,
the outlandish setting suiting Joaquim Splichal's esoteric Italian cooking. Among the starters are roasted
sweetbreads and sautéed foie gras; mains include
champagne and Tahitian vanilla bean risotto with
Maine lobster tail, and seared loin of hare. Push the
boat out with the six-course, $100 tasting menu.

Top tacos at **Yuca's Hut**. *See p157.*

Open all hours: Richard Riordan's **Original Pantry**. *See p159.*

Philippe the Original

1001 N Alameda Street, at Ord Street (1-213 628 3781/www.philippes.com). Metro Union Station/bus 45, 46, 81, 83, 84, 85/US 101, exit Alameda Street north. **Open** 6am-10pm daily. **Main courses** $3-$6. **No credit cards. Map** p315 D1 ● **Cafés & diners**
Philippe Mathieu invented the French Dip Sandwich in 1908: freshly carved roast beef, lamb, pork or turkey served on a soft bun dipped in the meat's juices. Almost a century later, it's served much as it was back then. The place gets packed at lunchtimes and in the early evenings, but staff keep the sandwiches coming apace. It's a veritable rip!

Pho

727 N Broadway, at Ord Street, Chinatown (1-213 625 7026). Metro Union Station/bus 45, 46, 81, 83, 84, 85/US 101, exit Hill Street east. **Open** 8.30am-6pm daily. **Main courses** $5-$7. **No credit cards. Map** p315 C1 ● **Vietnamese**
As the name suggests, this back-to-basics outpost specialises in Vietnamese noodle soup. The spring rolls are also excellent.

El Taurino

1104 S Hoover Street, at W 11th Street (1-213 738 9197). Bus 28, 603/I-110, exit Olympic Boulevard west. **Open** noon-2am Mon-Thur, Sun; 24hrs Fri, Sat. **Main courses** $5-$10. **No credit cards. Mexican**
Popular with in-the-know locals, this frill-free Mexican restaurant won't offer many surprises but it will serve you with a terrific taco at one in the morning for little more than pocket change.

Water Grill

544 S Grand Avenue, between 5th & 6th Streets (1-213 891 0900/www.watergrill.com). Metro Pershing Square/bus 14, 37, 76, 78, 79, 96/I-110, *exit 6th Street east.* **Open** 11.30am-8.30pm Mon, Tue; 11.30am-9.30pm Wed-Fri; 5-9.30pm Sat; 4.30-8.30pm Sun. **Main courses** $30-$50. **Credit** AmEx, Disc, MC, V. **Map** p315 B3 ● **Fish & seafood**
Long acknowledged as the best seafood restaurant in town, the Water Grill now has some competition following the defection of ex-chef Michael Cimarusti to open Providence (*see p151*). Still, it's risen to the challenge with dishes such as chilled, marinated Atlantic squid with mint, green heirloom tomatoes and rocket, or Ecuadorian Mahi Mahi steamed with peppercorns, green onions, napa cabbage and smoked eel pot stickers. Competition is a good thing.

Zucca

801 S Figueroa Street, at W 8th Street (1-213 614 7800/www.patinagroup.com). Metro 7th Street-Metro Center/bus 66, 81, 366, 381/I-110, exit 9th Street east. **Open** 11.30am-2.30pm, 5-9pm Mon-Thur; 11.30am-2.30pm, 5-11pm Fri; 5-10pm Sat; 5-9pm Sun. **Main courses** $12-$32. **Credit** AmEx, MC, V. **Map** p315 B4 ● **Italian**
Another in Joaquim Splichal's stellar array of Downtown eateries, Zucca serves up traditional Italian food with flair in a setting that takes its cues from a traditional Italian villa. Although it's smart, it doesn't have to be wallet-draining: there are even a few pizzas on the menu.

East LA

La Parilla

2126 E Cesar E Chavez Avenue, between Cummings & St Louis Streets (1-323 262 3434). Bus 68, 620/I-10, exit Cesar E Chavez Avenue east. **Open** 8am-11pm daily. **Main courses** $8-$10. **Credit** AmEx, Disc, MC, V. **Mexican**

Slap-bang in the middle of rundown Boyle Heights, La Parilla is the real thing. Its speciality is grilled meats – the sweet and spicy spare ribs are delicious – as well as seafood, mole sauce, cactus and sangria. Beware of the parillada for two: it's big. **Photo** *p162*.

La Serenata di Garibaldi

1842 E 1st Street, between N State Street & N Boyle Avenue (1-323 265 2887/www.laserenataonline.com). Bus 30, 31, 620/I-10, exit Boyle Avenue north. **Open** 11am-10pm daily. **Main courses** $8-$15. **Credit** DC, MC, V. **Mexican**

This small place in Boyle Heights – call in advance, get directions and park in the back – specialises in fresh fish in exquisite sauces. The atmosphere is great: Mexican families and Downtown artists collide at this upscale (foodwise) Mexican eaterie. **Other locations**: 1416 4th Street, Santa Monica (1-310 656 7017); La Serenata Gourmet, 10924 W Pico Boulevard, West LA (1-310 441 9667).

Tamales Liliana's

4619 E Cesar E Chavez Avenue, at N McDonnell Avenue (1-323 780 0989). Bus 253/I-5, exit Cesar E Chavez Avenue east. **Open** 11.30am-2pm, 5.30-9pm Mon-Fri; 5.30-9.30pm Sat. **Main courses** $10-$15. **No credit cards. Mexican**

Truly, madly, deeply wonderful Mexican food served in an unassuming spot out in East LA. Guess what the house speciality is?

El Tepeyac

812 N Evergreen Avenue, at Winter Street (1-323 267 8668). Bus 253/I-5, exit Cesar E Chavez Avenue east. **Open** 6am-9.45pm Mon, Wed, Thur, Sun; 6am-11pm Fri, Sat. **Main courses** $6-$10. **Credit** MC, V. **Mexican**

You'll find large portions and even larger lines at this simple Mexican mecca in Boyle Heights. You're on safe ground with more or less anything, but the burritos are particularly excellent.

South Central

Coley's Place

300 E Florence Avenue, at S La Brea Avenue, Inglewood (1-310 672 7474). Bus 40, 111, 115, 212, 315, 340, 711/I-10, exit La Brea Avenue south. **Open** 11am-9pm Mon-Thur; 11am-10pm Fri, Sat; 11am-8pm Sun. **Main courses** $9-$15. **Credit** AmEx, DC, Disc, MC, V. **Jamaican**

A hospitable Jamaican restaurant in Inglewood, Colye's does an out-of-this-world shrimp St James: tender shrimp, nestled in a coconut cream sauce. Don't leave before you've tried the peach cobbler.

Harold & Belle's

2920 W Jefferson Boulevard, between Arlington Avenue & Crenshaw Boulevard, Jefferson Park (1-323 735 9023). Bus 38, 210, 305, 710/I-10, exit Crenshaw Boulevard south. **Open** 11.30am-10pm Mon-Thur, Sun; 11.30am-11pm Fri, Sat. **Main courses** *Lunch* $13-$18. *Dinner* $16-$39. **Credit** AmEx, DC, MC, V. **American**

If you've a hankering for Southern food, you're in luck. Located in a down-at-heel neighbourhood, Harold & Belle's is a surprisingly elegant slice of the old South in the new West, both in terms of food – seafood platter and seafood gumbo are just the ticket – and the good ol' Southern hospitality.

Pann's

6710 La Tijera Boulevard, at S La Cienega Boulevard, Inglewood (1-310 670 1441/www.panns. com). Bus 62, 439/I-405, exit La Tijera Boulevard north. **Open** 7am-11pm daily. **Main courses** $5-$13. **Credit** MC, V. **American**

The food, while decent enough, is nothing out of the ordinary: pretty standard diner fare, with a few daily specials. The building, on the other hand, is a gem: all plate glass and swooping angles, it's one of the last remaining Googie structures in LA.

We ♥ LA Taco trucks

Forget the upscale restaurants, and skip the *taquerias* on every block from Highland Park to East LA: some of the best Latin American food in Los Angeles can be found in the distinctly more humble shape of the several thousand taco trucks that dot the city's streets. Some remain static during the day, while others cruise the boulevards and byways, constantly looking for trade.

As you'd expect, the peak hours are lunch time and after 7pm. Many trucks go beyond the usual tacos/ceviche/burrito menu items, representing cuisines from Guatemala and Honduras to Columbia and El Salvador. The foot is cheap, hot and – if you know where to go to find it – delicious.

Among the best are **El Pecas #2**, parked nightly at the corner of La Brea Avenue and Olympic Boulevard, which serves superior *carne asada* (charred steak), and the **unnamed white truck** at the corner of El Centro and Santa Monica Boulevard in Hollywood, which offers a $1 taco with 'fire in the hole' jalapeños. At the corner of Western and Lexington Avenues, **El Matador** offers the daring *burrito de sesos* (cow brains), while the truck that parks just north of the **Little Cave** bar in Highland Park (*see p178*) serves a *carnitas burrito* that's so big it might crush you. For more on the best tacos in town, see the useful and entertaining Great Taco Hunt blog at http://tacohunt.blogspot.com.

Comida auténtica mexicana at **La Parilla**. *See p160.*

The Valleys

San Fernando Valley

Art's Deli

12224 Ventura Boulevard, at Laurel Canyon Boulevard, Studio City (1-818 762 1221/www.artsdeli. com). Bus 150/US 101, exit Laurel Canyon Boulevard south. **Open** 7am-9pm daily. **Main courses** $10-$14. **Credit** AmEx, DC, Disc, MC, V. **Jewish**

Many people think that Art Ginsburg's 50-year-old joint is one of LA's best delis. Seating is mainly in booths, with photos of his famous sandwiches on the walls – try the corned beef and pastrami.

Hugo's

12851 Riverside Drive, at Coldwater Canyon Avenue, Studio City (1-818 761 8985/www.hugosrestaurant. com). Bus 96, 167/US 101, exit Coldwater Canyon Avenue north. **Open** 7.30am-10pm Mon-Fri; 8am-10pm Sat, Sun. **Main courses** $7-$15. **Credit** AmEx, MC, V. **Cafés & diners**

Don't think you have to eat breakfast before 9am. Hugo's healthy breakfast is available all day, as are many other wholesome dishes: from egg white omelettes to pasta dishes and lentil veggie meatloaf.

Max

13355 Ventura Boulevard, at Nagle Avenue, Sherman Oaks (1-818 784 2915/www.maxrestaurant.com). Bus 150, 240, 750/US 101, exit Woodman Avenue south. **Open** 5.30-10pm Mon-Thur, Sun; 5.30-11pm Fri, Sat. **Main courses** $9-$28. **Credit** AmEx, MC, V. **Pan-Asian**

This welcome addition to the Valley is headed up by André Guerrero, the former chef at Linq in West Hollywood. It's a noisy little place, but the California-Asian cuisine – pan-roasted butterfish, braised beef shortribs – is very sophisticated.

Minibar

3413 W Cahuenga Boulevard, at Lone Drive, Universal City (1-323 882 6965/www.minibar lounge.com). Bus 156/US 101, exit Lankershim Boulevard north. **Open** 5.30-11.30pm Mon-Thur, Sun; 5.30pm-1.30am Fri, Sat. **Main courses** $5-$16. **Credit** AmEx, MC, V. **Fusion**

Minibar is a slightly eccentric local eaterie that offers small plates or tapas, female valet service and good music on the stereo. Braised baby backs, chicken pibil and duck confit mini eggrolls are some of the items on the 'this, that and the other' menu.

Pinot Bistro

12969 Ventura Bouevard, at Coldwater Canyon Avenue, Studio City (1-818 990 0500/www.patina group.com). Bus 150, 167, 240, 750/US 101, exit Coldwater Canyon Avenue south **Open** noon-2pm Mon; noon-2pm, 6-9pm Tue-Fri; noon-2pm, 5.30-10pm Sat; noon-2pm, 5.30-9pm Sun. **Main courses** $18-$28. **Credit** AmEx, DC, Disc, MC, V. **French**

Another in Joachim Splichal's string of high-class French eateries, Pinot is a perfect balance of casual attitude and sophisticated cooking. The menu is stocked with bistro staples such as onion soup, and sautéed foie gras with apple butter packets.

Sushi Nozawa

11288 Ventura Boulevard, between Tujunga & Vineland Avenues, Studio City (1-818 508 7017). Bus 150, 240, 750/US 101, exit Vineland Avenue south. **Open** noon-2pm, 5.30-10pm Mon-Fri. **Sushi** $4-$6. **Credit** MC, V. **Japanese**

Hidden away in a strip mall, Sushi Nozawa is the Valley's best-kept secret. Chef Kazunori Nozawa has a reputation as a prickly character, but when he puts up a sign reading 'tonight's special: trust me', you should. In June 2006, Nozawa set up Sokyo in West Hollywood (8479 Melrose Avenue).

Zeke's Smokehouse

2209 Honolulu Avenue, at N Verdugo Road, Montrose (1-818 957 7045/www.zekessmokehouse. com). Bus 90, 91/I-210, exit Ocean View Boulevard south. **Open** 11am-10pm Mon-Sat; 11am-9pm Sun. **Main courses** $9-$21. **Credit** MC, V. **American**
This homage to barbecue is headed by Leonard Schwartz and Michael Rosen, who gave up their jobs at more prestigious restaurants to work here. As such, it's more expensive than your average 'cue joint, but the baby backs and spare ribs are lip-smackingly good, as are the pork sandwiches and the hush puppies. Worth the diversion.
Other locations: 7100 Santa Monica Boulevard, Hollywood (1-323 850 9353)

San Gabriel Valley

All India Café

39 S Fair Oaks Avenue, between E Green Street & E Colorado Boulevard, Pasadena (1-626 440 0309/www.allindiacafe.com). Metro Memorial Park/bus 180, 181, 256, 260, 361/I-110, exit Colorado Boulevard west. **Open** 11.30am-10pm Mon-Thur, Sun; 11.30am-11pm Fri, Sat. **Main courses** $7-$15. **Credit** AmEx, DC, Disc, MC, V. **Indian**
There's little in LA in the way of memorable Indian food, but this excellent restaurant offers distinguished curries and interesting vegetable dishes.
Other locations: 12113 Santa Monica Boulevard, West LA (1-310 442-5250).

Babita

1823 S San Gabriel Boulevard, at E Norwood Place, San Gabriel (1-626 288 7265). Bus 76, 489/I-10, exit San Gabriel Boulevard north. **Open** 11.30am-2.30pm, 5.30-9.30pm Tue-Thur; 11.30am-2.30pm, 5.30-10pm Fri; 5.30-10pm Sat, Sun. **Main courses** $10-$16. **Credit** AmEx, Disc, MC, V. **Mexican**
Babita offers a modern, almost gourmet spin on trad Mexican favourites, with an emphasis on Yucatan cuisine. It's all prepared with the panache of sophisticated French cooking, courtesy of chef Roberto Berrelleza. A real find.

Celestino Ristorante

141 S Lake Avenue, between E Green & Cordova Streets, Pasadena (1-626 795 4006/www.celestino pasadena.com). Metro Lake/bus 181, 485/I-210, exit Lake Aveune south. **Open** 11.30am-3pm, 5.30-11pm Mon-Fri; 5.30-11pm Sat. **Main courses** $15-$32. **Credit** AmEx, DC, Disc, MC, V. **Italian**
Yet another restaurant owned by one of the Drago family from Sicily (*see also p141 and p145*), and yet another good one. Here, Celestino serves up sophisticated but not overcomplicated dishes that find their origins in his homeland.

Empress Harbor

111 N Atlantic Boulevard, at W Garvey Avenue, Monterey Park (1-626 300 8833/www.empressharbor. com). Bus 20, 260, 361, 370/I-10, exit Atlantic Boulevard south. **Open** 9am-10pm daily. **Main courses** $9-$38. **Credit** AmEx, Disc, MC, V. **Chinese**
Empress Harbor serves what's arguably the best dim sum in the city, but only until 3pm. Main menu possibilities include shark fin soup and lobster.

Maison Akira

730 E Green Street, at S Oak Knoll Avenue, Pasadena (1-626 796 9501/www.maisonakira.com). Metro Memorial Park/bus 180, 181, 256, 260/I-710, exit Colorado Boulevard south. **Open** 11.30am-2pm, 6-9pm Tue-Thur; 11.30am-2pm, 6-9.30pm Fri; 5.30-9.30pm Sat; 11am-2pm, 5-8pm Sun. **Main courses** $24-$45. **Credit** AmEx, DC, Disc, MC, V. **French/Japanese**
Smart French cuisine and traditional Japanese food might seem to make unlikely bedfellows, but you'll be in good hands no matter which corner of the menu you favour. Lunch offers $20 bento boxes.

Saladang Song

383 S Fair Oaks Avenue, between E Bellevue Drive & E Del Mar Boulevard, Pasadena (1-626 793 5200). Metro Del Mar/bus 260, 361/I-110, exit Del Mar Boulevard west. **Open** 7am-10pm daily. **Main courses** $6-$16. **Credit** AmEx, DC, Disc, MC, V. **Thai**
The splendid setting looks more Moorish than Thai, until you spot the beautiful waitresses in their elaborate silk dresses. The inventiveness of the design is reflected in the creative nouvelle Thai food. Highlights include deep-fried spicy fishcakes, rice noodles dripping in coconut milk and pork spare ribs.

Heading south

South Bay & Long Beach

Il Boccaccio

39 Pier Avenue, at Beach Drive, Hermosa Beach (1-310 376 0211/www.ilboccaccio.com). Bus 130, 439B/I-405, exit Rosecrans Avenue west. **Open** 5.30-10.30pm Mon-Thur; 5.30-11.30pm Fri; 1-11.30pm Sat; 1-10pm Sun. **Main courses** $10-$26. **Credit** AmEx, Disc, MC, V. **Italian**
A mere skateboard hop to Hermosa Beach, Il Boccaccio's setting could be more modern, but the service and the food – the best lasagna al forno this side of Rome – is reason enough to ditch the board.

Chez Melange

Palos Verdes Inn, 1716 Pacific Coast Highway, between Palos Verdes Boulevard & Camino de las Colinas, Redondo Beach (1-310 540 1222/

> **Burger King (535 N Victory Boulevard, Burbank)**
> A skateboarding Michael J Fox hitches a ride on a truck in *Back to the Future*

www.chezmelange.com). Bus 225, 232/ I-405, exit Artesia Boulevard west. **Open** 7.30am-2.30pm, 5-10pm Mon-Thur, Sun; 7.30am-2.30pm, 5-11pm Fri, Sat. **Main courses** $8-$25. **Credit** AmEx, Disc, MC, V. **Californian**
In 1982, Michael Franks and Robert Bell walked into a bank, with no collateral, and left with a $200,000 loan to build Chez Melange; two decades later, we're pleased to say, the restaurant is still going strong. The food on offer might be called nouvelle eclectic, but it's not pretentious, and the 1950s diner decor is fab. There are also vodka, champagne and caviar bars. One of the better restaurants in the South Bay.

Michi
903 Manhattan Avenue, at 9th Street, Manhattan Beach (1-310 376 0613). Bus 126, 439/I-405,

Brunch bonanza

Today, lingering over meals is a near-forgotten luxury in LA, where there's always business to be done and traffic to be beaten. The sole exception is weekend brunch, when Angelenos feast on all those luxuries of which they've been depriving themselves all week.

The lap of luxury is available at a number of places across town. The all-you-can-eat champagne and seafood brunch buffet at **Cameron's Seafood & Market** (1978 E Colorado Boulevard, Pasadena, 1-626 793 3474, www.cameronsseafoods.com) is a winner, priced at a very reasonable $21.95. And a number of LA's smarter hotels also offer a posh brunch, among them **Gardens** at the Four Seasons (*see p52*).

After Miami Beach, LA is the most figure-conscious city in the US. As such, healthy brunches abound: go organic at **Literati** (*see p143*), or order the Healthy Joe Scramble (turkey, egg whites, spinach and mushrooms) at **Barefoot** (8722 W 3rd Street, 1-310 276 6223, www.barefootrestaurant.com). Conversely, food inhabiting its very own plane of decadence can be found at **Doughboys** (*see p153*): try the stuffed French toast filled with jam and cream cheese. For an authentic Mexican brunch, head to **La Serenata de Garibaldi** (*see p161*).

No one mixes things up better than chef Joe Miller at **Joe's** (*see p142*), and his brunch menu is no exception: try blue crab hash or salmon-and-chilli huevos rancheros. Also in Venice, weekend brunch at **Hal's** (1349 Abbot Kinney Boulevard, 1-310 396 3105, www. halsbarandgrill.com; *pictured*) is a winner.

Al fresco brunches abound in sunny SoCal; one of the best is in the leafy courtyard of **Alcove** in Los Feliz (1929 Hillhurst Avenue, 1-323 644 0100). All the seating at the **Firefly Bistro** (1009 El Centro Street, South Pasadena, 1-626 441 2443, www.eatat firefly.com) is outdoors on a festive, tented patio. And if you want your own beach house without a tiresome seven-figure mortgage, become a regular at **Dukes** (21150 Pacific Coast Highway, Malibu, 1-310 317 0777, www.dukesmalibu.com).

exit *Hawthorne Boulevard north.* **Open** 6-10.30pm Mon-Sat. **Main courses** $16-$43. **Credit** AmEx, DC, MC, V. **Californian**
Michi Takahashi is one of the Southland's hippest chefs, thanks to his cross-cultural – French, Italian and Japanese – culinary style. There's also a sushi bar and a hopping local bar scene.

Petros Greek Cuisine & Lounge

451 Manhattan Boulevard, at Morningside Drive, Manhattan Beach (1-310 545 4100/ www.petrosrestaurant.com). Bus 439B/I-405, exit Rosecrans Avenue west. **Open** 5.30-11pm Mon-Thur, Sun; 5pm-midnight Fri, Sat. **Main courses** $8-$22. **Credit** AmEx, Disc, MC, V. **Greek**
Manhattan Beach is a schlep for many Angelenos, but this place was packed within a week of opening. Calamari, saganaki (sautéed cheese with lemon and parsley) and fasalotha vegetable bean soup are meze delights; feta-crusted rack of lamb and grilled snapper are simple pleasures. Owner Petros Benekos also runs a vintage 501s store two doors down.

Samba Brazilian Steakhouse & Bar

207 N Harbor Drive, between Beryl Street & N Pacific Avenue, Redondo Beach (1-310 374 3411/ www.sambaredondo.com). Bus 130, OC205, exit 182nd Street west. **Open** 5-9pm Mon; 11am-3pm, 5-9pm Tue-Thur; 11am-3pm, 5-11pm Fri, Sat; 11am-9pm Sun. **Main courses** Lunch $17. Dinner $21-$27. **Credit** AmEx, Disc, MC, V. **Brazilian**
Redondo Beach collides head on with Rio de Janeiro and the result is declared a tie. The steakhouse is tricked out with colourful lights and paintings, the patio has views over the water, and samba dancers swing their hips. The food is all-you-can-eat barbecued meat, and fish cooked churrasco-style.

La Sosta

2700 Manhattan Avenue, at 27th Street, Manhattan Beach (1-310 318 1556). Bus 126, 439B/I-405, exit Rosecrans Avenue west. **Open** 6-10pm Tue-Sun. **Main courses** $18-$35. **Credit** AmEx, Disc, MC, V. **Italian**
A fair take on a traditional Italian enoteca, where the food is presented to show off a library of wines. Order a selection of artisanal cheeses and cold cuts to pair with fine bottle of Barolo or Barabara and you won't be disappointed. The entrèes are less original.

Orange County

Chakra Cuisine

4143 Campus Drive, at W Peltason Drive, Irvine (1-949 854 0009/www.chakracuisine.com). Bus OC59, OC79, OC175, OC178/I-405 south to Hwy 73. **Open** 11.30am-2.30pm, 5-10.30pm Mon-Fri; 11.30am-3pm, 5.30-10.30pm Sat, Sun. **Main courses** $16-$17. **Credit** AmEx, MC, V. **Indian**
The Irvine dining scene received a welcome injection of Indian spice when Chakra opened. Mind you, inculturation works both way in California, here no less than elsewhere. So you'll find traditional South Asian dishes with intriguing modern twists.

French 75

1464 Pacific Coast Highway, at Calliope Street, Laguna Beach (1-949 494 8444/www.culinary adventures.com). Bus OC1/Hwy 133, exit PCH south. **Open** 5.30-10pm Mon-Thur, Sun; 5-11pm Fri, Sat. **Main courses** $25-$36. **Credit** AmEx, Disc, MC, V. **French**
This little Parisian bistro is an elegant spot, with overstuffed chairs and art deco touches. If you crane your neck, you can see the ocean from the patio. Dishes run the gamut from heavenly seafood – langoustine and crayfish cappuccino – to rustic dishes.

Hush

858 S Coast Highway, at Shadow Lane, Laguna Beach (1-949 497 3616/www.hushrestaurant.com). Bus OC1/Hwy 133, exit PCH south. **Open** 5-11pm daily. **Main courses** $22-$32. **Credit** AmEx, DC, Disc, MC, V. **American**
The designer decor at Hush is Laguna Beach at its swankiest; there's even a patio, lit and heated with outdoor fireplaces, that is, of course, set overlooking the ocean. The food can't quite match the setting, but it's decent enough in its way: contemporary American with Asian and Mediterranean overtones.

El Misti Picanteria Arequipeña

3070 W Lincoln Avenue, at Beach Boulevard, Anaheim (1-714 995 5944). Bus OC29, OC42/I-405, exit Beach Boulevard north. **Open** 11am-9pm daily. **Main courses** $9-$42. **Credit** MC, V. **Peruvian**
Simple, rustic Peruvian dishes are the mainstay in this sweet and humble restaurant. If the food isn't enough to transport you south to the land of the Incas, take a look at the artwork on the walls depicting similar eateries around El Misti, a volcano that frowns down on Arequipa in Peru.

Napa Rose

Grand Californian Hotel, 1600 S Disneyland Drive, at Katella Avenue, Anaheim (1-714 300 7170). Bus 460, OC205, OC430/I-5, exit Harbor Boulevard south. **Open** 5.30-10pm daily. **Main courses** $27-$36. **Credit** AmEx, Disc, MC, V. **Californian**
It might be set inside a Disney-run hotel, but the cooking at Napa Rose is hardly of the Mickey Mouse variety. The food lives up to the Frank Lloyd Wright-style setting at what is possibly the best restaurant in Anaheim; the California wine list is truly astonishing.

Stonehill Tavern

St Regis Monarch Beach Resort, 1 Monarch Beach Resort, Dana Point (1-949 234 3318/www.stregis mb.com). I-5, exit Crown Valley Parkway south. **Open** 5.30-10pm Wed-Sun. **Main courses** $29-$38. **Credit** AmEx, DC, Disc, MC, V. **American**
Celebrated chef Michael Mina offers up his twist on modern tavern fare (the term is used in its lightest sense), employing seasonal products of the highest quality. Try the seasonal tasting menus and wine pairings for full effect. Set in the deluxe St Regis Resort and kitted out by designer Tony Chi, this is a very welcome addition to the OC.

Eat, Drink, Shop

Coffeehouses

The tastemakers.

Coffee has been kickstarting a nation of bleary-eyed Americans since the 1670s. With 54 per cent of the nation drinking coffee daily and a further 25 per cent supping it from time to time, it's clear that gasoline isn't the only liquid fuelling the US. LA's bar scene may not live up to expectations, but its coffee culture thrives.

Competition is fierce, with every spot looking for an edge. Some offer cheap eats, while others deal in expensive teas or offer Wi-Fi (see p169 **Get connected**). And the coffee comes with countless variations: soy milk, fudge swirls, cherries, boba… the list goes on. And on.

While the standard of coffee at the various chains is generally good, they otherwise tend to be rather bland places. We've reviewed a single branch of each of the town's big three chains (**Starbucks**, the **Coffee Bean & Tea Leaf** and the less famous **Peet's Coffee & Tea**), but you're never far from one or other of them.

Santa Monica & the beach towns

Santa Monica

Back on the Beach
445 Pacific Coast Highway, between Marguerita & Georgina Avenues (1-310 393 8282). Bus 20, SM4/I-10, exit 4th-5th Street north. **Open** 8am-2.30pm Mon-Fri; 8am-3pm Sat, Sun. **Credit** AmEx, MC, V. **Map** p310 A1 ❶
Plant your feet in the sand while you sip your coffee and sample the glorious, panoramic ocean views at this impossibly mellow café in Santa Monica.

Infuzion
1149 3rd Street, between California Avenue & Wilshire Boulevard (1-310 393 9985/www.infuzion cafe.com). Bus 33, 333, SM2, SM3, SM4, SM5, SM9/I-10, exit 4th-5th Street north. **Open** 6.30am-9pm Mon-Fri; 7am-9pm Sat; 8am-6pm Sun. **Credit** MC, V. **Map** p310 A2 ❷
This tiny coffee stop off the Third Street Promenade makes great coffee and offers an above-average selection of teas. However, the main attraction is that you get a free internet connection with any purchase.

❶ Orange numbers given in this chapter correspond to the location of each coffeehouse on the street maps.
See pp310-315.

Legal Grind
2640 Lincoln Boulevard, at Ocean Park Boulevard (1-310 452 8160/www.legalgrind.com). Bus SM3, SM8/I-10, exit Lincoln Boulevard south. **Open** 9am-6pm Mon-Tue, Thur; 9am-7pm Wed; 9am-1pm Fri; 10am-1pm Sat. **No credit cards. Map** p310 B4 ❸
Java justice is the order at this California State Bar-certified coffee-and-counselling café in Ocean Park, where you can get legal advice ($25 for 15mins) with your caffeine fix. Visiting lawyers dispense advice late on weekday afternoons and Saturday mornings. **Other locations**: 6816 S La Cienega Boulevard, Inglewood (1-310 645 3378).

Peet's Coffee & Tea
2439 Main Street, between Ocean Park Boulevard & Hollister Avenue (1-310 399 8117/www.peets.com). Bus 33, 333, SM2, SM8, SM10/I-10, exit Lincoln Boulevard south. **Open** 6am-7pm Mon-Fri; 6.30am-7pm Sat, Sun. **Credit** Disc, MC, V. **Map** p310 A4 ❹
Once a David against Starbucks' Goliath, Peet's is now almost as ubiquitous in LA. Still, aficionados claim it gives the best hit in town. This Ocean Park location is the hub of a stylish Gehry-designed mall. **Other locations**: throughout the city.

Venice

Abbot's Habit
1401 Abbot Kinney Boulevard, at California Avenue (1-310 399 1171). Bus 33, 333, C1, SM1, SM2/I-10, exit Lincoln Boulevard south. **Open** 6am-10pm Mon-Thur, Sun; 6am-11pm Fri, Sat. **Credit** MC, V. **Map** p310 A6 ❺
Venice generally attracts a eclectic crowd, and this established café is no exception. Affluent canal home-owners mix with artists responsible for the works on the walls, a mix of the delicious and the dreadful. Speaking of which, Sunday is open-mic night.

Cow's End
34 Washington Boulevard, at Pacific Avenue (1-310 574 1080). Bus 33, 333, C1, SM1, SM2/I-10, exit 4th-5th Street south. **Open** 6am-midnight daily. **No credit cards. Map** p310 A6 ❻
This neighbourly coffeehouse off Venice Beach is a fixture among locals, in part as a refuge from the visitor hordes, because few tourists wander in. There's Wi-Fi available, but it's not free.

Jin Patisserie
1202 Abbot Kinney Boulevard, between Aragon & Cadiz Courts (1-310 399 8801/www.jinpatisserie. com). Bus 33, 333, C1, SM1, SM2/I-10, exit 4th-5th Street north. **Open** 10.30am-7pm Tue-Sun. **Credit** AmEx, Disc, MC, V. **Map** p310 A5 ❼

Great coffee and over 20 types of tea are available at this Asian coffee spot, completely secluded from the bustle of the Venice streets. Smokers take note: there's a garden where you're welcome to puff away.

Brentwood to Beverly Hills

Beverly Hills

Le Pain Quotidien

9630 Santa Monica Boulevard, between N Bedford & N Camden Drives (1-310 859 1100/www.pain quotidien.com). Bus 4, 16, 304, 720/1-10, exit La Cienega Boulevard north. **Open** 7.30am-7pm daily. **Credit** AmEx, MC, V. **Map** p311 C3 ❽
'Rustic' is the keyword at this charming spot, which, from humble beginnings in Brussels, has grown into Europe's most successful bakery chain. The creamy café au lait is to die for, and the crusty bread and pastries will have you thinking you're in Paris.
Other locations: 11702 Barrington Court, Brentwood (1-310 476 0969); 8607 Melrose Avenue, West Hollywood (1-310 854 3700).

West Hollywood, Hollywood & Midtown

Our daily bread at **Le Pain Quotidien**.

West Hollywood

Buzz Coffee

8000 W Sunset Boulevard, at N Laurel Avenue (1-323 656 7460). Bus 4, 218, 304, LDHWH/I-10, exit Fairfax Avenue north. **Open** 6.30am-11pm Mon-Thur; 6.30am-midnight Fri-Sun. **Credit** AmEx, MC, V. **Map** p312 C1 ❾
Housed in a fashionable outdoor mall with the celeb-filled Crunch gym, this café is a vibrant spot. The coffee also lives up to the name: drink it later in the evening and expect to be awake into the wee hours.
Other locations: 8200 Santa Monica Boulevard, West Hollywood (1-323 650 7742); 7623 Beverly Boulevard, West Hollywood (1-323 634 7393).

Coffee Bean & Tea Leaf

8789 W Sunset Boulevard, at Sunset Plaza Drive (1-310 659 1890/www.coffeebean.com). Bus 2, 105, 302, LDHWH/I-10, exit La Cienega

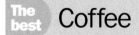

The best Coffee

Pour une tasse de café
Café Tartine. See p168.

Para una taza de café
Porto's Bakery. See p169.

For a cup o' joe
Abbot's Habit. See above.

Boulevard north. **Open** 6am-midnight Mon-Fri; 7am-midnight Sat, Sun. **Credit** MC, V. **Map** p312 A1 ❿
This branch of the Coffee Bean chain, which serves the best iced blended coffees in LA, has an enviably chichi Sunset Plaza location. For one of the cheapest shows in town, grab an outside table and clock the actors shopping at the designer boutiques next door.
Other locations: throughout the city.

Hugo's

8401 Santa Monica Boulevard, at N Kings Road (1-323 654 3993/www.hugosrestaurant.com). Bus 4, 304, LDHWH/I-10, exit La Cienega Boulevard north. **Open** 7.30am-10pm Mon-Fri; 8am-10pm Sat, Sun. **Credit** AmEx, DC, Disc, MC, V. **Map** p312 B2 ⓫
Located in the back of the venerable Italian-American eaterie, this is one of the best tea houses in town. It looks low-key, but appearances deceive: it actually draws the power breakfast/lunch crowd. Choose from more than 120 varieties of black, green, red and white tea, including yogi teas.
Other locations: 12851 Riverside Drive, Studio City (1-818 761 8985).

Kings Road Café

8361 Beverly Boulevard, at N Kings Road (1-323 655 9044). Bus 14, 105, LDF, LDHWH/I-10, exit La Cienega Boulevard north. **Open** 7.30am-10pm daily. **Credit** MC, V. **Map** p312 B3 ⓬
Despite more than a decade in business, the Kings Road Café has retained its original appeal. Some say it's the European feel; others appreciate the takeout pastry counter next door. But the crucial factor is the coffee, strong enough to drive an 18-wheeler.

Pull up a chair at the **Coffee Table**. *See p169.*

Urth Caffé

8565 Melrose Avenue, at N La Cienega Boulevard (1-310 659 0628/www.urthcaffe.com). Bus 10, 11, 105, LDF, LDHWH/I-10, exit La Cienega Boulevard north. **Open** 6.30am-midnight Mon-Sat; 7am-midnight Sun. **Credit** AmEx, DC, MC, V. **Map** p312 B2 ⑬
Organic coffee is the name of the game at this popular West Hollywood café, but don't pass over the incredible teas. Try to get a seat on the patio, where the people-watching is as superb as the drinks. **Other locations:** 267 S Beverly Drive, Beverly Hills (1-310 205 9311).

Hollywood

Bourgeois Pig

5931 Franklin Avenue, between Tamarind & N Bronson Avenues (1-323 464 6008/www.bourgeois pig.com). Bus 26, 180, 181, 217, LDH/US 101, exit Gower Street north. **Open** 8am-2am daily. **No credit cards. Map** p313 C1 ⑭
The shabby-chic aesthetic of this dimly lit, almost grungy joint is the antithesis of the normal La-La Land emphasis on showy style. However, the novelists and screenwriters who huddle over their laptops (the café has paid-for wireless access) don't seem to mind. The coffee is good and strong.

Fairfax District

Insomnia

7286 Beverly Boulevard, at N Poinsettia Place (1-323 931 4943). Bus 14/I-10, exit Fairfax Avenue north. **Open** 10am-1.30am daily. **No credit cards. Map** p312 D3 ⑮
A late-night café popular with laptop-toting writers, noteworthy for its extremely comfortable couches, high ceilings and the changing array of artworks. It's also become a notable place to go if you need to study: bring a script to blend in.

Starbucks

6333 W 3rd Street, at Fairfax Boulevard (1-323 965 9594/www.starbucks.com). Bus 316/I-10, exit Fairfax Avenue. **Open** 5.30am-10pm Mon-Thur; 5.30am-11pm Fri; 6am-11pm Sat; 6.30am-11pm Sun. **Credit** AmEx, MC, V. **Map** p312 C3 ⑯
Thanks to its location in the Farmers Market, this is one of the most happening Starbucks in town. Bring a book, but remember to look up from time to time: it's a great spot for people-watching. **Other locations:** throughout the city.

Miracle Mile & Midtown

Caffe Latte

6254 Wilshire Boulevard, at S Crescent Heights Boulevard (1-323 936 5213). Bus 20, 21, 217, 720, LDF/I-10, exit La Cienega Boulevard north. **Open** 7.30am-3pm, 5-8pm Mon-Fri; 8am-3pm Sat, Sun. **Credit** AmEx, MC, V. **Map** p312 C4 ⑰
Those who frequent this tucked-away spot swear by the homey atmosphere, the great food (try the muffins and French toast) and the coffee, roasted on the premises. The prices are as kind to your wallet as the food and drink are to your stomach.

Café Tartine

7385 Beverly Boulevard, at N Martel Avenue (1-323 938-1300). Bus 212/I-10, exit La Brea Avenue north. **Open** noon-10pm Tue-Thur; noon-11pm Fri; 9am-11pm Sat; 9am-5pm Sun. **Credit** MC, V. **Map** p312 D3 ⑱
A little piece of Paris in the heart of Los Angeles. The fresh, simple food includes bread shipped in from France daily; the coffee choices, naturally, are phenomenal. Popular with shoppers.

Chado Tea Room

8422½ W 3rd Street, at S Croft Avenue (1-800 442 4019/www.chadotea.com). Bus 16/I-10, exit La Cienega Boulevard north. **Open** 11.30am-6pm daily. **Credit** AmEx, MC, V. **Map** p312 B3 ⑲

The international menu at this quiet British Colonial jewel runs to 40 pages, so you might want to bring along a knowledgeable friend for 'tea guidance'. The $15 per person afternoon tea package offers a well-rounded array of rich scones, yummy finger sandwiches (the Punjab is highly popular) and fruit drenched in heavy cream.
Other locations: 79 N Raymond Avenue, Pasadena (1-310 431 2832).

Susina

7122 Beverly Boulevard, at N La Brea Avenue (1-323 934 7900/www.susinabakery.com). Bus 14, 212/1-10, exit La Brea Avenue north. **Open** 7am-11pm Mon- Fri; 8am-11pm Sat, Sun. **Credit** AmEx, MC, V. **Map** p312 D3 ⓴

A Paris-style patisserie and coffeeshop once known as the Sugar Plum Bakery, Susina was founded by a former Spago pastry chef. Perhaps predictably, its baked goods are insanely delicious.

Los Feliz, Silver Lake & Echo Park

Los Feliz

La Belle Epoque

2128 Hillhurst Avenue, at Avocado Street (1-323 669 7640). Bus 180, 181/I-5, exit Riverside Drive south. **Open** 10.30am-10pm Tue-Fri; 8am-8pm Sat, Sun. **Credit** AmEx, DC, Disc, MC, V. **Map** p314 B1 ㉑

The hipness of the Los Feliz neighbourhood has more than rubbed off on this café. It's a quaint place with an obvious French feel; be sure to try one of the amazing desserts from the bakery. The main café menu is more generically continental than French.

Silver Lake

Back Door Bakery & Café

1710 Silver Lake Boulevard, at Effie Street (1-323 662 7927). Bus 201/1-101, exit Silver Lake Boulevard north. **Open** 7am-6pm daily. **No credit cards. Map** p314 C3 ㉒

Home-made food coupled with huge cups of coffee makes for a little piece of heaven in Silver Lake. Touch wood, there'll be a sidewalk table free when you arrive, the perfect spot to take in the neighbourhood's comings and goings.

Coffee Table

2930 Rowena Avenue, between Avenal & Herkimer Streets (1-323 644 8111). Bus 180, 181/I-5, exit Los Feliz Boulevard south. **Open** 7am-11pm daily. **Credit** AmEx, Disc, MC, V. **Map** p314 C2 ㉓

A casual neighbourhood hangout, the Coffee Table has a gem of an outdoor patio, frequented by a mixed crowd of families, gays, industry types and artists. As for the food, the breakfast burritos are unsurpassed and the desserts scrumptious. **Photo** *p168.*

The Valleys

Porto's Bakery

315 N Brand Boulevard, at California Avenue, Glendale (1-818 956 5996/www.portosbakery.com). Bus 180/I-134, exit Brand Boulevard north. **Open** 7am-6pm Mon-Sat; 7am-3pm Sun. **Credit** MC, V.

This incredible Cuban bakery has expanded its café area of late. However, despite the extra space available, it's still packed almost every weekend, with Valley girls and boys who go nuts for the decadent pastries and fierce Cuban coffee.

Get connected

Los Angeles will never be as tech-friendly a town as its rival city up the Californian coast. However, getting online here is easier every day, with more and more coffeehouses now offering wireless access. Most of them, including all branches of Starbucks, still charge for the privilege. However, a few enlightened places offer free connections.

Out west, access is free at **Infuzion** (*see p166*), at Santa Monica's colourful **Velocity Café** (2127 Lincoln Boulevard, 1-310 314 3368, www.velocity-cafe.com), and at both branches of the literary-themed **Novel Café** in Santa Monica (212 Pier Avenue, 1-310 396 8566) and Westwood (1101 Gayley Avenue, 1-310 208 6410, www.novelcafe.com). In West Hollywood, you can log on for free at **Buzz Coffee** (*see p167*). In Hollywood, skip the paid-for access at Insomnia and the

Bourgeois Pig in favour of the free connection at **Solar de Cahuenga** (1847 N Cahuenga Boulevard, at Franklin Avenue, 1-323 467 7510). And on the Miracle Mile, connect for free over a monstrously good lunch at **Back Door Boba** (5484 Wilshire Boulevard, at S Dunsmuir Avenue, 1-323 933 4020).

On the east side of town, head to **Swork** (2160 Colorado Boulevard, Eagle Rock, 1-323 258 5600, www.swork.com), which offers free Wi-Fi and a cheap-to-rent computer. In Monterey Hills, there's the **Antigua Cultural Coffee House** (4836 Huntington Drive, 1-323 539 2233, www.antiguacoffeehouse.com), which has its own coffee plantation, while Glendale is home to the **Just Coffee Shop** (1010 N Glendale Avenue, Glendale, 1-818 291 0240).

For more on getting online in LA, *see p291.*

Eat, Drink, Shop

Bars

Just this once, leave the car at the hotel.

Angelenos have a reputation for fickleness, especially when it comes to bars. It's partially true, but the elusive pursuit of capital-c Cool isn't the only determinant. People who live in such a fractal city know that any night of imbibing connotes a night of arguing as to who, if anyone, is going to be the designated driver. As comedian Sam Kinison once put it: 'How are we supposed to get the car back to the house?'

As such, Angelenos need something to do besides sit and drink, which is why the city boasts so many different kinds of bars: tapas bars, dive bars, hotel bars, restaurant bars, illegal after-hours, DJ bars, nail bars. The (gradually) improving public transport system is making it easier to drink safely, especially in Metro-friendly Downtown and Hollywood, but there's still a little way to go. And the continued gentrification of decades-old dive bars into gone-in-60-seconds yuppie lounges also grates at times: Koreatown's beloved Escape Room, for example, is now a California fusion restaurant.

Still, despite all these problems, LA is more drinker-friendly now than it's been for years. Enjoy, and be safe after you do it: for a list of cab numbers, see p287.

BOOZE & THE LAW

All bars are subject to California's alcohol laws: you have to be 21 or over to buy and consume alcoholic drinks (take photo ID even if you look much older), and wine, beer or any other spirits can only be sold between 6am and 2am. Almost every bar calls last orders at around 1.45am; technically, staff are obliged to confiscate unconsumed alcohol after 2am.

Santa Monica & the beach towns

Santa Monica

Bar Copa

2810 Main Street, at Hill Street (1-310 452 2445/ www.barcopa.com). Bus 33, 333, SM1, SM2, SM8, SM10/I-10, exit 4th-5th Street south. **Open** 9am-2am Tue-Sun. **Credit** AmEx, MC, V. **Map** p310 A4 **❶**

> ❶ Pink numbers given in this chapter correspond to the location of each bar on the street maps. See pp310-315.

This clandestine, maroon-washed nook is part of the touted 'Main Street bar corridor' – essentially, the concept of Hollywood's Cahuenga bar corridor brought West. Our advice for the drinker seeking an intimate beach-style tête-à-tête sans Hollywood-style club beats: arrive early, claim one of the posh benches in the rear lounge and enjoy the eye candy.

Chez Jay

1657 Ocean Avenue, between Colorado Avenue & Pico Boulevard (1-310 395 1741/www.chezjays.com). Bus 33, 333, SM1, SM7, SM8, SM10/I-10, exit 4th-5th Street south. **Open** noon-2am Mon-Fri; 9am-2am Sat, Sun. **Credit** AmEx, MC, V. **Map** p310 A3 **❷**

This shambling, casually bohemian hole-in-the-wall offers a full menu, but it's better used as a bar, a no-nonsense watering hole in an area otherwise devoid of them. Jay Fiondella has presided over the place for some 40 years; the warm welcome he extends to all is well reflected in the cheery constitution of his customers. A better class of tavern.

Circle Bar

2926 Main Street, between Ashland & Pier Avenues (1-310 450 0508/www.thecirclebar.com). Bus 33, 333, SM1, SM2, SM10/I-10, exit 4th-5th Street south. **Open** 9pm-2am Mon-Wed, Sun; 8pm-2am Thur-Sat. **Credit** AmEx, DC, Disc, MC, V. **Map** p310 A4 **❸**

The poster establishment for the effects, beneficial or not, of beachside gentrification. When hotshot restaurateur Will Karges took over the Circle Bar, the employees of this once-dreary dive were so offended they trashed the place on their last night. Now, it's a grungey-chic social staple with Mao-red lighting and black velvet walls. Drinks prices, once the lowest on the Westside, have risen in turn.

Father's Office

1018 Montana Avenue, at 10th Street (1-310 393 2337). Bus SM3, SM11/I-10, exit Lincoln Boulevard north. **Open** 5pm-1am Mon-Thur; 4pm-2am Fri; 3pm-2am Sat; 3pm-midnight Sun. **Credit** MC, V. **Map** p310 B2 **❹**

The bar wall at the dimly lit Father's Office reads like an International Olympic Committee of micro-brews and draughts, while the tapas menu is a cosmopolitan mix of chorizo, cheeses, olive medleys and paprika-dusted almonds. The famed Office Burger is the not-to-be-missed offering.

Hideout

112 W Channel Road, at PCH (1-310 429 9920/ www.santamonicahideout.com). Bus 534, SM9/ I-10, exit PCH north. **Open** 7am-2am daily. **Credit** AmEx, MC, V. **Map** p310 A1 **❺**

Nestled in Santa Monica Canyon, this beachside lounge is a throwback to the sleepy hamlet that

Santa Monica was back in the 1920s. The dark lavender-blue walls, curtained lounge areas and old-fashioned red-cloth pool table practically invite indulgence in $12 Martinis and Cohiba Robustos. On Sundays, drinks are half-price all night.

Voda

1449 2nd Street, between Santa Monica Boulevard & Broadway (1-310 394 9774). Bus 33, 333, SM1, SM5, SM7, SM8, SM10/I-10, exit 4th-5th Street north. **Open** 6pm-2am Mon-Sat. **Credit** AmEx, DC, Disc, MC, V. **Map** p310 A3 **6**

Touted as 'the only vodka-themed bar to serve gourmet food', Voda is another signless, addressless wonder: easy to miss and even easier to get lost in, accented with intimate booths and chiaroscuro lighting. In insider jargon, this means 'very hip', but also, more interestingly, it means swell Martinis and Cosmopolitans of every race and creed.

Venice

Beechwood

822 W Washington Boulevard, at Abbot Kinney Boulevard (1-310 448 8884). Bus 108, C1/I-10, exit Lincoln Boulevard south. **Open** 6pm-midnight Mon-Wed, Sun; 6pm-2am Thur, Sat; 5pm-2am Fri. **Credit** AmEx, MC, V. **Map** p310 B6 **7**

Beechwood is a sparse, teak-adorned space that feels like a ski lodge which somehow mistakenly opened in a beachfront surf community. The chaotic bar scene has overtaken that of the smaller dining room, which may explain the long wait for service. Yes, those oblong couches look inviting, but the best bet is to remove yourself outside to the firepit atrium bar. There's yummy tapas available, too.

Brig

1515 Abbot Kinney Boulevard, at Milwood Avenue (1-310 399 7537). Bus 33, 333, SM2/I-10, exit Lincoln Boulevard south. **Open** 6pm-2am Mon-Thur, Sun; 7pm-2am Fri-Sat. **Credit** AmEx, MC, V. **Map** p310 A6 **8**

One wonders what the daytime drinkers who used to fuel up here would think of their favourite dive becoming a metallically sleek singles scene, not to mention the dance hothouse it is at weekends. Why they kept the pool table is anybody's guess, but we're glad for the old sign: a fighting image of pugilist Babe Brandelli, the joint's original owner.

Otheroom

1201 Abbot Kinney Boulevard, at San Juan Avenue, Venice (1-310 396 6230). Bus 33, 333, SM2/I-10, exit Lincoln Boulevard south. **Open** 5pm-2am daily. **Credit** AmEx, DC, Disc, MC, V. **Map** p310 A5 **9**

There's a line out the door nearly every night at this spacious candlelit brick-and-tin microbrewery, which stocks 15 taps and over 60 beers from Germany, Belgium and the UK as well as an international list of wines, sherries and ports. No food is served, but if you get hungry, they keep a stash of menus from local eateries who'll deliver right to your stool.

Formosa Café. *See p172.*

West LA

Irish Times

3267 Motor Avenue, between Irene Street and Rose Avenue (1-310 559 9648). Bus C3, SM12/I-10, exit National Boulevard west. **Open** 11am-2am Mon-Fri, Sun; 2pm-2am Sat. **Credit** AmEx, DC, Disc, MC, V.

Just what it sounds like, sort of: the Irish Times is actually an ex-German beer garden given a Gaelic twist. It's as popular for its food – bangers and mash, and steak and kidney pie, made to the family recipes of proprietors James and Dolores McGuerin – as for its ever-giving tap. They pour the finest pint of Guinness in the whole city: like sweet, dark candy.

UCLA & Westwood

Whiskey Blue

W Hotel, 930 Hilgard Avenue, at Le Conte Avenue (1-310 443 8232/www.starwoodhotels.com/whotels). Bus 2, 302, 305, 720, SM1, SM2, SM3, SM8, SM12/I-405, exit Wilshire Boulevard east. **Open** 5pm-1.30am daily. **Credit** AmEx, DC, Disc, MC, V.

This Polynesian-themed über-lounge has a scorching case of 'affluenza' yet charitably gives hotel guests priority-entrance. Even if you don't have a room key, it's still worth a visit for the famous faces who pop in on weekends and the eye-catching decor.

Eat, Drink, Shop

Beverly Hills

Avalon Hotel Lounge

Avalon Hotel, 9400 Olympic Boulevard, at S Canon Drive (1-310 277 5221/www.avalonbeverlyhills.com). Bus 28, 328, SM5/I-10, exit Overland Avenue. **Open** 7am-12.30am Mon-Thur, Sun; 7am-2am Fri, Sat. **Credit** AmEx, DC, MC, V. **Map** p311 D4 ❿
Compared to the ab-fab retro-'50s hotel that houses it (*see p56*), this lounge is small and reserved, at the back of the restaurant overlooking a kidney-shaped pool area ringed by cabanas. The theme is white. Evenings see an upper crust of mature sophisticates engaging in the ancient art of schmooze.

Bar on 4

Neiman Marcus, 9700 Wilshire Boulevard, at N Roxbury Drive (1-310 550 5900/www.neiman marcus.com). Bus 20, 21, 720/I-10, exit Robertson Boulevard north. **Open** 11.30am-5pm daily. **Credit** AmEx, DC, Disc, MC, V. **Map** p311 C3 ⓫
Should cocktails and shopping mix this well? Ponder the question here over a devilish white-chocolate Martini. You may even find yourself sitting near a Hollywood A-lister noshing on a $21 lobster club sandwich. The only drawback: small personal TVs that are bolted before each stool around the bar.

Nirvana

8689 Wilshire Boulevard, at S Robertson Boulevard (1-310 657 5040/www.nirvanabeverlyhills.com). Bus 20, 21, 220, 720/I-10, exit Robertson Boulevard north. **Open** 6pm-2am daily. **Credit** AmEx, MC, V. **Map** p312 B4 ⓬
The sexy vibe at this Indian-themed lounge might have something to do with the cushy canopied beds in the fireplace-lit back bar, or the Buddha fountain that gazes back at you from the wall, or even the tapas menu that's titled 'Foreplay'. The weeknight happy hours also screen Bollywood films.

Writer's Bar

Raffles L'Ermitage, 9291 Burton Way, between N Foothill Road & N Elm Drive (1-310 278 3344/www.lermitagehotel.com). Bus 16, 316/I-405, exit Wilshire Boulevard east. **Open** 11am-2am daily. **Credit** AmEx, DC, Disc, MC, V. **Map** p311 D2 ⓭

The best Bars

For the high life

SkyBar (*see p173*); **Tropicana Bar** (*see p174*); **Whiskey Blue** (*see p172*).

For the low life

Hank's Bar (*see p178*); **Power House** (*see p174* **Walk**); **Roost** (*see p176*).

For the easy life

Chez Jay (*see p170*); **Hideout** (*see p170*).

This lobby lounge is all mute taupe-tweeds and simple, curvaceous armchairs. Attire is casual couture, the customers young Hollywood types and hip-hop moguls sipping Dom or Cristal. It's not cheap, of course, but it does host a generous happy hour with an assortment of free treats (you heard us) and by-the-glass house wines for under $10.

West Hollywood, Hollywood & Midtown

West Hollywood

El Carmen

8138 W 3rd Street, between S La Jolla Avenue & S Crescent Heights Boulevard (1-323 852 1552). Bus 16, 217, 218, 316/I-10, exit La Cienega Boulevard north. **Open** 5pm-2am Mon-Fri; 7pm-2am Sat, Sun. **Credit** AmEx, MC, V. **Map** p312 C3 ⓮
Many Angelenos claim this is the city's best tequila bar, and when you're staring down the twin bulls that gaze out at you from this Frida Kahlo-coloured facsimile of a Tijuana roadhouse, you won't be in any position to argue. The bar has more than 100 tequilas and 25 mescals, so go easy, and save some room for the flautas.

Formosa Café

7156 Santa Monica Boulevard, at Formosa Avenue (1-323 850 9050). Bus 4, 212, 304, 312/I-10, exit La Brea Avenue north. **Open** noon-2am daily. **Credit** AmEx, DC, Disc, MC, V. **Map** p312 D2 ⓯
A seven-decade legend, this pan-Asian box retains the feel of old LA despite now drawing a hipster-heavy clientele, who come to ogle the pictures of former, hip-without-trying, regulars like Sinatra and Bogart, and tip down strong Martinis. It doesn't feel quite right without the cigarette smoke hanging in the air, but smokers at least have a very civilised back porch on which to puff. **Photo** *p171*.

Jones Hollywood

7201 Santa Monica Boulevard, at Formosa Avenue (1-323 850 1727). Bus 4, 212, 304, 312/I-10, exit La Brea Avenue north. **Open** 5pm-2am daily. **Credit** AmEx, DC, Disc, MC, V. **Map** p312 D2 ⓰
Home to one of LA's best jukeboxes, this modish rock 'n' roll roadhouse draws young Hollywoodties, messy-haired musicians and the young model-types who, for some reason, always seem to accompany them. The food, Italian in its inspiration, is better than you might expect – go for a pizza or hot apple pie dessert with your Joan Jett, Sid Vicious or Rodney Bingenheimer cocktail.

Monroe's

8623 Melrose Avenue, at Huntley Drive (1-310 360 0066/www.monroesbar.com). Bus 4, 10, 11, 105, 304, 305/I-10, exit Robertson Boulevard north. **Open** 5pm-2am Mon-Fri; 9pm-2am Sat, Sun. **Credit** AmEx, MC, V. **Map** p312 A2 ⓱
Monroe's comes off like a place John Waters would love for its kitsch value and the post-*Swingers* set

Eat, Drink, Shop

L'Scorpion. *See p174.*

would like for its Rat Pack cool. There's prodigious lounge room in the two-storey space, but we preferred to belly up at the majestic 30-foot bar and grab a signature Cosmo. Unfortunately, the parking isn't as inclusive as the co-ed restrooms.

SkyBar

Mondrian Hotel, 8440 W Sunset Boulevard, between N La Cienega Boulevard & N Olive Drive (1-213 848 6025/www.mondrianhotel.com). Bus 2, 302, LDHWH/I-10, exit La Cienega Boulevard north. **Open** 6pm-2am daily. **Credit** AmEx, DC, Disc, MC, V. **Map** p312 B1 ⑱

Its heyday may be behind it, but this lounge is still a great place for spotting celebrities, although it helps if you are one already. If not, call ahead and make a reservation. Despite its misleading name, the lounge is actually located on one of the Mondrian's lower floors, but it does give a good look out over the hotel's terrace and pool.

Hollywood

For **Boardner's**, the **Frolic Room, Musso & Frank Grill**, the **Pig & Whistle** and the **Power House**, *see p174* **Walk**.

Bar

5851 W Sunset Boulevard, at Bronson Avenue (1-323 468 9154). Bus 2, 302/US 101, exit Sunset Boulevard west. **Open** 9pm-2am Mon, Fri, Sat; 8pm-2am Tue-Thur, Sun. **Credit** AmEx, DC, Disc, MC, V. **Map** p313 C2 ⑲

A spot on Sunset where the hippest rockers and their willowy muses come to down pricey but potent drinks and see what everybody else is wearing. It's not easy to spot, so park your car near Bronson and Sunset and ask anyone with a Strokes-style haircut to point out the signless entrance.

Blu Monkey Lounge

5521 Hollywood Boulevard, at Western Avenue (1-323 957 9000/www.blumonkeylounge.com). Metro Hollywood-Western/bus 100, 101, 207, 217/US 101, exit Western Avenue north. **Open** 8pm-2am daily. **Credit** AmEx, DC, Disc, MC, V. **Map** p313 C1 ⑳

Awash in bright colors, this Mediterranean-style hideaway sports the serious simian groove implied by its name, right down to the plastic monkeys clinging to the side of your Martini. It's a high-end spot that bypasses exclusivity when it doesn't have to, and so, of course, it isn't cheap. At weekends, go with the valet, as street parking is next to impossible.

Cat & Fiddle

6530 W Sunset Boulevard, between Seward Street & Wilcox Avenue (1-323 468 3800/www.thecat andfiddle.com). Bus 2, 302/US 101, exit Sunset Boulevard west. **Open** 11.30am-2am daily. **Credit** AmEx, MC, V. **Map** p313 B2 ㉑

Formosa Café (p172)
Yes, that really is Lana Turner in *LA Confidential*. Isn't it?

Rather like Dick van Dyke's accent in *Mary Poppins*, Hollywood's take on pub culture doesn't exactly bring to mind England's green and pleasant hills. The beer is ordinary, the food is no better, and the staff, alternately sullen and sniffy, are pure LA. Despite all this, the place is still packed nightly. Most opt for a table in the attractive courtyard, which features a glowing fountain and overhanging trees.

L'Scorpion

6679 Hollywood Boulevard, at Las Palmas Avenue (1-323 464 3026). Metro Hollywood-Highland/bus 212, 217, LDH/US 101, exit Highland Avenue north. **Open** 6pm-2am Mon-Sat. **Credit** AmEx, DC, Disc, MC, V. **Map** p313 A1 ㉒

The Spanish Colonial interior of this tiny tequila bar is sexy and rustic, but the real draw is the tequilas, over 300 varieties, most of which run $12-$15 per shot (the Don Fulano is a cool $75). We urge care or you will feel the sting. **Photo** *p173.*

Red Buddha Lounge

6423 Yucca Street, at Cahuenga Boulevard (1-323 962 2913/www.theredbuddha.com). Metro Hollywood-Highland/bus 4, 156, 304, LDH, LDHWH/US 101, exit Highland Avenue south. **Open** 9.30pm-2am Tue-Sun. **Credit** AmEx, Disc, MC, V. **Map** p313 B1 ㉓

An upscale scarlet-and-black 'Zen den' that benefits from not shoving its styling at you. The space is long and narrow, with a small dance floor in back that leads to an outdoor patio. There's a cover charge at weekends, but no velvet rope policy. Keep an eye out for the 'Pink Pussy' drink specials.

Three Clubs

1123 Vine Street, at Santa Monica Boulevard (1-323 462 6441). Bus 4, 156, 304/US 101, exit Vine Street south. **Open** 6pm-2am daily. **Credit** AmEx, MC, V. **Map** p313 B2 ㉔

The Three Clubs might be an anonymous-looking spot – keep an eye out for the Bargain Clown Mart sign overhead or you'll miss it – but it nevertheless rewards the serious but genial drinker. Sip away in one of the dark booths, surrounded by flock wallpaper and a ceiling decorated like a sparkling night sky, away from LA's glare. Bands play regularly.

Tropicana Bar

Roosevelt Hotel, 7000 Hollywood Boulevard, at La Brea Avenue (1-323 769 8881/www.hollywood roosevelt.com). Metro Hollywood-Highland/bus 210, 212, 217, 710, LDHWH/US 101, exit Highland Avenue south. **Open** 7pm-2am Mon-Sat; 4-11pm Sun. **Credit** AmEx, DC, Disc, MC, V. **Map** p313 A1 ㉕

Walk Hollywood's vintage bars

The buckets of varnish applied to once-shady Hollywood have helped bring back the star-struck tourists. However, they haven't yet glossed over the drinking subculture that's thrived here for decades. In among the shiny new stores and the velvet rope-guarded nightclubs sit a number of great old bars: some historic, some simply old, but all very much part of a Hollywood that won't quite die.

Looking north from the corner of Hollywood and Highland is instructive, Hollywoods past and present facing off against each other with scarcely concealed antipathy. To the west stands the gleaming Hollywood & Highland complex; directly opposite slumps the **Power**

House (1714 N Highland Avenue, 1-323 463 9438), a squalorous hole in the wall that's somehow survived the renovations. This is a dive, pure and simple, but one with a heart of gold. Your welcome will be warm and your two-buck beer will be cold, all played out to sounds from an impeccably selected jukebox.

The **Pig & Whistle** (6714 Hollywood Boulevard, 1-323 463 0000) opened in 1927 as a restaurant to serve punters from the Egyptian Theatre next door, regular Joes chowing down alongside screen legends. There's now a buzzing bar and DJ scene to go along with the food trade. It's a historic place, but it's got nothing on the **Musso & Frank Grill** (6667 Hollywood Boulevard, 1-323 467 5123) The bar-restaurant has been open since 1919, serving everyone from Chaplin to Chandler, and wears its age with pride: some of the waiters appear to have been here since the silent era. The Martinis, served with weary panache, are as strong as an ox; no wonder Charles Bukowski drank here later in life.

The bar at 50-year-old **Boardner's** (1652 N Cherokee Avenue, 1-323 462 9621) buzzes, but with a different crowd. While Musso's draws a smart bunch, this handsome, atmospheric boozehouse, once favoured by

The slinky, stylish Trop is arguably the new centre for Hollywood's A-list: by night, it's as hard to get into as SkyBar was in the 1990s. If you don't know anyone famous, go before 5pm. *See also p60.*

La Velvet Margarita Cantina

1612 Cahuenga Boulevard, between Selma Avenue & Hollywood Boulevard (1-323 469 2000/www.velvet margarita.com). Metro Hollywood-Vine/bus 180, 181, 210, 212, 217, 710, LDH/US 101, exit Hollywood Boulevard west. **Open** 11.30am-2am Mon-Fri; 6pm-2am Sat, Sun. **Credit** AmEx, DC, Disc, MC, V. **Map** p313 B2 ⓱

If L'Scorpion is too restrained, hoof on down to this colour-dipped 'Tijuana Gothic' pop cathedral that resembles the vampire roadhouse in *From Dusk Till Dawn.* You'll either immediately flee the loud and boisterous vibe, or never leave. The wandering mariachis are a nice touch.

Fairfax District

Canter's Kibitz Room

419 N Fairfax Avenue, at Oakwood Avenue (1-323 651 2030/www.cantersdeli.com). Bus 14, 217, 218/ I-10, exit Fairfax Avenue north. **Open** 10am-2am daily. **Credit** MC, V. **Map** p312 C3 ⓯

An unlikely adjunct to the old-school Canter's Deli *(see p153),* this is an absolute peach of a dive. Early on in the evening it's usually pretty quiet, with little to interrupt the serious imbibing of alcohohol. But later on during the night you'll find bands showing up (some planned, some unannounced) and well and truly rousing the drunks from their stupor. The entertaining barkeeps act as though they're auditioning for a part in *Guns 'n Roses: The Movie.*

Miracle Mile & Midtown

Tom Bergin's

840 S Fairfax Avenue, between Wilshire & San Vicente Boulevards (1-323 936 7151/ www.tombergins.com). Bus 20, 21, 217, 720, LDF/I-10, exit Fairfax Avenue north. **Open** 11.30-2am daily. **Credit** AmEx, DC, Disc, MC, V. **Map** p312 C4 ⓰

Reportedly the bar that inspired *Cheers,* this 70-year-old pub could barely get any more Irish if the air was green mist. Behind the horseshoe-shaped bar is an array of shamrocks, each named after a regular, and gruff but lovable bartenders. St Patrick's Day here is more of a warm, reflective affair than elsewhere in the city.

Robert Mitchum and WC Fields, is a simpler place. Early-evening happy hour is a reflective time, solitary brothers taking the edge off the day with bottles and shots. The pace picks up later, but it's rarely frenetic. A humble landmark, but a landmark all the same.

It's a bit of a stagger down to the final stop in this little bar crawl, but your effort will be rewarded. The **Frolic Room** (6245 Hollywood Boulevard, 1-323 462 5890) has a walk-on

role in *LA Confidential*, its glorious sign lighting Kevin Spacey's way into the night, and has been favoured by a few wilfully debauched stars in recent years. But it remains what it's always been: a prince among dives, a neighbourhood hangout in a neighbourhood without many of them, and a bar not for dilettantes but for drinkers. Goes the song: hooray for Hollywood. Goes the other song: one more for the road...

Koreatown & around

Brass Monkey

659 S Mariposa Avenue, at Wilshire Boulevard,
Koreatown (1-213 381 7047). Metro Wilshire-
Normandie/bus 20, 21, 720/I-10, exit Normandie
Avenue north. **Open** 11am-2am daily. **Credit**
AmEx, Disc, MC, V. **Map** p313 D5 **㉙**

This '70s rumpus-room-cum-ski-lodge may not be
LA's first karaoke bar – that honour falls to Oiwake
in Little Tokyo – but it's certainly the best known. On
some nights, you may have to wait 45 minutes for the
spotlight; on others, you may get multiple shots to
pretend you're auditioning for *American Idol*.

HMS Bounty

3357 Wilshire Boulevard, at S Kenmore Avenue
(1-213 385 7275/http://hmsbounty.net). Metro
Wilshire-Normandie/bus 20, 21, 204, 720/I-10,
exit Western Avenue north. **Open** 11am-10pm Mon,
Sun; 11am-2am Tue-Sat. **Credit** AmEx, Disc, MC, V.
Map p313 D5 **㉚**

This nautical-themed treasure (it's 20 miles from the
ocean) wins for people-watching potential: office
drones, drag queens and hard rockers mingle with
folks from the residential hotel upstairs. The food's
pretty good, especially the big burgers and pork
chops, and the free jukebox is a nice touch. The most
important thing, though? Cheap drinks.

Prince

3198 W 7th Street, at S New Hampshire Avenue,
Koreatown (1-213 389 1586). Metro Wilshire-
Vermont/bus 20, 21, 720, LDWCK/I-10, exit
Vermont Avenue north. **Open** 4pm-2am daily.
Credit AmEx, DC, Disc, MC, V. Map p314 A6 **㉛**

You'll hear Korean easy listening music at this dimly
lit restaurant-lounge, but, strangely, the decor apes
that of a British gentlemen's club in St James (red-
velvet flecked wallpaper, figurine lamps, gilt-framed
oil paintings). Serious juicers nosh on the bar snacks;
you might just want to park yourself in one of the
blood-red booths with a Hite.

Los Feliz, Silver Lake & Echo Park

Los Feliz & Atwater Village

Bigfoot Lodge

3172 Los Feliz Boulevard, between Edenhurst
Avenue & Glenfeliz Boulevard (1-323 662 9227/
www.thebigfootlodge.com). Bus 180, 181/I-5, exit
Los Feliz Boulevard east. **Open** 5pm-2am daily.
Credit AmEx, Disc, MC, V.

A twisted lounge version of a Canadian fishing
lodge, the Bigfoot boasts an effigy of Smokey the
Bear and woodwork that replicates the great outdoors. There are comfy seats in the back lounge,
where you can sip on such staff-invented libations
as the Girl Scout Cookie and the Sasquatch. Rock 'n'
Roll Karaoke Mondays are a must.

Dresden Room

1760 N Vermont Avenue, between Franklin Avenue
& Hollywood Boulevard (1-213 665 4294/www.the
dresden.com). Bus 4, 156, 204, 754/US 101, exit
Vermont Avenue north. **Open** 11am-2am Mon-Sat;
3-10pm Sun. **Credit** AmEx, MC, V. **Map** p314 A2 **㉜**

Despite the cameo in *Swingers* made by house band
Marty and Elayne, who still make a quite unspeak-
able noise (9pm-1am Tue-Sat), this landmark tavern
hasn't changed to suit the times, retaining its tacky
white leather and corkboard interior. Come armed
with irony and earplugs.

Good Luck Bar

1514 N Hillhurst Avenue, at Hollywood Boulevard
(1-323 666 3524). Bus 4, 156, 204, 754/US 101,
exit Hollywood Boulevard east. **Open** 7pm-2am
Mon-Fri; 8pm-2am Sat, Sun. **Credit** MC, V.
Map p314 B3 **㉝**

Thanks to its gaudy, mock-Mandarin decor, the Good
Luck makes out like the secret Shanghai meeting
place for gangsters in a John Woo film. The bar stocks
Chinese liqueurs and brandies, and mixes a pretty
solid Singapore Sling; however, the predominantly
college-age crowd seems to prefer beer or shots.

Roost

3100 Los Feliz Boulevard, at Edenhurst Avenue
(1-323 664 7272). Bus 180, 181/I-5, exit Los
Feliz Boulevard east. **Open** 10am-2am daily.
No credit cards.

The Roost is a raggedy Western-themed dive that
always feels about ten years past its prime. Which
is why budget-conscious Atwater Village hipsters
(who once included the late punk-folk busker Elliott
Smith) come to fuel up on its cheap but strong drinks
and free baskets of peanuts and popcorn.

Silver Lake

4100 Bar

4100 Sunset Boulevard, between Fountain Avenue
& Santa Monica Boulevard (1-323 666 4460).
Bus 2, 26, 175, 302/US 101, exit Vermont Avenue
north. **Open** 8pm-2am daily. **Credit** AmEx, Disc,
MC, V. **Map** p314 B3 **㉞**

The 4100 started as a gay nightclub, but has since
morphed into a sleek urban hideaway with a killer
jukebox and a lack of attitude regarding dress code
and sexual preference. A lot of off-duty bartenders
stop by for a drink, which should tell you that the
mixologists here are top shelf.

Cha Cha Lounge

2375 Glendale Boulevard, at Silver Lake Boulevard
(1-323 660 7595). Bus 92/I-5, exit Glendale
Boulevard south. **Open** 4pm-1.30am Mon-Fri;
5pm-2am daily. **Credit** AmEx, DC, Disc, MC, V.
Map p314 D2 **㉟**

Prince (p176) Faye Dunaway meets
Jack Nicholson here in *Chinatown*

Slum it in style Downtown at the **Golden Gopher**. *See p178.*

The Cha Cha is a beer bar that really amps up the *Dia de los Muertos*-meets-Polynesia kitsch. The music is equally lo-fi: old vinyl LPs are played on a rickety turntable for maximum snap/crackle/pop effect. There's a big sandbox out at the front for ciggies and a tiny lot out back for parking.

Johnny's Cocktail Lounge

2939 W Sunset Boulevard, at Silver Lake Boulevard (1-323 660 2276). Bus 2, 4, 201, 302, 304/US 101, exit Silver Lake Boulevard north. **Open** 8pm-2am daily. **Credit** AmEx, DC, Disc, MC, V. **Map** p314 C4 **36**

Naturally, Johnny's black-as-pitch *boîte* has no sign outside the premises: look out for the neon Martini glass above the door. The interior is, of course, also sparse; the wine, champagne and port selections (served in globular snifter mugs) are better than in your usual lounge. In a twist, the sweet potato-based soju cocktails are named after local landmarks, including Car Wash on Sunset and Reservoir.

Smog Cutter

864 N Virgil Avenue, between Normal & Burns Avenues (1-323 660 4626). Bus 10, 11, 26/US 101, exit Vermont Avenue north. **Open** 1pm-2am daily. **No credit cards. Map** p314 B4 **37**

You'll notice this karaoke dive's sign in the opening frames of *Barfly*. Tough-talking Filipina barmaids, following the motto hung over the bar ('Hangovers installed and serviced!'), encourage you to imbibe, while everyone from Japanese businessmen to Silver Lake hipsters take their turn at the microphone.

Tiki-Ti

4427 W Sunset Boulevard, between Sunset Drive & Fountain Avenue (1-213 669 9381). Bus 2, 26, 175, 302/US 101, exit Vermont Avenue north. **Open** 6pm-1am Wed, Thur; 6pm-2am Fri, Sat. **No credit cards. Map** p314 B3 **38**

This outhouse-sized gem dares to ask the question: how many Polynesian-related knicknacks can you pack into a tiny box while still leaving room for customers? They take their sweet exotic drinks seriously: use caution when tangling with the Blood and Sand, the Stealth or the signature Ray's Mistake, named after the bar's late, much-loved founder.

Echo Park

Gold Room

1558 W Sunset Boulevard, at Echo Park Avenue (1-213 482 5259). Bus 2, 4, 302, 304/US 101, exit Glendale Boulevard. **Open** 11pm-2am Mon-Thur, Sun; 9pm-2am Fri, Sat. **Credit** AmEx, MC, V. **Map** p314 D5 **39**

This Mexican spot has withstood the hipsterisation of Echo Park: it's still a peanut-shell-on-the-floor kinda place, distinguished by a top shelf of tequilas and weekend mariachi band. On Sundays, it's packed with *futbol* fans watching Mexican League action on cable; but we wager the real sport is watching the waitresses, dolled up in red and white outfits that barely cover their crests and troughs.

Short Stop

1455 W Sunset Boulevard, between Sutherland & Portia Streets (1-213 482 4942). Bus 2, 4/I-110, exit Sunset Boulevard. **Open** 5pm-2am daily. **Credit** AmEx, Disc, MC, V. **Map** p314 D5 **40**

The Eastside renaissance got its watering hole when Afghan Whigs frontman Greg Dulli bought this old cop dive bar. The bar and singles scene is still hopping despite the ban on dancing: the club's famous photo booth more than makes up for a reason to canoodle. Still, it's a small, kinetic shebang, especially on weekends. If you're thirsty, be warned: you might be in for a lengthy wait at the three-deep bar.

Highland Park & Eagle Rock

Chalet
1630 Colorado Boulevard, at Townshend Avenue, Eagle Rock (1-323 258 8800). Bus 81, 180, 780/Hwy 2, exit Colorado Boulevard east. **Open** 7pm-2am daily. **Credit** AmEx, DC, Disc, MC, V.
As you get deeper into the valleys, you'll find more establishments going for some sort of Alpine ski lodge feel even though there hasn't been a significant snow-storm in LA in 73 years. Drinking a Gentleman Jack amid such splendour is like being on an idyllic snow retreat without the annoying time-share seminars.

Little Cave
5922 N Figueroa Street, at Avenue 59, Highland Park (1-323 255 6871/www.littlecave.com). Metro Highland Park/bus 81, 176/I-110, exit Avenue 43 north. **Open** 5pm-2am daily. **Credit** AmEx, DC, Disc, MC, V.
Jagged ersatz-brick walls, Hallowe'en-themed cocktails and the upside-down vampire bats that hang over the door makes this popular new grotto LA's first successful goth bar for years. But it ain't all black eyeliner and Robert Smith hairdos: on special music nights, electronica DJs and other local musicians invade the tiny space.

Downtown

Broadway Bar
830 S Broadway, at 8th Street (1-213 614 9909/www.thebroadwaybar.net). Metro Pershing Square/bus 10, 11, 38, 48, 81/I-110, exit 9th Street east. **Open** 5pm-2am Mon-Sat. **Credit** AmEx, DC, Disc, MC, V. **Map** p315 C4 ㊶
The Golden Gopher may be more popular with club-bers, but this glitzy Vegas-style palace is Downtown's newest ode to the art of tippling with a tough-talkin' moll on your arm. The *noir*-ishly lit space is huge, with a circular bar as the main attraction. Parking is no problem, partly due to the dodgy neighbourhood.

Gallery Bar
Millennium Biltmore Hotel, 506 S Grand Avenue, between W 5th & W 6th Streets (1-213 624 1011/www.millenniumhotels.com). Metro Pershing Square/bus 14, 37, 76, 78, 79, 96/I-110, exit 6th Street east. **Open** 4pm-1.30am daily. **Credit** AmEx, DC, MC, V. **Map** p315 B3 ㊷
The Gallery is largely frequented by financial dis-trict executives enjoying Martinis by the piano; a more interesting option is a Black Dahlia, named for the LA murder victim who was last seen alive in the hotel lobby. Check out the boss 1889 pool table (nets instead of slots) formerly owned by Willie Moscone.

Golden Gopher
417 W 8th Street, between Hill & Olive Streets (1-213 614 8001). Metro 7th Street-Metro Center/bus 10, 11, 38, 48, 81/I-110, exit 9th Street east. **Open** 5pm-2am Tue-Fri; 8pm-2am Sat. **Credit** AmEx, DC, Disc, MC, V. **Map** p315 C4 ㊸

This place started talk of barhopping in Downtown, although the winos who used to hang out here have been doing that for years. The new owners have kept the old name but refurbished with wraparound couches, bordello chandeliers, tenement-brick walls and a quirky mini-bodega selling mints, cigs and tiny 'Liquor to Go' bottles. It's still a shitty area, but this is what slumming is all about. **Photo** *p177*.

Hank's Bar
Stillwell Hotel, 840 S Grand Avenue, between W 8th & W 9th Streets (1-213 623 7718). Metro 7th Street-Metro Center/bus 14, 37, 76, 78, 79, 96/I-110, exit 9th Street east. **Open** 11am-2am daily. **Credit** MC, V. **Map** p315 B4 ㊹
One of Downtown's real old glories, this seedy, feck-less watering hole sits beneath a residential hotel, its inhabitants making up the bulk of the clientele. Failed writers sit next to old people in bathrobes; every half hour, someone strikes up a 'US of A ver-sus Everyone Else' argument. Try and avoid hitting on the long-legged mannequin, no matter how irre-sistible she looks after the seventh bottle of Bud.

Little Pedro's Blue Bongo
901 E 1st Street, at Vignes Street (1-213 687 3766). Metro Union Station-Gateway Transit Center/bus 30, 31, 330/US 101, exit Alameda Street south. **Open** 4pm-1.30am Mon-Fri; 4pm-2am Sat; 4-11pm Sun. **Credit** AmEx, Disc, MC, V.
Little Pedro's has been around since the late 1800s, but its new owners have installed a whole lotta crazy colourful crap – blue tablecloths, lavender carpets, a forest of frozen stuffed animals – to balance the lunchtime cops, happy-hour suits and after-dark bohos who seem to trade off in shifts. The live music and DJ nights are the best in the area.

Pete's Café & Bar
400 S Main Street, at W 4th Street (1-213 617 1000). Metro Pershing Square/bus 16, 316/I-110, exit 6th Street east. **Open** 11.30am-2am Mon-Sat; 11.30am-midnight Sun. **Credit** AmEx, DC, Disc, MC, V. **Map** p315 C3 ㊺
Head to Pete's and you may spot City Hall muckety-mucks engaging in empowerlunchment. Coral blinds, large windows and languorous fans draw down a high ceiling while mustard walls lighten the space. Half a dozen beers are available on tap, and there's also a worthwhile cocktail list and a solid menu of glorified pub food. Skid Row is nearby.

Roof at the Standard
Standard Downtown Hotel, 550 S Flower Street, between W 5th & W 6th Streets (1-213 892 8080/www.standardhotel.com). Metro 7th Street-Metro Center/bus 16, 18, 55, 60, 62, 316/I-110, exit 6th Street east. **Open** noon-2am daily. **Credit** AmEx, DC, Disc, MC, V. **Map** p315 B3 ㊻
This rooftop oasis looks like a design from *Rollerball*, and comes with an aggressively hip vibe that would suit the sport. Snag a seat by the pool, surrounded by NASA-meets-Arabian Nights cabana pods and Astroturf. Sunday afternoons are star-studded.

Shops & Services

Buy, buy, Miss American Pie.

The best retailers are budding within the **Grove**. *See p180.*

The diamond-studded boutiques of popular myth and legend are still very much in evidence here, especially on world-famous Rodeo Drive and the streets that surround it. However, LA's shopping scene goes far beyond such ostentation and luxury. From the bohemian boutiques of Venice to the bargain-bin knock-off stalls in the Fashion District, the variety is overwhelming. For more on the city's key shopping districts, *see p181* **Where to shop**.

Shop opening hours around Los Angeles are usually 10am to 7pm, though shops based in malls are usually open a couple of hours later. Return policies in the big chains are nearly always in the buyer's favour, but some smaller boutiques will go to the other end of the world to avoid giving you your money back. Parking is usually not too difficult. LA County adds an 8.25 per cent sales tax to the marked price of all merchandise and services; Orange County taxes at 7.75 per cent.

General

Department stores

LA has many branches of **Sears** (Hollywood store: 5601 Santa Monica Boulevard, 1-323 769 2600, www.sears.com) and **Robinsons-May** (Beverly Hills store: 9900 Wilshire Boulevard, 1-310 275 5464, www.robinsonsmay.com.

Barneys New York

9570 Wilshire Boulevard, at S Camden Drive, Beverly Hills (1-310 276 4400/www.barneys.com). Bus 20, 21, 720/I-10, exit Robertson Boulevard north. **Open** 10am-7pm Mon-Wed; 10am-8pm Thur-Sat; noon-6pm Sun. **Credit** AmEx, MC, V. **Map** p311 C3.

A good facsimile of the legendary New York store, Barneys offers four floors of cosmetics, jewellery, shoes, designer clothes (for both sexes), lingerie and home accessories. Above sits more elegance: Barney Greengrass, a classy rooftop restaurant and bar.

Bloomingdale's

Westfield Shoppingtown Century City, 10250 Santa Monica Boulevard, between Century Park W & Avenue of the Stars, Century City (1-310 772 2100/www.bloomingdales.com). Bus 4, 28, 304, 316, 328/I-405, exit Santa Monica Boulevard east. **Open** 10am-9pm Mon- Sat; 11am-7pm Sun. **Credit** AmEx, Disc, MC, V. **Map** p311 B4.

Known as Bloomies by its many fans, this upmarket store, doing business in Los Angeles since 1996, specialises in designer clothing, shoes, jewellery and accessories, along with its own-brand clothing. **Other locations**: throughout LA.

Macy's

Beverly Center, 8500 Beverly Boulevard, at S La Cienega Boulevard, West Hollywood (1-310 854 6655/www.macys.com). Bus 14, 16, 105, 316, LDF, LDHWH/I-10, exit La Cienega Boulevard north. **Open** 10am-9.30pm Mon-Sat; 11am-7pm Sun. **Credit** AmEx, MC, V. **Map** p312 B3.

Macy's has spent the past decade expanding from its original New York home right across the nation. Its wares include costly garments from mostly US designers, but also plenty of more affordable clothing lines, accessories and cosmetics. **Other locations**: throughout LA.

Neiman Marcus

9700 Wilshire Boulevard, at S Roxbury Drive, Beverly Hills (1-310 550 5900/www.neimanmarcus. com). Bus 20, 21, 720/I-10, exit Robertson Boulevard north. **Open** 10am-6pm Mon-Fri; 10am-7pm Sat; noon-6pm Sun. **Credit** AmEx. **Map** p311 C3.

Neiman Marcus may be widely nicknamed 'Needless Mark-ups', but nothing is really overpriced here; the goods here are simply top-of-the-line and you pay for the quality of products you purchase. The store has one of the best women's shoe departments in town and a good cosmetics section.

Nordstrom

Westside Pavilion, 10830 W Pico Boulevard, at Westwood Boulevard, West LA (1-310 470 6155/www.nordstrom.com). Bus C3, SM7, SM13/I-10, exit Overland Boulevard north. **Open** 10am-9pm Mon-Thur; 10am-9pm Fri; 10am-8pm Sat; 11am-7pm Sun. **Credit** AmEx, Disc, MC, V. **Map** p311 A5.

In the hierarchy of prestigious department stores, Nordstrom falls neatly into the middle: not as costly nor as swish as Neiman Marcus (is anywhere?), but both dearer and smarter than Macy's. The men's and women's shoe departments are uniformly excellent. **Other locations**: The Grove, 189 The Grove Drive, Fairfax District (1-323 930 2230); 200 W Broadway, Glendale (1-818 502 9922); *Nordstrom Rack* 6081 Center Drive, Culver City (1-310 641 4046).

Saks Fifth Avenue

9600 Wilshire Boulevard, at S Bedford Drive, Beverly Hills (1-310 275 4211/www.saksfifth avenue.com). Bus 20, 21, 720/I-405, exit Wilshire Boulevard east. **Open** 10am-6pm Mon-Wed, Fri; 10am-8pm Thur; 10am-7pm Sat; noon-6pm Sun. **Credit** AmEx, MC, V. **Map** p311 C3.

The byword for glamorous department stores, Saks opened its Beverly Hills branch in 1938 and continues to draw the city's biggest spenders with a classy selection of men's and women's clothing. **Other locations**: 35 N De Lacey Street, Pasadena (1-626 396 7100).

Target

7100 Santa Monica Boulevard, West Hollywood (1-323 603 0004/www.target.com). Bus 4, 212, 304, 312, LDHWH/I-10, exit La Brea Avenue north. **Open** 8am-10pm Mon-Sat; 8am-9pm Sun. **Credit** AmEx, MC, V.

Target has reinvented itself with the help of designers such as Isaac Mizrahi and Philippe Starck; locals jokingly pronounce the name 'Targée'. It's basically a good place to pick up low-cost designer labels, simple clothes, appliances and toys. **Other locations**: throughout LA.

Malls

Beverly Center

8500 Beverly Boulevard, at S La Cienega Boulevard, West Hollywood (1-310 854 0070/www.beverly center.com). Bus 14, 16, 105, 316, LDF, LDHWH/ I-10, exit La Cienega Boulevard north. **Open** 10am-9pm Mon-Fri; 10am-8pm Sat; 11am-6pm Sun. **Map** p312 B3.

It won't win any architectural awards, but this humungous mall, anchored by branches of Macy's and Bloomingdale's, is nonetheless a good one-stop all-rounder. Fashion retailers include Diesel, Banana Republic, Gap, Karen Millen, DKNY and, as of 2006, Ben Sherman; other popular shops include MAC Cosmetics and a huge Bed, Bath & Beyond. There's also a decent food court and a multi-screen cinema.

Glendale Galleria

N Central Avenue & W Broadway, Glendale (1-818 240 9481/www.glendalegalleria.com). Bus 180, 181, 183, 201/I-5, exit Colorado Street east. **Open** 10am-9pm Mon-Fri; 10am-8pm Sat; 11am-7pm Sun.

The largest shopping mall in the Valley boasts around 260 stores. There are four major department stores here: JC Penney, Robinsons-May, Macy's and Nordstrom; Timberland, Bebe, Abercrombie & Fitch and Lucky Brand Jeans are just a few of the innumerable fashion shops on site.

Grove

Farmers Market, 189 The Grove Drive, at W 3rd Street, Fairfax District (1-323 900 8080/www.the grovela.com). Bus 16, 217, 218, LDF/I-10, exit Fairfax Avenue north. **Open** 10am-9pm Mon-Thur; 10am-10pm Fri, Sat; 11am-7pm Sun. **Map** p312 C3.

In a town where most malls are housed inside bland, air-conditioned structures, this upscale open-air mall has been a hit. There are only some 50 retailers, but the selection is strong: an Apple Store, Anthropologie, and the West Coast's flagship Abercrombie & Fitch. There's also a decent movie theatre. Fears that it would kill the adjacent Farmers Market (*see p154*) have, happily, proven groundless. **Photo** *p179*.

Where to shop

SANTA MONICA & VENICE

Santa Monica's pedestrianised, chain-packed **Third Street Promenade** is popular, but there's more interesting shopping to be found north on **Montana Avenue**, tidily lined with upscale boutiques. South of Santa Monica, **Main Street** in Ocean Park has a variety of stores selling clothes and gifts. And in Venice, head first to the proudly independent gift, clothing and art stores on **Abbot Kinney Boulevard** before you think of heading to the **Boardwalk** for $2 shades and African masks.

BEVERLY HILLS

A few familiar chains have moved into the **Golden Triangle**, bounded by Santa Monica Boulevard, Wilshire Boulevard and Rexford Drive, but this is still swank central. As such, it's wonderful for window shopping, poor for actual purchasing. Chichi boutiques are also in abundance on the stretch of **Robertson Boulevard** south of Beverly Boulevard.

WEST HOLLYWOOD & HOLLYWOOD

The highlight of West Hollywood's shopping is to be found at **Sunset Plaza**, on Sunset Boulevard just east of La Cienega Boulevard. Shopping in Hollywood itself is scrappy, but the **Hollywood & Highland** complex does hold some worthwhile stores.

FAIRFAX & MELROSE DISTRICTS

There's plenty of stylish shopping on **Melrose Avenue** between Fairfax Avenue and San Vicente Boulevard. South and east of here, the pedestrian-friendly stretch of **W 3rd Street** between La Cienega and Crescent Heights Boulevards is also awash with great independent shops and cafés.

LOS FELIZ & SILVER LAKE

Both these East Side neighbourhoods offer a cultured, alt-slanted selection of stores. In Los Feliz, head to **Vermont Avenue** and **Hillhurst Avenue**; Silver Lake's shopping is concentrated around **Sunset Junction** and along Sunset Boulevard.

DOWNTOWN

Central **Downtown** doesn't offer much shopping of note, but its edges contain treasures. Both **Chinatown** and **Little Tokyo** have worthwhile multicultural shopping; further south, the **Fashion District** offers bargains galore, not all of them legitimate.

THE VALLEYS

Shopping in the Valleys is focused around malls, but Old Town in **Pasadena** breaks the mould. Centred around Colorado Boulevard, its old buildings have been modernised to form a handsome, strollable street.

Hollywood & Highland

6801 Hollywood Boulevard, at N Highland Avenue, Hollywood (1-323 817 0220/www.hollywoodand highland.com). Metro Hollywood-Highland/bus 210, 212, 217, 710, LDH, LDHWH/US 101, exit Highland Avenue south. **Open** 10am-10pm Mon-Sat; 10am-7pm Sun. **Map** p313 A1.

Initially blighted by the loss of tourist trade post 9/11 and not helped by a hopelessly confusing layout, this glitzy new mall has at last started to come into its own. The flagship retailer is a Virgin Megastore that attempts to reinvent its brand as a lifestyle shop; also present are Banana Republic, Express, and Swarovski. For the toddler who has everything, the Build-a-Bear Workshop allows the custom construction of the teddy of his dreams. Restaurants include two Wolfgang Puck eateries.

Westfield Shoppingtown Century City

10250 Santa Monica Boulevard, between Century Park W & Avenue of the Stars, Century City (1-310 277 3898/www.westfield.com). Bus 4, 28, 304, 316, 328/I-405, exit Santa Monica Boulevard east. **Open** 10am-9pm Mon-Sat; 11am-6pm Sun. **Map** p311 B4.

Management are hoping that a recent programme of renovations and refurbishments will reposition this outdoor mall as the main competitor to the Grove. Only time will tell, but the 130-plus strong collection of shops and restaurants is pretty strong: Brooks Brothers, Abercrombie & Fitch, Crabtree & Evelyn, and Louis Vuitton are tucked in alongside the inevitable Gaps and Banana Republics.

Westside Pavilion

10800 W Pico Boulevard, at Westwood Boulevard, West LA (1-310 474 6255/www.westsidepavilion. com). Bus C3, SM7, SM13/I-10, exit Overland Boulevard north. **Open** 10am-9pm Mon-Fri; 10am-8pm Sat; 11am-6pm Sun. **Map** p311 A5.

This glass-roofed Westside mall is also getting a renovation. The work will be completed in 2007, when a new cinema and a variety of long-promised and much-needed restaurants will finally open to the public. In the meantime, though, the likes of Nordstrom, Macy's Furniture Gallery, Robinsons-May, Lili's of Beverly Hills, Ann Taylor and Victoria's Secret remain open for business. Fans of Tom Petty might like to note that he filmed his video for *Free Fallin'* here while riding the escalators.

Eat, Drink, Shop

Speciality

Art supplies

Blick Art Materials in West Hollywood (7301 West Beverly Boulevard, 1-323 933 9284, www.blick.com) is a good source for everything from frames and portfolios to art books.

Aaron Brothers Art Mart

1645 Lincoln Boulevard, between Colorado Avenue & Olympic Boulevard, Santa Monica (1-310 450 6333/www.aaronbrothers.com). Bus 534, SM5/ I-10, exit Lincoln Boulevard north. **Open** 10am-9pm Mon-Sat; 10am-6pm Sun. **Credit** AmEx, Disc, MC, V. **Map** p310 B3.

The Westside's biggest art supply shop has a huge range of stuff, much of it at good prices. **Other locations**: throughout LA.

Books

There are branches of **Barnes & Noble** and **Borders** all over LA. To get you started, B&N has a shop at the Grove (1-323 525 0270, www. bn.com), and there's a Borders on the Third Street Promenade in Santa Monica (No.1415, 1-310 393 9290, www.borderstores.com). Call one or check online to find your nearest.

There are speciality bookstores all over LA. Aside from those listed below, there are stores devoted to comics (**Meltdown**, 7522 W Sunset Boulevard, Hollywood, 1-323 851 7223, www. meltcomics.com), food (**Cook's Library**, 8373 W 3rd Street, West Hollywood, 1-323 655 3141, www.cookslibrary.com; **photo** p183), African American interest (**Eso-Won**, 3655 S La Brea Avenue, Crenshaw, 1-323 294 0324, http:// esowon.booksense.com), spirituality (**Bodhi Tree**, 8585 Melrose Avenue, West Hollywood, 1-310 659 1733, www.bodhitree.com) and everything from sensory deprivation to serial killers (**Koma**, 814 S La Brea Avenue, between W 8th & W 9th Streets, Miracle Mile, 1-213 622 0501, www.komabookstore.com).

Acres of Books

240 N Long Beach Boulevard, at Maple Way, Long Beach (1-310 562 437 6980/www.acresofbooks.com). Metro 5th Street/I-710, exit Broadway east. **Open** 10am-9pm Mon-Sat; 10am-5pm Sun. **Credit** MC, V.

It may not be the best used bookshop in LA, but Acres of Books lives up to its name: it's easily the biggest.

Book Soup

8818 Sunset Boulevard, between Larabee Street & Horn Avenue, West Hollywood (1-310 659 3110/ www.booksoup.com). Bus 2, 105, 302/I-10, exit La Cienega Boulevard north. **Open** 9am-10pm Mon-Sat; 9am-7pm Sun. **Credit** AmEx, DC, Disc, MC, V. **Map** p312 A2.

The stock at Book Soup is huge and diverse, even if the space itself is cramped, and the newsstand is well stocked with domestic and international papers.

Children's Book World

10580½ W Pico Boulevard, between Prosser & Parnell Avenues, West LA (1-310 559 2665/www.childrens bookworld.com). Bus C3, SM7, SM13/I-10, exit Overland Avenue north. **Open** 10am-5.30pm Mon-Fri; 10am-5pm Sat. **Credit** MC, V. **Map** p311 B5.

A huge children's bookshop, with 80,000 titles and an incredibly knowledgeable staff. There are story-telling sessions three Saturdays a month.

A Different Light

8853 Santa Monica Boulevard, at N San Vicente Boulevard, West Hollywood (1-310 854 6601/ www.adlbooks.com). Bus 2, 105, 302/I-10, exit La Cienega Boulevard north. **Open** 10am-11pm daily. **Credit** MC, V. **Map** p312 A2.

America's most famous gay bookshop, A Different Light opened in 1979. In addition to selling books, vids and mags for gays, lesbians and transgendered people, the shop hosts readings and book signings.

Equator Books

1103 Abbot Kinney Boulevard, at Westminster Avenue, Venice (1-310 399 5544/www.equator books.com). Bus 33, 333, SM1, SM2/I-10, exit 4th-5th Street south. **Open** 11am-10pm Tue-Thur; 11am-11pm Fri, Sat; 11am-5pm Sun. **Credit** MC, V. **Map** p310 A5.

One of the highlights of Abbot Kinney Boulevard, Equator offers a gloriously esoteric selection of books, from chunky pictorial tomes on modern photography to drug abuse. The walls hold exhibitions.

Samuel French

7623 W Sunset Boulevard, at N Stanley Avenue, West Hollywood (1-323 876 0570/www.samuel french.com). Bus 2, 302, LDHWH/I-10, exit Fairfax Avenue north. **Open** 10am-6pm Mon-Fri; 10am-5pm Sat. **Credit** AmEx, Disc, MC, V. **Map** p312 C1.

From silver screen to printed page: Samuel French sells just about every film script in print, plus myriad theatre scripts and books about drama and film. **Other locations**: 11963 Ventura Boulevard, Studio City (1-818 762 0535).

Skylight Books

1818 N Vermont Avenue, at Melbourne Avenue, Los Feliz (1-323 660 1175/www.skylightbooks.com). Metro Vermont-Sunset/bus 204, 206, 754/US 101, exit Vermont Avenue north. **Open** 10am-10pm daily. **Credit** AmEx, MC, V. **Map** p314 A2.

This 'fiercely independent' (their words) bookstore in Los Feliz strikes a neat balance between intellectual crowd-pleasers and genuine esoterica.

Small World Books

1407 Ocean Front Walk, at Horizon Avenue, Venice (1-310 399 2360/www.smallworldbooks.com). Bus 33, 333, SM1, SM2/I-10, exit 4th-5th Street south. **Open** 10am-8pm daily. **Credit** AmEx, MC, V. **Map** p310 A5.

Tucked away amid the T-shirt hawkers, pamphleteers and jewellery makers on the Venice Boardwalk is this terrific indie bookseller. The stock carried is a suitably all-round mixture for this location, everything from pop fiction to scientific tomes.

Traveler's Bookcase

8375 W 3rd Street, at S King's Road, West Hollywood (1-323 655 0575/www.travelbooks.com). Bus 16/I-10, exit La Cienega Boulevard north. **Open** 10am-6pm Mon-Sat; 11am-5pm Sun. **Credit** AmEx, MC, V. **Map** p312 B3.

The best travel bookshop in the Los Angeles area – in fact, it's arguably the best to be found on the whole of the West Coast – offers a broad range of guide books and maps, along with an impeccably chosen selection of travel literature. The friendly staff are more than happy to offer recommendations.

Vroman's

695 E Colorado Boulevard, between N El Molino & N Oak Knoll Avenues, Pasadena (1-626 449 5320/www.vromansbookstore.com). Metro Lake/bus 181, 485/I-110, exit Colorado Boulevard east. **Open** 9am-9pm Mon-Thur; 9am-10pm Fri, Sat; 10am-8pm Sun. **Credit** AmEx, Disc, MC, V.

The largest independent bookshop in SoCal was founded over a century ago, and provides welcome competition to the big two up in the Valley. Watch out for the regular readings and book signings. **Other locations**: *Vroman's Hastings Ranch* 3729 E Foothill Boulevard, Pasadena (1-626 351 0828).

DVD sales & rentals

To find the nearest branch of the ubiquitous **Blockbuster** chain, see www.blockbuster.com. For **Amoeba Music**, *see p201.*

Rocket Video

726 N La Brea Avenue, between Melrose & Waring Avenues, Hollywood (1-323 965 1100/www.rocketvideo.com). Bus 10, 11, 212/I-10, exit La Brea Avenue north. **Open** 10am-11pm daily. **Credit** AmEx, MC, V. **Map** p313 A3.

The cinephile's video shop, Rocket is your best bet for finding that obscure foreign masterpiece.

Vidiots

302 Pico Boulevard, at 3rd Street, Santa Monica (1-310 392 8508/www.vidiotsvideo.com). Bus 33, 333, SM7, SM8/I-10, exit Lincoln Boulevard north. **Open** 10am-11pm Mon-Thur, Sun; 10am-midnight Fri, Sat. **Credit** AmEx, MC, V. **Map** p310 A3.

This wonderfully named store has all the usual commercial fare, but plenty more besides: foreign flicks, art-house videos and rare films, on DVD and video.

Electronics

There are **Circuit City** and **Best Buy** stores all over LA: the former's locations include 1839 S La Cienega Boulevard (1-310 280 0700, www.circuitcity.com), while the latter are at 1015 N La Brea Avenue in West Hollywood (1-323 883

Cook's Library. See p182.

Eat, Drink, Shop

0219, www.bestbuy.com). **Radio Shack** have a shop in West Hollywood (754 N Fairfax Avenue, 1-323 653 2767, www.radioshack. com), among other spots, while budget chain **Fry's** are in Burbank and Manhattan Beach (www.frys.com). **CompUSA** sell PCs and other gear in Burbank (761 N San Fernando Boulevard, 1-818 848 8588, www.compusa. com); Mac stalwarts should try the **Apple Store** at the Grove (*see p180*; 1-323 965 8400, www.apple.com).

Fashion

Children

There are branches of **Gap Kids** everywhere, including one on the Third Street Promenade in Santa Monica (No.1355, 1-310 393 0719, www.gap.com). Call 1-800 427 7895 to find your nearest.

Entertaining Elephants

12053½ Ventura Place, Studio City (1-818 766 9177/www.entertainingelephants.com). Bus 150, 240, 750/US 101, exit Laurel Canyon Boulevard south. **Open** 10am-6pm Tue-Sat; 9am-2pm Sun. **Credit** AmEx, Disc, MC, V.
Sophisticated, modern clothes and accessories, plus furniture and toys, from around the globe. There's an emphasis on natural and recycled materials: items can be bought in good conscience.

Flap Happy

2330 Michigan Avenue, at 24th Street, Santa Monica (1-310 453 3527/www.flaphappy.com). Bus SM5, SM7/I-10, exit Cloverfield Avenue north. **Open** 10am-5pm Mon-Sat. **Credit** Disc, MC, V. **Map** p310 C3.
Colourful, patterned cotton clothes, for children aged between one and ten.

Kitson Kids

108 S Robertson Boulevard, between Beverly Boulevard & W 3rd Street, Beverly Hills (1-310 246 3829/www.shopkitson.com). Bus 14, 16, 220, 305, 316, 550/I-10, exit Robertson Boulevard north. **Open** 10am-7pm daily. **Credit** AmEx, Disc, MC, V. **Map** p312 A3.
Family-minded hipsters love both the eye-popping design of this store and the goods on offer, from the likes of Stitches Jeans, Trunk and Great China Wall.

Paulina Quintana

1519 Griffith Park Boulevard, at Sunset Boulevard, Silver Lake (1-323 662 4010/www.paulinaquintana. com). Bus 2, 4, 302, 304/US 101, exit Silver Lake Boulevard north. **Open** 11am-5.30pm Mon-Fri, Sun; 9.30am-5.30pm Sat. **Credit** AmEx, MC, V. **Map** p314 C3.
Lounge pants, tank tops, T-shirts, leggings, frocks and shorts, for newborns up to six-year-olds. The clothes are embellished with modern designs.

Designer

You'll find every designer label under the sun in Los Angeles: the array of fashion shops here rivals those in better-known fashion cities like New York, London and Paris. Alongside the big names, LA also boasts a growing stable of home-grown designers, who mix Hollywood glitz, hippie chic and beachy sportswear.

The swankiest shopping area is Beverly Hills and, especially, the so-called Golden Triangle, bounded by Rexford Drive, Wilshire Boulevard and Santa Monica Boulevard. The starriest streets are **Rodeo Drive** and **Brighton Way**, which boast boutiques for most of fashion's premier names. In **Two Rodeo**, an outdoor complex at the corner of Rodeo Drive and Wilshire Boulevard, is **Versace** (No.248, 1-310 205 3921, www.versace.com); on Rodeo itself, designers include **Christian Dior** (No.309, 1-310 859 4700, www.dior.com), **Dolce & Gabbana** (No.312, 1-310 888 8701, www.dolce gabbana.it), **Gucci** (No.347, 1-310 278 3451, www.gucci.com), **Chanel** (No.400, 1-310 278 5500, www.chanel.com), **Hermès** (No.434, 1-310 278 6440, www.hermes.com), **Giorgio Armani** (No.436, 1-310 271 5555, www.giorgio armani.com), **Ralph Lauren** (No.444, 1-310 281 7200, www.polo.com), **Prada** (No.343, 1-310 278 8661, www.prada.com) and **Brioni** (No.337, 1-310 271 1300, www.brioni.com).

Cabaña

1511A Montana Avenue, between 15th & 16th Streets, Santa Monica (1-310 394 5123). Bus SM3, SM11/I-10, exit Lincoln Boulevard north. **Open** 10am-6pm Mon-Sat; noon-5pm Sun. **Credit** AmEx, Disc, MC, V. **Map** p310 C3.
The first West Coast store to carry Lilly Pulitzer's collection of summery, candy-coloured outfits for grown-ups and little girls.

Chrome Hearts

600 N Robertson Boulevard, at Melrose Avenue, West Hollywood (1-310 854 9800/www.chrome hearts.com). Bus 4, 220, 304/I-10, exit Robertson Boulevard north. **Open** 10am-7pm Mon-Sat. **Credit** AmEx, MC, V. **Map** p312 A2.
Does spending a lot of money on leather, black jeans and gothic jewellery qualify you as an authentic rock 'n' roll rebel? The shoppers here, who include Cher and P Diddy, think it does.

Costume National

8920 Melrose Avenue, between Robertson Boulevard & Doheny Drive, West Hollywood (1-310 273-0100/ www.costumenational.com). Bus 4, 220, 304/I-10, exit Robertson Boulevard north. **Open** 10am-6pm Mon-Sat. **Credit** AmEx, Disc, MC, V. **Map** p312 A2.
This chic shop looks more like a gallery or a mini-malist bar, an apt setting for the cool clothing and footwear produced by this hip Italian label.

Diane von Furstenberg

8100 Melrose Avenue, at N Crescent Heights Boulevard, West Hollywood (1-323 951 1947/www. dvf.com). Bus 10, 11, 217, 218, 717/I-10, exit Fairfax Avenue north. **Open** 11am-7pm Mon-Sat; noon-6pm Sun. **Credit** AmEx, Disc, MC, V. **Map** p312 C2.

Diane von Furstenberg invented the wrap dress, but her 1,700sq ft boutique shows there's much more to her designs. From evening gowns to sports gear, the clothes are chic but wearable.

James Perse

8914 Melrose Avenue, between Robertson Boulevard & Doheny Drive, West Hollywood (1-310 276 7277/www.jamesperse.com). Bus 4, 220, 304/I-10, exit Robertson Boulevard north. **Open** 10am-6pm Mon-Sat; noon-5pm Sun. **Credit** AmEx, Disc, MC, V. **Map** p312 A2.

Casually classic clothes, made from refined fabrics and featuring appropriately seasonal colours.

Ligia Morris/Eat My Leather

1-323 350 4100/eatmystyle@earthlink.net.

Morris is a costume designer for movies, theatre, ads and videos, but she also makes custom leather clothing for everyone from Iggy Pop to J-Lo. Expect to pay upwards of $700 for a pair of her intricate, hand-crafted trousers; call for an appointment.

Marc Jacobs

8400 Melrose Place, between La Cienega Boulevard & Melrose Avenue, West Hollywood (1-323 653 5100/www.marcjacobs.com). Bus 10, 105, LDHWH/I-10, exit La Cienega Boulevard north. **Open** 11am-7pm Mon-Sat; noon-6pm Sun. **Credit** AmEx, MC, V. **Map** p312 B2.

The collection that more than any other epitomises young Hollywood: Sofia Coppola was the unofficial spokesmodel for the colourful, seductive clothing.

Miu Miu

8025 Melrose Avenue, between N Fairfax Avenue & N Crescent Heights Boulevard, West Hollywood (1-323 651 0072/www.miumiu.com). Bus 10, 11, 217, 218, 717/I-10, exit Fairfax Avenue north. **Open** 11am-7pm Mon-Sat; noon-6pm Sun. **Credit** AmEx, Disc, MC, V. **Map** p312 C2.

The minimalist interior serves to display Muccia Prada's ready-to-wear, detailed couture.

Paul Smith

8221 Melrose Avenue, at N Crescent Heights Boulevard, West Hollywood (1-323 951 4800/www. paulsmith.co.uk). Bus 10, LDF/I-10, exit La Cienega Boulevard north. **Open** 11am-7pm Mon-Sat; noon-6pm Sun. **Credit** AmEx, MC, V. **Map** p312 C2.

The Nottingham-born style guru is now selling his clothes and lifestyle accessories to stylish Angelenos.

Stella McCartney

8821 Beverly Boulevard, at N Robertson Boulevard, West Hollywood (1-310 273 7051/www.stella mccartney.com). Bus 220, 550, LDHWH/I-10, exit Robertson Boulevard north. **Open** 11am-7pm Mon-Sat.* **Credit** AmEx, Disc, MC, V. **Map** p312 A3.

Stella McCartney's first store in the Los Angeles area sells much of her interesting clothing collection, plus shoes, sunglasses and perfume.

Discount

The nearest outlet malls to LA are **Premium Outlets** roughly 45 minutes north of LA (740 E Ventura Boulevard, Camarillo, 1-805 445 8520, www.premiumoutlets.com), where Banana Republic, Sunglass Hut and Nike are among the 150 outlets, and **Citadel Outlets** south-east of Downtown (100 Citadel Drive, Commerce, 1-323 888 1724, www.citadeloutlets.com), where you'll find the likes of Calvin Klein and Reebok.

In the **Fashion District** in Downtown (see p116), vendors hawk clothing, accessories and fabrics for shockingly low prices from 10am to 5pm daily. It's not exactly guilt-free shopping, though: LA has become an international manufacturing centre for fake designer accessories. For tours, see p71.

General

Branches of old reliables **Gap** (1355 Third Street Promenade, Santa Monica, 1-310 393 0719, www.gap.com), **Old Navy** (Beverly Connection, 8487 W 3rd Street, West Hollywood, 1-323 658 5292, www.oldnavy.com) and **Banana**

Go cheap in the **Fashion District**.

Republic (357 N Beverly Drive, Beverly Hills, 1-310 858 7900, www.bananarepublic.com) abound around town. You also won't have to travel too far to find an **Abercrombie & Fitch** store (The Grove, *see p180*; 1-323 954 1500, www.abercrombie.com), while there's a **French Connection** at the Beverly Center (*see p180*; 1-310 854 1965, www.frenchconnection.com). **Diesel** (www.diesel.com) can be found at the Third Street Promenade in Santa Monica (No.1340, 1-310 899 3055), in the Beverly Center (1-310 652 5504) or in Pasadena (1-626 304-0055). The Promenade also holds a branch of **Urban Outfitters** (No.1440, 1-310 394 1404, www.urbn.com), who've set up shop in West Hollywood, Burbank and Pasadena.

Alpha

8625 Melrose Avenue, between Huntley Drive & San Vicente Boulevard, West Hollywood (1-310 855 0775/www.alpha-man.com). Bus 220, 304, 705, LDHWH/I-10, exit La Cienega Boulevard north. **Open** 11am-6pm Mon-Sat; noon-5pm Sun. **Credit** AmEx, Disc, MC, V. **Map** p312 A2.
This metrosexual lifestyle store offers clothes from natives such as Band of Outsiders and approved outsiders including Paul Smith, plus the necessary grooming products to supplement the lifestyle, such as barbecues, iPod travel packs and vibrators.

American Apparel

2111 W Sunset Boulevard, at N Alvarado Street, Echo Park (1-213 484 6464/www.americanapparel. net). Bus 2, 200, 603/US 101, exit Alvarado Street north. **Open** 11am-9pm Mon-Sat; 11am-8pm Sun. **Credit** AmEx, Disc, MC, V. **Map** p314 D5.
Clothes to work up a sweat in – T-shirts, work-out pants, hoodies that come in a myriad colours – all made in Downtown LA and then advertised on billboards around town by the company's employees. Affordable and, for now at least, hip. **Other locations:** throughout LA.

Atmosphere

1728 N Vermont Avenue, at Hollywood Boulevard, Los Feliz (1-323 666 8420). Metro Vermont-Sunset/ bus 204, 206, 754/US 101, exit Vermont Avenue north. **Open** 11am-7pm Mon-Sat; noon-7pm Sun. **Credit** AmEx, Disc, MC, V. **Map** p314 A2.
Label hounds sniff out this Los Feliz store for its racks of upmarket brand names: Juicy Couture, Ben Sherman, Fred Perry, even Baby Juicy.

Curve

154 N Robertson Boulevard, between Beverly Boulevard & W 3rd Street, Beverly Hills (1-310 360 8008). Bus 20, 21, 220, 720/I-10, exit Robertson Boulevard north. **Open** 11am-7pm Mon-Sat; noon-6pm Sun. **Credit** AmEx, MC, V. **Map** p312 A3.
Delia Seaman and Nevena Borissova have combined their diverse sense of what makes for the best in fashion – Delia tends to the classic and conservative, while Nevena prefers the street-funky – at this women's clothing and accessories shop.

Fred Segal

8100 Melrose Avenue, at N Crescent Heights Boulevard, Melrose District (1-323 651 4129/www. fredsegalbeauty.com). Bus 10, 11, LDF/I-10, exit La Cienega Boulevard north. **Open** 10am-7pm Mon-Sat; noon-6pm Sun. **Credit** AmEx, MC, V. **Map** p312 C2.
A number of shops under one roof, Fred Segal sells hip casual wear and expensive designer gear, plus gifts, furniture and beauty goods. It's a great platform for local designers. The Santa Monica branch also has a state-of-the-art spa and hair salon. **Other locations:** 500 Broadway, Santa Monica (1-310 451 7178).

H Lorenzo

8660 W Sunset Boulevard, between N La Cienega Boulevard & Hancock Avenue, West Hollywood (1-310 659 1432/www.hlorenzo.com). Bus 2, 302, 305, LDHWH/I-10, exit La Cienega Boulevard north. **Open** 10am-7pm Mon-Sat; noon-7pm Sun. **Credit** AmEx, MC, V. **Map** p312 B1.
Highly imaginative, tasteful designer brands, all with a European touch: everything from day-to-day clothes to the perfect dress to highlight that Oscar acceptance speech.

Horn

140 S Robertson Boulevard, between Beverly Boulevard & W 3rd Street, West Hollywood (1-310 278 2052/ www.hornfashion.com). Bus 20, 21, 220, 720/I-10, exit Robertson Boulevard north. **Open** 10am-7pm Mon-Sat; noon-5pm Sun. **Credit** AmEx, Disc, MC, V. **Map** p312 A3.
A fine selection of designer and more casual clothes, from Missoni dresses to Henry Duarte jeans.

Kids Are Alright

2201 W Sunset Boulevard, between N Alvarado Street & N Rampart Boulevard, Echo Park (1-213 413 4014/www.thekidsarealright-shop.com). Bus 2, 200, 603/US 101, exit Alvarado Street north. **Open** noon-7pm Mon-Sat; noon-5pm Sun. **Credit** AmEx, Disc, MC, V. **Map** p314 D5.
Young local designers – Twinkle, Citizen of Humanity, Wooden Moustache – are displayed in a schoolroom setting. When will they graduate?

Lisa Kline

136 S Robertson Boulevard, between Beverly Boulevard & W 3rd Street, Beverly Hills (1-310 246 0907/www.lisakline.com). Bus 14, 16, 220, 316, 714/I-10, exit Robertson Boulevard north. **Open** 11am-7pm Mon-Sat; noon-6pm Sun. **Credit** AmEx, MC, V. **Map** p312 A3.
From humble beginnings, Kline's shop has become a major traffic-stopper in an area full of boutiques. Britney Spears, Reece Witherspoon and Jennifer Aniston have all thumbed through the racks.

Maxfield

8825 Melrose Avenue, at N Robertson Boulevard, West Hollywood (1-310 274 8800). Bus 10, 11, 220/I-10, exit Robertson Boulevard north. **Open** 11am-7pm Mon-Sat. **Credit** AmEx, Disc, MC, V. **Map** p312 A2.

Spotlight W 3rd Street

LA's two most celebrated shopping malls sit roughly a mile apart, south-east of Beverly Hills. At the corner of Beverly and La Cienega Boulevards is the huge **Beverly Center**; east of here, right by the Farmers Market, is the infinitely prettier, open-air **Grove**. Between them, the malls contain almost every major chain you might want to visit. And yet the best shopping in the area is on the stretch of road that links the two malls: **W 3rd Street**, the most agreeable concentration of independent boutiques, bookshops, cafés, gift stores and the like in LA.

Start just east of La Cienega, perhaps by stopping at one of the two branches of **Polkadots & Moonbeams** on W 3rd (No.8381, 1-323 655 3880). This one sells chic new modern clothes; in between here and its vintage counterpart (No.8367, 1-323 651 1746), there are two excellent bookstores, **Traveler's Bookcase** (No.8375; see p183) and the **Cook's Library** (No.8373; see p182). If you're in need of sustenance, stop at **Who's on Third?** (No.8369, 1-323 651 2928) for a smoothie.

It gets even more bijou down the road: the wonderful **Orchid Wrangler** (No.8365, 1-323 655 0855) is just next door to **Puppies & Babies** (No.8363, 1-323 653 3995), which sells gifts for dogs and toddlers. Well, why ever not? Across the road are four women's clothing stores where the wares range from old and glamorous (**Julian's Vintage**, No.8366½, 1-323 655 3011) to modern and

chic (Meghan Kinney's **Meg**, No.8362, 1-323 653 3972). And next door to Meg sit a pair of delightful gift stores, **Seaver** (No.8360, 1-323 653 8286) and **Raena** (No.8358, 1-323 951 0663). By now, you'll have earned a snack – let **Joan's on Third** (see p153) provide it.

Refilled, head back across on the north side of W 3rd for a string of interesting little operations. While the girls are browsing the exquisite toiletries in **Palmetto** (No.8321, 1-323 653 2470), the boys can rifle through the immaculate shirts at **Douglas Fir** (No.8309, 1-323 651 5445), before both meet up at **OK** (No.8303; see p200), which sells a cultured mix of books, art and housewares. Or continue heading east along the southern side of W 3rd, stopping to browse the European bath products at **Mistral** (No.8318½, 1-323 782 9463), the luxe furnishings at **Zipper** (No.8316, 1-323 951 0620), the antiquarian books at **Michael Thompson** (No.8312, 1-323 658 1901) or the gauzy clothes for designer waifs at **Kristin Londgren** (No.8308, 1-323 653 9200).

Past a couple more stores, cross the road and pick up some high-style travel goodies from **Flight 001** (No.8235, pictured; see p202). Just down the street, sample the funky kids' clothing at **Pip-Squeak** (No.8213, 1-323 6533250), the space-age furniture of **Plushpod** (No.8211, 1-323 951 0748) and the sexy T-shirts and jeans in **Milk** (No.8209, 1-323 951 0330). Hungry again? Don't worry: **Doughboys** (see p153) is close at hand.

Spotlight Abbot Kinney Boulevard

Barely a decade ago, Abbot Kinney Boulevard in Venice got its character from the many grungy antique stores that then lined it. Today, it could hardly be more different. On weekends, you'll find new, upwardly mobile Venetians strolling down the street, lattés in hand, soaking up the sun and window-shopping in the fashion boutiques, bookstores and gift shops that have opened in the last few years. It all stands in stark contrast to the cheap, touristy wares hawked nearby on the Boardwalk.

Abbot Kinney starts at Main Street and runs in a south-easterly direction to Washington Boulevard. Start at the northern end, perhaps with brunch at posh **Joe's** (No.1023; see p142) or affordable **Lilly's** (No.1031; see p142), before heading down to artsy **Equator Books** (No.1103; see p182) to browse the rare books and check out the art that's on the walls. The occasional art openings and parties attract much of the local bohemian crowd.

Across the street are a couple of nice little shops: **Brick Lane** (No.1132 1-310 392 2525), which sells only fashions by British designers, and the **Strange Invisible Perfumes** (No.1138; see p198). If you're already peckish, stop at **Jin Patisserie** (No.1202; see p166) for an aromatic tea and a chocolate. Further down on this side of the road are a few reminders of old Abbot Kinney: a couple of antique junk stores selling everything from furniture to books, and gay dive bar **Roosterfish** (No.1302; see p232 **Gay beaches**). Back across the street, a couple of more modish shops specialise in foot- and

eyewear: **Waraku** (No.1225; see p192), a speciality sneaker store, and **Microshapes** (No.1227, 1-310 314 4004), which sells only small spectacles.

A few yards away, it gets more glamorous at **Moulin Rouge** (No.1326; see p191), which sells expensive lingerie. Across the way is **Bountiful** (No.1335, 1-310 450 3620), which takes shabby chic to a whole new level: that beat-up old wicker recliner might look like it could disintegrate any minute, but for $3,500, you'd better make sure you get your money's worth.

Past more eating and drinking options – swanky **Hal's** (No.1349; see p164 **Brunch bonanza**), the cheaper **Tortilla Grill** (No.1357, 1-310 452 5751) and the **Abbot's Habit** (No.1401; see p166) – is **Firefly** (No.1413, 1-310 450 6288), a charming boutique gift store that sells presents for every occasion. **Enda King** (No.1419, 1-310 396 1242) and, across the street, **Collage** (No.1416, 1-310 482 3701), are the area's two best shops for men's clothes. A little further down is the **Green House** (No.1428, 1-310 450 6420), a smoking shop, before further evidence of Abbot Kinney's gentrification arrives: once a classic local dive complete with pool tables and knife fights, the **Brig** (No.1505, 1-310 399 7537) has now become a trendy DJ bar. Past more restaurants, another nod to the receding past is provided by **Board Gallery** (No.1639, 1-310 450 4114), the last surf shop standing on Abbot Kinney. And at the junction of Venice Boulevard, **Market Gourmet** (No.1800A; see p194) has delicious foods from around the world.

Just your average high fashion all-rounder, really, at least insofar as any store that stocks Gucci, Prada, Gaultier and Chanel can be termed 'average'. Sister shop Maxfield Bleu offers discounts on duds that are just so last season, darling.
Other locations: *Maxfield Bleu 151 N Robertson Boulevard, West Hollywood (1-310 275 7007).*

oOu

1764 N Vermont Avenue, between Kingswell & Melbourne Avenues, Los Feliz (1-323 665 6263). Metro Vermont-Sunset/bus 26, 204, 754/ I-5, exit Los Feliz Boulevard west. **Open** noon-7pm Mon-Sat; noon-6pm Sun. **Credit** AmEx, Disc, MC, V. **Map** p314 A2.
Funky and irreverent, tops, denims and dresses, and vintage women's clothing upstairs. A Los Feliz arche-type: hip and contemporary, with an eye on the past.

Planet Blue

3835 Cross Creek Road, at PCH, Malibu (1-310 317 9975). Bus 534/I-10, exit PCH north. **Open** 9.30am-6.30pm Mon-Sat; 10am-6.30pm Sun. **Credit** AmEx, MC, V.
Hilary Swank, Britney Spears and Jessica Simpson update their wardrobes here, calling in clothing rein-forcements from the likes of Cynthia Vincent, Burning Torch and True Religion.
Other locations: 800 14th Street, at Montana Avenue, Santa Monica (1-310 394 0135).

Pull My Daisy

3908 Sunset Boulevard, at Hyperion Avenue, Silver Lake (1-323 663 0608). Bus 2, 4, 302, 304/US 101, exit Silver Lake Boulevard north. **Open** 11am-7pm Mon-Sat; 11am-6pm Sun. **Credit** AmEx, MC, V. **Map** p314 B3.

If you'd like to investigate some clothes by local designers, then Pull My Daisy is your destination. 7 Diamonds and 191 do the numbers for the men, while Sound Girl and Dollhouse keep the women interested. But in truth the real fashionista comes here for one reason alone: to pay tribute to Bingo, the store's dachshund mascot.

Show Pony
1543 Echo Park Avenue, at Grafton Street, Echo Park (1-213 482 7676/www.lashowpony.com).
Bus 2, 4, 302, 304/US 101, exit Echo Park Avenue north. **Open** noon-6pm Wed-Sun. **Credit** AmEx, MC, V. **Map** p314 D4.
Show Pony celebrates soon-to-break designers and avant-garde artists; there are parties showcasing their work on the first Saturday of every month. The clothing, a mix of vintage and new, is cutting edge. Some of the designers are right out of school.

Theodore
189 The Grove Drive, at Fairfax Avenue & W 3rd Street (1-323 935 1636). Bus 16, 217, 218, 315, 717/I-10, exit Fairfax Avenue north.
Open 11am-7pm Mon-Wed, Sun; 11am-9am Thur-Sat. **Credit** AmEx, Disc, MC, V. **Map** p312 C3.
A haven, and outlet, for avant-garde designers, from Ann Demeulemeester to People of the Labyrinth, and sportswear from Plein Sud to Theory.

Tracey Ross
8595 Sunset Boulevard, between Alta Loma Road & N La Cienega Boulevard, West Hollywood (1-310 854 1996/www.traceyross.com). Bus 2, 105, 302, LDHWH/I-10, exit La Cienega Boulevard north.
Open 10am-7pm Mon-Sat; noon-5pm Sun.
Credit AmEx, Disc, MC, V. **Map** p312 B1.
Adored by celebrities and trust fund kids alike, Tracey Ross's boutique is a West Hollywood archetype. The designer items are carefully chosen, with prices naturally set to match.

Vintage & second-hand

American Rag
150 S La Brea Avenue, between W 1st & W 2nd Street, Fairfax District (1-323 935 3154). Bus 14, 16, 212/I-10, exit La Brea Avenue north.
Open 10am-9pm Mon-Sat; noon-7pm Sun.
Credit AmEx, MC, V. **Map** p312 D3.
One of the city's largest collections of vintage clothing, in a relaxed, warehouse setting. You can pick up anything from a 1960s leather mini to a second-hand, contemporary designer suit.

Decades
8214½ Melrose Avenue, between N Harper & N La Jolla Avenues, Melrose District (1-323 655 0223/www.decadesinc.com). Bus 10, 11, LDF/I-10, exit La Cienega Boulevard north. **Open** 11.30am-6pm Mon-Sat. **Credit** AmEx, Disc, MC, V. **Map** p312 B2.
America's most glamorous vintage shop sells couture classics from the 1960s and 1970s: chic outfits by the likes of Hermès, Pierre Cardin and Ossie Clark.

It's a Wrap!
3315 W Magnolia Boulevard, at N California Street, Burbank (1-818 567 7366/www.movieclothes.com).
Bus 163, 183/I-5, exit Olive Avenue west.
Open 11am-8pm Mon-Fri; 11am-6pm Sat, Sun.
Credit AmEx, Disc, MC, V.
Dress like a star, literally: this massive shop sells clothes worn by actors on film sets. Prices are surprisingly decent.
Other locations: 1164 S Robertson Boulevard, Beverly Hills (1-310 246 9727).

Lily et Cie
9044 Burton Way, between Doheny Drive & N Almont Drive, Beverly Hills (1-310 724 5757).
Bus 16, 316/I-10, exit Robertson Boulevard north. **Open** 10am-6pm Tue-Fri; 11am-5pm Sat.
Credit AmEx, MC, V. **Map** p311 D2.
A high-end boutique that outfits celebrities in old-school Hollywood glamour, suitable for the *Vanity Fair* post-Oscar party.

Lo-Fi
1038 N Fairfax Avenue, between Santa Monica Boulevard & Romaine Street, West Hollywood (1-323 654 5634/www.lofi.com). Bus 14, 217, 218, 714, 717/I-10, exit Fairfax Avenue north.
Open 11am-7pm Mon-Sat; noon-5pm Sun.
Credit AmEx, Disc, MC, V. **Map** p312 C2.
Fashion stylists and, sometimes, their celeb clients flock to this retail showroom for back-to-basics jeans, leather jackets, belts and T-shirts. Winona Ryder goes for the vintage T-shirts.

Tracey Ross, a WeHo favourite.

It's hip to be **Squaresville**.

Resurrection Vintage Clothing

8006 Melrose Avenue, at N Edinburgh Avenue, Melrose District (1-323 651 5516). Bus 10, 11, LDF/ I-10, exit Fairfax Avenue north. **Open** 11am-7pm Mon-Sat. **Credit** AmEx, MC, V. **Map** p312 C2.
Vintage clothes from the 1960s through the 1980s. There are clothes for both sexes, but evening gowns are a forte. Designers include Pucci and Ossie Clark.

Squaresville

1800 N Vermont Avenue, at Melbourne Avenue, Los Feliz (1-323 669 8464). Metro Vermont-Sunset/ bus 204, 206, 754/US 101, exit Vermont Avenue north. **Open** noon-7pm Mon, Sun; 11am-8pm Tue-Sat. **Credit** AmEx, MC, V. **Map** p314 A2.
A funky selection of old threads is offered at this Los Feliz favourite – some smart, but most casual and agreeably hipster-friendly. Prices are keen.

Fashion accessories & services

Clothing hire

After Hours Formal Wear

8621 Wilshire Boulevard, at N La Cienega Boulevard, Beverly Hills (1-310 659 7296/www.afterhours.com). Bus 20, 21, 105, 720/I-10, exit La Cienega Boulevard north. **Open** 10am-7pm Mon-Fri; 10am-6pm Sat; noon-5pm Sun. **Credit** AmEx, Disc, MC, V. **Map** p312 B4.
An excellent choice of tuxedos.
Other locations: throughout LA.

One Night Affair

1726 S Sepulveda Boulevard, at Santa Monica Boulevard, West LA (1-310 474 7808/www.one nightaffair.com). Bus 4, 304, C6, SM1/I-10, exit Santa Monica Boulevard east. **Open** by appt only. **Credit** AmEx, Disc, MC, V.
Everything from cocktail dresses to wedding gowns, designed by the likes of Versace and Bill Blass.

Dry cleaning

Brown's

1223 Montana Avenue, between 12th & Euclid Streets, Santa Monica (1-310 451 8531). Bus SM3, SM11/I-10, exit Lincoln Boulevard north. **Open** 7am-6pm Mon-Fri; 7am-noon Sat. **Credit** MC, V. **Map** p310 B2.
It's the most expensive dry cleaner in the Los Angeles area, but Brown's, run by the same family since 1939, is also a classic, and you certainly get what you pay for. Staff still box up shirts the old-fashioned way.

Glasses & sunglasses

There are several branches of **Sunglass Hut** in LA, including one at 7473 Melrose Avenue in West Hollywood (1-323 653 4914, www. sunglasshut.com). You can find cheap shades from street vendors all over the city, but particularly on the Boardwalk in Venice, or the Fashion District, Downtown.

Four Your Eyes

*12452 Venice Boulevard, at S Centinela Avenue,
Venice (1-310 306 5400/www.fouryoureyes.com).
Bus 33, 333, SM14/I-405, exit Venice Boulevard
west.* **Open** 9.30am-4pm Mon-Sat. **Credit** AmEx,
MC, V. **Map** p310 D6.

Get past the dreadful pun, and you'll find a terrific
range of vintage but unused frames, from 1950s cat-
eyes to the oversized spectacles of the 1970s.

LA Eyeworks

*7407 Melrose Avenue, at N Martel Avenue, Melrose
District (1-323 653 8255/www.laeyeworks.com). Bus
10, 11/I-10, exit La Brea Avenue north.* **Open** 10am-
7pm Mon-Sat. **Credit** AmEx, MC, V. **Map** p312 D2.

Not even the patronage of Elton John has tainted LA
Eyeworks: the frames here are so hip that people
with 20/20 vision have been known to wear them.
Other locations: 7386 Beverly Boulevard, Fairfax
District (1-323 931 7795).

Occhi Eyewear

*8615 Santa Monica Boulevard, between Westmount
Drive & Westbourne Drive, West Hollywood (1-310
360 8089/www.occhieyewear.com). Bus 4, 304, 105,
705, LDHWH/I-10, exit La Cienega Boulevard north.*
Open 8am-11.30pm daily. **Credit** AmEx, MC, V.
Map p312 B2.

Lorenzo Randisi and his relatives have been helping
people see, and be seen, for years, outfitting them
with glasses from the likes of Prada and Tom Ford.

Hats

Anita Hopkins Millinery

1-323 447 0428/www.anitahopkinsla.com.

Anita's highly original hats have been seen happily
perched atop noggins as varied as Christina Ricci's,
Omar Epps' and Damon Wayans'. Call to arrange
viewing at her studio in South Pasadena.

Jewellery

Arp

*8311½ W 3rd Street, between S Sweetzer & S
Flores Avenues, Melrose District (1-323 653 7764).
Bus 16, 316, LDF/I-10, exit La Cienega Boulevard
north.* **Open** noon-6pm Mon-Sat; noon-5pm Sun.
Credit AmEx, MC, V. **Map** p312 B3.

Restrained pieces of fine jewellery, mostly earrings,
are displayed here, most by Ted Muehling and
his protégés including Gabriella Kiss, Annette
Ferdinandsen and Nicole Landau. Prices from $100.

Me & Ro

*8405 Melrose Place, at Melrose Avenue, West
Hollywood (1-323 782 1071/www.meandrojewelry.
com). Bus 10, 11,105, 705, LDHWH/I-10, exit La
Cienega Boulevard north.* **Open** 11am-7pm Mon-Sat.
Credit AmEx, MC, V. **Map** p312 B2.

Me & Ro began when a dancer, Robin Renzi, and a
model, Michele Quan, threw in their day jobs and
began engraving messages in the beautifully elegant

Sanskrit and Chinese scripts on platinum, silver and
gold. Their devotees now include Julia Roberts, Kate
Capshaw and Meg Ryan.
Other locations: Bergamot Station, 2525 Michigan
Avenue, Santa Monica (1-310 315 1972).

Moondance Jewelry Gallery

*1530 Montana Avenue, between 15th & 16th Streets,
Santa Monica (1-310 395 5516/www.moondance
jewelry.com). Bus SM3, SM11/I-10, exit Lincoln
Boulevard north.* **Open** 10am-6pm Mon-Sat; 11am-
5pm Sun. **Credit** AmEx, Disc, MC, V. **Map** p310 C2.

Bold contemporary jewellery, designed by more
than 60 artists and supplemented by the occasional
vintage piece, is displayed in this gorgeous gallery.

Suzanne Felsen

*8332 Melrose Avenue, between N Flores Street & N
Sweetzer Street, West Hollywood (1-323 653 5400/
www.suzannefelsen.com). Bus 10, 11, LDF/I-10,
exit La Cienega Boulevard north.* **Open** 11am-6pm
Mon-Sat. **Credit** AmEx, MC, V. **Map** p312 B2.

Fine, modern jewellery: peridots with pink sapphires
or amethysts with rubies, set in 18ct white gold.

Tiffany & Co

*210 N Rodeo Drive, at Wilshire Boulevard, Beverly
Hills (1-310 273 8880/www.tiffany.com). Bus 20, 21,
720/I-405, exit Wilshire Boulevard north.* **Open**
10am-7pm Mon-Fri; 10pm-6pm Sat; 11am-6pm Sun.
Credit AmEx, Disc, MC, V. **Map** p311 C3.

The second-largest Tiffany in the country makes for
a quintessential Rodeo Drive window shopping
experience. Breakfast not available. There's a
branch of Harry Winston just up the street (No.310).

Lingerie

Nationwide lingerie chain **Victoria's Secret**
has branches everywhere in Los Angeles,
including one in the Beverly Center (*see p180*;
1-310 657 2958, www.victoriassecret.com).

Agent Provocateur

*7961 Melrose Avenue, between N Fairfax Avenue
& N Crescent Heights Boulevard, Melrose District
(1-323 653 0229/www.agentprovocateur.com). Bus
10, 11, 217, 218, LDF/I-10, exit Fairfax Avenue
north.* **Open** 11am-7pm Mon-Sat. **Credit** AmEx,
V. **Map** p312 C2.

Thanks to its saucy window displays and huge star
following, Brit chain Agent Provocateur has become
the most talked-about lingerie shop in the world.
Signature items include sexy corsets, half or quarter-
cup bras, open briefs and fluffy kitten-heeled mules.

Moulin Rouge

*1326 Abbot Kinney Boulevard, between Westminster
Avenue & California Avenue, Venice (1-310 452
1999). Bus 33, 333, SM1, SM2/I-10, exit 4th-5th
Street south.* **Open** noon-7pm Tue-Fri; noon-6pm Sat;
1-5pm Sun. **Credit** AmEx, Disc, MC, V. **Map** p310 A6.

This red craftsman's cottage has an intimate feel
and a French ambience. Stocked with imported lingerie from Europe, its wares are stylish and classy.

Eat, Drink, Shop

Panty Raid

2378½ Glendale Boulevard, at Brier Avenue, Silver Lake (1-323 668 1888/www.pantyraidshop.com).
Bus 92/US 101, exit Glendale Boulevard north. **Open** 11.30am-7pm Mon-Fri, noon-7pm Sat; noon-6pm Sun. **Credit** AmEx, Disc, MC, V. **Map** p314 D2.
A cornucopia of bras and panties strictly for women. Girls pore over the usual suspects, from Cosabella to Mary Green, in shades of pink to orange and back to blue again. There's a PlayStation out front for guys.

Trashy Lingerie

402 N La Cienega Boulevard, at Oakwood Avenue, West Hollywood (1-310 652 4543/www.trashy.com).
Bus 14, 105, LDF, LDHWH/I-10, exit La Cienega Boulevard north. **Open** 10am-7pm Mon-Sat.
Credit AmEx, Disc, MC, V. **Map** p312 B3.
'Who needs Viagra when you've got Trashy Lingerie?' So said Tony Curtis, who accompanies his wife here on shopping trips. You have to become a member, but it's only a formality.

Luggage

Beverly Hills Luggage

404 N Beverly Drive, at Brighton Way, Beverly Hills (1-310 273 5885/www.beverlyhillsluggage.com).
Bus 4, 16, 304, 720/I-10, exit Robertson Boulevard north. **Open** 9.30am-6pm Mon-Fri; 9.30am-5.30pm Sat. **Credit** AmEx, MC, V. **Map** p311 C3.
More than 100 years old, this shop sells all major brands of luggage and will repair anything.

Luggage 4 Less

11667 Wilshire Boulevard, at S Barrington Avenue, West LA (1-310 268 6698/www.luggage4less.com).
Bus 20, 720, SM2/I-405, exit Wilshire Boulevard west. **Open** 10am-8pm Mon-Fri; 10am-6pm Sat; 11am-6pm Sun. **Credit** AmEx, Disc, MC, V.
Low prices on brand-name luggage.
Other locations: 6 S Rosemead Boulevard, Pasadena (1-626 440 7411).

Shoes

Blu-82

2025 Sawtelle Boulevard, between Olympic Boulevard & Santa Monica Boulevard, West LA(1-310 445 0909). Bus 4, 304, SM1, SM4, SM5/I-405, exit Santa Monica Boulevard west. **Open** 11.30am-8pm Mon-Sat; 11.30am-6pm Sun. **Credit** AmEx, MC, V.
A veritable funhouse of sneakers, with a healthy helping of Japanese-inspired designs as well.

Camille Hudson Shoes

4685 Hollywood Boulevard, at N Vermont Avenue, Los Feliz (1-323 953 0377). Metro Vermont-Sunset/bus 2, 4, 26, 302, 304//US 101, exit Vermont Avenue north. **Open** noon-8pm Mon-Sat; noon-7pm Sun. **Credit** AmEx, MC, V. **Map** p314 A2.
Although unique international labels are sold at this tiny store, the most famous items are Camille's own distinctive pointy-toed flats and round-toe flats that put the focus squarely on comfort and function.

Kicks Sole Provider

141 N Larchmont Boulevard, between W 3rd Street & Beverly Boulevard, Hancock Park (1-323 468 9794).
Bus 14, 710/I-10, exit La Brea Avenue north. **Open** 11am-7pm daily. **Credit** AmEx, MC, V. **Map** p313 B4.
The punning name is on the mark: Vans, Lacoste, Dunks and Converse shoes are the deal.
Other locations: 3938 W Sunset Boulevard, Silver Lake (1-323 644 1272).

Re-Mix Shoe Company

7605½ Beverly Boulevard, between N Stanley & N Curson Avenues, Fairfax District (1-323 936 6210/www.remixvintageshoes.com). Bus 14/I-10, exit Fairfax Avenue north. **Open** noon-7pm Mon-Sat; noon-6pm Sun. **Credit** AmEx, Disc, MC, V.
Map p312 C3.
Despite its choice of URL, not everything at Re-Mix is old: besides the unworn vintage shoes is its own brand of retro shoes, from wingtips to slingbacks.

Silver Lake Shoes

3822 Sunset Boulevard, at Lucile Avenue, Silver Lake (1-323 663 7463). Bus 2, 4, 175, 302, 304/US 101, exit Silver Lake Boulevard north. **Open** 11am-7pm Mon-Sat; 11am-6pm Sun. **Credit** MC, V.
Map p314 B3.
The owners of Pull My Daisy (*see p188*) have opened a shoe store. The butter cream and military green interior, and the 1950s vibe, are lovely. The Irregular Choice, available for both sexes, is 'so totally rad, I'm worried people won't get it,' says co-owner, Sarah.

Waraku

1225 Abbot Kinney Boulevard, between Westminster Avenue & California Avenue, Venice (1-310 452 5300/www.warakuusa.com). Bus 33, 333, SM1, SM2/I-10, exit 4th-5th Street south. **Open** 10am-7pm Mon-Sat; 11am-7pm Sun. **Credit** AmEx, MC, V.
Map p310 A5.
This Japanese sneaker shop has some rare, striking varietals for the collector by the likes of Medium Namitatsu, Puma and Converse.

Food & drink

Bakeries

For **Breadbar**, **Dolce Forno** and the **La Brea Bakery**, three exceptional bakeries, *see p193* **Our daily bread**.

Boule

420 N La Cienega Boulevard, between Beverly Boulevard & Melrose Avenue (1-310 289 9977/www.boulela.com). Bus 14, 105, 705, LDF, LDHWH/I-10, exit La Cienega Boulevard north.
Open 10am-7pm Mon-Sat; 10am-5pm Sun.
Credit AmEx, Disc, MC, V. **Map** p312 B2.
Award-winning pastry chef Michelle Myers' contemporary interpretation of a traditional Parisian pastry shop. Indulge in artisanal pastries, confections and other exquisite desserts, including a Meyer lemon sorbet with saffron.

Our daily bread

A lot has happened in the 17 years since Nancy Silverton founded the phenomenally successful **La Brea Bakery** (624 S La Brea Avenue, Miracle Mile, 1-323 939 6813, www.labreabakery.com), single-handedly introducing Angelenos to the joys of the fresh, flavoursome loaf. The bread-free Atkins diet has risen and, slowly, hardened, leaving Angelenos free again to indulge their carbo cravings with the products of the artisanal bakeries that have sprung up everywhere. The alchemy of flour, salt and water has finally transformed the Californian diet.

Hans Röckenwagner, a German chef who set up a bakery in 1991 alongside his now-defunct restaurant in Santa Monica, believes locals have always loved bread, but they're only now being open about it. 'The Germans have always made the best bread,' says Röckenwagner. 'You just have to look at the bread-making equipment: it's all German.' It seems Angelenos agree: Röckenwagner's new **R Bakery** in Culver City (12835 Washington Boulevard, 1-310 578 8171, www.rockenwagner.com) supplies both trade and the public with everything from the popular Rudolph Steiner loaf (wholegrain with hazelnuts and sunflower seeds) to oversized bread sticks and pretzels. And in late 2006,

Röckenwagner plans to open the **3-Square Café & Bakery** on Abbot Kinney Boulevard in Venice, another outlet for his baked goods.

When pressed further as to German superiority in the bakery, Röckenwagner laughs. 'The only reason the French and Germans still speak,' he jokes, 'is the French use our bread for their cheese.' Don't tell Eric Kayser, a fourth-generation French baker from France who's just brought his **Breadbar** chain to West Hollywood (8718 W 3rd Street, 1-310 205 0124, www.breadbar.com). Since he opened in August 2005, the vast variety of breads has been selling like, er, hot cakes. Another popular chain selling high-quality artisanal breads is Belgium-based **Le Pain Quotidien** (*see p167*).

But – whisper it – the latest pretender to LA's baking crown hails not from France or even Germany, but from Italy. One of the godfathers of LA fine dining, Celestino Drago has run a commercial bakery for the last five years to service his own restaurants. But this year, he too answered the call, and opened his business to the public (**Dolce Forno**, 3828 Willat Avenue, Culver City, 1-310 280 6004). 'We try to make breads from different regions of Italy,' explains Drago. 'If I don't eat bread every day, something seems missing.'

Eat, Drink, Shop

Maison du Pain
5373 W Pico Boulevard, between Hauser Boulevard & La Brea Avenue, Midtown (1-323 934 5858). Bus SM5, SM7, SM12, SM13/I-10, exit La Brea Avenue north. **Open** 8am-6pm Mon-Sat. **Credit** AmEx, Disc, MC, V. **Map** p313 A6.
Two immigrant Filipino sisters with no baking experience decide to follow their dreams and start a French bakery, remortgaging their properties in order to fly in kitchen equipment and a young chef from France. The end result is the best croissants in the city.

Sprinkles Cupcakes
9635 Little Santa Monica Boulevard, at N Bedford Drive, Beverly Hills (1-310 274 8765/www.sprinkles cupcakes.com). Bus 4, 14, 16, 304, 316, 714/I-405, exit Santa Monica Boulevard east. **Open** 9am-7pm Mon-Sat. **Credit** AmEx, Disc, MC, V. **Map** p311 C3.
On Saturdays, there's often a queue around the block of this little storefront, as customers wait in line to stock up with colourful cupcakes in all manner of delectable and unusual flavours.

Sweet Lady Jane Bakery
8360 Melrose Avenue, at N Kings Road, West Hollywood (1-323 653 7145/ www.sweetladyjane.com). Bus 10, 105, LDHWH/

I-10, exit La Cienega Boulevard north. **Open** 8.30am-11.30pm Mon-Sat. **Credit** AmEx, Disc, MC, V. **Map** p312 B2.
Cakes, cheesecakes, croissants, fruit tarts, biscotti and a variety of breads are made daily with the finest freshest ingredients. There's a lovely café too.

Beer, wine & liquor

Du Vin
540 N San Vicente Boulevard, at Rangely Avenue, West Hollywood (1-310 855 1161/www.du-vin.net). Bus 4, 10, 11, 220, 304/I-10, exit Robertson Boulevard north. **Open** 10am-7pm Mon-Sat. **Credit** AmEx, Disc, MC, V. **Map** p312 A2.
The cobblestone courtyard entrance to Du Vin is more Europe than LA; inside, it's more wine cellar than shop. Californian, Italian and French wines are supplemented by grappas and eaux de vie.

Silverlake Wine
2395 Glendale Boulevard, at Brier Avenue, Silver Lake (1-323 662 9024/www.silverlakewine.com). Bus 92/US 101, exit Glendale Boulevard north. **Open** 11am-9pm Mon-Wed, Sun; 11am-10pm Thur-Sat. **Credit** AmEx, Disc, MC, V. **Map** p314 D2.

The get-fresh crew

The 1990s ended in a decadent Clintonian orgy of marbled steak, Martinis and cigars. Perhaps as a reaction, the first decade of the 21st century has seen a greater emphasis placed on healthy eating. Supermarkets and fast food outlets still make a tidy living pumping out junk, but many Angelenos are looking for fresher foods, prefererably sold through independent local businesses.

The most visible example of this trend is in the increased number of farmers' markets that have sprung up around the city. Some 25 years after the Santa Monica Farmers' Market made its debut as the first city-sponsored market in Southern California, everywhere from Chinatown to Long Beach has its own equivalent. For more, *see below*. Less well publicised are the two notable 'backyard' farms in Torrance just south of LAX. The Takahashi family's **Garden Patch** (25535 Hawthorne Boulevard, 1-310 375 0561) sells an unusual collection of greens grown on the family's nearby two-acre field, while the nearby **Ishibashi Farm Stand** (24955 Crenshaw Boulevard, Torrance, no phone) opens in late February for strawberry season and closes again after the pumpkin crop in October.

Health-food chains such as the **Whole Foods Market** (*see p195*) have a big following, but there are plenty of other smaller businesses out there, from health-nut standby **Erewhon Natural Foods Market** (*see p195*) to mom-and-pop organic stores. Up in Malibu, **Pacific Coast Greens** (22601 PCH, 1-310 456 0353) is an 'alternative grocery' notable for the fact that its stock is almost entirely top-grade organic produce. In Santa Monica, try **Mrs Winston's Green Grocery Store** (2901 Ocean Park Boulevard, 1-310 452 7770) or **Co-Opportunity** (*see p195*); Marina del Rey holds the pioneering **Rainbow Acres** (4756 Admiralty Way, 1-310 823 5373); and Inglewood is home to the excellent café-store **Simply Wholesome** (4448 W Slauson Avenue, 1-323 294 2144, www.simplywholesome.com).

The owners of this store take honest pleasure in making their favourite artisanal wines known to customers. Thrice-weekly tastings help to make this store a true oenophilic delight.

Farmers' markets

The city has a number of weekly markets where you can buy fresh, seasonal produce, some of it organic, directly from local farmers. Along with the food retailers, other stalls peddle flowers, fresh juices, coffee, hot food and knick-knacks.

There are farmers' markets in **West Hollywood** (9am-2pm Mon; Plummer Park, N Vista Street & Fountain Avenue), **Silver Lake** (8am-1pm Sat; 3700 W Sunset Boulevard, between Edgecliff & Maltman Avenues) **Hollywood** (8am-1pm Sun; Ivar & Selma Avenues) and **Downtown** (10am-4pm Thur-Sat; 7th & Figueroa Streets). **Santa Monica** has no fewer than four: on Wednesday at Arizona Avenue & 2rd Street (8.30am-1.30pm); on Saturday at Arizona & 3rd Street (8.30am-1pm) and at Virginia Park (corner of Pico & Cloverfield, 8am-1pm); and on Sunday at Main Street and Ocean Park Boulevard (9.30am-1pm). For details of others, see www.farmernet.com.

Gourmet

Market Gourmet
1800A Abbot Kinney Boulevard, between Venice Boulevard & Washington Boulevard, Venice (1-877 662 7538/www.marketgourmet.biz). Bus 33, 333/ I-405, exit Venice Boulevard west. **Open** 9am-7pm Mon-Fri; 10am-7pm Sat; noon-6pm Sun. **Credit** AmEx, MC, V. **Map** p310 B6.

The shelves of this food emporium are full of fine foods from all over the world. If you're unsure about a particular delicacy, chances are the friendly staff will open it up for you to have a taste!

Le Sanctuaire

2710 Main Street, at Hill Street, Santa Monica (1-310 581 8999/www.le-sanctuaire.com). Bus 33, 333, SM1, SM2, SM10/I-10, exit 4th-5th Street south. **Open** noon-6.30pm daily. **Credit** AmEx, MC, V. **Map** p310 A4.

This connoisseurs' delight, run by a discriminating Indonesian, offers an unashamedly elitist selection of the best foodstuffs (oils, pasta, risotto, nuts, chocolate, olives, green teas and myriad hard to find spices), as well as high-end cookery toys for chefs.

Surfas

8777 W Washington Boulevard, at National Boulevard, Culver City (1-310 559 4770/www. surfasonline.com). Bus 220, C5/I-10, exit Robertson Boulevard south. **Open** 9am-6.30pm Mon-Sat; 11am-6.30pm Sun. **Credit** AmEx, MC, V.

Surfas is coming up to 70 years as a family-owned business, which makes it positively prehistoric in Los Angeles time. The food at this huge gourmet food and restaurant supply emporium is as fresh and tasty as ever.

Organic & wholefoods

Co-Opportunity

1525 Broadway, at 16th Street, Santa Monica (1-310 451 8902/www.coopportunity.com). Bus 4, 304, SM1, SM10, SM11/I-10, exit Cloverfield Avenue-26th Street north. **Open** 7am-10pm daily. **Credit** AmEx, Disc, MC, V. **Map** p310 C3.

A range of macrobiotic and organic foods and complementary medicines is stocked at this likeable shop, owned and run by subscribing members (though you don't have to be a member to shop here).

Erewhon Natural Foods Market

7660 Beverly Boulevard, at The Grove Drive, Fairfax District (1-323 937 0777/www.erewhon market.com). Bus 14, 714/I-10, exit Fairfax Avenue north. **Open** 8am-10pm Mon-Sat; 9am-9pm Sun. **Credit** AmEx, Disc, MC, V. **Map** p312 C3.

The best organic supermarket in town sells a range of produce, food supplements, cosmetics and bath products. You can order fresh juices at the excellent hot- and cold-food counter.

Whole Foods Market

6350 W 3rd Street, at S Fairfax Avenue, Fairfax District (1-323 964 6800/www.wholefoods.com). Bus 16, 217, 218, LDF/I-10, exit Fairfax Avenue north. **Open** 7am-11pm daily. **Credit** AmEx, Disc, MC, V. **Map** p312 C3.

Whole Foods Market, a natural food favourite, is known for its great fish, organic meat, cheese and delicatessen counters, plus the excellent fresh pastas, all at prices as healthy as the food.
Other locations: throughout LA.

Speciality foods

Beverly Hills Juice

8382 Beverly Boulevard, between N Orlando Avenue & N Kings Road, Fairfax District (1-323 655 8300/www.beverlyhillsjuice.com). Bus 14, 714/ I-10, exit La Cienega Boulevard north. **Open** 7am-6pm Mon-Fri; 10am-6pm Sat. **No credit cards**. **Map** p312 B3.

Apple, papaya, coconut, carrot and any number of other fruits and vegetables (organic when possible) have 200lbs of pressure applied to squeeze out their natural juices. You get to drink them.

Cheese Store of Silverlake

3926 W Sunset Boulevard, at Sanborn Avenue, Silver Lake (1-323 644 7511/www.cheesestoresl. com). Bus 2, 4, 302, 304/US 101, exit Silver Lake Boulevard north. **Open** 10am-6pm Mon; 10am-6.45pm Tue-Sat; 11am-5am Sun. **Credit** AmEx, Disc, MC, V. **Map** p314 B3.

To go with the *fromage*, from cows, sheep and goats, there's an impressive array of epicurean treats: chocolates, cured meats, olives and teas, for example. A delightful shop.

Grand Central Market

317 S Broadway, between W 3rd & W 4th Streets, Downtown (1-213 624 2378/www.grand centralsquare.com). Metro Pershing Square/bus 2, 4, 30, 31, 40, 42, 45, 46, 302/I-110, exit 3rd Street east. **Open** 9am-6pm daily. **Credit** varies. **Map** p315 C3.

Running since 1917, this bustling Downtown market sells fruit, vegetables, meat, fish, herbs, spices and flowers. It's a real melting pot – Korean vendors who speak fluent Spanish, for example – and it makes for a lively way to pass a couple of hours.

K Chocolatier/Diane Krön

9606 Little Santa Monica Boulevard, at N Camden Drive, Beverly Hills (1-310 248 2626/ www.dianekronchocolates.com). Bus 4, 14, 16, 304, 316, 714/I-405, exit Santa Monica Boulevard east. **Open** 10am-6pm Mon-Fri. **Credit** AmEx, MC, V. **Map** p311 C3.

The K Sensual line of chocolates is designed to increase your libido, but the more usual ranges of truffles and chocolates are just as seductive to the tongue. The Brentwood store is open daily.
Other locations: 11677 San Vicente Boulevard, Brentwood (1-310 481 0388).

Petrossian Paris

321 N Robertson Boulevard, at Beverly Boulevard, West Hollywood (1-310 271 0576/www.petrossian. com). Bus 14, 16,220, 305, 316, 550/I-10, exit Robertson Boulevard north. **Open** 9am-6pm Mon-Sat. **Credit** AmEx, Disc, MC, V. **Map** p312 A3.

A French-owned and -run resource for those delights beloved by Francophiles: caviar, champagne, truffles, smoked salmon and foie gras. There's a charming café in which to enjoy all the good stuff on offer, and a refreshing lack of pretension throughout.

Eat, Drink, Shop

Arts & Letters.

Arts & Letters

*2665 Main Street, at Hill Street, Santa Monica
(1-310 392 9076). Bus 33, 333, SM1, SM2,
SM10/I-10, exit 4th-5th Street south.* **Open** 10am-
6pm Mon-Sat; noon-5pm Sun. **Credit** MC, V.
Map p310 A4.
When Hallmark's hackneyed rhymes and weary
illustrations won't do, head to this little boutique.
Greetings cards dominate, but there's also a pleasing range of stationery and a few surprises.

Chic-a-Boom

*6817 Melrose Avenue, at N Mansfield Avenue,
Melrose District (1-323 931 7441/www.chic-a-boom.
com). Bus 10, 11, 212/I-10, exit La Brea Avenue
north.* **Open** 11am-6pm Mon-Sat. **Credit** AmEx,
Disc, MC, V. **Map** p312 D2.
Toys, magazines, ads, lobby cards, movie posters,
bumper stickers and all kinds of other movie-relat-
ed ephemera from the 1930s to the 1970s.

8-Ball

*3806 W Magnolia Boulevard, at Holloway Way,
Burbank (1-818 845 1155/www.8ballwebstore.com).
I-5, exit Burbank Boulevard west.* **Open** 11am-7pm
Mon-Fri; 11am-6pm Sat; noon-5pm Sun. **Credit**
AmEx, Disc, MC, V.
Bowling shirts, Aloha outfits, Elvis playing cards
and pink flamingo cocktail shakers are among the
goodies at this kitschtastic store.

Elliot Salter

*7760 Santa Monica Boulevard, at N Genesee
Avenue, West Hollywood (1-323 656 9840). Bus
4, 217, 218, 304/I-10, exit Fairfax Avenue north.*
Open 9.30am-5.30pm Mon-Fri; 10am-4pm Sat.
Credit AmEx, MC, V. **Map** p312 C2.
Elliot Salter is less a pawn shop than a celebrity
hand-me-down museum. Its don't-ask, don't-tell policy has made it a firm celebrity favourite, though
you won't know who provided what stuff.

Farmacia Million Dollar

*301 S Broadway, at W 3rd Street, Downtown
(1-213 687 3688). Metro Pershing Square/bus 2, 4,
30, 31, 40, 42, 45, 46, 302/I-110, exit 3rd Street
east.* **Open** 9am-6pm daily. **No credit cards.**
Map p315 C3.
When witch doctors (*santeros*) go shopping, they
head to this *botánica*, which has all the herbs and
ingredients they need to make their potions. There's
lots of DIY hocus pocus, too: love potions, bath oil
that quells gossip, medallions to protect children.
What would Professor Snape say?

Panpipes Magickal Marketplace

*1641 N Cahuenga Boulevard, between Selma
Avenue & Hollywood Boulevard, Hollywood (1-323
462 7078/www.panpipes.com). Metro Hollywood-
Highland/bus 210, 212, 217, 710, LDH/US 101,
exit Cahuenga Boulevard south.* **Open** 11am-7pm
daily. **Credit** AmEx, MC, V. **Map** p313 B1.
Los Angeles' oldest occult shop, which has been open
since the early 1960s, sells everything from voodoo
dolls and mojo bags to crystal balls.

Santa Monica Seafood

*1205 Colorado Avenue, at 12th Street, Santa
Monica (1-310 393 5244/www.santamonicaseafood.
com). Bus 4, 304, SM5/I-10, exit Lincoln Boulevard
north.* **Open** 9am-7pm Mon-Fri; 9am-6pm Sat; 10am-
4pm Sun. **Credit** AmEx, MC, V. **Map** p310 B3.
The Cigliano family has run this wholesale and retail
enterprise since 1969, supplying restaurants all over
SoCal. The shop is beautiful: aquamarine tiles and
glistening silver light fixtures set off a heavenly
array of fish and shellfish.

Sorrento Italian Market

*5518 Sepulveda Boulevard, between Sawtelle &
Jefferson Boulevards, Culver City (1-310 391
7654). Bus C4, C6/I-405, exit Jefferson Boulevard
east.* **Open** 7am-7pm Mon-Sat; 7am-4pm Sun.
Credit AmEx, Disc, MC, V.
Go back to the old country, at least around the dinner table, with authentic Italian olive oils, balsamic
vinegars, breads, farm-fresh eggs and charcuterie.

Gifts

Museum shops are good for gifts. Try the
Getty Center (*see p83*), the **Japanese
American National Museum** (*see p111*),
LACMA (*see p100*) and **MoCA** (*see p115*).

Pleasure Chest

7733 Santa Monica Boulevard, at N Genesee Avenue, West Hollywood (1-310 860 9009/www.thepleasure chest.com). Bus 4, 217, 218, 304/I-10, exit Fairfax Avenue north. **Open** 10am-midnight Mon-Wed, Sun; 10am-1am Thur; 10am-2am Fri, Sat. **Credit** AmEx, MC, V. **Map** p312 C2.

Vibrators, dildos and all kinds of other things both unmentionable and, frankly, previously unimaginable are offered at this longstanding emporium of sauciness. It is open late, needless to say.

Skeletons in the Closet

LA County Department of the Coroner, 2nd Floor, 1140 N Mission Road, at Marengo Street, Downtown (1-323 343 0760/http://lacstores.co.la.ca.us/coroner). Bus 70, 71, 620/I-5, exit Mission Road. **Open** 8.30am-4.30pm Mon-Fri. **No credit cards.**

Gallows humour meets capitalism at this bizarre coroner's department shop. Gifts, 'to die or kill for', include beach towels, doormats and T-shirts emblazoned with corpse outlines.

Wacko

4633 Hollywood Boulevard, at N Vermont Avenue, Los Feliz (1-323 663 0122/www.soapplant.com). Metro Vermont-Sunset/bus 2, 4, 26, 302, 304/ I-10, exit Vermont Avenue north. **Open** 11am-7pm Mon-Wed; 11am-9pm Thur-Sat; noon-6pm Sun. **Credit** AmEx, MC, V. **Map** p314 A2.

A trip here is not just a shopping expedition: the curious building houses a trio of zany enterprises, namely the above mentioned Wacko, Soap Plant, and the La Luz de Jesus gallery (*see p226*). The emphasis, as you'd expect, is on the unusual: there's a varied and interesting mix of tchotchkes, cool art and unique gifts gathered under one roof.

Yamaguchi's

2057 Sawtelle Boulevard, between La Grange & Mississippi Avenues, West LA (1-310 479 9531). Bus SM4, SM5/I-405, exit Santa Monica Boulevard west. **Open** 9.30am-7pm Mon-Fri; 9.30am-6pm Sat. **Credit** MC, V.

A Japanese-style gift store in West LA. The colourful koi kites are particularly striking; Asian accessories, cookware and clothing make up the rest.

Health & beauty

Gary Motykie at Beverly Hills Body

9201 Sunset Boulevard, at Doheny Road, Beverly Hills (1-310 276 3183/www.beverlyhillsbody.com). Bus 2, 302, 305/I-405, exit Santa Monica Boulevard east. **Open** by appt only. **Credit** AmEx, Disc, MC, V. **Map** p311 D1.

One of the most skilled young plastic surgeons in a town where personal reconstruction is a sport.

Larchmont Beauty Centre

208 N Larchmont Boulevard, at Beverly Boulevard, Hancock Park (1-323 461 0162/www.larchmont beauty.com). Bus 14, 210, 710/I-10, exit La Brea Avenue north. **Open** 8.30am-8pm Mon-Sat; 11am-6pm Sun. **Credit** AmEx, Disc, MC, V. **Map** p313 B3.

All manner of prettifying products from high-end companies such as Decleor, Thymes Limited, JF Lazartigue and Shiseido.

Lather

106 W Colorado Boulevard, between S Pasadena & S De Lacey Avenues, Pasadena (1-626 396 9636/ www.latherup.com). Metro Memorial Park/bus 181,

Eat, Drink, Shop

LACMA. *See p196.*

Travel back to the space age at **Futurama**. *See p200.*

687/Hwy 134, exit Colorado Boulevard. **Open**
11am-9pm Mon-Thur; 11am-10pm Fri; 11am-11pm
Sat; 11am-7pm Sun. **Credit** AmEx, MC, V.
The emphasis at Lather, an elegant shop all the way
out in Pasadena, is on natural ingredients such as tea
tree and chamomile shampoo, oat-papaya face scrub,
and olive oil soaps, as well as cruelty-free products.
Aromatherapy items are also sold.

Strange Invisible Perfumes

*1138 Abbot Kinney Boulevard, at San Juan Avenue,
Venice (1-310 314 1555/www.siperfumes.com).
Bus 33, 333, SM1, SM2/I-10, exit 4th-5th Street
south.* **Open** 11am-7pm Tue-Sat; noon-6pm Sun.
Credit AmEx, Disc, MC, V. **Map** p 310 A5.
Alexandra Balahoutis weaves arcane stories into her
truly unique line of handmade organic perfumes,
with essences gathered from around the world.

Complementary & alternative medicine

Carolyn & David Cohen

*6404 Wilshire Boulevard, between N Crescent
Heights & San Vicente Boulevards, Fairfax District
(1-323 852 9704). Bus 20, 21, 720/I-10, exit
La Cienega Boulevard north.* **Open** by appt only.
Credit AmEx, MC, V. **Map** p312 B4.
This husband-and-wife team administer traditional
Chinese acupuncture and prescribe herbal medicine
with a great deal of passion, attention and humour.

Elixir

*8612 Melrose Avenue, between Westbourne &
Huntley Drives, West Hollywood (1-310 657 9300/
www.elixir.net). Bus 4, 304/I-10, exit La Cienega
Boulevard north.* **Open** 9am-10.30pm Mon-Thur;
9am-midnight Fri, Sat; 10am-10pm Sun. **Credit**
AmEx, MC, V. **Map** p312 B2.

Elixir, tucked away in West Hollywood, is a herbal
apothecary that doubles as an urban oasis. Along
with the exotic teas, Chinese tonics and potions,
there's a tranquil Zen-style garden. If you're lucky,
you might get an impromptu tarot card reading.

Healing Waters

*136 N Orlando Avenue, between W 1st Street
& Beverly Boulevard, Fairfax District (1-323 651
4656). Bus 14, 16, 218, 316, 714, LDF/I-10, exit
La Cienega Boulevard north.* **Open** 1-5pm Mon-Sat.
No credit cards. Map p312 B3.
In Jennifer Otto's store – which appears to the visitor as part laboratory and part witch's cauldron –
that most basic of health-giving substances, water,
comes in many therapeutic forms. Apart from
Adam's ale there are Bach flower remedies, oils and
holistic skincare products for sale.

Hairdressing

Argyle Salon & Spa

*Sunset Tower, 8358 Sunset Boulevard, at N
Sweetzer Avenue, West Hollywood (1-310 623 9000/
www.sunsettowerhotel.com). Bus 2, 302, LDHWH/
I-10, exit La Cienega Boulevard north.* **Open** 9am-
9pm Mon-Sat; 10am-7pm Sun. **Credit** AmEx, Disc,
MC, V. **Map** p312 B1.
The renovated Sunset Tower hotel now has a spa to
match its restored art deco splendour. The facilities
and practitioners are top notch, but notable even
among such talent is hair guru Gerald. There's also
a classic men's barber shop.

B2.V

*646 N Doheny Drive, between Harland Avenue
& Nemo Street, Beverly Hills (1-310 777 0345/
www.b2vsalon.com). Bus 2, 4, 302, 304, 305/I-10,
exit Robertson Boulevard north.* **Open** 8.30am-7pm
Tue- Sat. **Credit** AmEx, MC, V. **Map** p311 D1.

Everyone from Liv Tyler to Tim Curry comes here for highlights by Kim (*Extreme Makeover*) Vo, and cuts from tattooed surfer dude Mike D.

Rudy's Barber Shop Silver Lake

4451 W Sunset Boulevard, at Hollywood Boulevard, Los Feliz (1-323 661 6535/www.rudysbarbershop. com). Metro Vermont-Sunset/bus 2, 4, 26, 302, 304/ I-5, exit Los Feliz Boulevard west. **Open** 9am-9pm Mon-Sat; 11am-7pm Sun. **Credit** AmEx, Disc, MC, V. **Map** p314 B3.

Formerly a garage, this edgy Los Feliz salon is now one of the hippest places in LA to get coiffed. Check the art on the walls while you're being shorn.

Manicures & pedicures

Manicurists are as basic to LA life as gas stations; you'll see one on every high street, often run by Vietnamese or Korean women.

La Vie L'Orange

638½ N Robertson Boulevard, at Melrose Avenue, West Hollywood (1-310 289 2501/www.lavielorange. com). Bus 10, 11, 220, LDHWH/I-10, exit Robertson Boulevard north. **Open** 10am-5pm Tue, Sun; 10am-9pm Wed, Thur; 10am-6pm Fri; 9am-6pm Sat. **Credit** AmEx, MC, V. **Map** p312 A2.

One of the city's most hedonistic nail spas. Settle back, glass of wine or juice in hand, and enjoy one of the myriad manicures and pedicures on offer.

Paint Shop

319½ S Robertson Boulevard, between Olympic Boulevard & Gregory Way, Beverly Hills (1-310 652 5563/www.paintshopbeverlyhills.com). Bus 28, 220, 328/I-10, exit Robertson Boulevard north. **Open** 10am-7pm Tue, Wed; 10am-8pm Thur, Fri; 9am-6pm Sat; 10am-4pm Sun. **Credit** AmEx, MC, V. **Map** p312 A4.

Not your ordinary nail shop. The music is soothing, and there are even free cookies on weekends.

Pharmacies

There are branches of **Sav-On** (5510 W Sunset Boulevard, Hollywood, 1-323 464 2172, www. savon.com; for more, call 1-888 746 7252), **Rite Aid** (1132 N La Brea Avenue, West Hollywood, 1-323 463 8539, www.riteaid.com; for more, call 1-800 748 3243) and **Walgreens** (8770 W Pico Boulevard, Beverly Hills, 1-310 275 1344, www. walgreens.com) all over LA.

Skin & body care

Kate Somerville

8428 Melrose Place, between N La Cienega Boulevard & Melrose Avenue, West Hollywood (1-323 655 7546/www.katesomerville.com). Bus 10, 11,105, 705, LDHWH/I-10, exit La Cienega Boulevard north. **Open** 10am-7pm Mon-Sat. **Credit** AmEx, MC, V. **Map** p312 B2.

Luxurious potions and modern equipment like lasers combine to ensure the best medical care of your epidermis. The aestheticians are as skilled as they are charming; clients have included Lindsay Lohan and Halle Berry.

Pomp

1431 Ocean Avenue, between Santa Monica Boulevard & Broadway, Santa Monica (1-310 393 1543/www.pompsalon.com). Bus 3, 4, 304, 333, SM1/I-10, exit 4th-5th Street north. **Open** 10am-6pm Tue, Wed, Fri; 10am-9pm Thur; 9am-5pm Sat. **Credit** AmEx, MC, V. **Map** p310 A3.

British skincare expert Lisa Wilson is ensconced at this unfussy new salon with ocean views.

Spas & masseurs

For **Fred Segal**, *see p186*; for the **Argyle Salon & Spa**, *see p198*.

Amadeus Spa

799 E Green Street, at N Hudson Avenue, Pasadena (1-626 578 3404/www.amadeusspa.com). Bus 181, 485/I-210, exit Lake Avenue south. **Open** 9am-6pm Mon, Sun; 8am-8pm Tue; 8am-6pm Wed; 8am-9pm Thur, Fri; 7.30am-8pm Sat. **Credit** AmEx, Disc, MC, V.

Aside from all of the services you'd normally expect to find at a high-class spa, the highly regarded Amadeus also supplies a heavenly pumpkin-peel pedicure and foot reflexology. **Other locations**: throughout LA.

Burke Williams

8000 W Sunset Boulevard, at N Crescent Heights Boulevard, West Hollywood (1-323 822 9007/www. burkewilliamsspa.com). Bus 2, 218, 302, LDHWH/ I-10, exit Fairfax Avenue north. **Open** 8am-10pm daily. **Credit** AmEx, Disc, MC, V. **Map** p312 C1.

Treatments to uplift your body and spirit, from manicures to exotic herbal wraps. Create your own simple rejuvenation package: warm up in the jacuzzi, cool down in the plunge pool, then detox in the sauna. **Other locations**: throughout LA.

Ole Henrikson

8622 W Sunset Boulevard, at Sunset Plaza Drive, West Hollywood (1-310 854 7700/www.olefacebody. com). Bus 2, 302, LDHWH/I-10, exit La Cienega Boulevard north. **Open** 8.30am-5pm Mon; 8am-8pm Tue-Sat; 9.30am-4.30pm Sun. **Credit** AmEx, MC, V. **Map** p312 B1.

Ole Henrikson has been making faces glow and bodies gleam for three decades. The salon is a Zen-style retreat, where you can sip green tea as you soak in a Japanese tub. Briony Behets offers wonderful craniosacral massage.

Pho-Siam

1525 Pizarro Street, at Glendale Boulevard, Echo Park (1-213 664 8484/www.phosiam.com). Bus 92/US 101, exit Glendale Boulevard south. **Open** 9am-10.30pm daily. **No credit cards.** **Map** p314 D6.

A bare-bones Thai massage joint, where they charge $1 per minute to transform you into a pretzel of relaxed happiness.

Tattoos

Sunset Strip Tattoo

7524 W Sunset Boulevard, at N Gardner Street, West Hollywood (1-323 650 6530/www.sunsetstrip tattoo.com). Bus 2, 218, 302, LDHWH/I-10, exit Fairfax Avenue north. **Open** noon-midnight daily. **Credit** AmEx, MC, V. **Map** p312 D1.

One of the oldest tattoo parlours in town, where everyone from drunken girlfriends to legendary rockers come for the expert ink.

Homewares

Antiques

Most of LA's good antique shops are located in West Hollywood, along Robertson and Beverly Boulevards and La Brea Avenue. It's also worth looking near the Pacific Design Center on Melrose Avenue; on W 3rd Street east of La Cienega Boulevard; and on Echo Park's Antique Row, on the 2200 block of W Sunset Boulevard.

The **Pasadena Antique Center** (444 & 480 S Fair Oaks Avenue, Pasadena, 1-626 449 7706, www.pasadenaantiquecenter.com) boasts 130 dealers, who set up shop daily. Two markets merit mention: the **Long Beach Antique & Collectible Market** (Long Beach Veterans Memorial Stadium, Clark Avenue & E Conant Street, 1-562 655 5703, www.longbeach antiquemarket.com) on the third Sunday of the month from 5.30am, and the **Santa Monica Outdoor Antique Market**, on the fourth Sunday of the month at Santa Monica Airport.

Blackman Cruz

800 N La Cienega Boulevard, at Waring Avenue, West Hollywood (1-310 657 9228/www.blackman cruz.com). Bus 10, 11, 105, LDHWH/I-10, exit La Cienega Boulevard north. **Open** 10am-6pm Mon-Fri; noon-5pm Sat. **Credit** AmEx, Disc, MC, V. **Map** p312 B2.

Avant-garde antiques – furniture, lighting, trinkets – are the mainstay at Blackman/Cruz. There are some wonderfully bizarre pieces on offer: an old operating-room light fixture, say, or an animal-cage coffee table. Adored by celebs and decorators.

Emmerson Troop

8111 Beverly Boulevard, at N Crescent Heights Boulevard, West Hollywood (1-323 653 9763/www. emmersontroop.com). Bus 2, 218, 302, LDHWH/ I-10, exit Fairfax Avenue north. **Open** 11am-6pm Mon-Sat. **Credit** AmEx, MC, V **Map** p312 C3.

Period furniture, from Prouvé desks to Blenko glass, and contemporary art, gathered by dashing young Brit William Emmerson.

Liz's Antique Hardware

453 S La Brea Avenue, between W 4th & W 6th Streets, Miracle Mile (1-323 939 4403). Bus 20, 21, 212, 720/I-10, exit La Brea Avenue north. **Open** 10am-6pm Mon-Sat. **Credit** AmEx, MC, V. **Map** p312 D4.

With more than a million pieces of hardware (circa 1850 to 1970) for doors, windows and furniture, you're sure to find the right vintage handle here.

General & modern

Futurama

446 N La Brea Ave, at Oakwood Avenue, Hollywood (1-323 937 4522). Bus 10, 11, 212/I-10, exit La Brea Avenue north. **Open** noon-7pm daily. **Credit** AmEx, MC, V. **Map** p313 A3.

Some of the furniture at this long-standing La Brea Avenue store appears old, but don't be deceived: it's just fashionably retro. Got a space-age bachelor pad to furnish? Head here. **Photo** *p198*.

HD Buttercup

3225 Helms Avenue, at Venice Boulevard, Culver City (1-310 558 8900/www.hdbuttercup.com). Bus 3, 105, 333, 705, C1, C4/I-10, exit La Cienega Boulevard south. **Open** 10am-7pm Mon-Sat; 11am-6pm Sun. **Credit** AmEx, Disc, MC, V.

Within the 100,000sq ft of the former Helms Bakery manufacturers retail directly to customers at supposed discount prices. It's worth a wander to see the variety of things for sale, everything from antique Balinese day beds to eye-popping office furniture.

Jonathan Adler

8125 Melrose Avenue, at N Crescent Heights Boulevard, West Hollywood (1-323 658 8390/www. jonathanadler.com). Bus 10, 11, 217, 218,717/ I-10, exit Fairfax Avenue north. **Open** 10am-6pm Mon-Sat; noon-6pm Sun. **Credit** AmEx, MC, V. **Map** p312 C2.

Coolly creative pottery, pillows, rugs, chairs and table-top items from the legendary ceramicist turned all-round design guru.

OK

8303 W 3rd Street, at S Sweetzer Avenue, Fairfax District (1-323 653 3501). Bus 16, 316. LDF/I-10, exit La Cienega Boulevard north. **Open** noon-6pm daily. **Credit** AmEx, Disc, MC, V. **Map** p312 B3.

A stimulating store that sells beautifully crafted wares: small furniture items, jewellery and noguchi paper lamps, books on modern architecture and some well-picked hipster CDs.

Silho Furniture

142 N La Brea Avenue, at 1st Street, Hancock Park (1-323 935 9955/www.silhofurniture.com). Bus 212, 312/I-10, exit La Brea Avenue north. **Open** noon-5pm Mon; 10am-6pm Tue-Sat. **Credit** AmEx, MC, V. **Map** p313 A4.

Gifts and furniture that embrace modern forms and organic materials. Don't miss Kevin Ink's unique botanical mobiles.

Tortoise

*1208 Abbot Kinney Boulevard, between San Juan
& California Avenues, Venice (1-310 314 8448/
www.tortoiselife.com). Bus 33, 333, SM1, SM2/
I-10, exit 4th-5th Street south.* **Open** noon-6pm
Wed-Sun. **Credit** MC, V. **Map** p310 A5.
The tortoise is a symbol of longevity in Japan; it's
also the theme for this small store showcasing tra-
ditional Japanese crafts and items that are meant to
last such as stools made from the wood of the
Douglas fir and cast-iron ornaments.

Twentieth

*8057 Beverly Boulevard, at N Laurel Avenue, West
Hollywood (1-323 904 1200/www.twentieth.net).
Bus 2, 218, 302, LDHWH/I-10, exit Fairfax Avenue
north.* **Open** 10am-6pm Mon-Fri; noon-5pm Sat.
Credit AmEx, MC, V. **Map** p312 C3.
Classic, top-end 20th century furniture and acces-
sories, from Verner Panton chairs to Vladimir Kagan
sofas, plus more contemporary lines by the likes of
Marmol Radziner and Elizabeth Paige Smith.

Yolk

*1626 Silver Lake Boulevard, at Effie Street, Silver
Lake (1-323 660 4315/http://yolk-la.com). Bus 2, 4,
302, 304/US 101, exit Silver Lake Boulevard north.*
Open 11am-6pm Tue-Sun. **Credit** AmEx, Disc, MC,
V. **Map** p314 C3.
'New design is hatching all the time,' reads the sign
on the front: in this case, fresh, modern ideas for the
home, along with a lot of children's furniture and
accessories such as Not Neutral glassware.

Music

CDs & records

As well as the shops below, there's a flagship
Virgin Megastore in the Hollywood &
Highland mall (8000 W Sunset Boulevard,
1-323 769 8520, www.virgin.com), a mix of old-
style CD store and modern lifestyle shop.

Amoeba Music

*6400 W Sunset Boulevard, at N Cahuenga Boulevard,
Hollywood (1-323 245 6400/www.amoebamusic.com).
Metro Hollywood-Vine/bus 2, 302/US 101, exit Vine
Street south.* **Open** 10.30am-11pm Mon-Sat; 11am-
9pm Sun. **Credit** AmEx, MC, V. **Map** p313 B2.
The recent demise of Rhino (est.1973) and Aron's
(est.1965) was doubtless due in part to the internet,
but the knockout blow may in fact have been lev-
elled by this behemoth of a music shop, the largest
independent record store in the country. The ranges
of both new and used CDs and DVDs are exemplary,
the prices listed are fair, and there are frequent in-
store PAs. What's not to like?

Benway Records

*1600 Pacific Avenue, at Windward Avenue, Venice
(1-310 396 8898). Bus 33, 333, C1, SM1, SM2/
I-405, exit Venice Boulevard west.* **Open** 11am-8pm
daily. **Credit** AmEx, MC, V. **Map** p310 A5.

Ron and Kelly Benway, who own this used-CD and
vinyl shack, are the ultimate Venice fixtures. Drop
by to peruse the old and second-hand CDs, trashy
videos and shelves of cassettes, T-shirts, stickers
and posters. There are very occasional shows, too.

House of Records

*3328 Pico Boulevard, at 33rd Street, Santa Monica
(1-310 450 1222/www.houseofrecords.com).
Bus SM7/I-10, exit Centinela Boulevard south.*
Open 11am-7pm daily. **Credit** AmEx, Disc, MC, V.
Map p310 D4.
All kinds of used music, on vinyl and CD, are to be
found at this shop on the edge of Santa Monica.
Established in 1952, it's the oldest record shop in LA.

Music Man Murray

*5055 Exposition Boulevard, at S La Brea Avenue,
Crenshaw (1-323 734 9146/www.musicmanmurray.
com). Bus 38, 212/I-10, exit La Brea Avenue.* **Open**
noon-5pm Tue-Sat. **Credit** AmEx, Disc, MC, V.
'You name it, we find it!' runs Murray Gershenz's
tagline, and he usually does. At any one time,
Gershenz has over a million records (CDs, cassettes,
78s, 45s and 33s) in every genre imaginable.

Rockaway Records

*2395 Glendale Boulevard, at Silver Lake Boulevard,
Silver Lake (1-323 664 3232/www.rockaway.com).
Bus 92/I-5, exit Glendale Boulevard south.*
Open 11am-8pm Mon-Thur, Sun; 11am-9pm Fri,
Sat. **Credit** AmEx, MC, V. **Map** p314 D2.
Used CDs, rare vinyl, new alternative and LA-based
bands, 1960s memorabilia and videos are the spe-
cialities of this unassuming shop. Prices are keen.

Miles of aisles: **Amoeba Music**.

Musical instruments

If you want to make rather than listen to music, visit the **Guitar Center** in Hollywood (7425 W Sunset Boulevard, 1-323 874 1060, www.guitar center.com), which stocks most kinds of musical instruments alongside the axes. Two guitar shops merit mention: the wonderful **McCabe's Guitar Shop** in Santa Monica (3101 Pico Boulevard, 1-310 828 4497, www.mccabes guitar.com) is a favourite of folkies, while the Mexican instruments at East LA's **Candelas Guitars** (2427 E Cesar E Chavez Avenue, 1-323 261 2011, www.candelas.com) are favoured by everyone from Segovia to Ozomatli.

Photography

The pharmacies detailed on *p199* offer one-hour processing at the majority of their LA-area branches. There are branches of chain **Wolf Camera** around town, including one in Beverly Hills (270 N Beverly Drive, 1-310 285 9616, www.wolfcamera.com). For more stores selling photographic equipment, *see p183* **Electronics**.

Bel-Air Camera & Video

10925 Kinross Avenue, at Gayley Avenue, Westwood (1-310 208 5150/www.belaircamera.com). Bus 2, 302, 305, 720/I-405, exit Wilshire Boulevard east. **Open** 9am-7pm Mon-Fri; 9.30am-6pm Sat; noon-5pm Sun. **Credit** AmEx, Disc, MC, V.
Cameras of every conceivable style and in every conceivable specification. Prices are competitive.

Samy's Camera

431 S Fairfax Avenue, at Drexel Avenue, Fairfax District (1-323 938 2420/www.samyscamera.com). Bus 217, LDF/I-10, exit Fairfax Avenue north. **Open** 9am-7pm Mon-Fri; 9.30am-6pm Sat; 10am-5pm Sun. **Credit** AmEx, Disc, MC, V. **Map** p312 C3.
This huge showroom is photographic heaven for amateurs and professionals. There's also an excellent range of binoculars.
Other locations: throughout LA.

Sport & adventure

Two West Coast sporting chains have stores in LA. At 100 N La Cienega Boulevard sits one of several **Sport Chalets** (1-310 657 3210, www.sportchalet.com), while Santa Monica is home to a branch of **Big 5 Sporting Goods** (3121 Wilshire Boulevard, 1-310 453 1747, www.big5 sportinggoods.com). There's also a branch of **Niketown** in Beverly Hills (9560 Wilshire Boulevard, 1-310 275 9998, www.niketown.com).

Adventure 16

11161 W Pico Boulevard, between S Sepulveda Boulevard & I-405, West LA (1-310 473 4574/ www.adventure16.com). Bus C6, SM4, SM5/I-10,

exit Overland Boulevard north. **Open** 10am-9pm Mon-Fri; 10am-6pm Sat; 11am-6pm Sun. **Credit** AmEx, MC, V. **Map** p311 A6.
Whether you're off on an extended desert expedition or a little hillside hike, the city's best outward-bound shop will be able to kit you out.

ZJ Boarding House

2619 Main Street, at Ocean Park Boulevard, Santa Monica (1-310 559 9630/www.zjboardinghouse.com). Bus 33, 333, SM1, SM8, SM10/I-10, exit Lincoln Boulevard south. **Open** 10am-8pm Mon-Sat; 10am-6pm Sun. **Credit** AmEx, Disc, MC, V. **Map** p310 A4.
ZJ is widely acknowledged as the best surf shop in town. Sales are supplemented by a rental operation; snowboards are also stocked.

Toys

Lakeshore Learning Materials

8888 Venice Boulevard, at National Boulevard, West LA (1-310 559 9630/www.lakeshorelearning.com). Bus 33, 220, 333, 534, SM12/I-10, exit National Avenue south. **Open** 9am-7pm Mon-Fri; 9am-6pm Sat; 11am-5pm Sun. **Credit** AmEx, Disc, MC, V.
Fifty years old in 2004, this mini-chain retains a decidedly 1950s outlook: the toys sold here educate while they entertain.
Other locations: throughout LA.

Puzzle Zoo

1413 Third Street Promenade, at Santa Monica Boulevard, Santa Monica (1-310 393 9201/www. puzzlezoo.com). Bus 2, 4, 302, 304/I-10, exit 4th-5th Street north. **Open** 10am-10pm daily. **Credit** AmEx, Disc, MC, V. **Map** p310 A3.
Jigsaws remain a speciality at this Santa Monica favourite, but there's also tons of board games, models and whizz-bang modern goodies.
Other locations: throughout LA.

Travel

For **Traveler's Bookcase**, *see p183*.

Flight 001

8235 W 3rd Street, at S Harper Avenue, Fairfax District (1-323 966 0001/www.flight001.com). Bus 16/I-10, exit Fairfax Avenue north. **Open** 11am-7pm Mon-Sat; 11am-6pm Sun. **Credit** AmEx, MC, V. **Map** p312 C3.
The excellent Flight 001 harks back to a time when people travelled in style: pick up everything from inflatable neck rests to retro-styled luggage tags.

Travel Medicine Center & the One Stop Travel Shop

131 N Robertson Boulevard, at Wilshire Boulevard, Beverly Hills (1-310 360 1338/www.healthytravel. com). Bus 20, 21, 220, 720/I-10, exit Robertson Boulevard north. **Open** 9am-5pm Mon-Sat. **Credit** AmEx, DC, Disc, MC, V. **Map** p312 A4.
Vaccinations, customised first-aid kits, mosquito nets, travel-sized hairdryers and much more.

Eat, Drink, Shop

Arts & Entertainment

Festivals & Events	204
Children	210
Comedy & TV	215
Film	218
Galleries	222
Gay & Lesbian	228
Music	236
Nightclubs	245
Sports & Fitness	251
Theatre & Dance	260

Features

Festivals Music freebies	207
And the winner is…	208
The best Kids' stuff	210
Nanny knows best	213
The best Comedy	215
Come on down!	217
The best Cinema	218
Festivals Film	220
Festivals Art	225
The best Gay stuff	228
Straight eye for the queer guy	231
Gay beaches	232
Festivals Gay	234
Artists in residence	239
Festivals Music	242
Are you ready for your close-up?	247
We 🚫 **LA** Velvet ropes	248
A tale of two owners	252
The best Theatre	260

Circus Disco. *See p247.*

Festivals & Events

It's showtime…

TV weather reports in LA actually include a caption that describes the forecast as 'more of the same'. So how can you tell the season? The festivals. From spring's Cinco de Mayo celebration to winter's Hollywood Christmas Parade, somewhere in LA, there's usually a party going on. The *LA Times* and the *LA Weekly* are good sources of information; the former's website, www.calendarlive, and www.culturela.org are two good online guides.

Spring

Academy Awards
See p208 And the winner is….

Los Angeles Marathon
Starts & finishes Downtown (1-310 444 5544/ www.lamarathon.com). **Date** 1st Sun in Mar.
Every year, more than 23,000 runners and wheelchair racers take to the streets. But it's not a typical city marathon: this being Hollywood, the route is dotted with 1,000 cheerleaders. Visit the Quality of Life Expo at the LA Convention Center for sports gear and information prior to the race.

Blessing of the Animals
El Pueblo de Los Angeles Historical Monument, Olvera Street, Downtown (1-213 625 5045/ www.olvera-street.com). **Date** Sat before Easter.
Led by a cow festooned with flowers, this procession of farm animals and pets (and their owners), winds its way down the oldest street in LA. At the end, each animal is blessed with holy water by Cardinal Roger Mahony and even serpents get a blessing. The celebration dates back to the fourth century, when St Anthony of the Desert blessed the beasts, and honours animals' service to humanity.

Long Beach Grand Prix
Downtown Long Beach (1-888 827 7333/1-562 436 9953/www.longbeachgp.com). **Date** mid Apr.
Nicknamed the 'Southern California Official Spring Brake', this high-speed extravaganza features the cars and stars of the CART Champ Car World Series. The two-mile street circuit includes plenty of straights and curves; spectators should expect to spend the afternoon biting their nails.

► For **art festivals**, see p225.
► For **film festivals**, see p220.
► For **gay & lesbian events**, see p242.
► For **major music festivals**, see p234.

California Poppy Festival
Lancaster City Park, 43011 N 10th Street West, Lancaster (1-661 723 6077/www.poppyfestival.com). **Date** mid to late Apr.
This annual festival is a party for California's state flower. Pick up a free map to the poppy hot spots or browse the arts and crafts expo, farmers' market and Celtic Market Square, which features sheep and dog demonstrations and an English tea house.

LA Times Festival of Books
UCLA campus, Westwood (1-213 237 7335/ www.latimes.com/fob). **Date** late Apr.
Well over 100,000 people flock to the UCLA campus each spring to commune with authors giving readings and doing signings, and booksellers hawking their wares directly to the public.

Scandinavian Festival
California Lutheran University, 60 W Olsen Road, Thousand Oaks (1-805 493 3151). **Date** late Apr.
Dine like a Viking at an authentic smörgåsbord buffet, complete with Swedish meatballs, Viking sandwiches, pickled herring and *krumkake*, at a festival celebrating the Scandinavian heritage of the university and the surrounding Conejo Valley, settled by Norwegians in the 1890s.

Fiesta Broadway/Cinco de Mayo
Broadway Corridor, Olvera & Main Streets, Downtown (1-310 914 0015/www.fiestabroadway.la). **Date** last Sun in Apr.
Covering 36 square blocks Downtown, with crowds topping 500,000, this free fiesta lives up to its reputation as the largest Cinco de Mayo celebration in the world, pulling in Latin American pop superstars like Paulina Rubio, Chayanne and Celia Cruz. The festival commemorates the day in 1862 when Mexicans defeated French invaders, and is a blowout of music, piñata-breaking, clowns and food. The festival has become highly commercialised in recent years, so much so that cola and burger logos are now as prevalent as piñatas and clowns.

Santa Clarita Cowboy Poetry & Music Festival
Melody Ranch & Motion Picture Studio, and venues in the Santa Clarita Valley, just north of Hwy 14 (1-661 255 4910/www.santa-clarita.com). **Date** late Apr.
Get out your dude ranch duds for this Western hoedown. Among the attractions are the Walk of Western Stars gala, horseback rides, a cowboy couture fashion show, a casino and plenty of cowboy comedy, poetry and chow. The festival is the only time that Gene Autry's ranch opens to the public.

Arts & Entertainment

¡Ay Caramba! Downtown's **Cinco de Mayo** celebrations. *See p204.*

Ramona Pageant
Ramona Bowl, 27400 Ramona Bowl Road, Hemet, Riverside County (1-800 645 4465/1-909 658 3111/ www.ramonapageant.com). **Date** late Apr-early May.
A picturesque amphitheatre provides the backdrop for this flamboyant play, a love story about the forbidden romance between a Mexican woman and a Native American. Set in the 18th century, the production features a cast of 400; before she was famous, Raquel Welch appeared in the title role.

Summer

Pageant of the Masters
Festival of Arts, 650 Laguna Canyon Road, Laguna Beach (1-949 494 1145/www.foapom.com). **Date** early July-late Aug.
Life imitates art: classic paintings, statues and murals take on a new dimension as real people dress and pose to re-create original masterpieces. Helping to bring the works to life are a professional orchestra, live narration, intricate sets and lighting.

Long Beach Bayou Festival
Queen Mary Events Park, 1126 Queens Highway, next to RMS Queen Mary, Long Beach (1-562 981 1604/www.longbeachfestival.homestead.com). **Date** mid/late June.
Louisiana invades Southern California at this three-day, ocean-side festival. Expect zesty Creole cuisine and Cajun and Zydeco music; bring a mask and costume if you want to enter the Mardi Gras contest.

Absolut Chalk Street Painting Festival
Old Pasadena (1-626 440 7370/ www.absolutchalk.com). **Date** late June.

Hundreds of artists create temporary masterpieces in chalk on the streets of Pasadena, causing thousands of onlookers to watch carefully where they walk. Awards are presented in categories from Most Humorous to Best Rendition of a Master. You can test your talent in the Free Art Zone.

Independence Day
Across Los Angeles. **Date** 4 July.
The Hollywood Bowl hosts LA's most famous fireworks display, synchronised to music by the LA Phil. Celebrations are not limited to the Bowl by any means: Huntington Beach celebrates with a parade during the day, capped by fireworks at night. Then there's more patriotic razzle-dazzle to be found at Venice Beach, the Rose Bowl, Dodger Stadium and Disneyland's Magic Mountain.

Lotus Festival
Echo Park, between Glendale Avenue & Echo Park Boulevard, Echo Park (1-213 485 1310/ www.laparks.org). **Date** 2nd wknd in July.
Boasting the largest lotus bed in the US, this festival celebrates the cultures of Asia and the Pacific islands. Highlights include a market, dragon boat races, martial arts demos and carnival rides.

Blessing of the Cars
Hansen Dam Recreational Park, 11798 Foothill Boulevard (1-323 663 1265/www.blessingofthe cars.com). **Date** late July.
In this car-crazed city, it's no surprise that thousands of people roll in for a blessing of their own road warrior; pre-1968 preferred, please. The crowd is tattooed, the bands are punk and the priest is Catholic. Owners who ask nicely might even persuade Padre to put some holy water into their car's radiator.

Festival of the Chariots

From Santa Monica Civic Auditorium, down Main Street, to Ocean Front Walk Plaza, Venice (1-310 836 2676/www.festivalofchariots.com). **Date** late July/early Aug.

This 5,000-year-old Indian tradition, hosted by the Hare Krishnas, attracts 50,000 people who chant and cheer for the three honoured deities, Lord Jagannatha, Lord Balarama and Lady Subhadra, representations of whom are paraded through town on elaborately decorated chariots.

Nisei Week Japanese Festival

Little Tokyo, Downtown (1-213 687 7193/ www.niseiweek.org). **Date** mid Aug.

This eight-day event celebrates Japanese culture with displays of martial arts, tea ceremonies, flower arranging, calligraphy and more. It culminates with the coronation of the Nisei Week Queen (Nisei means the first generation of Japanese born in America).

US Open of Surfing

Huntington Beach Pier, at Main Street & Pacific Coast Highway, Huntington Beach, Orange County (1-310 473 0411/www.usopenofsurfing.com). **Date** end July/start Aug.

America's largest pro surfing competition attracts the world's elite, who compete for big money while wowing 200,000 beach boys and girls. Heating up the festivities are live bands and a sports expo.

Watts Summer Festival

109th Street Recreation Center, 10950 S Central Avenue, at 109th Street, Watts (1-323 789 7304/ www.wattsfestival.org). **Date** early/mid Aug.

First held in 1966, the year after the Watts Revolt, this black pride event is the oldest African American festival in the US, and has attracted the likes of James Brown, Stevie Wonder, Isaac Hayes and Nancy Wilson. Besides music, events include a fashion show, a film festival and a parade.

Sunset Junction Street Fair

3600-4400 blocks of Sunset Boulevard, between Edgecliff & Fountain Avenues, Silver Lake (1-323 661 7771/www.sunsetjunction.org). **Date** late Aug.

With three music stages situated along three miles of Sunset Boulevard, this street festival unites the disparate residents of the Silver Lake district of LA. And lots of them, too: 200,000 attend each year. In addition to the music, there are food stalls, arts and crafts, and carnival rides.

LA African Marketplace & Cultural Faire

Exposition Park, at Figueroa Street & W Martin Luther King Jr Boulevard (1-232 734 1164/ www.africanmarketplace.org). **Date** last three wknds in Aug.

This festival blends traditional African and Afro-Caribbean sights, sounds and flavours with contemporary African American culture. To keep the children entertained there are magicians and storytellers, plus a petting zoo for the zoophiles.

Fiesta Hermosa

Hermosa Beach, at Hermosa & Pier Avenues (1-310 376 0951/www.fiestahermosa.com). **Date** Labor Day.

Wear a swimsuit under your T-shirt and shorts: after roaming the 250 stalls at this arts and music festival, sampling the ethnic foods and listening to bands, you may want to take a dip in the ocean, handily placed next door to the beach. There's another Fiesta over Memorial Day weekend.

Port of Los Angeles Lobster Festival

Ports o' Call Village, San Pedro (1-310 798 7478/ www.lobsterfest.com). **Date** mid Sept.

Bizarre fact: although this weekend-long festival is held in the coastal town of San Pedro, all the lobsters eaten at it are actually flown in from Maine. Other attractions include live music and Saturday's deeply troubling LobsterDog Parade, at which people dress up their pet pooches as sea creatures.

LA County Fair

Pomona County Fairplex, 1101 W McKinley Avenue, at N White Avenue, Pomona (1-909 623 3111/www. lacountyfair.com). **Date** mid Sept-early Oct.

In keeping with the area's main business, back in 1921 when the LA County Fair was first held, it was an agricultural fair. Times, and LA's economy, have changed since then but the fair still has plenty of farm-friendly stuff including livestock beauty contests, displays of fruit and veg, and horse racing. However, there's now a blinding array of other attractions too: Ferris wheels, enchanted gardens, acrobats, vintage trains and wine-tasting.

Hart of the West Indian Powwow

William S Hart Park & Museum, 24151 N San Fernando Road, Newhall (1-661 255 9295/www. hart-friends.org). **Date** late Sept.

Regarded as the largest powwow in Los Angeles County, this two-day festival brings together some of the best Native American dancers, drummers, singers and artists.

Tarfest

Miracle Mile (www.tarfest.com). **Date** late Sept.

The area around LACMA and the LA Brea Tar Pits host a variety of events as part of this arty, weekend-long festival: film screenings, small concerts and even some performance art.

Grape Harvest Festival

Rancho Cucamonga Epicenter, Rochester Avenue, between Arrow Route & Foothill Boulevard, Rancho Cucamonga (1-909 987 1012/www.rcepicenter.com). **Date** early Oct.

Take off your shoes and join the traditional grape stomp at this festival, inspired by the planting of the first grapes at the Mission San Gabriel Archangel. The grape is also celebrated with pie-eating contests, a grape bake-off and plenty of wine tasting.

Arts & Entertainment

Festivals Music freebies

You don't have to spend big bucks to hear good music in LA – in fact, they're positively giving it away over here. Here's our guide on getting an earful for free. For detailed listings of the year's music events and festivals, many without charge, see www.culturela.org and www.experiencela.com.

Los Angeles County Museum of Art: Sundays Live
5905 Wilshire Boulevard, Miracle Mile (1-323 857 6000/www.lacma.org). **Date** year-round.
LACMA's year-round Sundays Live event (1-213 473 0625, www.sundayslive.org) offers weekly chamber music concerts in the Bing Theater, broadcast live on K-Mozart (105.1 FM). From April to December, there's Friday Night Jazz in the Central Court, from 5.30pm to 8.30pm.

Pershing Square Summer Concert Series
Pershing Square, 532 S Olive Street, Downtown (1-213 847 4968/www.laparks. org/pershingsquare). **Date** June-Sept noon-2pm Tue, Thur; 3-5pm third Sun of mth; 8pm Wed.
These free events feature acts from LA's local music scene, touring bands and the occasional national act. The programme has extended to include Salsa Sundays, swing bands on Wednesday evenings and, on Saturdays, Cinema under the Stars.

Grand Performances
California Plaza, 350 Grand Avenue, Downtown (1-213 687 2159/www.grand performances.org). **Date** June-Sept times vary.
More than 40 events (world music, dance and theatre) running through the summer, on weekday lunchtimes and at weekends. Bring a picnic and booze (red wine is not allowed as it might stain the granite).

Santa Monica Pier Twilight Dance Series
Santa Monica Pier, Santa Monica (1-310 458 8900/www.twilightdance.org). **Date** late June-early Sept 7.30pm Thur.
Reggae, folk, blues, pop, etc. If you don't want to stand in the crowd on the pier, bring a blanket and picnic and listen from the beach below or get drinks in one of the adjacent bars (you can't drink on the pier itself).

Marina Del Rey Summer Concerts
Burton Chace Park, 13650 Mindanao Way, Marina del Rey (1-310 305 9545/ www.labeaches.info). **Date** mid July-early Sept times vary.
Surrounded by water, this park is a delightful venue for a summer's evening picnic as the sun goes down. Classical concerts are held every other Thursday; there's soft jazz on alternating Saturdays at 7pm.

Day of the Drum & Watts Towers Simon Rodia Jazz Festival
Watts Towers Art Center Amphitheater, 1727 E 107th Street, Watts (1-213 847 4646/ www.trywatts.com). **Date** late Sept.
Two festivals on the same weekend: Saturday features an international mix of percussionists, while Sunday's fest offers a variety of jazz, gospel and R&B.

World City
WM Keck Foundation Children's Amphitheatre, Walt Disney Concert Hall, 111 S Grand Avenue, Downtown (1-213 972 7211/http://musiccenter.org). **Date** Sept-June times vary.
Roughly once a month, internationally renowned musicians perform in an outdoor amphitheatre at the Disney Hall. Free tickets are available from 10am on the day on Grand Avenue at 2nd Street, in front of Disney Hall.

Calabasas Pumpkin Festival
Juan Bautista De Anza Park, 3701 Lost Hills Road, Calabasas (1-818 222 5680/www.calabasaspumpkin festival.com). **Date** mid/late Oct.
The Calabasas festival proves there's more to pumpkins than jack-o'-lanterns: here you can try pumpkin bowling, pumpkin beer, pumpkin bread and, of course, pumpkin pie. Another reason to come to this festival is its location: it's held in Paramount's Western-themed studio in the Santa Monica mountains, the backdrop for such immortal television productions as *Dr Quinn, Medicine Woman*.

Halloween
Across Los Angeles. **Date** 31 Oct.
LA has its fair share of freaks, and they all come out on Halloween. Parties are held throughout the city, but the West Hollywood Halloween Carnival, held on the mile-long stretch of Santa Monica Boulevard between La Cienega and Doheny (1-800 368 6020, 1-323 848 6547), is where the real action takes place. More than 400,000 rowdy revellers are entertained by four stages of DJs, bands, costume contests, drag queen competitions and the crowning of the celebrity Honorary Mayor. *See also p234.*

Arts & Entertainment

Dia de Los Muertos
(Day of the Dead)

Self-Help Graphics, 3802 E Cesar E Chavez Avenue, at N Gage Avenue, East LA (1-323 881 6444).
Date 1st Sat in Nov.
LA's hip headquarters for Latin culture hosts this lively celebration. A month-long series of art workshops and events leads up to this day of dancing, theatrical performances and piñata-breaking, plus skeletons and skulls galore.

Mariachi Festival

Mariachi Plaza, at Boyle & Pleasant Streets, Boyle Heights (1-323 466 1156/www.nosotros.org).
Date mid Nov.
Mariachi derives from Spanish, Native American and African traditions, and its musicians are famously itinerant. Decked out in ruffled, rainbow-coloured splendour, musicians at the festival entertain in a range of mariachi styles. Tequila, tacos and other spicy Mexican specialties complete the festivities.

And the winner is…

The number of awards shows held every year in LA is getting out of hand; there are now so many that the already shaky concept of prize-giving is becoming even more devalued. But from a star-spotting point of view, they're a red-carpet must. MTV now has its Movie Awards (which move between LA and New York), VH1 has its Fashion Awards, and Latino Media and GLAAD (Gay & Lesbian Alliance Against Defamation) give out their prizes. But for the industry mogul and star-spotter alike, there are three that stand well above the pack.

It's hard to overemphasise the importance the **Academy Awards** have in LA. Oscar day is like LA's own Christmas. The ceremony is held on a Sunday in late February at the new Kodak Theatre on Hollywood Boulevard (*see p260*); fans queue for days to get places in the stands overlooking the red carpet. Still,

if you're in LA during Oscar week, you can't fail to star-spot. Everybody is in town, and we mean *everybody*.

For a glimpse of what you might expect come Oscar week, turn to the **Golden Globes**; held in late January (a month before the Oscars) and handed out by the Hollywood Foreign Press Association (pretty much the only thing for which it's known), they're the most significant precursor to the main event. The event is held at the Beverly Hills Hilton, and screened live on network TV.

The **Emmys**, essentially TV's Oscars, are held in early September. As with the Oscars, the days when celebs didn't bother to show up are long gone, so you'll be treated to a full raft of stars from the small screen, as well as film stars acting as presenters for the evening. The awards are usually dished out at the Shrine Auditorium (*see p121*).

Doodah Parade

Parade starts at Raymond Avenue & Holly Street, heads west on Colorado Boulevard, ends at Union Street, Pasadena (1-626 205 4029/www.pasadena doodahparade.com). **Date** Sun before Thanksgiving.
This bizarre spoof on the Rose Bowl Parade is pure mayhem. Anyone can take part: all that's required is a strange idea and a sense of humour. Acts range from the political to the puerile; past participants have included the Synchronised Briefcase Marching Drill Team, the Spawn of Captain James T Kirk and the Marching Lumberjacks.

Winter

Hollywood Christmas Parade

Parade starts at Mann's Chinese Theatre, travels east on Hollywood Boulevard, south on Van Ness Avenue, then east on Sunset Boulevard (1-323 469 2337/www.hollywoodchristmas.com). **Date** Sun after Thanksgiving.
The event that inspired Gene Autry to write 'Here Comes Santa Claus' is a glitzy, star-studded presentation that attracts a million fans. First held in 1928, the parade features elaborate floats, pop stars galore, celebs riding in antique cars, camels, equestrian shows and marching bands giving it the full razzle-dazzle. Even with reserved bleacher seats, early arrival is a must, and parking is a nightmare.

Glory of Christmas

Crystal Cathedral, 12141 Lewis Street, at Chapman Avenue, Garden Grove, Orange County (1-714 971 4000/reservations 1-714 544 5679/www.crystal cathedral.org). **Date** late Nov-Dec.
Set in the famous glass-and-steel, star-shaped cathedral, this holiday spectacular blends religion and showbiz in true Californian style. The 200-strong cast includes angels and camels.

Griffith Park Light Festival

Griffith Park, Crystal Springs Drive, between Los Feliz Boulevard & the Ventura Freeway (1-323 913 4688). **Date** late Nov-late Dec.
Brighten up your holidays with a drive along this mile-long stretch of lights. Highlights include a twinkling tunnel and flamboyant depictions of Holly-wood landmarks composed entirely of lights. Weekend nights can be bumper to bumper: park at the LA Zoo and stroll the mile instead.

Downtown Tree Lighting Ceremony

Citicorp Plaza, 777 S Figueroa Street, at W 8th Street, Downtown (1-213 236 3900). **Date** 1st wk of Dec.
Kick off the festive season with the lighting of this huge Christmas tree, LA's answer to Rockefeller Plaza. After that, get in the spirit with carolling, concerts, Christmas cookies and photos with Santa.

Marina del Rey Holiday Boat Parade

Marina del Rey, main channel (1-310 670 7130/www.mdrboatparade.org). **Date** mid Dec.

It's anchors aweigh, as more than 70 ornamented boats compete for prizes in this holiday festival. Watch from Fisherman's Village and Burton Chace Park.

Hannukah Family Festival

Skirball Cultural Center, 2701 N Sepulveda Boulevard, at I-405, West LA (1-310 440 4500/ www.skirball.org). **Date** mid/late Dec.
Enjoy the music, games, tales, tastes and traditions that celebrate the Jewish festival of lights. Everyone can participate in the Hannukah play, complete with costumes and songs.

Las Posadas

Olvera Street, at E Cesar E Chavez Avenue, Downtown (1-213 485 6855/www.olvera-street.com). **Date** 16-24 Dec.
This re-enactment of Mary and Joseph's journey to Bethlehem features a candlelit procession, songs, dancing and piñata-breaking, with free candy for children and adults.

Tournament of Roses Rose Parade

Parade starts in Pasadena at S Orange Grove Boulevard & Ellis Street, travels east on Colorado Boulevard and north on Sierra Madre Boulevard, ends at Paloma Street (1-626 449 4100/1-800 449 7673/www.tournamentofroses.com). **Date** 1 Jan.
The first Rose Parade in 1890 was staged to show off California's sun-kissed climate. And the elaborate floral floats, musical groups, marchers and horses, not to mention the crowning of the fresh-faced Rose Queen, are all still going strong.

Tet Festival

Garden Grove Park, 9301 Westminster Boulevard, at US 22 & Magnolia Street, Westminster, Orange County (1-714 890 1418/www.thsv.org). **Date** late Jan/early Feb.
Held in the city of Westminster, the heart of SoCal's Vietnamese community, this three-day festival celebrates the Lunar New Year, complete with music, food, dragon dancers and karaoke.

Riverside County Fair & National Date Festival

Riverside County Fairgrounds, 46-350 Arabia Street, at US 111, Indo, Riverside County (1-800 811 3247/ www.datefest.org). **Date** Feb.
A county fair with a Middle Eastern twist. There are the standard displays of animals and farm equipment, but things get a bit more exotic with the camel races, *Arabian Nights* pageant and alligator wrestling. As the name suggests, there's a host of date-related activities (date milkshakes, anyone?), topped off by a carnival and concerts.

Chinese New Year

Parade travels along N Broadway, between E Cesar E Chavez Avenue & Bernard Street, Downtown (1-213 617 0396/www.lagoldendragonparade.com). **Date** early Feb.
The spectacular Golden Dragon Parade through Chinatown highlights a two-day street fair, which also includes a carnival.

Children

In the city of eternal youth, children are in their element.

Some American metropolitan centres have recently seen a startling decline in the number of resident families. Not so LA. Although the sparsely populated streets don't always reveal as much, there are kids everywhere. From the affluent LA Basin to the poorer east side, there's a baby boom going on.

While a city planned for cars may not seem ideal for children, LA has a ton of activities. The main attractions are climatic and topographic – miles of seashore and mountains, bathed in balmy weather – but there's also a wide range of indoor attractions, from theme parks to child-friendly bookstores. LA's neighbourhoods each have their own entertainment, playgrounds, food and flavour. Want Johnny to hear a mariachi band? Take him to a park in East LA on a Saturday. Want Janet to ride horses? Head to Griffith Park.

For children's clothes shops, see p184; for toy shops, see p202.

Babysitters

Babysitters Agency of West LA
1-310 306 5437. **Open** *Office* 9am-5pm Mon-Sat. **No credit cards.**
Laurie Klein employs sitters over 21, but may even look after your kids herself. Sitters can take your kids for a bike ride, a swim or another activity. Fees start at $14/hr plus transport, with a four-hour minimum.

Babysitters Guild
1-310 837 1800). **Open** *Office* 8am-3pm Mon-Fri. **No credit cards.**
LA's largest and oldest babysitting service serves hotels all over the city for $10/hr and up plus travel. There's a four-hour minimum daily except Saturdays, when it's five hours. Staff require 24 hours' notice.

Restaurants & cafés

Most LA restaurants can accommodate kids. However, some actively welcome them: look for paper rather than cloth on the tables, and diversions such as fountains, fish tanks and crayons. The best bets are Chinese and Mexican restaurants: the service is fast, there's finger food for tiny hands and, in Mexican restaurants especially, the waiters are nuts about children. Other kid-friendly spots include the **Border Grill** (1445 4th Street, Santa Monica, 1-310 451 1655, www.bordergrill.com).

Angeli Caffe
7274 Melrose Avenue, between N Alta Vista Boulevard & N Poinsettia Place, West Hollywood (1-323 936 9086/www.angelicaffe.com). Bus 14, 212/I-10, exit La Brea Avenue north. **Open** 11.30am-10pm Tue-Fri; 5-10pm Sat, Sun. **Credit** AmEx, DC, Disc, MC, V. **Map** p312 D2.
The most child-friendly restaurant in town. The food here is fresh, simple Italian and moderately priced, and the setting is modern and comfortable. Crayons are available if the children want to scribble between courses, and the staff are as friendly as can be.

Café 50s
11623 Santa Monica Boulevard, between Barry & Federal Avenues, West LA (1-310 479 1955). Bus 4, 304, SM1, SM10/I-10, exit Bundy Drive north. **Open** 7am-midnight Mon, Thur, Sun; 7am-1am Fri; 8am-1am Sat; 8am-midnight Sun. **Credit** MC, V.
Kitschy dining fun for those weary of the Johnny Rockets chain but still craving the occasional old-fashioned burger, milkshake or egg-cream. Mini jukeboxes sit at each table; a house musician plays on Saturday and Sunday lunchtimes.

California Pizza Kitchen
Throughout the city (1-800 919 3227/www.cpk.com). The 15-plus kid-friendly branches of the California Pizza Kitchen are a favourite fallback among LA families. They're scattered all across the region, from Burbank to Santa Monica: call the above number or check online for your nearest.

Farmers Market
See p154 **Farmers Market favourites.**
No restaurant in the city surpasses the energy and variety of edibles on offer of the food court at the Farmers Market. While the children munch on pizza or burgers, adults can try more interesting fare – Brazilian food at Pampas Grill (1-323 931 1928), say, or cajun cooking at the Gumbo Pot (1-323 933 0358)

The best Kids' stuff

For bibliophiles
Storyopolis. See p212.

For running around
Griffith Park. See p214.

For Thomas fans
Allied Model Trains. See p211.

You're a really useful engine: **Allied Model Trains**.

– before all the generations reunite for a proper dessert at Gill's Old Fashioned Ice Cream (1-323 936 7986). Also located here is Du-Pars, a longtime family favourite that serves hearty comfort food and free ice-creams to the children. Aside from its Farmers Market location (1-323 933 8446), it has branches in Studio City and Thousand Oaks.

Newsroom Café

120 N Robertson Boulevard, between W 3rd Street & W Beverly Boulevard, Beverly Hills (1-310 652 4444). Bus 14, 16, 220, LDHWH, LDHWI/I-10, exit Robertson Boulevard north. **Open** 8am-9pm Mon-Thur; 8am-10pm Fri; 9am-10pm Sat; 9am-9pm Sun. **Credit** AmEx, DC, Disc, MC, V. **Map** p312 A3.
You won't have to worry about your offspring making too much noise in this big, boisterous restaurant. Set opposite children's bookstore and art gallery Storyopolis (*see p212*), the Newsroom has healthy and organic food, and tables outside. Overhead TV screens play news reports or music videos.

Wolfgang Puck Express

1315 Third Street Promenade, at Wilshire Boulevard, Santa Monica (1-310 576 4770/www.wolfgangpuck. com). Bus 20, 720, SM2, SM3, SM4, SM5, SM9/ I-10, exit 4th-5th Street north. **Open** 11am-9pm daily. **Credit** AmEx, MC, V. **Map** p310 A2.
Puck's top-end eateries, such as Spago of Beverly Hills (*see p147*) are not ideal, even leaving aside price, for the family. However, this casual and rather cheaper chain is very child-friendly.

Arts & entertainment

For details of what's on, check the 'Calendar' section of the Sunday *LA Times*, *LA Weekly* and the free monthly *LA Parent*, which can be found in any location that caters for children; for details, call 1-818 846 0400 or check http://losangeles.parenthood.com. The website www.gocitykids.com is a useful resource.

Activities

Allied Model Trains

4411 S Sepulveda Boulevard, between Barman Avenue and Braddock Drive, Culver City (1-310 313 9353/www.alliedmodeltrains.com). Bus 220, C5, C6, C437/I-405, exit Culver Boulevard east. **Open** 10am-6pm Mon-Sat. **Credit** Disc, MC, V.
Housed in a miniature replica of Union Station, this 12,000sq ft (1,115sq m) shop bills itself as the largest model train store in the world. Trains chug around the enormous displays through meticulously constructed scenes; even if you can't afford the models, Thomas fans are certain to be entertained.

Bright Child Children's Activity Center

1415 4th Street, at Santa Monica Boulevard, Santa Monica (1-310 393 4844/www.brightchild.com). Bus 4, 304, SM1, SM5, SM7, SM8, SM10/I-10, exit 4th-5th Street north. **Open** 10am-6pm Mon-Thur, Sun;

10am-8pm Fri, Sat. **Admission** $9.75/2hrs; $5/hr each additional hr. **Childcare** $12/hr (9mths-4yrs, Mon-Fri only). **Credit** AmEx, MC, V. **Map** p310 A3.

In addition to play structures such as ball pits, a wind tunnel and zip-line swings, this enormous indoor playground has a mini putting green, an art room and a basketball court with an adjustable rim. There's an invaluable toddler-only area with its own activities, so you don't have to worry about your three-year-old being mown down by the big boys.

Color Me Mine

1109 Montana Avenue, between 11th & 12th Streets, Santa Monica (1-310 393 0069/www.color memine.com). Bus 20, 720, SM3, SM11/I-10, exit Lincoln Boulevard north. **Open** 11am-9pm daily. **Rates** $10/session for adults; $6/session under-10s. **Credit** AmEx, Disc, MC, V. **Map** p310 B2.

For a few hours of creative fun, visit one of Color Me Mine's LA locations (check online for branches). Choose from a selection of ceramic plates, bowls, teapots or animals, which you then paint and have fired. The items themselves cost from $3 upwards. **Other locations**: throughout the city.

Storyopolis

12348 Ventura Boulevard, between Laurel Canyon Boulevard & Coldwater Canyon Avenue, Studio City (1-818 509 5600/www.storyopolis.com). Bus 150, 218, 240, 750/US 101, exit Laurel Canyon Boulevard south. **Open** 10am-6pm Mon-Sat; 11am-4pm Sun. **Credit** AmEx, Disc, MC, V.

This Studio City space, part children's bookstore and part gallery, exhibits original artwork from children's books, and hosts numerous family-friendly events (book signings, concerts and weekly storytimes for babies and toddlers).

Attractions & museums

Budget permitting – none is exactly a cheap day out – the various LA-area theme parks are all child-pleasers. For **Disneyland** and **Knott's Berry Farm** in Orange County, *see pp135-136*; for **Universal Studios** and **Six Flags California** in the San Fernando Valley, *see pp125-126*. If you're planning on driving to San Diego, there's **California Legoland**, off I-5 in Carlsbad (1-760 918 5346, www.lego.com).

Los Angeles has two children's museums; or, at least, it will have when the **Children's Museum of Los Angeles** reopens in 2007 on a new site in the San Fernando Valley; for more, call 1-818 786 2656 or see www.childrens museumla.org. The other is Pasadena's **Kidspace Children's Museum** (*see p129*), an inside-outside learn-while-you-play environment in a former botanical garden, with climbing towers, a mock bug food kitchen and a fake earthquake zone. For a look at real bugs, as well as other educational exhibits, visit Exposition Park, home to a pair of kid-friendly museums in the shape of the **Natural History Museum of Los Angeles County** and the **California ScienCenter** (for both, *see p120*).

Animal attractions are a favourite with youngsters, and LA's are no exception. As well as the **Los Angeles Zoo** (*see p105*), there's also the new **Star Eco Station** (*see p86*). The other main draws are marine-oriented – **Santa Monica Pier Aquarium** (*see p78*), San Pedro's **Cabrillo Marine Aquarium** (*see*

Griffith Park. *See p214.*

Nanny knows best

The most widely discussed play in Los Angeles during 2003 was Lisa Loomer's *Living Out*, a piece about affluent white mothers on the West Side and their Latina nannies. At one point, the nannies fantasised about what would happen if all the service workers in LA stayed home for a day. 'Los Americanos would be driving around in their dirty clothes, starving. Can't go to a restaurant – there's nobody to park the car! You get home, the house is a mess… They'd have to take care of their own kids!'

Taking care of one's own children is uncommon among LA's wealthy classes. Indeed, the super-rich often have one nanny per child. The substitute mothers are often Latinas who have likely left their own children at home in East LA with Grandma or, more poignantly, with relatives in their native Mexico or Guatemala or El Salvador, to whom they send as high a proportion of their wages as they're able to spare.

Latina nannies in LA typically work without contracts, timecards or any other records of employment. It suits both sides, to a point: the employers can count on flexibility and low wages, while the employees can find work without immigration documents. Only rarely does either side pay taxes. A few generous employers will help their nanny with learning English and, perhaps, getting a work visa. It's not known how many Latina women work over here, but it's certainly well into six figures.

The flip side to all this is a preponderance of labour violations. Stories abound of nannies working 12- or 13-hour days for a pittance, being let go without cause and even losing touch with their own children. And while the mothers enjoy the cheap labour and the TLC lavished on their kids, the service is not without its problems: their toddlers speak better Spanish than English and are more attached to nanny than to mummy. And, naturally, they also come to believe that Latinas are simply the hired help.

One might think that with so many Anglos and Latinas sharing such a precious commodity, there might be a growing mutual understanding. But the relationship between mother and nanny remains precarious, a complex brew of resentment, guilt, co-dependency and uneasy affection between the 'mistress' and 'servant' classes. Now, with the Latino population on the rise both in terms of pure numbers and the levels of economic and political power they wield, one wonders if the time may soon come when LA mothers are at last left holding the baby.

p131) and the **Aquarium of the Pacific** in Long Beach (*see p133*) – but there are a number of other attractions, such as the cutesy **Angels Attic Museum** (*see p77*), the **Travel Town Museum** in Griffith Park (*see p106*) and **Ripley's Believe it or Not!** (*see p97*).

If your kids love to paint, many of the museums here offer workshops; among them are **LACMA** (*see p100*), **MoCA** (*see p115*), the **Japanese American National Museum** (*see p111*), the **Getty Center** (*see p83*) and the new **Getty Villa** (*see p74*). For details, check individual websites or see www.gocitykids.com.

Bookstores & libraries

Much to the surprise of many visitors, LA is full of bibliophiles, and plenty of literary provision is made for kids. The children's section of the **Richard J Riordan Central Library** (*see p292*) has plenty of kids' books and a strong programme of events; among other diversions, the KLOS Story Theatre has weekly storytelling and puppet shows (2pm Sat). The unfortunately named Ronald McDonald Children's Charities

Southern California Multimedia Center features ten interactive workstations. Elsewhere, the city has spent the last eight years building new district libraries, all of which feature children's reading areas and special kids' programmes; see www.lapl.org for branches, or ask library staff for the *Children's Activities* pamphlet.

The LA region also boasts a wealth of children's booksellers that offer author and illustrator meet-and-greets, dress-up parties, crafts workshops, singalongs and story times. Listed below are some of the best-loved bookstores. Check their web sites or call them for special programmes.

Chevalier's Books *126 N Larchmont Boulevard, at W 1st Street, Hancock Park (1-323 465 1334). Bus 10, 11, 210, 720/US 101, exit Melrose Avenue west.* **Open** 10am-6pm Mon-Sat; 11am-5pm Sun. **Credit** MC, V. **Map** p313 B4.

Children's Book World *10580½ W Pico Boulevard, between Prosser & Parnell Avenues, West LA (1-310 559 2665/www.childrensbook world.com). Bus C3, SM7, SM13/I-10, exit Overland Avenue north.* **Open** 10am-5.30pm Mon-Fri; 10am-5pm Sat. **Credit** MC, V. **Map** p311 B5.

Once Upon a Story *3740 E 4th Street, between Loma & Grand Avenues, Long Beach (1-562 433 6856/www.onceuponastorybooks.com). I-405, exit Cherry Avenue south.* **Open** 10am-5.30pm Mon-Fri; 9am-5pm Sat; 9am-4pm Sun. **Credit** MC, V.

San Marino Toy & Book Shoppe
2424 Huntington Drive, between San Marino & Del Mar Avenues, San Marino (1-626 309 0222/ www.toysandbooks.com). Bus 79/I-110, exit Atlantic Boulevard north. **Open** 10am-6pm Mon-Sat; 11am-5pm Sun. **Credit** Disc, MC, V.

Storyopolis *See p212.*

Vroman's Bookstore *See p183.*

Music & theatre

On weekdays during July and August, the LA Philharmonic lays on performances and workshops for children under ten in a series called Summer Sounds at the **Hollywood Bowl** (*see p236*). During fall, winter and spring, take the young 'uns to a youth concert by the LA Philharmonic at the marvellous **Walt Disney Concert Hall** (*see p237*).

During long car journeys (and let's face it, there's going to be plenty of those), tune in to **KDIS** (1110 AM). Disney's 24-hour radio station features music, character voices and call-in contests, and should keep the kids quiet.

Bob Baker Marionette Theater

1345 W 1st Street, at Glendale Boulevard, Echo Park (1-213 250 9995/www.bobbakermarionettes. com). Bus 14/I-110, exit 3rd Street west. **Open** *Box office* 9am-5pm Tue-Fri. *Shows* 10.30am Tue-Fri; 2.30pm Sat, Sun. **Tickets** $12. **Credit** AmEx, MC, V. **Map** p314 D6.
Baker has been staging marionette shows for over four decades; booking for them is essential. Staff can also cater for children's parties.

Pasadena Symphony Musical Circus

Pasadena Civic Auditorium, 300 E Green Street, at Euclid Avenue, Pasadena (1-626 449 7360/Pasadena Symphony 1-626 793 7172/www.pasadenasymphony. org/circus). Metro Memorial Park/bus 181, 267, 687/I-110, exit Green Street east. **Open** *Box office* 10am-5pm Mon-Sat. **Tickets** free.
Musicians and teachers help children aged under ten discover the joy of music-making at these monthly sessions, held on Saturday mornings. After a musical petting zoo, where children get a close-up look at various instruments, there's a family concert.

Outdoors & nature

With picnic areas, miles of hiking and horse-riding trails, a 1920s merry-go-round and a zoo, the rolling hills of **Griffith Park** (*see p105*) make a great outdoor experience for kids. That said, most of LA's parks are good, the pick of them being **Will Rogers State Historic**

Park (*see p74*) and the **Kenneth Hahn State Recreation Area** (*see p123*).

The botanical gardens at the **Huntington Library** (*see p129*) now feature a children's garden, containing nine kinetic sculptures that explore the natural elements of earth, light, air and water. Children aged two and older can walk under a rainbow in a circle of mist, vanish into a sea of billowing fog, and feel sound waves moving through water in a sonic pool.

TreePeople

12601 Mulholland Drive, at Coldwater Canyon Drive, Beverly Hills (1-818 753 4600/www.treepeople.org). US 101, exit Coldwater Canyon Boulevard south. **Open** *Park* sunrise-sunset daily. *Nursery* 10am-noon Wed; 2-4pm Sat. **Admission** free.
This non-profit group plants and cares for native and exotic trees, and the environment. The centre is in the idyllic 45-acre Coldwater Canyon Park, a welcome break from the urban sprawl.

Playgrounds

On weekdays, LA playgrounds are usually just as full of nannies and babysitters as they are children, but the elusive parents are out in full force at weekends. Almost all of the major parks (including Griffith Park) contain playgrounds of varying shapes and sizes.

Clover Park

Ocean Park Boulevard, at 25th Street, Santa Monica (1-310 458 8311). Bus 33, 333, SM1, SM2, SM8, SM10/I-10, exit 4th-5th Street south. **Open** dawn-dusk daily. **Map** p310 D4.
In addition to a baseball field, two soccer fields, a sand volleyball court and a basketball court, this large park boasts barbecue rigs and one of the city's more thoughtfully designed playgrounds. A small bike path, often full of zig-zagging kids still using training wheels, connects the playground's sections, a 'tot lot', and a three-storey observation platform.

Beaches

On **Santa Monica Beach** and **Venice Beach**, between Santa Monica Pier to the north and Venice Pier to the south, there's sand, sea, bike and skate paths, with cycles and Rollerblades available for hire. Near the bike path are a number of mini-playparks; the largest is at the Venice Recreation Center, next door to basketball and racquetball courts for teens and adults. The aforementioned Santa Monica Pier itself holds plenty of amusement arcades, a big wheel and other fairground rides, including an old-fashioned carousel.

And why not learn to surf? There are regular surf camps for over-7s at Santa Monica and El Segundo Beaches. For more, call 1-310 663 2479 or check www.learntosurfla.com.

Comedy & TV

You're having a laugh.

Comedy

The comedy world in Los Angeles is split into two distinct sections. On the one hand are the world-famous clubs that charge steep two-drink minimums for the privilege of watching A-list stand-ups. On the other are the edgier theatres staging improv and sketch comedy at low prices. The twain rarely meet; for the full story, you'll need to sample both extremes.

Most of the action is in Hollywood and along the Sunset Strip, but quality laughs can be had as far afield as Pasadena and Hermosa Beach (respectively, the **Ice House** and the **Comedy & Magic Club**, two top hangouts). Reservations are encouraged – diners may get first dibs – and parking is often limited, so plan ahead and arrive early. After all, tonight's opening act might be tomorrow's star.

Venues

Acme Comedy Theatre

135 N La Brea Avenue, between Beverly Boulevard & W 1st Street, Hollywood (1-323 525 0202/www. acmecomedy.com). Bus 10, 11, 212/I-10, exit La Brea Avenue north. **Shows** 8pm Mon, Tue, Thur, Sun; 8pm, 10pm Wed, Sat; 8.30pm, 10pm Fri. **Admission** $5-$25. **Credit** AmEx, MC, V. **Map** p313 A4.
An enthusiastic group of jokesters, many of them up-and-comers, dish up a steady diet of cleverly written sketches with a dash of improvisation on the side. The troupe's freshness is shown in concepts such as an improvised radio show.

Bang

457 N Fairfax Avenue, between Rosewood & Oakwood Avenues, Fairfax District (1-323 653 6886/www.bangstudio.com). Bus 14, 217, 218, LDF/I-10, exit Fairfax Avenue north. **Shows** 8pm Thur, Fri; 8pm, 9pm, 10pm Sat. **Admission** $7-$10. **Credit** MC, V. **Map** p312 C3.
A writing and improv training centre, Bang is fast becoming a player on the LA comedy scene, helped in no small part by the lack of snobs on both the staff and the stage. The lobby of the intimate 49-seat theatre doubles as an art gallery.

Comedy & Magic Club

1018 Hermosa Avenue, between 10th Street & Pier Avenue, Hermosa Beach (1-310 372 1193/www. comedyandmagicclub.com). Bus 130, 439/I-405, exit Rosecrans Boulevard west. **Shows** 8pm Tue-Thur; 7.30pm, 10pm Sat; 7pm Sun. **Admission** $12.50-$30; 2-drink min. **Credit** AmEx, MC, V.

The classiest comedy club in SoCal. Jay Leno polishes his act here most Sundays; Jerry Seinfeld, Ray Romano and magician Harry Anderson are among those who also take the stage here semi-regularly.

Comedy Central Stage

6539 Santa Monica Boulevard, between Seward Street & Wilcox Avenue, Hollywood (1-323 960 5519/www.comedycentral.com). Bus 4, 156, 304/ US 101, exit Vine Street south. **Shows** 8pm, nights vary. **Admission** free. **Map** p313 B2.
The premier place for comedy on TV has quietly extended its reach to live theatre. At this small space, comics and actors workshop new shows and showcase one-of-a-kind performances before savvy audiences. Shows are free: try and book ahead.

Comedy Store

8433 W Sunset Boulevard, at N Olive Drive, West Hollywood (1-323 656 6225/www.thecomedystore. com). Bus 2, 302, LDHWH/I-10, exit La Cienega Boulevard north. **Shows** times vary. **Admission** $5-$20; 2-drink min. **Credit** AmEx, MC, V. **Map** p312 B1.
In its prime, this famous club hosted comics of the calibre of Richard Pryor and Robin Williams. These days, it's most famous for its starring role in reality TV show *Minding the Store* (hosted by Pauly Shore, son of club owner Mitzi), but still lures tourists in sufficient numbers to justify operating three stages.

Comedy Union

5040 W Pico Boulevard, between S Sycamore & S La Brea Avenues Midtown (1-323 934 9300/www.the comedyunion.com). Bus 212, 312/I-10, exit La Brea Avenue north. **Shows** 9pm Mon, Tue, Thur; 9.30pm Wed; 10pm Fri, Sat. **Admission** free-$12; 2-drink min. **Credit** MC, V. **Map** p312 D5.
Formerly a dentist's, this room on Pico is now a mecca for African American comics. Audiences often spar with the acts, especially at CU Fridays and Super Saturdayz. The likes of Eddie Murphy and Sinbad sometimes pop by to check out the new talent.

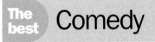

The best Comedy

For mainstream chuckles
Laugh Factory. *See p216.*

For indie giggles
Uncabaret at the M Bar. *See p216.*

For improv chortles
Improv Olympic West. *See p216.*

West Hollywood's **Improv**.

Groundlings Theatre

7307 Melrose Avenue, at N Poinsettia Place, West Hollywood (1-323 934 9700/www.groundlings.com). Bus 10, 11/I-10, exit Fairfax Avenue north. **Shows** 8pm Wed, Thur; 8pm, 10pm Fri, Sat; 7.30pm Sun. **Admission** $11-$20. **Credit** AmEx, Disc, MC, V. **Map** p312 D2.

The launching pad for comics such as Will Ferrell and Phil Hartman continues to hold its own with a range of quality, character-based sketch shows and improv. If broad, over-the-top humour is your particular thing, this is the place to be.

Ice House

24 N Mentor Avenue, at E Colorado Boulevard, Pasadena (1-626 577 1894/www.icehousecomedy.com). Metro Lake/bus 180, 181, 256, 485/I-210, exit Lake Avenue south. **Shows** 8.30pm Tue-Thur; 8.30pm, 10.30pm Fri; 7pm, 9pm, 11pm Sat. **Admission** $10-$15; 2-drink min. **Credit** AmEx, Disc, MC, V.

The oldest comedy club this side of the Mississippi, the Ice House has hosted virtually every great comic of the last three decades, from Steve Martin to Cheech and Chong. It's tamer than the Sunset Strip, but you could say the same thing about Pasadena itself.

Improv

8162 Melrose Avenue, between N Kildea Drive & N La Jolla Avenue, West Hollywood (1-323 651 2583/www.improv.com). Bus 10, 11, LDF/I-10, exit La Cienega Boulevard north. **Shows** 8pm Mon-Thur, Sun; 8.30pm, 10.30pm Fri, Sat. **Admission** $10-$20. **Credit** AmEx, MC, V. **Map** p312 C2.

There isn't much improv at Improv. There is, however, stand-up: lots of it, too, previously from the likes of Dave Chappelle. Budd Friedman's joint has delighted audiences for 40 years, and grown into a national chain in the process. Aside from the acts, the club stands out from its rivals in one other key way: the food served here is actually pretty good.

Improv Olympic West

6366 Hollywood Boulevard, at Ivar Avenue, Hollywood (1-323 962 7560/www.iowest.com). Metro Hollywood-Vine/bus 180, 181, 210, 212, 217, 710, LDH/US 101, exit Vine Street south. **Shows** call for details. **Admission** $5-$10. **Credit** MC, V. **Map** p313 B1.

The west coast branch of the influential Chicago theatre. The main event is the *Harold*, a long-form style that resembles a richly constructed one-act play more than a series of gags. *Scrubs* janitor Neil Flynn and *Curb Your Enthusiasm*'s Jeff Garlin both have weekly gigs. There are several shows nightly.

Laugh Factory

8001 W Sunset Boulevard, at Laurel Canyon Boulevard, West Hollywood (1-323 656 1336/www.laughfactory.com). Bus 2, 302, LDHWH/I-10, exit La Cienega Boulevard north. **Shows** 8pm Mon; 7.30pm, 9.30pm Tue; 8pm, 10pm Wed, Thur, Sun; 8pm, 10pm, midnight Fri, Sat. **Admission** $12-$17; 2-drink min. **Credit** (bar only) MC, V. **Map** p312 B1.

The stand-up equivalent to Carnegie Hall, and thus probably your best bet if you want to catch grade-A comics such as Dane Cook, Bob Saget and Jon Lovitz. Booking ahead is advisable. There's a sister club in Long Beach; check online for details.

M Bar

1253 N Vine Street, at Fountain Avenue, Hollywood (1-323 856 0036/www.mbarhollywood.com). Bus 210, 710/US 101, exit Vine Street south. **Shows** 8pm nightly. **Admission** free-$10; $10 food min. **Credit** AmEx, Disc, MC, V. **Map** p313 B2.

The unofficial hangout of the LA underground comedy scene. There's comedy nightly, but the main event is *Uncabaret* (fortnightly, Sat) when members of the indie elite – Patton Oswalt, David Cross, Bob Odenkirk – perform sketches and stand-up.

National Comedy Theatre

733 Seward Street, at Melrose Avenue, Hollywood (1-323 856 4796/www.comedysportzla.com). Bus 10, 11/US 101, exit Vine Street south. **Shows** 8pm Thur; 8pm, 10.30pm Fri, Sat. **Admission** $13-$15. **Credit** AmEx, DC, Disc, MC, V. **Map** p313 B3.

In ComedySportz LA (8pm Fri, Sat), two teams face off in a game-based improv similar in style to *Whose Line is it Anyway?*. The fast-paced antics are ideal for families: players have to wear a paper bag over their head if their material becomes too adult. *U-Sical* (10.30pm Fri, Sat) sees a team of comics improvise an entire musical about a single audience member.

Second City Studio Theatre

8156 Melrose Avenue, at N Kildea Drive, West Hollywood (1-323 658 8190/www.secondcity.com). Bus 10, 11, LDF/I-10, exit La Cienega Boulevard north. **Shows** times vary Tue-Sat. **Admission** $5-$15. **Credit** AmEx, MC, V. **Map** p312 C2.

It lacks the mystique of its original Chicago location, but Second City still cranks out top-notch shows. One of the strongest offerings is *Totally Looped*, in which a cast including Dan Castallaneta (aka Homer Simpson) create a live soundtrack to old movies.

Upright Citizens Brigade

5919 Franklin Avenue, at N Bronson Avenue, Hollywood (1-323 908 8702/www.ucbtheatre.com/la). Bus 26, 180, 181, 217, LDH/US 101, exit Gower Street north. **Shows** times vary, daily. **Admission** free-$8. **Credit** AmEx, Disc, MC, V. **Map** p313 C1.

Founded by Matt Besser, Ian Roberts and Matt Walsh from the Comedy Central show of the same name, the UCB is at the centre of avant-garde comedy. Citizens can exercise their right to free laughter on Sundays, when *Asssscat* hosts monologuers such as Sarah Silverman, Andy Richter and Tina Fey.

TV tapings

LA's self-described role as the centre of the entertainment industry is given credence by the massive number of TV shows filmed here. The packed shooting schedule means that tickets are surprisingly easy to get. You can apply online ahead of time, either through a specialist agency or, in some cases, through the TV network in question. However, if you haven't booked, clipboard-touting agents can be found at tourist hangouts such as Grauman's Chinese Theatre, Universal CityWalk, Third Street Promenade and Venice Beach, dispensing tickets for that week's shows.

Tickets for all shows are free, but be warned that the fulfilment of your TV dreams may involve three to four hours and a lot of sitting around. And check the fine print: tickets may not guarantee admission (early arrival is required), and every show has age restrictions. For tours of TV studios, *see p71*.

Agencies

Audience Associates
1-323 653 4105/www.tvtix.com.
The *Dr Phil Show*, *Real Time with Bill Maher* and *Jeopardy* are a few mouse clicks away. Audience Associates also enlists movie extras.

Audiences Unlimited
1-818 753 3470/www.tvtickets.com.
Audiences Unlimited deals exclusively with sitcoms, providing tickets to favourites such as *Two and a Half Men*, *That '70s Show* and *The King of Queens*.

Hollywood Tickets
1-818 688 3974/www.hollywoodtickets.com.
Hollywood Tickets' site is wonderfully straightforward: select the show you want to see, or the dates you're available, and up will spring a list of options.

Individual shows

Jimmy Kimmel Live
Tickets *1-866 546 6984/www.1iota.com.*
Shows 6.15pm Mon-Thur.
Having earned his stripes on *The Man Show*, Jimmy Kimmel is now a fixture on ABC's late-night line-up. The show, filmed at the El Capitan Entertainment Center in Hollywood, has a relaxed atmosphere, but still draws top-shelf guests. Don't be fooled by the name: it's filmed an hour before it airs out east.

The Price is Right
Tickets *1-323 575 2449/www.cbs.com/daytime/price.* **Shows** 1.30pm, 4.15pm Mon; 2.30pm Tue. *See below* **Come on down!**.

The Tonight Show with Jay Leno
Tickets *3000 W Alameda Avenue, Burbank, CA 91523 (details at www.nbc.com/The_Tonight_Show_with_Jay_Leno).* **Shows** 4.30pm Mon-Fri.
Getting in to this late-night staple takes persistence. Tickets are available at least six weeks in advance by mail only: check online for details of how to apply. A limited number of tickets is handed out for that day's show from 8am. You'll need to arrive by 2.30pm at the latest to guarantee entry.

Come on down!

For hardcore game show aficionados, nothing makes the pulse race faster than the fantasy of hearing Rich Fields call out their name, followed by the immortal invitation to, 'Come on down! You're the next contestant on *The Price is Right*'. Fantasists have had plenty of time to live their dreams: since relaunching in 1972 after a nine-year run between 1956 and 1965, *The Price is Right* has been on air for 35 seasons, making it the longest-running game show, and one of the most enduring programmes of any kind, in US TV history.

Hosted since '72 by the durable Bob Barker, *The Price is Right* owes much of its success to its simple format. If the contestants can guess the retail price of everyday household items, they win them.

As they continue to win, the items get more expensive and the competition get tougher.

Since anyone who's ever gone shopping can relate to the show, there's a never-ending supply of contestants. On any given weekday morning, scores of them line up outside CBS Television City, many wearing home-made T-shirts declaring their undying love for Barker. The show's format has remained unchanged since the 1970s, but so, crucially, has the set and the music; as such, the audience is a mix of housewives who've grown up adoring the show and college kids who venerate its kitsch appeal. To join them, contact the CBS ticket office (*see above*) or contact Hollywood Tickets, who operate a priority ticket service that minimises your wait at the studio.

Film

Be the first to see the blockbusters at LA's movie theatres.

Blue skies and easy living brought the first film-makers to LA, a world away from the snowy weather and tough patent laws of New York and the Midwest. By the start of World War I, Hollywood was jammed with film companies operating out of barns and warehouses, the scrappy origins of the world's largest dream factory.

From its inception, the movie business was built on star power. As early as 1915, executives were complaining about stars' salaries; Universal founder Carl Laemmle even took out an ad to claim he was the first producer to 'buck the star system – the ruinous practice that has been responsible for high-priced but low-grade features'. Still, the rising cost of top-drawer talent hardly proved Hollywood's undoing, as evidenced by the industry's first golden age, which began in the 1920s. The arrival of sound further consolidated the power of major studios.

The Great Depression reached Hollywood four years after the 1929 stock market crash, but it hit it hard. President Roosevelt came to the rescue with the National Industrial Recovery Act, allowing the studios to lock talent into long-term contracts that granted them huge salaries while ensuring they had no control over what they did. The studios were factories: actors and directors were assigned to projects whether they liked it or not, writers clocked in every day and an army of technicians kept the cameras rolling.

The 1940s saw the first cracks in the studio system; by the end of the '50s, competition from TV had more than halved the movie audience, and stars' desire to control their own destinies seemed to signal its demise. But after lean times in the late '60s and early '70s, Hollywood

bounced back, thanks in part to a generation of directors (Lucas, Spielberg, Scorsese) who made their names during this financially fallow but creatively rich era. After another slow period in the 1980s, the rise of so-called 'independent' film in the 1990s gave Hollywood another shot in the arm: nearly every major studio set up an art-house arm to develop less mainstream fare.

In terms of both profits and artistry, 2005 was the worst year for Hollywood studios since the mid-1980s. Executives blamed everything from bootleg DVDs to higher gas prices, conveniently overlooking the possibility that an endless stream of tired sequels, uninspired remakes and pointless adaptations of TV shows that were awful in the first place (*The Dukes of Hazzard*, anyone?) might have also had something to do with it.

However, the sheer pervasiveness of the movie industry in LA means that there are countless opportunities to be participant or observer. There are film courses aplenty at the local colleges, a couple of film festivals a month that welcome volunteers, and endless calls for extras. And if you wander Downtown, you're almost certain to come across a location shoot.

Movie theatres

The LA area is overrun with cinemas: some historic, some huge and some horrible. Movies occasionally play here in advance of their country- or worldwide release, often for just a week at a time in order to make them Oscar-eligible. US cinema dominates; European cinema is shown in retrospectives and special seasons, and not just in art-house cinemas.

INFORMATION & FILM RATINGS
The best sources for weekly film listings are the *LA Weekly*, *LA Citybeat* and the 'Calendar' section of the *LA Times*, all of which list festivals and special events as well as including information on standard screenings and reviews of movies currently in cinemas.

Producers pay the Motion Picture Association of America (MPAA) to protect the innocent by rating their movies. The NC-17 rating, which bars under-17s, is the toughest; the other guidelines are R (under-17s admitted only with an adult), PG-13 (under-13s admitted only with an adult), PG (parental guidance suggested) and G (unrestricted).

The best Cinema

For something old
American Cinematheque. *See p221*.

For something new
ArcLight. *See p219*.

For something massive
IMAX. *See p221*.

Watch like an Egyptian at the **American Cinematheque**. *See p221.*

PREVIEW SCREENINGS

As you read this, there's an industry screening taking place somewhere in LA. Getting tickets is very difficult. However, you may be accosted in the street by clipboard-toting recruiters offering free tickets to preview screenings. Such events are used either to test reaction to a completed film, or to spread word-of-mouth buzz about a movie due out in a couple of weeks. If you're approached, you'll be asked what you do for a living; if there's a whiff of 'industry' about you (that includes journalists), the invitation will be withdrawn. A few white lies won't go amiss: it's a standing joke that previews are full of social workers. Hang around on Hollywood Boulevard (especially by Grauman's Chinese Theatre), Santa Monica Pier or Universal CityWalk, and you're almost certain to be offered tickets to something.

Official sneak previews of movies opening the following week are open to everybody and are advertised in advance in the *LA Times* and the *LA Weekly*. Many are held at the **Mann Bruin** in Westwood (*see p220*).

Multiplexes

Multiplexes are everywhere in LA; below are four of the most popular and/or accessible. You can get show information and purchase tickets on MovieFone (1-323 777 3456).

AMC Century 15 *10250 Santa Monica Boulevard, between Century Park W & Avenue of the Stars, Century City (1-310 289 4262/www.amctheatres. com). Bus 4, 16, 304/I-405, exit Santa Monica*

Boulevard east. **Screens** 15. **Tickets** $10.50; $8.50 before 6pm; $7.50-$9.50 discounts. **Credit** AmEx, Disc, MC, V. **Map** p311 B4.
AMC Universal City Multiplex 100 *Universal City Plaza, Universal City (1-818 508 0588/www. amctheatres.com). Metro Universal City/bus 96, 156, 166/US 101, exit Universal Center Drive.* **Screens** 18. **Tickets** $9.75; $7.50 before 4pm; $6.75-$7.75 discounts. **Credit** AmEx, MC, V.
The Bridge: Cinema de Luxe/IMAX *The Promenade at Howard Hughes Center, 6081 Center Drive, at Sepulveda Boulevard, Westchester (1-310 568 3375/www.thebridgecinemas.com). Bus 429/I-405, exit Howard Hughes Parkway west.* **Screens** 17. **Tickets** $8.25-$11.50; $8 discounts. **Credit** MC, V.
Pacific Theaters at The Grove *6301 W 3rd Street, between N Fairfax Avenue & N Gardner Street, West Hollywood (1-323 692 0164/www. pacifictheatres.com). Bus 16, LDHWI/I-10, exit Fairfax Avenue north.* **Screens** 14. **Tickets** $10.50-$11.50; $8.50 discounts. **Credit** AmEx, MC, V. **Map** p312 C3.

Classic movie theatres

If you abhor multiplex culture, you're in luck: LA still has several classic movie houses screening big movies. The settings will (hopefully) make the trashiest blockbuster seem like high art.

ArcLight

6360 W Sunset Boulevard, between Ivar Avenue & Vine Street, Hollywood (1-323 464 1478/www. arclightcinemas.com). Bus 180, 181, 210, 212, 217, 310, LDH, LDHWI/US 101, exit Vine Street south. **Screens** 15. **Tickets** $14; $9.75 discounts. **Credit** AmEx, MC, V. **Map** p313 B2.

Festivals Film

Pan African Film Festival

1-323 295 1706/www.paff.org. **Date** Feb.
In addition to African-American films, this
festival spotlights movies from Africa and
from emigrant African communities.

Silver Lake Film Festival

*1-323 993 7225/www.silverlakefilm
festival.org.* **Date** Mar.
LA's own Sundance, surrounded by plenty of
scene-to-be-seen music events and parties.

Los Angeles Asian Pacific
Film & Video Festival

1-213 680 4462/www.vconline.org.
Date late April/early May.
What's coming out of the Pacific Rim.

IFP Los Angeles Film Festival

1-866 345 6337/www.lafilmfest.com.
Date late June/early July.
A ten-day event screening about 200 films,
ranging from features and shorts to
documentaries and music videos.

Last Remaining Seats

*1-213 623 2489/www.laconservancy.org/
remaining.* **Date** June.
Once a year, the LA Conservancy reopens
and screens classic films in the grand old
movie palaces on Broadway in Downtown LA,
among them the Palace (1911; No.630) and
the Orpheum (1926; No.842).

Los Angeles Latino
International Film Festival

1-323 469 9066/www.latinofilm.org.
Date July.
This festival, based at the Egyptian Theatre,
focuses on films from Mexico and Latin
America.

Outfest

1-213 480 7088/www.outfest.org. **Date** July.
A ten-day season of gay and lesbian movies,
held at a variety of venues.

Cinecon

1-800 411 0455/www.cinecon.org.
Date Labor Day wknd.
This five-day show, held at the Egyptian
Theatre, offers rarely seen classic films,
Q&As with actors and directors, and a
memorabilia sale.

RESfest

1-212 320 3750/www.resfest.com.
Date end Sept.
This salute to digital filmmaking is your best
bet to see obscure international short films
and music videos.

AFI Los Angeles
International Film Festival

1-866 234 3378/www.afifest.com. **Date** Nov.
The American Film Institute's festival screens
around 130 films from close to 40 countries.

Built in 1963, the formerly famous Cineramadome
has been given a luxury overhaul and has been reincarnated as the ArcLight, with wide, sofa-like seats,
top-of-the-line sound, and a café and bar. Arguably
the best place to catch a new movie in LA.

Grauman's Chinese Theatre

*6925 Hollywood Boulevard, between N Orange Drive
& N McCadden Place, Hollywood (1-323 464 8111/
www.manntheatres.com). Metro Hollywood-Highland/
bus 210, 212, 217, 310, LDHWH/US 101, exit
Highland Avenue south.* **Screens** 6. **Tickets**
$12; $9 discounts. **Credit** MC, V. **Map** p313 A1.
The most famous movie theatre in LA, and a tourist
attraction in its own right (*see p95*). In addition to
its regular programming, it hosts many premières.
Almost opposite is the Disney-owned **El Capitan**
(No.6838, 1-323 467 7674), another classic old theatre.

Mann Bruin

*948 Broxton Avenue, at Weyburn Avenue, Westwood
(1-310 248 6266/www.manntheatres.com). Bus 20,
21, 720, SM1, SM2, SM3, SM8, SM12/I-405, exit*

Wilshire Boulevard east. **Screens** 1. **Tickets** $9;
$6 before 6pm; $6-$6.50 discounts. **Credit** AmEx,
Disc, MC, V.
This handsome 1930s Streamline Moderne building
often has sneak previews of upcoming films.

Regent Showcase

*614 N La Brea Avenue, between Clinton Street
& Melrose Avenue, Hollywood (1-323 934 2944/
www.regenttheaters.com). Bus 10, 11, 212/I-10, exit
La Brea Avenue north.* **Screens** 1. **Tickets** $10; $7
discounts. **Credit** MC, V. **Map** p313 A3.
An old-fashioned movie theatre with a large screen.

Art houses

New Beverly Cinema

*7165 Beverly Boulevard, at N Detroit Street, Fairfax
District (1-323 938 4038/www.michaelwilliams.com/
beverlycinema). Bus 14, 212/I-10, exit La Brea
Avenue north.* **Screens** 1. **Tickets** $7; $4-$6
discounts. **No credit cards**. **Map** p312 D3.

The theatre might be dingy, but the double bills, a mix of recent art-house releases and beloved classics, are terrific. The building used to be a comedy club: Dean Martin and Jerry Lewis performed here.

Nuart
11272 Santa Monica Boulevard, at Sawtelle Boulevard, West LA (1-310 281 8223/www.landmarktheatres.com). Bus 4, 304, SM4/I-405, exit Santa Monica Boulevard west. **Screens** 1. **Tickets** $8.50; $5.50 concessions. **No credit cards.**
Considered to be one of the best repertory theatres in LA, the Nuart often gets exclusive engagements of independent and foreign movies, and also runs restored classics and documentaries.

Rialto
1023 Fair Oaks Avenue, at Oxly Avenue, South Pasadena (1-626 388 2122/www.landmarktheatres. com). Bus 176, 260, 361/I-110, exit Fair Oaks Avenue south. **Screens** 1. **Tickets** $7.75; $6 discounts. **No credit cards.**
Part of the same repertory chain as the Nuart, the good-looking Rialto also screens the latest art-house releases. There's a great balcony, though the sound isn't nearly as good as the view.

Sunset 5
8000 W Sunset Boulevard, at N Laurel Avenue, West Hollywood (1-323 848 3500/www.laemmle. com). Bus 2, 217, 218, 302, LDHWH/I-10, exit Fairfax Avenue north. **Screens** 5. **Tickets** $10; $8 before 6pm Mon-Fri; $5.50-$6.50 discounts. **Credit** MC, V. **Map** p312 C1.
The Laemmle group brings alternative fare to the masses. Sunset 5, a favourite with Academy voters, is the best of the bunch, showing the newest independents and smaller studio films. Other Laemmle cinemas include the **Monica 4-Plex** (1332 2nd Street, Santa Monica, 1-310 394 9741), the **Royal** (11523 Santa Monica Boulevard, West LA, 1-310 477 5581) and the **Music Hall** (9036 Wilshire Boulevard, Beverly Hills, 1-310 274 6869).

African American cinema

Magic Johnson Theatres
4020 Marlton Avenue, at Martin Luther King Jr Boulevard, Crenshaw (1-323 290 5900/www.magic johnsontheatres.com). Bus 40, 42, 210, 305, 310, 340, 608/I-10, exit Crenshaw Boulevard south. **Screens** 16. **Tickets** $9.25; $7.25 before 6pm; $7-$7.50 discounts. **Credit** AmEx, MC, V.
Owned by the former LA Lakers star, this venue specialises in African American films, both mainstream and underground. Worth attending just to experience the boisterous crowds.

Repertory & experimental

As part of their exhibitions, both **Museum of Contemporary Art** sites (*see p115*) screen a mixture of experimental and classic films, while

LACMA (*see p100*) runs regular seasons and tributes and, on Tuesday afternoons, classics for a mere $2. The **American Film Institute** (1-323 856 7600, www.afi.com) is dedicated to preserving old films and organises occasional screenings. For more info on alternative screenings in LA, see www.filmradar.com.

American Cinematheque
Egyptian Theatre, 6712 Hollywood Boulevard, between N Highland & N Las Palmas Avenues, Hollywood (1-323 466 3456/www.americancinema theque.com). Metro Hollywood-Highland/bus 210, 212, 217, 310, LDHWH/US 101, exit Highland Avenue south. **Screens** 1. **Tickets** $9; $6-$7 discounts. **Credit** AmEx, MC, V. **Map** p313 A1.
Specialising in retrospectives, the Cinematheque has accumulated a reputation for innovative programming. It's based in the beautifully restored Egyptian Theatre: the ticket price is worth it just to see the building. Some screenings have Q&As. **Photo** *p219*.

IMAX
California ScienCenter, 700 State Drive, between S Figueroa Street & S Vermont Avenue, Exposition Park (1-213 744 2014/www.casciencectr.org). Bus 40, 42, 102, 550/I-110, exit Exposition Boulevard west. **Screens** 1. **Tickets** $8; $4.75-$5.75 discounts. **Credit** AmEx, MC, V.
The seven-storey-high, 70ft-wide (21m) screen at the ScienCenter offers the requisite mix of nature documentaries and child-friendly entertainments.

Silent Movie Theatre
611 N Fairfax Avenue, at Clinton Street, Fairfax District (1-323 655 2520/www.silentmovietheater. com). Bus 10, 11, 217, 218, LDHWI/I-10, exit Fairfax Avenue north. **Tickets** $10; $8 discounts. **No credit cards.** **Map** p312 C2.
Silent-movie legends come alive again at this legendary theatre. Restored in 1999, it's the only cinema in the world devoted exclusively to silent movies. In the classic tradition, an organist provides the appropriate musical accompaniment.

UCLA Film & Television Archive
UCLA, 405 Hilgard Avenue, Westwood (1-310 206 3456/www.cinema.ucla.edu). Bus 20, 21, 720, SM1, SM2, SM3, SM8, SM12/I-10, exit Sunset Boulevard east. **Screens** 1. **Tickets** $8; $7 discounts. **Credit** AmEx, MC, V.
UCLA's massive archives are stuffed with a treasure trove of little-seen silents and classics from Hollywood's 1930s heyday. Newsreels and documentaries are also screened. It's not all old stuff: contemporary world cinema gets an airing, too.

Grauman's Chinese Theatre (p220)
Woman: 'Look, Herman, I'm
in Hedy Lamarr's shoes!'
Harvey Korman, walking briskly
past: 'HED-ley…'

Arts & Entertainment

Galleries

LA's art scene is beginning to give New York a run for its money.

The art world in LA has seen its highs and lows over the years, weathering the same extremes of boom and bust that routinely menace the art business around the world. But there's something special about the current explosion in the art scene here, a sense that this time it's serious – and there's no going back.

Gone are the leisurely strolls down a few well-appointed blocks of La Cienega or Wilshire Boulevards. Gone, too, is the nagging feeling of insularity borne of a lack of international fare. There are innumerable galleries here now, displaying every kind of fine art being made around the world. Not only is it selling, it's being covered in the international art press at an unprecedented level.

As in most major cities, it's been artists that have led the way in rediscovering and revitalising some of LA's seedier corners. There's a comparison here with Hoxton and Williamsburg, which began to attract artists a number of years ago: lofts got built, bars opened, people flocked in, and the artists started to move out. But unlike in London and New York, the powers-that-be seem interested in keeping their new bohemian neighbours. When Acuna-Hansen and Mary Goldman opened on an obscure Chinatown street, it should have been a fad, but the gallery population has doubled. When BLK/MRKT, d.e.n. and others signed leases in Culver City in 2005, you'd have thought they were building on Mars; today, it's the fastest-growing art district in town. And when Bert Green opened BGFA near Skid Row, he more or less single-handedly created the juggernaut of urban exuberance that has become the Downtown Arts District.

INFORMATION
LA has two free monthly art directories. Locals rely more on the exhaustive listings and previews of *Art Scene* (www.artscenecal.com), over and above the *Art Now Gallery Guide*. *LA Weekly* also provides extensive listings, as do the *LA Times*' Thursday and Sunday 'Calendar' sections. Of the web- or email-based coverage, Flavorpill (www.flavorpill.net) provides less comprehensive but more in-depth listings, while Fette's Flog (www.the-flog.com) does a good |job of documenting the shows and the scene.

Most (but not all) galleries are open from around 11am to 5pm, Tuesday to Saturday. However, call first to save a wasted trip.

Santa Monica & Venice

While sometimes maligned, the high-profile **Bergamot Station** (2525 Michigan Avenue, www.bergamotstation.com) has more than fulfilled its promise to attract new audiences for fine art in LA. The former trolley stop is a perfect setting for launch parties, performances, screenings and concerts that appeal to the silver- and chartreuse-haired alike. Most galleries here are open 10am-6pm Tuesday to Friday and 11.30am-5pm on Saturdays; the website has contact details for all residents.

Among the 30-plus galleries here are **Peter Fetterman**, a sophisticated, friendly purveyor of museum-level photography from Cartier-Bresson to Salgado. High-concept abstraction from LA and Europe is the mainstay at **Ruth Bachofner**; epic shows and experimental performances draw crowds at **Track 16**; and **Frank Lloyd** continues to be the single most important gallery of modern ceramics in the city. Robert Berman and William Turner, two standard-bearers of avant-garde West Coast abstraction, have joined forces to create **Berman/Turner Projects**, and now collectively occupy three spaces at the complex.

One-time It girl of the west side art world **Patricia Faure** is also here, with a young team lead by Dave Hickey protégé Heather Harmon abetting an exhilarating aesthetic. A similar dynamic, albeit more deliberately international, has sprung up at **Mark Moore Gallery**. **Patricia Correia** focuses on the passionate, vibrant and sometimes political traditions of Chicano art in Southern California; **Richard Heller** mounts exhibitions of post-illustration art with a potent mix of advanced draftsmanship and dark wit; and **Craig Krull** casts his eye wide enough to include photography by Julius Shulman and work by sculptors who draw inspiration from the natural and architectural world of LA.

East up Olympic, **Griffin Contemporary** (2902 Nebraska Avenue, 1-310 586 6886, www.griffincontemporary.com) strikes an academic, historical tone, showcasing rare modern and postmodern mixed media works from the likes of James Turrell, Joseph Beuys and Leon Golub. A bit further out is **GR2** (2062 Sawtelle Boulevard, 1-310 445 9276, www.gr2. net) the gallery spin-off of *Giant Robot*.

Arts & Entertainment

Berman/Turner Projects, one of many galleries at **Bergamot Station**. *See p222.*

West out of the Berg, it's just a short jog on Olympic to the galleries, theatre and studio spaces on the 1600 block of 18th Street, among them the **18th Street Arts Complex** (www. 18thstreet.org). Also in the area is **Christopher Grimes** (916 Colorado Avenue, 1-310 587 3373, www.cgrimes.com), which shows cutting-edge painting and video from North and South America. Turning south, you'll hit the cool aesthetic and international artists of **Angles** (2222 & 2230 Main Street, 1-310 396 5019).

In Venice, head first to the venerable **LA Louver** (55 Venice Boulevard, 1-310 822 4955, www.lalouver.com), which deals in LA's contemporary masters and younger artists from New York, South America and the UK. It's *de rigueur* on any LA art itinerary. Of course, Venice is also famous for its bohemian side, and for a taste of that you'll want to walk the length of Abbot Kinney Boulevard south from Main Street heading inland.

On Abbot Kinney, **Equator Books** (*see p182*) augments its art-heavy library with monthly exhibitions of art and photography with attitude. Down the block, **Jaxon House** (No.1337, 1-310 401 0080, www.jaxonhouse. com) shows emerging artists with a unique combination of urbanity and romanticism, and

Hamilton Press (No.1317, 1-310 396 8244, www.hamiltonpressgallery.com) is one of the country's most respected fine art lithographers. **Red House** (No.1224, 1-310 452 3264, www. trekkelly.com) and **Lightspace** (No.1732, 1-310 301 6969) are each run by artists, but go out of their way to support talented colleagues: the former with a dash of coiffed glitz, the latter with a hint of progressive spiritualism.

Had you turned east on Venice Boulevard, you'd be on your way to Culver City. Be sure not to pass **Cherry & Martin** (12611 Venice Boulevard, 1-310 398 7404, www.cherryand martin.com) or **Overtones** (11306 Venice Boulevard, 1-310 915 0346, www.overtones. org), which offer two of the city's most popular and engaging programmes of international contemporary painting, sculpture, video, installation and everything in between.

Culver City

The heart of Culver City's burgeoning gallery district is the intersection between S La Cienaga Boulevard and W Washington Boulevard. On Washington to the west of La Cienega are a few of the area's pioneers: among them are the **BLK/MRKT** (No.6009, 1-310 837 1989, www.blkmrktgallery.com), heavy on figurative painting and post-illustration with emotional depth. A few doors away, **d.e.n.** (No.6023, 1-310 559 3023, www.dencontemporaryart.com) offers a quirky, conceptual take on painting, drawing and installation; across the way is the party-friendly **Lab 101** (No.8530B, 1-310 558 0911, www.thelab101.com), a cheeky blend of photography, fashion, skate culture and music.

East on Washington is a cluster of galleries with very different aesthetics. **Sixspace** (No.5803, 1-323 932 6200, www.sixspace.com) offers graffiti-inspired art-school graduates; neighbour **Susanne Vielmetter** (No.5795, 1-323 933 2117, www.vielmetter.com) takes a more high-concept approach but still shows intense figurative work, ambitious installations and first-rate minimalist abstractions side by side. **Billy Shire Fine Arts** (No.5790, 1-323 297 0600, www.billyshirefinearts.com), from the man behind La Luz de Jesus, shows off the smart side of subversive with finely crafted works by rising stars such as Bari Kumar.

The stretch of S La Cienega north of Washington is jammed with contemporary art outfits. **Anna Helwing** (No.2766, 1-310 202 2213, www.annahelwinggallery.com), **Sandroni Rey** (No.2762, 1-310 280 0111, www.sandronirey.com) and Superflat godfathers **Blum & Poe** (No.2754, 1-310 836 2062, www.blumandpoe.com) all present self-consciously avant-garde painters, sculptors and photographers, with largely successful results. **Lizabeth Oliveria** (No.2712, 1-310 837 1073, www.lizabetholiveria.com) and **QED** (No.2622, 1-310 204 3334, www.qedgallery.com) have a predilection for off-beat, DIY-style mixed media installation, the kind that's fun to look at and impossible to decipher. **Lightbox** (No.2656, 1-310 559 1111, www.lightbox.tv) is the newest pet project of peripatetic impresario Kim Light, who has deep connections to some of LA's most aggressively cutting-edge artists.

A few other notable places sit along the edges of the circle thus charted. **Western Project** (3830 Main Street, 1-310 838 0609, www.western-project.com) has a lavish and baroque sense of visual narrative; the high-end **Denizen** (8600 Venice Boulevard, 838 1959, www.denizendesigngallery.com) brings together local and international design. A bit further out are the galleries at Otis College's **Ben Maltz Gallery** (9045 Lincoln Boulevard, 1-310 665 6905, www.otis.edu), Loyola Marymount's **Laband Art Gallery** (1 LMU Drive, 1-310 338 2880, www.lmu.edu/laband) and Pepperdine's **Frederick R Weisman Gallery** (24255 PCH, 1-310 506 4851, www. pepperdine.edu), which all offer a year-round schedule of group and solo exhibitions.

Beverly Hills

The galleries of Beverly Hills are among the most prestigious in the city. As ever, the **Gagosian Gallery** (456 N Camden Drive, 1-310 271 9400, www.gagosian.com) is the place to head for notable post-war painting, sculpture and photography (Stella, Koons, Sherman, Basquiat) and celebrity-studded openings. **Steve Turner** (275 S Beverly Drive, 1-310 271 3721, www.steveturnergallery.com) specialises in American art and design from the 19th and 20th centuries. **ACE** (9430 Wilshire Boulevard, 1-310 858 9090, www.acegallery.net) is a wondrous warren of rooms often filled with enormous photographs. **Marc Selwyn** (6222 Wilshire Boulevard, 1-323 933 9911, www.marcselwynfineart.com) keeps it simple with classy, straightforward abstract and representational exhibitions.

Miracle Mile & around

The centre of the action around here is the 6150 **Wilshire Boulevard Building**, whose family of galleries (ACME, Kontainer, Paul Kopeikin, Karyn Lovegrove, 1301PE, Marc Foxx and Roberts & Tilton, among others) is a breeding ground for emerging talent. Also on Wilshire, conceptual painting and avant-garde sculpture shine at **Carl Berg** (No.6018, 1-323 931 6060, www.carlberggallery.com); **Lawrence Asher** (No.5820, 1-323 935 9100, www.lawrence asher.com) mounts stylish group shows organised according to themes, always with a lively, youthful flair; and **Ace** (5514 Wilshire Boulevard, 1-323 935 4411, www.acegallery.net) regularly fills a whole floor of the landmark Desmond's art deco building with youngsters and modern masters. Shepard Fairey and crew operate **Subliminal Projects** (No.3780, 1-323 383 9299, www.subliminalprojects.com) as a kind of collective laboratory for off-beat ideas that have helped smooth the transition of the country's most gifted skate, deck, poster and graffiti artists from margins to mainstream.

Among the more notable galleries on nearby Beverly Boulevard are **Michael Kohn** (No.8071, 1-323 658 8088, www.kohngallery. com), a major dealer in representational and abstract art; the LA branch of New York's influential **Forum** (No.8069, 1-323 655 1550, www.forumgallery.com), one of the city's best bets for modern figurative art; and **Stephen Cohen** (No.7358, 1-323 937 5525, www.stephen cohengallery.com), which shows upscale photo-based works by stars and emerging talents. **Glü** (No.7424, 1-323 857 0510, www.glugallery. com) is a black sheep, injecting rough and tumble art into an otherwise clean-cut

Festivals Art

From monthly art walks to annual open studios, and late-night gallery crawls to multimedia festivals, all the neighbourhoods detailed in this chapter host some form of special event in order to attract Angelenos to the area. Most events are free, but some come with an admission charge.

The newly dense population of art galleries on and off Main Street in Downtown LA stay open until 9pm on the second Thursday of every month for the **Downtown Art Walk** (www.downtownartwalk.com). Many of them coordinate receptions for new shows with the event, and tours of the area are also available. In the same area, the Spring Arts Tower transforms itself into a multimedia mecca on the first Saturday of every other month for **Create Fixate** (www.createfixate. com), a late night art show and audio lounge. And twice a year, usually in May and October, the resident artists of the **Brewery Arts Complex** (*see p227*) open their doors to the public, with food and music, for the **Brewery Art Walk** (www.breweryartwalk.com).

Over at Bergamot Station in Santa Monica, **Berman/Turner Projects** (*see p227*) hosts the long-standing **Santa Monica Auctions** (www.smauctions.com) roughly twice a year, with great deals on A-list Los Angeles art released from private collections. Just down the road, May's weekend-long **Venice Art Walk** (www.venicefamilyclinic.org) offers unparalleled access to the studios of some

of the neighbourhood's most famous artists and architects, ancillary food and music events and a legendarily competitive silent auction. It's all in aid of the Venice Family Clinic; tickets run to about $50.

Beverly Hills takes a stab at the French *salon* tradition every May and October, but with a Californian twist: **Affaire in the Gardens** (www.beverlyhills.org) is held outdoors at Beverly Gardens, a stretch of fertile parkland along Santa Monica Boulevard. Not to be outdone, West Hollywood Avenues of Art & Design host an annual **Art & Design Walk** (www.avenues artdesign.com), at which shops and galleries throw parties, host talks, unveil new collections and hold special exhibitions.

The monthly **First Friday Artwalk** in Los Feliz (www.laluzdejesus.com) draws hipster crowds, as does the springtime **NoHo Theatre & Arts Festival** in North Hollywood (www.nohoartsdistrict.com) and the **NELAart Gallery Night** on the second Saturday of the month that takes place in and around Eagle Rock (www.nelaart.org). The galleries of **Culver City** hope to get a similar event off the ground in time for the summer of 2006: check www.ccgalleryguide.com for details. And in May, don't miss **SuperSonic** (www. soccas.org), a truly epic group show featuring the work of all the year's MFA graduates in California art schools gathered together under one roof.

neighbourhood, while **Richard Telles** (No.7380, 1-323 965 5578, www.tellesfineart. com) is a small but vital gallery devoted to cutting-edge work in all media.

West Hollywood & around

A cluster of galleries has taken root on Melrose Avenue, Robertson Boulevard and Almont Drive in West Hollywood. The businesses, which group themselves under the rubric of **Avenues of Art & Design** (www. avenuesartdesign.com), include numerous interior design shops and the hard-to-miss **Pacific Design Center** (*see p91*), which houses 130-plus showrooms for architects, decorators, dealers and designers in furniture, fabrics, lighting and flooring, among other items. The complex has a rooftop gallery overlooking the courtyard, which houses a design-oriented annexe of **MoCA** (*see p115*).

On Melrose Avenue, the hip, postmodern **Kantor/Feuer** (No.7025, 1-323 933 6976, www.kantorfeuer.com) has exhibited the likes of Haring, Lichtenstein and local hero Ed Ruscha. A stone's throw north of Melrose is **Manny Silverman** (619 N Almont Drive, 1-310 659 8256), specialising in American abstract expressionism; next door, **Regen Projects** (No.633, 1-310 276 5424, www.regenprojects. com) shows hipster darlings who've made it big (Raymond Pettibon, Lari Pittman). Several galleries in the neighbourhood are devoted to early Californian painting, a school synonymous with dramatic landscapes and American impressionism. Some good examples can be found on Melrose at **Edenhurst** (No.8920, 1-310 247 8151, www.edenhurstgallery.com) and **George Stern** (No.8920, 1-310 276 2600, www.sternfinearts.com). Galleries of note on N Robertson Boulevard include **Koplin Del Rio** (No.464, 1-310 657 9843, www.koplindelrio.com),

Arts & Entertainment

Peres Projects (left) and **4-F**, two galleries on Chinatown's Chung King Road. *See p227.*

which emphasises contemporary realism; **Margo Leavin** (No.812, 1-310 273 0603), which shows contemporary drawing, painting and sculpture; and **Earl McGrath** (No.454, 1-310 657 4257, www.earlmcgrathgallery.com), which displays bold contemporary art with a little bit of attitude.

Nearby N La Brea Avenue between Santa Monica Boulevard and W 3rd Street is dotted with photography galleries. The best of them include **Jan Kesner** (No.164, 1-323 938 6834, www.jankesnergallery.com) and **Fahey/Klein** (No.148, 1-323 934 2250, www.faheyklein gallery.com). **Jack Rutberg** (357 N La Brea Avenue, 1-323 938 5222, www.jackrutbergfine arts.com) deals in work by important modern European and American artists such as Jerome Witkin, Hans Hoffman and Alexander Calder, while **Merry Karnowsky** (170 S La Brea Avenue, 1-323 933 4408, www.mkgallery.com) offers masterfully rendered gory allegory from the likes of Becca, Alex Gross and Dean Karr. And the pick of the galleries on Santa Monica Boulevard are the hardcore alternative **Dirt** (No.7906, 1-323 822 9359, www.dirtgalleryla. com) and the underground star-makers at **New Image Art** (No.7908, 1-323 654 2192, www.newimageartgallery.com), whose walls have launched the careers of young guns such as Ed Templeton and Chris Johanson.

Hollywood

Many hoped that a new gallery scene would spring up in Hollywood following the relocation here of one of LA's most important alternative spaces, **Los Angeles Contemporary Exhibitions** (6522 Hollywood Boulevard, 1-323 957 1777, www.artleak.org). It hasn't happened but a couple of spaces are worth a look: **Newspace** (5241 Melrose Avenue, 1-323 469 9353, www.newspacela.com), which shines a light on local talents in painting, sculpture, video and conceptual art, and the **Advocate Gallery** (at the LA Gay & Lesbian Center; *see p290*), which promotes LGBT artists.

Silver Lake, Los Feliz & Echo Park

Galleries are a mainstay on the funky East Side, none more so than Los Feliz's **La Luz de Jesus** (4633 Hollywood Boulevard, 1-323 666

7667, www.laluzdejesus.com). Together with stores Wacko and Soap Plant, it offers a one-stop shopping experience with paintings, books and toys that reference high art, low art and everything in between. For nearby **Barnsdall Art Park**, *see p104*. Also in Los Feliz, Jim Fittipaldi displays the raw, powerful and ambitious work he's collected and shown for decades at the **Bedlam Art Salon** (1972 Hillhurst Avenue, 1-323 924 9000); just over the LA River in Atwater Village, **Black Maria** (3171 Glendale Boulevard, 1-323 660 9393, www.blackmariagallery.com) explores the rebellious sensibilities of outsider iconoclasm.

Silver Lake's **Ghetto Gloss** (2380 Glendale Boulevard, 1-323 912 0008, www.ghettogloss.com) is the premier East Side destination for artists both funky and punky. **Materials & Applications** (1619 Silver Lake Boulevard, 1-323 913 0915, www.emanate.org) is an outdoor space, open 24/7, that aims to combine art (architecture) and nature (landscape) in progressive conceptual experimentation; conversely, **Metro** (1835 Hyperion Avenue, 1-323 663 2787, www.metrogallery.org) is a straightforward room stocked with the work of local artists keeping it real, for better or worse. And in Echo Park, **Tropico de Nopal** (1665 Beverly Boulevard, 1-213 481 8112, www.tropicodenopal.com) describes itself as a 'swap-meet-church-machine-shop-chemistry-lab installation'.

Downtown

Artists have lived in Downtown's warehouses for a while; over the last few years, galleries have followed them. A handful have opened in the **Brewery Arts Complex** (2100 N Main Street, 1-213 694 2911, www.thebrewery.net), among them **Raid** (www.raidprojects.com) and **Abundant Sugar** (www.abundantsugar.com), but the real story of late has been the explosive success of **Gallery Row**, on Main and Spring Streets between 2nd and 9th Streets. Bert Green took the initiative when he relocated **Circle Elephant** to the area; first-rate outfits such as **Pharmaka**, **MJ Higgins**, **INMO** and **Kristi Engle** have helped make the gamble pay off. For details of galleries, see www.galleryrow.com; for the monthly Artwalk, *see p225* **Festivals**.

The other main concentration of galleries is in Chinatown, especially on pedestrianised Chung King Road. Perhaps emboldened by the decrepit charm of the mews, many tenants chose not to change the names of the import shops formerly in residence – look out for **China Art Objects** (No.933, 1-213 613 0384, www.chinaartobjects.com), where the spotlight is on local art school grads; **Black Dragon Society** (No.961, 1-213 620 0030, www.black-dragon-society.com), where

the shows take envelope-pushing seriously; **4-F** (No.977, 1-213 617 4948, www.4-fgallery.com); and **Happy Lion** (No. 963, 1-213 625 1360, www.thehappylion.com), where figurative allegory and advanced painting technique are the orders of the day. **Mary Goldman** (No.932, 1-213 617 8217, www.marygoldman.com) deals in more established artists with experimental natures; **Telic** (No.977, 1-213 344 6137, www.telic.info) runs hypnotic multimedia installations; and **Peres Projects** (No.969, 1-213 617 1100, www.peresprojects.com) is a kind of clearing house of difficult and often controversial work.

Just off this drag are a few more places. Chief among them is **Acuna-Hansen** (427 Bernard Street, 1-323 441 1624, www.ahgallery.com), which shows odd stuff by art fair darlings such as Tracy Nakayama, Carolee Schneemann and Bart Esposito. **Sister** (437 Gin Ling Way, 1-213 628 7000, www.sisterla.com) is a small but salient space with solo shows from some of LA's most in-demand artists. **L2k** (990 Hill Street, 1-323 225 1288, www.l2kontemporary.com) seems to be having all the fun in the world with its eccentric programming. Even SF stalwart **Jack Hanley** (945 Sun Mun Way, 1-213 626 0403, www.jackhanley.com) couldn't resist adding his brand of well-considered whimsy to the mix.

Other galleries are scattered from pillar to post. North, **La Mano Press** (1749 Main Street, 1-323 227 0650, www.lamanopress.com) doubles as a gallery and print shop run by Artemio Rodriguez. **Another Year in LA** (1-323 223 6867, www.anotheryearinla.com) mixes concept, craft, humour and open-mindedness; **Drkrm** (1-323 223 6867, www.drkrm.com) focuses on photographs that illuminate once-subversive subcultures. Both are housed in a former Capitol Records pressing plant just north of Downtown.

Out east, the new train-depot campus of the **Southern Californian Institute of Architecture** (960 E 3rd Street, 1-213 613 2200, www.sciarc.edu), offers lectures, screenings and shows. Further south, **Cirrus** (542 S Alameda Street, 1-213 680 3473, www.cirrusgallery.com) has promoted edgy, alternative art since 1971; nearby **Transport** (1308 Factory Place, 1-310 956 5344, www.transportgallery.com) displays powerful, timely and usually anti-establishment pieces; and both the **Hive** (729 S Spring Street, 1-213 955 9051, www.thehivegallery.com) and the **Hangar** (1018 S Santa Fe Avenue, 1-213 239 9060, www.hangar1018.com) are, in different ways, temples to designed disorder, mounting regular festivals of art, movement, sound and video. And over in Westlake, **Angela Hanley** (2404 Wilshire Boulevard, 1-323 356 2666, www.angelahanley.com) is looking to establish a discourse between east and west, high and low, gravitas and mad science.

Gay & Lesbian

Gay LA has undergone a renaissance and it's in the mood to party.

A not-so-subtle transformation has rocked urban gay LA recently. What was once a bland nightlife scene has become a queer mecca. Bars are busier, clubs are less segregated, and nightlife, overall, is bursting. Blame it on the influx of Hollywood's new publicity-hungry high society, its debauched crowd of shameless It Girls and Bad Boys Gone Wild; or, perhaps, on rebellion against the current government, mostly shunned by liberal, metropolitan USA. Like New York City in the 1980s, parts of Los Angeles are celebrating the decline of civilisation with dancing, drugs and Grey Goose... and gays, unsuprisingly, are at the forefront of the party.

As it's been for a while, the epicentre of this urban gay candy store is **West Hollywood**, glossier and livelier than ever. Out east in **Silver Lake** is an edgier, more alternative gay scene; in between sits **Hollywood**, home both to modish Martini joints and haunts from a glamorous yesteryear. Other gay locales outside the city centre include the Valleys (*see pp124-129*), the beaches (*see pp73-82*), Palm Springs (*see p272*) and San Diego's Hillcrest neighbourhood (*see p280*).

For details on gay and lesbian resources, among them the **LA Gay & Lesbian Center**, and for details on health clinics, *see pp290-291*. The *Gay & Lesbian Community Yellow Pages*, available from **A Different Light** (*see p182*), is LA's lesbian and gay phone book, listing everything from homo handymen to pink pet care. Admission to all bars and clubs in this chapter is free unless stated.

Shops & services

The sometimes cruisey WeHo branch of revered thrift chain **Out of the Closet** (8224 Santa Monica Boulevard, 1-323 848 9760, www.aids health.org/otc) offers free on-site HIV testing. For **A Different Light** bookstore, *see p182*.

Dorothy's Surrender
7985 Santa Monica Boulevard, at N Laurel Avenue, West Hollywood (1-323 650 4111). Bus 4, 218, 304/ I-10, exit La Cienega Boulevard north. **Open** 10am-11pm daily. **Credit** AmEx, MC, V. **Map** p312 C2.
This colourful store in the heart of West Hollywood sells all manner of gay and lesbian goodies and gifts, including books, postcards and novelty items. **Photo** *p229.*

Drake's
8932 Santa Monica Boulevard, between N Robertson & N San Vicente Boulevards, West Hollywood (1-310 289 8932). Bus 4, 105, 220, 304/I-10, exit La Cienega Boulevard north. **Open** 10am-2am daily. **Credit** AmEx, MC, V. **Map** p312 A2.
A surprisingly incognito sex shop located in the middle of WeHo's main strip. Everything a boy needs is here, including videos, toys, sex aids, novelty items and lots of glossy magazines.
Other locations: 7566 Melrose Avenue, West Hollywood (1-323 651 5600).

Los Angeles Sporting Club
8592 Santa Monica Boulevard, at N La Cienega Boulevard, West Hollywood (1-310 657 2858). Bus 4, 105, 304, LDHWH/I-10, exit La Cienega Boulevard north. **Open** 9am-9pm Mon-Sat; 10am-8pm Sun. **Credit** AmEx, Disc, MC, V. **Map** p312 B2.
LASC's clothing line has upped its stakes from clichéd gaywear to high-end brands (True Religion, Energie) and its own eponymous line, a WeHo staple. The store offers sporadic good-value sales, particularly on its swimwear.

Theatre

Although more high-profile productions originate here these days, LA's gay theatre scene remains intimate and accessible. The **Celebration Theatre** (7051 Santa Monica Boulevard, West Hollywood, 1-323 957 1884, www.celebrationtheatre.com) is the most renowned LGBT theatre in SoCal, showcasing both irreverent and socially conscious works; productions at **Highways** (1651 18th Street, Santa Monica, 1-310 315 1459, www.highways performance.org) are edgy for LA. The programme at the **Renberg Theatre** (1125 N McCadden Place, Hollywood, 1-323 860 7300,

The best Gay stuff

For a post-beach beer
Boom Boom Room. See *p232* Gay beaches.

For a naughty night out
Big Fat Cock at Fubar. See *p230.*

For boys... or are they girls?
Dragstrip. See *p233.*

After some valiant resistance, finally **Dorothy's Surrender**. *See p228.*

www.laglc.com) is varied: it staged the West Coast premiere of *The Vagina Monologues*, but also hosts drag queens, lesbian comics and new works by the likes of Larry Kramer. For a rawer, camper theatrical experience, head east to the **Cavern Club** nights at Silver Lake's **Casita Del Campo** (1920 Hyperion Avenue, 1-323 969 2530, www.cavernclubtheater.com), which showcases the likes of Bridgette of Madison County and local celebrity Jackie Beat.

Gay

As Elizabeth Taylor once remarked, 'Without homosexuals, there would be no Hollywood.' For years, gay men have flocked to the shores of Southern California to take all the sun and the sand they could handle. But they give as much as they take: today, the Hollywood star machine is run in no small part by a powerful coterie of gay agents, writers and actors.

West Hollywood gets all the headlines, but there's more variety than first appears, especially if you head across to Silver Lake. All manner of niche events thrive around the city: from line dancing nights to piano bars, high-octane raves to Asian-oriented sojourns. Want Monday-night football jocks who like beer and sports? Head to Santa Monica Boulevard. Seeking leather-clad daddies yearning for a public shoe-shining? Go east, young man. You'll find your own private LA eventually.

INFORMATION

To find out what's on, pick up one of the free gay magazines found in bars, cafés and shops in West Hollywood. Titles include *Frontiers* (www.frontiersnewsmagazine.com), *In Los Angeles* (www.inmagla.com) and *Edge*, all fortnightly; Latino-oriented bimonthly *qvMagazine* (www.qvmagazine.com); and quarterly *Circuit Noize* (www.circuitnoize.com). Locals soak up the social pages in *Odyssey*, as well as checking out the latest event nights. Online, www.westhollywood.com is a useful guide for news and events, while www.gay.com has hundreds of chat rooms.

West Hollywood

Equal parts urban party centre and residential neighbourhood, West Hollywood – or WeHo, as the locals say – basically is gay LA. The crime rate is low, the vibe is peaceful and the attitude is pro-gay. Cynics say it's vapid, homogenous and populated by body bimbos. It's all that, certainly, but it's also much more.

Main Street WeHo is **Santa Monica Boulevard** between N Doheny Drive and N Fairfax Avenue, a notorious stretch of bars, clubs and über-gay coffee houses (you'll find at least three 'GayBucks' here). The heart of WeHo, however, belongs to **Robertson Boulevard**, where gym boys and lipstick lesbians spill out from bars and cafés on to the streets each night. Soak up the gorgeous bodies and try to sip up the ostentation without judgment.

Accommodation

Gay-friendly hotels include **Le Montrose Suite Hotel** and the **Ramada West Hollywood**. For both, *see p59.*

San Vicente Inn-Resort

845 N San Vicente Boulevard, between Cynthia Street & Santa Monica Boulevard (1-800 577 6915/ 1-310 854 6915/www.gayresort.com). Bus 4, 105, 220, 304/I-10, exit La Cienega Boulevard north. **Rates** $69-$209. **Credit** AmEx, Disc, MC, V. **Map** p312 A2.

There's excitement on Santa Monica Boulevard, sure, but there's also plenty of action to be had at this steamy oasis with a pool and jacuzzi, a tropical garden, nude sunbathing and a high sexual temperature. Clothing is optional but rarely encouraged.

Bars & clubs

In addition to the venues detailed below, try the hip hop- and house-dominated **Boytrade** (www.boytrade.com), held on the last Friday of the month at the El Rey Theatre (*see p240*) and every Thursday at Marketplace (7969 Santa Monica Boulevard). Tuesdays in LA see the Falcon (7213 Sunset Boulevard, 1-323 850 5350) host **Beige**, which draws a Hollywood crowd of directors, producers and A-list celebs.

Factory/Ultra Suede

652 N La Peer Drive, between Santa Monica Boulevard & Melrose Avenue (1-310 659 4551/ www.factorynightclubla.com). Bus 4, 105, 220, 304/ I-10, exit Robertson Boulevard north. **Open** 9pm-2am Wed-Sat. **Admission** $3-$15. **Credit** Bar only AmEx, MC, V. **Map** p312 A2.

Two venues for the price of one, run by the same team and almost sharing a building. The Factory's Saturday-nighter is huge; Ultra Suede's line-up is highlighted by Friday's top 40 Popstarz party and a 1980s night on the last Wednesday of the month.

Fubar

7994 Santa Monica Boulevard, between N Laurel & N Edinburgh Avenues (1-323 654 0396/www.fubar la.com). Bus 4, 218, 304/I-10, exit La Cienega Boulevard north. **Open** 5pm-2am daily. **Credit** MC, V. **Map** p312 C2.

Fubar is LA's slightly more tepid equivalent of NYC bar the Cock. Wild times abound, particularly at Thursday night's Big Fat Cock soirée: genitalia flashes and celebs swarm to California electro-trash.

Here Lounge

696 N Robertson Boulevard, at Santa Monica Boulevard (1-310 360-8455/www.herelounge.com). Bus 4, 105, 220, 304/I-10, exit La Cienega Boulevard north. **Open** 4pm-2am daily. **Credit** MC, V. **Map** p312 A2.

The minimalist, upscale Here Lounge, located off the Santa Monica Boulevard main drag, accommodates a large crowd comprised of the scene's prettiest – and cruisiest – guys. Sunday afternoon/early evening is when the locals come out.

Hot Dog at 7969

7969 Santa Monica Boulevard, at Laurel Avenue (1-323 654 0280). Bus 4, 218, 304/I-10, exit La Cienega Boulevard north. **Open** 10pm-2am daily. **Admission** $10-$15. **Credit** MC, V. **Map** p312 C2.

Formerly Peanuts, 7969 is usually LA's capital of cross-dressing, but Saturdays are when the hottest boys come out to play. Arrive early to escape the inevitable fire marshalls pulling out drunken boys.

Mark's. *See p232.*

Straight eye for the queer guy

A curious fashion phenomenon has evolved within homo subculture over the past five years, nowhere more so than in LA. Increasingly, gay men are dressing like straight dudes, and their heterosexual counterparts have begun dressing exceedingly – how does one say it? – GAY. Designer spandex and form-fitting fabrics were once the staple of a queer closet, but the LA gay of today is eschewing Donna and Calvi for the fashion-forward aesthetic of frat-boy, keg-ready lads. The un-ironed, inexpensive lines of Abercrombie are de rigueur and thrift-store retro has replaced vintage couture. While the heteros hop around town shopping for the latest 'It' button-down, the gays are playing volleyball at Will Rogers Beach. So, to help you avoid sticking out like a gay sore thumb, we've put together some tips for the LA-bound boy. (Thanks to Botox and brow lifts, 'most everyone here is considered a 'boy'.)

Basically, keep it simple. In sunny SoCal, where lawyers litigate in flip-flops and baseball caps, you should never look like you're trying too hard. Generally, a dressy night in West Hollywood entails jeans, a T-shirt (or tank-top) and flip-flops or trainers. The jeans, of course, should be alternative-designer du jour, which in 2006 meant True Religion, Energie or Antiq Denim (Diesel? *So* yesterday). **Fred Segal** (*see p186*) and **Barneys** (*see p179*) are two worthwhile stores; WeHo boys on a budget head to **American Rag** (*see p189*) and **Crossroads** (8315 Santa Monica Boulevard, 1-323 654 0505), the area's best consignment store.

I Candy

7929 Santa Monica Boulevard, between N Fairfax & N Hayworth Avenues (1-323 656 4000/www.icandy lounge.com). Bus 4, 218, 304/I-10, exit La Cienega Boulevard north. **Open** 6pm-2am Tue-Sat. **Credit** AmEx, MC, V. **Map** p312 C2.

Famous for launching as a reality show on Logo, America's first gay TV network, I Candy is WeHo's bar du jour. The crowd lives up to the name.

Mother Lode

8944 Santa Monica Boulevard, at San Vicente Boulevard (1-310 659 9700). Bus 4, 105, 220, 304/I-10, exit La Cienega Boulevard north. **Open** 3pm-2am Mon-Fri; noon-2am Sat, Sun. **No credit cards. Map** p312 A2.

Everyone's favourite beer bash is held on Sunday afternoons at LA's friendliest gay bar, where guys gather to shoot pool and shoot the breeze. Nearby is Micky's, another old favourite (No.8857, 1-310 657 1176, www.mickys.com).

Numbers

8741 Santa Monica Boulevard, at Hancock Avenue (1-310 652 7700). Bus 4, 105, 220, 304/I-10, exit La Cienega Boulevard north. **Open** 5pm-2am daily. **Credit** AmEx, DC, Disc, MC, V. **Map** p312 A2.

An LA institution, Numbers is an elegant supper club doubling up as an upscale hustler joint. Tuxedoed waiters serve up some of the meanest burgers in town to porn stars and their elderly admirers.

O-Bar

8279 Santa Monica Boulevard, between N Sweetzer & N Harper Avenues (1-323 822 3300/www.obar restaurant.com). Bus 4, 304, LDHWH/I-10, exit La Cienega Boulevard north. **Open** 6pm-midnight Mon, Sun; 6pm-1am Tue, Wed; 6pm-2am Thur-Sat. **Credit** AmEx, MC, V. **Map** p312 B2.

Every gay metropolis has a hot spot where locals kick off the weekend, and this restaurant-bar is LA's. Tom Whitman's popular Smack party on Thursday features a five-minute cocktail free-for-all at the stroke of 11pm and midnight, but the clientele aren't cheap: the atmosphere here is more upscale than at most of WeHo's other bars. Dress the part.

Rage

8911 Santa Monica Boulevard, between Hilldale Avenue & N San Vicente Boulevard (1-310 652 7055/www.ragewesthollywood.com). Bus 4, 105, 220, 304/I-10, exit La Cienega Boulevard north. **Open** noon-2am daily. **Admission** free-$10. **Credit** *Bar only* AmEx, MC, V. **Map** p312 A2.

The quintessential WeHo gay club hosts a range of themed nights, from its refreshing alternative club on Mondays to techno and diva house at the weekend. A favourite among the younger crowd.

Restaurants & coffeehouses

Health-conscious food and hip crowds are an absolute prerequisite for any restaurant to endure in West Hollywood, but, given the Darwinian struggle for survival, the ones that do last really deliver. The best way to get up to speed with the many happy hours and dining specials is to pick up a local gay guide: like the diet books on the shelves of their buff patrons, they change rapidly.

In addition to the venues detailed below, others merit mention. **Basix Café** (8333 Santa Monica Boulevard, 1-323 848 2460, www.basix cafe.com) does a mean Sunday brunch; just down the street, **Marix** (1108 N Flores Avenue, 1-323 650 0507, www.marixtexmex.com) serves

Gay beaches

Many of southern California's beaches (for more, see p76 Life's a beach) are gay-friendly, but those listed below are three of the best. Gay men and lesbians head here, but the scenes are male-dominated.

Laguna Beach

Laguna Beach: off PCH, 30 miles south of Long Beach. Gay beach: just past the pier; look for the rainbow flag.

It's a long drive from LA on congested Saturdays, but the water is clean and the beach is hot. After the beach, try the **Boom Boom Room** (1401 S Coast Highway, 1-800 653 2697, www.boom boomroom.com), which offers dancing, drinks specials and plenty of guys who've somehow forgotten their shirts.

Venice Beach

Venice: see p79. Gay beach: where Windward Avenue meets the beach, next to the wall, just down from Muscle Beach.

It figures that Los Angeles' most bohemian and liberal neighbourhood should also welcome the gay community to its territory. The quasi-legendary **Roosterfish** (1302 Abbot Kinney Boulevard, 1-310 392 2123, www.roosterfishbar.com) is a must-see for the guys.

Will Rogers State Beach

Will Rogers State Beach: on the Pacific Coast Highway, just over two miles north of Santa Monica Pier, in front of the Beach Club.

This cruisey beach is packed on sunny weekends, and it's easy to see why: it's free, it's got tons of guys playing volleyball and it lasts until sunset. Parking can be a drag: it's best to pay to park in the lot.

healthier-than-most Tex-Mex food and what some swear are the best Margaritas in town. **Hamburger Mary's** (8288 Santa Monica Boulevard, 1-323 654 3800) is a lively spot; **Irv's Burgers** (8289 Santa Monica Boulevard, 1-323 650 2456) is a tiny mainstay of the strip. The neighbourhood muscle Marys get their protein intake from chicken chain **Koo Koo Roo** (8520 Santa Monica Boulevard, 1-310 657 3300, www.kookooroo.com). But if all you want to do is sit down and relax with a grande latte, head to **Urth Caffé** (see p168), which serves delicious, inexpensive food, unbeatable coffee and prime people-watching.

Abbey

692 N Robertson Boulevard, at Santa Monica Boulevard (1-310 289 8410/www.abbeyfood andbar.com). Bus 4, 105, 220, 304/I-10, exit Robertson Boulevard north. **Open** 8am-2am daily. **Main courses** $8-$13. **Credit** AmEx, MC, V. **Map** p312 A2.

This expansive restaurant/cocktail bar is a popular spot, and it more than deserves the crowds it attracts. The setting, a large outdoor patio with statues and fairy lights, is altogether pleasant; the food is superb and won't break the bank; and the various Martinis on offer are beyond reproach. And unlike the rest of WeHo's stereotypically white bread scene, it attracts an ethnically diverse crowd.

Bossa Nova

685 N Robertson Boulevard, at Santa Monica Boulevard (1-310 657 5070). Bus 4, 105, 220, 304/I-10, exit Robertson Boulevard north. **Open** 11am-midnight Mon-Thur, Sun; 11am-1am Fri, Sat. **Main courses** $9-$17. **Credit** AmEx, Disc, MC, V. **Map** p312 A2.

The tables at this Brazilian restaurant are highly sought after, but the passing eye-candy outside makes the time fly by as you wait for your order, and the food when it arrives is worth the wait. **Other locations**: 7181 W Sunset Boulevard, West Hollywood (1-323 436 7999).

French Quarter

7985 Santa Monica Boulevard, between N Laurel & N Edinburgh Avenues (1-323 654 0898/www.french quarterwest.com). Bus 4, 218, 304/I-10, exit Fairfax Avenue north. **Open** 7am-midnight Mon-Thur, Sun; 7am-3.30am Fri, Sat. **Main courses** $12-$17. **Credit** AmEx, DC, Disc, MC, V. **Map** p312 C2.

This neighbourhood staple has an eclectic menu and a lively, older crowd. The flamboyant interior is a little slice of Bourbon Street translated to the West Coast; there's a terrace for outside dining.

Mark's

861 N La Cienega Boulevard, between Santa Monica Boulevard and Melrose Avenue (1-310 652 5252/ www.marksrestaurant.com). Bus 4, 105, 304, LDHWH/I-10, exit La Cienega Boulevard north. **Open** 6pm-2am Mon-Sat; 11am-2pm, 6pm-2am Sun. **Main courses** $12-$30. **Credit** AmEx, Disc, MC, V. **Map** p312 B2.

There's never a shortage of eye-candy at Mark's, but one doesn't have to sacrifice gastronomy to guys-tronomy: the food's excellent, a Cal-American jumble of healthy and indulgent dishes. On Mondays, the Dish it Out promotion slashes prices. **Photo** p230.

Gyms

Gay-friendly gyms in the area include **24-Hour Fitness** (see p259), distinguished by its great pool and cruisey atmosphere, and **Gold's Gym** (1016 Cole Avenue, 1-323 462 7012; see p259), a fantasyland of porn performers, prom queens and soap stars.

Crunch

*8000 W Sunset Boulevard, at N Laurel Avenue
(1-323 654 4550/www.crunch.com). Bus 4, 218,
304/I-10, exit Fairfax Avenue north.* **Open** 5am-
midnight Mon-Fri; 7am-10pm Sat, Sun. **Rates**
$24/day. **Credit** AmEx, Disc, MC, V. **Map** p312 C1.
It's hard to know which is the more breathtaking:
the view of the Hollywood Hills, or the Adonises who
choose it as a backdrop to work out in front of.
Flirtation can easily be part of the workout: wash up
inside the oft-discussed 'peek-a-boo' see-through
showers. A popular gay meeting place.

Bathhouses & sex clubs

Melrose Spa

*7269 Melrose Avenue, at N La Brea Boulevard
(1-323 937 2122/www.midtowne.com). Bus 10, 11,
212/I-10, exit La Brea Avenue north.* **Open** 24hrs
daily. **Admission** *Per 8hrs* $28 room; $16 locker.
Credit AmEx, MC, V. **Map** p312 D2.
This two-storey spa close to WeHo attracts a varied
clientele. Amenities of note include a rooftop patio,
a huge adult movie room and a darkened maze for
anonymous action. In case all of this screws you up,
the spa has its own resident sex therapist.

Hollywood

Hollywood's gritty gay scene is not for the
faint-hearted. Neither as friendly nor as visible
as the West Hollywood scene, this is the place to
slide into the underbelly of gay nightlife.

Bars & clubs

Gay nights are held at **Arena**, which boasts a
popular Latin night on Saturday, and trendy
teenybopper crowd on Thursday (Tigerheat).
Also, check out **Circus Disco**, particularly
Boys Night Out every Tuesday and the mixed
night Spundae on Saturday (for both, *see p247*).

Spotlight Bar

*1601 N Cahuenga Boulevard, at Selma Avenue
(1-323 467 2425). Metro Hollywood-Highland/bus
4, 156, 304, LDH, LDHWH/US 101, exit Highland
Avenue south.* **Open** 6am-2am daily. **No credit
cards. Map** p313 B2.
For a drink on the darker side, check out LA's oldest gay bar, the Spotlight. Trannies abound mid-
week, and there's a diverse clientele most nights and
days. Thursday night's Sexual Outlaw attracts a
younger, more alternative crowd.

Bathhouses & sex clubs

Hollywood Spa

*1650 N Ivar Avenue, between Hollywood Boulevard
& Selma Avenue (1-800 772 2582/1-323 464 0445/
www.hollywoodspa.com). Metro Hollywood-Vine/
bus 2, 210, 212, 217, 302, 310, LDH/US 101, exit*

Hollywood Boulevard west. **Open** 24hrs daily.
Admission *Per 8hrs* $16-$33/room; $23/locker.
Credit AmEx, Disc, MC, V. **Map** p313 B2.
The best-known bathhouse in the city has a good
gym, although that's not the main reason why peo-
ple come here. At weekends, a live DJ provides a
soundtrack to the shenanigans until 6am.
Other locations: 5636 Vineland Avenue, North
Hollywood (1-818 760 6969).

Silver Lake

Though it's recently seen an influx by straights
sniffing after some excellent real estate deals,
Silver Lake remains LA's most diverse gay
neighbourhood. The alternative homo scene
here is less twink and more kink; it's the best
known gay 'hood after WeHo.

Bars & clubs

Gender-bending, glamour-loving Dragstrip 66
(www.dragstrip66.com) is the east side's most
fun night: it's held on the third Saturday of the
month at **Echo** (1151 Glendale Boulevard).
For gay-friendly **Akbar**, *see p246*.

Cuffs

*1941 Hyperion Avenue, between Fountain &
Lyric Avenues (1-323 660 2649/www.cuffsla.com).
Bus 175/US 101, exit Sunset Boulevard east.*
Open 2am-2am Mon-Thur, Sun; 4pm-3am Fri, Sat.
No credit cards. Map p314 C2.
This light-deprived leather speakeasy, which
celebrated its 25th anniversary in 2006, is a quin-
tessential part of Silver Lake's alternative scene.
A must, at least for the butcher cruisers.

Eagle

*4219 Santa Monica Boulevard, at Myra Avenue,
Silver Lake (1-323 669 9472/www.eaglela.com).
Metro Vermont-Santa Monica/bus 2, 4, 302, 304/
US 101, exit Vermont Avenue north.* **Open** 4pm-
2am daily. **Admission** free-$10. **No credit cards.**
Map p314 B3.
Formerly the Gauntlet, the Eagle spins some of the
coolest rock/alternative tunes in town. Porn plays
alluringly on the monitors as the leather daddies
swarm and get their boots polished.

Faultline

*4216 Melrose Avenue, at N Vermont Avenue
(1-323 660 0889/www.faultlinebar.com). Bus 10,
11, 204, 754/US 101, exit Vermont Avenue north.*
Open 6pm-2am Tue; 5pm-2amWed-Fri; 2pm-2am
Sat; 2pm-1am Sun. **Admission** $5-$10. **No credit
cards. Map** p314 A4.
Leather men and their followers hold Faultline in the
highest regard, but other fetishes are catered for, too:
bikers, bodybuilders, HIV-positive guys and body
piercers are all regulars. The DJs have a strict 'no
divas' music policy, instead spinning an edgy mix
of electronica and rock.

Arts & Entertainment

MJs

2810 Hyperion Avenue, at Monon Street (1-323 660 1503). Bus 175/US 101, exit Silver Lake Boulevard east. **Open** 4pm-2am Mon-Sat; 2pm-2am Sun. **Credit** MC, V. **Map** p314 C2.

Is the ascent of MJs the decline of edgy Silver Lake as we know it? The bar is more West Hollywood than Slakers (slang for the locals) care to enjoy, but there's an array of outlandish theme nights that tries to keep everyone happy. Friday night even brings together go-go dancers and hard rock.

Other Side

2538 Hyperion Avenue, between Evans & Tracy Streets (1-323 661 4233). Bus 175/US 101, exit Silver Lake Boulevard east. **Open** noon-2am Mon-Fri; 9am-2am Sat, Sun. **Credit** AmEx, MC, V. **Map** p314 C2.

LA kitsch at its finest. The average age here may be 70-plus, but the talent performing at this classy piano bar is terrific: some of the regulars performed on the Great White Way in the 1940s and '50s.

Bathhouses & sex clubs

Slammer

3688 Beverly Boulevard, between N Madison & N Westmoreland Avenues (1-213 388 8040/www.slammerclub.com). Metro Vermont-Beverly/bus 14/US 101, exit Beverly Boulevard west. **Open** 8pm-late Mon-Fri; 2pm-late Sat, Sun. **Admission** $20. **No credit cards. Map** p314 B5.

Silver Lake's only sex club caters mostly to the leather crowd. Monday nights are a fetish fest, Tuesdays are for gym buffs and Wet Wednesdays attract those into watersports. Don't expect many of Hollywood Spa's pretty guys. Free HIV testing is available.

Festivals Gay

June's **LA Gay Pride** (www.lapride.org) is one of the biggest pride events in the US. As many as 350,000 people watch the often raucous three-hour Sunday parade make its way down Santa Monica Boulevard; tens of thousands attend the nearby two-day festival, renowned for its diva headliners, drag starlets and top DJs.

The area's three Circuit parties are **Masterbeat** (New Year's Eve, Downtown), **White Party** (April, Palm Springs; *see p272*) and **Pride** (June, Downtown). Santa Monica Boulevard is home to October's wild **Hallowe'en** festivities (*see p208*), while August is **Lesbian Visibility Month**, which means lots of lesbian dances, comedy nights and social forums. For **Outfest**, LA's gay and lesbian film festival, *see p220* **Festivals**.

Lesbian

As proved by the success of *The L Word*, a soap-like LA-set Sapphic confection, West Hollywood celebrates girls, whether they be gay, straight or gay hangers-on. You'll find lesbians of all demographics here, from power lunchers to good-time WeHo party girls.

The LA lesbian is a lot harder to reduce to caricature than her gay male counterpart. If you're looking for the flannel-and-Birkenstock stereotype, you'll be disappointed, even in granola-friendly Silver Lake. And though the clubs don't devote themselves each night to a strictly-female crowd, there are event nights that bring the women out in droves.

INFORMATION

Pick up free monthly mag *Lesbian News* (www. lesbiannews.com) from local shops. *Frontiers* is mainly a men's magazine (*see p229*), but covers women's interests. **A Different Light** bookstore (*see p182*) is a good source of lesbian literature. For the LA Sparks, a women's basketball team popular among lesbians, *see p253*; for lesbian resources, *see pp290-291*.

Bars & clubs

An old prophet once opined that LA lesbians don't grow old, they just retire to the Valley. There remains a prolific female presence across the San Fernando hill, but most girl action happens in West Hollywood and Silver Lake.

With the exception of the venues detailed below, few LA bars or clubs devote themselves to lesbians seven days a week, so pick your events carefully. On the first Wednesday of each month, the team behind Girl Bar (*see below*) promote Girls' Night Out at **Mark's** (*see p232*), a more elegant soirée. Thursdays see the loungey Fuse, LA's best-known lesbian night, at **Here Lounge** (*see p230*). Arrive early and beat the long lines. **Encounters** (203 N Sierra Madre Boulevard, Pasadena, www.encounters niteclub.com) offers an alternative to Thursday night WeHo madness. And on Fridays the Factory (*see p230*), **Girl Bar** offers the finest beats and the finest women.

Benvenuto

8512 Santa Monica Boulevard, at N La Cienega Boulevard, West Hollywood (1-310 659 8635). Bus 4, 105, 304, LDHWH/I-10, exit La Cienega Boulevard north. **Open** 11.30am-2.30pm Tue-Fri; 5.30-10.30pm Tue-Thur; 5.30-11pm Fri, Sat. **Credit** AmEx, Disc, MC, V. **Map** p312 B2.

After closing temporarily for renovations in 2006, this long-running lesbian favourite is back on course, offering a full bar and decent food.

The dancers at **Girl Bar** are poles apart. *See p234.*

Jewel's Catch One

4067 W Pico Boulevard, at S Norton Avenue, Midtown (1-323 734 8849/www.jewelscatchone.com). Bus 30, 31, 210/I-10, exit Crenshaw Boulevard north. **Open** 9pm-2am daily. **Admission** $7-$15. **Credit** AmEx, Disc, MC, V. **Map** p313 B6.
Jewel's Catch One is LA's lesbian superclub. The huge dancefloor draws a mixed but predominantly African-American crowd. To keep the crowds happy, the DJs spin a mix of R&B, hip hop and house. Special events include strippers and karaoke. Get there early, as it fills up fast.

Normandie Room

8737 Santa Monica Boulevard, between Hancock Avenue & Huntley Drive, West Hollywood (1-310 659 6204). Bus 4, 105, 304/I-10, exit La Cienega Boulevard north. **Open** 5pm-2am daily. **No credit cards.** **Map** p312 A2.
This popular neighbourhood bar draws an eclectic crowd, but Saturday is the best night for the ladies. The bar's motto reads: 'No homophobes, no heterophobes, no assholes.'

Oil Can Harry's

11502 Ventura Boulevard, between Colfax Avenue & Tujunga Avenue, Studio City (1-818 760 9749/www.oilcanharrysla.com). Bus 150/US 101, exit Tujunga Boulevard south. **Open** 7.30pm-12.30am Tue, Thur; 9pm-2am Fri; 8pm-2am Sat. **Admission** varies. **Credit** AmEx, MC, V.

Bring your cowboy boots and affect your best country twang at this femme-dominated line-dancing joint. Whether you go solo or with a group, there's always someone with whom to dance. Lessons are held on Tuesdays and Thursdays (7.45-9.15pm).

Palms

8572 Santa Monica Boulevard, between Westbourne Drive & W Knoll Drive, West Hollywood (1-310 652 6188/www.thepalmsbar.com). Bus 4, 105, 304, LDHWH/I-10, exit La Cienega Boulevard north. **Open** 8pm-2am Mon-Fri; 4pm-2am Sat, Sun. **Admission** free. **Credit** AmEx, MC, V. **Map** p312 B2.
The oldest lesbian bar in LA, with dancing, a pool table and a patio. The Sunday beer bust and trendy new dance event, Cream on Saturday nights, are both very popular. Check out the go-go girls.

Restaurants & coffeehouses

Gay venues popular with lesbians include the **Abbey** (*see p232*), **French Quarter** (*see p232*), **Marix** (*see p231*), the **Coffee Bean & Tea Leaf** (*see p167*) at 8735 Santa Monica Boulevard in West Hollywood and the **Highland Grounds** (742 N Highland Avenue, Hollywood, 1-323 466 1507, www.highlandgrounds.com). The latter often gets crowded in the evenings, when there's often live music. In Silver Lake, try the **Coffee Table** (*see p169*).

Music

It's not just Disney Hall.

It has its landmark venues, not to mention its great bands and ensembles, but Los Angeles' greatest musical asset is size. The urban sprawl, along with its cultural and racial mix, throws up an amazing variety of music in virtually every corner of the city, performed before surprisingly devoted audiences. What's more, LA's status as the second largest conurbation in the US and a de facto music business hub means that every touring act worth its salt passes through from time to time, hawking a new album or ploughing through a well-travelled back catalogue. In short, from superstars to the next Next Big Thing, there's plenty here to see.

TICKETS & INFORMATION

Big-name concerts, both classical and rock, often sell out, so try and buy tickets in advance. It's worth checking with the box office on the day of the show, when the promoters sometimes release extra seats. Try to get tickets directly from the venue – by phone, online or in person – to save on fees. At smaller venues, you can usually pay at the door. Otherwise, you're stuck with the booking fees charged by Ticketmaster (1-213 480 3232, www.ticketmaster.com).

The most comprehensive listings appear in the *LA Weekly*. The *LA Times*' 'Calendar' section on Sundays is a good source, while the LA edition of cool-kid newsletter flavorpill.net spotlights the town's hottest tickets.

Classical

LA's classical circuit is one of the strongest in the US. The LA Philharmonic has had an excellent reputation for a number of years, but the opening of Disney Hall has boosted interest in classical music to unprecedented heights.

Ensembles

Los Angeles Master Chorale

1-213 972 7282/www.lamc.org.
Described by Sir Simon Rattle as 'one of the finest choruses in the world', the 120-voice LA Master Chorale is the largest choir of its kind in the US. Founded in 1962, the Chorale performs regularly with the LA Phil. Its crowd-pleasing repertoire ranges from Mozart and Bach to Cole Porter; its Christmas events – including Handel's *Messiah* – remain justifiably very popular.

Los Angeles Opera

1-213 972 8001/www.losangelesopera.com.
The LA Opera made its debut in 1986 with an acclaimed production of Verdi's *Otello*. Now led by Plácido Domingo and Kent Nagano, the company specialises in high-concept stagings of works both old and new. Recent productions have included Wagner's *Parsifal*, the world premiere of Deborah Dratell and Nicholas Von Hoffman's *Nicholas and Alexandra*, and Puccini's *Madama Butterfly* as staged by controversial avant-gardist Robert Wilson. Performances are held at the Dorothy Chandler Pavilion (*see p237*).

Los Angeles Philharmonic

1-323 850 2000/www.laphil.org.
An institution. Established in 1919 by local tycoon William Andrews Clarke, the LA Phil has long served as proof that LA isn't a cultural wasteland. After the orchestra's 1964 move to the Dorothy Chandler Pavilion, and the concurrent tenure of Zubin 'Macho Maestro' Mehta as musical director, the Philharmonic began to attract international attention. But since the orchestra's move to Disney Hall a few years ago, its reputation has soared further; so much so, in fact, that the *New York Times* has described it as the best orchestra in the US.

Thanks to its tenth and present music director – the justifiably acclaimed, dynamic Finn Esa-Pekka Salonen – the Phil's programming includes a large contemporary repertoire, along with the standard warhorses. Zubin Mehta and Sir Simon Rattle still appear regularly as guest conductors. For more insight, the Phil offers UpBeat Live, a lecture series that starts one hour before each concert. The majority of the Philharmonic's concerts are staged at Disney Hall (Oct-May), though the summer sees them move outside in the Hollywood Bowl (June-Sept). For both, *see p237*. **Photo p237**.

Also recommended

The **Los Angeles Chamber Orchestra** (1-213 622 7001, www.laco.org) is LA's foremost chamber orchestra, performing works from the 17th to the 20th centuries at venues including UCLA's Royce Hall, Glendale's Alex Theatre and Disney Hall. The **Da Camera Society**'s Chamber Music in Historic Sites (1-310 477 2929, www.dacamera.org) presents concerts by first-rate ensembles and soloists in some of the city's more interesting buildings.

Outside LA, the **Pasadena Symphony** (1-626 793 7172, www.pasadenasymphony.org) plays at the Pasadena Civic Auditorium, and both the **Long Beach Symphony** (1-562 436 3203, www.lbso.org) and the daring **Long Beach Opera** (1-562 439 2580, www.longbeachopera.org) are based at the Long Beach Convention & Entertainment Center.

In the shape of the **LA Philharmonic**, Disney Hall has the orchestra it deserves. *See p236.*

Major venues

For the weekly concerts at LACMA's Leo S Bing Theatre, *see p207* **Festivals**.

Dorothy Chandler Pavilion

Performing Arts Center of Los Angeles County, 135 N Grand Avenue, between W 1st & W Temple Streets, Downtown (1-213 972 7211/www.music center.org). Metro Civic Center/bus 2, 4, 10, 11, 14, 48, 92, 302, 714/I-110, exit 4th Street east. **Box office** 10am-6pm Mon-Sat. **Tickets** $8-$150. **Credit** AmEx, MC, V. **Map** p315 B2.

The grey lady of LA's classical music venues, the Chandler has declined in stature in recent years due to the LA Phil moving to Disney Hall and the relocation of the Academy Awards ceremony to the Kodak Theatre. Still, the LA Opera remains in situ. The theatre seats 3,200 amid dark wood panelling and crystal chandeliers; the sound is best appreciated from the upper floors, although the view from the top balcony can be vertigo-inducing.

Hollywood Bowl

2301 N Highland Avenue, at US 101 (1-323 850 2000/www.hollywoodbowl.org). Bus 156/US 101, exit Highland Avenue north. **Box office** *June-Sept* 10am-6pm Mon-Sat; noon-8pm Sun. **Tickets** $1-$95. **Credit** AmEx, Disc, MC, V.

This jewel of an outdoor amphitheatre has been hosting concerts since its first LA Philharmonic performance at Easter 1921. Nestled in an aesthetically blessed fold up in the Hollywood Hills, the 18,000-seat venue can bring out the romantic in the terminally cynical (the glorious setting almost makes up for the somewhat dodgy acoustics). The summer home of the LA Philharmonic, it's hosted everyone from the Beatles to Big Bird. Shows – classical, rock, jazz or country – are sometimes followed by fireworks. The Bowl's bandshell was designed by Lloyd Wright in 1928, and later updated by Frank Gehry.

Walt Disney Concert Hall

111 S Grand Avenue, between W 2nd & W 3rd Streets, Downtown (1-213 972 7211/http://wdch. laphil.org). Metro Civic Center/bus 2, 4, 10, 11, 14, 48, 92, 302, 714/I-110, exit 4th Street east. **Box office** noon-6pm Tue-Sun. **Tickets** $35-$120. **Credit** AmEx, Disc, MC, V. **Map** p315 B2.

The $274-million crown jewel of the LA Music Center, Disney Hall opened in 2003 to rave reviews. Several years later, the novelty hasn't yet worn off: both inside and out, this is a terrific venue. Designed by Frank Gehry, the hall features a 2,265-capacity auditorium with an open platform stage. Chief acoustican Yasuhisa Toyota combined the best aspects of orchestral halls in Tokyo, Berlin, Amsterdam and Boston in a bid to provide aural warmth and clarity; the result of his endeavours is a virtually perfect acoustic that works almost as well for amplified events as for orchestral performances. The hall is the new home of the LA Philharmonic and the LA Master Chorale, but the programme is surprisingly varied throughout the year. The complex also includes the 250-seat Roy and Edna Disney/CalArts Theatre, and an art gallery. For tours of the building, call 1-213 972 7483. *See also p28 and p113.*

College venues

College venues include **Schoenberg Hall** and the beautiful **Royce Hall** at UCLA (1-310 825 2101, www.uclalive.org); **Norris Auditorium** at USC (1-213 740 7111, www.usc.edu); the **Harriet & Charles Luckman Fine Arts Complex** at Cal State LA (1-323 343 6600, www.luckmanfineartscomplex.org); Zipper Hall at the Colburn School for the Performing Arts (200 S Grand Avenue, www.colburnschool.edu) and the **Gindi Auditorium** at the University of Judaism (1-310 476 9777, www.uj.edu).

Arts & Entertainment

Rock & pop

LA's music scene, like that of most major cities, rolls in waves. It's ridden some big surf over the last four decades: in the 1960s, when the Sunset Strip was at its fashionable peak; in the 1970s, when local labels such as Elektra and A&M racked up hit after hit and the city became the de facto centre of the American music industry; in the 1980s, when hair metal acts from Mötley Crüe to Guns 'n Roses ruled the roost; and in the 1990s, when West Coast hip hop went global. In between times, to continue the metaphor, LA has sometimes struggled to mount its board. The 1990s, in particular, were very lacklustre. But LA is once more showing signs of musical life. Acts such as Moving Units and Dirty Little Secret are picking up plaudits, and a few noted East Coast acts are even moving out here: Karen O, lead singer of Brooklyn archetypes the Yeah Yeah Yeahs, now calls the city home.

Be sure to bring photo ID to every music venue: some shows are open only to over-18s or over-21s, and you'll need to be 21 or older to get served at the bar. For major festivals, see p242; for free events, see p207.

Major venues

The **Summer Nights at the Ford** series is held at the John Anson Ford Amphitheatre (see p260). The **Henry Fonda Music Box Theatre** (6126 Hollywood Boulevard, Hollywood, 1-323 464 0808, www.henryfonda theater.com) hosts everyone from Josh Rouse to Felix Da Housecat. For the 1,200-seat **Avalon**, which stages gigs in between its club nights, see p246; for the **Pantages Theatre**, which hosts some concerts in between its runs of musical theatre, see p260; for the **Wadsworth Theatre**, which offers some world music and experimental pop shows, see p262.

Great Western Forum

3900 Manchester Boulevard, at Prairie Avenue, Inglewood (1-310 673 1300/www.thelaforum.com). Bus 115, 211, 212, 315, 442/I-405, exit Manchester Boulevard east. **Box office** 10am-6pm, show days only. **Tickets** $10-$70. **Credit** AmEx, MC, V.
The 18,000-seat, acoustically challenged Forum was once *the* place to play in LA: the venue housed some of Guns 'n Roses' most infamous concerts. Since the opening of the Staples Center, it's no longer the city's premier enormodome, but world-class acts still perform here, from classic rock legends such as AC/DC to modern pretenders like Coldplay.

Greek Theatre

2700 N Vermont Avenue, Griffith Park (1-323 665 1927/www.greektheatrela.com). Bus 180, 181/ US 101, exit Vermont Avenue north. **Box office**

noon-6pm Mon-Fri; 10am-4pm Sat, Sun. *Closed* winter. **Tickets** $15-$100. **Credit** AmEx, MC, V. **Map** p314 A1.
This bucolic, open-air, 6,000-seat theatre, immortalised by Neil Diamond's *Hot August Night* LP, is a great place to catch big names in summer from the likes of Franz Ferdinand. The 'stacked' parking means getting out of the car park often takes longer than the show; if you can, stump up for VIP parking.

Gibson Amphitheatre

Universal CityWalk, 100 Universal City Plaza, Universal City (1-818 777 3931/www.hob.com). Metro Universal City/bus 96, 156, 166/US 101, exit Universal Center Drive. **Box office** Amphitheatre 1-9pm Mon, Thur-Sun. *CityWalk* 1-9pm Mon-Thur, Sun; 1-10.30pm Fri, Sat. **Tickets** $20-$150. **Credit** AmEx, MC, V.
This slick, semi-circular room serves major pop, R&B and Latin acts (David Gray, Mary J Blige et al) wanting a slightly more intimate, classy venue. The slightly showbizzy environment isn't what God had in mind when He invented rock 'n' roll, but clean sightlines and good sonics make this a popular spot. Warning: parking is both inconvenient and dear.

Hollywood Palladium

6215 W Sunset Boulevard, between N Argyle & N El Centro Avenues, Hollywood (1-323 962 7600/www. hollywoodpalladium.com). Metro Hollywood-Vine/bus 2, 212, 217, 302, LDHWI/US 101, exit Vine Street south. **Box office** from 7pm, show days only. **Tickets** $10-$50. **No credit cards. Map** p313 B2.
Once ruled by the big band sounds of Glenn Miller and Tommy Dorsey, this faded ballroom now hosts hip hop shows, punk bands (the reunion of hardcore innovators Black Flag) and indie faves like Interpol.

Staples Center

1111 S Figueroa Street, at 11th Street, Downtown (1-213 742 7340/www.staplescenter.com). Metro Pico/bus 81, 381, 442, 444, 445, 446, 447, 460/I-110, exit Olympic Boulevard. **Box office** 9am-6pm Mon-Sat; 10am-6pm Sun. **Tickets** $50-$150. **Credit** AmEx, Disc, MC, V. **Map** p315 A5.
Downtown's sports shrine (see p253) also hosts big musical acts, such as the Eagles and U2. A plush, modern facility, the purple-seated, 20,000-capacity stadium is miles from the old-school funkiness of the Great Western Forum, although the sound quality is just as variable. At the concession stand, don't miss the nachos camachos, an LA favourite.

Wiltern LG

3790 Wilshire Boulevard, at S Western Avenue, Koreatown (1-213 380 5005/www.thewiltern.com). Metro Wilshire-Western/bus 20, 21, 207, 209, 720, LDHWI/I-10, exit Western Avenue north. **Box office** 10am-4pm Sat; also from 3hrs before show. **Tickets** $20-$60. **Credit** MC, V. **Map** p313 D5.
Located in Koreatown, this classy art deco gem – now named for the Korean company that sponsors it – draws crowds for shows from the likes of Death Cab for Cutie, Belle & Sebastian and Van Morrison, as well as the odd comic act like Eddie Izzard and

Artists in residence

As the West Coast hub of America's music industry, LA is host to a constant turnover of touring acts, passing through the city for a one-night-stand here or a three-day stint there. But some acts become resident.

The best-known residency in LA is Jon Brion's anything-can-happen Friday-night session at **Largo** (see p241). Brion (pictured), a wildly talented songwriter, performer and producer who's worked with everyone from Aimee Mann to Kanye West, plays two sets, using a multitude of instruments and looping devices to create perfect power-pop arrangements all on his lonesome. Look out for the regular unannounced guests, who might leap up and join Brion to play a few songs at the end of the night. But be sure to book well in advance.

Other week-in-week-out events are a little more low-key. **Room 5** (143 N La Brea Avenue, 1-323 938 2504, www.room5 lounge.com), an acoustic lounge located above a restaurant, hosts a regular Songwriters' Night on Mondays, featuring Jay Nash, Garrison Starr and a number of other local singer-songwriters. Bill Clark & the Mighty Balls of Fire play their high-octane blues each weekend at **Babe & Ricky's Inn** (see p243), which also hosts a regular jam night on Mondays, while local blues belter Mickey Champion holds court Tuesday nights at **Little Pedro's Blue Bongo** (see p178).

A number of venues offer short-term residencies: artists playing weekly for a month or two, perhaps a well-known act trying out new material. Monday nights at **Spaceland** (see p242) and the **Echo** (see p240) have operated along these lines, while the residences programmed by intimate, nouveau-hip **Hotel Café** (see p240), involving

artists such as Imogen Heap and Butch Walker, have spawned a new singer-songwriter scene and even a cross-country group tour. But residencies aren't restricted to sensitive young folk strumming an acoustic guitar. The **Key Club** (see p239) has featured Video Star, a New Romantic cover band, as well as potty-mouthed heavy metal hellraisers Metal Skool. Outlandish '80s covers act the Spazmatics play each Sunday at the **Dragonfly** (see p240), while Cubensis pay tribute to the Grateful Dead each Sunday at **14 Below** in Santa Monica (see p240).

Brion aside, music residencies are constantly in flux here. The best way to keep track is to consult the club listings in *LA Weekly* or to check individual club websites.

Tenacious D. The venue's comfy seating (in the balcony; the floor is standing room only), relatively elegant decor and democratic sightlines are draws.

Rock clubs

In addition to clubs below, other venues in the city stage live music. The **Key Club** (9039 W Sunset Boulevard, West Hollywood, 1-310 274 5800, www.keyclub.com) offers occasional shows alongside its club programming. For the **Bigfoot Lodge**, which books punk, garage and rockabilly acts, *see p176*.

Conga Room
5634 Wilshire Boulevard, between Hauser Boulevard & S Ridgeley Drive, Miracle Mile (1-323-938 1696/ www.congaroom.com). Bus 20, 21, 212, 720, LDF/ I-10, exit La Brea Avenue north. **Open** 9pm-1.30am Thur, Fri; 8pm-2am Sat. **Admission** $15-$20. **Credit** AmEx, MC, V. **Map** p312 D4.
The place for lovers of Latin sounds, bossa nova to salsa and all sorts of sashaying in between. Club DJs sometimes do their thing, too – check online for the schedule to see who's playing when. For those unsure of what to do with feet and hips, there are salsa lessons on Thursday and Saturday nights, 8-9pm ($15 Thur, $20 Sat).

A gorgeous art deco relic, the El Rey has accommodated everyone from the indie hip-hop of Madlib's Stones Throw posse via old schoolers such as Tom Tom Club to cool-kid underground buzz-binners like Dizzee Rascal. The sound and sightlines are excellent. It also hosts highly popular gay club night Boytrade (*see p230*).

Fais Do-Do
5257 W Adams Boulevard, at Cloverdale Avenue, West LA (1-323 954 8080/www.faisdodo.com). Bus 37/I-10, exit La Brea Avenue south. **Open** 7pm-midnight Mon-Wed, Sun; 7pm-2am Thur-Sat. **Admission** $5-$8. **Credit** MC, V.
Once mostly the province of blues and zydeco acts, Fais Do-Do (Cajun dialect for 'dance party') now stages a wild variety of events, anything from rockabilly and Brazilian bands to hip hop turntablists. The club offers an impressive array of beers and decent Southern-style cooking; the opulent interior and the desolate West Side location add to the exotic vibe.

14 Below
1348 14th Street, at Santa Monica Boulevard, Santa Monica (1-310 451 5040/www.14below.com). Bus 4, 304, SM1, SM10, SM11/I-10, exit 26th Street north. **Open** 3pm-2am Mon-Fri; 4pm-2am Sat; 7pm-2am Sun. **Admission** $7-$30. **Credit** MC, V. **Map** p310 B3.
Wannabes, washed-up '80s acts and tributes to major stadium-fillers from days of yore make up the bill at this Santa Monica venue. The volume is deafening; to save your ears, watch the show on TV from the pool room.

Hotel Café
1623½ N Cahuenga Boulevard, between Hollywood Boulevard & Selma Avenue, Hollywood (1-323 461 2040/www.hotelcafe.com). Metro Hollywood-Vine/ bus 156, 210, 212, 217, 710, LDH/US 101, exit Hollywood Boulevard west. **Open** from 7pm nightly. **Admission** varies. **Credit** MC, V. **Map** p313 B1.
Where cool-kid singer-songwriters of the upcoming variety make their mark. Cary Brothers (of *Garden State* soundtrack fame), Alaskan troubadour Kate Earl and edgy French chanteuse Keren Ann are typical of the consistently excellent roster.

House of Blues
8430 W Sunset Boulevard, at N Olive Drive, West Hollywood (hotline 1-323 650 1451/box office 1-323 848 5100/www.hob.com). Bus 2, 302, LDHWH/I-10, exit La Cienega Boulevard north. **Box office** 10am-9pm Mon-Sat; 9am-9pm Sun. **Shows** 8pm or 9pm daily. **Admission** $10-$35. **Credit** AmEx, DC, Disc, MC, V. **Map** p312 B1.
While some blues aficionados cringe at the sight of this club's faux blues-shack exterior, the HOB bookers do a great job of mixing major blues, rap, country and rock acts (Kanye West did some of his breakout shows here). The cramped conditions, bad parking, traffic-laden Sunset Strip location and surly staff are annoying, but the food is excellent, and the sound is above average (except under the balcony).

Echo Echo Echo Echo Echo Echo Echo Echo Echo Echo Echo ▪

Dragonfly
6510 Santa Monica Boulevard, at Wilcox Avenue, Hollywood (1-323 466 6111/www.dragonfly.com). Bus 4, 156, 304/I-10, exit La Brea Avenue north. **Open** 9pm-2am daily. **Admission** $5-$15. **Credit** AmEx, MC, V. **Map** p313 B2.
A club masquerading as a Middle Eastern harem, this slightly glam, somewhat trashy spot hosts local bands, tattooed Hollywood fromage and, at weekends, club nights. The sound is excellent, although the club's tendency to spin 1990s electronics between sets can irritate. Every Sunday, the Spazmatics pay unwarranted tribute to '80s new wave acts whose very existence you've spent 15 years trying to forget.

Echo
1822 W Sunset Boulevard, at Glendale Boulevard, Echo Park (1-213 413 8200/www.attheecho.com). Bus 2, 4, 96, 302, 304/US 101, exit Glendale Boulevard north. **Open** 8pm-2am daily. **Admission** free-$25. **Credit** AmEx, MC, V. Map p314 D4.
This funky room out in Echo Park can get a little too funky at times: on busy nights, the walls practically sweat from to the hipster bodies crammed inside it. Shows range from edgy rap, dub reggae and electronica acts to up-and-comers on the indie circuit: TV on the Radio and Cut Copy played early LA shows here.

El Rey Theatre
5515 Wilshire Boulevard, between Burnside & Dunsmuir Avenues, Miracle Mile (1-323 936 6400/ www.theelrey.com). Bus 20, 21, 720, LDF/I-10, exit La Brea Avenue north. **Open** varies. **Admission** $10-$30. **No credit cards.** Map p312 D4.

Joint

8771 W Pico Boulevard, at S Robertson Boulevard, Beverly Hills (1-310 275 2619). Bus 28, 220/ I-10, exit Robertson Avenue north. **Open** 8pm-2am daily. **Admission** $5-$10. **Credit** MC, V. **Map** p312 A5.

This interesting club has a chaotic booking policy, encompassing everything from hip hop DJs to folk singers and local wannabe bands. Check the schedule for the club's jam sessions, where you might catch anyone from Slash to Robert Plant letting rip.

Knitting Factory

7021 Hollywood Boulevard, at N Sycamore Avenue, Hollywood (1-323 463 0204/www.knittingfactory. com). Metro Hollywood-Highland/bus 212, 217, LDHWH/US 101, exit Hollywood Boulevard west. **Open** varies. **Admission** $5-$25. **Credit** AmEx, MC, V. **Map** p313 A1.

This offshoot of the famed New York club doesn't have much personality in the way of its room and touristy mall setting. Still, it makes up for its shortcomings with an adventurous booking policy that offers stage space to alternative touring and local acts on three stages: think buzz bands such as the Books, punk as played by the Subhumans, or classic indie rockers such as Teenage Fanclub.

Largo

432 N Fairfax Avenue, between Rosewood & Oakwood Avenues, Fairfax District (1-323 852 1073/www.largo-la.com). Bus 217, 218, LDF/ I-10, exit Fairfax Avenue north. **Shows** from 8pm Mon-Thur; from 8.30pm Fri, Sat. **Admission** $10-$20. **Credit** AmEx, MC, V. **Map** p312 C3.

The speciality at this intimate room is singer-songwriters: Aimee Mann, John Doe, Grant Lee Phillips, Jill Sobule and, every Friday, perennial hot ticket/head-scratching Kanye West collaborator Jon Brion. There's also occasional comedy, with stars like Louis CK and Patton Oswalt performing in an unusually intimate environment. The food leaves a lot to be desired; you're better off eating across the street at Canter's Deli (*see p153*).

Mint

6010 W Pico Boulevard, at Stearns Drive, Midtown (1-323 954 9400/www.themintla.com). Bus 217/ I-10, exit Fairfax Avenue north. **Open** from 7pm daily. **Admission** $7-$15. **Credit** AmEx, MC, V. **Map** p312 C5.

A large part of the Mint's charm resides in the fact that the decor doesn't seem to have changed since it opened in the 1930s. The other part of its appeal lies in its unpredictability: Harry Dean Stanton singing country one night, the next a local band that'll likely stay that way. Jazz and blues also figure in the schedule, together with the odd impromptu performance from stars of the calibre of Bonnie Raitt.

Mr T's Bowl

5621 N Figueroa Avenue, between Avenues 56 & 57, Highland Park (1-323 256 7561/http:// mrtsbowl.tripod.com). Metro Highland Park/bus 83/ Hwy 110, exit Avenue 52. **Open** 10am-2am daily. **Shows** 9pm-2am Tue-Sun. **Admission** free-$5. **Credit** AmEx, MC, V.

An unlikely amalgam of young punks and old locals, mixing in a former bowling alley in a tough Highland Park neighbourhood. Despite the edgy surroundings, the food is delicious.

Roxy

9009 W Sunset Boulevard, between San Vincente Boulevard & Doheny Drive, West Hollywood (1-310 276 2222/www.theroxyonsunset.com). Bus 2, 105, 302/I-10, exit La Cienega Boulevard north. **Open** from 8pm daily. **Admission** $10-$20. **Credit** AmEx, DC, Disc, MC, V. **Map** p312 A2.

Get there early, snag a table, and reflect that 30 years ago you might have been watching Springsteen on its stage. Even today, an occasional surprise gig from the likes of Courtney Love or Billy Idol can turn your evening upside down. If not, prepare for a night of metal or indie from the likes of Hot Hot Heat.

Safari Sam's

5214 W Sunset Boulevard, at N Kingsley Drive, Hollywood (1-323 666 7267/www.safari-sams.com). Metro Hollywood-Western/bus 2, 302/US 101, exit Western Avenue north. **Open** varies. **Admission** $5-$10. **No credit cards**. **Map** p313 D1.

A 1980s Huntington Beach punk institution, Safari Sam's has moved to Sunset Boulevard on the East Side, but still majors in old-school punk/alternative nostalgia from the likes of the Blasters, as well as some artier sounds and tribute bands.

Sweet **Molly Malone's**. *See p243.*

Festivals Music

Coachella

Empire Polo Field, Indio (www.coachella.com).
Date late Apr.
The biggest rock festival in the US takes place over a weekend in the Coachella Valley, where a *Spin*-tastic line-up of acts entertain crowds well into five figures. The 2006 event featured Depeche Mode, Franz Ferdinand, Madonna and Cat Power, among others.

Topanga Banjo Fiddle Contest, Dance & Folk Arts Festival

Paramount Ranch, 2813 Cornell Road, off Mulholland Hwy, Agoura (1-818 382 4819/ www.topangabanjofiddle.org). **Date** mid May.
Running annually since 1961, this homey little event brings together folk musicians, dancers and artists for a variety of performances, lessons and competitions.

Playboy Jazz Festival

Hollywood Bowl, 2301 N Highland Avenue, at Odin Street, Hollywood (1-310 450 1173/ www.playboy.com). **Date** June.
Hugh Hefner might drop by, but you can ignore the sponsorship in favour of a high-profile slate of Latin, fusion, bebop, big band and Dixieland acts.

Woodland Hills Concerts in the Park

Warner Ranch Park, 5800 Topanga Canyon Boulevard, between Califa & Marylee Streets, Woodland Hills (1-818 704 1358/www.valley cultural.org). **Date** Jun-Aug.

Grab a blanket, pack a picnic and settle in for a free night of music at the Lou Bredlow Pavilion. Held on 13 Sundays during summer, the programme includes top pop, classical, folk and world music performers.

Central Avenue Jazz Festival

Around the Dunbar Hotel, 4225 S Central Avenue, between 42nd & 43rd Streets, South Central (1-323 234 7882). **Date** late July.
Two days of music, discussion and art. The venue adds resonance: the historic Dunbar, built in 1928, was America's first luxury hotel for blacks, and hosted the likes of Billie Holiday and Louis Armstrong.

Arthurfest

Barnsdall Art Park, 4800 Hollywood Boulevard, Los Feliz (www.arthurmag.com).
Date Sept.
The first of what will hopefully become an annual festival was held in 2005, and was a roaring success. Programmed by estimable magazine *Arthur*, the line-up is devoted to art-rock, psychedelia, noise-rock and all sorts of other unimaginable dins.

Catalina Island JazzTrax Festival

Avalon Casino Ballroom, 1 Casino Way, Avalon, Santa Catalina Island (1-760 323 1171/www.jazztrax.com). **Date** early-mid Oct.
The already middlebrow Santa Catalina Island is made even more so by the arrival of this festival of smooth jazz, held over three weekends in the landmark Avalon Ballroom.

Silverlake Lounge

2906 W Sunset Boulevard, at Parkman Avenue, Silver Lake (1-323 663 9636/www.foldsilverlake.com). Bus 2, 4, 302, 304/US 101, exit Silver Lake Boulevard north. **Open** 8pm-2am Tue-Thur.
Admission $5-$10. **No credit cards. Map** p314 C4.
Depending on which night you visit, this hangout will either be a grungy watering hole favoured by transvestites or a grungy club favoured by indie bands and the women that love (and probably feed) them. Although the sound is dire and the beer smell is sometimes overpowering, ascendant indie rockers (Fiery Furnaces, Devendra Banhart) or local acts (Wiskey Biscuit, Helen Stellar) usually deliver.

Smell

247 S Main Street, between 2nd & 3rd Streets, Downtown (www.thesmell.org). Metro Pershing Square/bus 16, 316/I-110, exit 4th Street east. **Open** from 9pm daily. **Admission** $5. **Credit** AmEx, MC, V. **Map** p315 C3.

The closest thing to a European squat-style venue in LA, this stark, hard-to-find warehouse-like space near Skid Row hosts the latest in indie-noise, political art-punk and the like. The Smell doesn't serve booze, and thus attracts an all-ages crowd skewed young. Veggie-friendly snacks are available.

Spaceland

1717 Silver Lake Boulevard, at Effie Street, Silver Lake (1-323 661 4380/www.clubspaceland.com). Bus 201/US 101, exit Silver Lake Boulevard north. **Open** from 9pm daily. **Admission** $7-$20. **Credit** AmEx, MC, V. **Map** p314 C3.
Spaceland remains the leading LA shrine to all things indie, with industry showcases introducing the likes of Nine Black Alps and Test Icicles to local audiences. The sound isn't great and parking is a combat sport, but at least there's a patio for smokers. The Monday-night programme features free monthly residencies for local buzz bands on their way up.

Tangier

2138 Hillhurst Avenue, at Avocado Street, Los Feliz (1-323 666 8666/www.foldsilverlake.com). Bus 180, 181/US 101, exit Hollywood Boulevard east. **Open** *varies.* **Admission** *$5-$10.* **No credit cards.** **Map** p314 B1.

Despite the North African name, this intimate boite on a cool street in the hip Los Feliz area favours genre-defying chamber-indie sounds such as Devics, Great Northern and local fave Eleni Mandell, a smokily eccentric songstress with elastic pipes. The venue typically draws a very cool East Side crowd.

Temple Bar

1026 Wilshire Boulevard, at 11th Street, Santa Monica (1-310 393 6611/www.templebarlive.com). Bus 20, 720, SM2/I-10, exit Lincoln Boulevard north. **Open** *8pm-2am daily.* **Admission** *$5-$10.* **Credit** *AmEx, MC, V.* **Map** p310 B2.

This Santa Monica neo-souled-out lounge mixes things up with an Afrocentric roster of shows that takes in largely laid-back indie hip hop, funk, dance (King Britt is a fave) and the odd bit of organic rock.

Troubadour

9081 Santa Monica Boulevard, at N Doheny Drive, West Hollywood (1-310 276 6168/www.troubadour. com). Bus 4, 304/I-405, exit Santa Monica Boulevard east. **Open** *varies.* **Admission** *free-$30.* **Credit** *AmEx, MC, V.* **Map** p312 A2.

Elton John made his US debut at the Troub during the club's salad days, when it nurtured the careers of Jackson Browne, Warren Zevon and Tom Waits. The thrillingly intimate venue hosts acts of taste and substance: the schedule featured early shows from Arcade Fire and Bloc Party, while Franz Ferdinand made its LA debut here. The sound system is one of the strongest in town.

Viper Room

8852 W Sunset Boulevard, at Larrabee Street, West Hollywood (1-310 358 1880/www.viperroom.com). Bus 2, 105, 302/I-10, exit La Cienega Boulevard east. **Open** *hrs vary, daily.* **Admission** *free-$20.* **Credit** *AmEx, MC, V.* **Map** p312 A2.

Clumsy punk acts and Hollywood detritus of varying vintage play this scrappy little hole on the Sunset Strip, once owned by Johnny Depp and forever notorious as the venue at which River Phoenix keeled over and died.

Whisky A Go-Go

8901 W Sunset Boulevard, at N San Vicente Boulevard, West Hollywood (1-310 652 4202/www. whiskyagogo.com). Bus 2, 105, 302/I-10, exit La Cienega Boulevard north. **Open** *6.30pm-2am daily.* **Admission** *$10-$15.* **Credit** *MC, V.* **Map** p312 A2.

The Doors were once the house band at the Whisky, until the owner objected to the lyrics of 'The End' and banned the group. Its place in Sunset Strip lore can't be denied, but these days, the music comes mostly from classic-rock tribute acts (Led Zepagain, anyone?) and young acts of the punk/metal variety, few of whom you'll ever hear of again. Or want to.

Roots & blues

Country, folk and – yes – Irish music join imported beers on the menu at **Molly Malone's** (575 S Fairfax Avenue, Miracle Mile, 1-323 935 1577, www.mollymalonesla.com). Despite the recent shaky status of its lease, the **Derby** (4500 Los Feliz Boulevard, Los Feliz, 1-323 663 8979, www.the-derby.com) offers swing bands every week. For the **Conga Room**, where you can catch Latin acts, *see p239.*

Babe & Ricky's Inn

4339 Leimert Boulevard, at 43rd Street, Leimert Park (1-323 295 9112/www.bluesbar.com). Bus 42, 210, 305, 608, 710/I-10, exit Crenshaw Boulevard south. **Open** *10am-2am Mon, Thur-Sat.* **Tickets** *$5-$10.* **Credit** *AmEx, MC, V.*

Both an established blues club, one of the oldest in LA, and an authentic one, in its acts and its location in the African-American neighbourhood of Leimert Park. The vibe is friendly and the acts are smokin' (don't miss house band Bill Clark & the Mighty Balls of Fire), and Mama Laura's fried chicken is magic.

BB King's Blues Club

Universal CityWalk, 1000 Universal Studios Boulevard, Universal City (1-818 622 5464/www. bbkingclubs.com). Metro Universal City/bus 96, 156, 166/US 101, exit Universal Center Drive. **Open** *5pm-1am Mon-Thur; 5pm-2am Fri, Sat; Sun varies.* **Admission** *$10-$30.* **Credit** *AmEx, DC, Disc, MC, V.*

Local guitar slingers and the odd national R&B name ply their trade at the LA branch of King's Memphis supper club, the most down-to-earth joint on Universal City's hideously plastic CityWalk.

Catalina Bar & Grill. *See p244.*

Harvelle's

1432 4th Street, between Broadway & Santa Monica Boulevard, Santa Monica (1-310 395 1676/www. harvelles.com). Bus 4, 304, SM1, SM2, SM3, SM4, SM10/I-10, exit 4th-5th Street north.
Open 8pm-2am daily. **Admission** $3-$10; 2-drink min. **No credit cards. Map** p310 A3.

Santa Monica's self-styled home of the blues – though you'll catch a little funk and jazz here too – is often smokin'. The comfy bar/lounge setting is packed at weekends; it pays to show up early.

McCabe's

3101 Pico Boulevard, at 31st Street, Santa Monica (1-310 828 4497/www.mccabesguitar.com). Bus SM7/I-10, exit Centinela Avenue south.
Open varies. **Admission** $5-$30. **Credit** AmEx, DC, Disc, MC, V. **Map** p310 A4.

By day a revered guitar shop, McCabe's doubles as an intimate performance space. The roster includes rootsy singers such as Rosanne Cash and Ralph Stanley, but also includes curveballs such as Will Oldham's Superwolf. Gigs are usually held on Fridays, Saturdays and Sundays.

Jazz

The city's jazz circuit is scattered from pillar to post. Aside from the venues below, all manner of bars, hotels and restaurants host jazz acts, many of them top-notch sessioneers playing as much for pleasure as for pay. In addition, a few club nights feature prime talent from the avant-garde jazz scene: **Rocco** (www.roccinla.com), which sets up shop Downtown at Café Metropol (923 E 3rd Street, 1-213 614 1357, www.cafe metropol.com), **Cryptonight/Cryptonoche** (www.cryptonight.com) at Club Tropical (8641 Washington Boulevard, Culver City, 1-310 559 1127); and bassist Nick Rosen's **Monday Jazz Night** at the Temple Bar (*see p243*).

Baked Potato

3787 N Cahuenga Boulevard, at Lankershim Boulevard, North Hollywood (1-818 980 1615/www. thebakedpotato.com). Bus 96, 150, 156, 240, 750/ US 101 north, exit Lankershim Boulevard south.
Open 7pm-2am daily. **Shows** 9.30pm, 11.30pm daily. **Admission** $10-$30; 2-drink min. **Credit** AmEx, Disc, MC, V.

Don Randi's pint-sized room spawned the LA jazz fusion sound in the 1970s. It's still the site of synth-driven romps, though Latin jazz acts appear too (as, in the past, has onetime MC5er Wayne Kramer). Famous session sidemen show up incessantly – if you've always wanted to see the guitar player from Toto solo on into the night, this is your joint. The menu is full of – yes! – spuds.

Catalina Bar & Grill

6725 W Sunset Boulevard, between N Highland & N Las Palmas Avenues, Hollywood (1-323 466 2210/ www.catalinajazzclub.com). Metro Hollywood-Highland/
bus 2, 156, 302, LDH, LDHWH/US 101, exit Vine Street south. **Open** 8.30pm-1am Mon-Sat; 7.30pm-1am Sun. **Admission** $10-$30; 2-drink min except for diners. **Credit** AmEx, DC, Disc, MC, V. **Map** p313 A2.

Catalina Popescu pulls jazz's heaviest hitters to her civilised Hollywood establishment. The venue attracts old-timers such as Jimmy Smith, McCoy Tyner and Pharoah Sanders, plus newer stars of the calibre of Branford Marsalis and Joshua Redman. The food isn't as good as the music. **Photo** *p243*.

Jazz Bakery

3233 Helms Avenue, at Venice Boulevard, Culver City (1-310 271 9039/www.jazzbakery.org). Bus 33, 333/I-10, exit La Cienega Boulevard south.
Open Shows 8pm, 9.30pm Mon-Sat; 4pm, 8.30pm Sun. **Admission** $10-$35. **Credit** AmEx, MC, V.

Although iconoclasts such as Bill Frisell sometimes wrest the stage from players such as Mose Allison and Dave Grusin, this extremely cultured, not-for-profit aficionados' hangout in Culver City generally plays it straight ahead. The name comes from its location in the old Helms Bakery building.

La Ve Lee

12514 Ventura Boulevard, at Whitsett Avenue, Studio City (1-818 980 8158/www.laveleejazzclub. com). Bus 150, 240, 750/US 101, exit Laurel Canyon Boulevard south. **Open** 7-11pm Tue-Sat. **Shows** 8.30pm & 10.30pm Tue-Sat. **Admission** varies; 2-drink min. **Credit** MC, V.

A Studio City institution, La Ve Lee serves up everything from hardcore fusion to Latin funk to full-on Steely Dan tributes; you might even see ex-Prince percussionist Sheila E glamorously jamming the night away. The Mediterranean food ain't bad, either.

Vibrato

2940 Beverly Glen Circle, at Beverly Glen Boulevard, Bel Air (1-310 474 9400/www.vibratogrilljazz.com). I-405, exit Sunset Boulevard east. **Open** 5.30-11pm Tue-Sat. **Shows** times vary, nightly. **Credit** AmEx, MC, V.

Co-owned by Herb Alpert, this high-end steakhouse books better talent than one could ever expect for a Westside crowd who probably think jazz begins and ends with Diana Krall. The food is terrific, too, and you might catch Will Smith or LAPD Police Chief William Bratton nodding their heads to the likes of Bobby Hutcherson, Kenny Barron and local bass legend John Heard. Reservations are recommended.

World Stage

4344 Degnan Boulevard, between 43rd Street & 43rd Place, Leimert Park (1-323 293 2451/www. theworldstage.org). Bus 40, 210, 305, 710/I-10, exit Crenshaw Boulevard north. **Open** varies. **Admission** $5-$10. **No credit cards.**

Strictly for the hardcore jazz fan, this Leimert Park space, founded by drummer Billy Higgins, is where local cats come to hone their chops. It really is all about the music here: there's no food, no booze and no dancefloor. Big names sometimes sit in, but it's the young unknowns who'll knock you out.

Nightclubs

Flash? Dance.

Circus Disco. *See p246.*

Nowhere is LA's fascination with glamour and beauty more evident than on its nightclub circuit, which grows glammier almost by the day. And nowhere is this attitude more obvious than in Hollywood: formerly scuzzy around the edges, it's now awash with super-glitzy, mega-stylish and hyper-hip clubs that fit the Angeleno archetype to a tee.

As such, the scene is by no means vibrantly trend-setting, in terms of either nightclub decor or music. No matter: entrepeneurs continue to open and reopen venues at a terrifying rate, and promoters shimmy and shuffle their nights to make the most of crowds desperate to be one step ahead of the pack. LA's latest nightlife boom mirrors the bigger-is-better, spectacle-driven vogue in Las Vegas casinos, in its eye-popping race to excess. But you want originality? C'mon: this is Hollywood, the land of a thousand sequels.

The contest to be the brightest and the biggest means that what's new and hip today can become old hat tomorrow. One strategy

Bliss (3465 W 6th Street, Koreatown) Vincent and Max go clubbing in *Collateral*

employed by a number of movers and shakers to combat this predicament has been to build a buzz by holding invitation-only celebutante soirées for the first months of a club's existence. When Joe Public is finally allowed to come in, the pent-up demand will keep the club rammed, even though the stars have moved elsewhere. A newer crop of spots, among them Rokbar and the Red Buddha Lounge, have attempted to be high-end while creating a more inclusive vibe, welcoming proles along with A-listers. But whichever venue you favour, a Lohan, Simpson or Hilton twin will likely have been there first.

Apart from the clubs listed here, many bars – especially in Hollywood – host DJs, spinning everything from microhouse to Bollywood. For gay-oriented clubs, *see pp228-235*.

PRACTICAL INFORMATION

While venues come and go regularly, individual club nights chop and change almost weekly. See *LA Weekly* for details of what's on when you're here. Some venues are open seven days a week, but most operate a more limited schedule, with a scattering of weekday nights warming up the venue for the big events on Fridays and Saturdays. Don't leave home without photo ID: all clubs 'card' people at the door, and if you can't prove you're 21 (a few venues are open to over-18s), you won't be allowed inside. Arrive before 11pm for a better chance of entry.

Admission prices vary just as much as opening times. Some gigs early in the week come with free admission; on weekends, you'll likely end up paying upwards of $20 in most of the big Hollywood clubs. Tickets are available in advance from some venue websites or from www.ticketmaster.com. The situation is complicated further by the prevalence of guest lists at many venues. Some are accessible via an email to the promoters (check club websites or www.la.com), others may be accessible if you tip a wink to your hotel's concierge, while others still are genuinely exclusive. Speaking of which, any clubgoer in LA is likely to run into the dreaded velvet rope at some point; *see p248*. You'll be able to pay for your drinks with a card (given the prices, it's a necessity), but few clubs accept credit cards at the door.

After a series of busts from the Drug Enforcement Agency (DEA), club owners have tightened security. Suffice to say, that hash pipe carelessly left in a pocket or the bottle of champagne brought for your friend's birthday will be confiscated. If you make it past the rope, you may be given a wristband or a hand stamp, which will allow you to get served at the bar. And always carry the number of a reliable, affordable cab firm; you can't just flag one down on the street here. *See p287* for details.

Akbar

4356 W Sunset Boulevard, at Fountain Avenue, Silver Lake (1-323 665 6810). Bus 2, 26, 175, 302/ US 101, exit Vermont Avenue north. **Open** 7pm-2am Mon-Thur, Sat, Sun; 6pm-2am Fri. **Admission** free-$5. **Credit** AmEx, MC, V. **Map** p314 B3.
This Moroccan-themed dive is currently enjoying a rebirth after adding a second bar and a dancefloor.

Surprisingly, the casual vibe isn't ruined by the dance scene, which attracts a comfortably mixed crowd of gays and straights as well as the usual Silver Lake bohemians. Thursdays are memorable for the rump-bumpin' Dirty Dirty House Club.

Avalon

1735 N Vine Street, at Hollywood Boulevard, Hollywood (1-323 462 8900/www.avalonhollywood. com). Metro Hollywood-Vine/bus 180, 181, 210, 212, 217, 710, LDH/US 101, exit Hollywood Boulevard west. **Open** 10pm-6am Sat. **Admission** $15-$35. **Credit** AmEx, MC, V. **Map** p313 B1.
The longtime residency of Giant (www.giantclub. com) kickstarted the local dance scene in the 1990s, but the hipness quotient hasn't evaporated from this capacious venue despite the span of years that have elapsed. The music policy remains house-heavy, but don't be surprised to see the superstar DJs toss some techno and trance into the mix.

Basque

1707 Vine Street, at Hollywood Boulevard, Hollywood (1-323 464 1654/www.basquehollywood. com). Metro Hollywood-Vine/bus 180, 181, 210, 212, 217, 710, LDH/US 101, exit Hollywood Boulevard west. **Open** varies. **Admission** free-$20. **Credit** AmEx, MC, V. **Map** p313 B1.
The sexy decor of this space draws equally sexy clubbers, and the Berlin Wall of bouncers like to keep it that way: even by LA's standards, this is a highly exclusive club. Hip hop and R&B are the staples here, though Sunday offers a very Hollywood mix of alt-rock and house. Bring a credit card.

Cabana Club

1439 N Ivar Avenue, at Sunset Boulevard, Hollywood (1-323 463 0005/www.cabanaclub hollywood.com). Metro Hollywood-Vine/bus 180, 181, 210, 212, 217, 710, LDH/US 101, exit Sunset Boulevard west. **Open** 9pm-2am Wed-Sat. **Admission** free-$20. **Credit** AmEx, MC, V. **Map** p313 B2.

Highlands. *See p248.*

Are you ready for your close-up?

American tabloids are stuffed with pictures of celebrities stumbling out of nightclubs in the small hours, shot by pavement-lurking paparazzi who'll go to any lengths to get the snap that'll pay their mortgage. But a new breed of club photographer is lurking around the clubs of LA, and, unlike the paparazzi, they don't have to lurk out front: they're inside, invited to all the hottest parties and very much part of the scene. And, what's more, they want pictures of you.

Promoters are constantly on the lookout for new, non-traditional ways to increase awareness of their events, and their latest tool is photo-blogging. There are plenty of websites dedicated to people's pictures of their previous night's adventures: www.clubzone.com, www.inlist.com, www.liquidexposure.com, www.lastnights party.com and www.clubplanet.com, to name only a few of the many out there. But 21-year-old photographer Mark Hunter, aka the Cobra Snake, is a photoblogger with a difference: he makes a living from it.

Where once he sneaked into parties, Hunter now gets invited to them: by hipsters, by promoters, even by corporations. Once inside, he points and shoots; the next morning, he uploads images of the night's drunken festivities to his www.thecobrasnake.com.

Around the clubs, he's shot Paris and Nicky Hilton, Beck, André 3000, and Jarvis Cocker. But in fact celebrities aren't his focus, nor the focus of the promoters and marketing people who throw the parties: a ground-level, word-of-mouth buzz is worth its weight in publicity gold. We, the punters the publicists are pursuing, might just be looking for a good laugh on the morning after, but the promoters are seeing their brand or club virally connecting with a wider audience.

Even if you weren't there, these websites are fun to scan: you can vicariously experience the hipster scene through them. The Cobra Snake site is unedited and uncensored, and comes with something of a deliberately amateurish look. However, in this age of reality TV, its candidness has struck a chord: so much so, in fact, that the producers of *The Real World* and *The Simple Life* are planning a reality show around Hunter, who already has a book deal and a column in *LA Weekly*.

So when someone asks to take your picture at the latest club, it's worth remembering that no matter where in the world your nearest and dearest live, they can see exactly what you got up to the previous evening by clicking on these photoblog sites. Fame or infamy? Your call.

The scenery at this Sardinian-styled oasis is far removed from the blaring horns and hot dog carts on nearby Sunset: 10-foot waterfalls, 40-foot palm trees and 16 eponymous tented cabanas are centred around a shimmering pool. You may pay wildly for the privilege – there's dreaded bottle service for the best tables – but that's the A-list for you.

CineSpace

6356 Hollywood Boulevard, at Ivar Avenue, Hollywood (1-323 817 3456/www.cine-space.com). Metro Hollywood-Vine/bus 180, 181, 210, 212, 217, 710, LDH/US 101, exit Hollywood Boulevard west. **Open** 6pm-2am daily. **Admission** varies. **Credit** AmEx, MC, V. **Map** p313 B1.

The film capital of the world is the perfect home for this multimedia venue. Start your evening with dinner and a movie in the dining/screeing room at the back, then head into the club and make the scene to a soundtrack that could cover hip hop, alt-rock or fashionable electronica.

Circus Disco

6655 Santa Monica Boulevard, between N Las Palmas Avenue & Seward Street, Hollywood (1-323 462 5508/www.circusdisco.com). Bus 4, 156, 304/ US 101, exit Santa Monica Boulevard west. **Open** *Club 9am-2pm Mon, Tue, Fri, Sun; 9pm-4am Sat.* **Admission** $20. **No credit cards. Map** p313 A2.

At a massive 22,000sq ft (2,000sq m), there's room for you, all your friends and just about everyone else at Circus, where the promotional roster is highlighted by Saturday's Spundae. Designed with one eye on the European superclubs, the club attracts a fine roster of top international DJs who spin funk, house, trance, disco and more. Adjacent is the gay-slanted Arena (www.arenanightclub.com)

El Centro

6202 Santa Monica Boulevard, at N El Centro Avenue, Hollywood (1-323 957 1066/www.elcentrola. com). Bus 4, 156, 304/US 101, exit Santa Monica Boulevard west. **Open** varies. **Admission** varies. **Credit** AmEx, MC, V. **Map** p313 B2.

After the skeeziness of the neighbourhood and the back alley entrance (off Eleanor Avenue) this sleek mahogany and brick-adorned club comes as a pleasant surprise, although that surprise doesn't extend to the degraded stone floors. Although it has specific DJ nights, the club stands out for its Thursday night residency of live R&B band Funkin Pie.

We 🚫 LA Velvet ropes

The use of the velvet rope outside nightclubs, barring entry to the common folk unless the all-powerful bouncer approves of your haircut/shoes/bosoms (delete as applicable), rises and falls with the years. Unfortunately, in 21st-century LA, the damn things are everywhere, thanks in no small part to the extraordinary value currently placed on celebrity. Hollywood has always ensured that the ropes go up if there are stars in the house – indeed, the concept evolved from using red-velvet matinée barriers to keep the press and public at bay at Hollywood premières. The technique has spun off a variety of approaches, from special 'passwords' to signless, phoneless anonymity, but the bouncer-manned rope out front remains the default method of imbuing some high-priced, fly-by-night cocktail bars with a little exclusivity.

But how do you get past the red barrier to the nirvana within? If you're a well-groomed woman in your twenties with most of your teeth, you've got it made. If you're a gentleman, the requirements are similar to those for breaking into the porno-film industry: dress smart, tan weekly, work out daily, moisturise hourly and turn up with a sexy lady on each arm, each wearing enough jewellery – and, for that matter, silicone – to distort their spinal columns.

While the Red Buddha Lounge (*see p174*), the Blu Monkey Lounge (*see p173*) and

RokBar (*see p249*) have declared themselves open to everyone, a terrifying number of nightclubs rely on their door staff to flavour the scene just *so*. Among them are Guy's, Basque, the Tropicana at the Roosevelt, El Centro and LAX. When you see big beefy guys in black suits and walkie-talkie headsets holding clipboards, start smiling and give no lip: honey, no matter how artificial, goes further than vinegar. Or you could always just go drink somewhere else.

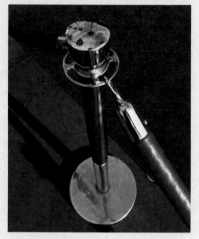

Gabah

4658 Melrose Avenue, at Ardmore Avenue, Hollywood (1-323 664 8913/www.gabah.net). Bus 10, 11, 206/ US 101, exit Melrose Avenue west. **Open** 7pm-2am Mon-Thur, Sat, Sun; 6pm-2am Fri. **Admission** varies. **Credit** AmEx, MC, V. **Map** p313 D3.
Gabah (Arabic for 'jungle') mixes up the people more than the music: you may hear snatches of Latin, acid jazz and funk, but hip hop is the main ingredient in the mix. Weekends bring live shows, with artists such as Ozomatli and the Breakestra occasionally dropping by to perform at the Chocolate Bar, LA's longest running hip hop club.

Guy's

8713 Beverly Boulevard, at San Vincente Boulevard, West Hollywood (1-310 360 0290). Bus 14, 16, 105, 316, LDF, LDHWH/I-10, exit La Cienega Boulevard north. **Open** varies. **Admission** varies. **Credit** AmEx, MC, V. **Map** p312 B3.
Located on the edge of Beverly Hills, this is one LA's hottest new clubs, and thus, of course, one of its most

exclusive. The place boasts the sort of Bogartian vibe that is appropriate for the lexically challenged gangstas who normally frequent the place. Actor Danny Masterson attempts to create a Harlem renaissance jazz club vibe on Sundays.
Other locations: Guy's North, 12655 Ventura Boulevard, Studio City (1-818 766 8311).

Highlands

6801 Hollywood Boulevard, at N Highland Avenue, Hollywood (1-323 461 9800/www.thehigh landsla.com). Metro Hollywood-Highland/bus 156, 210, 212, 217, 710, LDH/US 101, exit Hollywood Boulevard west. **Open** varies. **Admission** free-$20. **Credit** AmEx, Disc, MC, V. **Map** p313 A1.
Live like a movie star for an evening at this palace. The vistas are absolutely breathtaking, the LA skyline in immense panorama. It's a big place: over 25,000 square feet, with a huge dancefloor and – hello smokers! – three outdoor decks. The music policy tends towards hip hop, but you won't find out for yourself unless you dress up.

Ivar

6356 Hollywood Boulevard, between N Cahuenga Boulevard & Ivar Avenue, Hollywood (1-323 465 4827/www.ivar.cc). Metro Hollywood-Vine/bus 180, 181, 210, 212, 217, 710, LDH/US 101, exit Hollywood Boulevard west. **Open** 9pm-2am Fri, Sat. **Admission** varies. **Credit** AmEx, Disc, MC, V. **Map** p313 B1.

The look is *Starship Enterprise* meets industrial warehouse, with 25ft ceilings, plush red seats, four bars, an outdoor patio and a tiny dancefloor. However, you're not at the Ivar to dance but to people-watch, and the buff and beautiful LA archetypes who head here make staring a pleasure. Dress up.

Joseph's Café

1775 Ivar Avenue, at Yucca Street, Hollywood (1-323 462 8697/www.josephscafe.com). Metro Hollywood-Vine/bus 180, 181, 210, 212, 217, 710, LDH/US 101, exit Hollywood Boulevard west. **Open** *Lounge/nightclub* 7pm-2am Mon-Thur, Sat, Sun; 6pm-2am Fri. **Credit** AmEx, MC, V. **Map** p313 B1.

This vintage slice of Hollywood history, in business since the 1940s, has been reborn in recent years. It still serves food (for breakfast and lunch, as well as in the evenings), but it's also now a lounge and, later at night, a swank club with a varied programme.

LAX

1714 N Las Palmas Avenue, at Hollywood Boulevard, Hollywood (1-323 464 0171/www.laxhollywood.com). Metro Hollywood-Highland/bus 156, 210, 212, 217, 710, LDH/US 101, exit Hollywood Boulevard west. **Open** 10pm-2am Wed, Fri-Sat. **Admission** varies. **Credit** AmEx, MC, V. **Map** p313 A1.

Happily, the name is a clue not to the location (it's in Hollywood) but the decor: LAX carries an airport-lounge theme, albeit without the hordes of screaming infants and solitary fat businessmen slumped over laptops. The music policy varies, but the door policy is unwavering: if they don't know who you are, you'll face an uphill battle simply to get in.

Mayan Theatre

1038 S Hill Street, at W Olympic Boulevard, Downtown (1-213 746 4287/www.clubmayan.com). Bus 2, 4, 30, 31, 40, 42, 45, 56, 58, 302/I-110, exit Olympic Boulevard east. **Open** varies. **Admission** $10-$25. **Credit** AmEx, MC, V. **Map** p315 B4.

Not all of Downtown's grand old theatres are in such good shape these days, but the Mayan, built in 1927, is doing quite nicely, thank you. There are occasional gigs here, but the real action is on weekends: Mixxx on Friday offers glamour-friendly house sounds, while Saturday's Tropical is one of the biggest salsa nights in the city.

Mood

6623 Hollywood Boulevard, at Cherokee Avenue, Hollywood (1-323 464 6663). Metro Hollywood-Highland/bus 156, 210, 212, 217, 710, LDH/US 101, exit Hollywood Boulevard west. **Open** 9pm-2am Tue-Sun. **Admission** $20. **Credit** AmEx, MC, V. **Map** p313 A1.

The bold and the beautiful of Hollywood's after-hours circuit flock to this impossibly hip hangout, blessed with a location that's come into its own in recent years. The decor is exotic in a modish way, which is more than can be said for the largely mainstream music. Still, celebs love it, and where they go, the rest of us can only follow.

Mor Bar

2941 Main Street, at Ashland Avenue, Ocean Park (1-310 455 6720/www.themorbar.com). Bus 33, 333/I-10, exit 4th-5th Street south. **Open** 5pm-2am daily. **Admission** varies. **Credit** AmEx, MC, V. **Map** p310 A4.

The nightclub scene in Santa Monica has never been exciting, to put it mildly, but this recent arrival has injected it with some much-needed pep. Earlier in the week sees the venue draw a younger collegiate crowd, while weekends yield an older but equally cool clientele of Hollywoodites who come to the beach to hear the likes of Miguel Migs.

Naçional

1645 Wilcox Avenue, at Hollywood Boulevard, Hollywood (1-323 962 7712/www.nacional.cc). Metro Hollywood-Vine/bus 180, 181, 210, 212, 217, 710, LDH/US 101, exit Hollywood Boulevard west. **Open** 7pm-2am Mon-Thur, Sat, Sun; 6pm-2am Fri. **Admission** free-$20. **Credit** AmEx, MC, V. **Map** p313 B1.

This intimate Cuban-themed lounge is the latest home for the Bud Brothers' Monday Social, a venerable house club that draws big names for guest slots on the decks from time to time. The rest of the week sees rather more hip hop on the agenda, but the crowd remains much as it is on Monday: stylish, rich and, occasionally, famous.

Privilege

8117 W Sunset Boulevard, at Crescent Heights Boulevard, West Hollywood (1-323 654 0030/www.sbeent.com). Bus 2, 302, LDHWH/I-10, exit La Cienega Boulevard north. **Open** varies. **Admission** varies. **Credit** AmEx, MC, V. **Map** p312 C1.

Located in former heavy-metal hangout the Coconut Teaszer, this swanky place lives up to its name. This is velvet rope territory: if your name's not down, you may not be coming in. The look is a WeHo take on art deco. The schedule changes regularly.

RokBar

1710 N Las Palmas Avenue, at Hollywood Boulevard, Hollywood (1-323 461 5600/www.rokbaronline.com). Metro Hollywood-Highland/bus 156, 210, 212, 217, 710, LDH/US 101, exit Hollywood Boulevard west. **Open** 7pm-2am daily. **Credit** AmEx, MC, V. **Map** p313 A1.

With a fashionable Hollywood location and an ownership coterie that includes Tommy Lee and Dave Navarro, a celeb-studded clientele is only to be expected at this foxy lounge. Naturally enough, glossy rock music features heavily on the sound system, but the fashions draped over the clientele wouldn't go down too well at CBGB.

Arts & Entertainment

Vanguard

6021 Hollywood Boulevard, at Bronson Avenue, Hollywood (1-323-463-3331/www.vanguardla.com). Metro Hollywood-Vine/bus 180, 181, 210, 212, 217, 710, LDH/US 101, exit Hollywood Boulevard west. **Open** 9pm-2am Mon-Thur, **Admission** $10. **Credit** AmEx, MC, V. **Map** p313 B1.

You may need a *Thomas Map Guide* to negotiate this massive venue, but it's worth the effort. The posh sound system pumps out a pleasingly egalitarian selection of music over the various themed nights, everything from danceable electro and drum 'n' bass (remember that?) to headier rock tunes.

Vine Street Lounge

1708 N Vine Street, at Hollywood Boulevard, Hollywood (1-323 464 0404/www.vinestreetlounge. com). Metro Hollywood-Vine/bus 180, 181, 210, 212, 217, 710, LDH/US 101, exit Hollywood Boulevard west. **Open** varies. **Admission** varies. **Credit** AmEx, MC, V. **Map** p313 B1.

This corner hotspot was hip even before it opened, thanks in no small part to its enviable location at the centre of the T-town nightlife. DJs spin everything from funk to rock, with occasional live spots.

White Lotus

1743 N Cahuenga Boulevard, at Hollywood Boulevard, Hollywood (1-323 463 0060/www.white lotushollywood.com). Metro Hollywood-Vine/bus 156, 210, 212, 217, 710, LDH/US 101, exit Cahuenga Boulevard south. **Open** *Club* 9pm-2am Tue-Sat. *Restaurant* 6pm-12.30am Tue-Sat. **Credit** *Bar & restuarant only* AmEx, MC, V. **Map** p313 B1.

This Asian-themed club opened in 2003 and almost immediately started a big buzz that hasn't wholly evaporated. Here's a tip: go for dinner early in the evening and you'll avoid the large queues that start around 10pm. Another tip: dress to impress to get past the velvet rope.

XES

1716 N Cahuenga Blvd, at Hollywood Boulevard, Hollywood (1-323 461 8190). Metro Hollywood-Vine/bus 156, 210, 212, 217, 710, LDH/US 101, exit Cahuenga Boulevard south. **Open** varies. **Admission** varies. **Credit** AmEx, MC, V. **Map** p313 B1.

Pronounced 'excess', the name of this dimly lit decadanceteria on the Cahuenga Corridor pretty much demands you lower your inhibitions. Go-go dancers work the poles to a soundtrack largely built around hip hop and R&B, with a little yacht rock thrown in on mock-trashy Truck Stop Thursdays.

Strip clubs

With America under a conservative leadership, strip clubs don't have the draw they did during the excesses of the Clinton years. Most clubs run newspaper ads offering free or discounted admission, and some have free lunch buffets. To find out who's performing, check the listings at the back of the *LA Times*' sports pages, the *LA Weekly* and local adult-happenings rag *LA XPress* (available in bins along many major streets). Most clubs are topless only, chiefly because clubs licensed for full nudity are barred from serving alcohol.

Body Shop

8250 W Sunset Boulevard, at N Harper Avenue, West Hollywood (1-323 656 1401/www.thebodyshop clubla.com). Bus 2, 302, LDHWH/I-10, exit La Cienega Boulevard north. **Open** noon-4.30am daily. **Admission** $10; 2-drink min. **No credit cards.** **Map** p312 B1.

This club on the Sunset Strip – in the city of West Hollywood, and so not affected by some of the stricter laws regarding nudity and alcohol – is a venerable showgirl palace. Totally nude, and late opening too.

Crazy Girls

1433 N La Brea Avenue, between W Sunset Boulevard & De Longpre Avenue, Hollywood (1-323 969 0055). Metro Hollywood-Highland/bus 2, 156, 212, 302, 304, LDH, LDHWH/US 101, exit Highland Avenue south. **Open** noon-2am daily. **Admission** $5 after 6pm; 2-drink min. **Credit** AmEx, Disc, MC, V. **Map** p313 A2.

Crazy Girls is something of a multi-tasker: as well as dancers, it offers pool tables and televised sports. But most people are here to look at the girls.

Forty Deuce

5574 Melrose Avenue, at N Gower Street, Hollywood (1-323 465 4242/www.fortydeuce.com). Bus 10, 11, LDHWI/US 101, exit Gower Street south. **Open** 9pm-2am Wed-Sat. **Admission** $10. **Credit** AmEx, Disc, MC, V. **Map** p313 B3.

Ivan Kane's burlesque club is for people too scared, chic, ironic, famous or fashionable to go to strip clubs. Forty Deuce (the name's a nod to *42nd Street*) has girls swooping and shimmying to a jazz trio in plush surroundings. Rather ironically, you have to dress up to get in.

Hollywood Tropicana

1250 N Western Avenue, at La Mirada Avenue, Hollywood (1-323 464 1653). Bus 156, 207/US 101, exit Santa Monica Boulevard west. **Open** 8pm-2am Tue-Sat. **Admission** $10; 2-drink minimum. **No credit cards.** **Map** p313 C2.

Lingerie and mud wrestling are on the menu at this infamous strip club in the shadow of US 101, made famous by the Mötley Crüe song 'Girls, Girls, Girls'.

Jumbo's Clown Room

5153 Hollywood Boulevard, between N Winona Boulevard Drive & N Normandie Avenue, Hollywood (1-323 666 1187/www.jumbos.com). Bus 180, 181, 206/US 101, exit Hollywood Boulevard west. **Open** 3pm-2am daily. **Admission** free. **Credit** AmEx, Disc, MC, V. **Map** p313 D1.

Female-run Jumbo's has been in business for over 30 years (licensed as a 'bikini bar', which means the dancers wear pasties) and is as much bar as strip joint. There's a goodly number of women punters, drawn by the anything-but-identikit dancers.

Sports & Fitness

Just for a change, get out of the car.

Even in a city built around the car, you don't always need four wheels. *See p255.*

Blessed with a climate that simply demands outdoor activities, Southern Californians are legendary for indulging in everything under the gorgeous Californian sun when it comes to getting physical. Sure, people spend hours each week in their cars, the terrible air quality challenges even the most hardy set of lungs and there's not much of a pedestrian culture, but don't be fooled: this is still one of the healthiest cities in America.

For sporting goods stores, *see p202.*

Spectator sports

As the second-largest sports market in the United States (after New York), Los Angeles features an abundance of athletic franchises, most of which have a passionate and devoted followings. A great number of them – including the town's hockey team, its arena football outfit and all three of its basketball franchises – are based at the state-of-the-art 19,000-seat **Staples Center** in Downtown, which also hosts everything from concerts (*see p238*) to political conventions.

INFORMATION & TICKETS

The sports section in the *LA Times* lists the teams' games and broadcast schedules each day. If you want to look further ahead, check each team's individual websites, or the comprehensive and easy-to-navigate site run by sports TV network ESPN at www.espn.com.

As a first step, it's best to approach individual teams' box offices for advance individual-game tickets, but prepare to be disappointed. LA Lakers games routinely sell out, for example, while the very best seats at LA Dodgers matches are sold as part of season-ticket packages. If that approach fails, then try the ubiquitous if rather expensive **Ticketmaster** (1-213 480 3232, www.ticketmaster.com). An even riskier approach is to buy tickets from unauthorised touts – aka scalpers – who wait outside the venue before the game starts. If you do decide to buy tickets from them, be sure to double-check the date before you hand over your money. Selling tickets for games that have already happened is the oldest trick in the scalper's book, but people still fall for it.

A tale of two owners

For more than four decades, the rivalry between the Dodgers and Angels baseball clubs was profoundly one-sided. Quite simply, the Dodgers were LA's team, drawing over three million fans a season while their less-glamorous cousins out in Anaheim were lucky to attract half that number. But since 2002, when the Angels won their first World Series championship, popular sentiment among local baseball fans has begun to shift. And if new Angels owner Arte Moreno has his way, the Angels will soon be the number one team in the Southern California market.

The first Latino owner in baseball history, Moreno purchased the Angels from the Walt Disney Company in 2003, and immediately won favour with fans by reducing the price of beer at Angels Stadium. Historically, the Angels' players and followers were both predominantly white, but since seizing the reins, Moreno has aggressively marketed the team to Southern California's sizeable Latino

community, and stocked the team's roster with such talented Latino players as Vladimir Guerrero and Bartolo Colon. Under Moreno's watch, the Angels have been one of the best teams in the American League, with attendance figures to match: they drew 3.4 million fans during the 2005 season, the fourth best in major league baseball.

The Dodgers, on the other hand, have lost much of their lustre in the eight years since longtime owners the O'Malley family sold the team to Rupert Murdoch's Fox News Corporation. The Fox tenure was marked by an endless series of poor management and personnel decisions, but things haven't exactly improved under Boston real estate developer Frank McCourt, who bought the team from Fox in 2004 and has already presided over some dreadful trades and signings. Some observers have wondered if McCourt is really more interested in the development possibilities of the Chavez Ravine area surrounding Dodger Stadium.

But while Dodger fans have grown frustrated with the chaos surrounding their club, the team still drew 3.6 million fans during 2005, a season in which the team posted its second worst win-loss record since the team moved to LA from Brooklyn in 1958. Clearly, the Dodgers' popular dominance will be hard to supplant, and Moreno's decision to change his team's name from the Anaheim Angels to the Los Angeles Angels of Anaheim – a move that resulted in a local fan backlash, a lawsuit from the city of Anaheim and tons of negative PR – will probably hold him back in the short term. But if the Angels continue to dominate their division, and the Dodgers continue squandering the goodwill of fans, Los Angeles could really be Angel City before too long.

Baseball

The Major League Baseball (MLB) season runs from April until late September/early October, whereupon the top four teams from each of the two leagues (the American and the National) begin four weeks of play-off games. *See also above* **A tale of two owners**.

Los Angeles Angels of Anaheim

Angel Stadium of Anaheim, 2000 Gene Autry Way, between Katella & Orangewood Avenues, Anaheim, Orange County (information 1-888 796 4256/

tickets 1-714 634-2000/www.angelsbaseball.com). *Bus OC50, OC57/I-5, exit Katella Avenue east.* **Tickets** $5-$110. **Credit** AmEx, MC, V.
The Angels' surprise World Series victory in 2002 is now very much in the rear-view mirror. Indeed, in one regard, the team is literally unrecognisable: new owner Arte Moreno, who bought the team in 2003, changed its name from the Anaheim Angels to the peculiarly tautological Los Angeles Angels of Anaheim in a bid to draw more fans. A very successful 2005 season, in which they topped the standings in the American League West, was followed by defeat in the ALCS by the Chicago White Sox, who

Arts & Entertainment

went on to win the World Series. Competition in the AL West will always be fierce, most of it coming from the over-achieving Oakland A's. But though the Angels' minor-league system isn't stacked with talent, the major-league roster, led by pitcher Bartolo Colon and outfielder Vladimir Guerrero, is strong enough that the Angels ought to contend for the forseeable future. The team's ballpark might lack character in comparison to Dodger Stadium, but it's still an entirely pleasant place to take in a game.

Los Angeles Dodgers

Dodger Stadium, 1000 Elysian Park, at Stadium Way, Echo Park (1-323 224 1448/www.dodgers. com). Bus 2, 4, 302, 304/I-110, exit Dodger Stadium north. **Tickets** $10-$80. **Credit** AmEx, Disc, MC, V.
While the Angels are stuck in a tough division, the Dodgers have it relatively easy: in 2005, the National League West was shocking, a black hole of under-achievement topped ('won' seems too strong a word) by the San Diego Padres. The Dodgers, meanwhile, struggled to one of their worst seasons in years; spurred on by a witch-hunt orchestrated by a handful of local sportswriters who won't be happy until wizened old geezer Tommy Lasorda is rehired to run the club, owner Frank McCourt fired manager Jim Tracy and general manager Paul DePodesta.

Lured down from San Francisco, new GM Ned Colletti proceeded to stock the 2006 roster with ageing former Giants. Placed next to some of DePodesta's more dubious signings (always-injured outfielder JD Drew and erratic pitcher Derek Lowe were granted ridiculously lucrative contracts under his watch), Colletti's team looks set to struggle. But in such a weak division, they still might have enough talent to make the postseason. And regardless, the fans will keep coming: understandably so, since Dodger Stadium is one of the nicest venues in the major leagues. If you can't make a game, at least tune in to hear Vin Scully, the greatest broadcaster in baseball, call one on TV or radio.

Basketball

The National Basketball Association (NBA) season starts in late October/early November and runs until mid April. Then the league's best teams enter the playoffs, which end in mid June.

When the regular season is finished, the WNBA hoves into view, beginning in May and wrapping up in September. Led by hometown hero Lisa Leslie, the **Los Angeles Sparks** draw pretty good crowds to their games at the Staples Center; for tickets, call 1-877 447 7275 or see www.wnba.com/sparks.

Los Angeles Clippers

Staples Center, 1111 S Figueroa Street, at 11th Street, Downtown (1-800 462 2849/ www.nba.com/clippers). Metro Pico/Downtown buses/I-110, exit Olympic Boulevard east. **Tickets** $10-$1,000. **Credit** AmEx, Disc, MC, V. **Map** p315 A5.

To suggest that the Clippers have been slightly over-shadowed in the last decade by the rival Lakers (*see below*) is akin to offering that LA might have a slight traffic problem. The Clippers have stunk for as long as anyone can remember: going into the 2005-06 season, they'd won just four playoff games in three decades and hadn't finished the regular season with a winning record since 1991-92. Perhaps understandably, few owners are more loathed by the fans of his team than Donald Sterling ('quixotic and capricious', say ESPN, clearly in a generous mood).

At last, though, things may just be changing. The Lakers' lacklustre play during the 2005-06 regular season was coupled with a wholly unexpected but entirely welcome Clipper resurgence, led by Sam Cassell and the estimable Elton Brand. With young point guard Shaun Livingston primed for brilliance in years to come, the future looks bright. No wonder the crowds are finally beginning to show up.

Los Angeles Lakers

Details as per LA Clippers above, except: www.nba.com/lakers. **Tickets** $10-$2,100.
While baseball has the New York Yankees and soccer has Manchester United, the Los Angeles Lakers are the team everybody loves to hate in the NBA. For 'hate', read 'beat': there's not a player in the league who doesn't enjoy putting one over on arguably the most glamorous team in American sports.

It's rarely been easier to do so: following years of dominance, the Lakers have suffered through a couple of decidedly lacklustre seasons, missing the playoffs entirely in 2004-05 and only just squeaking into the post-season the following year. The departure of iconic centre Shaquille O'Neal has hit the team extremely hard: though Kobe Bryant regularly puts up splashy numbers, scoring a preposterous 81 points in a single game against the Toronto Raptors in 2006, he's hardly a team leader, and the team has struggled to find a way to play around him.

Like the Clippers, the team play at the Staples Center. Unlike the Clippers, they draw a crowd packed with Hollywood stars (including, courtside, a permanently sunglassed Jack Nicholson).

Football

Despite being the second city of the United States, Los Angeles has been without an NFL team since the Raiders returned to Oakland in 1996. However things may be about to change. The NFL has been in discussion with various consortiums about possible methods by which to bring a team to the city, either by moving a struggling franchise across the country or by adding a 33rd team to the league. It's hoped that, one way or another, there'll finally be some NFL action in LA for the 2008 season, though no one's sure exactly where that action is likely to take place: the Coliseum looks the most likely venue, but both Carson and Anaheim are possibilities.

Arts & Entertainment

The **Los Angeles Avengers** (1-310 788 7744, www.laavengers.com) bring a little rough and tumble to the Staples Center between February and June in the Arena Football League (AFL), but interest is greater in the college game. Under head coach Pete Carroll, the storied **USC Trojans** (1-213 740 4672, www.usctrojans.com) have become one of the greatest teams in college football history; they play at the Los Angeles Coliseum (3911 S Figueroa Street). The **UCLA Bruins** (1-310 825 2101, www.uclabruins.com), who play at the Rose Bowl in Pasadena (1001 Rose Bowl Drive), struggle by comparison, but still draw passionate crowds. The college season runs September to November; the grand finale is the bevy of bowl games played across the country on New Year's Day, of which the most famous is at the Rose Bowl.

Horse racing

There are three racetracks in the LA area, all of which feature flat racing. Call or check online for post times; expect to pay around $5 to get in.

Hollywood Park Race Track & Casino *1050 S Prairie Avenue, between 90th Street & Century Boulevard, Inglewood (1-310 419 1500/www. hollywoodpark.com). Bus 211, 212/I-405, exit Manchester Avenue east.*
Los Alamitos Race Course *4961 Katella Avenue, at Walker Street, Los Alamitos, Orange County (1-714 995 1234/www.losalamitos.com). Bus OC50/I-5, exit Katella Avenue west.*
Santa Anita Park *285 W Huntington Drive, between Baldwin & Santa Anita Avenues, Arcadia (1-626 574 7223/www.santaanita.com). Bus 79, 264/I-210, exit Baldwin Avenue south.*

Hockey

The National Hockey League (NHL) regular season runs from October to early April, and is followed by two months of playoffs.

Los Angeles Kings

Staples Center, 1111 S Figueroa Street, at 11th Street, Downtown (1-888 546 4752/www.lakings. com). Metro Pico/Downtown buses/I-110, exit Ninth Street or Olympic Boulevard. Tickets $24.50-$385.50. Credit AmEx, Disc, MC, V. Map p315 A5.
Ice hockey in Southern California may seem slightly ridiculous, but the Kings try their darnedest to get the locals interested. The crowds they draw to the Staples Center are decent and surprisingly enthusiastic; it's just a pity the team's not up to much.

Mighty Ducks of Anaheim

Arrowhead Pond, 2695 Katella Avenue, at Douglass Road, Anaheim (information 1-877 945 3946/tickets 1-714 703 2545/www.mightyducks.com). Bus OC50, OC53/I-5, exit Katella Avenue east. Tickets $15-$85. Credit AmEx, MC, V.

It's not only their name – perhaps the most ridiculous in all of sports, though the oxymoronic Utah Jazz basketball team provides some stiff competition – that garners the Mighty Ducks of Anaheim attention from locals. The team has long been competitive, progressing all the way to the Stanley Cup Finals in 2003 and comfortably making the playoffs in 2006, thus proving that the idea of ice hockey under the Southern Californian sun is not so odd after all.

Motor racing

The annual glamour event is the **Long Beach Grand Prix**, held on a street circuit in April (*see p200*). The **California Speedway** in Fontana (1-909 429 5000, www.california speedway.com), 90 minutes east of LA just off I-10, hosts an assortment of Nascar and Superbike events between April and October.

Irwindale Speedway

13300 E Live Oak Avenue, at I-605, Irwindale (1-626 358 1100/www.irwindalespeedway.com). Bus FT492/I-605 north, exit E Live Oak Avenue west. Tickets varies. Credit MC, V.
This half-mile paved oval in the San Gabriel Valley, which opened in 1999, is California's first new short track for 20 years. The 6,500-seat venue features a variety of racing from Feb to Nov.

Soccer

Aided by the significant and steadily growing Latino population in Los Angeles, soccer is slowly but surely catching on as a spectator sport. The **LA Galaxy** (1-310 630 2200, 1-877 342 5299, www.lagalaxy.com), which plays at the Home Depot Center in Carson (take I-110 south, exit at 190th Street), has a solid fan base and a team that usually proves competitive in MLS (Major League Soccer). The season runs from April to October.

With that Latino population providing the basis for the thriving 'futbol' culture, there is therefore plenty of opportunities for the many millions of European-Americans living here to get their fix. There is a huge number of amateur teams and leagues, often organised according to native country, which can be seen in action evenings and weekends at high schools, sports grounds and public parks.

Numerous bars and cafés around town show overseas matches on satellite TV; check the sports section of the Spanish newspaper *La Opinion* for Spanish-speaking coverage. If you want to watch catch up on the English Premiership, try the **Cock & Bull** in Santa Monica (2947 Lincoln Boulevard, at Pier Avenue, 1-310 399 9696), which shows several games live or as-live each week when they're beamed in on pay-per-view.

Unleash your inner Tiger on LA's public courses. *See p256.*

Participation sports

Baseball batting cages

More Major Leaguers hail from California than any other US state. Small wonder, then, that batting cages abound in Los Angeles and its environs. Whatever your skill level – whether you're ready to take a swing at a fastball or are striving to work on hitting the curve – there are plenty of batting cages with multi-speed automated pitching machines. Among the most popular are **Batcade** in Burbank (220 N Victory Boulevard, 1-818 842 6455, http://batcade.com) and the long-established **Batting Cages** in Glendale (620 E Colorado Street, 1-818 243 2363). Both are open daily (usually until around 10pm); expect to pay around $8 for 15 minutes in a cage, or $23-$25 for an hour. Bats and helmets are provided.

Bowling

Bowling is popular in LA. Check the phone book or ask your concierge for one near you.

AMF Bay Shore Lanes

234 Pico Boulevard, between Main & 3rd Streets, Santa Monica (1-310 399 7731/www.amf.com). Bus 33, 333, SM1, SM2, SM7, SM8, SM10/I-10, exit 4th-5th Street south. **Open** 9am-midnight Mon-Thur, Sun; 9am-2am Fri, Sat. **Rates** $4.75/person; $4.25 shoe rental. **No credit cards. Map** p310 A3.
Santa Monica's main bowling alley has a bar that's a favourite with local cops.

Lucky Strike Lanes

Hollywood & Highland, 6801 Hollywood Boulevard, at N Highland Avenue, Hollywood (1-323 467 7776/www.bowlluckystrike.com). Metro Hollywood-Highland/bus 210, 212, 217, 710, LDH, LDHWH/US 101, exit Highland Avenue south. **Open** 11am-2am daily. **Rates** $4.95-$7.95/person; $3.95 shoe rental. **Credit** MC, V. **Map** p313 A1.
This 12-lane alley is a homage to bowling alleys of the past, with cartoon-sexy wait staff and a dress code (no athletic or baggy clothes) that aims to get bowlers into the spirit of the age.

Cycling

It's easy to bike long distances in Los Angeles, but be sure to take plenty of water and some sunscreen. Riding off-road isn't actually legal, but there haven't been any efforts to stop the cyclists who weave through the **Santa Monica Mountains**, home to the most popular and accessible mountain biking areas: numerous fire trails jut off Mulholland Boulevard from Beverly Hills to Topanga and Malibu. You may have to squeeze under a gate or two, but keep pedalling until you reach the peaks. Bear in mind that while the wilds are generally safe, there are dangers out there: in 2004, two cyclists were attacked, one fatally, by a mountain lion in Orange County. **Topanga State Park** in Topanga (1-310 454 8212, www.parks.ca.gov) and **Malibu Creek State Park** in Calabasas (1-818 880 0367, www.parks.ca.gov) may seem out of the way, but the tracks are well worth it.

The most appealing bike trails in the city, both for scenery and lack of traffic, run along the beaches. The **South Bay Bicycle Trail**, more commonly known as the **Strand**, runs 22 miles from Will Rogers State Beach to Torrance, while the **Huntington Beach Bicycle Trail** extends eight miles south from Sunset Beach. Many oceanfront stalls in Santa Monica and Venice rent beach bikes, usually with one gear and pedal brakes; for anything more serious, visit a proper bicycle shop, such as **Spokes 'n' Stuff** (1715 Ocean Front Walk, Santa Monica, 1-310 395 4748). Expect to pay $15-$25 a day.

Inland, **Griffith Park** has more than 14 miles of bike trails, but some are MTB-accessible only and many are quite hilly. Visit **Woody's Bicycle World** (3157 Los Feliz Boulevard, 1-323 661 6665) for information.

Fishing

Free public fishing is popular at the piers of many local beaches: try **Santa Monica Pier** (the nearest), **Seal Beach**, **Redondo Beach** or **Manhattan Beach**. A licence is not required. For freshwater fishing, try the public park system's **Echo Park Lake** (1-213 250 3578) and **Lincoln Park Lake** in Lincoln Heights (1-213 237 1726). A much bigger lake is **Castaic Lake** in the Los Angeles National Forest north of LA. Fishing parties are a good way to get out and do some deep-sea fishing at a spot where the fish are biting.

Redondo Sport Fishing

233 N Harbor Drive, at W Beryl Street, Redondo Beach (1-310 372 2111/www.redondosport fishing.com). Bus 130, 439/I-405, exit Artesia Boulevard west. **Open** *Office* 5am-8pm daily. **Rates per person** *Half-day trip* $32; $27 children. *Full-day trip* $50; $35 children. **Credit** AmEx, MC, V. Call for exact trip departure times, which vary with the seasons, and for details of boat charters. The company also hosts whale-watching trips running from late Dec.

Golf

The City of Los Angeles Department of Recreation & Parks runs 13 municipal courses around the city: seven 18-hole courses, three nine-hole circuits and three nine-hole par-three

set-ups. In order to book a tee time in advance, you'll need a registration card, available at any public course, from 1-818 291 9980, or at www.laparks.org. The card costs $20/year for LA residents and $40 for non-residents. Without a card, it's a case of turning up at the course and taking your chances. Always call ahead to find out your chances before setting out.

For a full list of municipal courses, see www.laparks.org. Among them are a nine-hole, par-three course in **Los Feliz** (reservations not required; 3207 Los Feliz Boulevard, 1-323 663 7758); a popular complex containing a 18-hole course and a nine-hole, par-three course in **Rancho Park** (10460 W Pico Boulevard, 18-hole: 1-310 838 7373, nine-hole: 1-310 838-7561); the 36-hole **Sepulveda Golf Complex** in Encino (16821 Burbank Boulevard, 1-818 995 1170); and the **Harding** and **Wilson** courses in Griffith Park (4730 Crystal Springs Drive, 1-323 663 2555). Rates run from $4 in Los Feliz up to $28.50 for a weekend round on an 18-hole course.

Hiking

LA has some fantastic places to hike, from Griffith Park and the Santa Monica Mountains (including the Hollywood Hills) to the San Gabriel Mountains. All are quickly and easily accessible, at least if you have a car). The local chapter of the venerable **Sierra Club** (1-213 387 4287, http://angeles.sierraclub.org) runs an astonishing 4,000 outings each year in the area; check their website for details.

Horse riding

LA still taps into the Old West archetype of the cowboy, and horse riding is concomitantly popular. In Griffith Park, you can rent horses from the **Los Angeles Equestrian Center** (480 Riverside Drive, Burbank, 1-818 840 9063, www.la-equestriancenter.com); for riding in the Hollywood Hills, try **Sunset Ranch** (3400 Beachwood Drive, 1-323 464 9612, www.sunset ranchhollywood.com). Expect to pay around $20 an hour at both. Both offer lessons.

Pool & billiards

Hollywood Billiards

5750 Hollywood Boulevard, at N Wilton Place, Hollywood (1-323 465 0115/www.hollywoodbilliards. com). Metro Hollywood-Western/bus 180, 181, 217/ US 101, exit Hollywood Boulevard east. **Open** 11am-2am daily. **Rates** $8-$17/hr. **Credit** AmEx, MC, V. **Map** p313 C1.
There are almost as many draft beers as pool tables in this smart Hollywood fixture: 30 of the former, 32 of the latter. DJs play on weekend evenings.

Yankee Doodles

1410 Third Street Promenade, between Broadway &
Santa Monica Boulevard, Santa Monica (1-310 394
4632). Bus 4, 304, SM1, SM3, SM4, SM5/I-10, exit
4th-5th Street north. **Open** 11am-2am daily. **Rates**
$8-$16/hr. **Credit** AmEx, Disc, MC, V. **Map** p310 A3.
This sports bar has 26 pool tables and assorted
arcade games (foosball, air hockey, soft-tip darts).
Big-screen TVs complete the sporting picture.

Rock climbing

With places like El Capitan in Yosemite National
Park within easy reach, it's no surprise there
are plenty of climbing facilities available in the
city. One of the best outdoor climbing areas is
at the south end of Point Dume at **Zuma
Beach** (*see p77*), while **Will Rogers State
Historic Park** in Pacific Palisades (*see p74*)
includes the famed Inspiration Point, one of the
highest peaks in the Santa Monica Mountains.

Rockreation

11866 La Grange Avenue, at S Westgate Avenue,
West LA (1-310 207 7199/www.rockreation.com).
Bus SM10, SM14/I-10, exit Bundy Drive north.
Open noon-11pm Mon, Wed; 6am-11pm Tue, Thur;
noon-10pm Fri; 10am-6pm Sat, Sun. **Credit** AmEx,
MC, V.
Use of the facilities here, at one of LA's better indoor
climbing walls, costs $16 a day. There are classes
available for everyone from beginners to experts.

Rollerblading & skateboarding

For rollerbladers, there's no place like the
Strand, an immaculate, paved path stretching
along the coast. Public parks along the beach
also serve as gathering points for quality
skaters who like to rehearse their tricks before
an audience. Other tranquil spots include
Griffith Park, **Ocean Front Walk** in Venice
Beach and **Sepulveda Dam Recreation
Center** in the San Fernando Valley.

SkateLab Skate Park

4226 Valley Fair Street, between Vanessa & Winifred
Streets, Simi Valley (1-805 578 0040/www.skatelab.
com). US 118, exit Stearns Street south. **Open** times
vary. **Admission** $6-$13. **No credit cards**.
Owned by former Dodger pitcher Scott Radinsky,
SkateLab is a mecca for boarders and BMXers, with
two half-pipes and numerous smaller ramps and
obstacles. You'll need to sign a waiver form to skate;
under-18s will need a parent's signature. If you've
time, check the museum.

Rollerskating

Pick-up games of rollerhockey can – and
frequently do – take place on open stretches of
pavement virtually anywhere in Los Angeles.

Venice's legendary **Muscle Beach**.

If you've come with rollerskates and are looking
for some action, good places to look include the
beach parking lot just north of Ocean Park in
Santa Monica, and at the **West Hollywood
Park & Recreation Center** (647 N San
Vicente Boulevard).

Moonlight Rollerway

5110 San Fernando Road, at Hawthorne Street,
Glendale (1-818 241 3630/www.moonlightrollerway.
com). Bus 94, 394/US 134, exit San Fernando Road
south. **Open** times vary. **Admission** $6; $3 skate
rental. **No credit cards**.
This longstanding rink up in Glendale holds a variety of events: Saturdays, for example, are for children only, while Sunday nights are only open to
over-30s. Moonlight has rollerskates for hire, but not
blades or inline skates.

Scuba-diving

The best places to dive are off **Leo Carillo
State Beach**, **Laguna Beach**, **Redondo
Beach** and **Palos Verdes**, but if you're really
serious, head to **Santa Catalina Island** (*see
p278*) or the **Channel Islands** (*see p267*).
As a cursory acquaintance with TV will tell
you (*Baywatch* comes to mind), most of the LA
coastline consists of miles of sloping sand, but
the coastal islands have rocky shores with plenty
of kelp beds, fish and shipwrecks to explore.

Arts & Entertainment

Surfing

Those miles of golden sand that make up Southern California's world-famous beaches are used for more than just sunbathing and posing. If you really want to hook into the California lifestyle, you need to get on a surfboard. But don't expect to ride a wave quickly: it can take weeks just to learn to sit on the board properly, let alone negotiate the whitewash standing up. Windsurfing is even harder.

Most novice surfers opt for the easier-to-learn alternatives: boogie-boards (aka bodyboards), body surfing and skim-boarding. If you're learning to surf, choose a wide-open beach break such as **Zuma Beach** (*see p77*), **Will Rogers State Beach** (*see p74*; the surfing is best where Sunset Boulevard meets the Pacific Coast Highway), **Santa Monica Beach** (*see p77*) or El Porto at **Manhattan Beach** (*see p79*). Intermediate surfers can find excellent beach breaks at **Manhattan, Hermosa, Redondo** and **Huntington Beaches** (*see p131*). Only experienced surfers should test their skill at the competitive, surfers-only point breaks, such as **Topanga State Beach** (near the intersection of PCH and Topanga Canyon Road), **Surfrider Beach** (by PCH and Cross Creek Road, just north of Malibu Pier), and the **Wedge**, an extremely dangerous break at the end of Balboa and Ocean Boulevards at the top of the Balboa Peninsula in Orange County.

Plenty of places hire surfboards, among them the excellent **ZJ Boardinghouse** in Santa Monica (*see p202*), **ET Surf** in Hermosa Beach (904 Aviation Boulevard, 1-310 379 7660, www.etsurf.com) and **Malibu Ocean Sports** in Malibu (22935 PCH, 1-310 456 6302, www.malibuoceansports.com). Expect to pay anywhere from $10 an hour up to around $25-$30 a day for board hire. The seriously keen, though, may care to investigate the **Paskowitz Surfing Camps** in San Diego, a series of relatively expensive but highly regarded five-day training camps held weekly from June to Labor Day. For details, call 1-949 728 1000 or check www.paskowitz.com.

For surfing and beach conditions, call the Surfing Conditions Hotline on 1-310 578 0478, check with the Department of Beaches & Harbors on 1-310 305 9503 or see http:// beaches. co.la.ca.us. There's more on surfing at www.surfdiva.com, www.surfersvillage.com and, especially, www.surfline.com. For a round-up of the best beaches in Los Angeles, *see p202* **Life's a beach**.

Swimming

For the best beaches for swimming, *see p68* **Life's a beach**. There are also a number of freshwater alternatives. At **Echo Park Recreation Center** (1632 Bellevue Avenue, at Glendale Boulevard, 1-213 250 3578), there's an outdoor swimming pool at the lake, though the lake itself is for fishing, not swimming. The majority of the city's YMCAs (*see p259*) also contain swimming pools.

Surfing USA.

Tennis & racquetball

There are a number of tennis courts scattered around the parks of LA. For a full list, see www.laparks.org. **Griffith Park** has tennis courts ($5-$8/hour) at two sites: 12 lit ones at Griffith/Riverside (1-323 661 5318) and 12 unlit ones at Griffith/Vermont Canyon (1-323 664 3521). On weekdays before 4pm, they're available on a first come, first served basis; after 5pm, you can book if you have a registration card. Cards cost $15 for residents and $30 for non-residents; see the above website or call 1-323 644 3536 for details.

You can find tennis and racquetball courts at most gyms in LA; book a couple of days in advance. Or try the tennis centres, such as the **La Cienega Tennis Center** (325 N La Cienega Boulevard, West Hollywood, 1-310 550 4765), the **Burbank Tennis Center** (1515 N Glenoaks Boulevard, Burbank, 1-818 843 4105, www.burbanktenniscenter.com) and the **Studio City Golf & Tennis Center** (4141 Whitsett Avenue, Studio City, 1-818 761 3250); ask your hotel concierge to recommend others.

Whale-watching

Whale-watching provides California's most extraordinary wildlife experience. The annual season, off the Southern California coastline, is in winter (December to March), following the migratory habits of the gray and wright whales, the two most common species. In **Santa Barbara** (*see p268*), whale-watching reaches its peak in summer, ending in mid-September. Most marinas have numerous boats offering whale-watching trips and many operate on a 'sightings guaranteed' basis: if you don't see any whales, your money is refunded, or you're given a pass to go free on a subsequent trip.

Sea Landing

Santa Barbara Harbor, off Harbor Way, Santa Barbara (1-805 963 3564/www.condorcruises.com). US 101, exit Cabrillo Way west. **Rates** $35-$75; $18-$30 children; free under-5s. **Credit** Disc, MC, V.
Board the *Condor* to view the whales feeding off Santa Barbara. Expeditions incorporate the Painted Cave, the world's largest underwater sea cave.

Fitness

Dance & fitness classes

Arthur Murray Studio

262 N Beverly Drive, between Dayton Way & Wilshire Boulevard, Beverly Hills (1-310 274 8867/www.dancestudios.com). Bus 20, 21, 720/I-10, exit Robertson Boulevard north. **Open** 1-10pm Mon-Fri. **Credit** AmEx, MC, V. **Map** p311 D3.

A conservative dance studio that will teach you just about any step from ballroom to swing.
Other locations: throughout the city.

Gyms

There are gyms all over LA; the following are open to non-members. YMCAs often have gyms. For gay-friendly gyms, *see p232*.

Gold's Gym

360 Hampton Drive, at Rose Avenue, Venice (1-310 392 6004/www.goldsgym.com). Bus 33, 333, SM1, SM2/I-10, exit Lincoln Boulevard south. **Open** 4am-midnight Mon-Fri; 5am-11pm Sat, Sun. **Rates** *Non-members* $20/day; $70/wk. **Credit** AmEx, Disc, MC, V. **Map** p310 A5.
Gold's bills itself as 'the mecca of bodybuilding', and perhaps with some justification: this is where the Governor of California honed and toned his body.
Other locations: throughout the city.

24-Hour Fitness

8612 Santa Monica Boulevard, at N La Cienega Boulevard, West Hollywood (1-310 652 7440/www.24hourfitness.com). Bus 4, 105, 304, LDHWH/I-10, exit La Cienega Boulevard north. **Open** 5am-midnight Mon-Fri; 7am-11pm Sat, Sun. **Rates** *Non-members* $15/day. **Credit** AmEx, MC, V. **Map** p312 B2.
Right in the heart of West Hollywood, this branch offers a pool, sauna, weights, aerobics and even cardio kick-boxing.
Other locations: throughout the city.

YMCAs

Santa Monica Family YMCA

1332 6th Street, between Santa Monica Boulevard & Arizona Avenue, Santa Monica (1-310 393 2721/www.ymcasm.org). Bus 4, 304, SM1, SM8, SM10/I-10, exit 4th-5th Street north. **Open** 6am-10pm Mon-Fri; 7am-8pm Sat; 8am-8pm Sun. **Rates** *Non-members* $15/day. **Credit** AmEx, Disc, MC, V. **Map** p310 B3.
Racquetball and handball, weights, a lap pool, spa, aerobics, volleyball and a running track on the roof.
Other locations: throughout the city.

Yoga

Yoga shows few signs of waning in popularity. Below are two good studios, both of which run a variety of classes. Call for details.

Exhale Center for Sacred Movement *245 S Main Street, between Rose Avenue & Navy Street, Venice (1-310 450 7676/www.sacredmovement.com). Bus 33, 333, SM1, SM2/I-10, exit Lincoln Boulevard south.* **Classes** $16. **Credit** MC, V. **Map** p310 A5.
Yoga Works *230½ N Larchmont Boulevard, between Beverly Boulevard & 3rd Street, Hollywood (1-323 464 1276/www.yogaworks.com). Bus 14, 210, 710, 714/I-10, exit La Brea Avenue north.* **Classes** $17. **Credit** AmEx, MC, V. **Map** p311 B4.
Other locations: throughout LA

Theatre & Dance

High culture where you least expect it.

It turns out that not every performer in LA is aiming to make it on screen. The theatre scene here is lively and varied, offering everything from star-studded musicals to small-scale dramas. There's less dance, but the calendar is still liberally scattered with enticing events.

Advance ticket purchase is recommended. The box office hours given are for days without performances; hours are longer on show days. For details of what's on, see *LA Weekly*; useful websites include www.theatrela.org, www.laplayz.com and www.broadwayla.org.

Theatre

Much to the surprise of many visitors, LA's theatre scene is strong. The movie and TV industries certainly help, their concomitant communities of directors and actors investing time and effort on stage as well as screen. But lest you think that actors treat live theatre as merely a way station to the bright lights and fat cheques of film and television, you'll be amazed at the number of A-listers who emerge from behind the curtain. Productions abound: from full-scale musicals to readings of old radio plays to a dizzying number of one-person shows (LA attracts talent; it also breeds narcissism).

Major venues

John Anson Ford Amphitheatre

2580 Cahuenga Boulevard east, north of Cahuenga Terrace, Hollywood (1-323 461 3673/www.ford amphitheatre.com). Bus 156/US 101, exit Cahuenga Boulevard north. **Box office** *May-Oct* noon-7pm Tue-Sun. *Nov-Apr* 1-6pm Wed-Sun. **Tickets** $7-$35. **Credit** AmEx, Disc, MC, V.

The best Theatre

For homegrown shows
Performing Arts Center. *See right.*

For foreign imports
UCLA Live. *See p264.*

For making a point
Actors' Gang Theatre. *See p263.*

Set against a backdrop of cypress trees, this intimate amphitheatre is a glorious place to hear classical, world music or jazz concerts, or, from June to October, to choose from the variety of dance and theatre events that makes up Summer Nights at the Ford. In autumn and winter, activities move indoors to [Inside] the Ford, a tiny renovated theatre. **Photo** *p261.*

Kodak Theatre

6801 Hollywood Boulevard, at N Highland Avenue, Hollywood (1-323 308 6363/www.kodaktheatre.com). Metro Hollywood-Highland/bus 156, 212, 217, LDH, LDHWH/US 101, exit Highland Avenue south. **Box office** 10am-6pm Mon-Sat; 10am-2.30pm Sun. **Tickets** $30-$99. **Credit** AmEx, MC, V. **Map** p313 A1.

Though it was built with acoustics and sightlines to suit TV (it hosts the Academy Awards), the Kodak also hosts touring Broadway musicals and major dance companies. Half-hour tours of the facility ($15; $10 discounts) are held between 10.30am and 2.30pm daily, depending on the theatre's schedule.

Pantages Theatre

6233 Hollywood Boulevard, between Argyle Avenue & Vine Street, Hollywood (1-213 468 1770/www.nederlander.com/wc). Metro Hollywood-Vine/bus 180, 181, 210, 212, 217, 710, LDH/US 101, exit Vine Street south. **Box office** 10am-6pm daily. **Tickets** $15-$125. **Credit** AmEx, MC, V. **Map** p313 B1.

The art deco beauty of the Pantages was chosen as a suitable backdrop for the first televised Oscar ceremony in 1953, since when it's continued to stage big-budget plays and musicals. If the ornate decor doesn't leave you speechless, perhaps the ghost of eccentric movie mogul Howard Hughes, rumoured to roam the halls, will give you a thrill.

Performing Arts Center of Los Angeles County

135 N Grand Avenue, between W 1st & W Temple Streets, Downtown (Ahmanson & Taper 1-213 628 2772/Chandler 1-213 972 0711/www.musiccenter. org). Metro Civic Center/bus 2, 4, 10, 11, 14, 48, 92, 302, 714/I-110, exit 4th Street east. **Box office** 10am-6pm Mon-Sat. **Tickets** $10-$100. **Credit** AmEx, Disc, MC, V. **Map** p315 B2.

The closest thing LA has to New York's Lincoln Center, this complex (also known as the Music Center) houses several performance spaces. The Ahmanson Theatre seats 2,000 and is one of the city's main venues for big musicals; the 'thrust' stage at the 760-seat Mark Taper Forum features plays by the likes of August Wilson and Neil Simon. The Dorothy Chandler Pavilion and the Walt Disney Concert Hall (for both, *see p237*) are largely devoted to classical

John Anson Ford Amphitheatre.
See p260.

music, but the Chandler does stage dance events from time to time. Leave time to have a drink or a meal in the huge outdoor plaza.

Smaller venues

For **UCLA Live**, which stages a very strong International Theatre Festival in the autumn, *see p264*. Look out, too, for site-specific shows from the likes of the **Zoo District Theatre Company** (www.zoodistrict.org), known for 'unstaging' classic plays in subway terminals, banks and lobbies of old picture palaces.

Carlson Memorial Park

Braddock Drive, between Overland & Motor Avenues, Culver City (1-310 712 5482/www.ccpt. org). Bus C3, C5/I-10, exit Overland Avenue south. **Box office** *varies.* **Tickets** *free.*
This outdoor theatre may not be as lush as the Theatricum Botanicum (*see p262*), but it does add a bit of sparkle to Culver City. In July and August, it's home to the Culver City Public Theatre, which specialises in classical theatre productions.

Coronet Theatre

366 N La Cienega Boulevard, between Beverly Boulevard & Oakwood Avenue, West Hollywood (1-310 657 7377/www.coronet-theatrela.com). Bus 14, 105, LDF, LDHWH/I-10, exit La Cienega Boulevard north. **Box office** *10.30am-5pm Mon-Fri; 12.30-8pm Sat; 12.30-7pm Sun.* **Tickets** $28-$45. **Credit** *AmEx, MC, V.* **Map** *p312 B3.*

This 284-capacity institution has seen its share of celebrities since first opening as long ago as 1947 (prehistoric by LA standards). These days, it hosts local and touring productions, including some Off-Broadway works, plus popular writers' and actors' labs, where homegrown talent gets more talented.

Edgemar Center for the Arts

2437 Main Street, between Hollister Avenue & Norman Place, Santa Monica (1-310 399 3666/www. edgemarcenter.org). Bus 33, SM1, SM8, SM10/I-10, exit Lincoln Boulevard east. **Box office** *9am-6pm Mon-Fri.* **Tickets** $20. **Credit** *MC, V.* **Map** *p310 A4.*
This Frank Gehry-designed venue opened in 2003, hoping to establish itself as the hub of the Santa Monica arts scene. It's begun well. The programming in its two theatres (one with 99 seats, the other with 65) is made up of dance, theatre, stand-up, music and workshops. There's also an art gallery.

Geffen Playhouse

10886 Le Conte Avenue, between Tiverton Avenue & Westwood Boulevard, Westwood (1-310 208 5454/www.geffenplayhouse.com). Bus 2, 302, 305, C6/I-405, exit Wilshire Boulevard east. **Box office** *10am-6pm Mon-Fri; 11am-6pm Sat, Sun.* **Tickets** $24-$46. **Credit** *AmEx, MC, V.*
This charming little theatre, funded in part by entertainment mogul David Geffen, stages works as precious and stylish as its intimate patio, a prime people-watching spot. Plays are a smart selection of classic and contemporary pieces by the likes of Margulies, McPherson and Mamet.

Arts & Entertainment

Kirk Douglas Theatre

9820 W Washington Boulevard, at Culver Boulevard, Culver City (1-213 628 2772/www.taperahmanson. org). Bus 33, 220, 333, C1, C4, C5/I-10, exit Robertson Boulevard south. **Box office** *By phone* 10am-6pm Mon; 10am-8pm Tue-Fri; noon-8pm Sat, Sun. **Tickets** $20-$40. **Credit** AmEx, MC, V.

The highbrow Center Theatre Group adopted this Streamline Moderne movie house in 2004; it's already become a crucial part of the burgeoning Culver City arts scene. The diverse repertoire, including full-scale and in-house minority-promoting workshop productions, makes it a worthy stop.

Pasadena Playhouse

39 S El Molino Avenue, at E Green Street, Pasadena (1-626 792 8672/box office 1-626 356 7529/www. pasadenaplayhouse.org). Bus 180, 181, 401, 402/ I-110 to Arroyo Parkway, exit Colorado Boulevard east. **Box office** noon-6pm daily. **Tickets** $29-$100. **Credit** AmEx, Disc, MC, V.

A Pasadena landmark, the Playhouse opened in 1924; having fallen on hard times in the 1970s, it reopened in 1986 following a painstaking restoration. Plays run the gamut from classic works by Nöel Coward and Tennessee Williams to contemporary pieces by the likes of Kenneth Lonergan.

Reuben Cordova Theatre at Beverly Hills High School

Beverly Hills High School, 241 S Moreno Drive, between Robbins & Young Drives, Beverly Hills (1-310 364 3606/box office 1-310 364 0535/www. theatre40.org). Bus 4, 16, 304/I-405, exit Santa Monica Boulevard east. **Box office** varies. **Tickets** $15-$25. **Credit** AmEx, Disc, MC, V. **Map** p311 C3.

Fans of trashy TV are not usually known for their love of community theatre, but some make a special effort to visit this stage: it's located in Beverly Hills High, the setting for *Beverly Hills 90210*. The repertoire is wide, and you may catch former Hollywood notables treading the boards. Main plays run Thur-Sat, plus a matinee on Sunday.

Santa Monica Playhouse

1211 4th Street, between Wilshire Boulevard & Arizona Avenue, Santa Monica (1-310 394 9779/ www.santamonicaplayhouse.com). Bus 20, 720, SM2, SM3, SM5, SM9/I-10, exit 4th Street north. **Box office** varies. **Tickets** $10-$20. **Credit** MC, V. **Map** p310 A2.

Although it's one of LA's most respected theatres, the Santa Monica Playhouse is currently fighting for survival after a series of rent hikes. Its two theatres present a mix of family shows, European classics – Molière, Strindberg, Ionesco – and experimental works. Performances tend to be on weekends only.

Skirball Cultural Center

2701 N Sepulveda Boulevard, at Skirball Center Drive, Beverly Hills (1-310 440 4500/box office 1-323 655 8587/www.skirball.org). Bus 761/ I-405, exit Skirball Center Drive north. **Box office** noon-5pm Tue, Wed, Fri, Sat; noon-9pm Thur; 11am-5pm Sun. **Tickets** vary. **Credit** AmEx, Disc, MC, V.

The Jewish-American experience is the focus at this multifaceted facility. Most events are one-offs and short runs, but there's also jazz, films, lectures and performance art, and regular taped-for-radio productions by LA Theatre Works in their ongoing 'The Play's the Thing' series (www.latw.org).

Wadsworth Theatre

11301 Wilshire Boulevard, at W San Vicente Boulevard, Brentwood (1-310 479 3003/www.rich markent.com). Bus 20, 720/I-405, exit Wilshire Boulevard west. **Box office** 10am-5.30pm daily. **Tickets** $20-$90. **Credit** AmEx, MC, V.

Since its 2002 renovation, this Mission Revival structure has hosted everything from ballet to *The Good Body*, a one-woman show by *Vagina Monologues* author Eve Ensler. Schedules can be erratic.

Will Geer Theatricum Botanicum

1419 N Topanga Canyon Boulevard, at Cheney Drive, Topanga (1-310 455 3723/www.theatricum.com). Bus 534/I-10, exit PCH north. **Box office** noon-6pm Wed-Fri; 11am-7.30pm Sat, Sun. **Tickets** $15-$25; $12-$15 discounts; free under-6s. **Credit** MC, V.

Better known as Grandpa on *The Waltons*, the late Geer founded this theatre as a haven for blacklisted artists in the 1950s; the outdoor venue is situated in what was his backyard. The resident company has a penchant for Shakespeare and other classic works; its season runs June-Oct.

Wilshire Theatre

8440 Wilshire Boulevard, at N Hamilton Drive, Beverly Hills (1-323 468 1770/www.broadwayla.com/ wilshire). Bus 20, 21, 105, 720/I-10, exit La Cienega north. **Box office** 10am-6pm daily. **Tickets** $20-$200. **Credit** AmEx, Disc, MC, V. **Map** p312 B4.

A fabulous 1920s art deco structure at the edge of Beverly Hills. Whatever the show – religious lectures, Sigur Ros gigs, Jerry Hall disrobing in *The Graduate* – the atmosphere is always intimate.

99-seat theatres

The prevalence and popularity of small theatres in LA stems from the 99-Seat Equity Waiver Agreement, which means theatres with fewer than 100 seats don't have to pay full Equity wages. While some attract big names who don't need the money but could use the extra cred, others deal in experimental works. In addition to those listed below, check out the theatres in North Hollywood for shows in the Off- and Off-Off-Broadway vein (www.nohoartsdistrict. com). If you're in town during October, you can sample the small theatre scene at the Edge of the World Theater Festival ('Edgefest' at www.edgeoftheworld.org), which runs for two weeks with around 50 troupes.

Most theatres are dark on Mondays and Tuesdays; others shut on Wednesdays. Check online for full details of show times. For gay and lesbian theatre, *see p228*.

Actors' Gang Theatre

9070 Venice Boulevard, between Culver & Robertson Boulevards, Culver City (1-323 838-4264/www.theactorsgang.com). Bus 33, 220, 333, C1, C4, C5/I-10, exit Robertson Boulevard south. **Tickets** $6-$25. **Credit** AmEx, MC, V.

Tim Robbins is the artistic director of this theatre, which should give you an idea as to its political tone. The company moved to the Ivy Substation Theatre in Culver City in 2005. Robbins isn't involved with every production, but in 2006 he took the director's chair for a new adaptation of Orwell's *1984*.

Company of Angels Theatre

2106 Hyperion Avenue, at Lyric Avenue, Silver Lake (1-323 883 1717/www.companyofangels.org). Bus 175/US 101, exit Silver Lake Boulevard east. **Box office** *Recorded ticketline* 24hrs daily. **Tickets** $10-$20. **Credit** MC, V. **Map** p314 C3.

This 50-seat theatre, the oldest non-profit repertory company in LA, produces a wealth of superior, socially conscious shows. All are wholly created by its in-house membership troupe.

Electric Lodge

1416 Electric Avenue, at California Avenue, Venice (1-310 306 1854/box office 1-310 823 0710/www.electriclodge.org). Bus 33, 333, C1, SM2/I-10, exit Lincoln Boulevard south. **Box office** *Recorded ticketline* 24hrs daily. **Tickets** $6-$20. **Credit** AmEx, MC, V. **Map** p310 A6.

The Lodge is a solar-powered theatre, presenting low-budget, unusual plays and dance productions typically underscored by social and political themes.

Evidence Room

2220 Beverly Boulevard, at N Alvarado Street, Westlake (1-213 381 7118/www.evidenceroom.com). Bus 14, 200/US 101, exit Alvarado Street south. **Box office** from 1hr before start of performance. **Tickets** $10-$25. **No credit cards**. **Map** p314 C6.

Set up in a rundown Culver City warehouse in 1995, the Evidence Room is one of LA's most daring companies. It's since moved to a grand warehouse, but the shows – from difficult German works to pulp thrillers – have retained their edge.

Hudson Theatres

6539 Santa Monica Boulevard, at N Hudson Avenue, Hollywood (box office 1-323 856 4200/information 1-323 856 4252/www.hudsontheatre.com). Bus 4, 156, 304/US 101, exit Highland Avenue south. **Box office** 24hrs daily. **Tickets** $12-$25. **Credit** MC, V. **Map** p313 A3.

This group of four theatres, housed in an industrial building on Hollywood's so-called Theatre Row, almost never has a bad show. Works run the gamut from musicals to sketch comedy.

MET Theatre

1089 N Oxford Avenue, at Santa Monica Boulevard, Hollywood (1-323 957 1152/www.themettheatre.com). Bus 4, 156, 207, 304/I-10, exit Western Avenue north. **Box office** *Recorded ticketline* 24hrs daily. **Tickets** $20-$25. **Credit** MC, V. **Map** p313 D2.

This company carries with it some serious celeb credentials: A-list founding benefactors include Bette Midler, Kevin Costner and James Cameron, while the productions of classics and contemporary fare have featured the likes of Bill Pullman and Holly Hunter. Look for the annual On the Verge festival, a showcase of new plays and works-in-development.

A Noise Within

234 S Brand Boulevard, between E Colorado & E Harvard Streets, Glendale (1-818 240 0910/www.anoisewithin.org). Bus 92, GB1, GB2, GB4/I-5, exit Colorado Street east. **Box office** 2-6pm Tue-Fri. **Tickets** $20-$40. **Credit** MC, V.

Founded in 1991, this classical theatre company stages quality productions of works by the likes of Shakespeare, Molière and George Bernard Shaw. Look out for occasional special events.

Odyssey Theatre Ensemble

2055 S Sepulveda Boulevard, between La Grange & Mississippi Avenues, West LA (1-310 477 2055/www.odysseytheatre.com). Bus C6, SM5/I-405, exit Santa Monica Boulevard east. **Box office** 1-6pm Tue, Sun; 1-8pm Wed-Sat. **Tickets** $20-$25. **Credit** AmEx, MC, V.

Its exterior is unattractive and in need of a paint job; the lobby is just as uninspiring. But it's what's inside that counts, and the Odyssey delivers. Three small stages host new American plays, international works, political lectures and classics with a twist.

Open Fist Theatre

6209 Santa Monica Boulevard, at Vine Street, Hollywood (1-323 882 6912/www.openfist.org). Bus 4, 156, 304/US 101, exit Vine Street south. **Box office** 24hr answerphone. **Tickets** $15-$25. **Credit** MC, V. **Map** p313 B2.

Founded in 1989, Open Fist focuses on modern works from Arrabal to Brecht. Artistic director Martha Demson has been behind recent triumphs, including Caryl Churchill's *Fen* and the one-man Hemingway show *Papa*. The Directors' Festival in August features four diverse plays in two nights.

Sacred Fools Theatre

660 N Heliotrope Drive, between Melrose Avenue & Clinton Street, Hollywood (1-310 281 8337/www.sacredfools.org). Bus 10, 11, 206/US 101, exit Melrose Avenue east. **Box office** *Recorded ticketline* 24hrs daily. **Shows** 8pm Wed-Sat; 7pm Sun. **Tickets** $5-$25. **Credit** MC, V. **Map** p314 A4.

This witty and wise theatre company is known for its original works, many of them comic: irreverent Christmas shows, political parodies, musicals (such as *Bukowsica!*, a jaunty show about the booze-soaked *Barfly* author) and odd versions of classics.

Theatre of NOTE

1517 N Cahuenga Boulevard, at W Sunset Boulevard (1-323 856 8611/www.theatreofnote.com). Metro Hollywood-Highland/bus 4, 156, 304, LDH, LDHWH/US 101, exit Highland Avenue south. **Box office** *Recorded ticketline* 24hrs daily. **Shows** 8pm, days vary. **Tickets** $15-$20. **Credit** MC, V. **Map** p313 B2.

This 'little theatre that could' celebrated its 25th year of live productions in 2006. The signature shows Late Night Five-Minute One-Act Play Series, plus other maverick works, make Theatre of NOTE a theatrical landmark of sorts in an area of town already surprisingly full of them.

Dance

Major national and international dance companies warm their muscular tootsies in LA all year round, but most come here in autumn and winter. Between times, the homegrown talent fills theatres: Burbank's trad **Media City Ballet** (www.mediacityballet.org), the multi-culti **Lula Washington Dance Theatre** (www.lulawashington.com), the intensely physical **Benita Bike DanceArt Company** (www.danceart.org), the site-specific dance and performance art shows by Heidi Duckler's **Collage Dance Theatre** (www.collagedance theatre.org) and the oft-nude duo **Osseus Labyrint** (www.osseuslabyrint.net).

The graduate dance programmes of **UCLA** (www.ucla.edu; within the Department of World Arts and Cultures), **USC** (www.usc.edu) and **CalArts** (www.calarts.org) turn out performers with a strong grasp of dance history, beyond the boundaries of which they then often deftly advance. Visiting artists find a receptive audience at these schools: small concerts by big figures are common. Look out, too, for dance events in music clubs: Meg Wolfe's monthly showcase Anatomy Riot (www.dancemeg wolfe.org) may set a trend that increases the accessibility of modern dance.

Venues

For the dance-oriented **Dorothy Chandler Pavilion**, *see p237*. For the **Kodak Theatre** and the **Skirball Cultural Center**, *see p260* and *p84* respectively.

Alex Theatre

216 N Brand Boulevard, at E Wilson Avenue, Glendale (1-818 243 2539/www.alextheatre.org). Bus 92, GB1, GB2/I-5, exit Glendale Boulevard north. **Box office** noon-6pm daily. **Tickets** $5-$70. **Credit** MC, V.
The events calendar at this restored movie house takes in all sorts of events, with a fair amount of dance among them.

Carpenter Performing Arts Center

6200 Atherton Street, at Snowden Avenue, Long Beach (1-562 985 7000/www.carpenterarts.org). I-405, exit Palo Verde Avenue south. **Box office** 11am-6pm Mon-Fri; noon-4pm Sat. **Tickets** $20-$50. **Credit** AmEx, MC, V.
Named after 1970s brother-sister pop duo Richard and Karen Carpenter (and funded in part by the surviving Richard), this Long Beach venue presents music concerts, theatre, and great dance. The Diavolo Dance Theatre was a recent worthy visitor.

Grand Performances at California Plaza

Watercourt, 350 S Grand Avenue, between W 3rd & W 4th Streets, Downtown (1-213 687 2159/ www.grandperformances.org). Metro Pershing Square/bus 14, 37, 76, 78, 79, 96/I-110, exit 4th Street east. **Tickets** free. **Map** p315 C2.
Located between high-rises in Downtown LA, this space runs a worthwhile programme of summer presentations, usually a mix of multicultural music and dance performances (and some during lunch hour).

Harriet & Charles Luckman Fine Arts Complex at Cal State LA

5151 State University Drive, between the I-710 & the I-10, Alhambra (1-323 343 6611/box office 1-323 343 6600/www.luckmanfineartscomplex.org). Bus 256, 258/I-10, exit Eastern Avenue north. **Box office** noon-6pm Tue; 10am-6pm Wed-Fri; noon-4pm Sat. **Tickets** $20-$40. **Credit** AmEx, MC, V.
Colleges and universities are always good for the off-beat stuff, and this state-of-the-art theatre doesn't disappoint. Check online for performance details.

Highways at the 18th Street Arts Complex

1651 18th Street, at Olympic Boulevard, Santa Monica (1-310 453 1755/box office 1-310 315 1459/www.highwaysperformance.org). Bus SM5, SM11/I-10, exit 20th Street north. **Box office** Recorded ticketline 24hrs daily. **Tickets** $5-$20. **Credit** MC, V. **Map** p310 C3.
Some really weird stuff happens on the Highways stage. More performance art than strictly dance, the presentations are often incredibly personal and sometimes downright pretentious.

REDCAT (Roy & Edna Disney Cal Arts Theater)

Walt Disney Concert Hall, 631 W 2nd Street, at Hope Street, Downtown (1-213 237 2800/www. redcatweb.org). Metro Civic Center/bus 2, 4, 10, 11, 14, 48, 92, 302, 714/US 101, exit Grand Avenue south. **Box office** noon-6pm Tue-Sat. **Tickets** free-$40. **Credit** AmEx, Disc, MC, V. **Map** p315 B2.
This 270-seat black box theatre at the back of Disney Hall has quickly established itself as the city's hot test venue for avant-garde dance. CalArts graduate students also perform quality concerts here.

UCLA Royce Hall

Royce Drive, between Wilshire Boulevard & Hilgard Avenue, Westwood (1-310 825 4401/box office 1-213 825 2101/www.uclalive.org). Bus 2, 302, 305, 761/I-405, exit Wilshire Boulevard east. **Box office** 10am-4pm Mon-Fri; 10am-2pm Sat, Sun. **Tickets** $20-$100. **Credit** AmEx, Disc, MC, V.
The gloriously refurbished Royce Hall, one of UCLA's original buildings, regularly presents internationally acclaimed dance artists as part of its prestigious UCLA Live arts schedule.

Trips Out of Town

Getting Started	**266**
Heading North	**267**
Heading Inland	**269**
Heading South	**278**

Features

Meet George Jetson…	273
Springs eternal	274
On a mission	281
Over the border	282

Map

Trips Out of Town	266

Joshua Tree National Park.
See p276.

Getting Started

Get out of town!

As you've doubtless realised by now, the Los Angeles urban area has an overwhelming quantity and variety of attractions. But LA is also the gateway to some stunning sights and scenery elsewhere in California and even beyond it. Leave early to beat the traffic, and you'll be away from the smog before you can say 'Hit the road, Jack'.

From LA, you've really got three main options, a fact reflected in the way we've divided this section of the book. Travelling north up the coast will lead you to the undervalued **Channel Islands National Park** and the well-dressed but easygoing town of **Santa Barbara** (Heading North, *pp267-268*). Taking the coast road in the opposite direction will bring you to sunbleached **San Diego** and, across the border, the berserk border town of **Tijuana** (Heading South, *pp278-282*). And if you head east, you'll soon be in the desert, whether isolated in **Joshua Tree** or **Death Valley National Parks**, or crammed into **Palm Springs** and the Coachella Valley (Heading Inland, *pp269-277*).

The easiest – and sometimes the only – way to get to the places listed in this chapter is by car. On some trips, such as those up US 101

towards San Francisco or through the desert, the scenery is so jaw-dropping that the drive itself is as notable as the destination. Reaching all the destinations involves a drive of at least an hour and a half and usually more, depending on whether or not you stick to the speed limit. For information on car hire and tips on driving, *see pp284-286*. It is also possible to travel by plane, train or bus to larger destinations such as Palm Springs and San Diego.

Further gems sit even further from LA. To the north are the natural glories of Big Sur and the buzzing town of San Francisco, LA's polar opposite in so many ways. To the north-east lie the photogenic wonders of Sequoia National Park and Yosemite National Park, not to mention the delightful B&Bs of the Gold Country. And north-east – nearly 300 miles away, makeable in less than four hours if you're lucky with both traffic and police – is the incomparable Nevadan city of Las Vegas. All are featured in the 416-page **Time Out California** (UK: Ebury, £13.99; US: PGW, $19.95), a full guide to the state; also available are **Time Out San Francisco** and **Time Out Las Vegas**, a pair of comprehensive city guides (both – UK: Ebury, £13.99; US: PGW, $19.95).

Trips Out of Town

Heading North

The coast road to riches.

Los Angeles to Ojai

The drive north from LA is a gorgeous one, however you choose to begin it. If you take US 101 from Hollywood, cut down through the untamed **Santa Monica Mountains**. Taking route N1 (aka Las Virgenes Road) will bring you down via the start of the Las Virgenes View Trail: this two-and-a-half-mile uphill hike, which begins at the junction of N1 and the Mulholland Highway, affords gorgeous vistas.

But it's the coastal road that really appeals. The stretch of **Route 1** from Malibu to the plain little town of **Oxnard** is dotted with surfer-friendly beaches. **Leo Carillo State Beach** is popular, as are the beaches that form rugged **Point Mugu State Park** (1-818 880 0350, www.parks.ca.gov). Close by sits **Ventura**, a largely unspoilt piece of well-preserved Middle America by the sea.

Ventura is the jumping-off point for the **Channel Islands National Park**, a wildlife sanctuary on a five-island archipelago. Diving, hiking, fishing, kayaking and simple wildlife observation are all on offer; **Santa Rosa** is the best island for an extended stay. Boat transport from Ventura to the islands is organised by **Island Packers Cruises** (1-805 642 1393, www.islandpackers.com); for more on the islands themselves, see www.nps.gov/chis.

Located a dozen miles north of Ventura, **Ojai** initially looks to be nothing more than a sweet village in a gorgeous setting. But all is not quite as it seems. The cinema is flanked by a psychic; there are two racks of new age CDs at the local music store. And so it goes: Ojai has long been a magnet for those of a spiritual bent, a fact borne witness by the galleries of **Ojai Avenue** and the esoteric businesses on the fringes of the town, such as the **Krotona Institute of Theosophy**. Those who've already found themselves should instead go looking for bargains at fabulously chaotic **Bart's Books** (302 W Matilija Street, 1-805 646 3755).

Where to eat & drink

Ventura beats Oxnard for food. **71 Palm** (71 N Palm Street, 1-805 653 7222, www.71palm.com, closed Sun & lunch Sat, mains $12-$29) dishes up solid French cuisine; the **Anacapa Brewing Company** (472 E Main Street, 1-805 643 0350,

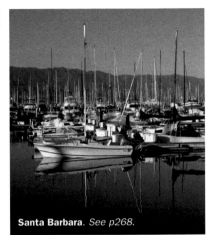

Santa Barbara. See p268.

www.anacapabrewing.com, mains $9-$15) offers bar food to go with the brews. In Ojai, there are worthwhile restaurants on Ojai Avenue, among them French-esque **Suzanne's Cuisine** (No.502, 1-805 640 1961, www.suzannescuisine. com, closed Tue, mains $8-$16). However, the most esteemed eatery is a short drive from the centre: at the **Ranch House** (S Lomita Avenue, www.theranchhouse.com, 1-805 646 2360, closed Mon, mains $23-$30), in-the-know locals dine on high-class Californian cuisine.

Ojai lodgings are above par. The cottages at the **Emerald Iguana** (Blanche Street, 1-805 646 5277, www.emeraldiguana.com, rates $189-$249) are individually decorated; the same owners run the more traditional **Blue Iguana** (11794 N Ventura Avenue, 1-805 646 5277, www.blueiguanainn.com, rates $95-$145).

Tourist information

Ojai *Ojai Visitors Bureau, St Thomas Aquinas Chapel, 150 W Ojai Avenue (1-805 646 8126/ www.ojaichamber.org).* **Open** 9.30am-4.30pm Mon, Wed-Fri; 10am-4pm Sat, Sun.
Oxnard *Oxnard CVB, 200 W 7th Street (1-800 269 6273/1-805 385 7545/www.visitoxnard.com).* **Open** 8.30am-12.30pm, 1.30pm-5.30pm Mon-Fri.
Ventura *Ventura CVB, Suite C, 89 S California Street (1-800 483 6214/1-805 648 2075/www. ventura-usa.com).* **Open** 8am-5pm Mon-Fri; 9am-5pm Sat; 10am-4pm Sun.

Santa Barbara

The wealthy resort town of **Santa Barbara** is almost too perfect to be true. And boy, does it know it. A well-heeled, conservation-minded coterie works hard to keep it handsome, almost immaculate: the only edge you'll get here is the oceanfront. Still, you don't come to Santa Barbara for urban thrills, but history, culture, top-end eating and an old-world aesthetic.

Sheltered between towering green mountains and deep blue ocean, this has long been sought-after land. The local Chumash Indians lived here for 5,000 years, before the Spanish arrived in 1786 and set about building the **Santa Barbara Mission** (2201 Laguna Street, 1-805 682 4713, www.sbmission.org, $4), one of the loveliest in the state. The current building dates from 1870 and is still an active Catholic Church, though parts of it are run as a museum.

For a different historical perspective on the region, try the **Museum of Natural History** (2559 Puesta del Sol Road, 1-805 682 4711, www.sbnature.org, $4-$7), or go Downtown to the **Santa Barbara Historical Society** (100 E De La Guerra Street, 1-805 966 1601, www.santabarbaramuseum.com, closed Mon). Just down De la Guerra Street from here is historic **De la Guerra Plaza**, flanked by **City Hall** and the site of the raucous Old Spanish Days Fiesta (first weekend in August). Nearby is what's left of the **Presidio** (123 E Canon Perdido, 1-805 965 0095), now a state park in the process of restoration.

Perhaps the finest example of the town's Spanish-Moorish colonial architectural heritage is the **County Courthouse** (11 Anacapa Street, www.sbcourts.org), a veritable castle of the law, complete with lofty towers, an interior covered with murals and sprawling grounds. It's worth taking the elevator up to the top to breathe in the billion-dollar views, from the 4,000-foot tips of the Santa Ynez Mountains all the way to the beach.

Two blocks away is the main drag of **State Street**, a strip of uppity boutiques, decent restaurants and upscale bars. Near the top of the Downtown core is the **Museum of Art** (1130 State Street, 1-805 884 6476, www.sbmuseart.org), a worthwhile display of ancient creativity and modern-day artistic pretenders. In the other direction, State Street ends at **Stearns Wharf**, where there's wine tasting, seaside dining and ocean views galore. Up the coast, soft waves make **Leadbetter Beach** the perfect littoral playground; down the coast is the sweet and sandy East Beach.

Where to eat & drink

There's plenty of variety here, and plenty of quality. **Bouchon** (9 W Victoria Street, 1-805 730 1160, www.bouchonsantabarbara.com, mains $24-$34) and **Downey's** (1305 State Street, 1-805 966 5006, www.downeyssb.com, mains $27-$37) both serve upscale menus of Californian cuisine with a number of local wines; at **Sage & Onion** (34 E Ortega Street, 1-805 963 1012, www.sageandonion.com, closed lunch Mon-Thur & Sun, mains $12-$15), Brit chef Steven Giles serves what he calls European-American cuisine with an English twist. At the harbour, long-time fave **Brophy Bros** (119 Harbor Way, 1-805 966 4418, http://brophybros.com, mains $8-$18) turns out fresh fish and justly celebrated bowls of clam chowder. More affordable fare can be found at the **Sojourner** (134 E Canon Perdido Street, 1-805 965 7922, closed Sun, mains $8-$16), the organic old-timers' favourite. Try N Milpas Street for Mexican food. **La Super-Rica** (No.622, 1-805 963 4940, mains $4-$9) draws the raves, but our favourite is **Julian's** (No.421, 1-805 564 2322, mains $5-$10).

The bars scene is busy but not especially interesting. State Street and its surrounds are split between the loud college bars and the wannabe-sophisticated venues such as **Blue Agave** (20 E Cota Street, 1-805 899 4694). **Joe's Café** (536 State Street, 1-805 966 4638) is a friendly, low-key place for a quiet drink.

Where to stay

Unless you're staying at the **Santa Barbara Tourist Hostel** (134 Chapala Street, 1-805 963 0154, www.sbhostel.com, rates $55-$65), expect to spend a healthy sum. The best Downtown option is the **Hotel Santa Barbara** (533 State Street, 1-800 549 9869, www.hotelsantabarbara.com, rates $149-$229), within walking distance of the beach. The ritzy **Biltmore** (1260 Channel Drive, 1-805 969 2261, www.fourseasons.com, rates $450-$550) is adjacent to Butterfly Beach, the region's choicest cove. You'll find cheaper deals further out of town, among them **El Prado Inn** (1601 State Street, 1-805 966 0807, rates $70-$150).

Tourist information

Santa Barbara *Santa Barbara CVB, 1 Garden Street (1-805 966 9222/www.sbchamber.org).* **Open** 9am-5pm Mon-Sat; 10am-5pm Sun.

Kalyra Winery (Santa Ynez, north-west of Santa Barbara) Where Jack meets Stephanie in *Sideways*

Heading Inland

Into the great wide open.

Yea, though I walk through the **Valley** of the shadow of **Death**, I will fear no evil. *See p270.*

Nature played a cruel trick on the early Western pioneers. Just where the barrier of the Sierra Mountains peters out in the south, a great desert swathe cuts across to the coast. Technically, much of southern California is desert, receiving less than ten inches of rain a year. Were it not for irrigation, air-con and the automobile, large areas would be close on uninhabitable for modern man.

Inhospitable, perhaps, but also spectacular. **Death Valley** and **Joshua Tree National Parks** are both breathtaking; the drive to the former is one of the state's most undervalued road trips. In the middle of this alien landscape, in what's known as the **Coachella Valley**, sit a cluster of sunbleached resort towns, of which **Palm Springs** is easily the most notable. Despite the heat, however, there's skiing close by at **Big Bear Lake** and **Lake Arrowhead**.

The desert is beautiful when seen from behind the wheel of a car, but engaging with it more closely, preferably on foot, pays large dividends. Go on an interpreted or ranger-led trail to familiarise yourself with some of the basics of geology, flora and fauna. *A Sierra Club Naturalist's Guide to the Deserts of the Southwest* by Peggy Larson, and the National Audubon Society's *Deserts* are good field guides; see also www.desertusa.com.

LA to Death Valley

The quickest and most popular of the two routes from Los Angeles to Death Valley is along I-15 via bleak **Barstow** and beautiful **Rainbow Basin Natural Area** (1-760 252 6000) to **Baker**, and then continuing north on Highway 127 to Death Valley Junction. The alternative route, though, is more the more beguiling one to take.

Leave LA on I-5, I-210 or I-405, then pick up Highway 14 north of Sylmar. From here, it's 35 miles north to **Edwards Air Force Base** (1-661 277 8050, www.edwards.af.mil) in **Palmdale**, home of *The Right Stuff*. If you're not here for the open house and air show in October, take one of the regular tours (apply online) or visit the museum. It's a further 35 miles north to **Mojave**, a barely extant town populated by more old planes (stored here, in the dry air, until they find buyers) than people.

Around 30 miles north of Mojave, you'll pass the erosion-carved formations of **Red Rock Canyon State Park** made famous by *Jurassic Park*. However, the entire stretch of road from Mojave to Death Valley (Highway 14/395, then Highway 190) is desert driving at its best, a scintillating, otherworldly rainbow of subtly changing reds, oranges, yellows and browns beneath immense, clear skies.

Death Valley National Park

Death Valley is the largest national park outside Alaska, covering more than 5,000 square miles. Famously, it's one of the hottest places on the planet: air temperatures regularly top 120°F (49°C) in July and August (ground temperatures can be 50 per cent higher). The real meaning of heat is apparent when the wind blows: it feels like someone has pointed a giant hairdryer at you. The park usually gets less than two inches of rain a year; as such, the flash floods of August 2004, which killed two people and destroyed parts of the park road, were devastating.

The drive in from Death Valley Junction takes you past the turn-off to **Dante's View**, reached via a winding 13-mile road. The landscape, some 5,475 feet (1,669 metres) above sea level, is drab and barren yet oddly beautiful. Returning to Route 190, you'll pass **Zabriskie Point**, famed to cinephiles for the eponymous 1970 Antonioni film but recognisable to all by its ragged, rumpled appearance.

Five miles down the road, you'll reach the Death Valley Visitor Center (*see below*) at **Furnace Creek**, which contains an excellent bookshop, decent exhibits, a useful orientation film and helpful staff. Ask for advice on current weather and road conditions (some tracks are only accessible to 4WD vehicles), pay your fee of $20 per car (valid for seven days) and fill up at one of the park's three gas stations.

From Furnace Creek, you've two choices. The road south will take you first past **Golden Canyon**, a straightforward two-mile round-trip hike; in the late afternoon sunlight, you'll see how it got its name. Nine miles down the road is the **Devil's Golf Course**, a striking, scrappy landscape formed by salt crystallising and expanding; a few miles further is bleak, eerie **Badwater**, just two miles as the crow flies

from Dante's View but more than 5,000 feet (1,500 metres) lower. Nearby but inaccessible is the lowest point in the Western Hemisphere, 282 feet (86 metres) below sea level.

Heading north from Furnace Creek offers a greater variety of sights. The remains of the **Harmony Borax Works** have been casually converted into a short trail; there's a similarly simple walk at nearby **Salt Creek** (look out for pupfish in the stream in spring). Following the road around to the left will lead you past the eerie **Devil's Cornfield**, the immense **Sand Dunes** and on to the small settlement at **Stovepipe Wells**; taking a right and driving 36 miles will take you to the extravagant **Scotty's Castle** (1-760 786 2392), built in the 1920s for Chicago millionaire Albert Johnson but named after Walter Scott, his eccentric chancer of a friend. Costumed rangers tell the story during 50-minute tours from 9am to 5pm, usually hourly ($11; $6-$9 discounts).

It's often too hot to hike in Death Valley, but there are plenty of trails, short and long. Among the options is the 14-mile round-trip to the 11,000-foot (3,300-metre) summit of **Telescope Peak**, a good summer hike (the higher you climb, the cooler it gets). Starting at Mahogany Flat campground, you climb 3,000 feet (900 metres) for spectacular views of Mount Whitney. In winter, only experienced climbers with ice axes and crampons should attempt it.

Where to eat, drink & stay

There are restaurants at Furnace Creek Ranch, Stovepipe Wells Village and Panamint Springs, but the food tends to the ordinary. The exception is the dining room at the **Furnace Creek Inn** (*see below*; closed mid May-mid Oct, mains $11-$30), where the upscale Californian food is considerably better than it has any right to be.

Set into the hillside above Furnace Creek Wash, 1930s **Furnace Creek Inn** (1-760 786 2345, www.furnacecreekresort.com, closed mid May-mid Oct, rates $250-$375) is the luxury option, while the attached **Furnace Creek Ranch** (rates $105-$179) has 200 motel-style rooms and cabins, with a pool, tennis courts and the world's lowest golf course. **Stovepipe Wells Village** has 83 rooms (1-760 786 2837, www.stovepipewells.com, closed May-mid Oct, rates $87-$107). The park's nine campgrounds cost $10-$25 a night; Furnace Creek (1-800 365 2267) and a few others are open all year.

Tourist information

Death Valley *Death Valley Visitor Center, Furnace Creek (1-760 786 3200/www.nps.gov/deva).* **Open** 8am-6pm daily.

Stovepipe Wells sand dunes, Death Valley National Park (p270)
C3PO lands here in *Star Wars*

$139-$239). The large **Lake Arrowhead Resort** (27984 Hwy 189, 1-866 794 3732, www. laresort.com, rates $139-$209) is near the village.

Tourist information

Lake Arrowhead *Lake Arrowhead Chamber of Commerce, 28200 Hwy 189 (1-909 337 3715/ www.lakearrowhead.net)*. **Open** 9am-5pm Mon-Fri.

Big Bear Lake

Big Bear Lake offers a less charming and more rugged experience than its near-neighbour. But there's also a greater variety of activities available here all year-round, and no need to rely on the fake snow that is often required at Lake Arrowhead.

Unlike at Arrowhead, visitors can swim in the lake. It's also a first-rate fishery, where you can find rainbow trout, large and small mouth bass, catfish and blue gill. Many hiking trailheads are easily accessible, with most providing fine views. The **Big Bear Lake Visitor Center** (*see below*) offers maps and advice.

During the winter, **Snow Summit** (1-800 232 7686, www.bigbearmountainresorts.com) is one of the most popular ski/snowboard resorts in Southern California. In summer, its East Mountain Express high-speed chairlift is converted into the **Scenic Sky Chair** (1-800 232 7686); running to an 8,200-foot (2,500-metre) summit, it offers magnificent views of the San Gorgonio Mountains.

Where to eat, drink & stay

The restaurants along Big Bear Boulevard include **Marisco's La Bamba** (No.40199, 1-909 866 2350, mains $3-$12), which specialises in Mexican seafood. Traditional B&Bs around the lake include the **Windy Point Inn** (39015 North Shore Drive, 1-909 866 2746, www.windy pointinn.com, rates $145-$195). A variety of chains can be found Downtown.

Tourist information

Big Bear Lake *Big Bear Lake Visitor Center, 630 Bartlett Road (1-909 866 6190/www.bigbear.com)*. **Open** 8am-5pm Mon-Fri; 9am-5pm Sat, Sun.

Getting there

By car

Take I-10 and then I-215 to San Bernardino, before picking up Highway 30 eastbound for a mile and then heading north on Highway 18; the Lake Arrowhead turn-off is around 30-40 minutes before Big Bear Lake. The journey from LA should take around two hours.

Getting there

By car

To reach Death Valley, take I-10 west to Ontario, follow I-15 north to Baker, drive on Highway 127 to Death Valley Junction and then take Highway 190 west into the park. Alternatively, leave LA to the north-west and, at Sylmar, pick up Highway 14. This eventually turns into Highway 395; from here, take Highway 190 west into the park at Olancha. Both journeys are around 300 miles; allow 5-6hrs.

Lake Arrowhead & Big Bear Lake

Lake Arrowhead

Nestled atop one of Southern California's few mountain ranges, two small towns and a handful of scattered neighbourhoods make up the community of Lake Arrowhead. **Blue Jay**, at the west side of the region, is made up of a number of small but forgettable shops. **Lake Arrowhead Village**, meanwhile, offers gift and outlet shops on a water-ringed peninsula.

Though the boat tours on the **Arrowhead Queen** (1-909 336 6992, $12) offer a little history, sightseeing is largely usurped by the sports and activities. In summer, water sports are king at **McKenzie's Water Ski School** in Arrowhead Village (1-909 337 3814, http://mckenzieskischool.com), the oldest water-ski school in the United States. The main disappointment, apart from the plethora of speedboats buzzing about, is the lack of swimming: the lake is privately owned.

Winter sees skiers from the Los Angeles conurbation descend on the area. The Arrowhead Ranger Station (1-909 337 2444) can offer guidance on current conditions for cross-country skiing and snow-shoeing. About ten miles up from Lake Arrowhead on US 18 is the **Snow Valley** resort (1-800 680 7669), where you can buy a range of ski and snowboarding passes. The resort is located at a low altitude, but makes its own snow to ensure that the slopes are always in service.

Where to eat, drink & stay

Variety is limited, but if you're looking for something quaint and home cooked, try the tiny, family-owned **Casual Elegance** (26848 Hwy 189, 1-909 337 8932, www.casualelegance restaurant.com, mains $18-$36). The most notable of the few B&Bs is the quaint little **Fleur de Lac European Inn** (285 Hwy 173, 1-909 336 4612, www.fleurdelac.com, rates

Trips Out of Town

Coachella Valley

Palm Springs

Tucked into an abutment of the San Jacinto and Santa Rosa mountain ranges, **Palm Springs** first found fame as a destination for the infirm and the tubercular, who were able to soothe their aches and pains at the town's eponymous natural springs. However, Hollywood began filming silent westerns and Arabian-themed romances in the deserts during the 1920s, and the town transformed itself into a winter playground for the Hollywood elite. By the 1950s and '60s, nearly every major American entertainer owned a home in Palm Springs.

When the same stars moved on to more lavish spreads elsewhere in the Valley, the town itself metamorphosised into a tawdry tourist trap. However, it's turned itself around once more. Though late mayor Sonny Bono gets most of the credit, the town's resurgence is really due to the combination of a strong economy and an active gay community. Renewed interest in mid-century modernist architecture and the opulent trappings of the leisure-obsessed Rat Pack era have also proved welcome shots in the arm.

Still, the future of the city remains somewhat cloudy. Current mayor Ron Oden has been portrayed (with some accuracy) as having never met a developer he didn't like; under his tenure, the council has signed off one ugly, sprawling housing development after another, destroying many of Palm Springs' scenic vistas in its desperation to appear 'business-friendly' and favouring tacky Spanish style over modernism. Thankfully, the non-profit **Palm Springs Modern Committee** (www.psmodcom.com) has been sounding the alarm about these issues, as part of its continuing mission to preserve Palm Springs' architectural aesthetic and keep the still lovely city from mutating into another ugly, anonymous Riverside Country exurb.

The city consists simply of a commercial spine: **N Palm Canyon Drive**, home to most of the town's eating, drinking and shopping options. Mid-century antiques shops abound on Palm Canyon and the parallel N Indian Canyon Drive; while bargains are no longer easy to find, you can score a lucite table for less than you would pay on LA's Beverly Boulevard. On Thursday nights, a mile-long stretch of Palm Canyon is closed to traffic for **Villagefest**, when shops open late and stalls line the road. The scene is played out to the accompaniment of some high-concept, low-taste street musicians.

Though it takes less than an hour to traverse the lengths of Palm Canyon and Indian Canyon by car, don't keep driving in a straight line. Nearly every turn opens up yet another eye-popping mountain view, as well as striking examples of mid-century modern architecture, from simple tract homes to Jetsonian structures. The aforementioned Palm Springs Modern Committee publish a map, available for $5 from their website or from the visitor centre (*see p275*), that details the most notable buildings in the city; for more, *see p273* **Meet George Jetson…**.

The town is dotted with small attractions. In the heart of Palm Springs sits the impressive **Palm Springs Art Museum** (101 Museum Drive, 1-760 325 7186, www.psmuseum.org, $13), which supplements selections from its permanent collection with temporary shows. Across from the airport, the **Palm Springs Air Museum** (1-760 778 6262, www.palm springsairmuseum.org, $4-$8) boasts a collection of propeller-driven World War II aircraft, many still in flying condition. South of town sits the wilfully eccentric **Moorten Botanical Garden** (1701 S Palm Canyon Drive, 1-760 327 6555, $1-$2.50), a living museum with nature trails, sculpture, rusted-out cars, dinosaur footprints and 3,000 varieties of cacti, succulents and flowers.

Outdoor types are well served. There are hundreds of hiking trails throughout the San Jacintos and Santa Rosas, but the **Indian Canyons** (1-760 325 3400, www.indian-canyons.com, $8), located five miles south of Downtown on S Palm Canyon Drive, are a must-see. Owned and preserved by the Agua Caliente Indians, the Canyons contain miles of hiking trails that wind through an unspoiled wilderness of palm groves, barrel cacti, waterfalls and dramatic rock formations.

For a change of ecosystem, take the **Palm Springs Aerial Tramway** (1-760 325 1391, www.pstramway.com, $22) to the crest of San Jacinto. The rotating tram cars lift you 5,873 feet (1,791 metres) through four different 'life zones' into a lush pine forest that's typically 30°F to 40°F (18°C to 24°C) cooler than on the desert floor. Aside from the sheer scenic beauty, it's worth the journey just to enjoy a drink or a meal at E Stewart William's **Tramway Mountain Station**. From here, you can also walk a mile to Idyllwild, a mountain retreat housing a small artsy community and school.

Where to eat

Palm Springs' cuisine is improving, but many restaurants are still geared to elderly locals. Mediocre Mexican food dominates, and there

Meet George Jetson...

It has been said that what art deco did for Miami Beach in the 1980s, modernism is doing today for Palm Springs, making visitors feel as though they've travelled 40 or 50 years back in time. Though many of the city's great structures have been razed or changed, invariably in pseudo-Spanish style, beyond recognition, you can still find gems by such modernist architects as William Cody, Richard

Neutra, John Lautner, Donald Wexler, E Stuart Williams and Albert Frey in the area. Indeed, Frey's classic 1963 **Tramway Gas Station**, a dramatically angled structure at the town entrance that came perilously close to demolition, has been renovated to serve as the Palm Springs Bureau of Tourism's Visitor Information Center (*see p275*).

It's far from the only must-see modernist site. The upside-down arches of E Stewart Williams' **Washington Mutual Bank** (499 S Palm Canyon Drive; *pictured*) were built in 1961 across the street from Rudy Baumfeld's blue-tiled 1959 **Bank of America Building** (588 S Palm Canyon Drive). William Cody's sensually curved **St Theresa's Church** (2800 E Ramon Road), built in 1968, is a quick drive from the equally fantastic **Palm Springs City Hall** at 3200 E Taghuitz Canyon Way (Albert Frey, 1952) and the nearby **Palm Springs International Airport** (Donald Wexler, 1965).

A map to more than 50 significant structures is published by the **Palm Springs Modern Committee**, and available at the Visitor Information Center. But it's also fun to just get lost in the winding streets of the ritzy Las Palmas and Little Tuscany locales west of Palm Canyon Drive at the foot of Mount San Jacinto, where hundreds of ranch-style modern mansions have been preserved in all of their space-age glory. Famous homes include Frank Sinatra's **Twin Palms** (1148 E Alejo Road), where Ol' Blue Eyes lived and fought with Ava Gardner; Liberace's Spanish-style **Casa de Liberace** (501 N Belardo Road), still adorned with the pianist's trademark 'L' logo; and two John Lautner buildings on Southridge Drive, the **Elrod House** and Bob Hope's **Flying Saucer House**.

are more lousy Italian joints than you can shake a breadstick at; one exception to the latter rule is **Al Dente** (491 N Palm Canyon Drive, 1-760 325 1160, www.aldente-palmsprings.com, mains $6-$18). Also on N Palm Canyon Drive, the **Blue Coyote** (No.445, 1-760 327 1196, mains $10-$22) serves decent Southwestern cuisine, while **Thai Smile** (No.651, 1-760 320 5503, mains $8-$15) is the best Thai restaurant in a town that's overrun with them.

On S Palm Canyon, try the **Kaiser Grille** (No.205, 1-760 323 1003, www.kaisergrille.com, mains $8-$32), which serves reliable continental favourites in a sleek setting, or an amazing burger at **Tyler's** (No.149, 1-760 325 2990,

burgers $3-$8). For breakfast, head to **More Than a Mouthful** (134 E Tahquitz Canyon Way, 1-760 322 3776, mains $6-$15), a welcome addition to the Downtown dining scene.

Where to drink

The town goes pretty quiet around 9pm. The **Village Pub** (266 S Palm Canyon Drive, 1-760 323 3265) can get lively, while the Casablanca Lounge at the **Ingleside Inn** (200 W Ramon Road, 1-760 325 0046, www.inglesideinn.com) is good for old-school lounge entertainment. But nights belong to the city's gay contingent, at bars such as **Badlands** (200 S Indian Canyon,

Trips Out of Town

Springs eternal

There are an abundance of natural hot springs in California. Just as naturally, an abundance of spas and resorts has sprung up wherever warm water leaks out of the rocks, from five-star resorts to national parks. Some are just a quick drive from LA, making overnight trips feasible, while others are further out and best reserved for a weekend trip. Here are some of the best.

Beverly Hot Springs

308 N Oxford Avenue, at Beverly Boulevard, Midtown (1-323 734 7000/www.beverlyhot springs.com). **Open** 9.30am-9pm daily. **Rates** $40-$50. *Treatments* $50-$240. **Credit** AmEx, MC, V. **Map** p313 D4.
In the heart of LA, this spot draws its water from a well with a natural mineral spring. All the usual spa treatments are offered. The site has separate facilities for men and women; there's a 'swimsuit optional' policy.

Deep Creek Hot Springs

6221 Bowen Ranch Road, Apple Valley (no phone). I-15, exit Bear Valley; head east for about 10 miles until it turns into a two-lane road. At first stop sign, turn right on Central for 3 miles, then left on Ocotillo Way. The road turns into a dirt road for about 6 miles to Bowen Ranch (4WD recommended). **Rates** $4-$5.
It's a good 45-minute hike down to the creek from the parking lot, but worth it: these are probably the best springs in SoCal. Wade through cold water to three pools of hot, mineral water running out of the mountain. You can camp on the ranch land but not at the springs; clothing is optional, but it's a good idea to have warm clothes and a torch after the sun sets. Hiking boots are recommended. There are no facilities: bring food and plenty of water.

Glen Ivy Hot Springs Spa

25000 Glen Ivy Road, at Temescal Canyon Road, Corona (1-888 258 2683/1-909 277 3529/www.glenivy.com). I-15, exit Temescal Canyon Road west. **Open** Aug-Oct 9.30am-6pm daily. Nov-Mar 9.30am-5pm daily. **Rates** $35-$48. *Treatments* $30-$260. **Credit** AmEx, Disc, MC, V.
Less than two hours drive from the city, this recently upgraded spa resort is a favourite with Angelenos. The facilities include mineral baths, steam rooms, saunas, salt-water pools and the signature 'Club Mud', where you cover yourself with locally mined red clay (it stains, so wear an old or dark swimming costume that you don't mind sacrificing). Bring your own towel, robe and slippers.

Sycamore Mineral Springs Resort

1215 Avila Beach Drive, at US 101, San Luis Obispo, CA 93405 (1-800 234 5831/1-805 595 7302/www.sycamoresprings.com). US 101, exit Avila Beach Drive west. **Open** Spa 7am-2am daily. **Rates** $20 1st hr, then $10/hr. *Massages* $45-$90. *Rooms* $169-$795. **Credit** AmEx, Disc, MC, V.
Stop to soak in one of the mineral hot tubs by the hour (reservations recommended), or check into the resort, book yourself a massage and take a class at the Healing Arts Institute. Most rooms have their own hot tub and the decor is more home-grown than swanky resort. To stop yourself turning into a water-soaked prune, there are lots of trails for hiking the coastline.

Tecopa Hot Springs

Tecopa Hot Springs Road, at Noonday Road, Tecopa (1-760 852 4420/www.tecopa springs.org). Hwy 127 north from Baker for 48 miles, right at Old Spanish Trail, left on Tecopa Hot Springs Road.
Tecopa Hot Springs is primarily a campground with some RV hookups, rather than a proper spa. There are basic accommodations available and two private, enclosed baths. They recently turned the convenience store into an art gallery. There are other hot springs in the area including the public baths and a natural, outdoor spring. A relatively convenient stop on the way to Vegas.

Two Bunch Palms

67425 Two Bunch Palms Trail, Desert Hot Springs (1-800 472 4334/1-760 329 8791/www.twobunchpalms.com). I-10, exit Palm Drive north. **Open** 8am-10pm Mon-Thur, Sat, Sun; 8am-11pm Fri. Closed 2wks Aug. **Rates** *Treatments* $50-$200. *Rooms* $195-$725 (2-night min). **Credit** AmEx, MC, V.
Thought to be one of the best resort spas in the country, this exclusive, adult-only facility was patronised by Al Capone before his run-in with the IRS. The grounds are extensive, complete with a serene man-made lake. Guests are requested to speak softly to maintain the tranquil atmosphere.

1-760 778 4326), **Hunter's Video Bar** (302 E Arenas Road, 1-760 323 0700) and the tropical-themed **Toucan's Tiki Lounge** (2100 N Palm Canyon Drive, 1-760 416 7584).

Where to stay

Palm Springs has seen a massive upsurge in the quality of its lodgings in recent years. The mid-century **Orbit In** (562 W Arenas Road, 1-760 323 3585, www.orbitin.com, rates $179-$289) has been funkily appointed with furniture by Eames et al. The chic **Movie Colony** (726 N Indian Canyon Drive, 1-760 320 6340, www.moviecolonyhotel.com, rates $129-$309) is, if anything, even more handsome: a 1935 Albert Frey construction with a lovely pool area.

The **Caliente Tropics** (411 E Palm Canyon Drive, 1-760 327 1391, www.calientetropics.com, rates $60-$160) is a faux-Polynesian playground regenerated in 2001. Moving from the ridiculous to the sublime, the historic **Parker** (4200 E Palm Canyon Drive, 1-760 770 5000, www.theparkerpalmsprings.com, rates $125-$5,000) is the town's most stylish spot, a modish spa resort popular with celebs and the local in-crowd. Gay lodgings include the smart **East Canyon Hotel** (288 E Camino Monte Vista, 1-760 320 1928, www.eastcanyonhotel.com, rates $109-$359), the only gay men's hotel in town with a full-service pool, and **Inndulge** (601 Grenfall Road, 1-760 327 1408, www.inndulge.com, rates $125-$190), a clothing-optional hotel with a pool and a ten-man jacuzzi.

The waters that lend their name to the neighbouring town of Desert Hot Springs have naturally been exploited by several hotels in the town, each with their own natural mineral pools. The **Desert Hot Springs Resort** (10805 Palm Drive, 1-760 329 6000, www.dhsspa.com, rates $90-$139) offers good value, but the best bet is the gorgeous **Hope Springs** motel (68075 Club Circle Drive, 1-760 329 4003, www.hopespringsresort.com, rates $175-$190). If you don't require a therapeutic soak, then the **Desert Hot Springs Motel** (cnr of Yerxa Road & San Antonio Street, 1-760 288 2280, www.lautnermotel.com, rates $135-$150), a lovingly restored treasure built in 1947 by John Lautner, makes an excellent choice, or the beatnik-themed sister operation the **Beat Hotel** (67840 Hacienda Drive, 1-760 288 2280, www.dhsbeathotel.com, rates $150-$300).

Tourist information

Palm Springs *Palm Springs Visitor Information Center, 2901 N Palm Canyon Drive (1-800 347 7746/1-760 778 8418/www.palm-springs.org).* **Open** 9am-5pm daily.

Tahquitz Canyon, Palm Springs (www.tahquitzcanyon.com) Home of the waterfall in Frank Capra's *Lost Horizons*

Other Coachella towns

The climate remains just as delicious elsewhere in the Coachella Valley. However, outside the recuperative waters of **Desert Hot Springs** (*see left*), there's not much of interest here. **Cathedral City** is notable only as the last resting place of Frank Sinatra (at the **Desert Memorial Park** cemetery, 69-920 E Ramon Road); **Rancho Mirage**'s sole claim to fame is the Betty Ford Clinic.

Palm Desert's appeal rests on the **Living Desert Zoo & Gardens** (47-900 Portola Avenue, 1-760 346 5694, www.livingdesert.org, $8-$12), a 1,200-acre wildlife and botanical park with animals from local and African deserts. Nearby **Indio** is home to the annual **Coachella Music Festival** (www.coachella.com) and a date industry that thrives all year. The **Shields Date Gardens** (80-225 Highway 111, 1-760 347 0996, free) is one of the area's oldest tourist traditions: stop by for a date shake. All you'll find in **Indian Wells** and **La Quinta**, though, are gated communities and golf courses.

Getting there

By bus
Greyhound (1-800 229 9424, www.greyhound.com) runs 7 buses a day. The 3-hour trip from LA costs $40 (round trip).

By car
To reach Palm Springs from LA, take I-10 eastbound for just over 100 miles. The journey can take anywhere between two and three hours, depending on the traffic and your starting location.

East to Joshua Tree

Whether you're approaching from LA or Palm Springs, Joshua Tree National Park is best entered from the north via Highway 62: many of the park's highlights are in this northern section. En route, you'll pass **Yucca Valley**, the gateway to **Pioneertown** (www.pioneertown.com). Originally a set for movies and TV shows (*The Cisco Kid*, among many others), this better-than-average tourist trap retains an Old West feel; its dirt roads make you realise why so many cowboys were called Dusty.

Those who prefer their nature unmediated should head to the **Pipes Canyon Preserve**, owned by a private conservation group and every bit as wild as a national park. Ask at the visitor centre (*see below*) for information about cougars, bears and bobcats, petroglyphs and active springs. Admission is free.

East of Yucca Valley are two smaller settlements, both of which offer entrances into Joshua Tree National Park. The town of **Joshua Tree** itself and, around 16 miles further along Highway 62, **Twentynine Palms** are both small, rather plain towns with a few hotels and restaurants but not much else.

Joshua Tree National Park

North of Palm Springs, the desert valley gives way to massive granite monoliths and strange, jagged trees with spiky blooms. These are Joshua trees, a form of cactus named by early Mormon settlers after the prophet Joshua, which they believed pointed the way to the Promised Land. The trees lend their name to the 794,000-acre **Joshua Tree National Park**, a mecca for modern-day explorers that's home to 17 different types of cactus, palm-studded oases, ancient petroglyphs, spectacular rock formations and all manner of wildlife. The park straddles two desert ecosystems, the Mojave and Colorado. The remote eastern half is dominated by cholla cactus, small creosote bushes and some adrenaline-pumping 4WD routes. The cooler and wetter western section is what the Joshua tree tourists come to see.

Entering via the West Entrance at the town of Joshua Tree (the $10/car fee is valid for seven days), you'll soon come to **Hidden Valley**, a cornucopia of climbs, hikes and picnic spots stretching as far as the eye can see. The most popular of the park's 4,500 climbing routes are located here: **Sports Challenge Rock** is a favourite of experienced climbers; **Echo Rock** is where rookie rappellers test their mettle. There's walking, too, with more than a dozen trails revisiting remnants of the gold mining era. The **Hidden Valley** mile-long loop winds around a dramatic, rock-enclosed valley. Nearby **Barker Dam Trail** leads to a lake built by early ranchers; at dusk, it's possible to spot bighorn sheep taking a sip. Try to take at least one of the trails during your visit.

Keys View, due south of Hidden Valley, is worth a side trip; on a clear day, you can see all the way to Mexico. Here you can also pick up 18-mile **Geology Tour Road** (high clearance vehicles are a must) showing off some of Joshua Tree's most dramatic landscapes. Off-road adventures continue on **Berdoo Canyon Road,** which intersects Geology Tour Road and passes the ruins of a camp constructed in the '30s by builders of the California Aqueduct.

Where to eat, drink & stay

Once a cantina set for numerous westerns, **Pappy & Harriet's Pioneertown Palace** (53688 Pioneertown Road, 1-760 365 5956, www.pappyandharriets.com, closed Tue & Wed, $3-$25) in Yucca Valley is now a popular local hangout serving heaped portions of mesquite BBQ and live country music. In Joshua Tree, locals swear by the **Crossroads Café** (61715 Twentynine Palms Highway, 1-760 366 5414, closed Wed, $6-$8), a hippy-ish eaterie that serves huge salads, veggie burgers and smoothies; the new-ish **Park Visitor Café** (6554 Park Boulevard, 1-760 366 3622, $6-$8) is a great place to stock up on take-out. The best of a so-so bunch of restaurants in Twentynine Palms is the **Twentynine Palms Inn** (*see below*; $6-$30), which serves steaks, chops and veggies from its own garden (yes, in the desert).

Lodgings are cheap and characterful. Yucca Valley's **Pioneertown Motel** (5040 Curtis Road, 1-760 365 4879, www.pioneertownmotel. com, rates $55-$75) hosted actors, such as Barbara Stanwyck, when they filmed in the area. In Joshua Tree, try the hacienda-style **Joshua Tree Inn** (61259 Twentynine Palms Highway, Joshua Tree, 1-760 366 1188, www.joshuatreeinn.com, rates $75-$145). Built in the 1950s as a getaway for movie stars, it then drew rock star guests such as the Rolling Stones and the Eagles during the 1960s; Gram Parsons spent his final hours in room 8. Over in Twentynine Palms, skip the vanilla motels on Highway 62 in favour of funky, old-school **Twentynine Palms Inn** (73950 Inn Avenue, 1-760 367 3505, www.29palmsinn.com, rates $95-$170), or the 1950s-style **Harmony Motel** (711661 Twentynine Palms Highway, 1-760 367 3351, www.harmonymotel.com, rates $65-$80), where U2 stayed while recording *The Joshua Tree*. In the national park itself, there are nine campsites available, but only two of those have water. Remember to carry two litres a day.

Tourist information

Joshua Tree National Park *Oasis of Mara, Twentynine Palms (1-760 367 5500/www.nps. gov/jotr).* **Open** 8am-5pm daily. There's a smaller visitor centre (9am-3pm daily) at the Cottonwood Spring entrance to the park.

Pipes Canyon Preserve *51010 Pipes Canyon Road (1-760 369 7105).* **Open** dawn-dusk daily.

Getting there

By car

Joshua Tree National Park can be reached from the south via I-10, or from the north via Highway 62 in the towns of Joshua Tree and Twentynine Palms.

Easy riders, hard climbers and prickly cacti: **Joshua Tree National Park**.

Trips Out of Town

Heading South

Welcome to Pleasantville.

Ocean Beach. *See p281.*

Santa Catalina Island

The most Mediterranean island in North America, **Santa Catalina Island** juts more than 2,000 feet (600 metres) above the Pacific Ocean at its highest point, a mere 22 miles off Long Beach. Privately owned for two centuries and now 86 per cent owned and run by the **Santa Catalina Island Conservancy** (125 Claressa Avenue, Avalon, 1-310 510 2595, www.catalinaconservancy.org), it's protected from overdevelopment.

The first street you walk will be **Crescent Avenue** in the tiny town of **Avalon**. Riddled with shops and restaurants, the street curves along a postcard-perfect harbour towards the art deco **Casino** building, which houses a theatre, a ballroom and the **Santa Catalina Island Museum** (1 Casino Way, Avalon, 1-310 510 2414, $1-$3). Crowded, wave-free **Crescent Beach** is a big draw, though the **Descanso Beach Club** (1-310 510 7410, closed Nov-Apr, $1.50), a ten-minute walk north along Via Casino from Avalon, is a less busy alternative.

From the north end of Crescent Avenue, it's a half-hour stroll (or low-cost shuttle ride) along

Avalon Canyon to the **Wrigley Memorial & Botanical Gardens** (1400 Avalon Canyon Road, 1-310 510 2288, $3). The 1934 memorial recognises Chicagoan gum magnate William Wrigley Jr, who bought the island in 1915. The harbour views are beautiful.

You'll need a permit from the Conservancy to either hike (free) or bike ($60/year) outside Avalon or Two Harbours, the rustic settlement at the island's northern isthmus. There's good skin and scuba diving; try **Catalina Divers Supply** (1-800 353 0330, www.catalinadivers supply.com). The less adventurous can enjoy one of a variety of boat trips; call **Discovery Tours** (1-800 626 1496, www.scico.com).

Where to eat, drink & stay

Most eating options are in Avalon. For fairly-priced fish, try **Armstong's Seafood** (306 Crescent Avenue, 1-310 510 0113, mains $8-$21) on the harbour; those seeking an elegant meal should opt for the **Channel House** (205 Crescent Avenue, 1-310 510 1617, mains $8-$33). Among more relaxed options, the dockside **Busy Bee** (306 Crescent Avenue, 1-310 510 1983, mains $10-$25) is the locals' fave. Want to know where everyone is scoring those saliva-inducing, ice-cream-packed waffle cones? **Big Olaf's** (220 Crescent Avenue, 1-310 510 0798).

It's no wonder most visitors are day-trippers: lodging is scarce and expensive. You'll pay to be in the thick of things, but the casual elegance of **Hotel Vista del Mar** (1-800 601 3836, rates $145-$395), steps from the beach, is worth it. Down Crescent Avenue is the mid-century modern **Pavilion Lodge** (1-800 626 1496, $94-$279), a classic motor court without the motors (Catalina is car-free). If cost is no concern, try the **Inn at Mt Ada** (1-310 510 2030, www.catalina.com/mtada, rates $320-$560). **Hermit Gulch** is the only one of five campgrounds near Avalon (reservations/permits required; call 1-310 510 8368, pitches $12); for the others, such as the stunning seaside hike-in at **Little Harbour**, call 1-310 510 0303 (www.scico.com).

Tourist information

Avalon *Catalina Island Chamber of Commerce & Visitors Bureau, 1 Green Pleasure Pier, Avalon (1-310 510 1520/www.catalina.com).* **Open** 8am-5pm Mon-Sat; 9am-3pm Sun.

Getting there

By boat

For the hour-long boat journey from Long Beach or San Pedro, call **Catalina Express** (1-800 481 3470, www.catalinaexpress.com). For the 75-minute trip from Newport Beach, call the less regular **Catalina Flyer** (1-949 673 5245, www.catalinainfo.com). Fares are $23-$25 one-way and $44-$50 return; reservations are recommended but not always necessary.

San Diego

To the casual visitor, San Diego might initially come across as a little bland. It lacks the boho earthiness that defines San Francisco (despite an active gay community). It lacks the cascade of competing cultures that makes up the LA urban sprawl. Most of all, it lacks character.

Of course, one man's character is another man's freak show, which explains how San Diego has grown into America's sixth largest city. Once known for its naval base and its climate, it's blossomed into a cheery centre of business, academia and tourism of late. It's unashamedly a nice kind of place, as sunny as the day is long, Californian conservatism at its brightest and most approachable.

The town is quietly changing. The ever-expanding Mexican and gay communities have shaken the town out of its pleasant, woozy stasis, and a slew of unlikely political scandals – most famously, the 2005 resignation of mayor

Dick Murphy after a run of appalling financial troubles – put the city in the spotlight across the nation. Still, you don't come here for an edgy urban experience. Indeed, you don't really come here for an urban experience at all. You come here to find Middle America under Southern Californian skies.

DOWNTOWN SAN DIEGO

The heart of San Diego is its well-scrubbed, thriving Downtown, which combines a high-rise business district with a commercial core that locals actually use. The area, like Downtowns in many major US cities, had become moribund, but has been revived in the last 20 years by a combination of commercial development and high-quality in-fill urban housing. Start at **Horton Plaza**, a complex of shops and restaurants on six open-air levels.

Surrounding Horton Plaza is the historic, 16-block **Gaslamp Quarter**. Built in the 19th century, the area had fallen on hard times before the construction of Horton Plaza in the 1980s. However, it's since been transformed into a thriving entertainment district, home to a number of neat, tidy and rather predictable bars and restaurants. Much of the street furniture, such as the mock-Victorian street lamps and brick sidewalks, is modern; conversely, many of the buildings are original. A walking tour of the area departs from the **William Davis Heath House** (410 Island Avenue, 1-619 233 4692), which was built in 1850 and is the city's oldest building, every saturday at 11am and cost $8.

West on Broadway, just a stone's throw from the waterfront stands one of San Diego's most recognisable landmarks, the **Santa Fe Depot** (1050 Kettner Boulevard). Constructed in 1915, the Spanish Mission-Colonial Revival building is still an important travel hub. Across the street is the futuristic, two-storey **Museum of Contemporary Art** (1001 Kettner Boulevard, 1-619 234 1001, www.mcasd.org), the sister to the original venue in La Jolla (*see p281*).

Continue west, and you'll reach the tree-lined **Embarcadero**, which affords panoramic views of the city and numerous reminders of San Diego's naval history: the excellent **Maritime Museum** (1492 N Harbor Drive, 1-619 234 9153, www.sdmaritime.com, $7-$10) has been joined by **Midway: San Diego's Aircraft Carrier Museum** (910 N Harbor Drive, 1-619 544 9600, www.midway.org, $8-$15). Some visitors choose to experience San Diego's water at closer quarters: **San Diego Harbor Excursions** (1050 N Harbor Drive, 1-619 234 4111, www.harborexcursion.com, rates $8-$22) offers one- and two-hour tours from Broadway Pier.

A little further south, along Downtown's waterfront, are the town's huge **Convention**

Center; the massively conventional **Seaport Village** mall; and **Petco Park**, home to the San Diego Padres baseball team since 2004.

BALBOA PARK

Like Central Park in New York, 1,200-acre **Balboa Park** occupies a prominent piece of real estate at the centre of town. But unlike its Manhattan equivalent, San Diego's city park is dotted with around two dozen fine cultural institutions. Stop by the **Visitor Centre** (1549 El Prado, 1-619 239 0512, www.balboapark.org) for a map and other orientation aids. If you're planning on visiting a number of attractions, ask about the Balboa Park Passport, which entitles the bearer to entry to many of the park's attractions. If $30 is too dear, come on Tuesday, when some of the park's attractions are free.

Where to start? With the park itself: it's a gorgeous place, handsomely landscaped and smartly kept. Though most tourists just swing by and whistle-stop through a handful of the park's museums, it's worth taking a time-out to wander away from the crowds.

Culture vultures will want to take in the temporary exhibitions and permanent displays in the decent **San Diego Museum of Art** (1-619 232 7931, www.sdmart.com, $4-$10), the involving **Museum of Photographic Arts** (1-619 238 7559, www.mopa.org, $4-$6), the low-key **Timken Museum of Art** (1-619 239 5548, www.timkenmuseum.org) and the **Mingei**

Riding the rails in **Mission Bay**. *See p281*.

International Museum of folk art and crafts (1-619 239 0003, www.mingei.org, $3-$6). Families, meanwhile, would be better served by the **Reuben H Fleet Science Center** (1-619 238 1233, www. rhfleet.org, $5-$15), the **Natural History Museum** (1-619 232 3821, www.sdnhm.org, $5-$9) or the **San Diego Aerospace Museum** (1-619 234 8291, www.aerospacemuseum.org, $4-$9).

However, the park's real highlight is **San Diego Zoo** (1-619 234 3153, www.sandiego zoo.org, $15-$32). At the 100-acre site, staff have employed pioneering techniques to help create themed, naturalistic habitats for the 4,000 residents. Start by taking a 40-minute bus tour of the highlights, or riding the aerial Skytram across the park. The pandas and tigers are very popular, as are the polar bears; the calming hummingbird exhibit is the best place to avoid the crowds. And do notice the fabulous plant life: the site is a botanical garden of no little repute. (The zoo also runs the safari-style **Wild Animal Park** in the otherwise uninteresting town of Escondido, 30 miles north of San Diego. Check online for details.)

HILLCREST & OLD TOWN

San Diego's two most famous neighbourhoods have little in common save their interest for the casual visitor. A short drive north of Downtown sits **Hillcrest**, a few pretty streets lined with vintage shops, old-fashioned cafés and gay bars; after the somewhat predictable nightlife Downtown, it'll come as a relief.

A little to the west of Hillcrest, meanwhile, is **Old Town**, the first Spanish settlement in California and the original centre of San Diego. The two dozen original buildings now comprise a State Historic Park, albeit one dotted with a number of rather ordinary restaurants. The visitor centre in the Robinson-Rose building offers further information (1-619 220 5422, www.oldtownsandiego.org); two-hour trolley tours run every half-hour, 9am-4pm daily.

CORONADO

You can get a sense of the might of the US Navy driving across the two-mile Coronado Bay Bridge, which swoops over the harbour from Downtown to the 'island' (actually a peninsula) of Coronado: it yields a dramatic view of the cruisers, destroyers and other vessels anchored in the bay. Most of Coronado is military, but it's also home to a comfortable downtown area and the 1888 **Hotel del Coronado** (1500 Orange Avenue, 1-800 468 3533, www.hoteldel.com), one of the US's largest all-wood structures and a tourist attraction in its own right. The hotel overlooks a lovely beach, neatly tying together the sum total of Coronado's other attractions.

On a mission

In 1767, King Carlos III expelled the Jesuits from Spain's colonies, and asked Junípero Serra, a 54-year-old missionary from Majorca, to take over the missions in Baja California. When Carlos claimed the west coast of America for Spain the following year, Serra trudged up the coast to convert the locals.

Over the course of six decades, Serra and his cohorts founded a string of 21 missions. Their aim was to convert the tribal peoples and establish self-sustaining communities, but they succeeded only in creating wealthy farms while many of the Native American converts died from disease and malnutrition. History, though, was quick to forget, thanks to the Spanish padres' architectural legacy: the white, sometimes Moorish buildings spawned Mission-style architecture and decor, a popular branch of Californian design.

The 21 missions – some original, others reconstructed – are near US 101, which loosely follows the old El Camino Real ('Royal Road', named for Carlos). The first mission, **San Diego de Alcalá** (1-619 281 8449, www. missionsandiego.com), was founded in what is now San Diego; a few miles north sits the 18th, **San Luis Rey de Francia** (1-760 757 3651, www.sanluisrey.org). The remains of **San Juan Capistrano** (1-949 234 1300, www. missionsjc.com) lie in San Juan Capistrano, 40 miles south of Long Beach. LA County itself holds **San Gabriel** (428 S Mission Drive, San Gabriel, 1-626 457 3035) and **San Fernando Rey de España** (15151 San Fernando Mission Boulevard, Mission Hills, 1-818 361 0186), the largest free-standing adobe structure in California. In Ventura is the mission of **San Buenaventura** (1-805 643 4318, www.sanbuenaventuramission.org); slightly further north is **Santa Barbara** (*see p268*). The string continues up the coast as far as Monterey Bay.

HEADING NORTH

The Pacific Ocean sits a ten-minute drive from Old Town, and facing it are a number of beaches and resorts. **Ocean Beach** is surf-bum central, an amusing fusion of Venice and Surfrider Beach up in LA. A few miles north, **Mission Beach** is a little tidier, adding a punctuation point to the **Mission Bay** aquatic resort. The beach is home to the **Belmont Park** amusement park; the resort as a whole, meanwhile, offers watersports and **SeaWorld Adventure Park** (1720 South Shores Drive, 1-619 226 3901, www.seaworld.com, $43-$53), a wildly popular family attraction that includes all manner of watery fun and games.

A ten-minute drive north of here, **La Jolla** (say 'La *Hoy*-a') is Beverly-Hills-on-Sea. The **Museum of Contemporary Art** (700 Prospect Street, 1-858 454 3541, www. mcasd.org, $2-$6) features more than 3,000 post-1950 works, including impressive collections of pop art and Latin American art. Scattered around La Jolla are some elegant modern buildings, among them Louis Kahn's **Salk Institute for Biological Studies** (10010 N Torrey Pines Road). There's more important architecture at the **Scripps Institute of Oceanography** (2300 Expedition Way, 1-858 534 3474, www.aquarium.ucsd.edu, $8-$11): some of its buildings were designed by early California Modernist Irving Gill. The Birch Aquarium here is an excellent place to get acquainted with the local marine life.

Where to eat & drink

Downtown in general and the Gaslamp Quarter in particular are packed with restaurants and bars. **Croce's** restaurant and jazz bar (802 5th Avenue, 1-619 233 4355, www.croces.com, mains $12-$33) is the place that started the revival in the mid 1980s; **Star of the Sea** (1360 N Harbor Drive, 1-619 232 7408, www.starofthesea.com, mains $27-$40) is the town's finest seafood restaurant; and **Kiyo's** (531 F Street, 1-619 238 1726) is tops for sushi. **Confidential** (901 4th Avenue, 1-619 696 8888, www.confidentialsd. com, mains $4-$13), opened in 2005 and has picked up raves for its tapas. Having enjoyed success with **Chive** (558 4th Avenue, 1-619 232 4483, www.chiverestaurant.com, mains $8-$32), Tracy Borkum has now opened the posh but approachable **Laurel** (505 Laurel Street, 1-619 239 2222, $18-$30).

Elsewhere, in Balboa Park, **Prado** (1549 El Prado, 1-619 557 9441, www.pradobalboa. com, mains $8-$32), in the House of Hospitality building, serves Latin-inflected American cuisine. Among the eating options in Hillcrest are **Kemo Sabe** (3958 5th Avenue, 1-619 220 6802, mains $7-$26), where the Southwest meets south-east Asian. On Prospect Street in La Jolla, **George's on the Cove** (No.1250, 1-858 454 4244, www.georgesatthecove.com, mains $15-$42) sets the standards for California cuisine; **Alfonso's** (No.1251, 1-858 454 2232, mains $8-$25) is good for top-of-the-line Mexican meals.

Trips Out of Town

Over the border

After squeaky-clean San Diego, **Tijuana** smacks you upside the head like the third Margarita of the evening. A classic border town, it's loud, messy, edgy and gaudy, an intoxicating if inauthentic taste of the land beyond the border and a vibrant reminder of the ongoing tensions between the mutually dependent gringo north and impoverished south. You can stay without a visa for up to 72 hours but, particularly for non-US or Canadian citizens, it's important to take a passport in case you're asked for proof of nationality on your return.

The main attraction for the daytripper is the tourist-oriented **Avenida Revolución**, a pulsing strip of bars, restaurants, shops and street vendors selling everything from religious kitsch to cheap cigarettes. In recent years, Burger King and the Hard Rock Café have arrived, catering to some of the least adventurous tourists on earth. Nightfall brings boozy exuberance: the legal drinking age is 18, which makes the town popular with San Diego students.

Still, there's more to the place than dodgy tacos and drunk teens. Built in 1928, **Agua Caliente** (on Bulevar Agua Caliente) was once a fabulous Prohibition playground. It's mostly ruined now, and the few remaining bungalows are all private residences, but it's worth a wander. Meanwhile, bullfights are held here in a pair of stadia: **El Toreo** (Bulevar Agua Caliente, +52 664 686 1510) and **Plaza de Toros Monumental** (Calle Rafael Rodríguez s/n, esq López Mateos, +52 664 680 1808), aka the Bullring-by-the-Sea, on Sundays from May to September.

To reach Tijuana, drive south on I-5 or I-805 from San Diego for 25 miles to the San Ysidro International Border. You're best off parking here, then walking, riding the bus or taking a taxi into Tijuana. Alternatively, from Downtown San Diego, take the San Ysidro trolley (1-619 233 3004, www.sdcommute.com), which runs until 1am daily and all night on Saturdays; a one-way fare is a mere $2.50.

The liveliest drinking scene is Downtown, though it can be touristy. Boasting the city's oldest liquor licence, the **Waterfront Bar & Grill** (2044 Kettner Boulevard, 1-619 232 9656) is still one of Downtown's best taps. The **US Grant Bar** (326 Broadway, 1-619 232 3121) is a real old-school classic. Hillcrest also has a number of good bars, among them crowded **Alibi** (1403 University Avenue, 1-619 295 0881), civilised **Live Wire** (2103 El Cajon Boulevard, 1-619 291 7450) and retro-cool **Nu Nu's** (3537 5th Avenue, 1-619 295 2878).

Where to stay

There's a decent choice of accommodation in San Diego. Downtown offers everything from the high-end, stately luxury of the **US Grant** (326 Broadway, 1-619 232 3121, www.usgrant. net, call for rates), due to reopen in late 2006, to **Hotel International San Diego**'s low-budget creature comforts (521 Market Street, 1-619 223 4778, www.sandiegohostels.org, rates $20-$80). The ultra-modern **W Hotel** (421 West B Street, 1-619 231 8220, www.whotels.com, rates $199-$299) is the hipsters' choice, but the area's landmark property is the immaculate **Hotel del Coronado** (*see p280*; rates $315-$550). In La Jolla, the boutiquey, 28-room **Hotel Parisi** (1111 Prospect Street, 1-858 454 1511, www.hotelparisi.com, rates $265-$325) offers a little modish East Coast style.

Tourist information

Balboa Park Visitors Center *House of Hospitality, 1549 El Prado (1-619 239 0512/ www.balboapark.org)*. **Open** 9am-4pm daily.
San Diego Convention & Visitors Bureau *11 Horton Plaza (1-619 236 1212/www.sandiego. org)*. **Open** 8.30am-5pm Mon-Sat.

Getting there

By car
From Downtown LA, take the I-5 south. From West LA, take the I-405 south and then join the I-5. From LA, it takes about 2hrs with no traffic.

By bus
Greyhound (1-800 231 2222, www.greyhound.com) runs around 25 buses a day: fare $25, time 3hrs.

By train
Amtrak (1-800 872 7245, www.amtrak.com) runs about ten trains per day. A round trip costs about $50; journey time is 2hrs 40mins.

Getting around

Although the car is the most efficient way to take it all in, you can also get around the metropolitan area on San Diego Transit Corporation buses or use the San Diego Trolley between Downtown and Old Town to the north or Tijuana to the south. For information on public transport, visit the Transit Store (102 Broadway, 1-619 234 1060, www.sd commute.com). For bus route information, call 1-619 233 3004; for trolley information, call 1-619 231 8549.

Directory

Getting Around	**284**
Resources A-Z	**289**
Further Reference	**297**
Index	**299**
Advertisers' Index	**306**

Features

Travel advice	289
Passport update	293
Monthly climate	296

Santa Monica Pier. *See p77.*

Directory

Getting Around

Arriving & leaving

By air

Los Angeles International Airport (LAX)

1-310 646 5252/www.lawa.org/lax.
LAX is situated on the Westside and has eight terminals. Flying in or out of here is rarely enjoyable: signage is poor and the staff are brusque at best. Most flights from Europe arrive at the Tom Bradley International Terminal; Virgin Atlantic, based at Terminal 2, are the main exception.

The cheapest and most time-consuming way to reach your hotel from LAX is by **public transport**. From the airport, take either the C or G shuttle buses, both free. The C will ferry you to the MTA Bus Center at Vicksburg Avenue and 96th Street, from where you can take a bus; the G heads to the Aviation station on the Metro's Green line (*see p287*). This route, though, isn't recommended.

A fleet of **shuttles** flits between LAX and every neighbourhood in LA. Most will drop you at your hotel; fares start around $25. Pick them up outside the arrival terminals. Many of the same companies will pick you up from your hotel and take you back to LAX when you leave town, given 24 hours' notice. Firms serving LAX include **Golden West Express** (1-800 917 5656, 1-818 679 679 5569, www.goldenwestexpress.com); and **SuperShuttle** (1-800 258 3826, 1-949 776 6601, www.supershuttle.com).

Taxis can be found outside arrivals. Fares from LAX come with a $2.50 surcharge. If you're staying on the Westside, a taxi from LAX will cost $20-$25 plus tip; to Hollywood or beyond, expect to pay twice that. There's a flat rate of $38 ($40.50 including surcharge) between LAX and Downtown. For firms, *see p287*.

Burbank–Glendale–Pasadena Airport

1-818 840 8840/www.burbank airport.com.
If you're flying from a US airport, you may land at Burbank. As with its larger competitor, there are many ways to travel from Burbank to your hotel: by **public transport** (a free

shuttle will take you to the MTA bus stop at Hollywood Way and Thornton Avenue; the airport is also served by Metrolink rail), by **shuttle** (firms are numerous) and by **taxi**.

Major airlines

Air Canada *1-888 247 2262/ www.aircanada.com.*
Air New Zealand *1-800 262 1234/ www.airnewzealand.com.*
Alaska Air *1-800 252 7522/ www.alaskaair.com.*
America West *1-800 235 9292/ www.americawest.com.*
American Airlines *1-800 433 7300/www.aa.com.*
British Airways *1-800 247 9297/ www.britishairways.com.*
Continental Airlines *domestic 1-800 523 3273/international 1-800 231 0856/www.continental.com.*
Delta *domestic 1-800 221 1212/ international 1-800 241 4141/ www.delta.com.*
Lufthansa *1-800 399 5838/ www.lufthansa.com.*
Northwest *domestic 1-800 225 2525/international 1-800 447 4747/ www.nwa.com.*
Southwest Airlines *1-800 435 9792/www.iflyswa.com.*
United Airlines *domestic 1-800 864 8331/international 1-800 538 2929/www.united.com.*
US Air *domestic 1-800 428 4322/ international 1-800 622 1015/ www.usair.com.*
Virgin Atlantic *1-800 862 8621/ www.virgin-atlantic.com.*

By bus

LA's main **Greyhound** station is Downtown, at 1716 E 7th Street. However, Greyhound buses arriving in LA stop at several smaller stations around town. For more on Greyhound, call 1-800 231 2222 or check www.greyhound.com.

By rail

Trains to LA terminate at **Union Station**, at 800 N Alameda Street in Downtown. From here, you can take the Red or Gold lines on Metra to

your destination, or connect with any number of buses. For more on **Amtrak**, which runs services from LA to all corners of the US, call 1-800 872 7245 or see www.amtrak.com.

Driving

Although public transport in LA is improving, it's a brave soul who chooses to tackle the town without a car. LA's sprawl is best negotiated, and enjoyed, from behind the wheel of an automobile.

Driving in LA presents its own challenges. Those used to driving in towns or smaller cities may initially blanche at the five-lane freeways. But LA is far less terrifying for drivers than, say, London or New York, not least because the traffic often moves at a snail's pace. But late at night, when the freeways are quieter, driving can be a true pleasure.

Freeways in LA are referred to by their numbers (10, 110, 405, etc) but also, fairly often, by their names: the I-10 (I stands for Interstate) west of Downtown, for example, is known as the Santa Monica Freeway. For more explanation of the freeway system, *see p70* **Street talk**. There's a speed limit of 65mph on the freeways, but you'll see cars going much faster. Don't expect people to indicate when they change lanes. The outside lanes are the fast lanes, though it's normal to overtake on the inside. It's best to stay in the middle lanes until you need to exit.

Freeways often have a car-pool lane, which only cars carrying at least two or three people (depending on the signs) can use. This is not a members-only scheme; if you fit the criterion, you can use the lane, but make sure you get out of it well before your exit. On your own? Keep out of car-pool lanes. Fines are steep.

All non-freeways are known as surface streets. When you merge on to a freeway from a surface street, accelerate to freeway speed; similarly, be prepared to brake sharply when exiting. Exits are marked by the name of the surface street with which they link; for all businesses listed in this guide, we've included a convenient freeway route and its nearest exit.

Plan your route before you leave. The freeway system can be tricky to negotiate; if you don't know your entrance and exit and the direction you need to go when you find it (north, south, east or west), you may find yourself being sucked off at the wrong exit.

On surface streets, driving is much the same as in any US city. You can turn right on a red light if your way is clear, and the speed limit is 35mph. At four-way stop signs, 'courtesy driving' is expected: cars cross in the order they arrive at the junction. Seatbelts are compulsory.

Large and potentially dangerous intersections, where you should take special care, include the following:

West LA Santa Monica Boulevard at Westwood Avenue; Bundy Drive at Pico Boulevard; Sepulveda Boulevard at National Avenue.
Westwood Wilshire Boulevard at Westwood Avenue.
Century City Santa Monica Boulevard at Avenue of the Stars.
Beverly Hills Wilshire Boulevard at Santa Monica Boulevard.
West Hollywood W Sunset Boulevard at N Crescent Heights Boulevard, N Harper Avenue, N Gardner Avenue.
Hollywood W Sunset Boulevard at N La Brea Avenue, N Highland Avenue.
Downtown S Alvarado Street at W 3rd Street; S Broadway at W 7th Street; Aliso at N Los Angeles Street; S Hill Street at W Jefferson Boulevard; S Main Street at E 2nd Street.

American Automobile Association (AAA)

2601 S Figueroa Street, at W Adams Boulevard, Downtown, Los Angeles, CA 90007 (1-213 741 3686/www. aaa-calif.com). I-110, exit Adams Boulevard west. **Open** 9am-5pm Mon-Fri.
The Triple A has many maps and guides, which won't cost you a penny if you're a member or belong to an affiliated club, such as the British AA. Many hotels offer discounts to AAA members. There are offices all over the city; check online for details.

Car rental

To rent a car, you'll need a credit card and a driver's licence (British licences are valid). Most firms won't rent to anyone under 25; those that do often add a surcharge. The national rental firms, which tend to offer the best deals, have 1-800 numbers and offer online booking (*see below*).

Rates seesaw wildly. It can pay to book weeks ahead: you can put a hold on a car without committing yourself to pay for it. You may qualify for a discount: members of the AAA and affiliated foreign clubs are eligible, and corporate deals are often available. As a rule, you won't be allowed to take a hired car into Mexico.

All quotes from US websites will exclude insurance. US travellers may be covered by your car rental insurance at home; always check before setting out. If not, you'll need to take out liability insurance (SLI) and collision damage waiver (CDW) with the rental firm, which together usually total around $20-$25 a day.

Travellers from outside the US have several choices. The simplest is to book via the firm's US website and pay the expensive insurance premiums details above. One alternative is to head to the separate UK-based websites maintained by a few firms, where the quotes include insurance. A third option for UK travellers who regularly hire cars in the US is

www.insurance4carhire.com, whose comprehensive annual policies can save drivers a fortune over the rates levied by the rental firms themselves.

Car rental companies
Alamo *US: 1-800 462 5266/ www.goalamo.com. UK: 0870 400 4562/www.alamo.co.uk.*
Avis *US: 1-800 230 4898/ www.avis.com. UK: 0870 606 0100/ www.avis.co.uk.*
Budget *US: 1-800 527 0700/ www.budget.com. UK: 0870 153 9170/www.budget.co.uk.*
Dollar *US: 1-866 434 2226/ www.dollar.com. UK: 0800 085 4578/www.dollar.co.uk.*
Eagle Rider Motorcycle Rental *1-310 536 6777/www.eaglerider.com.*
Enterprise *US: 1-800 261 7331/ www.enterprise.com. UK: 0870 350 3000/www.enterprise.com/uk.*
Hertz *US: 1-800 654 3131/ www.hertz.com. UK: 0870 844 8844/ www.hertz.co.uk.*
National *US: 1-800 227 7368. UK: 0116 217 3884. Both: www.nationalcar.com.*
Rent-A-Wreck *1-800 944 7501/ www.rent-a-wreck.com.*
Thrifty *US: 1-800 847 4389/ www.thrifty.com. UK: 01494 751600/www.thrifty.co.uk.*

Highway information

For traffic information, call the **CalTrans Traffic Hotline** on 1-800 427 7623, or check www.dot.ca.gov/hq/roadinfo. Radio station KNX (1070 AM) has traffic reports every six minutes during the day; KFWB (980 AM) gives traffic reports every ten minutes, 24-7.

Parking

Parking restrictions vary from street to street, and the signs detailing them are far from clear. Don't block driveways or fire hydrants, and pay attention to kerb markings: if they're red, you're at risk of getting hit up for a big fine, and you could get towed. Check signs on your side of the block, which should detail parking laws. Most streets have street-cleaning days when parking is illegal; others allow permit parking only after 6pm and at

Directory

weekends. All parking tickets accrued while in a rented vehicle are your responsibility.

Parking meters and free or cheap car parks are plentiful. Most parking meters take quarters (25¢), dimes (10¢) and nickels (5¢). In some bars and restaurants, you can use valet parking; you'll need to tip the valet (usually $1-$2) but it's cheaper than paying a parking fine. If you do get nabbed, call the phone number listed on the ticket; you should be able to pay with a credit card.

The LAPD suggests you keep your rental agreement with you at all times in case your car gets towed or stolen (most people stick it in the glove compartment – bad idea). If you do get towed, call the nearest police precinct to find out where the car has been taken. To reclaim it, you'll need your rental papers, the car's licence number, your passport or driving licence and cash to pay the parking ticket, anywhere from $100 upwards.

Roadside service

There are yellow call boxes on the sides of all the major freeways and some roads in LA County. Still, a cellphone provides more security.

Public transport

LA's public transport system is run by the **Metropolitan Transportation Authority (MTA)**. For information on the network, see **www.metro.net**; here you'll find full system maps and timetables, information on fares, and an interactive journey planner. If you can't get online, a journey-planner service is available by calling 1-800 266 6883.

We've listed a variety of bus routes for almost every venue featured in this book. Note, though, that Downtown is served by innumerable buses. We've listed a variety of buses

for these venues, but if you catch any bus that passes through central Downtown and your destination is also in central Downtown, you'll be no more than a 15-minute walk from your destination.

Buses in LA run every 5-10 minutes on the main routes, less often at night. On main crosstown routes, the service is 24-hour, but there's only one bus an hour after 11pm.

MTA information centres

Miracle Mile *5301 Wilshire Boulevard, at S La Brea Avenue, Miracle Mile. Bus 20, 21, 212, 720/I-10, exit La Brea Avenue north.* **Open** 9am-5pm Mon-Fri. **Map** p312 D4.
Union Station *800 N Alameda Street, at Los Angeles Street. Metro Union Station/bus 33, 38, 40, 42, 68, 70, 71, 78, 79/US 101, exit Alameda Street north.* **Open** 6am-6.30pm Mon-Fri. **Map** p315 D1.
East LA *4501B Whittier Boulevard, at S Ford Boulevard. Bus 18, 65, 720/I-5, exit Olympic Boulevard east.* **Open** 10am-6pm Tue-Sat.
Baldwin Hills *3650 Martin Luther King Boulevard, at Crenshaw Boulevard. Bus 40, 42, 210, 710, 740/I-10, exit Crenshaw Boulevard south.* **Open** 10am-6pm Tue-Sat.

MTA buses

The main mode of public transport in LA are the 2,000-plus white-and-orange MTA buses, which cover over 180 routes throughout the area. The fare on all MTA routes is $1.25; a further 25¢ is required for a transfer to a bus run by a separate agency (for example, Culver City buses; *see p287*). An all-day pass is $3. All MTA bus routes in LA are given a number according to the areas they cover:

1-99	Local services to and from Downtown
100-199	Local east–west services that don't pass through Downtown
200-299	Local north–south services that don't pass through Downtown
300-399	Limited-stop services, usually on routes also served by local services; for example, the 302, which takes the same

	route along Sunset Boulevard as the 2 but makes fewer stops
400-499	Express services to and from Downtown
500-599	Express services in other areas
600-699	Special services (such as the 605, a shuttle bus to the LA County/USC Medical Center
700-799	Rapid bus services (similar to limited-stop services detailed above)

The following are among LA's more useful crosstown bus services. For full details on routes and services, download maps from www.metro.net.

2	Runs along Sunset Boulevard from its junction with the PCH in Castellammare to Westwood, whereupon it runs along the southern border of the UCLA campus. It then takes Sunset Boulevard through West Hollywood, Hollywood, Silver Lake and Echo Park to Downtown, where it picks up Hill Street south as far as Venice Boulevard. The return route is identical save for the fact that it heads north through Downtown on Broadway rather than Hill Street, and that at Pacific Palisades, it takes a left on to Temescal Avenue to the PCH. The 302 takes an identical route as far as the northern edge of Downtown, but makes fewer stops.
4	Runs along Santa Monica Boulevard from Santa Monica to the junction with Sunset Boulevard in Silver Lake, whereupon it follows the same route as the 2. The 304 is its limited-stop version.
20	Runs the length of Wilshire Boulevard from Santa Monica to Downtown, whereupon it takes 6th Street (east) or 7th Street (west). Between Westwood and Downtown, its route is mimicked by the 21. The 720 offers a limited-stop alternative.
156	Runs from the Vermont-Santa Monica Metro station west along Santa Monica Boulevard, then north up Highland Avenue and Cahuenga Boulevard (past the Hollywood Bowl and Universal Studios) into Van Nuys.
212	Runs between the Hollywood-Vine Metro station and Inglewood, along Hollywood Boulevard and La Brea Avenue.
217	Runs between the Vermont-Sunset Metro station and the West LA Transit Center, along Hollywood Boulevard and Fairfax Avenue.

LA DASH buses

DASH stands for Downtown Area Short Hop; its six express shuttles (A, B, C, D, E and F) run every 5-20 minutes and serve many of Downtown's important sites, including the Convention Center, City Hall, USC, Union Station, Exposition Park and Disney Hall.

Despite its name, there are a number of DASH shuttles in other areas of LA. Fares on all DASH routes are 25¢, one of the best bargains in town. For more, see www.ladottransit. com or call either 1-310 808 2273 or 1-323 808 2273. The following are among the most useful routes:

Fairfax (abbreviated in our listings to LDF) Links the Beverly Center with the Melrose District, the Fairfax District and the Miracle Mile.
Hollywood (LDH) Loops around Hollywood, chiefly (but not exclusively) on Highland, Franklin, Fountain and Vermont Avenues.
Hollywood-West Hollywood (LDHWH) Runs between the Beverly Center and the Hollywood-Highland Metro station, via La Cienega and Sunset Boulevards.
Hollywood-Wilshire (LDHWI) Runs between the Hollywood-Vine and Wilshire-Western Metro stations, via Vine Street, Sunset Boulevard, Gower Street, Melrose Avenue and Western Avenue.

Municipal buses

Some areas have their own municipal bus services that complement the MTA services. Among them are the following:
Santa Monica (denoted with prefix 'SM' in this book; SM1, SM2, etc) The Big Blue Bus company serves Santa Monica, Venice and parts of West LA. The fare on all routes is 75¢, with a 25¢ inter-agency transfer. For more, call 1-310 451 5444 or see www.bigbluebus.com.
Culver City (denoted with prefix 'C') Fares on all Culver City's bus routes are 75¢, with inter-agency transfers costing 25¢. Call 1-310 253 6500 or see www.culvercity.org/bus for details.
West Hollywood Cityline is a shuttle service that covers 18 locations in West Hollywood. The service runs only 9am-6pm Mon-Fri, 10am-7.30pm Sat. The fare is 50¢. For more, call 1-800 447 2189.

San Gabriel Valley The Foothill Transit service mostly serves the San Gabriel and Pomona Valleys. Fares are $1-$3.75. For details, call 1-626 967 3147 or see www.foothilltransit.org.
Orange County (denoted with prefix 'OC') For details, call 1-714 636 7433 or see www.octa.net. Most fares are $1.25.

Trains

While LA's **Metro** subway system only covers a limited area of the city, it can be a convenient way to get around, especially from Downtown. One trip costs $1.25. Trains run approximately 5am to 12.30am daily. There's a map of the network on *p320*; below is a summary of its four lines.

Red Line The most useful line for visitors, the Red Line starts at Union Station, crosses Downtown and forks into two branches at Wilshire-Vermont. One continues west to Wilshire-Western; the other heads through Hollywood to Universal Studios. At North Hollywood, you can connect to the Orange Line: it's actually a bus service, but it looks and acts like a train line, running in its own dedicated busway between North Hollywood and Canoga Park.
Gold Line The newest of the Metro lines begins at Union Station (where it connects with the Red Line) and heads north-east through Monterey Hills and Pasadena to Sierra Madre.
Blue Line Starting at the Red Line station at 7th and Figueroa, the Blue Line heads south through South Central all the way to Long Beach.
Green Line This overground route links the area around LAX (there is no station at the airport) with South Central and Norwalk to the east.

Taxis & limos

Because of the city's size, taxis are not a cheap way of getting around LA. Nor are they convenient (there are some taxi ranks, but you can't hail taxis on the street) or especially straightforward (you may well have to give the driver directions). The basic fare is $2; each additional mile will cost you a further $2. There's a $2.50 surcharge on all fares leaving LAX. Large, licensed firms include **Bell Cab** (1-888 235 5222, www.bellcab.com),

Checker Cab (1-800 300 5007, www.lacheckercab.com), **Independent Taxi** (1-800 521 8294, www.taxi4u.com), **United Taxi** (1-800 411 0303, www.unitedtaxi.com) and **Yellow Cab Co** (1-877 733 3305,www.layellowcab.com). For more details, see www.taxicabsla.org.

If you're really flush, you might want to consider hiring a limousine. The limo is the quintessential LA form of transport: you'll see more limos here than just about anywhere else in the world. The cost of hiring one starts at around $50-$60 an hour, usually with a three- to four-hour minimum; on top of this, the driver will expect a decent tip. Companies include **Alliance** (1-800 679 5466, www.alliancelimo.net) and **Everest** (1-866 308 8089, www.everestla.com).

Cycling

There are bike paths down the coast through Santa Monica and Venice, and there are bike lanes in other parts of LA; you can also and mountain bike in Griffith Park and Topanga Canyon. Otherwise, though the volume of traffic and distances involved make cycling difficult (but not impossible) in LA. For more information on bike paths and rentals, *see p255*.

Walking

Certain sections of LA – Santa Monica and Venice, Beverly Hills, parts of West Hollywood, a good chunk of central Hollywood, the commercial centres of Los Feliz and Silver Lake, pretty much all of Downtown – are easily covered on foot. Jaywalking – crossing the street anywhere except at a designated pedestrian crossing – can get you a $100 ticket; police don't generally enforce the penalty on tourists, but it's best to be on the safe side.

Directory

*LHR – LAX**

The online guide to the world's greatest cities
timeout.com

Resources A-Z

Addresses

Written addresses in LA follow the standard US format. Where applicable, the apartment and/or suite number usually appears after the street address, followed on the next line by the city name and the zip code. For more on street-numbering and orientation in Los Angeles, *see p70* **Street talk**.

Age restrictions

Buying alcohol 21
Drinking alcohol 21
Driving 16
Sex (heterosexual couples) 18
Sex (homosexual couples) 18
Smoking 18

Attitude & etiquette

California is famously casual, but there are distinct codes within that bracket in LA. If you're here on business, make it expensive, stylish casual; if you're here to go out, dress up (even in a casual way) rather than down. Few restaurants operate a specific dress code, but nor do the posher places approve of (for example) torn jeans and scruffy sneakers. Pay attention to social pleasantries.

Business

Angelenos work hard. The city's working day starts early and finishes late, influenced by the need of the film industry to start shooting as soon as it gets light and not shout 'cut' until sundown. And ambition fuels overtime. Long car commutes mean there's little drinking culture, so business is more often done over still or sparkling, not red or white.

Don't worry if a meeting is postponed several times. The LA affliction of 'flaking' (making and then rescheduling appointments) occurs both in business and socially; it's nothing personal. That said, if you're here with cap in hand, don't do the flaking yourself. Make sure you know your route and leave time to park, and when you arrive, don't be afraid to sell your wares. Don't be shy about name-dropping, and don't be ashamed to talk about money. Make sure you get everything in writing.

Conventions

The vast **LA Convention Center** (1201 S Figueroa Street, at W 12th Street, Downtown, 1-213 741 1151, www.lacclink.com) is a giant building at the intersection of I-10 and I-110. The facilities are OK, but until the LA Live plans reach fruition (*see p21* **Live and direct**), local amenities are limited to the Hotel Figueroa and the Original Pantry. Allow a ten-minute wait for parking.

Couriers & shippers

DHL *1-800 225 5345/www.dhl.com.* **Credit** AmEx, Disc, MC, V.
Federal Express *1-800 463 3339/ www.federalexpress.com.* **Credit** AmEx, DC, Disc, MC, V.
UPS *1-800 742 5877/www.ups.com.* **Credit** AmEx, MC, V.

Office services & useful organisations

For **Mail Boxes Etc**, *see p294*.

Kinko's *7630 W Sunset Boulevard, at N Stanley Avenue, West Hollywood (1-323 845 4501/www. kinkos.com). Bus 2, 302, LDHWH/ I-10, exit Fairfax Avenue north.* **Open** 24hrs daily. **Credit** AmEx, Disc, MC, V. **Map** p312 C1.
Other locations: throughout LA.
Office Depot *2020 Figueroa Street, at 20th Street, Downtown (1-213 741 0576/www.officedepot.com). Metro Grand/bus 65, 68, 81/I-110, exit Adams Boulevard.* **Open** 8am-8pm Mon-Fri; 9am-7pm Sat; 10am-7pm Sun. **Credit** AmEx, Disc, MC, V. **Other locations**: throughout LA.
Los Angeles Area Chamber of Commerce *350 S Bixel Street, at W 3rd Street, Downtown 90017 (1-213 580 7500/www.lachamber. org). Bus 14, 16, 316, 714/ I-110, exit 3rd-4th Street west.* **Open** 8.30am-5pm Mon-Fri.

Consulates

Australia *2049 Century Park East, at W Olympic Boulevard, West LA (1-310 229 4800). I-405, exit Olympic Boulevard east.*
Canada *550 S Hope Street, between W 5th & W 6th Streets, Downtown (1-213 346 2700). I-110, exit 6th Street east.*
New Zealand *12400 Wilshire Boulevard, at S Carmelina Avenue, West LA (1-310 207 1605). I-405, exit Wilshire Boulevard west.*

Travel advice

For up-to-date information on travel to a specific country – including the latest news on safety and security, health issues, local laws and customs – contact your home country government's department of foreign affairs. Most have websites packed with useful advice for would-be travellers.

Australia
www.smartraveller.gov.au

Canada
www.voyage.gc.ca

New Zealand
www.mfat.govt.nz/travel

Republic of Ireland
http://foreignaffairs.gov.ie

UK
www.fco.gov.uk/travel

USA
http://travel.state.gov

Republic of Ireland *5657 Wilshire Boulevard, at Hauser Boulevard, West LA (1-323 634 6474). I-10, exit Washington Boulevard east.*
United Kingdom *11766 Wilshire Boulevard, Suite 400, at S Carmelina Avenue, West LA (1-310 481 0031/ visas 1-310 481 2900). I-405, exit Wilshire Boulevard west.*

Consumer

Department of Consumer Affairs *1-800 952 5210/deaf callers 1-916 322 1700/www.dca.ca.gov.* Investigates complaints and gives information on consumer rights.
Better Business Bureau of the Southland *1-909 825 7280/ www.bbbsouthland.org.* Good for filing complaints against businesses. Has information on reliable businesses in your area.

Customs

International travellers go through US Customs directly after Immigration. Give the official the filled-in white form you were given on the plane.

Foreign visitors can import the following items duty-free: 200 cigarettes or 50 cigars (not Cuban; over-18s) or 2kg of smoking tobacco; one litre of wine or spirits (over-21s); and up to $100 in gifts ($800 for returning Americans). You can take up to $10,000 in cash, travellers' cheques or endorsed bank drafts in or out of the country tax-free. You must declare and possibly forfeit plants or foodstuffs. Check the **US Customs** website (www.cbp.gov/xp/cgov/travel) for more. **UK Customs & Excise** allows returning travellers to bring in £145 worth of goods tax-free.

Disabled travellers

For over 20 years, California's strict building codes have ensured equal disabled access to all city facilities, businesses, parking lots, restaurants, hotels and other public places. Only older buildings are likely to present problems, and many of those have been retrofitted. The MTA has reduced fares

and specific 'lift' buses. For more, call the **Disabled Riders** line on 1-800 621 7828.

Dial-A-Ride *1-800 827 0829/www. asila.org.* Refers mobility-impaired people and senior citizens to door-to-door transportation services.
Department on Disability *1-213 485 6334/www.lacity.org/dod.* Information and resources. Also has a copy of the Junior League's now-defunct 'Around Town with Ease' booklet: staff can photocopy sections and send them to you.
Society for the Advancement of Travel for the Handicapped *1-212 447 7284/fax 1-212 725 8253/www.sath.org.* Advice and referrals for disabled travellers planning trips to all parts of the US.

Electricity

The US uses a 110-120V, 60-cycle AC voltage. Except for dual-voltage flat-pin shavers, most foreign visitors will need to run appliances through an adaptor. Note that DVDs purchased here will only work in DVD players equipped with multi-region capabilities.

Emergencies

Police, fire, ambulance *911.*
Coast Guard *1-310 215 2112.*
Poison Information Center *1-800 876 4766.*

Gay & lesbian

The **West Hollywood CVB** (1-800 368 6020, 1-310 289 2525, www.visitwest hollywood.com) is another useful source of information. For Progressive Health Services, which runs special clinics for the LGBT communities, *see p291.*

LA Gay & Lesbian Center
1625 N Schrader Boulevard, between Hollywood Boulevard & Selma Avenue, Hollywood (1-323 993 7400/www.lagaycenter.org). Metro Hollywood-Vine/bus 210, 212, 217, 710, LDH/US 101, exit Highland Avenue south. **Open** 9am-8pm Mon-Fri; 9am-1pm Sat (mental health and pharmacy only). **Map** p313 B2.
The largest centre of its type in the world offers myriad resources for LA's LGBT communities.

Health & medical

Health treatment in LA can be pricey even by US standards. Make sure you have full insurance, preferably the kind that pays upfront. Emergency rooms are obliged by law to treat genuine emergencies, though they will do all they can to make you pay. If your medical problem is not an emergency and you do not have insurance, try the **LA Free Clinic** (*see below*), but don't expect an immediate appointment. Also, please bear in mind it's there to provide basic health care to those Americans who can't afford adequate insurance, so don't abuse the service.

Accident & emergency

The hospitals listed below have emergency rooms, and are open 24 hours daily.

Cedars-Sinai Medical Center *8700 Beverly Boulevard, at George Burns Road, West Hollywood (1-310 423 3277/www.csmc.edu). Bus 14, 105, LDHWH, LDF/I-10, exit La Cienega Boulevard north.* **Map** p312 A3.
Century City Doctors' Hospital *2070 Century Park E, between Constellation & Olympic Boulevards, Century City (1-310 772 4000/ www.ccdoctorshospital.com). Bus 28, 316, 328/I-405, exit Santa Monica Boulevard east.* **Map** p311 C4.
Children's Hospital of Los Angeles *4650 W Sunset Boulevard, at N Vermont Avenue, Los Feliz (1-323 660 2450/www.chla.org). Metro Vermont-Sunset/bus 2, 204, 302, 754/US 101, exit Vermont Avenue north.* **Map** p314 A3.
St John's Health Center *1328 22nd Street, at Santa Monica Boulevard, Santa Monica (310 829 5511/www.stjohns.org). Bus 4, 304, SM1, SM10/I-10, exit 26th Street north.* **Map** p310 C3.

Clinics

LA Free Clinic
8405 Beverly Boulevard, at N Orlando Avenue, West Hollywood (1-323 653 1990/www.lafreeclinic. org). Bus 14/I-10, exit La Cienega Boulevard north. **Open** 9am-5pm Mon-Fri. **Map** p312 B3.

Free medical and dental care.
There are other locations at 6043
Hollywood Boulevard in Hollywood
and at 5205 Melrose Avenue.

Progressive Health Services

*8240 Santa Monica Boulevard,
between N Harper & N La Jolla
Avenues, West Hollywood (1-323
650 1508/www.progressivehealth.
org). Bus 4, 218, 304/I-10, exit La
Cienega Boulevard north.* **Open**
11am-6pm Mon-Thur; 11am-5pm Fri.
Map p312 B2.
Founded as a women's health clinic
in the 1980s, this centre now offers a
wide range of medical services, with
a number of clinics devoted to the
LGBT communities.

THE Clinic, Inc

*Ruth Temple Health Center, 3834
S Western Avenue, at W 38th Place
(1-323 730 3502/www.theclinicinc.
org. Bus 102, 207, 757/I-10,
exit Western Avenue south.*
Open 8.30am-5pm Mon-Fri.
A non-profit health centre (the
acronym in the name is 'To Help
Everyone') that offers a number of
different medical services.

Contraception & abortion

Family Planning Associates
Medical Group
*12304 Santa
Monica Boulevard, at Wellesley
Avenue, West LA (1-800 492 3764/
1-310 820 8084/www.fpamg.net).
Bus 4, 304, SM1, SM10/I-405, exit
Santa Monica Boulevard west.* **Open**
8am-4.30pm Mon-Fri; 7am-2pm Sat.
Other locations: 6000 W San
Vincente Boulevard, at W Olympic
Boulevard, West Hollywood (1-323
937 1390).

Dentists

LA Dental Society
*1-213 380 7669/www.ladental
society.com.* **Open** 8.30am-4.30pm
Mon-Thur; 8.30am-4pm Fri.
Referrals to approved practices.

HIV & AIDS

THE Clinic, Inc and
**Progressive Health
Services** (for both, *see above*)
operate HIV/AIDS clinics.

AIDS Healthcare Foundation Clinic
*Suite 200, 99 S La Cienega
Boulevard, at S San Vicente
Boulevard, West Hollywood (24hr*

hotline 1-800 797 1717/1-310 657
9353/www.aidshealth.org). Bus 16,
105/I-10, exit La Cienega Boulevard
north.* **Open** 8.30am-5.30pm
Mon-Thur; 10.30am-5.30pm Fri.
Map p312 B3.
This HIV/AIDS medical provider
offers quality care regardless of the
patient's ability to pay. For other
LA-area locations, see its website.

CDC National STD & AIDS Hotline
1-800 342 2437. **Open** 24hrs daily.
Advice on HIV, AIDS and other
sexually transmitted illnesses.

Jeffrey Goodman Special Care Clinic
*1625 Schrader Boulevard, at
Hollywood Boulevard, Hollywood
(1-323 993 7500/www.laglc.org).
Metro Hollywood-Vine/bus 210,
212, 217, 710, LDH/US 101, exit
Highland Avenue south.* **Open** 9am-
1pm, 2-6pm Mon-Fri. **Map** p313 B2.
Based at the LA Gay & Lesbian
Center, the Goodman Clinic offers
AIDS testing and a comprehensive
HIV/AIDS care programme.

Pharmacies

See p199.

Helplines

Alcoholics Anonymous
*1-323 936 4343/www.alcoholics-
anonymous.org.*
Child Abuse Hotline
1-800 540 4000.
Gamblers Anonymous
*1-877 423 6752/www.gamblers
anonymous.org.*
**LA Commission on Assaults
Against Women/Rape Hotline**
*Central LA 1-213 626 3393/
LA County 1-310 392 8381/
www.lacaaw.org.*
**LA County Department of
Mental Health** *1-800 854 7771/
www.dmh.co.la.ca.us.*
LA Suicide Prevention Hotline
*1-877 727 4747/www.suicide
preventioncenter.org.*
Narcotics Anonymous NA
1-310 390 0279/www.todayna.org.
**Shelter for Victims of
Domestic Violence**
1-800 978 3600/1-805 259 4357.

ID

Even if you look 30, you may
need a photo ID – preferably
a drivers' licence with a photo
included – to get served in
some of the city's bars.

Immigration

Immigration regulations apply
to all visitors to the US. During
the flight, you'll be issued with
an immigration form, which
you need to present to an
official upon landing. You'll
also have your photograph
and fingerprints taken. If you
have a foreign passport, expect
close questioning. For more on
passports, *see p293* **Passport
update**; for visas, *see p296*.

Insurance

Non-nationals should arrange
comprehensive baggage,
trip-cancellation and medical
insurance before they leave
home. Medical centres will ask
for details of your insurance
company and your policy
number if you require
treatment; keep the details
with you at all times.

Internet access

Getting online in LA is
increasingly straightforward.
Most hotels now offer some
form of in-room, high-speed
access for travellers with
laptops, either via cable or via
a wireless network; many also
have a communal computer on
which guests can get online.

A number of bars and cafés
offer wireless access to anyone
with a laptop. *See p169* **Get
connected**; http://metrofree
fi.com is also a useful resource.
If you don't have your own
laptop, a number of locations
have open terminals; among
them are numerous branches
in the LA Public Library chain.
And wireless 'Hot Zones' have
been set up in parts of **Culver
City** (www.culvercitywifi.org),
Hermosa Beach (www.wifi
hermosabeach.com) and **Long
Beach** (www.longbeach
portals.com), and in **Pershing
Square** in Downtown (www.
experiencela.com/pershingwifi).
Anyone with a laptop can
connect for free in these areas.

Directory

Left luggage

Due to security concerns, LAX has suspended its lockers. However, the **LAX International Baggage Service**, while unrelated to the airport itself, does offer storage of baggage outside the airport. For details, call 1-310 863 4109. There are no locker facilities at Union Station.

Legal help

Los Angeles is a ridiculously litigious city. If you get sued, or if you think you have a claim against someone else, there are hundreds of attorneys listed in the *Yellow Pages*, but you're best off getting a recommendation from a trusted friend or colleague. Legal fees are high but most attorneys will work for a percentage of any settlement. If you are arrested and held in custody, call your insurer's emergency number or contact your consulate for assistance (*see p289*).

Libraries

Richard J Riordan Central Library

630 W 5th Street, between Grand Avenue & Flower Street, Downtown (1-213 228 7000/www.lapl.org). *Metro Pershing Square/bus 14, 37, 76, 78, 79, 96/I-110, exit 6th Street east.* **Open** 10am-8pm Mon-Thur; 10am-6pm Fri, Sat; 1-5pm Sun. **Map** p315 B3.
This is the most comprehensive library in the city, with excellent facilities and a very knowledgeable reference staff. For details of the Los Angeles Public Library's other branches, check the website above.

Lost property

If you've lost something at LAX, try your airline, then the general lost property number (1-310 417 0440). For goods lost on MTA buses or trains, call 1-323 937 8920. For items left in taxis, call the firm in question (*see p287*).

Media

Newspapers & magazines

The **Los Angeles Times** (www.latimes.com, 50¢) has been the only big newspaper in town for years. Despite a lack of competition, its coverage of local and worldwide events is often excellent. The Sunday 'Calendar' section covers the arts; one section spotlights Hollywood films and locally produced TV shows, while the other covers architecture, art and performing arts. Its main weakness is its sports coverage.

The monthly **Los Angeles Magazine** (www.lamag.com) has tried to fashion itself as a West Coast *Vanity Fair* without success, though it has improved and often offers good articles about the city. Two dailies, the **Hollywood Reporter** (www.hollywood reporter.com) and **Daily Variety** (www.variety.com) have the scoop on industry deals; both are $1.50.

LA Weekly (www.la weekly.com) is the biggest of the town's free weeklies, though the writing lurches from the inspired to the insipid and the listings could hardly be more convoluted. The scrappy **LA Citybeat** (www.lacitybeat. com) offers a little competition. Both are available in bars and clubs, and from distribution boxes on streetcorners.

Television

LA has affiliates of the three major networks: CBS (**KCBS**, channel 2), NBC (**KNBC**, channel 4) and ABC (**KABC**, channel 7). Competition comes from Fox (**KTTV**, channel 11), WB (**KTLA**, channel 5) and UPN (**KCOP**, channel 13). **KWHY** (channel 22), **KMEX** (channel 34) and **KVEA** (channel 52) serve the city's Latino population, while **KSCI**

(channel 18) and **KDOC** (channel 56) offer a mix of Japanese, Korean, Chinese and Armenian programming.

Various cable firms provide different services to different neighbourhoods. Some networks, such as **E!** and **Comedy Central**, are limited to half- day programming or are unavailable in parts of the city. **KCET** (channel 28) is LA's local PBS affiliate.

Radio

Thanks to the ubiquity of cars, radio plays a crucial role in LA life. As such, it's a shock to find the airwaves are awash with rubbish: from blustery phone-ins to over-familiar classic rock, LA radio is largely awful (public radio stations excepted).

MUSIC RADIO
LA's two major dance and hip hop stations are the Beat (**KKBT**, 100.3 FM, www.the beatla.com) and the popular Power 106 (**KPWR**, 105.9 FM, www.power106.fm). **KCMG** (92.3 FM, www.mega923.com) serves up old-school R&B; alt-rock comes courtesy of **KROQ** (106.7 FM, www.kroq.com). **KLOS** (95.5 FM, www.955 klos.com) mixes soft and hard rock from the 1950s onwards. Classical fans should tune into **KUSC** (91.5 FM, www.kusc. org), **KCSN** (88.5 FM, www. kcsn.org) or **KKGO** (105.1 FM, www.kkgofm.com).

PUBLIC & COLLEGE RADIO
Loyola Marymount's **KXLU** (88.9 FM, www.kxlu.com) provides noisy and nice indie sounds. USC's **KUSC** (91.5 FM, www.kusc.org) mixes classical music and talk. Public stations include **KPFK** (90.7 FM, www.kpfk.org), **KPCC** (89.3 FM, www.scpr.org) and **KCRW** (89.9 FM, www.kcrw. com), which mixes talk shows, news, world music, alt rock,

jazz and classical. Supported by a dedicated subscriber base, it's the standout station in LA.

TALK RADIO

All talk, all the time. **KFI** (640 AM, www.kfi640.com) hosts Rush Limbaugh (9am-noon Mon-Fri) and pop psychologist Dr Laura (noon-3pm Mon-Fri). More moderate is Larry Elder (3-6pm Mon-Fri) on **KABC** (790 AM, www.kabc.com), but the same station also hosts the outspoken Bill O'Reilly (9-11am Mon-Fri). Liberals have KCRW's Warren Olney, whose 'Which Way LA?' (7-7.30pm Mon-Thur) and national 'To the Point' (noon-1pm Mon-Fri) are the best issues-forum radio shows in California.

For news, **KNX** (1070 AM, www.knx1070.com), **KFWB** (980 AM, www.kfwb.com) and **KNNZ** (540 AM) offer 24-hour, up-to-the-minute coverage.

Money

The US dollar ($) is divided into 100 cents (¢). Coins run from the copper penny (1¢) to the silver nickel (5¢), dime (10¢), quarter (25¢) and the less-common half-dollar (50¢). There are also two $1 coins, though neither are common. Notes or 'bills' are all the same green colour and size; they come in denominations of $1, $5, $10, $20, $50 and $100. You will find both old-style and new-style notes in circulation.

ATMs

There are ATMs all over LA: in banks, in some stores and even in the occasional bar. ATMs accept Visa, Mastercard and American Express, as well as Cirrus, Maestro and other debit cards. However, almost all will charge the user a fee.

Banks

Banks in LA are usually open from 9am or 10am to 4.30pm Monday to Thursday; until 6pm on Friday; and from 9am or 10am until 2pm or 3pm on Saturday. Some, but not all, have bureaux de change. Call the numbers below to locate your nearest bank branch.

Bank of America *1-800 944 0404/www.bankofamerica.com.* **Citibank** *1-800 374 9700/ www.citibank.com.* **Wells Fargo** *1-800 869 3557/ www.wellsfargo.com.*

Bureaux de change

There are a number of bureaux de change at LAX. However, you may get a better rate away from the airport.

If you need money wired to you, **Western Union** (1-800 325 6000, www.westernunion.com) can receive funds from anywhere in the world; high commission underscores their 'emergency' status.

American Express Travel Services *327 N Beverly Drive, between Brighton & Dayton Ways, Beverly Hills (1-310 274 8277/ lost & stolen cheques 1-800 221 7282/http://travel.americanexpress. com). Bus 4, 16, 20, 21, 304, 720/ I-10, exit Robertson Boulevard north.* **Open** 10am-6pm Mon-Fri; 10am-3pm Sat. **Map** p311 C3. **Other locations:** 8493 W 3rd Street, West Hollywood (1-310 659 1682); 269 S Lake Avenue, Pasadena (1-626 449 2281).

Travelex *421 N Rodeo Drive, between Brighton Way and Little Santa Monica Boulevard, Beverly Hills (1-310 247 0892/www. travelex.com). Bus 4, 16, 20, 21, 304, 720/I-10, exit Robertson Boulevard north.* **Open** 9.30am-5.30pm Mon-Fri. **Map** p311 C3. **Other locations:** throughout LA.

Credit & charge cards

MasterCard and **Visa** are accepted almost universally; **American Express** is also prominent. Less common cards include **Carte Blanche**, **Diners Club** and **Discover**. For lost or stolen cards, call the numbers over the page.

Passport update

People of all ages who enter the US on the Visa Waiver Scheme (*see p281*) are now required to carry their own machine-readable passport, or MRP. MRPs are recognisable by the double row of characters along the foot of the data page. All burgundy EU and EU-lookalike passports issued in the UK since 1991 (and still valid) should be machine readable. Some of those issued outside the country may not be, however; in this case, holders should apply for a replacement even if the passport has not expired. Check at your local passport-issuing post office if in any doubt at all.

The US requirement for passports to contain a 'biometric' chip applies only to those issued from 26 October 2006. By then, all new and replacement UK passports should be compliant, following a gradual phase-in. The biometric chip contains a facial scan and biographical data.

Though it is being considered for 2008 (when ID cards may be introduced), there is no current requirement for UK passports to contain fingerprint or iris data. The application process remains as it was, except for new guidelines that ensure the photograph you submit can be used to generate the facial scan in the chip.

Further information for UK citizens is available at www.passport.gov.uk or 0870 521 0410. Nationals of other countries should check well in advance of their trip whether their passport meets the requirements for the time of their trip, at http://travel.state.gov/visa and with the issuing authorities of their home country.

Directory

American Express 1-800 992 3404/www.americanexpress.com.
Diners Club 1-800 234 6377/ www.dinersclub.com.
Discover 1-800 347 2683/ www.discovercard.com.
MasterCard 1-800 622 7747/ www.mastercard.com.
Visa 1-800 847 2911/www.visa.com.

Travellers' cheques

Although they're less common than they were a decade ago, travellers' cheques are still accepted in a majority of shops and restaurants, albeit with some proof of identity (such as a passport). Draw the cheques in US dollars before your trip.

Opening times

Though many establishments in the LA region open at 8am or 9am, the magic hour for shoppers is 10am, when most businesses open. Shops are usually open until 6pm, with malls open until 9pm or later. Museums generally welcome visitors until 6pm, though many are open later on one or two days during the week.

Postal services

Post offices are usually open 9am to 5pm, but often have last collections at 6pm. Many are open on Saturdays from 9am to 1pm or 2pm. Stamps for postcards within the US cost 23¢; for Europe, the charge is 70¢. Below are listed several post offices around the city; for others, dial 1-800 275 8777 or check www.usps.com.

Beverly Hills 325 N Maple Drive, between Burton Way & W 3rd Street. Bus 16/I-10, exit Robertson Boulevard north. **Open** 8.30am-5.30pm Mon-Fri. **Map** p311 D2.
Downtown 505 S Flower Street, at W 5th Street. Metro 7th Street-Metro Center/bus 14, 37, 76, 78, 79/I-110, exit 6th Street east. **Open** 8.30am-5.30pm Mon-Fri. **Map** p315 B3.
Santa Monica 1248 5th Street, at Arizona Avenue. Bus 4, 304, SM2, SM3, SM4, SM5, SM9/ I-10, exit 4th-5th Street north. **Open** 9am-6pm Mon-Fri; 9am-3pm Sat. **Map** p310 B2.

West Hollywood 1125 N Fairfax Avenue, at Santa Monica Boulevard. Bus 4, 217, 218, 304/I-10, exit Fairfax Avenue north. **Open** 8.30am-5.30pm Mon-Sat. **Map** p312 C2.

Poste restante

If you need to receive mail but don't know what your address will be, have it sent to: General Delivery, [your name], Los Angeles, CA 90086/9999, USA. You can then pick it up at the main Downtown post office at 760 N Main Street.

Private mail services

Mail Boxes Etc

1-800 789 4623/www.mbe.com. **Open** hours vary by location. **Credit** AmEx, Disc, MC, V. One of many LA mail forwarding services, Mail Boxes Etc also offers shipping and business services.

Religion

Whether established religion or cult, if it exists, then it's here. For more, see p39 **Have a little faith**.

Places of worship

Aatzei Chaim Synagogue 8018 W 3rd Street, at S Laurel Avenue, Fairfax District (1-323 782 1321). Bus 16, 217, 218/I-10, exit La Cienega Boulevard north. **Map** p312 C3.
All Saints Episcopal Church 504 N Camden Drive, at Santa Monica Boulevard, Beverly Hills (1-310 275 0123/www.allsaintsbh.org). Bus 4, 16, 304/I-10, exit Robertson Boulevard north. **Map** p311 C3.
Beverly Hills Presbyterian Church 505 N Rodeo Drive, at Santa Monica Boulevard, Beverly Hills (1-310 271 5194/www.bhpc. org). Bus 4, 16, 304/I-10, exit Robertson Boulevard north. **Map** p311 C3.
Congregation Beth Israel Synagogue 8056 Beverly Boulevard, at S Crescent Heights Boulevard, West Hollywood (1-323 651 4022). Bus 14/I-10, exit La Cienega Boulevard north. **Map** p312 C3.
First Baptist Church of Hollywood 6682 Selma Avenue, at Las Palmas Avenue, Hollywood (1-323 464 7343). Metro Hollywood-Highland/bus 2, 156, 302/US 101, exit Hollywood Boulevard west. **Map** p313 A2.

Hope Lutheran Church of Hollywood 6720 Melrose Avenue, at N Citrus Avenue, Hollywood (1-323 938 9135/www.hopelutheran church.net). Bus 10, 11/I-10, exit La Brea Avenue north. **Map** p313 A3.
Islamic Cultural Centre 434 S Vermont Avenue, between W 4th & W 5th Streets, Koreatown (1-213 382 9200). Metro Wilshire-Vermont/bus 204, 754/I-10, exit Vermont Avenue north.
St Mary of the Angels Anglican Church 4510 Finley Avenue, at Hillhurst Avenu, Los Feliz (1-323 660 2700/www.stmaryoftheangels. org). Bus 26, 180, 181/I-5, exit Los Feliz Boulevard east. **Map** p314 B2.
St Monica's Roman Catholic Church 725 California Avenue, at Lincoln Boulevard, Santa Monica (1-310 393 9287). Bus 20, 720, SM2/I-10, exit Lincoln Boulevard north. **Map** p310 B2.
Wat Thai Buddhist Temple 8225 Coldwater Canyon Avenue, at Roscoe Boulevard, North Hollywood (1-818 785 9552/www.watthaiusa. org). Bus 147, 152, 167/I-405, exit Roscoe Boulevard east.
Westwood United Methodist Church 10497 Wilshire Boulevard, at Warner Avenue, Westwood (1-310 474 4511). Bus 20, 21, 720/ I-405, Wilshire Boulevard east. **Map** p311 A3.

Safety

LA is generally a safe city, but it still pays to be cautious: don't fumble with your wallet or a map in public; avoid walking alone at night; keep your car doors locked while driving; and avoid parking in questionable areas.

As a pedestrian, walk with confidence. As a motorist, avoid coming off the freeway in unfamiliar areas, never drive too slowly or too quickly, and always carry a map and a cellphone. Areas where you should be careful at night include parts of Silver Lake, Hollywood, Koreatown, Watts, Compton, Echo Park, Highland Park, Downtown and Venice.

Smoking

Smoking is banned in all enclosed public areas: shops, restaurants, cinemas, hotels (except some private rooms) and bars. Some bars and restaurants have terraces where smoking is allowed. However, the city of Calabasas, has banned smoking in all public places, inside and out.

Study

There's no better place to study movies than LA. USC's **School of Cinema-TV** (1-213 740 2235, www-cntv.usc.edu) has a great reputation, as does the **School of Theater, Film and Television** at UCLA (1-310 825 5761, www.tft.ucla.edu). The **American Film Institute** (1-323 856 7600, www.afi.com), the **Art Center College of Design** in Pasadena (1-626 396 2200, www.artcenter.edu) and the graduate programme at Chapman University's **School of Film & Television** in Orange County (1-714 997 6765, www.ftv.chapman.edu) are also smart choices.

Telephones

Dialling

Collect/reverse-charge calls *0*.
Local enquiries *411*.
National enquiries *1 + [area code] + 555 1212 (if you don't know the area code, dial 0 for the operator)*.
International calls *011 + [country code] + [area code] + [number]*.
Police, fire or medical emergencies *911*.

Area codes

LA is covered by several area codes. Calling outside your local area code from your hotel can be costly; you're generally better off using a payphone or even your cellphone (*see below*).

Local area codes

213 Downtown
310 Malibu, Santa Monica, Venice, Culver City, West LA, Westwood, Beverly Hills, parts of West Hollywood, Inglewood
323 parts of West Hollywood, Hollywood, East LA, South Central
562 Long Beach
626 San Gabriel Valley
818 San Fernando Valley
949 Laguna & Newport Beaches

Long-distance codes

415 San Francisco
619 San Diego
702 Las Vegas
714 Orange County
805 Santa Barbara

Free codes

1-800, 1-888, 1-877, 1-866

Making a call

If you're calling a number with the same code as the phone from which you're calling, dial the (seven-digit) number without the area code. If you're calling a different area code, dial **1** + **three-digit area code** + **seven-digit number**. All phone numbers in this guidebook have been listed in this eleven-digit format.

For international calls, dial **011** followed by the country code (UK **44**; New Zealand **64**; Australia **61**; Germany **49**; Japan **81**). If you need operator assistance with international calls, dial **00**.

Public & hotel phones

On a hotel phone, you may have to dial **0** or **9** before dialling the number. Check rates before you call: using a phonecard, credit card or payphone may work out cheaper, especially on long-distance or international calls (though you'll be charged a flat rate, usually a dollar for even free calls). Smaller hotels and motels may not allow you to call long-distance unless you call collect or use a credit card.

Payphones are plentiful in LA. They vary in appearance, but all work in the same way: simply pick up the receiver, listen for a dialling tone and feed it change. Operator and directory calls are free. Local calls cost 35¢, with the cost increasing with the distance (a recorded voice will tell you to feed in more quarters). Make sure you have plenty of change: payphones take only nickels, dimes and quarters.

It's nigh on impossible to make international calls using cash at a payphone, but you can use your MasterCard credit card with **AT&T** (1-800 225 5288) or **MCI** (1-800 950 5555). Alternatively, buy a phonecard from large stores such as Rite-Aid, Sav-On and Walgreens. The card will give you a fixed amount of time anywhere in the US and abroad.

Mobile/cellular phones

LA operates on the 1900mHz GSM frequency. Travellers with tri-band handsets should be able to connect to one of the networks here, assuming their service provider at home has an arrangement with a local network; the majority do, but it's worth checking before you depart. European visitors with only dual-band phones will need to rent a handset on arrival from a company such as **TripTel** (*see below*).

Check the price of calls with your home service provider before you arrive. Rates may be hefty and, unlike in the UK, you'll be charged for receiving as well as making calls.

TripTel

Tom Bradley International Terminal, LAX (1-310 645 3500/www.triptel. com). **Open** 7am-10pm daily. **Credit** AmEx, DC, Disc, MC, V.
Cellphone rental costs from $3 a day.

Time & dates

California operates on **Pacific Standard Time**, eight hours behind GMT (London), three hours behind Eastern Standard Time (New York), two hours behind Central Time (Chicago) and one hour behind Mountain Time (Denver). Clocks go forward by an hour on the last Sunday in April, and back on the last Sunday in October.

In the US, dates are written in the order of month, day, year; 5.1.06 is the first of May.

Tipping

Unlike in Europe, tipping is a way of life in the US. Many locals in service industries rely on gratuities for the lion's share of their income, so be sure to tip fairly. In general, tip bellhops and baggage handlers $1-$2 a bag; tip cab drivers, wait staff, hairdressers and food delivery agents 15-20 per cent of the total tab; tip valets $2-$3; and tip counter staff 25¢ to ten per cent of the order, depending on its size. In restaurants, tip at least 15 per cent and usually nearer 20 per cent of the total. In bars, bank on tipping a buck a drink, especially if you plan on hanging around. If you look after the bartender, he or she will look after you.

Tourist information

The LACVB provides a wealth of information on the city, both online and at its Downtown information centre. For local tourist offices (in the likes of Santa Monica and Long Beach), see the relevant Sightseeing chapter (*pp68-136*).

Los Angeles Convention & Visitors Bureau *685 S Figueroa Street, at Wilshire Boulevard, Downtown (1-213 689-8822/www. lacvb.com). Metro 7th Street-Metro Center/bus 66, 81, 366, 381/I-110, exit 6th Street east.* **Open** 8.30am-5pm Mon-Fri. **Map** p315 B3.

Visas

Under the **Visa Waiver Scheme**, citizens of 27 countries – including the UK, Ireland, Australia and New Zealand – do not need a visa for stays in the US of less than 90 days (business or pleasure). Visitors are required to have a machine-readable passport that's valid for the full 90-day period (longer is safer) and a return or open standby ticket. Canadians and Mexicans do not need visas but must have legal proof of residency. All other travellers need visas.

Monthly climate

	Average high	Average low	Average rain
Jan	68°F (20°C)	48°F (9°C)	3.3in (8.5cm)
Feb	70°F (21°C)	50°F (10°C)	3.7in (9.4cm)
Mar	70°F (21°C)	52°F (11°C)	3.1in (8.0cm)
Apr	73°F (23°C)	54°F (12°C)	0.8in (2.1cm)
May	75°F (24°C)	58°F (14°C)	0.3in (0.8cm)
June	80°F (27°C)	61°F (16°C)	0.1in (0.2cm)
July	84°F (29°C)	65°F (18°C)	0.0in (0.1cm)
Aug	85°F (29°C)	66°F (19°C)	0.1in (0.3cm)
Sept	83°F (28°C)	65°F (18°C)	0.3in (0.8cm)
Oct	79°F (26°C)	60°F (16°C)	0.4in (0.9cm)
Nov	73°F (23°C)	53°F (12°C)	1.1in (2.7cm)
Dec	69°F (21°C)	48°F (9°C)	1.9in (4.9cm)

However, given current security fears, all travellers are advised to double-check current requirements in advance of their trip. Full information, as well as visa application forms, can be obtained from your nearest US embassy or consulate. If you need to apply for a visa, allow plenty of time for officials to process your application.

For more on passports, *see p293* **Passport update**. For details on visa requirements, see http://travel.state.gov. UK citizens can find information at www.usembassy.org.uk, or by calling the embassy's Visa Information Hotline on 09042 450100; calls cost £1.20 a minute from BT landlines.

When to go

With an annual average of 300 clear days, LA offers generally idyllic weather. However, the smog can be awful, especially when combined with the summer heat and, in July/August and October/November, the Santa Ana winds.

The best times to visit LA are between September and November, and between March and May, when temperatures are cooler and the air is nicer. June and July are best avoided: the coastal cities are swathed in sea mist, referred to as 'June gloom', and temperatures inland soar. In comparison to the averages in the chart to the left, summer temperatures are generally around 5-8°F (3-5°C) warmer in the Valleys, and 3-5°F (2-3°C) cooler on the coast.

For the weather, call 1-213 554 1212. For 24-hour smog and air-quality checks, contact **South Coast Air Quality Management District** (1-800 288 7664, www.aqmd.gov).

Public holidays

New Year's Day (1 Jan); **Martin Luther King Jr Day** (3rd Mon in Jan); **President's Day** (3rd Mon in Feb); **Memorial Day** (last Mon in May); **Independence Day** (4 July); **Labor Day** (1st Mon in Sept); **Columbus Day** (2nd Mon in Oct); **Veterans' Day** (11 Nov); **Thanksgiving Day** (4th Thur in Nov); **Christmas Day** (25 Dec).

Working in LA

Working in the US has become increasingly difficult for non-nationals in the years since 11 September 2001. Contact the US embassy in your home country for details on visas; working here without one isn't recommended.

Directory

Further Reference

Books

Non-fiction

Kenneth Anger *Hollywood Babylon*
The dark side of Tinseltown.
Reyner Banham *Los Angeles: The Architecture of Four Ecologies*
Architectural history and paean to life in the fast lanes.
Leon Bing *Do or Die*
History of LA gang culture.
Donald Bogle
Bright Boulevards, Bold Dreams
Long-overdue history of black Hollywood.
Carolyn Cole & Kathy Kobayashi *Shades of LA: Pictures from Ethnic Family Albums*
Beautifully rendered scrapbook of the ethnic family in LA.
Mike Davis *City of Quartz; Ecology of Fear; Magical Urbanism: Latinos Reinvent the US City*
Exhilarating Marxist critique of LA's city 'planning'; more apocalyptic LA-bashing, this time focusing on LA's precarious ecology; Davis's view of Latino influence on modern cities.
Douglas Flamming
Bound for Freedom
The history of African-Americans in LA from its birth to Jim Crow.
Hampton Hawes with Don Asher *Raise Up Off Me*
Portrait of a troubled LA jazz genius.
Barney Hoskyns *Waiting for the Sun; Hotel California*
Californian music in the 1960s
Steven Isoardi *The Dark Tree: Jazz and the Community Arts in LA*
A history of the South Central arts movement of the 1960s and '70s.
Jenna Jameson with Neil Strauss *How to Make Love Like a Porn Star*
Nobel Prize for Literature runner-up.
Norman Klein *The History of Forgetting: Los Angeles and the Erasure of Memory*
Part factual, part fictional analysis of LA's myth creation by eccentric cultural critic.
Chris Kraus, Jan Tumlir & Jane McFadden *LA Artland*
Contemporary update of LA's art scenes.
Tommy Lee et al *The Dirt*
Sunset Strip's 'hair metal' days, from those who survived.
Carey McWilliams *Southern California: An Island on the Land; North From Mexico: The Spanish-Speaking People of Los Angeles*
A history of LA's sinfulness and scandals; pioneering celebration of the Mexican heritage in the Southwest (written in 1948).

Leonard Pitt & Dale Pitt
Los Angeles A-Z
An interesting encyclopaedia of LA's people, places and institutions.
David Reyes & Tom Waldman *Land of A Thousand Dances*
History of East LA music, from 'Brown-Eyed Soul' to Los Lobos.
Michael Jacob Rochlin *Ancient LA*
Architecture and archeology.
Luis J Rodriguez *Always Running: La Vida Loca – Gang Days in LA*
Autobiog of a Latino gang member.
Josh Sides *LA City Limits*
History of African-Americans in LA from the Depression to the present.
Marc Spitz & Brendan Mullen
We Got the Neutron Bomb
Lovingly stinky oral history of the LA punk movement.
Randall Sullivan *LAbyrinth*
The murders of Biggie and Tupac investigated by an LA cop
Paul Theroux *Translating LA*
Around the neighbourhoods with the great traveller.
David Thomson
The Whole Equation
An engaging history of Hollywood.

Fiction

Charles Bukowski *Hollywood*
The legendarily drunk poet's musings on making a movie in Tinseltown.
James M Cain *Double Indemnity, Mildred Pierce*
Classic 1930s/'40s noir.
Raymond Chandler
The Big Sleep; Farewell, My Lovely; The Long Goodbye
Philip Marlowe in the classic hard-boiled detective novels.
Bret Easton Ellis *Less Than Zero*
1980s coke-spoon-chic novel about being young and fast on both coasts.
James Ellroy *The Black Dahlia, The Big Nowhere, LA Confidential, White Jazz*
Ellroy's LA Quartet is a masterpiece of contemporary noir; the black and compelling *My Dark Places* recounts his search for his mother's killer.
John Fante *Ask the Dust*
Depression-era Los Angeles as seen by an Italian emigré.
David Fine (ed)
Los Angeles in Fiction
Anthology including work by Walter Mosely, Norman Mailer, Thomas Pynchon and James M Cain.
F Scott Fitzgerald
The Pat Hobby Stories
Short stories about Hollywood from a writer who died there.
Dennis Hensley
Misadventures in the 213
A laugh-out-loud romp through gay Hollywood.

Elmore Leonard *Get Shorty*
Miami loan shark turns movie producer in gutsy thriller.
John Miller (ed)
Los Angeles Stories
Fiction and essays by Henry Miller, Fitzgerald, Chandler et al.
Walter Mosely
The Easy Rawlins Mystery Series
The heir apparent to Marlowe, Easy Rawlins is an African-American PI in post-war LA. Also *Always Outnumbered, Always Outgunned*, with ex-con Socrates Fowler.
Budd Schulberg
What Makes Sammy Run?
Furious attack on the studio system by one of its employees.
Bruce Wagner *I'm Losing You; I'll Let You Go; Still Holding*
Biting Hollywood satire.
Nathaniel West
The Day of the Locust
Classic, apocalyptic raspberry blown at the movie industry.
Evelyn Waugh *The Loved One*
Hilarious and accurate satire on the American way of death.

Film

The Aviator (2004)
Glory days of Old Hollywood and Howard Hughes.
Barfly (1987)
Anti-hero meets anti-hero, as Mickey Rourke takes a Bukowski script and runs with it. Or stumbles drunkenly.
The Big Lebowski (1998)
John Goodman. Jeff Bridges. Dude.
Boogie Nights (1997)
The 1970s and '80s San Fernando Valley porn industry uncovered.
Boyz N the Hood (1991)
Can a right-thinking father stop his son falling prey to the culture of gang violence in South Central LA?
Bulworth (1998)
Hilarious political satire starring and co-scripted by Warren Beatty, who plays a rapping Democrat senator.
Chinatown (1974)
Roman Polanski's dark portrait of corruption in 1940s LA.
City of Angels (1998)
LA has never looked more dreamily beautiful than in this remake of Wim Wenders' *Wings of Desire*.
Clueless (1995)
Satirical portrait of LA rich kids and their lives at Beverly Hills High.
Collateral (2004)
Jamie Foxx gives Tom Cruise the runaround in this after-dark thriller.
Colors (1988)
Gritty locations, plausible dialogue and a laudable lack of sensationalism in Dennis Hopper's take on cops versus LA's murderous gangs.

Crash (2005)
Altmanian, Oscar-winning run around 48 hours in LA.
A Day Without a Mexican (2004)
Inventive illegal immigration mockumentary.
Double Indemnity (1944)
Billy Wilder's sexy, sweaty, classic film noir, with dialogue by Chandler.
Earth Girls are Easy (1988)
The complexities of being a Valley Girl, explored through the eyes of three aliens.
Echo Park (1986)
Obscure indie movie of neighborhood weirdos, Tom Hulce among them!
Edgeplay (2004)
Gloriously seedy doc about punk jailbait girl group the Runaways.
El Norte (1983)
Life as part of the LA underbelly of illegal immigrants searching for a better life in the north.
The End of Violence (1997)
The Griffith Observatory has a starring role in Wim Wenders' love-hate letter to Hollywood.
Falling Down (1992)
Michael Douglas turns vigilante terrorist in a hellish LA.
Get Shorty (1995)
John Travolta as a Miami loan shark who ends up in Hollywood.
Heat (1995)
Sprawling crime drama starring Pacino and De Niro.
The Hours (2002)
Julianne Moore struggles to cope in 1950s suburban LA.
Jackie Brown (1997)
Quentin Tarantino's mature adaptation of Elmore Leonard's *Rum Punch*: Pam Grier in sterling form.
LA Confidential (1997)
The film version of Ellroy's novel.
LA Story (1991)
Steve Martin's love letter to LA: a sentimental but sweet look at a group of affluent Angelenos.
The Limey (1999)
Terence Stamp heads to LA in a vengeful state of mind.
The Long Goodbye (1973)
Robert Altman's superb homage to Chandler, with Elliott Gould playing Marlowe as a shambling slob.
Los Angeles Plays Itself (2003)
Epic bootleg history of the world's most filmed city is worth finding.
Mayor of Sunset the Strip (2003)
Bio-documentary on legendary KROQ DJ Rodney Bingenheimer.
Million Dollar Baby (2004)
Good pastiche of the city's gritty downtown boxing world.
Mulholland Dr. (2001)
David Lynch's compelling *noir*.
The People vs Larry Flynt (1996)
Engaging portrayal of LA's very own porn king.
Pretty Woman (1990)
Richard Gere and Julia Roberts in an unlikely, if rather glossy, Hollywood love story.

Pulp Fiction (1994)
Tarantino's witty, vivid, violent interweaving of three LA stories.
Seabiscuit (2003)
A horse is a horse, of course…
Shampoo (1975)
In which Warren Beatty single-handedly takes on womankind and almost wins.
Short Cuts (1993)
More Altman, this time a epic series of interconnected lives, adapted from stories by Raymond Carver.
Singin' in the Rain (1952)
The best ever movie about Hollywood.
Strange Days (1995)
Kathryn Bigelow's dystopian view of Los Angeles on the eve of 2000.
Sunset Boulevard (1950)
Gloria Swanson and William Holden star in a still-relevant tale of faded fame, creative ambition and ego in Hollywood.
Swingers (1996)
An out-of-work actor and his pals trawl the town looking for honeys.
Terminator 2: Judgment Day (1991)
Arnie as a caring cyborg. Really.
Timecode (2000)
Mike Figgis's inventive, four-screen piece of LA realism.
Training Day (2001)
Denzel Washington plays bad cop to Ethan Hawke's rookie.
We Jam Econo (2005)
Wild and woolly history of San Pedro avant-punks the Minutemen.

Music

Bicycle Thief
You Come and Go Like a Pop Song
Ex-Thelonius Monster fuck-up Bob Morris' blue valentine to his fucked-up city.
Dr Dre *The Chronic*
Released in 1992, *The Chronic* flipped hip hop on its head. Snoop Doggy Dogg has never been on better form.
The Doors *LA Woman*
The last album from the Los Angeles quartet.
The Eagles *Hotel California*
The defining album of the 1970s, for better or worse.
Earlimart *Treble & Tremble*
Haunting ode to late singer Elliott Smith.
Elliott Smith
From a Basement on a Hill
Echo Park hermit Elliott Smith's haunting ode to himself.
Hole *Celebrity Skin*
'This album is dedicated to all the stolen water of Los Angeles.'
LA Free Music Society
The Lowest Form of Music
Mammoth 10-disc retrospective of influential Pasadena weirdos.
Mötley Crüe *Girls, Girls, Girls*
The girls! The guitars! The spandex! The haircuts!

Nels Cline with Devin Sarno
Buried on Bunker Hill
Avant-garde paean to a vanished LA neighbourhood.
Randy Newman
Trouble in Paradise
The closest LA's finest songwriter has come to making an LA album.
NWA *Straight Outta Compton*
The moment at which gangsta rap went mainstream. Tough to overestimate its influence.
X *Los Angeles*
A punk classic, still fresh.
Tom Waits *Small Change*
Streetcorner balladry from the longtime resident of the Tropicana.

Websites

City of Los Angeles
www.ci.la.ca.us
The LA government's home page.
Curbed LA
http://curbed.la.com
Urban planning, culture, gossip, architecture… You name it, really. A terrific website.
Defamer *www.defamer.com*
'The LA gossip rag', runs the subtitle, but it's far rather better written than that description might suggest.
Experience LA
www.experiencela.com
Produced by a variety of groups, including MTA and the LACVB.
Flavorpill *http://la.flavorpill.net*
The hipster's guide to what's on in LA, tidily presented online but also available for free on email.
LA Cowboy
http://lacowboy.blogspot.com
The blog of influential Downtown booster Brady Westwater.
LA Observed *www.laobserved.com*
What's happening, and what's going to happen, in LA.
LA Times *www.latimes.com*
You'll need to register to access much of the archive. The *Times* also runs Calendar Live (*www.calendarlive.com*).
LA Weekly *www.laweekly.com*
Listings information for bars, clubs, music venues and the like.
LA.com *www.la.com*
A fine guide to bars, shops, restaurants and after-hours culture.
LACVB *www.lacvb.com*
Tourist information.
MTA *www.metro.net*
Public transportation information.
Public Art in LA
www.publicartinla.com
An excellent guide.
Seeing Stars
www.seeing-stars.com
Not the best-looking site on the net, by any means, but there's plenty of good celeb-related stuff buried here.
Traffic News *http://cad.chp.ca.gov*
The latest incidents on the road.
Yahoo! Maps *http://maps.yahoo.com*
Get around town.

Index

Note: page numbers in **bold** indicate section(s) giving key information on a topic; *italics* indicate photographs.

a

A + D Museum 99
A Noise Within 263
Abbot Kinney Boulevard 188
Absolut Chalk Street Painting Festival 205
Academy Awards 208
Accelerated Charter School 29
accommodation 44-66
 by price
  budget 46, 48, 50, 55, 57, 59, 61, 63, 66
  expensive 45-47, 50, 52, 53, 55, 57, 64, 65, 66
  moderate 44, 47, 48, 50, 51, 52, 56, 58, 59, 60, 62, 63, 64, 65, 66
 camping 65
 chains 46
 gay 230
 hostels 55
 prices & services 44
 see also p305 Accommodation index
Actors' Gang Theatre 263
Adamson House 73
addresses & street names 289
AFI Los Angeles International Film Festival 220
African American LA 119
 festival 206
 literary 32
age restrictions 289
Ahmanson Theatre 113
airlines 284
airports 284
 accommodation 65
Al Kramers 89
Alex Theatre 264
Alhambra 128
Allied Model Trains 211, *211*
American Cinematheque 218, *219*, 221

Amoeba Music 97
Anaheim 135
 visitor centre 135
Angels Attic Museum 77
Angels Flight 114
Angels of Anaheim 252
antique shops 200-201
aquariums 78, 131, 133
Aquarium of the Pacific 132, *132*, 133
Arcadia 128
architecture 23-29
 Googie style **27**, 99
 modernism 29, 273
 tours 71
 vernacular 28
ArcLight cinema 97, 218, 219
art 222-227
 festivals 225
 galleries 222-227
 public art 80, 110, 126
 supplies 182
ATMs 293
attitude & etiquette 289
Autry Museum of the American West 105
Autry Southwest Museum of the American Indian 107
Avalon 27
Avila Adobe 109

b

babysitters 210
Baca, Judith 126
Baja California missions 281
bakeries 192, **193**
Baldwin Hills Crenshaw Plaza 123
Ballona Wetlands 81
Barker, Bob 217
Barneys New York 179
Barnsdall Art Park 103, 104, *104*
bars 170-178
 best 172
 gay 230
 vintage 174-175
 see also p306 Bars index
baseball 252-253
 batting cages 255
basketball 253
Baxter Steps 107
Baywatch 73
beaches **76-79**
 beach towns 73-82

gay 232
 information 76
 Orange County 133
 parking 77
beauty parlours 197-200
beer, wine & liquor 193
Bel Air 88
 accommodation 52
 restaurants 145
Bell, Al 16
Bergamot Station 78, 222
Beverly Center 180
Beverly Drive 89
Beverly Gardens 88
Beverly Hills 83-90
 accommodation 52-57
 bars 171-172
 coffeehouses 168
 galleries 224
 restaurants 145-147
 shopping 181
 visitor centre 89
Beverly Hills Cop 90
Bicycle Rack 110
Big Bear Lake 269, **271**
Big Picture 126
birdwatching 81
Blessing of the Animals 109, 204
Blessing of the Cars 205
Bloomingdale's 180
Boardner's 174
Bob Baker Marionette Theater 214
Boogie Nights 124
books
 about LA 30-32, 297
 literary LA 30-31
 shops 182-183
 for children 214
border, Mexico 282
Borofsky, Jonathan 110
botanical garden 128, 129
bowling 255
Box 28, 85
Bradbury Building 24, 115
Bradley, Tom 17, 18, 19
Brea Tar Pits, La **99**, *100*, **101**
Brentwood 87-90
 bars 171-172
 restaurants 143
Bright Child Children's Activity Center 211
Brighton Way 89
Broadway **115-116**, 117
Brown Derby Plaza 28
brunch 164

Buddhism 39
Bullocks Wilshire 24
Bunker Hill 113-114
Bunker Hill Steps 114
Burbank 124
Burbank-Glendale-Pasadena Airport 284
bureaux de change 293
bus 284
 LA DASH 287
 MTA 286-287
 municipal 287
business information 289

c

Cabrillo Marine Aquarium 131
cafés *see* coffeehouses
Calabas Pumpkin Festival 207
California Heritage Museum 79
California Market Center 116
California Plaza 113
California Poppy Festival 204
California ScienCenter 119, 120, *120*
Californian African American Museum 119
Caltrans Building 113
Caltrans District 7 HQ 29
camping 65
Canter's Deli 98
Canter's Kibitz Room 98
Capitan Theatre, El 24, 220
Capitol Records Building 28, 97
Carison Memorial Park 261
Carpenter Performing Arts Center 264
Carroll Avenue 23
cars & driving **284-285**
 car rental 285
 highway information 285
 parking 285-286
 roadside assistance 286
Catholic Cathedral of Our Lady of Angels 28
CBS Televsion City 98
celebrity LA 36-39
 celebrity politicians 37
 celebrity religions 39
 hotels 51

star-spotting 38, 90
see also film
cellphones see mobile
phones
cemetery 97, 99
Central Avenue 121
Central Library 24
Century City 88
accommodation 52
restaurants 145
Chandler, Raymond
33, 83
Chateau Marmont 91
Cheaper By the Dozen
102
Chemosphere 25, 26
Chiat/Day Building 81
childcare 213
children 210-214
aquarium 78, 131
arts & entertainments
211
attractions &
museums 212
babysitters 210
beaches 214
best attractions 210
bookstores &
libraries 213
clothes shops 184
family walks 71
Kidspace Museum 129
music & theatre 214
playgrounds 214
restaurants & cafés
210-211
toy shops 202
zoo 105
Chinatown 108-109, *109*
Chinatown 124, 176
Chinese American
Museum 108, 110
Chinese LA 128
Chinese New Year 108,
209
Chung King Road 109
churches 109, 294
Cinco de Mayo 204
cinema *see* film
City Hall 24, 113
City Walk II 26
Citypass 69-70
Civic Center & around
89, **113**
Claremont 128
climate 296
Clippers, Los Angeles
253
Clooney, George 37, 38
clothing hire 190
Clover Park 214
clubs *see* nightclubs
clubs, rock 239-243
Coachella Valley 269,
272-275
Coca-Cola Building 116

coffeehouses 166-169
best 167
wireless access 169
see also p306
Coffeehouses index
Collateral 245
Color Me Mine 212
Colorado Court 29
Comedy & Magic Club
215
comedy & TV 15-17
best 15
venues 15-16
Comedy Central Stage
215
Comedy Store 91, 215
Comedy Union 215
community 22
Company of Angels
Theatre 263
construction, post-war 17
consulates 289
consumer information
290
Convention Center 21
conventions 289
Cook's Library 182, *183*
Coronet Theatre 261
couriers 289
Craft & Folk Art
Museum 99
Crash 88
credit & charge cards
293
Crenshaw 123
Crossroads of the World
28
Cruise, Tom 39
Crystal Cathedral 135
Culver City 85-86
galleries 223-224
restaurants 143-144
Culver Hotel 85
customs 290
cycling 255-256, 287

d
Dana, Richard Henry 11
dance 264
classes 259
see also theatre
Danziger Studio/
Residence 27
Day of the Drum &
Watts Towers Simon
Rodia Jazz Festival 207
Dayton Way 89
Death Valley **269-270**,
269
demographics 14, 19, 21
Descanso Gardens 127,
128
designer shops 184-185
Dia de Los Muertos 108
dialling codes 295

Diamond Ranch High
School 29
disabled travellers
290
discount shopping 185
Disney Ice Arena 28
Disneyland **135-136**
accommodation 66
history 17
Dodger Stadium 107
Doheny Drive 88
Doheny Library 121
Doheny, Edward L 89
Doodah Parade 127, 209
Dorothy Chandler
Pavilion 113, **237**
Downtown 108-116
accommodation 62-64
bars 178
Chinatown 108-109,
109
farmers' market 115
galleries 227
history 109
public art 110
restaurants 158-160
shopping 181
Tree Lighting
Ceremony 209
visitor centre 109
walking tours 108
driving *see* cars
dry cleaning 190
DVD sales & rentals 182

e
Eames House 25, 74
Eames Office Gallery 78
earthquakes
1933 15
East LA 117-118
restaurants 160-161
Eastern Columbia
Building 29, **116**
Eastwood, Clint 37
Echo Park 106-107
bars 177
galleries 226
map 314
restaurants 158
Ed Ruscha Monument
110
Edgemar Center for the
Arts 27, **78**, *166*, 261
Egyptian Theatre 95, 221
Ehrlich, Stephen 81
Eizenberg, Koning 81
Electric Lodge 263
electricity 290
electronics shops 183-184
emergencies 290
Emmys 108
Ennis-Brown House 24,
103
Erotic Museum 95

etiquette 289
Evergreen Cemetery 118
Evidence Room 263
Exposition Park 119, *120*

f
Fairfax Avenue 98
Fairfax District 98-99
accommodation 61-62
bars 175
coffeehouses 168
restaurants 153-154
shopping 181
Falling Down 81
Fargo Street 107
Farmers Market 154
farmers' markets 77, 98,
115
Fashion District 116
fashion shopping 184-190
Feliz, José 103
festivals & events
204-209
art 225
autumn 206-209
awards ceremonies
209
Chinese New Year 108
film 220
gay 234
music 207, 242
spring 204
summer 205-206
winter 209
Festival of the Chariots
206
Fiesta Broadway 204
Fiesta Hermosa 206
Fight Club 113
film 218-221
cinemas 218-221
African-American
221
art-house 220-221
best 218
classic movie
theatres 219
information 218
multiplexes 219
repertory 221
festivals 220
history 32-35
LA in the movies 32-35,
297-298
movie studios 85
screenings 219
studio tours 71
Universal Studios 126
see also celebrity LA
Financial District 113-114
Fisher, Fred 81
fishing 256
fitness 259
Flower District 116
Flower Market 116

food & drink
bakeries 192, 193
farmer's markets 77,
98, 115, **154**
healthy eating 194
organic & wholefoods
195
shops 192-196
*see also restaurants &
coffeehouses*
football 253-254
Forest Lawn Memorial
Park 105, 124
Formosa Café 172, 173
Fowler Museum of
Cultural History 86
Friendship Knot 110
Frolic Room 97, 174, 175

g

galleries 222-227
art scene 222
Bergamot Station
222, *223*
information 222
Gamble House 24, **127,
129**
gay & lesbian 228-235
accommodation 230
bars & clubs 230-231
bathhouses & sex
clubs 232
beaches 232
best places 228
fashion 231
festivals 234
gyms 232
information 229, 290
lesbian bars &
restaurants
234-235
restaurants 230-232
shops & services 228
Geffen Contemporary 28,
115
Geffen Playhouse 261
Gehry House 26, 27
Gehry, Frank **27, 28**,
75, 81
Getty Center 27, **83**, *84*
Getty Museum 27
Getty Villa 74
Getty, J Paul 74
Gibson Amphitheatre
238
Gibson, Mel 39
gift shops 196-197
glasses & sunglasses
190-191
Glendale 124
Glendale Galleria 180
Glory of Christmas 209
Go for Broke Monument
111
Gold's 81, 259

Golden Globe awards 108
Golden Triangle 89
golf 256
Googie style **27**, 99
Graetz, Gidon 110
Graham, Robert 110
Grand Avenue Authority
113
Grand Avenue Project 29
Grand Central Market
115, 195
Grand Hope Park 116
Grand Performances
207, 264
Grape Harvest Festival
206
Grapes of Wrath, The 15
Graumann's Chinese
Theatre 24, **93**, **95**, 220
Grease 81
Great Western Forum
123, 238
Greek Theatre 238
Greystone Mansion
85, 89
gridlock 22
Grier Musser Museum
102
Griffith Observatory
29, **105**
Griffith Park 103, *103*,
105, *212*, 214
Griffith Park Light
Festival 209
Ground Zero 27
Grove, The *179*, 180
Guitar Center 97
gyms 259

h

hairdressing 198
Halloween Festival 207
Hammering Man 110
Hampton Studio Lofts 81
Hancock Park 101-102
restaurants 155
Hannukah Family
Festival 209
Happy Days 91
Harriet & Charles
Luckman Fine Arts
Complex at Cal State
LA 264
Hart of the West Indian
Powwow 206
hat shops 191
Hayden Avenue 85
Hayden Tract 85
health & beauty parlours
197-200
health & medical
290-291
accident & emergency
290
alternative 198

clinics 290
contraception &
abortion 291
dentists 291
HIV & AIDS 291
pharmacies 199, 291
Helms Bakery 85
helplines 291
Herald Examiner
Building 29, 116
Hermosa Beach 79, 131
Higashi Honganji
Buddhist Temple 111
Highways at the 18th
Street Arts Complex
264
hiking 256
history 10-18
architecture 23-24
movies 12, 85
race relations 15-18
20th century 12-18
hockey 254
holiday, public 296
Hollenbeck Park 118
Hollyhock House 24, **104**
Hollywood 92-98
accommodation 60-61
bars 173-175
celebrity LA 36-39
coffeehouses 168
galleries 226
gay scene 233
Hollywood Hills 98
Information Center 96
LA on film 32-35,
297-298
restaurants 150-153
shopping 181
sign 13
Walk of Fame 93
Hollywood & Highland
Center 93
Hollywood Boulevard 92
Hollywood Bowl 29,
98, 237
Hollywood Christmas
Parade 209
Hollywood Entertainment
District 92
Hollywood Entertainment
Museum 95
Hollywood Forever
Cemetery 97, *99*
Hollywood Museum
95, 96
Hollywood Palladium 238
Hollywood Park Race
Track & Casino 123
Hollywood Pop Academy
93
Hollywood Reservoir &
Dog Park 98
Hollywood Roosevelt 95
Hollywood Wax Museum
95, 96

homeware shops 200-201
Hopper House 81
horse racing 254
horse riding 256
hospitals 290
hostels 55
hotels *see*
accommodation
House of Blues 91
Hudson Theatres 263
Huntington Beach 79, 133
Huntington Library,
Art Collections &
Botanical Garden
128, 129
Huntington, Henry
127, 129
Hustler Casino 26
Hyatt West Hollywood
51, *51*
Hyde Park Miriam
Matthews Branch
Library 29

i

Ice House 216
ID 291
IMAX 218, 221
immigration 117, 291
Improv 216
Improv Olympic West
216, *216*
Indecent Proposal 89
Independence Day 205
information, tourist 296
Inglewood 123
Inner City Arts 25
In-n-Out Burger 26
insurance 291
International Surfing
Museum 131
internet access 291
in cafés 169

j

Jackson, Helen Hunt 11
James Irvine Gardens 111
Japanese American
National Museum 111
Japanese LA 111
festival 206
Jazz Bakery 85
Jet Propulsion
Laboratory 127, **130**
jewellery shops 191
Jewelry District 116
John Anson Ford
Amphitheatre 260, *261*
Johnie's Coffee Shop 99
Jolla, La 281
Joshua Tree National
Park 269, **275-276**,
277
Julian CC 15

Index

k

Kabbalah 39
Kenneth Hahn State
    Recreation Area 123
Kidspace 127, 129
King, Rodney 18
Kinney, Abbot 81
Kirk Douglas Theatre
    85, 262
Knott's Berry Farm 135,
    135, 136
Kodak Theatre **93**, 260
Koreatown 102
    bars 176
    restaurants 155-156

l

LA African Marketplace
    & Cultural Faire 206
LA Confidential 103
LA Convention Center
    116, 289
LA County Fair 128, 206
LA DASH buses 287
LA Gay & Lesbian
    Center 290
LA Live 21
LA Times Festival of
    Books 204
LACMA 99
Laguna Beach gay 232
Lake Arrowhead 269,
    271
Lakers, Los Angeles 253
Larchmont Village 102
Largo 98
Last Remaining Seats
    festival 115, 220
Latino LA 106, 177, 118
Laugh Factory 216
Lautner, John 27
left luggage 292
legal help 292
Leimert Park 123
lesbian LA 234-235
    see also gay & lesbian
Less Than Zero 106
Lexton-MacCarthy
    House 26
libraries 213, 292
limos 287
Lincoln Park 118
lingerie shops 191
literary Los Angeles
    30-32
Little Tokyo 111
Living Out 213
Lloyd Wright Home &
    Studio 92
Lloyd Wright, Frank 24,
    25, 27
Long Beach 132-133
    accommodation 65
    Bayou Festival 205

Grand Prix 132, 204
Museum of Art 132,
    133
Opera 132
visitor centre 133
Lords of Dogtown 76
Los Angeles Clippers
    253
Los Angeles Coliseum
    119
Los Angeles Conservancy
    28, 71, 115
Los Angeles Convention
    Center 28
Los Angeles County
    Arboretum &
    Botanical Garden
    128, 129
Los Angeles County
    Museum of Art 99, 100
    Sundays Live 207
Los Angeles Court House
    113
Los Angeles Dodgers 253
Los Angeles
    International Airport
    (LAX) 284
Los Angeles Lakers 253
Los Angeles Marathon
    204
Los Angeles Maritime
    Museum 132
Los Angeles Master
    Chorale 236
Los Angeles Opera 236
Los Angeles
    Philharmonic 236, *237*
Los Angeles Police
    Academy 107
Los Angeles River 104
Los Angeles Theatre 116
Los Angeles Times 30
Los Angeles Zoo 104, 105
Los Feliz 103-106
    bars 176
    coffeehouses 169
    galleries 226
    restaurants 156-157
    shopping 181
lost property 292
Lotus Festival 205
Lovell Beach House
    24, *25*
Lovell House 24, **103**
Loyola Law School 27
luggage shops 192

m

Mack, Mark 81
Macy's 180
magazines 292
Magic Johnson Theaters
    123, 221
Main Street 10
Maison 140 27

MAK Center for Art &
    Architecture 24, 92, *92*
Malibu 73
    accommodation 44-45
    beaches 78
    Chamber of Commerce
    73
    restaurants 139
Manhattan Beach 79, 131
    accommodation 65
manicures 199
Manson, Charles 17
maps, star-spotting 90
Mariachi Festival 108
Mariachi Plaza 117, *118*
Marina del Rey 81
    accommodation 50
    boat parade 209
    harbor & sailing 81
    restaurants 142-143
    summer concerts 207
Mark Taper Forum
    113
markets 115
Marlowe, Philip 33
masseurs 199-200
Matador, El State Beach
    77
Mathias Botanical
    Gardens 87
Mayan Theate 116
Mayo, Morrow 11
McKinley Residence 29
media 292
Media Park 85
Melrose Place 105
MET Theatre 263
Metropolitan Detention
    Center 113
Mexican LA 115
    festival 108, 204
    literary 32
Mexican-American War
    11
Mexico, day trip 282
Midtown 99-101
    bars 175
    coffeehouses 168-169
    restaurants 155
Million Dollar Baby 116
Million Dollar Theatre
    115
Mind, Body & Spirit
    110
Miracle Mile 99-101
    bars 175
    coffeehouses 168-169
    galleries 224
    restaurants 155
Mission Hills 124
missions 281
Mitchell, Dodd 148
mobile phones 150, 295
MoCA 91
modernism 29, 273
Mondrian 26

money 293-294
Monroe, Marilyn 83
Monrovia 128
Monterey Park 118, 128
Moreno, Arte 252
Mormon Temple 87
Moss, Eric Owen 85
motor racing 254
Mount Hollywood 105
Mount St Mary College
    83
movie studios 85
movies *see* film
MTA buses 286-287
Mulholland, William 12
Murphy, Brian 81
Murphy, George 37
Muscle Beach, Venice 81
museums
    art: A + D Museum 99;
    Craft & Folk Art
    Museum 99; Geffen
    Contemporary 115;
    Getty Center 83;
    Long Beach Museum
    of Art 132, 133; Los
    Angeles County
    Museum of Art 99,
    100; Museum of
    Contemporary Art
    111, 115; Museum of
    Latin American Art
    132, 133; Museum of
    Neon Art 116; Norton
    Simon Museum 127,
    127, 129; Pacific
    Asia Museum 127,
    130; Pasadena
    Museum of California
    Art 127, 130; Santa
    Monica Museum of
    Art 78, 79; UCLA
    Hammer Museum 88
    children's interest:
    212; Kidspace
    Museum 129
    cultural: California
    Heritage Museum
    79; Californian
    African American
    Museum 119;
    Chinese American
    Museum 108, 110;
    Erotic Museum
    95; Hollywood
    Entertainment
    Museum 95;
    Japanese American
    National Museum
    111; Museum of
    Television &
    Radio 89
    history: Autry Museum
    of the American
    West 105; Autry
    Southwest Museum

of the American
Indian 107; Fowler
Museum of Cultural
History 86;
Hollywood Museum
95, 96; Museum of
Tolerance at the
Simon Wiesenthal
Center for Holocaust
Studies 90; Ronald
Reagan Museum 125;
Santa Monica
Historical Society
Museum 77
science: California
ScienCenter 119, 120,
120; Natural History
Museum of LA
County 119, 120;
Los Angeles
Maritime Museum
132; Page Museum
at the La Brea Tar
Pits *100*, 101
transport: Petersen
Automative
Museum 99, 101;
Museum of Flying
79; Travel Town
Museum 106
unusual: Angels
Attic Museum 77;
Grier Musser
Museum 102;
Hollywood Wax
Museum 95, 96;
International
Surfing Museum 131;
Museum of Jurassic
Technology 85
Museum of
Contemporary Art
27, 111, 115
Museum of Flying 79
Museum of Jurassic
Technology 85
Museum of Latin
American Art 132, 133
Museum of Neon Art 116
Museum of Television &
Radio 27
Museum of Television &
Radio 89
Museum of Tolerance at
the Simon Wiesenthal
Center for Holocaust
Studies 90
music 236-244
children's 214
classical 236-237
ensembles 236
venues 237
festivals 242
free 207
from/about LA 298
jazz 244

opera 236
rock & pop 238-243
major venues
238-239
artists in residence
239
rock clubs 239-243
roots & blues 243-244
shops 201-202
tickets & information
236
Musso & Frank 174
Muybridge, Eadward 37

n

nannies, Latina 213
Nate 'n Al's 89
National Boulevard 85
National Center for the
Preservation of
Democracy 111
Natural History Museum
of LA County 119, 120
Neiman Marcus 180
Nethercutt Collection
124
Neve, Felipe de 11
Newport Beach 133
newspapers 292
nightclubs 245-250
bouncers & door policy
248
gay 230-231
information 245
paparazzi 247
photo-blogging 247
strip clubs 250
Nisei Week Japanese
Festival 206
Nixon Library &
Birthplace 135, 136
Nordstron 180
Northridge 124
Norton House 81
Norton Simon Museum
127, *127*, 129

o

O'Herlihy, Lorcan 26
Odyssey Theatre
Ensemble 263
office services 289
off-licences 193
oil business 14
Ojai 267
'Okies' 15
Oliver, Henry 24
Olvera Street 109
Olympic Games, 1932
14
Olympic Games, 1984
18
Open Fist Theatre 263
opening times 294

opera 132, 236
Orange County 133-135
accommodation 65-66
Anaheim & inland 135
beaches 133
Disneyland 135-136
restaurants 165
visitor centre 135
Orpheum 116
Oscars 208
Our Lady, Queen of
Angels 109
Owens River 12
Oxnard 267

p

Pacific Asia Museum
127, 130
Pacific Pallisades 73-74
Page Museum at the La
Brea Tar Pits *100*, 101
Pageant of the Masters
205
Palm Springs 269,
272-275
Palos Verdes 131
Pantages Theatre 24,
116, **260**
paparazzi 247
Paramount Ranch 124
Paramount Studios 71, 97
Pasadena Convention &
visitor centre 130
Pasadena Museum of
California Art 127, 130
Pasadena Playhouse 262
Pasadena Symphony
Musical Circus 214
Paseo of Peace 117
passports 293
payphones 295
pedestrians 287
Pegasus Apartments 28
Pegasus Lofts 115
Peninsula Beverly Hills
89
Performing Arts Center
of Los Angeles County
260
Pershing Square 114
Summer Concert Series
207
Petersen Automative
Museum 99, 101
pharmacies 199, 291
Philharmonic orchestra
236, *237*
Phoenix, River 243
photo-blogging 247
photography shops 202
Pico House 24
Pig & Whistle 174
Pioneertown 275
Pipes Canyon Preserve
275, 276

Playa del Rey 81
playgrounds 214
Plaza 109
politicians, celebrity 37
Pomona 128
pool & billiards 256
Port of Los Angeles
Lobster Festival 206
Posadas, Las 109, 209
postal services 294
Powerhouse 174
Price is Right, The 98,
217
Prince 176, 178
Prospect Park 118
public art 80
Pueblo de Los Angeles
Historical Monument,
El 109

q

Queen Mary 132, 133

r

race relations 14, 15-18, 21
racing 254
radio 292
rail travel 284
railroad expansion 11
Ramirez Canyon Park 73
Ramona Pageant 205
Randy's Donuts 28, 123
Reagan, Ronald 17, 37
REDCAT 264
religion 294
celebrity 39
Relondo Beach 131
reservoir 98
Reservoir Dogs 99
restaurants 138-165
best 139
brunch 164
chefs 139
for children 210
designer 148-149
farmer's market 154
gay 231
information 139
taco trucks 161
vegetarian 139
*see also p306
Restaurants index*
Reuben Cordova Theatre
at Beverly Hills High
School 262
Richard J Riordan Central
Library 114, *114*
riots, Rodney King 18
Ripley's Believe it or Not!
95, *95*, **97**
river, Los Angeles 104
Riverside County Fair
& National Date
Festival 209

Robert F Maguire
 Gardens 114
Robertson Library 26
Robinsons-May 179
rock climbing 257
Rodeo Drive 89, *89*
Rodia, Simon 122
rollerblading 257
rollerskating 257
Ronald Reagan Library
 & Museum 124, 125
Rose Bowl 11
Rose Garden 119
Rose Parade 11, 127, **130**
Roxy 91
Runyon Canyon Park 98
Rush Hour 108
Rustic Canyon Park 73

S

Sacred Fools Theatre 263
safety, public 294
sailing 81
Saks Fifth Avenue 180
Salazar Park 118
Samitaur 28, 85
San Diego 279-282
 Balboa Park 280, 282
 zoo 280
San Fernando Valley
 124-126
 accommodation 64
 restaurants 162-163
San Gabriel Valley
 127-129
 accommodation 64
 restaurants 163
San Marino 127
San Pedro 131
San Vincente Boulevard
 83
Santa Anita Park 128
Santa Barbara *267*, **268**
Santa Catalina Island
 278-279
Santa Clarita 124
 Cowboy Poetry &
 Music Festival 204
 restaurants 163
**Santa Monica & the
 beach towns** 73-82
 accommodation 45-47
 aquarium 78
 Art Museum 79
 bars 170-171
 Beach 76, 77-78
 coffeehouses 166
 galleries 222
 inland 78-79
 mountains 124, *125*,
 267
 public art 80
 restaurants 139-142
 shopping 181
 visitor center 79

Santa Monica Boulevard
 88, **91**
Santa Monica Historical
 Society Museum 77
Santa Monica Museum of
 Art 78, 79
Santa Monica Pier *75*, 77
 Aquarium 78
 Twilight Dance Series
 207
Santa Monica Place 27
Santa Monica Playhouse
 262
Santa Rosa 267
Scandinavian Festival
 204
Schindler, Rudolf 92, 106
Schoenberg Hall 87
Schoenberg, Arnold 87
schools 295
Schwarzenegger, Arnold
 18, 37, 38
ScienCenter School 29
scientology 39
scuba-diving 257
Seal Beach 133
Sears 179
SeaWorld 281
second-hand clothes
 189-190
Segundo, El 131
Self-Realization
 Fellowship Lake Shrine
 73
Sepulveda House 109
Serra, Junipero 281
Sherman Oaks 124
shoe shops 192
shops & services
 179-202
 Abbot Kinney
 Boulevard 188
 by district 181
 department stores
 179-180
 fashion 184-190
 gay 228
 malls 180-181
 opening hours 179
 sales tax 179
 W 3rd Street 187
Shrine Auditorium 121
Shutters on the Beach 46,
 77
Sierra Madre 128
sightseeing 68-71
 best attractions
 by district 68
 CityPass 69-70
 guided tours 70-71
 street names &
 numbers 70
 studio tours 71
Silver Lake 106, *107*
 bars 176-177
 coffeehouses 169

film festival 220
galleries 226
gay scene 232
 restaurants 157-158
 shopping 181
Simi Valley 124
Simon Wiesenthal Center
 90
Simpson OJ 83
Simpson, Nicole Brown 83
Sinclair, Upton 15
Six Flags park 124, 125
skateboarding 257
Skid Row 111
skin & body care 199
Skirball Cultural Center
 84, 262
smoking 294
soccer 254
Solar Umbrella House 29
Sony Studios 85
Source Figure 110, *110*
**South Bay & Long
 Beach** 131-133
 restaurants 163-165
South Central LA
 119-123
 on film 35
 restaurants 161
South Coast Botanic
 Garden 131
South Park 116
South Pasadena 128
Spadena House 24, **88**
spas 199-200
 outside LA 274
Spiller House 81
sport & fitness 251-259
 fitness & yoga 259
 participation sports
 255-259
 shops 202
 spectator sports
 251-254
 baseball 252-253
 basketball 252-253
 football 253-254
 hockey 254
 information & tickets
 251
 soccer 254
Sprinkles 89
Standard 62, 114
Stanford, Leland 37
Staples Center 116, **238**,
 239, **251**, 253
Star Eco Station **86**
Starck, Philippe 26
Stealth 85
Stick House 75
Stockton, R F 11
Storyopolis 212
Strathmore Apartments
 24
street names & numbers
 70

strip clubs 250
studio tours 71
study & learning 295
Sturges House 25
Sunset Boulevard 88
Sunset Boulevard 95
Sunset Junction 106
street fair 206
Sunset Plaza 91
Sunset Plaza Drive 91
Sunset Strip 91
surfing 258
SWAT 123
swimming 258
Sylmar 124
synagogues 294

T

taco trucks 161
Tail-o'-the-Pup 28
Tajiri, Shinkichi 110
Tarfest 206
Target 180
tattoos 200
taxis 287
 airport 284
Taylor, Henry 106
Team Disney office 27
telephones 295
television 292
Temescal Canyon Park
 73
tennis & racquetball
 259
Tet Festival 209
theatre & dance
 260-264
 best theatre 260
 for children 214
 dance 264
 gay 228-229
 major theatre venues
 260
 99-seat theatres 262
theme parks
 Disneyland 135-136
 Knott's Berry Farm 136
 Six Flags California
 125
 Universal Studios 126
ticket agencies 217
Tijuana 282
times & dates 295
Times-Mirror Building
 113
tipping 296
*Tonight Show with Jay
 Leno, The* 217
tourist information 296
Tournament of Roses
 Rose Parade 209
tours
 architecture 29
 Downtown 108
 family walks 71

guided 70-71
studio 71
Tower Theatre 116
Town Plaza 85
toy shops 202
traffic 22
trains 284, **287**
Transamerica Building
29
transport, disabled 290
transport, public 286-287
travel advice 289
travel agents 202
Travel Town Museum
106
travellers' cheques 294
Travolta, John 39
Truman Show, The 124
TV shows, filming of 217
Twitchell, Kent 110

U

UCLA 86-87
accommodation 50-52
restaurants 145
UCLA Hammer Museum
88
UCLA Royce Hall 264
Umbrella 85
Union 76 gas station 89
Union Station 24, 25, **110**
United Artists Theatre
116
Universal City Walk 26
Universal Studios 124,
126
University of California
at Los Angeles *see*
UCLA
University of Southern
California 121
US Bank Tower 114
US Open Surfing 206
USC 120

V

Valley Girls 124
Valleys, The 124-130
accommodation 64
coffeehouses 169
restaurants 162-163
shopping 181
Venice 79-82
accommodation
48-50
architecture 29
bars 171
boardwalk *82*
Beach 78, 232
coffeehouses 166-167
galleries 222
public art 80
restaurants 142
shopping 181

Venice Beach Loft 81
Venice Pier 81
Ventura 267
Vertical House 26
Vibiana Place 111
Viceroy 27, **46**, 77
Villaraigosa, Antonio
18, *19*, 21
vintage shopping 189-190
Viper Room 243
visas 293, 296

W

Wadsworth Theatre 262
Walden Drive 88
Walk of Fame 93
walking 287
Wall Street 111
Walt Disney Concert Hall
28, 113, **237**
Watts 121-122
riots 17
summer festival 206
Watts Towers 24, 121,
122
Wattstax 16
Wayfarer's Chapel 131
Wearstler, Kelly 27
weather 296
websites, useful 298
Wells Fargo Center 114
West Angeles Church of
God in Christ 123
West Hollywood
91-92
accommodation 57-60
bars 172-173
coffeehouses 167-168
galleries 225
gay & lesbian 229-233
map 312
restaurants 147-150
shopping 181
visitor centre 92
Westlake 102
Westside Pavilion 87
Westwood 86-88
accommodation 50-52
restaurants 145
whale-watching 259
Whisky A Go-Go 91
Whittier Boulevard 118
Will Geer Theatricum
Botanicum 262
Will Rogers Memorial
Park 89
Will Rogers State Beach
73, 232
Will Rogers State
Historic Park 73, 74
Wilshire Electric
Fountain 88
Wilshire Theatre 262
Wilson, Randall 110
Wiltern LG 238

Wiltern Theatre 24
*Witches of Eastwick,
The* 89
work visas 296
World City 207
World Gym 81

Y

YMCAs 259
yoga 259
Youngwood Park 101,
101
Yucca Valley 275

Z

zoo 105, 106
San Diego 280
Zuma Beach 78

Accommodation

Ambrose 47
Angeleno 50
Avalon 56
Banana Bungalow
Hollywood 55
Bayside 49
Best Western Hollywood
Hills 61
Beverly Hills Hotel &
Bungalows 52, *53*, 88
Beverly Laurel Motor
Hotel 61
Beverly Terrace 57
Cadillac 50
Candy Cane Inn 66
Casa del Mar 45
Casa Malibu Inn on the
Beach 44
Chamberlain West
Hollywood *56*, 58
Channel Road Inn 47
Chateau Marmont 57
Crescent 56
Delfina 47, *47*
Disney's Grand
California Hotel 65
Disney's Paradise Pier
Hotel 66
Disneyland Hotel 66
Élan 58
Fairmont Miramar 45
Farmer's Daughter 62
Four Seasons LA at
Beverly Hills 52
Georgian 49
Grafton on Sunset 58
HI Santa Monica 55
Highland Gardens 61
Hilgard House 51
Hotel Bamboo 60
Hotel Bel-Air **52**, 88, 145
Hotel California 49
Hotel Carmel by the Sea
49

Hotel Figueroa 63, *63*
Hotel Oceana 46
Hyatt Century Plaza
Hotel & Spa 52
Inn at 657 62
Inn at Playa del Rey 50
Loews Beverly Hills 56
Loews Santa Monica
Beach Hotel 46
Luxe Hotel Rodeo Drive
52
Magic Castle 60
Maison 140 57
Malibu Beach Inn 45
Meridien, Le at Beverly
Hills 53
Merigot, Le 46
Millennium Biltmore 62,
114
Mondrian 57
Montage Resort & Spa 66
Montrose Suite Hotel,
Le 59
Mosaic 53
Orlando Hotel *58*, 59
Omni Los Angeles 62
Peninsula Beverly Hills 55
Queen Mary 64, *65*
Raffles L'Ermitage
Beverly Hills 55
Ramada West
Hollywood 59
Regent Beverly
Wilshire 55
Renaissance
Hollywood 60
Ritz Milner 64
Ritz-Carlton Huntington
Hotel & Spa 64
Ritz-Carlton Laguna
Niguel 66
Ritz-Carlton Marina del
Rey 50
Roosevelt 60
Secret Garden B&B 60
Shade 65
Shangri-La **49**, 75
Sheraton Gateway 65
Shutters on the Beach
45, 46
Sofitel Los Angeles 59
Sportsmen's Lodge 64
St Regis Monarch Beach
Resort & Spa 66
Standard Downtown 62
Standard Hollywood 59
Sunset Marquis Hotel &
Villas 57
Sunset Tower 59, *61*
Venice Beach House
Historic Inn 49
Viceroy 46
W 50
Westin Bonaventure
62, 114
Wilshire Grand 63

Restaurants

25 Degrees 151
Ago 147
All India Café 163
Allegria 139
Ammo 150
Angelini Osteria 153
AOC 153
Apple Pan 144, *144*
Art's Deli 162
Aunty Kizzy's Back
    Porch 142
Axe 142
Babita 163
Beacon 143
Blue Bamboo 147
Boccaccio, Il 165
Bombay Café 144
Brick House 142
Brite Spot 158
Cachette, La 145
Café Brasil 144
Café del Rey 143
Café Stella 157
Campanile 155
Canter's Deli 153
Cassell's 155
Celestino Ristorante 163
Chakra Cuisine 165
Chano's 158
Chez Melange 164
Choio, El 156
Ciudad 158
Cliff's Edge 157
Cobras & Matadors 153
Coley's Place 161
Counter 139
Dakota 150
Dan Tana's 147
Delicias Chapinas, Las
    156
Dominick's 147
Dong Il Jang 156
Doughboys 153
Drago 141
Edendale Grill 157
Electric Lotus 156
Empress Harbor 163
Empress Pavilion 159
Engine Co No.28 159
Ford's Filling Station 144
Fountain Coffee Shop at
    Beverly Hills Hotel 145
Fred 62 156
French 75, 165
Geisha House 150
Geoffrey's 139
Gingergrass 158
Giorgio Baidi 141
Girasole 155
Grace 153
Griddle Café 147
Grill on the Alley 146
Guelaguetza 156
Harold & Belle's 161
Hirozen 148

Hotel Bel-Air 145
Hugo's 162
Hump 141
Hungry Cat 151, *151*
Hush 165
Inaka 155
India Sweet House 153
Ivy 148
Jade Café 158
Jar 148
Joan's on Third 153
Joe's 142
Josie 141
Kate Mantillini 146
Kendall's Brasserie &
    Bar 159
Koi 149
Koshiji 159
Leaf Cuisine 144
Lemon Moon 141
Lilly's French Café &
    Wine Bar 142
Literati II 143
Lucques 149
M Café de Chaya 153
Maio 158
Maison Akira 163
Mao's Kitchen 142
Marlo's Peruvian
    Seafood 151
Mastro's Steakhouse 146
Matsuhisa 146
Max 162
Mélisse 141
Memphis 151
Meson G 154
Mexico City 156
Michi 165
Millie's 158
Minibar 162
Misti Picanteria
    Arequipeña, El 165
Monte Alban 145
Moonshadows 139
Mori Sushi 145
Nanbankan 145
Napa Rose 165
Nate 'n Al's 146, *146*
Native Foods 145
Nic's 146
Nobu 139
Ocean Seafood 159
Orchid 141
Original Pantry 159, *160*
Orso 149
Ortolan 154, *155*
Palm 149
Pann's 161
Parilla, La 160, *162*
Patina 159
Pecorino 143, *143*
Petros Greek Cuisine &
    Lounge 163
Philippe the Original 160
Pho 160
Pho Café 158

Pinot Bistro 162
Polo Lounge 147
Porta Via 147
Prado 155
Providence 151
Roscoe's House of
    Chicken & Waffles
    151
Sakura House 143
Saladang Song 163
Sarnba Brazilian
    Steakhouse & Bar 165
Serenata di Garibaldi, La
    161
Sole, Il 148
Sona 150
Soot Bull Jeep 156
Sosta, La 165
Spago of Beverly Hills
    147
Stonehill Tavern 165
Sushi Nozawa 162
Sushi Roku 141
Table 8 154
Takao 143
Tamales Liliana's 161
Tanino 145
Tantra 158
Taurino, El 160
Taylor's Steak House
    156, *157*
Tepeyac, EL 161
Tiapazola Grill 145
Toast 154
Vermont 156
Versailles 155
Vincenti 143
Violet 141
Wabi Sabi 142
Water Grill 160
Wilshire *138*, 142
Yuca's Hut 157, *159*
Zeke's Smokehouse 163
Zucca 160

Coffeehouses

Abbot's Habit 166
Back on the Beach 166
Belle Epoque, La 169
Black Door Bakery &
    Café 169
Bourgeois Pig 168
Buzz Coffee 167
Café Tartine 168
Caffe Latte 168
Chado Tea Room 168
Coffee Bean & Tea Leaf
    167
Coffee Table *168*, 169
Cow's End 166
Hugo's 167
Infuzion 166
Insomnia 168
Jin Patisserie 166
King's Road Café 167
Legal Grind 166

Pain Quotodien, Le 167,
    167
Peet's Coffee & Tea 166
Porto's Bakery 169
Starbucks 168
Susina 169
Urth Caffé 168

Bars

4100 Bar 176
Avalon Hotel Lounge
    172
Bar 173
Bar Copa 170
Bar on 4 172
Beechwood 171
Bigfoot Lodge 176
Blu Monkey Lounge 173
Brass Monkey 176
Brig 171
Broadway Bar 178
Canter's Kibitz Room 175
Carmen, El 172
Cat & Fiddle 173
Cha Cha Lounge 176
Chalet 178
Chez Jay 170
Circle Bar 170
Dresden Room 176
Father's Office 170
Formosa Café 172
Gallery Bar 178
Gold Room 177
Golden Gopher 178
Good Luck Bar 176
Hank's Bar 178
Hideout 170
HMS Bounty 176
Irish Times 171
Johnny's Cocktail
    Lounge 177
Jones Hollywood 172
L'Scorpion 174
Little Cave 178
Little Pedro's Blue
    Bongo 178
Monroe's 172
Nirvana 172
Otheroom 171
Pete's Café & Bar 178
Prince 176
Red Buddha Lounge 174
Roof at the Standard 178
Roost 176
Short Stop 177
SkyBar 173
Smog Cutter 177
Three Clubs 174
Tiki-Ti 177
Tom Bergin's 175
Tropicana Bar 174
Velvet Margarita
    Cantina, La 175
Voda 171
Whiskey Blue 171
Writer's Bar 172

Place of interest and/or entertainment	▊
Hospital or college	▊
Railway station	▊
Parks	▊
River	▊
Interstate highway	🛡110
US highway	🛡101
State or provincial highway	①1
Main road	
Airport	✈
Metro stop	Ⓜ Ⓜ
Area name	VENICE
Hotel	❶
Restaurant	❶
Coffeehouse	❶
Bar	❶

Maps

LA Overview	**308**
Santa Monica & Venice	**310**
Beverly Hills & Around	**311**
West Hollywood	
& Around	**312**
Hollywood & Midtown	**313**
East of Hollywood	**314**
Downtown	**315**
Street Index	**316**
Metro Rail Network	**319**
LA by Area	**320**

LA Overview

118
RONALD REAGAN FREEWAY

SIMI VALLEY

NORTHRIDGE

TOPANGA CANYON BLVD

RESEDA

5

405

San Fernando Valley

170

VAN NUYS

NORTH HOLLYWOOD

STUDIO CITY

Burbank-Glendale-Pasadena Airport

101

134

UNIVERSAL CITY

AGOURA HILLS

101

CALABASAS

VENTURA FREEWAY

27

SHERMAN OAKS

Hollywood Hill

Santa Monica Mountains

BEL AIR

See p311

HOLLYWOOD

See p31

WEST HOLLYWOOD

SANTA MONICA BLVD

BRENTWOOD

BEVERLY HILLS

PACIFIC PALISADES

SUNSET BLVD

SAN DIEGO

CENTURY CITY

See p312

MALIBU BEACH

PACIFIC COAST HIGHWAY

1

SANTA MONICA

WEST LA

SANTA MONICA FREEWAY

CRENSHAW

MALIBU

VENICE

SANTA MONICA FREEWAY

CULVER CITY

See p310

LINCOLN BLVD

MARINA DEL REY

405

INGLEWOOD

Pacific

PLAYA DEL REY

Los Angeles International Airport

Ocean

EL SEGUNDO

1

HAWTHORNE

MANHATTAN BEACH

HERMOSA BEACH

REDONDO BEACH

107

PALOS VERDES ESTATES

0   6 miles
0   10 km

© Copyright Time Out Group 2006

RANCHO PALOS VERDES

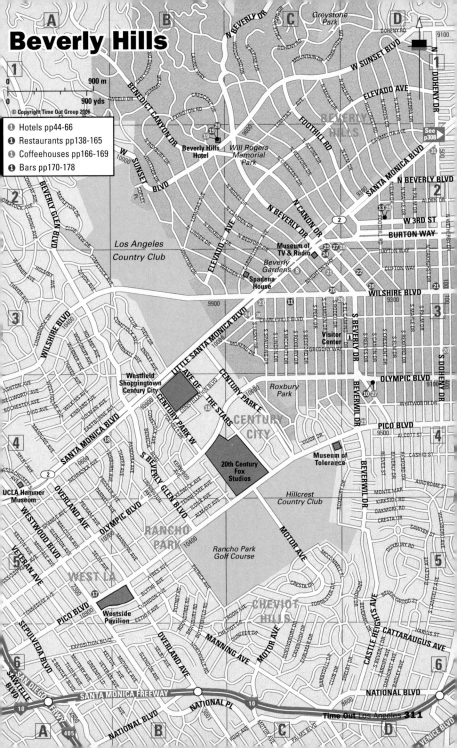

Beverly Hills

Hollywood & Midtown

① Hotels pp44-66
① Restaurants pp138-165
① Coffeehouses pp166-169
① Bars pp170-178

© Copyright Time Out Group 2006

East of Hollywood

Griffith Park
Griffith Observatory
Ennis Brown House
Greek Theatre

A 1 **B** **C** **D**

N VERMONT AVE
N COMMONWEALTH AVE
LOS FELIZ BLVD
RIVERSIDE DR
GOLDEN STATE FREEWAY
FLETCHER DR

LOS FELIZ BLVD
HILLHURST AVE
ST GEORGE ST
ROWENA AVE

LOS FELIZ
FRANKLIN AVE
N VERMONT AVE
ABC TV Center
GLENDALE BLVD

HOLLYWOOD BLVD
Barnsdall Park
Silver Lake Reservoir

W SUNSET BLVD
Vermont/Sunset
DE LONGPRE AVE
FOUNTAIN AVE
LA MIRADA AVE
GRIFFITH PARK BLVD
HYPERION AVE
SILVER LAKE BLVD

LEXINGTON AVE
Vermont/Santa Monica
SANTA MONICA BLVD
SILVER LAKE

WILLOW BROOK AVE
LOCKWOOD AVE
BURNS AVE
NORMAL AVE
MONROE ST
MARATHON ST

ROMAINE ST
Bellevue Park

MELROSE AVE
CLINTON ST
ECHO PARK

ROSEWOOD AVE
OAKWOOD AVE

BEVERLY BLVD
Vermont/Beverly
SILVER LAKE BLVD
W SUNSET BLVD

W 1ST ST
Echo Park & Lake

TEMPLE ST
HOLLYWOOD FREEWAY
RAMPART BLVD
ALVARADO ST
GLENDALE BLVD

W 3RD ST
N NORMANDIE AVE
S VERMONT AVE
S VIRGIL AVE

W 6TH ST
WILSHIRE BLVD
Wilshire/Vermont
Lafayette Park
WESTLAKE

Wilshire/Normandie
SUNSET PL
MacArthur Park
W 6TH ST

❶	Hotels pp44-66
❶	Restaurants pp138-165
❶	Coffeehouses pp166-169
❶	Bars pp170-178

900 m
900 yds

© Copyright Time Out Group 2006

← See p309

Downtown

❶ Hotels pp44-66
❶ Restaurants pp138-165
❶ Coffeehouses pp166-169
❶ Bars pp170-178

© Copyright Time Out Group 2006

Street Index

Note: the numbered streets
in Santa Monica (2nd St,
3rd St, and so on) have
been differentiated from the
numbered streets elsewhere
in LA with the label 'SM'.

1st Ct (SM) - p310 A2
E 1st St - p315 C2/D2
W 1st St - p312 B3/C3/D3,
p313 A4/B4/C4/D4, p314
A5/B5, p315 A2/B2/C2
2nd Ct (SM) - p310 A2
2nd St (SM) - p310 A2
E 2nd St - p315 C2/D2/3
W 2nd St - p312 D3, p313 A4/
B4/C4/D4, p313 A5/B6,
p315 A2/B2/C2
3rd Ave - p313 C5/6
3rd St (SM) - p310 A2-5
E 3rd St - p315 C3/D3
W 3rd St - p311 D2, p312 A3/
B3/C3/D3, p313 A4/B4/
C4/D4, p314 A5/B5/6/
C6/D6, p315 A2/B3/C3
4th Ave (SM) - p310 A4/5
4th Ct (SM) - p310 B2
4th St (SM) - p310 A2
E 4th St - p315 C3/D3
W 4th St - p312 B3/C3, p314
A6/B6, p315 A3/B3/C3
5th Ave - p313 C5/6
5th Ave (SM) - p310 A5
5th Ct (SM) - p310 B2
5th St (SM) - p310 B2
E 5th St - p315 C3/D3
W 5th St - p312 B3/C4, p314
A6/B6, p315 A3/B3/C3
6th Ct (SM) - p310 B2
6th St (SM) - p310 B2
E 6th St - p315 C3/D3/4
W 6th St - p312 C4/D4, p313
A5/B5/C5/D5, p314 A6/
B6/C6, p315 A3/B3/C3
7th St (SM) - p310 B1-3
E 7th St - p315 C4/D4
W 7th St - p313 C5/D5, p314
B6, p315 A4/B4/C4
W 8th Pl - p315 A4
E 8th St - p315 C4/D4
W 8th St - p312 C4/D4, p313
A5/B5/C5/D5, p314 B6,
p315 A4/B4/C4
9th Ct (SM) - p310 B2
9th St (SM) - p310 B1/2
E 9th St - p315 C4/D4/5
W 9th St - p312 D4, p313 A5/
B5/C5/D5, p315 A4/B4/C4
10th St (SM) - p310 B1-3
E 10th St - p315 D5
W 10th St - p315 A4
11th Ct (SM) - p310 B2
11th St (SM) - p310 B1-3
W 11th St - p313 C6/D6,
p315 A5/B5/C5
12th Ct (SM) - p310 B2
12th St (SM) - p310 B1/2
E 12th St - p315 C5/D5
W 12th St - p312 D5, p313 A6/
B6/C6/D6, p315 A5/B5/C5
14th St (SM) - p310 B1-3
E 14th Pl - p315 D6
E 14th St - p315 D5
W 14th St - p315 B5/C5
15th St (SM) - p310 C1-3
E 15th St - p315 C6/D6
W 15th St - p313 C6/D6,
p315 B6/C6
16th St (SM) - p310 C1-4
E 16th St - p315 C6/D6
17th St (SM) - p310 C1-4
W 17th St - p315 A6/B6/C6

18th St (SM) - p310 C1-3
E 18th St - p315 C6/D6
W 18th St - p312 A5/B6,
p315 B6
19th St (SM) - p310 C1-3
20th St (SM) - p310 C1-4
E 20th St - p315 D6
21st Ct (SM) - p310 C2
21st Pl (SM) - p310 C1/2
21st St (SM) - p310 C1-4
E 21st St - p315 C6/D6
22nd St (SM) - p310 C1-4
23rd St (SM) - p310 C1-5
W 23rd St - p312 D6
24th St (SM) - p310 C2/D1/2
W 24th St - p312 A6
25th St (SM) - p310 D1/2
W 25th St - p312 A6
26th St (SM) - p310 D1-3
28th Ave (SM) - p310 A6
28th St (SM) - p310 D4
29th St (SM) - p310 D4
31st St (SM) - p310 D4
33rd St (SM) - p310 D4

**Abbot Kinney Blvd -
p310 A5/6/B6**
Adelaide Dr - p310 A1/B1
Agatha St - p315 D4
Airdrome St - p311 D4, p312
A5/B5/C5/6
Airport Dr - p310 C5/D5
N Alameda St - p315 D1/2
Albany St - p315 A5/6
Alcott St - p311 D4,
p312 A5/B5
Alden Dr - p311 D2, p312 A3
N Alexandria Ave - p313 D1-3,
p314 A2-5
S Alexandria Ave - p313 D4/5
S Alfred St - p312 B4/5
Allesandro St - p314 D3/4
Almayo Ave - p311 B5
N Almont Dr - p311 C1/2/D2/3
S Almont Dr - p312 A4/5
Aloha St - p314 C2
Alpine St - p315 B1/C1
Alta Ave - p310 A1/B1/C1/D1
N Alta Dr - p311 D1/2
Alta Loma Rd - p312 B1/2
N Alta Vista Blvd - p312 D1-3
Alvarado St - p314 C5/6/D3/4
Alvira St - p312 B4/5
Ambrose Ave - p314 A2
Ames St - p314 B1/2
Amesbury Rd - p314 B1
Amoroso Pl - p310 B6
Anchor Dr - p311 D5
Angelina St - p315 A1/B1
Angelo Dr - p311 A1/B1
Appleton Way - p310 C5
N Arden Blvd - p313 B3/4
S Arden Blvd - p313 B5/6
N Arden Dr - p311 D2
N Ardmore Ave - p313 D3
S Ardmore Ave - p313 D5/6
N Argyle Ave - p313 B1/2
Arizona Ave - p310 A2/B2/
C2/D2
Armstrong Ave - p314 C2/D2
N Arnaz Dr - p312 A3/4
Ashcroft Ave - p312 A3
Ashland Ave - p310 A4/B4/C4
Ashton Ave - p311 A4
Ashwood Ave - p310 C5/6
Ave of the Stars - p311 B4/C4
Avenel St - p314 C1/2
Avocado St - p314 B1
Ayres Ave - p311 B5

Bagley Ave - p311 D5/6
Bangor St - p312 D6

Barbydell Dr - p311 C6
Barton Ave - p313 A3/B3
Baxter St - p314 D3
Bay St - p310 A3/B3
Beachwood Dr - p313 B1/C3/4
N Beaudry Ave - p315 B1/2
S Beaudry Ave - p315 A3/B3
N Bedford Dr - p311 B2/C2/3
S Bedford Dr - p311 C3/4
S Bedford St - p312 B5
Beethoven St - p310 C6
Bellevue Ave - p313 B4/C5/
D5, p315 A1/B1
Belmont Ave - p314 D6
Benecia Blvd - p311 B4
Benedict Canyon Dr - p311 A1/
B1/2
S Bentley Blvd - p311 A6
N Benton Ave - p314 C4
N Benton Way - p314 C4/5
S Benton Way - p314 B5
Benvenue St - p310 D1
N Berendo St - p314 A2-5
Berkeley Ave - p314 C4/D4
Berkeley St - p310 D2/3
Beverleywood St - p312 A6
Beverly Blvd - p311 D2, p312
A3/B3/C3/D3, p313 A4/
B4/C4/D4, p314 A5/B5/
C5/6/D6
N Beverly Dr - p311 C1-3
S Beverly Dr - p311 D3-6
Beverly Glen Blvd - p311 A2/3/
B4/5
Beverlywood St - p311 D5
Beverwil Dr - p311 D4-6
Bicknell St - p310 A4
Bimini Pl - p314 A5
N Bixel St - p315 A1/A2
S Bixel St - p315 A4/5
Blackburn Ave - p312 B3/C3
Blaine St - p315 A4/5
Blythe Ave - p311 B5
Boise Ave - p310 D6
Bonita Ave - p312 C5
N Bonnie Brae St - p314 C6/D5
S Bonnie Brae St - p314 C6
Boston St - p315 B1
Boyd St - p315 D3
N Boylston St - p315 A1/2
S Boylston St - p315 A3
Bradbury Rd - p311 B5/6
Braeburn Way - p314 B1
Brighton Way - p311 C3
Broadway - p310 A3/B3/C3/D3
N Broadway - p315 C1/2
S Broadway - p315 B5/6/C2-4
N Bronson Ave - p313 C1-4
S Bronson Ave - p313 B6/C5/6
Brooks Ave - p310 A5/B5
Bunker Hill Ave - p315 B1/C1
Burlingame Ave - p310 D1
N Burlington Ave - p314 D5
S Burlington Ave - p314 D5
Burns Ave - p314 A4/B4
S Burnside Ave - p312 D4/5
Burton Way - p311 D2,
p312 A3/B3
Butterfield Rd - p311 B5/6

Cabrillo Ave - p310 A5/6
Cadillac Ave - p312 A6/B6
N Cahuenga Blvd - p313 B1-3
California Ave - p310 A2/B2/
C2, p310 B5/6
California Plaza - p315 B2/C2
Calle Vista Dr - p311 C1
Calumet Ave - p315 A1
N Camden Dr - p311 B2/C2
S Camden Dr - p311 C3/4
Camerford Ave - p313 B3
Camero Ave - p314 B2

Cameron Lane - p315 B5
Canal St - p310 A6
S Canfield Ave - p311 D5/6
N Canon Dr - p311 C2/3/D3
S Canon Dr - p311 D3/4
Cardiff Ave - p311 D6, p312 A5
Carlos Ave - p313 B1/C1
Carlton Way - p313 C2
Carlyle Ave - p310 B1/C1/D1
Carmelina Ave - p310 D2/3
Carmelita Ave - p311 D2
Carmona Ave - p312 C5
N Carolwood Dr - p311
A1/2/B2
S Carondelet St - p314 C5/6
Carroll Ave - p315 A1
N Carson Rd - p312 B3/4
Cashio St - p311 D4, p312
A5/B5
Castle Heights Ave - p311 D5/6
Catalina St - p314 A1
Cattaraugus Ave - p311 D6
Cavendish Dr - p311 C5/6
Cecilia St - p315 C4
Cedar St - p310 B4
Centinela Ave - p310 D2-6
N Central Ave - p315 D2/3
Century Park E - p311 B3/C4
Century Park W - p311 B4
Ceres Ave - p315 D4
Cesar E Chavez Ave - p315
B1/C1/D1
Chalmers Dr - p312 B4
Channel Rd - p310 A1/B1
Chariton St - p312 B6
Charleville Blvd - p311 C3,
p312 A4/B4
Chelsea Ave - p310 C2/3
N Cherokee Ave - p313 A2/3
Cherry St - p315 A5
Cheviot Dr - p311 B6/C5/6
Citrus Ave - p313 A3/4
S Citrus Ave - p313 A5/6
Clarissa Ave - p314 B2
S Clark Dr - p312 A4/5
Clayton Ave - p314 B2
Clifton Way - p311 D3, p312
A3/B3
Clinton St - p312 C2/D2, p313
A3/B3, p314 A4/B4/C4/D5
Cloverdale Ave - p312 D4/5
Cloverfield Blvd - p310 C4
Club Dr - p311 C6
Club View Dr - p311 B3
S Cochran Ave - p312 D4/5
Colgate Ave - p312 B3/C3
Cologne St - p312 C6
Colorado Ave - p310 A3/B3/
C3/D3
Colorado Pl - p310 D3
E Commercial St - p315 D1/2
N Commonwealth Ave - p314
B1/4/5
Comstock Ave - p311 A2/3/B3
Constellation Blvd - p311 B4
Conway Ave - p311 A2
Copley Pl - p311 B2
S Corning St - p312 B4/5
N Coronado St - p314 C4/5
S Coronado St - p314 B6/C6
Council St - p314 A5/B5/C5,
p315 A2
Country Club Dr - p313 C6
Court St - p314 D6, p315 A1
Courtney Ave - p312 C1
Crenshaw Blvd - p313 B6/C5
N Crescent Dr - p311 B1/C2
S Crescent Dr - p311 D3/4
Crescent Heights Blvd - p312
B5/6/C2-4
Cresta Dr - p311 C5/D5,
p312 A5

Crocker St - p315 D3-5
N Croft Ave - p312 B1/2
Cromwell Ave - p314 A1/B1
Crystal Springs Dr - p314 C1
Cumberland Ave - p314 B3
N Curson Ave - p312 C2/3
S Curson Ave - p312 C5
Cushdon Ave - p311 B5
Cynthia St - p312 A2

David Ave - p312 A6
Dawson St - p314 D6
Dayton Way - p311 D3, p312 A3/B3
De Longpre Ave - p313 C2/D2, p314 A3/B3
Delaware Ave - p310 C3/D3/4
Delfern Dr - p311 A1/2
Descanso Dr - p314 C4
N Detroit St - p312 D1-3, p313 A3/4
S Detroit St - p312 D4/5
Devon Ave - p311 A2/3
Dewey Ave - p310 A5/B5/C5/D5
N Dillon St - p314 B5
Dockweiler St - p313 A6/B6
N Doheny Dr - p311 D1/2, p312 A2/3
S Doheny Dr - p311 D3/4, p312 A4/5
Doheny Rd - p311 C1/D1
Donald Douglas Loop - p310 D5
Doreen Pl - p310 B5
Dorrington Ave - p312 A3
Douglas St - p315 A1
Drexel Ave - p312 B3/C3
Dryad Rd - p310 B1
Duane St - p314 D3
Ducommun St - p315 D2
Dudley Ave - p310 A5
Dunleer Dr - p311 C6
S Dunsmuir Ave - p312 D4/5
Duxbury Rd - p311 D5

Earl St - p314 D3
Earlmar Dr - p311 C5/6
Eastborne Ave - p311 A4
Easterly Terr - p314 C3/4
Echo Park Ave - p314 D4/5
Edgecliffe Dr - p314 B3/4/C3
N Edgemont St - p314 A4/5
S Edgemont St - p314 A1-3
E Edgeware Rd - p315 A1
Edgewood Pl - p313 A5/6
N Edinburgh Ave - p312 C2/3
Effie St - p314 B3/C3
S El Camino Dr - p311 D3/4
El Centro Ave - p313 B2/3
Eleanor Ave - p313 B2
Electric Ave - p310 A5/6
Elevado Ave - p311 B2/3/C2
N Elm Dr - p311 D2/3
S Elm Dr - p311 D3/4
Emerald St - p315 A2
Ensley Ave - p311 B3
Entrada Dr - p310 B1
Esther Ave - p311 B5
Euclid Ct - p310 B2
Euclid St - p310 B1-3
Evans St - p314 C2
Ewing St - p314 D3
Exposition Blvd - p310 D3/4, p311 A6

Fairburn Ave - p311 A4
N Fairfax Ave - p312 C1/2
S Fairfax Ave - p312 B6/C3-5
Fargo St - p314 D3
Figueroa St - p315 A5/6/B2-4
Finley Ave - p314 A2/B2
Firmin St - p315 A1
Fletcher Dr - p314 D2
N Flores St - p312 B1
Flower Ave - p310 B5
S Flower St - p315 B2-6
Foothill Rd - p311 C1/2/D2/3
N Formosa Ave - p312 D1-3, p313 A2/3
S Formosa Ave - p312 D3
Forrester Dr - p311 C5

Fountain Ave - p312 C1/D1, p313 A2/B2/C2/D2, p314 A2/3/B2/3/C2
Fox Hills Dr - p311 B4
Francis Ave - p313 B5
Francisco St - p315 A4
Frank Ct - p315 C3/C4
Franklin Ave - p313 A1/B1/C1/D1
Franklin Ct - p310 D3
Franklin St - p310 D2/3
N Fremont Ave - p315 B1/2
N Fuller Ave - p312 D1/2
S Fuller Ave - p312 D3

Garden Ave - p314 D1
N Gardner St - p312 D1-3
Garfield Ave - p310 B6
Garfield Pl - p313 C1
Garland Ave - 315 A4
S Garth Ave - p312 B5
N Genesee Ave - p312 C1-3
S Genesee Ave - p312 C5
Georgia St - p315 A4/5
Georgina Ave - p310 A1/B1
Gibson St - p312 A6
Gladys Ave - p315 D4
Glencoe Ave - p310 C6
Glendale Blvd - p314 D2-6, p315 A2
Glendon Ave - p311 A5/B6
Glenhurst Ave - p314 D1
Glenville Dr - p312 A5
Glyndon Ave - p310 C6
Golden Gate Ave - p314 C3
N Gower St - p313 B1-3
Gramercy Pl - p313 C1-6
Grand Ave - p315 B2-6/C1
Grand Blvd - p310 A6
Grand Canal Ct - p310 A6
Grange Ave - p311 A5
Grant St - p310 B4
Greenfield Ave - p311 A6/B6
Greenwood Ave - p310 C6
Gregory Ave - p313 B3
Gregory Way - p311 C3/D3, p312 A4/B4
Griffith Ave - p315 D5/6
Griffith Park Blvd - p314 C1-3
The Grove Dr - p312 C3
Guthrie St - p312 A6/B6/D3

N Hamel Rd - p312 A3/4
Hamilton Dr - p312 B4
Hammond St - p312 A2
N Hampshire St - p314 A2
Hampton Ave - p312 C1/D1
Hampton Dr - p310 A5
Hancock Ave - p312 A2
Harbor St - p310 A6
Hargis St - p311 D6
Harlem Pl - p315 C3
Harold Way - p313 C2
N Harper Ave - p312 B2/3
Hartford Ave - p315 A3/A4
Harvard Ave - p310 D2/3
N Harvard Blvd - p313 D1-4
Harvard Ct - p310 D2
Hauser Blvd - p312 C5/6/D3-5
Havenhurst Dr - p312 B1/C1
Hawthorn Ave - p312 C1/D1, p313 A2
N Hayworth Ave - p312 C1-3
S Hayworth Ave - p312 B5/6
Heliotrope Dr - p314 A3/4
Hidalgo Ave - p314 D2/3
N Highland Ave - p313 A2/3
S Highland Ave - p312 D5/6, p313 A4/5
N Hill Pl - p315 C1
Hill Pl N - p310 B4/C4
Hill St - p315 B4-6/C2/3
Hill St (SM) - p310 A4/B4/C4
Hillcrest Rd - p311 D2
Hillhurst Ave - p314 B1/2
Hillsboro Ave - p311 D5
Hillside Ave - p312 C1
Hobart Blvd - p313 D1-6
Hollister Ave - p310 A4/B4
Holloway Dr - p312 A2/B2

Hollydale Dr - p314 D1/2
Hollywood Blvd - p312 C1/D1, p313 A1/B1/C1/D1, p314 A2
Holman Ave - p311 A4
Holmby Ave - p311 A3/4
S Holt Ave - p312 B4/5
N Hoover St - p314 B3/4
S Hope St - p315 B2-5
Horn Ave - p312 A1/2
Horner St - p312 B5
Hudson Ave - p313 A6/B4/5
Huntley Dr - p312 B2/3, p315 A2
Hyperion Ave - p314 B3/4/C2/3

Idaho Ave - p310 A2/B2/C2
Ilona Ave - p311 B4/5
Indiana Ave - p310 A5/B5
Ingraham St - p313 C5, p315 A3
Iowa Ave - p310 D3
Irolo St - p313 D5/6
N Irving Blvd - p313 C3/4
S Irving Blvd - p313 C4/5
Ivar Ave - p313 B2

N June St - p313 B3

Kansas Ave - p310 C4/D4
Keith Ave - p312 A2
Kelton Ave - p311 A5/6/B6
Kenilworth Ave - p314 C2/3
Keniston Ave - p313 A5/6
N Kenmore Ave - p314 A2-5, p313 D1-3
S Kenmore Ave - p314 A4
W Kensington Rd - p314 D5
Kent St - p314 C5
Kerwood Ave - p311 B4
Keswick Ave - p311 B4
N Kilkea Dr - p312 C2/3
Kingman Ave - p310 B1
N Kingsley Dr - p313 D1-3
S Kingsley Dr - p313 D4/5
N Kings Rd - p312 B1-3
Kingswell Ave - p314 A2/B2
Kinnard Ave - p311 A4
Kirkside Rd - p311 D5
W Knoll Dr - p312 B2

N La Brea Ave - p312 D1/2, p313 A2/3
S La Brea Ave - p312 D3-6
N La Cienega Blvd - p312 B2/3
S La Cienega Blvd - p312 B5/6
N Lafayette Park Pl - p314 C4/5
S Lafayette Park Pl - p314 B5/6
N La Jolla Ave - p312 B2/3
S La Jolla Ave - p312 B2-5
La Mirada Ave - p313 B2/C2/D2, p314 A3/B3
Lake Ave - p310 B5/C5
Lake Shore Ave - p314 D3/4
Lake St - p310 C5
S Lake St - p314 C5/6
Lake View Ave - p314 D2/3
Lanewood Ave - p313 A2
N La Peer Dr - p312 A2
S La Peer Dr - p312 A4/5
N Larchmont Blvd - p313 B3/4
Larrabee St - p312 A2
N Las Palmas Ave - p313 A2/3
S Lasky Dr - p311 C3
N Laurel Ave - p312 C1-3
Laurel Way - p311 B1
Laveta Terr - p314 D5
N Le Doux Rd - p312 B2/3
Lebanon St - p315 B5/6
Leeward Ave - p313 C5, p314 B6
Leland Way - p313 A2/B2
Lemon Grove Ave - p313 D3
Lemoyne St - p314 D4
Lexington Ave - p312 C1/D1, p313 A2/B2/C2/D2, p314 A3/B3
Lexington Rd - p311 B1
Lillian Way - p313 B2/3
Lincoln Blvd - p310 B6

Lincoln Ct - p310 B2
Lindbrook Dr - p311 A3
N Linden Dr - p311 B2/C3
S Linden Dr - p311 C3
Lindley Pl - p315 C3/4
Linnington Ave - p311 B4/5
Locksley Pl - p314 D2
Lockwood Ave - p314 A4/B4
Loma Vista Dr - p311 C1/D1
Lomitas Ave - p311 B2/C1/2
Longpre Ave - p312 C1/D1
S Longwood Dr - p313 A5/6
Loring Ave - p311 A2/3
Lorraine Blvd - p313 C4/5
S Los Angeles St - p315 C2-6/D1/2
Los Feliz Blvd - p314 A1/2/B1/C1
Lovella Ave - p310 C6
Lowry Rd - p314 B1
Lucas Ave - p315 A3
N Lucerne Blvd - p313 B3/4
S Lucerne Blvd - p313 B4/5
Lucille Ave - p310 C6
Lyman Pl - p313 B3/4
Lyric Ave - p314 C2

Mabery Rd - p310 A1
Madera Ave - p314 D1
N Madison Ave - p314 B4
Main St - p310 A5
S Main St - p315 C1-6
Malcolm Ave - p311 A5
Maltman Ave - p314 B4/C3
S Manhattan Pl - p313 C4/5
Manning Ave - p311 A4/B5/6/C6
Mansfield Ave - p313 A2/3
Manzanita Pl - p314 B3
Maple Ave - p315 C4-6
N Maple Dr - p311 C1/D2/3
S Maple Dr - p311 D3/4, p312 A4/5
Maple St - p310 B4
Mapleton Dr - p311 A2
Maplewood Ave - p310 C5/6
Marathon St - p313 C3, p314 A4/B4/C4/5
Marco Pl - p310 B6
Margo St - p315 B5
Marguerita Ave - p310 A1/B1/C1/D1
Marine St - p310 A4/B5/C5
N Mariposa Ave - p313 D1-3, p314 A2-5
S Mariposa Ave - p313 D4-6, p314 A6
Market St - p310 A5
N Martel Ave - p312 D2/3
Maryland Dr - p312 B4/C4
Maryland St - p315 A3
Massachusetts Ave - p311 A4
S Masselin Ave - p312 C5
May St - p310 D6
N McCadden Place - p313 A2/3
S McCarty Dr - p311 C3
McCollum St - p314 C4/D4
McConnell Pl - p311 C5
Meier St - p310 C6/D6
Melbourne Ave - p314 A2/B2
Melrose Ave - p312 B2/C2/D2, p313 A3/B3/C3/D3, p314 A4/B4
Micheltorena St - p314 B4/C2-4
Michigan Ave - p310 B3/C3
Midvale Ave - p311 A5/6/B6
Mildred Ave - p310 A6
Military Ave - p311 A5
Milwood Ave - p310 B6
Miramar St - p315 A2
Mississippi Ave - p311 A5
Mohawk St - p314 D4/5
Monon St - p314 C2
Monroe St - p314 A4/B4
Montana Ave - p310 A2/B2/C2/D2
Montana Pl - p310 A2/B2
Montana St - p314 C4/D4
Monte Mar - p311 D4
Moore St - p310 C6/D6

Moreno Ave - p310 D1
Moreno Dr - p311 C3, p314 C2
Morningside Way - p310 C5
N Morton Ave - p313 C3/4
Motor Ave - p311 C5/6
Mountain Dr - p311 C1
N Mountain View Ave - p314 C5/6
S Muirfield Rd - p313 B5
S Mullen Ave - p313 B5
Myra Ave - p313 B3
Myrtle St - p315 C5/6

National Blvd - p311 A6/B6/C6/D6
National Pl - p311 B6/C6
Navy St - p310 C5
Nebraska Ave - p310 D3, p311 A4
Neilson St - p310 A3-5
N New Hampshire Ave - p314 A4/5
New High St - p315 C1
Normal Ave - p314 A4/B4
N Normandie Ave - p313 D1-3, p314 A2-6
S Normandie Ave - p313 D4-6
Northvale Rd - p311 B6/C6
Norton Ave - p312 C1/D1
S Norton Ave - p313 B6/C5/6
Norwich Dr - p312 A2/B3
Nowita Ct - p310 B6

Oak St - p310 B4/C4
Oakhurst Ave - p311 D6
Oakhurst Dr - p311 D2/3, p312 A2-5
Oakmore Rd - p311 D5
Oakwood Ave - p312 B3/C3/D3, p313 A3/4, p314 A5/B5
N Occidental Blvd - p314 C4/5
S Occidental Blvd - p314 B5/6
Ocean Ave - p310 A1-6
Ocean Front Walk - p310 A5
Ocean Park Blvd - p310 A4/B4/C4/D4
Ocean Park Pl S - p310 B4/C4
Ocean View Ave - p314 B6/C6
Ocean Way - p310 A1
Ogden Dr - p312 C1/2/4/5
Ohio Ave - p311 A4
Olive Ave - p310 A6
S Olive St - p315 B3-5/C2/3
Olvera St - p315 D1
Olympic Blvd - p310 B3/C3/D3, p311 A5/B4/5/C4/D4, p312 A4/B4/C4/D4, p313 A5/B5/6/C6/D6, p315 A4/B4/C4
Orange Dr - p312 D1-3, p313 A2-5
Orange Grove Ave - p312 C1-5
Ord St - p315 C1
N Orlando Ave - p312 B2/3
S Orlando Ave - p312 B3-5
Overland Ave - p311 A4/5/B5/6
N Oxford Ave - p313 D3/4

Pacific Ave - p310 A5/6
Pacific St - p310 B4
Packard St - p312 B5/C5/D5
Palisades Ave - p310 A1/B1
Palisades Beach Rd - p310 A1-3
N Palm Dr - p311 D1-3, p312 A3/4
S Palm Dr - p311 D3/4, p312 A4/5
Palms Blvd - p310 B6/C6/D6, p311 C6
Paloma St - p315 D5/6
Pandora Ave - p311 B4
Parkman Ave - p314 C4/5
N Park View - p314 C5
Parnell Ave - p311 A4/5/B5
Patrick Ave - p311 B5
Patton St - p315 A1
Pearl St - p310 B4/C4
S Peck Dr - p311 C3/4

Pelham Ave - p311 A4/5
S Pembroke Lane - p315 B4/5
Penmar Ave - p310 B6/C5/6
Penn Ave - p310 D3
Pershing Sq - p315 C3
Pickford St - p312 A5/B5/C5/D6
Pico Blvd - p310 C4/D4, p311 A5/6/B5/C4/D4, p312 A5/B5/C5/D5, p313 A6/B6/C6/D6, p315 A5/B5/C5/D5
Pier Ave - p310 A4/B4
Pine St - p310 B4
N Plymouth Blvd - p313 C3/4
S Plymouth Blvd - p313 B4/5
Poinsettia Dr - p312 D1
N Poinsetta Pl - p312 D1/2
S Point View St - p312 B5
Preston Way - p310 C5
S Preuss Rd - p312 A5/6
Princeton Ave - p310 D2/3
Prospect Ave - p314 A2/B2
Prosser Ave - p311 A4/B5
Putney Rd - p311 B5

Queen Anne Pl - p313 B6
Queensbury Dr - p311 C5/6

Rampart Blvd - p314 B6/C5
Rangely Ave - p312 A3
Raymond Ave - p310 A4/B4
Redcliff St - p314 C13
S Redondo Blvd - p312 D5/6
Redwood Ave - p310 C5/6
S Reeves Dr - p311 D3/4
Reeves St - p311 D4
Reno St - p314 B5
Reservoir St - p314 C4/D4
N Rexford Dr - p311 C1/2
S Rexford Dr - p311 D3/4, p312 A4/5
Richland Ave - p314 B1
S Ridgeley Dr - p312 D4/5
N Ridgewood Pl - p313 C4
Rimpau Blvd - p313 B5
Riverside Dr - p314 C1/D1/2
Riviera Ave - p310 A6
N Robertson Blvd - p312 A3/4
S Robertson Blvd - p312 A4-6
Robinson St - p314 B4/5
Rochester Ave - p311 A4
N Rodeo Dr - p311 B2/C2
S Rodeo Dr - p311 C3/4
Rodney Dr - p314 A2
Romaine St - p312 B2/C2/D2, p313 A3/B3/C3/D3, p314 A4
Rose Ave - p310 A5/B5/C5, p311 C6
Rose St - p315 D2
Roselake Ave - p314 C5
Rosemont Ave - p314 C5
Rosewood Ave - p310 C5/6, p312 A3/B2/3/C2/D2, p313 A3/B3, p314 A4
S Rossmore Ave - p313 B4/5
Roundtree Rd - p311 B5/6
Rowena Ave - p314 B1/C1/2/D2
Roxbury Dr - p311 B2/C2-5/D4
Rugby Dr - p312 B2
Russell Ave - p313 D1, p314 A2/B2

St Andrews Pl - p313 C1-5
St George St - p314 B2/C2
St Josephs Pl - p315 C5/6
San Juan Ave - p310 A5/B5
San Julian St - p315 C5/D4/5
San Lorenzo St - p310 B1
S San Pedro St - p315 D2-6
San Vicente Blvd - p310 A1/B1/C1/D1, p312 A2/3/B3/4/C4/5/D5
San Ysidro Dr - p311 B1
Sanborn Ave - p313 B3
Santa Monica Blvd - p310 A4/B3/C3/D3, p311 A4/B3/4/C2/3/D2, p312 A2/B2/C2/D2, p313 A2/B2/C2/D2, p314 A3/B3
Little Santa Monica Blvd - p311 A4/B3/4/C3/2/D2
Santee St - p315 C4-6
Saturn St - p312 B5/C5
Sawtelle Blvd - p311 A6
Sawyer St - p311 D5, p312 A6/B6
Schrader Blvd - p313 B2
Scott Ave - p314 C4/D4
Selby Ave - p311 A4/5/B6
Selma Ave - p312 C1, p313 A2/B2
Sepulveda Blvd - p311 A5/6
N Serrano Ave - p313 D1/2
S Serrano Blvd - p313 D3/4
Seward St - p313 B2/3
Shatto Pl - p314 A6/B6
Shelby Dr - p311 D6
S Shenandoah St - p312 A5/6
Sherbourne Dr - p312 A1
N Sierra Bonita Ave - p312 D2/3
S Sierra Dr - p311 D1/2
Silver Lake Blvd - p314 B4/5/C4/D2/3
W Silver Lake Dr - p314 C2/3
Silver Ridge Ave - p314 D2/3
N Spaulding Ave - p312 C2/3
S Spaulding Ave - p312 C5
S Spalding Dr - p311 C3
Speedway - p310 A5
N Spring St - p315 C1-3
S Spring St - p315 C3/4
Stanford Ave - p315 D3-6
N Stanley Ave - p312 C1-3
S Stanley Ave - p312 C5
N Stanley Dr - p312 B3/4
Stearns Dr - p312 B5/6
Stewart Ave - p310 D5/6
Stewart St - p310 D4
Strand St - p310 A4/B4
Summit Dr - p311 B1
Sunbury St - p315 A4
Sunset Ave - p310 A5/B4/5
W Sunset Blvd - p311 A2/B2/C1/D1, p312 A1/B1/C1/D1, p313 A2/B2/C2/D2, p314 A3/B3/C3/4, p315 B1
Sunset Dr - p313 B3
Sunset Pl - p314 B6
Sunset Plaza Drive - p312 A1/B1
Superba Ave - p310 B6
S Swall Dr - p312 A4/5
Sweetzer Ave - p312 B1-3
Sycamore Ave - p312 D1-3, p313 A1-5

Taft Ave - p313 C1
Temple St - p314 B5/C5/D5, p315 A1/B1/C2/D2
Tikosciuszko Way - p315 B2/C2
Tilden Ave - p311 A6
N Toluca St - p315 A2
Towne Ave - p315 D3-5
Tracy St - p314 B2/C2
Trinity St - p315 C6
Troon Ave - p311 B5/C5
Tularosa Dr - p313 B4
Talmadge St - p314 B2/3
Teviot St - p314 D2/3
Thayer Ave - p311 A3/4/B4
Tennessee Ave - p311 A5/B4/5
S Tremaine Ave - p313 A5/6

N Union Ave - p314 C6/D6
Urban Ave - p310 D4

Valita St - p310 B5
N Van Ness Ave - p313 C1-4
N Vendome St - p314 B5
S Vendome St - p314 B5
Venezia Ave - p310 B6
Venice Blvd - p310 A6/B6/C6/D6, p311 D6, p312 B6/C6/D5, p313 A6/B6, p315 A5/B5/C6

D2, p313 A2/B2/C2/D2, p314 A3/B3
Little Santa Monica Blvd - p311 A4/B3/4/C3/2/D2
N Vermont Ave - p314 A1-4
S Vermont Ave - p314 A5/6
Vernon Ave - p310 A5/B5
Veteran Ave - p311 A5/6/B6
S Victoria Ave - p313 B5/6
Vidor Dr - p311 C4
N Vignes St - p315 D1
Vine St - p313 B2/3
N Virgil Ave - p314 B3/4
S Virgil Ave - p314 B6
Virginia Ave - p310 C4/D4
Virginia Ave - p313 C2
Vista Del Mar - p313 B1
Vista Dr - p314 C2
Vista St - p312 D1-3

Wade St - p310 D6
Walden Dr - p311 B3/C3
Walgrove Ave - p310 C5/6
Wall St - p315 C4-6
Walnut Ave - p310 C6
Warden Ave - p310 B5
Waring Ave - p312 B2/C2/D2
Waring Ave - p313 A3/B3
Warnall Ave - p311 B3
Warner Ave - p311 A3/4
Warren Ave - p310 C5/D5/6
Washington Ave - p310 A2/B2/C2/D2
E Washington Blvd - p315 C6/D6
W Washington Blvd - p310 A6/B6, p312 C6/D6
Waterloo St - p314 D3
Waverley Dr - p314 C1
Waverly Dr - p314 C1/D2
Wayne Ave - p314 B1
Welcome St - p314 D6
Wellworth Ave - p311 A4
Werdin Pl - p315 C3/C4
Westbourne Dr - p312 B2
Westchester Pl - p313 C5/6
Westerley Terr - p314 C3/4
N Western Ave - p313 C1-3
S Western Ave - p313 D5/6
Westholme Ave - p311 A4
N Westlake Ave - p314 C5/6
S Westlake Ave - p314 C6
Westminster Ave - p310 A5/B5, p313 C4/5
N Westmorland Ave - p314 B4
S Westmorland Ave - p314 B6
Westmount Dr - p312 B2
Westwood Blvd - p311 A5/B6
N Wetherby Dr - p311 D2/3
N Wetherly Dr - p312 A3/4
Whiteley Ave - p313 B1
Whittier Dr - p311 B2/3
Whitworth Dr - p311 D4, p312 A4/B4/C4/D4/D5
Wilcox Ave - p313 B1/2
Wilkins Ave - p311 A4
N Willaman Dr - p312 B3/4
Willoughby Ave - p312 B2/C2/D2, p313 A3/B2/C3/D3
Willow Brook Ave - p314 A2/B3
Wilshire Blvd - p310 A2/B2/C2/D2, p311 A3/B3/C3/D3, p312 A4/B4/C4/D4, p313 A5/B5/C5/D5, p314 A6/B6, p315 A3/B3
N Wilton Pl - p313 C1-3
S Wilton Pl - p313 C5/6
N Windsor Blvd - p313 C3/4
S Windsor Blvd - p313 B5/6/C4/5
Windward Ave - p310 A5
Winona Blvd - p313 D1/2
Winston St - p315 C3/D3
Witmer St - p315 A3
Woodbine St - p311 C6
Woodland Dr - p311 C1
Woodruff Ave - p311 A3/4
S Wooster St - p312 A5/6

Yale Ave - p310 D2/3
Yucca St - p313 A1/B1

Zanja St - p310 B6/C6